THE MISSIONARY
MOVEMENT
IN AMERICAN
CATHOLIC HISTORY

The American Society of Missiology Series, in collaboration with Orbis Books, seeks to publish scholarly works of high merit and wide interest on numerous aspects of Missiology — the study of mission. Able presentations on new and creative approaches to the practice and understanding of mission will receive close attention.

Previously published in
the American Society of Missiology Series

American Society of Missiology Series, No. 26

THE MISSIONARY MOVEMENT IN AMERICAN CATHOLIC HISTORY

Angelyn Dries, OSF

ORBIS BOOKS

Maryknoll, New York 10545

The Catholic Foreign Mission Society of America (Maryknoll) recruits and trains people for overseas missionary service. Through Orbis Books, Maryknoll aims to foster the international dialogue that is essential to mission. The books published, however, reflect the opinions of their authors and are not meant to represent the official position of the society.

Library of Congress Cataloging-in-Publication Data

Dries, Angelyn.
    The missionary movement in American Catholic history / Angelyn Dries.
        p.   cm. — (American Society of Missiology series ; no. 26)
    Includes bibliographical references and index.
    ISBN 1-57075-167-6 (alk. paper)
    1. Catholic Church—Missions—North America—History.
  2. Missions—North America—History.   3. Immigrants—North America—
Religious life.   I. Title.   II. Series.
  BV2240.N7D75   1998
    266'.273–dc21   97–32083

This book is affectionately dedicated to

Luise Ahrens, MM,
Joseph Chinnici, OFM,
Dick Pankratz, SSC,
and Bill Sweeney, SSC,

each of whom has contributed immeasurably
to my life and understanding of mission.

Contents

Illustrations

Preface to the Series

The purpose of the American Society of Missiology (ASM) Series is to publish — without regard for disciplinary, national, or denominational boundaries — scholarly works of high quality and wide interest on missiological themes from the entire spectrum of scholarly pursuits relevant to Christian Mission, which is always the focus of books in the Series.

By "mission" is meant the effort to effect passage over the boundary between faith in Jesus Christ and its absence. In this understanding of mission, the basic functions of Christian proclamation, dialogue, witness, service, worship, liberation, and nurture are of special concern. And in that context questions arise, including, How does the transition from one cultural context to another influence the shape and interaction between these dynamic functions, especially in regard to the cultural and religious plurality that comprise the global context of Christian mission?

The promotion of scholarly dialogue among missiologists and among missiologists and scholars in other fields of inquiry may involve the publication of views that some missiologists cannot accept, and with which members of the Editorial Committee do not agree. Manuscripts published in the Series reflect the opinions of their authors and are not understood to represent the position of the American Society of Missiology or of the Editorial Committee. Selection is guided by such criteria as intrinsic worth, readability, and accessibility to a range of interested persons and not merely to experts or specialists.

The ASM Series Editorial Committee
James A. Scherer
Mary Motte, FMM
Charles Taber

Acknowledgments

The history of the U.S. foundations for Catholic missionary work abroad could not have been written without the assistance and cooperation of many persons and groups. In 1990, two advisory meetings were held at the Overseas Ministries Study Center in New Haven, Connecticut, to discuss the possibilities and parameters of writing a comprehensive U.S. Catholic mission history. The project had been on the minds of the research committee of the United States Catholic Mission Association for some time and the gracious hospitality of Dr. Gerald H. Anderson, director of the OMSC, provided the space for discussion in two gatherings of about twenty missionaries, mission historians, and theologians. A Mission History Project Board was formed and I, having completed my doctoral dissertation on the topic at the Graduate Theological Union, Berkeley, California, was commissioned to do the research and writing. Work began in the fall of 1993.

Thus, first among the people who deserve recognition are the History Project Board of the United States Catholic Mission Association, whose members have included USCMA Executive Directors Margaret F. Loftus, SND, Lou McNeil, and Rosanne Rustemeyer, SSND. Other members include Dolores Liptak, RSM, Janet Carroll, MM, Christopher Kauffman, Robert Schreiter, CPPS, Jean-Paul Wiest, Dana Robert, William R. Burrows, and Mary Motte, FMM. Another History Board member who deserves special recognition is Dr. Gerald H. Anderson, executive director of the Overseas Ministries Study Center, New Haven, Connecticut. His outstanding encouragement and support moved the mission history from an idea to a reality.

A second group to whom thanks is due provided finances for extensive research. Funding for research leading to this publication was provided by the Research Enablement Program, a grant program for mission scholarship supported by the Pew Charitable Trusts, Philadelphia, Pennsylvania, U.S.A., and administered by the Overseas Study Center, New Haven, Connecticut, U.S.A. Other groups and persons who provided funding are The Our Sunday Visitor Institute; the Divine Word Missionaries; Missionary Sisters of the Holy Spirit; the Maryknoll Society; Maryknoll Sisters; Holy Spirit Missionaries; the Society of St. Columban; the Franciscan Missionaries of Mary; Xaverian Fathers and Brothers; Glenmary Home Missioners; Sisters of St. Francis of Assisi, Milwaukee; Sisters of Mercy of the Americas; Missionhurst Fathers; Jesuits International Ministries; Holy Cross Mission Center; Sisters of the Holy Cross; Sisters of Charity – St. Elizabeth; Sisters of St. Joseph of Carondelet; School Sisters of Notre Dame; Sisters of Charity – Mount St. Vincent on Hudson; Missionary Association of Catholic Women; Sisters of Providence – St. Mary of the Woods; Bishop William J. McCormack; Jerome and Marion Dries; Lora Cronin; and Audrey Meske.

I am grateful to Dolores Liptak, RSM, who provided excellent editing of all draft chapters, the History Project Board, which provided comments on several chapters, Louis J. Luzbetak, SVD, Stanley Uroda, SVD, Ernest Brandewie, Jean-Paul Wiest, Barbara Hendricks, MM, and William D. McCarthy, MM, who provided extensive critiques of all the chapters. Thanks also to Lawrence Nemer, SVD, Jeremy Quinn, CSA, and Simon J. Smith, SJ, who commented on particular chapters.

I am grateful to archivists and others who provided exceptional service and/or accommodations while I perused materials: Jeremy Quinn, CSA, the Sisters of St. Agnes, Fond du Lac, Wisconsin; Sisters of Charity of Halifax, Brooklyn; Carl Hoegerl, CSSR, Redemptorist Fathers and Brothers, Baltimore Province; the archival staff of the Society of the Divine Word Fathers and Brothers at Techny, Illinois, and the SVD formation community in Chicago; the Sisters of Charity, Mount St. Vincent on Hudson, New York; the Maryknoll Sisters, Fathers, and Brothers, especially Dolores Rosso, MM, and Mary Grace Krieger, MM; Blaithin Sullivan, CSJ, and the Sisters of St. Joseph, Brighton, Massachusetts, with whom I stayed while using many of the archives in the Boston area; Gloria Fournier, SMSM, and the Marist Missionary Sisters, Waltham, Massachusetts; the Sisters of Notre Dame de Namur at the Julie Billiart Residence in Washington, D.C.; Anthony Zito, John Shepherd, and David Richardson, OSC, at The Catholic University of America Archives; Paul Casey, SSC, and the Columban Fathers, Omaha, Nebraska; and Robert Johnson Lally and Phyllis Danehy of the archives of the archdiocese of Boston.

Finally, heartfelt thanks go to my colleagues at Cardinal Stritch University, Milwaukee, for their support and for the use of the resources of the Religious Studies Department; to the Milwaukee Korean Catholic community, who for six years have shared their lives with me; to my family; and to the Sisters of St. Francis of Assisi, with whom I have been in mission many years.

Abbreviations

AABoston	Archives, Archdiocese of Boston
AANY	Archives, Archdiocese of New York
ABCM	American Board of Catholic Missions
ACUA	Archives, The Catholic University of America
AID	Association for International Development
CA	*Catholic Action*
CAL	Pontifical Commission for Latin America
CELAM	Regional Conference of Latin American Bishops
CFA	Columban Fathers Archives
CICOP	Catholic Inter-American Cooperation Program
CIF	Center for Intercultural Formation, Cuernavaca, Mexico
CM	*Catholic Missions*
CMMB	Catholic Medical Mission Board
CSAA	Sisters of St. Agnes Archives
CSMC	Catholic Students Mission Crusade
FA	*The Field Afar*
FE	*The Far East*
FSPAA	Franciscan Sisters of Perpetual Adoration Archives
LAB	Latin American Bureau
MMA	Maryknoll Mission Archives
NCCB	National Council of Catholic Bishops
NCCW	National Council of Catholic Women
NCWC	National Catholic Welfare Council (1919–69)
PAVLA	Papal Volunteers for Latin America
RFBA	Redemptorist Fathers and Brothers Archives
SFC	Sister Formation Conference
SPF	Society for the Propagation of the Faith
SVDA	Divine Word Missionary Archives
SVM	Student Volunteer Movement for Foreign Missions
USCC	United States Catholic Conference (1969–present)
USCMA	United States Catholic Mission Association (1982–present)
USCMC	United States Catholic Mission Council (1970–81)

Abbreviations of Societies and Congregations of Women and Men Religious

CFX	Brothers of St. Francis Xavier
CHM	Congregation of the Humility of Mary
CICM	Missionhurst (Congregation of the Immaculate Heart of Mary)
CM	Congregation of the Mission (Vincentians)
CND	Congregation of Notre Dame
CP	Congregation of the Passion (Passionists)
CPPS	Society of the Precious Blood
CSA	Sisters of St. Agnes
CSC	Congregation of the Holy Cross
CSJ or SSJ	Sisters of St. Joseph
CSP	Missionary Society of St. Paul the Apostle (Paulists)
CSSp	Congregation of the Holy Spirit (Spiritans)
CSSR	Congregation of the Most Holy Redeemer (Redemptorists)
FMM	Franciscan Missionaries of Mary
FSC	Brothers of the Christian Schools (Christian Brothers)
IMC	Consolata Missionaries
MAfr	Missionaries of Africa
MM	Maryknoll Missioners (Catholic Foreign Mission Society of America); Maryknoll Sisters of St. Dominic
MSBT	Missionary Servants of the Most Blessed Trinity
MSC	Missionary Sisters of the Sacred Heart of Jesus
OFM	Order of Friars Minor
OFMCap	Orders of Friars Minor Capuchins
OFMConv	Order of Friars Minor Conventual
OMI	Oblates of Mary Immaculate
OP	Order of Preachers (Dominicans)
OSF	Order of St. Francis
OSM	Order of Friar Servants of Mary (Servites)
OSU	Order of St. Ursula (Ursulines)
PBVM	Sisters of the Presentation of the Blessed Virgin Mary
PIME	Pontifical Institute for Foreign Missions
RSM	Sisters of Mercy of the Americas

SBS	Sisters of the Blessed Sacrament for Indians and Colored People
SC	Sisters of Charity
SCL	Sisters of Charity of Leavenworth
SCMM	Society of Catholic Medical Missionaries (Medical Mission Sisters)
SJ	Society of Jesus (Jesuits)
SM	Society of Mary (Marianists)
SM	Society of Mary (Marists)
SMSM	Missionary Sisters of the Society of Mary
SND	Sisters of Notre Dame de Namur
SPS	St. Patrick's Missionary Society
SSC	Society of St. Columban (Columban Fathers)
SSF	Sisters of the Holy Family
SSJ	Josephites (St. Joseph's Society of the Sacred Heart)
SSJ	Sisters of St. Joseph
SSND	School Sisters of Notre Dame
SSpS	Holy Spirit Missionary Sisters
SSSF	School Sisters of St. Francis
SVD	Society of the Divine Word
WF	White Fathers (after 1984: Missionaries of Africa)

Introduction

The Missionary Movement of the United States Catholic Church, 1841–1980

The energetic and kaleidoscopic narrative of the U.S. Catholic missionary movement overseas not only includes the missionaries themselves but an entire network of individuals and groups of laity, clergy, religious, bishops, interacting clusters of strategists, fund-raisers, promoters, theoreticians, organizers, and pray-ers. This monograph of their story might be compared with the maps of the "New World" drawn by Jacques Marquette, Louis Hennepin, Eusebio Kino, and other missionaries. Their cartography provided depictions of land shapes, major rivers, and other geographic detail in order to construct, as best they could, the parameters of a land unknown to Europeans. Compared with twentieth-century maps, the earlier ones are amazingly accurate and, yet, exaggerated the shape of certain land masses and lack details we know today. New map projections have resulted both from better instruments and from actually living on that land.

In a similar fashion, this book outlines the main contours of the mission movement by identifying representatives of various themes. The narrative does not name every person or group who contributed to the mission endeavor but focuses on the interaction of various mission groups who illustrate the meaning and significance of the mission movement. While we will follow some missionaries as they begin their work in other countries, we will not treat the growth of the Church there as much as we will observe the religious, social, and economic constructions missionaries brought with them. Some persons, such as Maryknoll luminaries Mother Mary Joseph Rogers and Bishop James A. Walsh, have had their stories told. Much more could be said about each organization or person identified here or about the heroes and heroines important to various mission societies. That task can be left to other historians, who will benefit, hopefully, from the resources I have identified and compiled. The abundance of sources in the footnotes is convincing evidence that U.S. Catholic mission history is a new field needing further exploration.

Missionary maps piqued the interest of a variety of groups in Europe. Future explorers, business and commercial entrepreneurs, adventurers and travelers, as well as missionaries themselves, had reasons for reading the maps. Similarly, my narrative will interest those in several fields, including those studying religion in America, the history of world Christianity, women's history, and mission studies. Our subject has not been treated by these historians in any significant way.[1]

The narrative has attempted to

- establish the historical record and elucidate the meaning of the diverse U.S. Catholic efforts within global Christianity;

- identify key themes and issues;

- analyze the gender factor in missionary consciousness;

- indicate the interaction of Catholic and Protestant mission theory and practice; and

- examine the cross-cultural bridges constructed through the effect of missionary encounter on Americans and on the U.S. Catholic community.

In so doing, I have placed mission history in a broader political and cultural context and have made available a new database for historians of the American mission experience and of world Christianity. I am also interested in having missionaries themselves see the wider picture in which they were vital constituents.

Among the questions I have considered in my examination of the broad base of primary resources are:

- What were the social, political, cultural, and religious factors which gave rise to mission efforts toward particular areas of the world at various times in U.S. history?

- What presuppositions lay at the foundation of American Catholic thought and practice of world evangelization?

- What were similarities and differences between genders in the perception of the nature and practice of world evangelization?

- To what extent did American missionaries contribute to the shift in mission theory and practice?

This history does not give equal attention to all the geographic locations where U.S. Catholics were sent. For example, a substantial increase in missionaries to sub-Saharan countries occurred between 1940 (108 missionaries) and 1963 (1,025), the greatest increase occurring after World War II and after a papal encyclical calling for missionaries to that continent. My narrative notes this briefly. While I provide possible reasons for lack of interest in the topic in the United States, much more needs to be said about the mission movement toward African countries. This is true for New Guinea, as well, where the United States Province of the Divine Word Missionaries assumed a significant role in the development of the local church and in the recording of life and language in island tribal communities.[2]

Many other topics need to be studied in the historical mapping of American Catholic missions, as we continue to plumb their riches. Women's studies can be further enhanced through a study of the impact of U.S. missionary women on international women's history and on the globalization of feminism as a result of missionary activity.

Asian American studies can be augmented through oral histories and the preservation of documents concerning Asian immigrants, especially those who arrived in the United States after 1950. Asian groups experienced some of the same problems as those who preceded them from Europe, but the fact that Asian religious culture differed from European culture provides important material for observing what Buddhist, Confucian, and Christian elements Asian Americans were able to use in adjusting to the American way of life. Virtually no historical study has been done on the experience of Asian Catholics in the United States. What has been the role of missionaries on both sides of the Pacific as the immigrants arrived on American shores?

How have missionaries and the federal government interacted on such issues as release of prisoners, Central Intelligence Agency activity, and the transfer of bodies of missionaries killed abroad? Because missionaries interpreted other religions and cultures for those in the United States, what do the objects sent home — artistic renderings and other forms of material culture — indicate about missionary attitudes?

Other mission emphases need to be treated as part of American Catholic experience, including the use of technology (airplane and radio missionaries), the development of Catholic presses,[3] and the placement of those with "no overt mission" or "faith mission," such as the American Jesuit mission to Baghdad from 1932 to 1968.[4] What do missionaries' letters and diaries depicting their travel from the United States to their mission say about the anthropologic themes of *journey?* How do missionaries compare themselves to other travelers?

These are just some of the topics needing further exploration. Hopefully, this book will encourage historians' use of U.S. Catholic missionary archives in an under-researched field. Along the same lines, I hope that dioceses and regions locate and make available their resources for examining missionary life. Why, for example, did the state of New York have the greatest number of priest and religious missionaries in the 1950s and the Midwest, in the same decade, have the largest number of lay missionaries?

A word about the use of the word *American.* Technically, of course, the word refers to both the northern and southern hemispheres in the Western world. Our story, however, treats missionaries sent from the United States. In some cases, a missionary might first have been an immigrant here before being sent overseas by a group located in the United States. In other cases, the person may have been born in the United States but joined a European or Canadian province before being sent overseas to represent that group. Thus, the word *American* is slippery, but, except for some cases where noted, I use it as it is commonly understood; i.e., to refer to the United States.

   To demonstrate the continuity of mission throughout American Catholic history, the narrative begins in 1492. To highlight the main emphasis of the book's examination of the missionary movement overseas from the United States, the beginning date in this introduction, 1841, is the year the U.S. Catholic Church was formally commissioned to send missionaries to Liberia. The closer we get to our own times, the more difficult it is to understand the impact and long-range force of particular events. Our narrative closes in 1980, the year that four American Catholic missionary women were killed in El Salvador, an event which echoed again in the life of Sister Maureen Courtney, CSA, in Nicaragua, the last story of our book. In a work this size, there are bound to be factual errors, for which I take responsibility, though, occasionally, I have found disagreements about facts in the sources themselves.

Chapter 1

Mission in the Colonial Period, 1492–1775

Until fairly recently, the historiography of the Catholic Church in the United States focused on the colonial missions, the Federal period, and the key figures of American ecclesiastical history. Pioneer historians of Catholicism in the United States concentrated on collecting documents which related to the life and interaction of Catholics and Native Americans. John Gilmary Shea (1824–92) spent his few hours after work in the evenings translating original sources, collecting documents, and writing a history of Catholic missions among the First Nations. One aim of Shea's work was to demonstrate that the work of Catholic missions resulted in the perpetuation of tribes, whereas the efforts of Protestant missionaries resulted in the tribes' demise.[1]

John Tracy Ellis (1905–92), the "dean of American Catholic History," examined the documents of the Federal period and the work of James Cardinal Gibbons and provided much more of an interpretive framework for the documents than did Shea. More recent interest in ethnic groups, women's history, and regional history has illuminated the nineteenth- and twentieth-century experience of whole groups of people not examined by early historians of American religious experience, but has also diverted attention from the colonial period. In beginning this narrative of the Catholic overseas mission movement in the United States, we start in that earlier time to note the threads of mission woven throughout the history of people who would often be referred to as "the Americans," though in reality that designation applies to all those in North and South America.[2]

Mission to the peoples of the land, which after 1776 became known as the United States of America, coincided with European expansion, exploration, colonization, and commercial ventures. The countries having the most impact, Spain, France, and England, each brought a distinctive approach to mission with particular perceptions about the people to whom they came. The missionaries arrived in the New World at specific moments in the historical and cultural development of the diverse First Nations. Both European and native cultures had been changed over the centuries through wars, reshuffling of territorial boundaries, introduction of various technologies, and developments in spiritual forces. Spanish missions and colonization affected the life and growth of the Church and society in the lower tip of Florida, Texas, California, and the Southwest. French influence is seen to this day in parts of the northeastern and upper midwestern United States, along the Mississippi River, and in Louisiana. English colonization produced very little by way of mission to Native Americans, especially among Roman Catholics, but from these colonists came the philosophical and political foundations of the United States of America.

As many studies have been written about the colonial period, we will briefly highlight a few perspectives on mission which each of these major European groups brought with them to North America.

Patronato Real and Propaganda Fide

The division of the world by Pope Alexander VI's bull *Inter cetera* (4 May 1493) charged Portugal and the newly united Castile and Aragon with responsibility for the instruction of natives in the Catholic faith.[3] Having driven the Moors from their land, Ferdinand and Isabella were ready for the last great crusade, the evangelization of the native peoples in Spain's newly discovered lands. Responsibility for the spiritual life of the Indians was part of the right of *patronato real* (1508), which included the Crown's authority to oversee Christianity and the Church both in Spain and in its colonies. King Philip II (r. 1556–98) also interpreted his monarchical role to include concern for things religious.[4]

Not all rulers or local governors took this religious responsibility seriously. Vast areas of the world were left with vacancies in the bishop's office for decades at a time because the ruler or governor did not appoint a person to the position. Large geographic sectors, which were the responsibility of one bishop, were completely unmanageable pastorally due to a lack of clergy or inadequate finances.

On 22 June 1622, Pope Gregory XV (r. 1621–23) established the last of the Congregations, the Propaganda Fide, as part of the overall change in and centralization of the administration of the Catholic Church offices. The purpose of the congregation was to seek the return of Protestants to the Catholic Church and to make new converts in the many lands newly discovered by Europeans.[5] Five years later, Pope Urban VIII established the Collegium Urbanum in Rome to train missionaries under papal auspices.[6] The Jesuits were sent to the mission fields, including North America, through their superiors by request of Propaganda Fide. In 1659, in the attempt to bypass the right of *patronato*, Propaganda Fide created vicars apostolic (one who acts as a vicar of the pope) in mission territories.

Missions in New Spain

When the Franciscans came to the New World authorized by the Crown, their ecclesial environment was undergoing various religious and spiritual reforms.[7] In the 1480s, Cardinal Jiménez de Cisneros attempted to revitalize religious institutions through appointment of reform-minded pastors and through confrontation on the practice of concubinage. On this latter point, some friars preferred to emigrate to Morocco and become Muslim rather than to give up their women. Francisco Osuna's *Third Spiritual Alphabet* (1527) emphasized growth in religious knowledge for lay persons in the middle and upper social groups. Reform leaders emerged among the Carmelites and Franciscans to renew their respective orders. This was the century of renewed interest in the written word, the Golden Age of Spanish literature. The University of Alcala was founded (1502–8) and became a center of Catholic humanism and Bible study.

An extension of European power and the discovery of new peoples led to the emergence of the field of international law. Dominican Francisco de Vitoria and Jesuit Francisco Suarez, who followed his methods, discussed issues of freedom and the law, elaborating on the role of the will and conscience, as well as that of authority. Suarez put forth the idea of a natural community of all nations, held together in a moral unity and a quasi-political identity. In this atmosphere, clergy, religious, the Crown, theologians, bishops, and lawyers entertained spirited debates about the nature of the Indian, about war and peace, and about the relationship among the political, ecclesiastical, and economic realms during a lively exploration of the significance of these new peoples for the Crown, for the Church, and for legitimating Spain's claims to internationalism. Juan Ginés de Sepúlveda and Vitoria were well-known participants in the debate. Bartolomé de Las Casas (1474–1566), a Dominican and former secular priest, persuasively defended the rights of the Indian.[8] Pope Paul III's decree *Sublimis Deus*, issued 2 June 1537, which affirmed the spiritual equality of the indigenous peoples and showed Las Casas's influence, contained the Spanish definition of what it meant to be a human being:

> Since man, according to the testimony of the scriptures, has been created to enjoy eternal life and happiness, which none may obtain save through faith in our Lord Jesus Christ, it is necessary that he should possess the nature and faculties enabling him to receive that faith.... Nor is it credible that anyone should possess so little understanding as to desire the faith and yet be destitute of the most necessary faculty to enable him to receive it.... All are capable of receiving the doctrines of the faith. Indians are truly men and they are not only capable of understanding the Catholic Faith but, according to our information, they desire exceedingly to receive it.... The Indians and all other people who may later be discovered by Christians, are by no means to be deprived of their liberty or the possession of their property, even though they be outside the faith of Jesus Christ.[9]

Though they had this sublime doctrine in hand, the Crown's plan was that missionaries could make the natives docile to the Spanish government. More important, converted Indians would become a source of tithes and tribute to the throne.

The stages of Spanish mendicant missions in the sixteenth-century Americas can be roughly charted:

1493–1522: mission centered in the Caribbean,

1524–1560: mission emanating from Mexico and Peru,

1551–1620: church planting from the centers in Mexico and Uma.

The first permanent Spanish settlement in what is now the United States was at St. Augustine, a mission from Spain and the Caribbean. The collective presence of Franciscans and their methodical approach to mission began in 1524 when the "Twelve Apostles" arrived in Mexico under the direction of Fray Martín de Valencia to form the Province of the Holy Gospel. Twelve Dominicans came to Mexico in 1526; the Augustinians arrived in 1533. By 1559, the Franciscans had 380 missionaries in Mexico, the Dominicans had 210, and the Augustinians had 212.[10]

The Franciscans' encounter with the rituals of Aztec civilization and its religious practices led to the destruction of native temples and of objects which in the friars' minds symbolized idolatry. Temples, however, were also used as Aztec fortresses, and Spanish soldiers probably destroyed them after Cortés conquered Mexico.[11] The religious culture and worldview of the First Nations was filled with daily and cyclic references to nature, with communal storytelling, and with sacrifices, sometimes human sacrifices.

Nevertheless, the Franciscans, up until about 1550, tried approaches which reflected their Spanish and Franciscan heritage. They were influenced by the social experiments of Vasco de Quiroga, bishop of Michoacán, a man steeped in Spanish humanist thought. His model of urban communities, based on Thomas More's *Utopia*, was applied to the missions by having potential and new converts live together. Property was held in common, and living expenses were provided through crafts and agriculture.[12]

These sixteenth-century friars also perceived their mission in the context of a millennial background, which they characterized in thematic time frames. In retrospect, there were three time periods: an eschatological framework for the conquest of the New World, which stemmed back to the thirteenth century; the golden age of the Indian Church (1524–64); and the Babylonian captivity of the Indian Church (1564–96).[13] Devoted to the ideal of holy poverty, the friars came to Mexico from a spiritual climate influenced by the teachings of the mystic Joachim of Fiore (1130–1201), who saw the present age as the era of the Holy Spirit, a time when the Church would act under the guidance of mendicants. This attitude might partially explain the reason the friars did not advance a local church under native leaders.

The Franciscan view of the native peoples supported the theoretical presuppositions of *Sublimis Deus,* that the Indians were capable of responding to the message of God. These mendicants noted the religious orientation of the people but saw the worship as misplaced. Because the Indians' ancestors were wise enough to figure out calendar systems and demonstrated other quasi-scientific ideas, the natives were also capable of understanding God, "if they had counseled well among themselves."[14]

The Indians' capacity for the reception of the Faith was also posited from their simple lifestyle, a theme dear to the heart of the Franciscans. Bernardino de Sahagún's description of the Indians' simplicity reads like the life of an observant Franciscan:

> There is hardly anything to hinder the Indians from reaching heaven, nothing like the obstacles which hinder us Spaniards and which submerge us. The Indians live in contentment, though what they possess is so little that they have hardly enough to clothe and nourish themselves. Their meal is extremely poor and the same is true of their clothing; for sleep the majority of them have not even a whole mat. They lose no sleep over acquiring and guarding riches, nor do they kill themselves trying to obtain ranks and dignities.... Their dwellings are very small.... The riches that suffice to fill such dwellings show what treasures the Indians have. These Indians live in their little houses — the parents, the children, and the grandchildren. They eat and drink without much noise and talking. They spend their days peacefully and amicably. They seek only what is necessary to sustain life.[15]

Toribio de Motolinía, one of the "Twelve Apostles" and historian of the Spanish missions, on hearing the oft-spoken Indian word *motolinea*, inquired about its meaning. When told that it meant "poor," he declared, "That shall be my name."[16] This mindset allowed the missionary to identify immediately with those to whom he came. The Indians seemed to possess the angelic spirit and the innocence of Adam and the early church. This innocence was further manifested in the construction of single-nave churches, which, unlike the ornate, many-naved European churches, resembled the church of the apostles.

The friars seemed to want to keep the Indians in a pre-parish or *doctrinero* situation, which meant the Indians would not pay taxes to the Crown and the mission would not come under the jurisdiction of the bishop. After the mid-1600s, the bishops remonstrated with the friars about this situation.

The sixteenth-century friars learned the native language and wrote dictionaries and grammar books for the indigenous dialects. Bernardino de Sahagún (1499–1590) spent his life in the study of the religion, language, traditions, and history of the native peoples of Mexico and published his impressive, encyclopedic *Historia general de las cosas de Nueva España* (1583) in defense of indigenous culture. Knowledge of the religious worldview of the peoples was necessary, he maintained, in order for the physician to "treat his patient properly."

And just as it is necessary for the physician to have a perfect knowledge of remedies and maladies in order to apply to each of the latter that which tends to counteract it, in like manner it is necessary for preachers and confessors, who are the true physicians of souls in spiritual sicknesses, to gain a knowledge of spiritual maladies and the medicines they require. The preacher must know the vices of the country to exercise his zeal there, and the confessor must be no less conversant with those vices, to the end that he may make them the basis of his questions and understand what his penitents are accusing themselves of in their confessions.[17]

The book was compiled with the help of Indians and was written in Nahuatl and in Spanish. This ethno-linguistic treatment of First Nation experience demonstrated the latter's capacity for commerce, art, religion, and leadership, and was meant to show the natives "the manner in which they had been led astray and thus appropriate their Indian identity in a Christian context."[18]

Such creative steps were less common among the Franciscans after 1555, the year of the first ecclesiastical synod of Mexico. Over the next ten years, an almost anti-native spirit seemed to dominate the church dignitaries. The original "Twelve" had died and early enthusiasm seemed far away. Translation of sacred texts into native languages was forbidden, and Philip II forbade writing about native customs.[19] Spanish surnames were given to Indian converts. The concern for orthodoxy, the establishment of the Inquisition, and the embroilments around Protestantism soon found their way across the Atlantic Ocean.

After 1768, when Spain expelled the Jesuits, the Franciscan mission presence extended from the mission College of San Fernando to the southwestern parts of the present United States.[20] The leader of this new venture was Junipero Serra (1713–84), who had come from his birthplace in Majorca as a missionary to the Americas in 1750. He worked among the Indians in Sierra Gorda for nine years and then returned to the college,[21] preaching missions among the Mexicans for seven years. On 14 July 1767, after the Viceroy had requested the Franciscans to take responsibility for the missions left vacant by the Jesuits, Serra set out with eight friars for California and Sonora. Over the succeeding years he established the first nine of the missions, which eventually stretched from San Diego de Alcala to Sonoma, California.

Serra still carried remnants of the millennial thinking of the "Twelve Apostles" to Mexico. In his *Diary,* the missionary remarked on hearing of the conversion of a "Gentile Captain" and forty-four men, women, and children on his *ranchería:*

I was infinitely rejoiced, and wrote to the Father a thousand congratulations. I begged him that so honest a Captain should be the first he baptized, and should be called Francisco, in reverence to our Father St. Francis, from whose intercession I devoutly believe this happy novelty proceeded, which is in fulfillment of the word which God has given in these last centuries, and is affirmed by the Venerable Mother Maria de Jesus de Agreda, that, at only the sight of the sons of St. Francis, the Gentiles shall be converted to our Holy Faith.[22]

Serra maintained an optimistic attitude, hoping "that the [Indians] would fall shortly into the apostolic and evangelic net."[23] The policy in California became more militant, paternalistic, and rigid in discipline than had been true in earlier times and in other parts of the Spanish New World. Franciscan response to the indigenous population, who to the friars appeared less than diligent, kept the missionaries from accepting the natives as "adults." Their place in the Church would be as catechumen or laity, but not as ordained ministers. Whether the natives could receive the Eucharist continued to be a matter of disagreement among the friars. Many friars no longer sought to learn the native language but taught the natives Spanish.

The friars' approach to mission in California brought the catechumens together for significant periods of time. The friars thought that if the Indians remained among their families they would be tempted to return to former customs and practices. Grouped together, the natives would also be kept from the harmful influences of the Spanish soldiers. The missions became beehives of social, economic, and artistic activity as friars taught the Indians various trades and skills needed to create mission buildings and accouterments. It seemed ironic that while the friars of the sixteenth century had praised the simple lifestyle of the Nahuatl Indians, the friars of the eighteenth century sought to upgrade the natives' economic life.

While the Franciscans, Dominicans, Augustinians, and Mercedarians had entered the New World under the patronage of the Spanish Crown, Jesuits embarked under the authority of the superiors on the request of Propaganda Fide, the mission-sending agency of the Catholic Church in Rome. The first Jesuit mission in North America was in Florida, though that mission was abandoned after several murders of soldiers and missionaries in 1566.[24] The first missionary efforts in what is now Arizona were the work of the remarkable Jesuit Eusebio Kino (1644–1711), who had come to Mexico from Tyrol in 1681.[25] His Sonora and Arizona mission work, which started in 1687, included cartography, the introduction of stock cattle, and the founding of several missions. After his death, however, these missions began to languish, and when the Franciscans came to the area, only three modest missions were in operation.

The "Blackrobes," who arrived in New Spain, were educated in a southern European "renaissance curriculum," the *ratio studiorum* of Jesuit education. Music, literature, and visual arts were offered alongside science, astronomy, and arithmetic. The Jesuit "reductions," which brought the Indians together in mission areas, became models of well-managed property, with surplus products sold for the purchase of items not available at the mission.[26] An official visitor to a Sonora mission commented that, while the mission area was remote from other reductions, the music, singing, and liturgical celebrations were excellent and provided a sort of witness to the natives.

Like the early group of Franciscans before them, the Jesuits developed a facility for native languages. Seminarians who sought ordination could not pass their exams without knowledge of at least one Indian dialect. The Jesuits sent promising sons of chiefs to a regional college for education.

Much of all the missionaries' efforts under Spanish rule was thwarted because of wars, both European and Indian, uprisings among native peoples, lack of understanding of those whom the missionaries visited, and through unjust and cruel treatment of the Indians by the government and sometimes by the missionaries. In many cases, mission work was abandoned after Indian attacks; many years often passed before missionaries tried again to evangelize the First Nations. The California missions dwindled in influence during the Mexican period, from 1821 to 1846, and the buildings themselves started to decay. However, in some cases, church people of various cultural backgrounds continued to form parish and diocesan churches.[27]

French Missions[28]

Seventeenth-century ecclesiastical France had two evident theological currents: Jansenism, characterized by a pessimistic view of the human person and moral rigorism, and Gallicanism, which attempted to make the French Church independent of the papacy and subservient to the French Crown.[29] Both circles were suspicious of the Jesuits, the first viewing them as lax, the second not appreciating their ultramontanist views which stressed the rights and independence of Rome in dealing with the Church in France. The French held little respect for both lower and higher clergy, and leaders of the French School of Spirituality sought reforms in priestly formation. Among the leaders were Pierre de Bérulle (the Oratory), Jean Jacques Olier (the Company of Saint Sulpice), and John Eudes (the Congregation of Jesus and Mary), all of whom emphasized interior holiness in tandem with evangelization. The same century witnessed the formation of several mission congregations, including the Paris Foreign Mission Society and the Congregation of the Mission. However, in the attempt to "raise up" the importance of the priesthood, Bérulle saw the priest as distant from the people:

> In the order established by God, there are two types of people: those who receive and those who communicate Christ's spirit, light and grace. The former are all the faithful; the latter are the priests and superiors, who exert an influence on their inferiors and who themselves must imitate the angels above.[30]

It was amidst this ecclesiastical and spiritual atmosphere that missionaries went overseas.

In the course of French exploration of the New World, settlements appeared in Canada, Maine, upstate New York, Upper Michigan, Wisconsin, and Illinois, as well as up and down the Mississippi River. The charting of the land and of the river courses was the task of explorers, such as Samuel de Champlain, Robert Cavelier de la Salle, and Antoine de la Mothe Cadillac, and missionaries or chaplains, such as Jacques Marquette and Louis Hennepin. Seventeenth-century French missions to native peoples were influenced by France's economic policies in the colonies and by their location, often on the rim between English and French territorial claims and, therefore, frequently subject to the effects of war between the two European powers.[31]

While Jacques Cartier had reached the Gaspé Peninsula in 1534 and preached to the native peoples through interpreters, no settlement occurred in the area until Samuel de Champlain arrived in 1604. Four years later he founded Québec and invited four Recollect Franciscans to instruct the French young boys and to evangelize the Indians. After the restoration of the French colonies, the Jesuits returned to French Canada in 1632 and the Recollects arrived in 1670 on the advice of a governor antagonistic toward the Jesuits. The Company of One Hundred Associates, who settled Ville-Marie (Québec), had hoped to create a family environment for Christians based on the model of the apostolic community in Jerusalem. One Company member, Ursuline Sister Marie de l'Incarnation, founded Canada's first school for girls in 1639 and remained an important advisor for both men and women.[32] Marguerite Bourgeoys (1620–1700) opened a school for girls and, eventually, one for indigenous people. In 1658 she founded the Sisters of the Congregation of Notre Dame. Four Sulpician priests came to Montreal in 1657 and established a seminary there in 1672. In 1659, Bishop François de Montmorency Laval erected a "foreign missions" seminary in Québec. Graduates were sent to the tribes in the southern Mississippi valley in 1689 and made Cahokia, Illinois, their mission center.

Present-day Maine, the border area between the French and English colonies, was in turmoil frequently throughout the 1600s. Both European groups sought Indian assistance in their wars, and the two countries encouraged brutality and destruction of villages in the process. In this geographic area, the Jesuits worked among the Abenakis, who became a Catholic tribe. The Jesuits also traveled with Samuel de Champlain to New York. Champlain had devised a policy of aligning the colonies with one set of Indians (the Ontario Hurons, Montagnais, Algonquins), which he thought would guarantee the development of the fur trade. In the process, the Iroquois became the colonies' enemies. This economic strategy caused grave problems when the Jesuits tried to work among the Iroquois, a confederacy of five Nations throughout New York. The death of Isaac Jogues and four other Jesuits near Auriesville, New York, between 1642 and 1649 was part of the general Huron conflagration initiated by the Iroquois, the Hurons' enemies. The Hurons were the main conduit for the French fur industry.[33] After this massacre, many Christian Hurons fled north to Canada. Reflecting on the deaths of his Jesuit companions, J. M. Chaumonot wrote to the Québec mission superior, whose nephew had also been killed by Indians earlier that month:

> Precious burnt-offering of those virtuous Fathers! ... We all, as many Fathers as we are here, have never loved our vocation more, than after having seen that it can raise us even to the glory of martyrdom; there is nothing by my imperfections which can make me give up my part. ... I have been for a month at Ahwendoe, on the Island of St. Joseph, where most of our poor Hurons have taken refuge; it is here that I see a part of the miseries which war and famine have caused to this poor desolate people.[34]

These unstable conditions also presented a problem for Jesuit mission strategy in their new situation among the Hurons:

> It is difficult for the faith to remain alive in these countries, unless we have a place which may be, as it were, the center of all our Missions; whence we can send the Preachers of the Gospel into the Nations who are spread abroad in all these regions; and where we can assemble from time to time, in order to confer there on the means which God will supply to us for procuring his glory, and on the light that he shall give us for that purpose. This house of Sainte Marie, where we have been until now, was at the most advantageous location that we could have chosen for this purpose, wherever we might have been. But, affairs being in the condition in which we see them now, it would be but rashness in us to dwell in a forsaken place, whence the Hurons had retired, and where the Algonquins were unable to have further trade; not one would come to see us there, unless the Enemies, who would discharge upon us alone the whole weight of their hostility. Consequently, we are resolved to follow our flock, and to flee with the fleeing, since we do not live here for ourselves, but for the salvation of souls, and for the conversion of these Peoples.[35]

Jean de Brébeuf, one of those martyred in 1649, had written guidelines for the kind of missionary who should be sent to work with the tribes. After noting that the missionary must have a "sincere affection for the Savages," who were "ransomed by the blood of the Son of God" and who were "brothers" to the Jesuits, Brébeuf gave specific advice based on his experience. When traveling, missionaries were not to be late or to be troublesome to the Indians, were to carry their own canoes, to keep silent in difficult times, and to keep comforts few. He wrote that Indians did not care for philosophy or theology. What made for a "gentleman" in France was despicable to the natives, who valued physical strength.

> If you go naked and carry the load of a horse upon your back, as they do, then you would be wise according to their doctrine, and would be recognized as a great man, otherwise not. Jesus Christ is our true greatness;

it is He alone and His cross that should be sought in running after these people, for if you strive for anything else, you will find naught but bodily and spiritual affliction. But having found Jesus Christ in His Cross, you have found the roses in the thorns, sweetness in bitterness, all in nothing.[36]

These prescriptions served as a warning that French manners and customs and the French way of being a priest of the First Estate of the Realm would not suffice in this wilderness situation. But one would have the strength to adopt new manners by focusing on the crucified Jesus, presumably through the use of the Spiritual Exercises, requiring the active use of imagination to place oneself in the various scenes in Christ's life.

Louisiana's cosmopolitan area was served by Québec seminary clergy, after the foundation of Biloxi (1699) and New Orleans (1718). In 1722, the vast area controlled by France in what is now the United States was divided among four religious groups: the Jesuits and Québec priests in the Midwest, the Capuchins in the lower Mississippi, and the Carmelites in Mobile. In 1726, the Jesuits took responsibility for all the Indian missions. One attempt was made by the Oneida Indians, apparently at the instigation of a Frenchman, Pierre Penet, to request a separate episcopal jurisdiction for the Six Nations in upstate New York. This occurred between 1779 and 1780 and was not successful, probably because the move was politically motivated.[37]

Jacques Marquette was among the more well-known Jesuits in the upper Midwest,[38] while Louis Hennepin became known among the Recollects because of his writings about the people and places of the French colonies. Hennepin (1625–c. 1701), Belgian by birth, joined the Recollects in France and preached missions in Holland. This friar's "inclination to travel" found fulfillment when he came as one of four chaplains with the La Salle expeditions. While he himself did not spend much time evangelizing the Indians, he wrote down his many impressions of what he observed. His *Description of Louisiana* identifies what he saw as obstacles to the conversion of the Indians. These included what he termed complacency, "superstitions," and a migratory lifestyle.[39] Further difficulties were the acquisition by missionaries of native dialects, diverse opinions about the best method of evangelizing the Indians, and the Dutch and English "spirit of lucre." He did not note the last attribute as a problem among the French, nor did he mention the problems the French themselves brought: the use of Indian women for prostitution, promotion of liquor trade with the Indians, and laws prohibiting Indian widows from inheriting their husbands' property.[40]

The royal Code Noir (1724) sought to rectify some of the abuses of slavery in Louisiana but required owners' permission for slaves to marry one another. Religions besides Roman Catholicism were outlawed and Jews were ordered out of the area, legislation based on the principle in France of the union of church and state.

The French Jesuits' organized mission work ended in 1763 with the dissolution of the society.[41] Tribal wars and the loss of French colonies reduced the missions considerably. Secular priests took over some of the work in French areas after the Jesuits left, and a few priests from the Québec seminary served the area. But the French mission to natives faded away, especially as the Indians were pushed farther west.

Six Ursuline nuns, one novice, and two Ursuline lay Sisters sailed from France to New Orleans in August 1727 under contract with the Dutch West India Company and on the persistent appeal of the Jesuit superior general of the Louisiana missions.[42] The women were to "relieve the sick poor" and provide especially for the education of young, adept Creole girls. Within nine months, the Ursulines' school contained twenty boarders, three "lady" boarders, and seven slave boarders. They also taught a large number of "day-scholars and negresses and savages who come two hours a day to be instructed."[43] The Sisters received two black boarders, one six years old, the other seventeen, who were to serve the Sisters while gaining instruction in religion. With all their boarders the Sisters were quite successful, and many of the young women wished to become Ursuline Sisters. However, the Jesuit superior thought it more expedient for these young ladies to become "Christian mothers, in order to establish religion in this country by their good example."[44] The Ursulines' work at the Royal Hospital in the eighteenth century blended spiritual and physical healing with the introduction of prayer to Our Lady of Prompt Succor, a shrine which became an important devotional center in New Orleans.

The French Sulpicians in October 1791 began a seminary in Baltimore. At that time, Gabriel Richard (1767–1832), a Sulpician emigré from the political turmoil in France, arrived at the seminary and received an assignment to work in Detroit, Upper Michigan, and Wisconsin.[45] In addition to his mission work over a vast geographic area, he became a pioneer in education, a publisher, and an elected representative in the U.S. Congress (1823). The last French mission came under the jurisdiction of the diocese of Baltimore on 1 June 1796, twenty years after the English colonies gained their independence.[46]

English Missions

The formation of the Church of England after King Henry VIII's break with Rome and rival political powers Catholic Spain and France was just one reason for the antipathy between English Protestants and Catholics. Few Catholics came to the English colonies. The largest Catholic population lived in Maryland, though other Catholics settled along the Atlantic coast, as far south as Virginia and west into Pennsylvania. George Calvert brought the first two English secular priests to Newfoundland in 1627.

As members of the first permanent settlement of English colonists, Andrew White, SJ, and two other Jesuits arrived among the Catholic and Protestant passengers of the *Ark and Dove,* which docked along the Potomac River in March 1634.[47] They purchased land from King Yaocomico, whose tribe was being invaded in that area by the Susquehanoes. The transaction helped both Indians and settlers, because Yaocomico's tribe wanted to move away from its Indian adversaries. After the Catholics established themselves, having endured much sickness and epidemics spawned by the marshy lands, they became relatively well-to-do. Their economic situation was hampered, however, by various penal laws issued against them by the royal government and by anti-Catholic harassment. Economically and professionally they were a diverse group, ranging from plantation owners to those who worked the tobacco fields along with the more numerous black slaves. The majority of priests who came to the English colonies belonged to the Society of Jesus. From 1634 to 1776, over 130 Jesuit priests and Brothers settled in Maryland and Pennsylvania; the largest number at one time was twenty, in 1773.[48]

White came to the colonies as a missionary to Indians. After slowly acquiring the native language, both he and Roger Rigby, SJ, wrote a grammar, catechism, and dictionary in Piscataway. To do this, the Jesuits set up the first printing press in the English colonies.[49] The first chapel in what would become the seat of the American Catholic Church after the Revolution was the chapel the natives used.[50] It had taken about five years since their arrival for the two priests to go among the Indians beyond their immediate area, due to periodic Indian attacks on farms farther away from St. Mary's City. White and four Jesuits (three priests and one Brother) then ventured to the main Piscataway village, where Chief Chitomachen, his family, and some of his tribe were converted. White had been living in this Tayac's abode. The chief sent his daughter to St. Mary's City for her education, where she became a ward of Margaret Brent and married her brother, Giles.[51] White then moved about fifty miles to Port Tobacco, where a young queen of the Indians there was baptized along with a number of her subjects.

Other Jesuits traveled the rivers of Maryland to additional tribes, though the priests needed interpreters for their work. The mission to the Indians in Maryland ceased after Richard Ingle's rebellion, when the missions were looted and White and fellow Jesuit Thomas Copley were captured and sent to England for trial. The English Jesuits thereafter worked with the colonists.[52]

The Federal Period

Eighteenth-century English Catholicism gradually became centered on the manors of the landed gentry and was generally characterized in Maryland by tolerance toward Protestants. The Jesuit farms became the hub of religious activity, changing from centers for mission activity into parishes,[53] and the values and perspectives of the landed gentry came to characterize the Catholic Church after the American Revolution. Its new leader, John Carroll (1735–

1815),[54] was born in Maryland, educated and ordained in Europe, and had been a Jesuit until the society's dissolution in 1773. Technically, the Catholic Church in America fell under the spiritual authority of the vicar apostolic of the London District. After the Revolution, Carroll and his confreres argued for a Church authority independent of England. Carroll pressed Rome about the uniqueness of the American situation. He saw the country not as a mission (and therefore under the governance of Propaganda Fide's authority) but as a Church with "regular clergy," not missionary clergy. As he noted to Ferdinand Farmer in Pennsylvania,

> We form not a fluctuating body of labourers in Christ's vineyard, sent hither and removeable at the will of a Superior; but a permanent body of national Clergy, with sufficient powers to form our own system of internal government, and I think, to chuse [sic] our own Superior, and a very just claim to have all necessary Spiritual authority communicated to him, on his being presented as regularly and canonically chosen by us.[55]

In 1784 Carroll was appointed superior of the Mission of the United States and in 1790 became the first bishop of the Catholic Church in the new country. His first report to Propaganda Fide on 1 March 1785 noted the numbers of Catholics who were settlers and "negroes," but made no mention of the number of Catholic Indians.

A single effort at mission work overseas began almost immediately after the Revolution. Born in Port Tobacco, Maryland, and educated in England, Leonard Neale (1746–1817), an austere Jesuit, appears to be the first Roman Catholic from the United States who worked as a missionary overseas. He received authorization from Propaganda Fide to work among the settlers and natives in Demerara, British Guiana, from 1780 to 1782. He found the natives more amenable to his message than the settlers, who harbored animosity toward Jesuits. Neale returned to the United States and subsequently became rector of Georgetown College (1798) and the second archbishop of Baltimore (1815).[56] The French-founded Ursuline Sisters in Louisiana, then under Spanish rule in New Orleans, sent some Sisters to Cuba to found a school in 1802 in the event that their New Orleans foundation were closed. This occurred the year before the Louisiana Purchase. The superior of this Louisiana convent wrote to Thomas Jefferson in 1804 to inquire what impact the administration of a "Protestant" United States government might have on their property and religion.[57]

The first Catholic overseas mission effort from the established United States occurred during the administration of John Carroll, who was given jurisdiction of the Virgin Islands in 1804. Two priests of the Congregation of the Holy Ghost, Henry Kendal and Matthew Hérard, who had been working there since 1793, were named prefect and vice prefect, respectively. Hérard continued to work in the Islands until 1819.[58]

Conclusions

The success or failure of the missionary movement in colonial times depended more often on the economic and political nature of the relationship between a European church and state than on the strength of Indian conversions or the zeal or methods of particular missionaries. The message of salvation came along with economic assumptions. Both Spanish and French governments viewed missionaries' relationships with the First Nations as significant for the royal coffers or for business. While missionaries decried the "filthy lucre" motives of Spanish and French settlers, Franciscan friars in New Spain often characterized the natives as "lax," and sought to have them work and store up food and other products for the future. Among the Hurons, the fur industry made individual Indians more wealthy, but the use of that wealth illustrated the natives' different social values. That Indians "gave away" accumulated wealth to tribal members seemed not in keeping with the aims of French economics.[59] The dual roles of the French clergy, who served as agents for French commerce and French interests as well as missionaries, were often in conflict.

Mission incorporated a holistic framework and mindset. The spiritual imagery of the "Twelve Apostles" influenced their interpretation of those they came to evangelize, their manner of setting up the mission, and their architecture. The creation of "middle spaces" — mission compounds — between the tribes and the conquistadors was meant to keep Indians distant from the unsavory witness of both groups. Generally, missionaries preached individual salvation amidst Indian values that honored the collective.[60] Jesuits, for the most part, lived among the natives and followed them in their itinerancy, even though the Jesuits hoped for reductions, as they had in Paraguay.[61] In keeping with the Ignatian notion of leadership, more chiefs seem to have been converted in Jesuit missions than by the Franciscans.

One explanation for failures in the Spanish missions is that the missionaries came from an intellectual climate of literacy and reason, whereas the First Nations were an oral and visual culture. For Europeans, the understanding of religious truth was primarily rational. The description of the Indian, given in *Sublimis Deus,* emphasized this aspect of the human person. The missionaries reasoned that the natives would want to learn Spanish, the language of "civilization," even as the Spanish had learned Latin, the language of Roman culture. By destroying some of the pictographs and other visual "memory" of the tribes, missionaries were actually "erasing" a key link in Indian oral culture.[62]

Nevertheless, significant developments in mission occurred in colonial times. First, several of the men became historians and ethnologists of the First Nations. Though their mindset was limited and prejudiced according to modern standards, Mendieta's four-volume *Historia eclesiástica indiana,* Motolinía's *Historia de los indios de la Nueva España,* Las Casas's *Historia de las in-*

dias, and Sahagún's *Historia general de las cosas de Nueva España* provide an outside view of the First Nations and much insight and understanding of the interior world and life of these people.

In comparison with the reports of the explorers, the missionaries provided Europe with a fairly large body of literature about a land and people unknown to the majority of the Spanish, French, and English. Publication of *The Jesuit Relations* started in 1632 and was an inexpensive way to raise support for the missions. In 1673 publication ceased due to the debate over the Chinese rites. Pope Clement X forbade any publication of mission literature without Propaganda Fide approval. However, descriptions of the First Nations over the course of the seventeenth century provided a body of literature and evoked images that in the following century led Jean Jacques Rousseau (1712–78) to construct his symbolic "noble savage" as a critique of French manners. The philosopher presented the romantic conception that this natural, "pristine" existence was characteristic of humans, who became corrupted only when they were exposed to "civilization." In addition to the popular mission documents, objects sent home by missionaries, such as headdresses, hatchets, and pipes, also fed the European imagination.

Jesuits, particularly skilled in mapmaking, used cartography to send theological messages to European Catholics. Surrounding the delineation of rivers, mountains, and plains, the men frequently drew figures and symbols reflecting the motifs of enlightenment. One map, for example, which pictures the martyrdom of John de Brébeuf and Gabriel Lalemant, displays the light of the cross rebuffing the darkness, and "through representation of their death into the grid of Euclidean space" the map universalizes the martyrdom theme. America was a new area of the world in which the forces of good and evil, of light and darkness, would play out.[63]

Lay persons also took an active role in evangelization. In the Jesuit New York missions, at least three people among the First Nations provided significant religious leadership. Daniel Garacontié was an Onondaga chief who strove to make peace among the Iroquois tribes. A woman from the Erie tribe, adopted as an Oneida, aided Jacques Bruyas in his study of their language. She converted to Catholicism and, after her baptism as Catherine Ganneaktena, was responsible for the conversion of many Indians in the village of La Prairie. Kateri Tekakwitha (1656–80), daughter of a Mohawk father and a Christian Algonquin mother, engaged in catechetical work among her people.[64]

Not surprisingly, with adverse political and ecclesial feelings running high in Europe and the New World throughout the colonial period, the rift of the Reformation had effects on the American Catholic Church and on the missions. French missionary Sébastien Râle, who had spent thirty years among the Abenaki, was killed in 1724 by New England militia and Indians; his scalp and those of some Indians were paraded in Boston.

The increase in the size of the United States after 1803 meant that ecclesiastical responsibilities would multiply, as well. In addition, the number of immigrants, especially from Ireland and Germany, would occupy the pastoral concern of the bishops and of the men and women who formed religious congregations, who assisted the new arrivals. Meanwhile, the mission to Native Americans and black Americans continued with diminished priority for the American Catholic Church.

Chapter 2

Mission within the United States, 1820–1920

Four significant trends and events affected the mission movement within the United States in the nineteenth century: the acquisition of new land; the increased numbers of immigrants, especially after the 1840s; the Civil War; and government policies toward Native Americans. On 17 September 1789, the vicariate of Baltimore was raised to the status of a diocese, and became an archdiocese in 1808. The United States acquired vast holdings beyond the old Northwest Territory, including land gained from the Louisiana Purchase (1803); the Red River basin (1818); Florida (1819); Texas (1845); southern areas of present-day New Mexico and Arizona, acquired in the Gadsden Purchase (1845); the Oregon Territory (1846); territory ceded by Mexico (1848); Alaska (1867); and Hawaii (1898). These areas eventually came under the jurisdiction of U.S. bishops or vicars apostolic. Much of nineteenth-century Catholicism was really frontier Catholicism, and a litany of its missionary names would include the missionary in Kentucky, Charles Nerinckx (1761–1824), who brought the first Jesuits to the West, including Pierre Jean De Smet (1801–73), Rose Philippine Duchesne (1769–1852) in St. Charles, Missouri,[1] and Samuel Mazzuchelli, OP (1806–64), who established the first Catholic Church in Wisconsin, and who opened a school for Menominee Indian children.[2]

Mission to Immigrants

For the first seven decades of the nineteenth century, a number of bishops were responsible for people spread throughout the expansive land masses, which could only be termed *missions*. This was particularly true in the South, parts of the Midwest, and the West.[3]

John England was among the notable missionary bishops before the Civil War. Born in Cork, Ireland, England (1786–1842) was ordained on 21 September 1840 and worked first at the Cathedral of St. Mary's, then as a pastor in Bandon. He had taken a mission vow and had first requested Propaganda Fide to send him to Australia, but, later, he asked to be sent to the United States. He was appointed bishop of Charleston, South Carolina, in 1820.[4] Well known today for the constitution he wrote for his diocese, which comprised North and South Carolina and Georgia, England displayed an ecclesiology which was consultative and collaborative. The constitution called for a "House" of the laity and a "House" of the clergy to be convened annually, giving "voice and vote" in building the local church. Because the Church members (about eleven thousand Catholics, of whom one thousand were slaves) were scattered throughout the diocese, he saw the importance of the "visibility" of members, each to the other, as a means of support and encouragement in the faith.[5] This was no small task, as his diocese was not only far-flung and racially diverse, but elements of lay trusteeism were present, too.[6] He traveled around his diocese, drawing the small groups together for prayer, study, and conversation, while seeing himself as "embodying" the geographically dispersed members.[7] He further promoted unity in the small Catholic community by editing the first Catholic newspaper printed in the United States, the *United States Catholic Miscellany,* which brought the members of the diocese in touch with each other and with the Church around the world. He urged this same sense of collaboration among the bishops, and, through his efforts, the first provincial councils of Baltimore were held. In 1829 he founded the Sisters of Our Lady of Mercy in Charleston to educate black and poor white girls. He later inaugurated the missionary Society of Saint John the Baptist to provide financial aid to missionaries working throughout the diocese. He hoped a seminary could be founded for such purposes. England died after an illness he contracted while preaching in Philadelphia and Baltimore to raise money for the U.S. Catholic mission to Liberia.

By far the greatest amount of the American Catholic Church's effort, time, and money provided for the pastoral care and social needs of nineteenth-century immigrants, mainly from Ireland and Germany. The ports of the North Atlantic seaboard swelled with greater numbers as the century passed.[8] The documents of the six provincial councils of Baltimore (1829–46) and the three Baltimore Plenary Councils (1852–84) bear out a state of solicitude. However, in almost all parts of the country, bishops were working in regions which were mixed racially and ethnically, even though one group might have predominated in a given diocese. Leadership among bishops and laity in the nineteenth century forged a Church distinctive in important ways from the European Church. The story is important and has already been well told.[9] Rather than aim at completeness in telling the story of the nineteenth century, this chapter will highlight a few representative persons or groups who worked with immigrants, African Americans, and Native Americans and identify the approaches to mission they took to meet the needs they found.

Irish and Germans had been immigrating to America since the seventeenth century. After 1820, however, the numbers increased, and soon the tapestry of the Catholic Church in the United States showed signs of tangling due to the immigrants' cultural differences. Political disagreements between bishops and laity over the control of Church property (trusteeism) led to attacks that Catholics were "foreign" and, hence, not American, because the head of the Church government was in Rome. Attendance at public schools, where the Protestant version of the Bible was read daily, seemed to promote a loss of Catholic faith. Many of the immigrants who arrived, first at Castle Garden, then at Ellis Island and Angel Island in San Francisco Bay, seemed religiously illiterate. National parishes sprang up in cities, with membership defined by the language spoken. Immigrant mutual-aid associations, such as the German Catholic Central Verein (1855), the Irish Catholic Benevolence Union (1869), the Polish Roman Catholic Union (1874), and the Catholic Slovak Union (1890), formed representative organizations for economic protection, especially if a family worker were injured or ill, and also provided a location to discuss other topics relative to the needs of immigrants.[10] The Catholic Church, like other groups, endured periodic attacks from nativists or from other anti-Catholic propagandists.

The Practice of Bishops

Between 1829 and 1846 the American bishops held six provincial councils in Baltimore; between 1852 and 1884 they held three plenary councils. At these latter gatherings, archbishops and bishops from around the country shared their experience, wisdom, and concerns about the Church in their part of the land. Immediate pastoral care of Catholics who had little or no religious education, the spiritual and intellectual life of the clergy, and the administration of sacraments were priorities. But the bishops' agenda was as varied as the people in their dioceses.

In 1829, the Baltimore Council urged priests to be men of prayer and effective preachers, who sought "not to exhibit the individual or gain applause but [are] reminded that we are preaching the doctrines of a crucified Redeemer." Pastors were to "have a few good books and keep them in constant use."[11] Clergy and laity were urged to study the Scriptures. The American Church was informed of the need to educate its own clergy rather than to rely on clergy from Europe, some of whom were renegade priests or in disrepute. The pastoral letter of the Second Provincial Council (1833) again exhorted clergy and laity to study the Bible. Sections of the pastoral spoke of missions to Native Americans and of the Lyons (Society for the Propagation of the Faith) and Vienna (Leopoldine) mission agencies, which were sending funds to bishops in Louisiana, Kentucky, Boston, and to other parts of the United States. The first Plenary Council of Baltimore (1852) requested the establishment of a sodality to pray for the conversion of non-Catholics.

Difficulties arose often between the Irish and Germans, especially in acculturating to American society, a phenomenon which appeared in various ways into the twentieth century. By the end of the century, bishops with Irish surnames predominated among the hierarchy. Not only were there political and cultural adjustments for all immigrants, but changes in language and religious expression were closely related as well. The slogan "language saves faith" was attributed to Swiss-born John Martin Henni (1805–81), a man who championed the voice of German immigrants in their new surroundings. He had studied at St. Gall, Lucerne, and in Rome and arrived at the Bardstown, Kentucky, seminary in 1829 to finish his priestly preparation.[12] Ordained for the Cincinnati Archdiocese, he took a census of the Germans in Ohio and learned firsthand about their needs in the new country. In 1834 he became the vicar general and pastor for Germans in Cincinnati and developed a varied program for the immigrants. He began English classes for adults, founded a newspaper, *Der Wahrheitsfreund,* introduced better liturgical music, wrote a German catechism for children, and planned for a bilingual seminary to educate native clergy. As a reminder to German immigrants and as a notice to those who attacked immigrants for their "foreignness," Henni often reprinted the "Creed of a Nineteenth Century Citizen" in his newspaper. Items included belief in the "brotherhood of all," love of God and of one's neighbor as the core of religion, and the importance of all kinds of work, including agriculture, trade, and manufacturing, to benefit the good of society. He added:

> I believe in tolerance, and that persecution because of religious belief is one of the most abominable scourges on earth, like the plague, small-pox, famine, and war....
>
> I believe that diligence, the social virtues, and good morals are far more useful than religious wrangling....
>
> I believe that the best of all governments is one wherein all abide by the laws, and that the laws themselves can be no better enforced than by the will of an upright and virtuous people....
>
> I believe that courage, valor, and love of country are the first foundations of mankind and are the most useful to the State.[13]

In 1843, Henni became Milwaukee's first bishop and in 1875 its first archbishop. In his first year in Milwaukee the Catholic population was concentrated mainly in the northern part of Wisconsin around Green Bay and consisted largely of Native Americans, the result of the work of the Dominican Samuel Mazzuchelli and Frederic Baraga. Northern Wisconsin had a parish of seven hundred Indians and those of mixed ancestry. Henni visited these native groups, though he never learned any of their languages. He was well known to the Ludwig Missionsverein in Munich, which supplied funds for his diocese's Native Americans and immigrants.[14] Within two years of his arrival in Milwaukee, the composition of the diocese drastically changed. The number of German Catholic residents increased from seven thousand to nineteen thousand, a figure which continued to rise over the next years. Wisconsin became the northern point of the "German triangle" in the United States. For his defense of German Catholics in the face of nativism and for his pastoral care, he acquired the accolades "Apostle of the Germans" and "the Las Casas of the German immigrants."

The consecration of the Milwaukee diocesan cathedral in 1853 was solemnized through a mission given to the priests and laity. Henni encouraged appropriate liturgical music, promoted fine art, and developed an excellent personal library. Among the many journals he kept were *Brownson's Quarterly Review* and the *Catholic World*. Henni edited and published the works of John England and founded St. Francis de Sales Seminary (1856), which provided clergy for Wisconsin, Minnesota, and the Middle West. The graduates went on to assume significant leadership in liturgical practice and to promote social-justice teachings. Through pastoral leadership, such as that of John Martin Henni, large numbers of immigrants became active members of the Catholic Church in their adopted country.

Women Religious

The number of women's religious congregations increased steadily over the century, with a noticeable expansion after the Irish potato famine and the *Kulturkampf*.[15] Widespread poverty, especially among Irish women, the problems of alcoholism and prostitution, the accidents that came with increasing industrialization, and premature death were part of many urban immigrants' lives. Religious communities in the East responded to these social problems. New York's archbishop, John Hughes, invited the Mercy Sisters to open a House of Mercy in 1846 to "protect" Irish immigrant women. The Sisters of Charity, Mount St. Vincent on Hudson, New York, began a foundling asylum in which babies were admitted irrespective of the physical condition or the marital status of the mother.[16] Women religious opened fledgling hospitals, which, by the end of the century, became city landmarks. Some women's congregations opened schools for well-to-do young ladies and used some of that tuition money to fund schools for poorer children. Parish schools, staffed by Sisters and, sometimes, by Brothers, became more of a norm, especially after the Third Baltimore Council. The Irish, though, tended to favor the public schools.

Such responses to social problems typified the Midwest and the West as well. The cholera epidemic in 1849 left many children without parents, and that year the Sisters of St. Francis of Assisi, Milwaukee, started St. Aemilian's Orphanage to care for them. The institution continues to the present, though with an emphasis on assisting emotionally disturbed and delinquent young people. The first hospital in Kansas was established by Sister Joanna Bruner in 1864.[17] In 1880 the Sisters of St. Joseph of Carondelet started St. Mary's Hospital in Tucson, Arizona. By the 1880s, when new ethnic groups from eastern Europe and the Mediterranean area had started arriving in New York, another generation of women, such as Frances Xavier Cabrini (1850–1917), were responding to their needs by establishing hospitals, orphanages, and schools.[18]

Parish Missions

The bishops at their Baltimore Council meetings sought various ways to keep in touch with their growing flock and to add to their followers' knowledge of the faith. The hierarchy urged the preaching of missions, especially during Advent and Lent, for the renewal of faith and for greater religious knowledge.[19] The Redemptorists were particularly noted for their week-long parish missions, which emphasized both doctrine and devotion in the Catholic revival. As the introduction to the classic Redemptorist manual on preaching these missions indicated,

> Catholic missions are of two kinds: the Foreign and the Home Missions. The object of the Foreign Mission is to carry the glad tidings of salvation to the nations that sit in the shadow of death, to plant the cross of Christ in heathen lands. The Home Mission finds its field of activity among those who already possess the faith. Hence, a Home Mission, or simply a Mission, consists of a series of Sermons and instructions preached, in connection with the administration of the Sacraments, to an organized congregation, for the purpose of making them better Catholics.[20]

These missions became very popular and reached many Catholics, especially after the 1840s. A full mission would consist of a week for the women and then one week for the men. The idea was that the women, having seen the value for themselves, would convince the men to attend. Sermons were accompanied by drama, including the planting of a large cross, either in front of the church or in the church. Missions emphasized one's sinfulness, the confession of sins, and the ways one could live a Catholic life. These "religious revivals" bolstered devotional life and helped develop a "Catholic ethos."[21] Leaflets were distributed at the close of the mission to remind Catholics of their obligations as parishioners. The mission priests then went on to another parish to repeat the process. In some ways, this practice marked the beginning of missionaries as "specialists."

Mission to African Americans

Albert Raboteau, a leading authority on black American history, has identified three periods covering the presence of blacks in the United States.[22] The first period (1440–1808), the "Atlantic World," began with contact between the Portuguese merchants and sub-Saharan black Africans, and the transport of slaves from the coast of western Africa over the Atlantic Ocean to the Caribbean and eastern coast of what became the United States. As the sugar plantation traveled west over the Atlantic, so, too, did African slave labor. Raboteau points out that more Africans than European immigrants crossed the ocean before the middle of the nineteenth century. Some of the slaves ended up in the houses and on the property of Catholics. The year 1808 marked the end of legal slave trade to the United States.

The second phase of African American history (1808–1906), the "Continental Phase," was characterized by the influence of the land and the religious interpretations given to North American space, using the themes of Egypt, the exodus, and the Promised Land. Organizationally, several major black evangelical denominations arose.

The third period (1906–present), the "Global Phase," was characterized by the links between black Americans and blacks in the Caribbean and around the world, as well as a reconnection with African roots. Membership in pentecostal groups grew after a black preacher organized the Azusa Street Revival in 1906 in Los Angeles. Black Pentecostals spoke and preached in more global terms. Afro-Americans became members of Islam and produced new forms of that religion.

Cyprian Davis, a historian of the black Catholic experience in the United States, begins his narrative in the West with the first black Catholic, a Spanish-speaking slave, Esteban, who arrived in 1536 with four Spanish soldiers in Mexican territory.[23] While not a missionary in any sense of the term, Esteban was ultimately murdered by Native Americans because they could not believe that he would be trusted by the Spaniards. The eleven families who founded Los Angeles were black, Indian, and Spanish. On the East Coast, a population of free and slave blacks and black soldiers from Cuba formed part of St. Augustine, Florida, and a settlement just north of that area. This Spanish period in Florida ended in 1763, when the land was turned over to England after the Treaty of Paris. The second Spanish period covered from 1784 to 1821, near the end of which Florida was annexed to the United States.

In the English colonies several leading Catholics, including the Jesuits who came to Maryland in 1634, owned slaves for work on their tobacco plantations. In 1633, Matthias Sousa, a mulatto, was the first black person of record baptized in the province of Maryland. In 1641, he was the first black to serve in the Maryland Assembly.[24]

Since the country's founding, several bishops and six of the eight first women's religious congregations have also held slaves.[25] Though the Jesuits were debating whether to sell their slaves in the early 1830s, the formation of the first black Sisters' congregation, the Oblate Sisters of Providence, already had taken place in 1829 through the efforts of Sulpician James Hector Joubert (1777–1843) and Mary Elizabeth Lange (1812–62) in Baltimore. Lange was born in Cuba of Haitian parents.[26] A second black congregation of women religious, the Sisters of the Holy Family, was founded in 1842 in New Orleans by two free women of color, Juliet Gaudin (1808–87) and Henrietta Delille (1813–62).[27] Both groups of women taught black children. The Oblate Sisters of Providence opened a home for black orphans.

Pope Gregory XVI had condemned the slave trade in 1839, but the U.S. hierarchy took no official stand on the slavery issue before the Civil War. John England, bishop of Charleston, South Carolina, in an incomplete treatise on the topic, used arguments from Scripture and Church law to justify slavery. Two French-born bishops, Auguste Marie Martin and Augustin Verot, received Rome's disapproval for their endorsement of slavery. At the Second Plenary Council in Baltimore (1866), the bishops called for the education of emancipated slaves, but they perceived the issue as a "local" concern of bishops who lived in dioceses where slaves had been newly emancipated:

> We urge upon the Clergy and people of our charge the most generous cooperation with the plans which may be adopted by the Bishops of the dioceses in which they are, to extend to [emancipated slaves] that Christian education and moral restraint which they so much stand in need of.[28]

Their statement reflected stereotypical images of black Americans. At the time of this council, the Catholic Church had three black clergy, who were more or less uncomfortable with their color. The Healy brothers, James Augustine (1830–1900), Alexander Sherwood (1836–75), and Patrick Francis (1834–1919), were three of the ten children Michael Morris Healy had by one of his slaves, Mary Eliza.[29] Two years before this council, the Jesuits had established the first black Catholic parish, St. Francis Xavier, which had grown from the small community in the basement of St. Mary's Seminary, Baltimore, toward the end of the eighteenth century.[30]

The Propaganda Fide office in Rome urged the Third Baltimore Council (1884) to deal with "the negro problem," but, again, the bishops viewed the reality as a local situation and did not corporately address ecclesial or social inequities toward black Catholics. W. H. Gross of Savannah, Georgia, addressed his brother bishops on the topic of "Missions for the Colored People." While on the one hand he reminded the hierarchy that all were created by the same God and all had a common Father, he also judged blacks to have very little morality. The role of the Church in their evangelization was to make "honest men, chaste women, obedient, law-abiding citizens." The burden of evangelization to effect these virtues, especially chastity, rested with women, for, Gross noted, "The Catholic Church can alone give to the colored woman her proper elevation and make her influence widespread for good." He noted that the Sisters of Providence in Baltimore were proof of that influence.[31] The bishop thus manifested a double stereotype of race and gender. He clearly articulated the prevailing Catholic assumption that, without the saving influence of women, men would resort to barbarism.

Unlike black Protestant groups, which grew out of the slavery experience and which freely employed music and actions from that culture as part of the gospel idiom, black Catholicism was slow to grow. In a Church structurally oriented toward clergy and hierarchy, U.S. Catholic male leadership generally acted unfavorably to the development of black clergy.

There were a few exceptions, however. The Society of St. Joseph of Mill Hill, founded in England by then-Bishop Herbert Vaughan in 1866, had arrived in 1871 to minister to emancipated blacks in the United States. The missionaries' first assignment was St. Francis Xavier Church in Baltimore, which had been relinquished by the Jesuits. John R. Slattery (1851–1926), son of a wealthy New York family in the construction business, became pastor and reduced the parish debt that the Jesuits had incurred. Slattery became provincial but was ousted in 1883. The society separated into two groups in 1893, and the American foundation became known as the St. Joseph's Society of the Sacred Heart (Josephites). Slattery was reinstated as superior until his resignation in 1904. At the same time as his ardent advocacy for black Americans, he was also attracted to the views of the modernists Alfred Loissy and Adolf von Harnack, both of whom he met in Europe in 1902. In Slattery's famous "Dorsey sermon" preached at the ordination of Josephite John Dorsey, the second black priest educated and ordained in the United States, Slattery condemned the American Catholic clergy for their discouragement of priestly vocations among black Catholics. The *Catholic World* published his talk on the same theme, "The Negro Race: Their Condition, Present, and Future," which he gave at the Columbian Catholic Congress in 1893.[32]

The Josephite missionary spoke vigorously for the education of black seminarians and hoped that the college for black catechists in Montgomery, Alabama, which opened in 1900, would become a source for priestly vocations. Slattery's model for mission was Charles Cardinal Lavigerie (1825–92), founder of the Missionaries of Africa and the Missionary Sisters of Our Lady of Africa, whose work in Africa was based on the importance of adapting to the mentality and life of the Africans. Slattery held that blacks eventually would return to evangelize Africa.[33] He favored industrial training for blacks, as well as the inculcation of the virtues of sobriety and thrift. In advocating such virtues, Slattery held to some of the same stereotypes as the bishops at the Second Baltimore Council. Because he also thought of blacks as a group, he was not able to see the emergence of strong black leaders in the 1890s. This advocate for integration of black men into the seminaries eventually left the Catholic Church in 1906, affected by the ideas of modernism.

At the time of the Louisiana Purchase, all the blacks in St. Louis were Catholics.[34] At about the same time black Catholic laity had become members of the Confraternity of the Rosary at Holy Trinity Church, St. Thomas Manor, Maryland. Black Catholics published the *Journal of the Society of Colored People — The Holy Family Society* in Baltimore between 1843 and 1845. Black Catholic leadership gained national attention in the five Afro-American Congresses held from 1889 to 1894, under the leadership of a former slave, Daniel Rudd, founder in Springfield, Ohio, of a black Catholic newspaper, the *American Catholic Tribune*. The gatherings opened in ecumenical fashion with the presence of significant black Protestant leadership at the inaugural Mass and at the banquet on the evening of the first congress.[35] Among the issues the congresses addressed were the injustices and discrimination that black Catholics were experiencing in the Church and the need for the evangelization of their own race by black Catholics.[36]

Other groups responded to the call to mission among African Americans in the late nineteenth century and early decades of the twentieth century. The Congregation of the Holy Ghost Fathers and Brothers arrived in the United

States in 1872, having been driven from Germany after the *Kulturkampf.* They tended to the needs of German immigrants, but they also accepted a corporate mission with African Americans.[37] The Divine Word Missionaries were invited to work with southern blacks shortly after the founding of the U.S. provincial headquarters outside of Chicago.[38] One of their significant foundations was St. Augustine's Seminary, Bay St. Louis, Mississippi, opened in 1923 for African American candidates to the priesthood. Graduates went on to become bishops in the United States (Bishop Dominic Carmon, SVD, Auxiliary of New Orleans and missionary in Papua, New Guinea) as well as in West Africa (Bishop Joseph Bowers, SVD, Ordinary of Accra, Ghana), the Republic of Panama (Bishop Carlos Lewis, SVD, Co-adjutor of David), and New Guinea (Bishop Raymond Caesar, SVD, Ordinary of Goroka, Papua).

The society's founder, Arnold Janssen, also began a women's congregation, the Missionary Sisters of the Holy Spirit. Some of the Sisters arrived in the United States in 1901, and on 17 September 1906 four of the women, all of German birth, one of them an American citizen, set off for Vicksburg, Mississippi. They began a school for black children, the first of several schools they would begin in that state and in Arkansas. Through the years of financial struggle and anti-Catholic and Ku Klux Klan harassment, the Divine Word Missionaries and the Missionary Sisters benefited from the monetary assistance and kindly advice of Mother Katharine Drexel (1858–1955). This dynamic and enterprising woman, heir of the Philadelphia Drexel family fortune, had traveled extensively with her father and saw firsthand the plight of both blacks and Native Americans. In 1891 she founded the Sisters of the Blessed Sacrament for Indians and Colored People. In her constitution for the community, she noted that the special aim of the Sisters was "to lead the Indian & Colored Races to the knowledge & love of God, & so make of them living temples of Our Lord's Divinity."[39] Her financial assistance provided for black and Indian missions in Africa, British Honduras, Cuba, the Canal Zone, the British West Indies, and Canada, as well as for those in the United States. Her Sisters staffed missions in the southwest and southeastern parts of the United States and continue to do so today.[40]

Two other groups of Anglo women religious formed in the early twentieth century for mission to and education of black Americans, especially in the South, were the Missionary Servants of the Most Blessed Trinity, which began in 1912,[41] and the Franciscan Handmaids of the Most Pure Heart of Mary, who began their work in Savannah, Georgia, in 1916.

Mission to Native Americans

Four Missionary Styles

Most of the land which the United States acquired in the nineteenth century was considered "mission" ecclesiastically and "frontier" geographically. Some of this area, particularly in the Oregon Territory and Upper Michigan, was originally administered from the archdiocese of Québec. Settlers were pushing farther west of the Mississippi, sometimes through government sponsored "land grabs" or through colonization programs. Much of this land had been taken from the Indians, who were forcibly put onto reservations. Antipathies also grew between the farmers and the cattle ranchers. In many areas, "justice" was decided with firearms.[42] The "wild and wooly West" could still be found into the twentieth century, and stories such as Sister Blandina Segal's encounter with Billy the Kid provided colorful narratives of a frontier world.[43] Sulpician Abbé Magnien had traveled from Baltimore in 1902 to visit fellow Sulpician missionary Henry Granjon (1863–1922), bishop of Tucson, Arizona. In a letter to Cardinal Gibbons, Granjon wrote,

> Magnien was with me 24 hours and was, I hope, well pleased with his visit. I gave him a driver, across the sandy plains, to the old mission church of San Xavier del Bac, in the Papago Indian Reservation. The entire experience was a revelation to the Doctor; it took him an effort to believe that he was still in the United States.[44]

Missionaries continued to be active among both settlers and Native Americans. Frederic Baraga, Pierre Jean De Smet, Francis Norbert Blanchet, and Sarah Theresa Dunne (Mother Amadeus) approached their mission to the Indians in slightly different ways.

Frederic Baraga (1798–1868).[45]   The first bishop of Marquette, Michigan (originally the diocesan headquarters was at Sault Sainte Marie), Baraga was born in Slovenia, educated in Ljubljana and Vienna, and received a doctorate in law. He became proficient in several European languages. Student meetings with the Redemptorist Clement Hofbauer greatly influenced Baraga, who decided to enter the seminary after his studies. He was ordained in 1823.

While working as a parish priest for seven years he published a Slovenian prayerbook, *The Pasture of the Soul*. In an ecclesiastical environment of Jansenism and Josephinism, he was accused of exaggerated devotion to the Blessed Sacrament and of introducing devotion to the Sacred Heart and the Assumption of Mary, and was distrusted by the local curia. Baraga had read the Propaganda Fide reports from Bishop Edward Fenwick's Cincinnati Diocese and decided to become a missionary to the Native Americans. He arrived in the United States in 1830 and stayed with Fenwick, who had several Ottawa Indian boys living at his residence, preparing them for the priesthood. He accompanied the bishop to Arbre Croche,[46] where he gained still greater facility in the language and wrote a dictionary and grammar as he became proficient in the language. Fifteen months after he arrived, he published the first of many devotional books, catechisms, and Bible histories in the Indian language. In a report to the Leopoldine mission-funding foundation five years after arriving among the Indians, Baraga wrote:

It seems very strange to me to be now in a parish of whites. I, of course, could live comfortably, but not contentedly and in peace, if I were not to go to the Indian mission again. I now have learned the Indian language fairly well, and hope soon to perfect myself in it, and therefore I am firmly resolved to spend my remaining days in the Indian mission, if it be God's will.[47]

The missionary also learned and translated works into Ojibwa during his years at Grand Rapids, La Pointe, Wisconsin, and L'Anse, Michigan, before becoming bishop in 1853. In 1857 three neighboring bishops ceded their Indian territories to Baraga. He was a prodigious writer, compiler, and translator, the printing of books often underwritten by the Leopoldine foundation. Of particular interest are his catechetical works and the approach which he employed in their use. Well aware of the Indians' love for song, Baraga learned many of the Indian songs, composed some of his own, and translated many European songs into Indian languages. When the Indians gathered for any occasion, such as the illness of a family member, Baraga began singing an appropriate hymn, and the Indians all joined in, continuing throughout the night to provide comfort to the sick person. Catechetical lessons followed these hymns, which contained the doctrinal lesson for the day. The hymns in their books seemed to have more frayed edges than the catechetical pages. Baraga's books provided a pattern for other missionaries to use with Indians. After gaining this background and experience, Baraga was one of the participants at the Second Baltimore Plenary Council in 1866.

Francis Norbert Blanchet (1795–1883).   Farther west, Blanchet was another missionary bishop who exercised much of his ministry before the Civil War.[48] He attended Baltimore II as the archbishop of Oregon City. In 1838, Blanchet and Father Modeste Demers were sent by the bishop of Québec to Fort Vancouver on the Columbia River, where the Hudson Bay company had their headquarters. They arrived mainly to work among the Indians, but they also served the white settlers in the area. The missionaries generally spent a week or two with each group of Indians, much of this time with the chief. It became clear to Blanchet after his first contact with Chief Tslalakum and some of his followers at Cowlitz that a visual aid would be necessary to overcome language barriers. In April 1839, Blanchet used a Sahale stick with forty marks to represent the thirty-three years of Christ's life and other facets of Christian history. Soon the stick developed into "The Catholic Ladder," a chart with pictures illustrating many aspects of Christian history and doctrine. This device became popular among the Indians; they used it to teach interested people in their settlements. The success of this tool among the Indians of the Northwest prompted the Methodist preachers in the area to adapt it as well.[49]

Pierre Jean De Smet (1801–73).   A Belgian Jesuit who became well known in Europe for his letters about mission life in the western United States, De

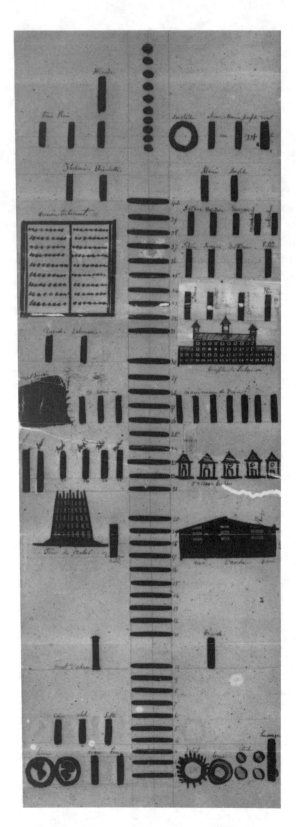

The Catholic Ladder: Designed by Fr. Francis Norbert Blanchet, "the Catholic Ladder" illustrated aspects of Christian history and doctrine. The Ladder was also use by Indians to teach in the settlements and was adapted by Methodist missionaries as well. (Courtesy, Oregon Historical Society)

Smet worked closely with Blanchet to organize the Church in the Oregon Territory.[50] As a young man, De Smet had met the missionary from Kentucky, Charles Nerinckx, in Europe and came to the United States to work as a missionary, especially among the Indians. The Belgian's first mission after his seminary formation in Florissant, Missouri, was in Council Bluffs, Iowa, from 1837 to 1839. In his work among the Potawatomi, he saw the debilitating effects of alcohol on the Indians. After two Flathead Indians came through the area on their way to St. Louis, seeking priests to instruct their people, De Smet visited the Rocky Mountains and returned to that area in 1841 with five more Jesuits. They founded St. Mary's Mission, near Missoula, Montana.

In spring of 1842, on a visit still farther west, he, Blanchet, and Modeste Demers charted the region for the growth of the Church in the Northwest. After recruiting five European Jesuits and six Notre Dame de Namur Sisters, he opened a mission headquarters along the Willamette River, in 1844. De Smet had been there for only a short time when he was asked to return to St. Louis for mission promotion and administration in the Jesuit Society. His work continued among the Indians in the next decades, however, as an agent of the federal government. He acted as a peacemaker among several Indian tribes, and, while the government sought his advice, it seldom followed it.

Sarah Theresa Dunne (1846–1919). De Smet had visited Miles City, Montana, in 1841, and three Jesuits opened a mission there in 1858. The men sent requests to eastern dioceses for assistance, especially in teaching the native children. One of those who responded was Dunne, a daughter of Irish immigrants. As a young girl she had imagined herself as a missionary in the Rocky Mountain area and in Alaska. Born in Akron, Ohio, Sarah entered the Ursuline community in Toledo and took her religious vows in 1864, receiving the name Amadeus. She taught school, had responsibility for the congregational finances, and was eventually elected the superior of the province. At one point she traveled to the Québec convent founded by Marie of the Incarnation to examine Ursuline life there.[51] In 1883, when Bishop Gilmour of Cleveland advertised for some religious who were willing to serve with the Jesuits in Montana, Mother Amadeus finally had the opportunity to go West. She and four companions established a boarding school in Miles City and subsequent missions among the Cheyenne between 1884 and 1899.[52] The women had been preceded by the chaplain of the Toledo convent, Father Eberschweiler, SJ. The Ursulines hoped to begin the formation of a religious congregation of Native American women who could catechize their own people, but this did not come to pass. Small schools were begun among the Native American girls. On a trip to Rome in November 1900, Amadeus took along her companion, Angela Pretty Eagle, to meet Pope Leo XIII. A few years after their return from Europe, Dunne traveled to Alaska several times to scout areas for mission work and opened her first mission among the Inuits and Aleuts

in 1908. Though she remained in ill health for much of her life due to an ac-
cidental poisoning in her early years, she remained intrepid until her death in
Alaska.[53]

"Chief Lady Black Robe," as she was called by the Indians, possessed a keen
appreciation for the intuitive Native American sense, which she saw as more
valuable in many cases than the prevailing European scientific approach to nature. Her personal style of mission was to be present among the native women
and to prepare them in a holistic manner, with attention to their education and
physical and spiritual development. Dunne was carrying on the Ursuline mission tradition, which Marie of the Incarnation had exemplified in teaching the
Indians of Canada and which the Ursulines in Louisiana had started with Indian
and black children after the Ursulines' arrival in 1727.

Bureau of Catholic Indian Missions and
the Third Plenary Council of Baltimore

Structural changes on the part of the American government toward Native
Americans had advanced sharply after the Civil War. Two years after the Second Baltimore Council (1866), the first Sioux War ended in Wyoming; the
following year, on 10 April 1869, an act of Congress created a Board of Indian Commissioners. Legislation over the next decade continued to subdue the
Indians and force them onto reservations. In March 1871 Grant's "Peace Policy" virtually made Native Americans wards of the government and turned
back George Washington's policy of making the tribes distinct and independent political realities. The government divided the tribes among the various
denominations as a way to pacify the Indians. In the 1880s and early 1890s,
"land grabs" in Oklahoma and South Dakota took more and more land belonging to the Indians. In 1892, more Indian reservation lands were opened
to white settlers. It seemed ironic that in that year the first Gideon Bible was
placed in an Iron Mountain, Montana, hotel, which stood on what had once
been Indian land.

During these decades the Oregon clergy, the Ladies' Catholic Indian Missionary Association, and the missionaries of the West brought the needs of the
Indians to the Third Plenary Council of Baltimore in 1884. The Oregon clergy
had published an address to Catholics in 1874 summarizing Grant's Indian policy and arguing against that course of action.[54] This sixteen-page document
presented the issue as an experiment in "Church/State-ism," an example of sec-
tarian influence in the distribution of supplies to the Indians. The clergy pointed
out that under the new "Christian policy (as they call it)," Protestants were to
have the entire jurisdiction of a reservation without any interference of other denominations. Such a policy hindered religious liberty and opposed the rights of
the individual conscience. "Our Red brethren in the faith" have a right "under
the Constitution, to full enjoyment of liberty of conscience." The clergy proposed four courses of action: that Catholics obtain a correct understanding of

the problem, that there be unity about the situation in the Catholic press in order to influence public opinion, that Catholics use the ballot box to obtain a change of policy, and that a Catholic Indian fund be raised "to rescue our Catholic Indians from spiritual bondage, and thereby indirectly protect our own liberty of conscience."[55]

One response to this appeal was the Ladies' Catholic Indian Missionary Association, formed in Washington, D.C., in 1875, after Archbishop James Roosevelt Bayley of Baltimore had appointed General Charles Ewing as Catholic Commissioner for Indian Missions. Ewing's wife was a member of the association, as were several of the Carroll relatives and Mrs. Agnes Caldwell. Consternation among Catholics arose because the government's policy toward the Indians seemed to favor Protestants and Protestants appeared eager to work among the Indians, especially among those who, heretofore, had been under Catholic auspices. Recognizing the zeal of Protestants and the work of Protestant women, the Catholic Ladies raised money to support Ewing's office, to supplement government aid at missions assigned by the government to the care of Catholics, and to "furnish such spiritual and material aid to all Indians that profess the Catholic faith or desire to be taught in it, wherever such Indians may be asserting their right, under all circumstances, to profess and practice the faith of their choice."[56] The Bureau of Catholic Indian Missions was formed in 1874 to represent the Catholic Church before the federal government in matters relating to Indian missions. The bureau became permanent ten years later at the Third Baltimore Plenary Council. In the twentieth century Katharine Drexel provided over $1.5 million to Native American work and more than half the budget of the Bureau of Catholic Indian Missions.

The Catholic Ladies and the Oregon clergy did not see the situation as an example of government injustice toward the Indians in general. Rather, they stated their case on the democratic principle of freedom of religion, on the right of Indians to practice their (Catholic) faith. The injustices committed against Native Americans were related to the bishops in 1883 by Archbishop Charles John Seghers, who was resigning his See of Oregon and was newly entrusted with Vancouver Island and Alaska. In his speech to the bishops during their month-long meeting, Seghers reminded them that

> We are in possession of the red man's country, we occupy his hunting ground, we are masters of the soil where his wigwam stood.... [I]f instead of bringing them the olive branch of civilization, we have followed towards them a policy of extermination, let at least those that remain be an object of our charity.[57]

He described what he learned from his own experience among the Indians and then appealed to the bishops to send missionaries and funds to Alaska and Vancouver Island.

Catholic Indian Congresses

On the banks of the Missouri River, where Pierre De Smet had set foot on his first visit to the Sioux nation, Father Philip Gordon addressed the Catholic Indian Congress in 1915.[58] Gordon was the second Native American ordained as a Roman Catholic clergyman. He had grown up in northern Wisconsin and had been encouraged by the reservation's Franciscan friars (St. Louis Province) to consider ordination. After being refused admission to St. Francis Seminary in Milwaukee, Gordon began his studies for the priesthood in Germany. The congress had been part of Northern Plains' Catholic Indian experience since 1880, when Martin Marty,[59] the Benedictine abbot responsible for the Dakota Territory, had called together a sodality for men (St. Joseph) and one for women (St. Mary) just after the Battle of Wounded Knee. These congresses were a tool for evangelization, meant to accelerate the momentum of conversions. Prayers, readings, and catechetical topics were led by the Indian men and women. Song, dance, and drama were also part of the outdoor gatherings, which lasted several days. They took place around the Fourth of July, a time when the Sun Dance, now condemned by the federal government, had been held. In a declining native culture subsequent to wars and resettlement on reservations, the sodalities provided, especially for men, a new opportunity for status in the tribe. These sodality meetings became the source of the Catholic Sioux Congresses, the first of which was held on 4 July 1883. Though the U.S. government felt the gatherings were unpatriotic, the congress concluded with three resolutions: "Gratitude for their calling to the true Church, concern for mutual aid to needy Catholics, and striving to become good citizens."[60]

The Mission to America

In the last three decades of the nineteenth century, a new voice for a mission to America arrived in the person of Isaac Hecker, founder of the society of Missionary Priests of St. Paul the Apostle (Paulists) in 1858. Hecker, a spiritual pilgrim through the Transcendentalists' Brook Farm, Protestantism, and the mainly German-speaking Redemptorists (1845–57), felt a call to convert America. He believed that the unity of Catholicism, which was able to hold together such disparate groups of people in varied economic and social situations, could provide the answer for an increasingly multicultural America.[61] Hecker's evangelical principles emphasized the Holy Spirit, who dwelt within all persons and was the source of the "aspirations of their hearts." This was evident in two of his popular works, *Questions of the Soul* (1855) and *Aspirations of Nature* (1857). This spiritual foundation coupled with a providential sense of the role of America and with Hecker's promotion of the values found in the American experiment, including the democratic value of the freedom of the individual. Methodologically, Hecker emphasized what Protestants and

Catholics held in common and stressed the principle of "non-controversy." He thought that polemics could convince no one of anything, much less bring about "conversion."[62] After Hecker's death, these "missions to non-Catholics" continued through fellow Paulist Walter Elliott and through the Catholic Missionary Union, which Elliott and Alexander Doyle founded to train diocesan clergy for this work (see chapter 4).

In this era of the "common man," evangelization by the laity surfaced on the agenda of the various lay congresses held between 1889 and 1893, including, as we have seen, Daniel Rudd's Afro-American Catholic Congresses. One person who had rallied around some of Isaac Hecker's ideas, especially the compatibility of democratic principles, a republican form of government, and a monarchical Roman Catholic Church, was Orestes Brownson (1803–76), a convert to Catholicism from Presbyterianism, Universalism, and Transcendentalism. As editor of *Brownson's Quarterly Review,* he became one of the most influential lay Catholics in the United States. He, too, spoke on the theme of the mission to America, the need for continual renewal in the Church, and the importance of the laity in that mission. He argued that while American roots originated mainly in the evangelical Protestant tradition, an emphasis on private illumination, subjectivity, and a theology which viewed human nature as totally depraved (which was Brownson's assessment of Protestantism) could not provide the foundations for a new world culture in "modern" times. Rather, Catholicism brought the supernatural to bear on the natural, had a positive perspective on the nature of the human person, and was able to hold together a variety of races and cultures. The American mission, neither exclusive nor strictly nationalist, was to absorb all distinctive nationalities by creating one family in the natural order, as Catholicism had done in the supernatural order. Thus, while America might save the world, Catholics could save America.[63]

In his later years, Orestes Brownson became less jubilant about a Catholicism wedded to America. But his son, Henry F. Brownson, carried forward plans for a lay Catholic congress, which emphasized the need for the laity to become involved in the mainstream of American life. Such persons could correct any prejudices Protestants might have about Catholics. In his 1889 congress speech, "Lay Action in the Church," the younger Brownson reminded his audience of the many laity who had been engaged in preaching, evangelization, and other missionary endeavors throughout Church history. Modern American Catholics could participate in such regeneration and reconversion of society by inserting themselves effectively into the political and social spheres.[64]

Walter Elliott told his audience at the 1893 World's Columbian Catholic Congress in Chicago that the "problem is how to place this virtue of Catholic faith in a missionary attitude and secure it a hearing; how to turn all the organic and personal force of Catholic faith into apostolic zeal for the eternal salvation of the entire nation."[65] The end of the century brought to the fore several groups of articulate, lay black, Indian, Anglo-, and German American Catholics, who were interested in mission and evangelization as they understood them. At their congresses and annual meetings, resolutions passed on many social issues, including the need for evangelization among Native and African American people.[66]

Focus and Characteristics of Mission in the Nineteenth Century

The great achievement of American Catholicism in the nineteenth century was the growth in Church membership and participation, especially among immigrant groups, through vigorous pastoral presence and effective evangelization on the part of women and men religious, bishops, clergy, and laity. Differences arose among Catholics as to the amount of "acculturation" to be made in what some viewed as a Protestant America. Money from European mission groups financed a number of projects and persons in the United States, though by the beginning of the new century American contributions to the Society for the Propagation of the Faith had notably increased. The U.S. Catholic Church received $4,582 from the society in 1822. By 1902, U.S. Catholics were sending $100,000 to the society. The United States was officially removed in 1908 from its status as a mission country, both because of an organizational move in Church government in Rome and because, by that time, America had become a world power and American Catholics were contributing toward missions elsewhere.

Compared to the colonial and Federal periods, the number of women missionaries in the United States had increased considerably. Highly visible reminders of Catholicism because of their distinctive dress, these women drew both the ire of anti-Catholic groups (there were several convent burnings) and ameliorated the faulty impressions Protestants had of Catholics through public works of mercy such as nursing Civil War wounded and caring for cholera victims. Women religious laid the groundwork for the social infrastructures of twentieth-century American Catholicism through hospitals, education, and social work. Even though black women experienced discrimination and injustice, they formed religious congregations well before seminaries accepted black or Native American candidates for the priesthood. While persistently urged by Propaganda Fide to support the ordination of black Americans, the U.S. Bishops and many other Catholic groups failed to comply with those directives. Often discriminated against as a corporate body themselves, the majority of Catholics did not embrace other groups, such as black Americans, who endured similar and worse plights. Aside from approving an annual fund for "Negroes and Indians," the bishops generally left the evangelization and education of these groups to religious congregations. With few exceptions, the American Catholic defense of the Indian, when the federal government stepped in to provide funds, rested more on fear that discrimination in this area might lead to disparity in other areas for immigrant Catholics, rather than on defense of the tribes against injustice done to them. Individual missionaries such as Samuel Mazzuchelli and Pierre De Smet made known to the government the injustices toward the Indians.

Evangelization among the Native Americans was largely the work of the Jesuits, Benedictines, and women religious communities, such as the Ursulines. A number of missionaries continued the pattern of colonial times by constructing grammars, dictionaries, and translations into native languages. While these latter put European devotions and the expression of doctrine into the Indian vocabulary, several missionaries, like Blanchet, attempted to link expressions in indigenous experience with Christianity. Visuals, as media for evangelization, bridged the gap between less clearly understood spoken languages.

Black, Indian, Anglo, and German lay Catholics toward the end of the century served as articulate spokespersons for the need for lay leadership in American evangelization. In 1902, the Society for the Propagation of the Faith indicated this need by identifying three mission periods in history. The first mission period was the time of the apostles. The second was the "union and protectorship," when the "temporal powers of the world united and established the Kingdom of Jesus Christ." The third was the "popular" era of missions, when "Providence substituted the people for the kings."[67] While the American hierarchy looked to laity for financial support for missions, it would be quite some time before they trusted laity to engage directly in mission and evangelization, except in the catechetical instruction of American Catholics. The formation of the American Federation of Catholic Societies in 1901 encouraged lay leadership in society but placed those efforts under control of the bishops in church affairs.[68]

With much attention being paid to urban immigrants, little energy was left for "home missions." Emphases in this direction in the twentieth century would come through the Catholic Church Extension Society, founded by Francis Clement Kelley (see chapter 4) and through the bishop of Fort Wayne, Indiana, John Francis Noll (1875–1956). Noll had received some of his preparation in the Cleveland Diocese by using the mission methods of Walter Elliott and the Catholic Missionary Union. Work among non-Catholics led him to use publication as a form of evangelization, especially for clarifying for Protestants what Catholics believed. In an environment of anti-Catholicism in Indiana, he published *Our Sunday Visitor* in 1912, a newspaper which gained a national following and which continues to the present. Though concentrating on mission in the United States, the newspaper raised fifty thousand dollars for overseas missions at a critical point in 1917 and has provided funds for and awareness of all missions. Still later, Father Howard Bishop (1885–1953), who had extensive experience in rural leadership, in 1937 founded the Glenmary Society of Priests, Brothers, and Sisters for rural areas with minimal Catholic presence.[69] Eventually this society aided some areas of India and Colombia in setting up their own home mission societies. Religious congregations of American women founded specifically for home mission work included the Mission Helpers of the

Sacred Heart, established in Baltimore (1890). These women, who also served in Puerto Rico, were influenced in their formation by the work of the Josephite Fathers and Brothers. Another women's congregation formed for home missions was the Religious of Our Lady of Christian Doctrine, founded in 1910.

The American Catholic Church in the nineteenth century was diverse locally and nationally. It prided itself at century's end that the witness of Catholic unity amidst distinctiveness (in spite of internal ethnic feuds) could become a pattern for American social and political life. As the country became more "settled," fewer mission bishops were part of the conciliar proceedings. As the new century dawned, the hierarchy started to regularize, systematize, and centralize, a process that blossomed in 1919 with coordinated Catholic efforts to assist in the First World War.

Chapter 3

Missions Overseas, 1820–93

With such intense mission activity and pastoral care within the United States, was there any effort during the nineteenth century to send missionaries overseas? If so, what circumstances provided the context for these missions? What perspective did these persons have about "mission"? What were the focus and characteristics of mission that they put into action? We will examine the corporate response of the U.S. Bishops to two requests by the Vatican office of the Propaganda Fide, and requests from representative congregations of women and men religious, in order to identify the first burgeonings of the overseas thrust by U.S. Catholics.

Appeals to Bishops for Missions Overseas

Mission to Liberia

During a visit to Rome in 1830, John England spoke with Pope Gregory XVI about the various mission needs the bishop of Charleston perceived in the United States. He expressed the importance of fostering the sacramental life of African American Catholics who had gone to Liberia. While the idea behind the American Colonization Society existed before 1816, that was the year that Robert Finley, a black Presbyterian minister in Washington, D.C., sought to resettle freed blacks in western Africa. Some of the first colonists had been Catholics from Maryland and, at one point, Charles Carroll was president of the society. John England brought the matter of pastoral care to the First Provincial Council of Baltimore (1829) and again to the Second Provincial Council (1833). At the latter gathering, the bishops recommended the Liberian mission be placed in the hands of the Jesuits. The Society of Jesus did not accept this mission, however. They were already responsible for several native American missions in the West, where they had been applying themselves vigorously. They could hardly accept the Liberian mission, when the Maryland Province was growing in disfavor among Catholics on account of actions which would lead to the decision to sell the Jesuit slaves.[1]

Nothing further happened until 1841, when Propaganda Fide issued an appeal to the U.S. Bishops for their assistance in missions beyond the shores of the United States. When the request came from Rome to send missionaries to Liberia, Bishop England, in one of the last public appearances before his untimely death, spoke at the Baltimore Cathedral in December 1841 to raise interest and financial support for the mission. Irish-born Edward Barron (1801–54), vicar general of the Philadelphia Diocese, John Kelly, an Albany, New York, priest, and Denis Pindar, a lay catechist from Baltimore, offered to go. They arrived at Cape Palmas, Liberia, on 31 January 1842. Within the year, Barron received ecclesiastical jurisdiction as vicar apostolic for Upper Guinea, a region from Liberia south to Angola.

The missionaries sent from the United States translated some prayers and the Creed into the Grebo language. One of their first mission goals was to have the Greboes observe the sabbath, for the people worked in the bush every day of the week and were thus unable to attend a Sunday liturgy. Apparently this was a novel idea, and one which appealed to the local tribal leader. Barron purchased land for a church and school, though these were not built. He requested additional clergy, some of whom could speak either Spanish or Portuguese since these countries had colonists in the area, though many of them had fallen from the practices of Catholicism. The mission was discussed at the Fifth Provincial Council of Baltimore (1843), and a subsequent letter to Pope Gregory XVI praised the work being done.

The Liberian population to whom the missionaries were sent turned out to be more than Maryland Catholics transplanted to the continent of their origins. The mixed populations both in the United States and Liberia represented a wide spectrum of cultural and social backgrounds, presenting an impossible task for this small group of U.S. Catholics. Adding to this complexity, Barron, when he received his papers naming him the vicar apostolic, was reminded by Propaganda Fide to look over his shoulder for Protestant proselytizing: "Spare no pains to make that people remain in the hall of the true faith, and thus bring to naught the efforts of those who threaten their spiritual good."[2]

This mission also provided the first contact with people from Africa, about which little was known to U.S. Catholics in the 1840s. But they received Barron's impressions when he wrote an article for the Philadelphia Catholic *Herald*, which was published in other newspapers as well. The Liberians, who had no houses (and thus, in the mind of the writer, no civilization), were like Christians in that they acknowledged the presence of a Supreme Being, but they gave way to superstition. "They worship demons; they practice polygamy; they bury their slaves with their deceased masters. They are, in a word, immersed in all those worst vices which must accompany the most barbarous ignorance." Yet, Barron acknowledged, converts were being made and were showing "attachment to [the Church's] ministers, the first fruits of that heavenly grace, which seems to have chosen this as the line of their conversion."[3] In recounting his encounter with indigenous religions, Barron presented the Africans as benighted, but capable of the illumination of faith. His standard for religious orthodoxy implied particular theological convictions and European/American cultural and social tenets.

The mission was short-lived. On 2 January 1844, Pindar died of sunstroke at

Cape Palmas, and Kelly went back to the United States within the month. Barron solicited the help of seven French priests from Francis Liebermann's newly founded Society of the Immaculate Heart of Mary. Poor health afflicted Barron, who also returned to the United States. He died assisting victims of yellow fever in Savannah, Georgia, in September 1854. The mission continued until 1884 under the leadership of the Society of the Immaculate Heart of Mary, which soon amalgamated with the Holy Ghost Fathers.

Mission to the Bahamas

Another request for ecclesiastical jurisdiction of an area came in 1860, just before the start of the Civil War, when Propaganda Fide invited the Charleston Diocese to look after the spiritual needs of the few Catholics in the Bahamas. In the vicinity where Spanish explorers had sailed, the islands were now under the control of the British. The bishop of Charleston, caught in the trauma and defeat of the Southern states in the Civil War and hindered by the difficulty of ship passage to the Bahamas, was unable to take full responsibility for this mission. Instead, Timothy Bermingham, a diocesan priest who lived in Barnwell, South Carolina, and tended several mission stations throughout that part of the state while on vacation once a year, ministered to the spiritual needs of the relatively small population of Catholics at Nassau.

The New York Archdiocese was asked to take over the mission. The archdiocese could offer little practical assistance in the first years, though St. Francis Xavier Church was built for the small group of English-speaking Catholics in the area in 1885. Archbishop Michael Corrigan (1839–1902) made a pastoral visit to Nassau in 1887 to assess needs, but could not induce mainly Irish New York clergy to accept an assignment of any length in this British colony. While an attractive spot for a short vacation, the Bahamas offered poverty, isolation, and tropical heat that further dissuaded other than volunteers from coming. Considering the primary responsibility New York felt to the influx of immigrants, it is not surprising that in the annual Sadlier Directory of Catholic institutions for these early years the Bahamas were listed as "Country Churches" at the end of the New York Archdiocese entry, though Nassau itself was a port city and somewhat cosmopolitan. By 1890 Father Denis Paul O'Flynn and, after him, Father Bernard J. Reilly occasionally pastored the small congregation in Nassau, New Providence.

Corrigan then turned for assistance to Mother Mary Ambrosia Sweeney (1830–1904) of the Sisters of Charity, Mount St. Vincent on Hudson, and to the Benedictine men of Newark. He specifically asked them for missionaries. However, as the Benedictines from St. John's, Collegeville, Minnesota, were interested in starting a foundation in New York at the time, Corrigan, in effect, bargained that they send someone to the Bahamas as part of his acquiescence to the foundation in his archdiocese. These transactions took some time, so the Sisters arrived first on New Providence Island in 1889. Thirty-six-year-old Father

Chrysostom Schreiner (1859–1928), a history professor and recently retired vice president of St. John's College, arrived in 1892 and became the resident pastor of St. Francis Xavier Church in Nassau and eventually vicar forane of the Islands.[4]

Among the many Sisters of Charity who volunteered, five women were chosen. Sister Marie Dolores Van Rensselaer (1843–1914), a member of a long-established New York family, had spent twelve years as director of the medical department of the New York Foundling Hospital. She was named superior of the mission and traveled with four teachers, Sisters Teresa Alacoque Nagle, Casilda Saunders, Mary Mercedes Donovan, and Maria Corsini Gallagher. Mother Ambrosia Sweeney sent some of her most qualified Sisters to the mission. Each brought valuable experience to mission work. She sailed with Sisters Mary Irene Fitzgibbon of the New York Foundling Hospital, Teresa Gonzaga Battell, the procuratrix of the motherhouse, and Maria Dodge, the directress of the Academy of Mount St. Vincent. These persons stayed for a few weeks to offer suggestions and to assess the new mission. Two recent graduates of the Academy of Mount St. Vincent came along, as did a lay woman, Margaret Wohlfert, who taught kindergarten, first at St. Francis, then on Andros Island.

The governor general of the Islands was on board the *Santiago* carrying the women on their four-day trip, so the Sisters' entrance to the mission was accompanied by bands, streamers, and lanterns on display for the dignitaries. The Sisters noted the "colored element lining one side of the road in sharp contrast to the gay party group to meet His Excellency the Governor."[5] After docking they made their way to their small home. "As soon as the altar was placed and the room arranged as a chapel, all felt at home; the mission was really commenced."[6]

By the end of their first week they had set up two schools in Nassau: St. Francis Xavier Academy, a tuition-paying school, which had sixteen girls and two boys, and St. Francis Xavier School for Colored Children, a free school, which enrolled two hundred children in its first year. By 1896 the latter had almost three hundred students and the academy remained steady at twenty-two. The intention of this plan was to use profits from tuition to fund the free school, a strategy many congregations of Sisters had used in the United States in order to provide an income for themselves and also to make education affordable for persons in a lower economic bracket.[7]

Though the mission was technically the responsibility of the New York Archdiocese, the Sisters received no financial assistance from them. In addition to a small tuition, the Sisters solicited funds through a literary magazine, *Children of Providence,* produced by the Sisters at the motherhouse in the Bronx. They also advertised in this periodical for boarders. Sister Mercedes, in addition to teaching her primary eighth in the British educational system on the Islands, taught music students and raised chickens to supplement their income. Life became particularly difficult in the wake of periodic hurricanes, which drove up prices on foodstuffs and destroyed many buildings and homes.

The summer after the Sisters arrived they inaugurated a sewing class to make contact with those persons "out east" on the island. Twenty-five young girls and women showed up for the first class. The women expressed a desire to have an "everyday school," and the house rented for this purpose soon became too small. This group eventually became Sacred Heart Parish; its school was one of the only two parochial schools in the Islands for thirty years. The Sisters found the conditions primitive and, in spite of great natural beauty all around, destitute. However, Sister Veronica Mary remarked, "We have nothing to work with, no place to store any equipment, no plans, but we are happy in the realization that under such conditions the work will really and truly be God's and not ours."[8]

On their arrival, and especially when they began to work on Harbor Island, the Sisters met with a great deal of bigotry from the mainly Protestant population. The Sisters gradually dissolved much of this antipathy, however, through their patience, charity, and work. While the Benedictine Fathers were zealous in their preaching and ministry, "it is a fact that the [Islands were] won by the daily efforts of the Sisters of Charity."[9] The first converts in the Bahamian Catholic Church in this period were six native children, students at the free school, along with their mother.

Over the years, as the population increased in these and other newly opened schools, the Sisters offered three-week summer courses for native women who were volunteer teachers but who had little formal academic training. The Sisters were carrying on the tradition of Mother Ambrosia, who had counseled them in principles of education. Among her maxims was, "We must aim to educate the whole child, mind and body, heart and soul."[10] This "holistic" postulate moved beyond the classroom and the children when the Sisters, in addition to their teaching, assumed many other aspects of mission work. The Sisters visited the homes of the villagers and led Sunday services through hymn singing and by reading the sermon from a homiletics book in the absence of the priest, who was away at other towns about a third of the year. In a location with few doctors, people frequently sent for the Sisters to provide for the sick and the dying.

Close as they were to the islanders, the Sisters realized that in the part of Bahamian life closest to the people's African roots there still was a domain in which the people kept them distant. In a letter from the 1920s one of the Sisters remarked:

> It is difficult for white people, even those living in Nassau, to penetrate into the racial life of the negro, but a dear old black mammy, whose affections I have won, occasionally talks to me as "she nebber did talk to no oder white pusson 'cept you, honey chile." Her confidence even in me, however, has its limitations and no amount of persuasion can draw from her any information as to the annual election of a queen, a custom which still prevails, I have been told, among the real Africans living in Nassau or on the so-called out-islands.[11]

The Sisters were educating more persons of color (and more young girls) than colonists from Europe. The Sisters' view of the native Bahamians can be seen against the background of their publication that raised funds for the mission. Each month one article featured the Sisters' and Benedictines' work in the Bahamas. *The Children of Providence* was a vehicle for the League of Divine Providence, whose object was the "conversion of the Colored People of the Bahamas and the spiritual and temporal welfare of all subscribers." Leading Catholic writers of the day, such as Louise Imogene Guiney, Eliza Allen Starr, and James J. Walsh, wrote for the periodical, which was published from 1894 to 1922. A major theme was the contribution of educated women to the intellectual and spiritual life of the Church and society, a theme also supported in the pages of the *Catholic World.* Catholic African Americans were featured within this same philosophical framework. Articles on Pierre Toussaint, the Oblate Sisters of Providence, and New York's Catholic Negroes presented a view of educated black Americans, such as those who organized and attended the Afro-American Catholic Congresses of the late 1880s and 1890s.

The Benedictines, under the leadership of Abbot Bernard Locknikar at St. John's, Collegeville, were reluctant to support the Bahamian mission, a substantial distance from Minnesota. Father Schreiner himself remained in Nassau, largely due to his near drowning as he sailed to another island. As he thrashed about in the waters, he vowed that were he saved, he would remain. The first men sent to aid Schreiner from 1891 to 1893 came to restore their health. They started a short-lived preparatory school for sons of businessmen, to ready the boys for education in Europe. Periodically Schreiner returned to New York to raise funds. Archbishop Corrigan, who was going through his own troubles with the Americanists and was not known as a man particularly interested in missions or in making converts, did provide a thousand dollars. Other diocesan priests who came for vacations contributed money toward the parish. The Negro and Indian Mission Board eventually provided $750 a year.

Schreiner lacked, however, a sustaining community of Benedictines. Newly ordained Fathers Gabriel Roerig (1870–1950) and Melchior Bahner joined Schreiner in 1894. Sensitive to the importance of English in the Bahamas, Schreiner changed Melchior's name to Austin, a sound more tuneful to British ears. Melchior labored at Sacred Heart Chapel in eastern Nassau and set about building a church there. Gabriel, who came in ill health, worked with the people on Andros Island where he, too, constructed a church. He stayed to serve the Church in the Bahamas for fifty-six years. The previous year James Martin, a catechist from Brooklyn, had arrived, characterized by Gabriel as "a lame violinist, teacher, and an all around genius except for making money."[12] Martin stayed on for five years, until the Benedictines gave him a ticket back to New York. Until 1920 the Church, pastored by three Benedictines, largely centered its work in these three parishes, with some evangelization of the "out islands." While the priests were dedicated preachers and ministers, they relied on the work of the Sisters for growth in the mission. The mainly German-speaking

Benedictines had difficulty breaking into English social circles, which generally harbored anti-Catholic sentiments. This was particularly difficult for Schreiner, who yearned to share intellectual pursuits and who keenly missed the academy. While he tutored some of the young men of the island, his contact with the Bahamians was primarily liturgical.

Schreiner's perception of mission revolved around a traditional Benedictine framework of liturgical prayer and working the land. His sacramental ministry and his Benedictine life had been his main preparation for the mission. He wrote to Abbot Bernard:

> You seem to think that I have very little to do here. Well, as far as work is concerned I have not too much to do, yet I have enough to keep me occupied. I preach two sermons a week (in Lent three) — and prepare for them — and can profitably spend an hour or two a day in the schools. . . . I am opening up a vegetable garden, looking after the sisal plantation, etc.[13]

In spring, he led daily May devotions and gave a Thursday evening sermon.

The Sisters appreciated the good Benedictine liturgies. Sister Felicitas remarked to Mother Rose:

> All the other sisters are well and some very happy — for after all, dear Mother, we are far better off here than we would be in some of the houses north — we have far more privileges, I mean in a spiritual way — Mass regularly every morning and Benediction twice a week and, as for Father's [Schreiner's] kindness, I am sure he cannot do enough for us.[14]

The Benedictine liturgical tradition would reach maturity in the new century, when the island exhibited the fruits of liturgical renewal as proposed by Virgil Michel, OSB, who volunteered in 1923 to serve in the Bahamas, and Godfrey Diekmann, OSB, in the 1940s.

The New York Archdiocese was thus able initially to fulfill its missionary responsibility through the services of these two religious congregations. The Bahamas remained in the jurisdiction of the New York Archdiocese until 1931.

Third Plenary Council of Baltimore (1884)

Another ecclesiastical response to missions overseas in the nineteenth century came when the bishops gathered in Baltimore at their Third Plenary Council (1884). In addition to discussion about home missions, the bishops took up the topic of foreign missions. As a body, the bishops acknowledged that the U.S. Church needed to look beyond its shores and contribute toward Christianity in other parts of the world. Such mission work would expand the ecclesial perspective of the country. The motive for this apostolic ardor sprang from the appreciation Catholics had for their own faith.

> The charity and zeal in [the Christian's] heart must be like that in the heart of the Church, whose very name is Catholic, like that in the heart of

Christ, who "died for all men, and gave Himself a redemption for all...."
The more we appreciate the gift of faith, the more must we long to have
it imparted to others.... The missionary spirit is one of the glories of the
Church and one of the chief characteristics of Christian zeal.[15]

The pastoral letter, which followed that council, had a section on "Home
and Foreign Missions." Having seen themselves "mature" as a body, due to
their participation at the First Vatican Council and to the relatively successful growth of the Catholic Church in the United States, in spite of nativism
and anti-Catholic sentiment, the bishops reminded themselves and all American
Catholics:

> Heretofor[e] we have had to strain every nerve in order to carry on the
> missions of our own country, and we were unable to take any impor-
> tant part in aiding the missions abroad. But we must beware lest our local
> burdens should make our zeal narrow and uncatholic.[16]

At the council the bishops approved the establishment of the Society for the
Propagation of the Faith for every parish and diocese. However, the U.S. branch
of the SPF did not start until 1896, when San Francisco Archbishop Patrick Riordan recommended a proposal from the Sulpician general superior, Arthur J.
Captier, to appoint an SPF director and to locate the headquarters at the Sulpician seminary in Baltimore. The rector, Alphonse Magnien (1837–1902), was
invited to be the delegate of the Central Council of the SPF, and the society was
incorporated in Maryland.[17]

Religious Congregations

Even earlier than the Third Plenary Council of Baltimore, religious congregations were responding to the call to mission overseas in the nineteenth century.
The American Province of the Society of the Redemptorist Fathers and Brothers
was asked by the superior general to take on a mission in the Antilles. Initially
Pope Pius IX enjoined the Redemptorists to take on a near schismatic parish
in the Danish Virgin Islands of St. Thomas and St. Croix. In July 1856 the superior general, Father Nicholaus Mauron, asked the American superior to send
three of his men to St. Thomas. The year 1856 was difficult, partly because
Isaac Hecker had recently left the congregation along with several other priests
to form the Paulist Fathers.

However, at the same time as the request from the Redemptorist superior
general, Father Joseph Prost (1804–85), a pioneer in the foundation of the
American Redemptorists, had written from Vienna and offered to help the
American Province found the St. Thomas mission. He arrived on 1 March
1858, and on 23 May Father Louis Dold (1821–82) and Brother Henry Voss
(1817–69) joined him in Christiansted, St. Croix, to form the first Redemptorist community outside of North America and Europe. Their plan was that

the Redemptorists would provide retreats and missions to Catholics on other islands in the area, in addition to serving the Church on St. Thomas.[18] The mission was difficult because of the potential schism; in addition, one of the three Redemptorists who had joined them from Naples died of typhus in 1869, and Dold seemed near a nervous breakdown. Nevertheless, the Redemptorists retained the mission "to touch the lives of the more neglected and abandoned and...to do this through the proclamation of the Word of God and the change of life that it brings about."[19] Practically speaking, the mission tried to regularize church attendance and the practice of the sacraments and sermons, and to promote devotions, especially to Our Lady of Perpetual Help.

Other religious congregations with European roots and North American provinces also sent personnel to overseas missions in the nineteenth century. The Passionist Fathers, through the work of Father Dominic Tarlattine and Father Peter Maganatto, established a foundation in Mexico City in 1865. Over the next few years, twelve more Passionists joined them in Tepotzotlán, near the capital.[20] After 1881, the Passionists also began foundations in Buenos Aires, La Planta, Sarmiento, and Valparaiso. Behind the Argentinian and, later, Chilean foundations was a Boston-born convert to Catholicism, James Kent Stone (1840–1921), whose religious name was Father Fidelis. A Harvard graduate and president of Hobart College in Ohio, Stone's spiritual journey led him first to the Paulists and then to the Passionists.

Three Franciscan Sisters from Allegany, New York, sailed to Jamaica in 1879 to assist a congregation with the development of those who had vocations to religious life. They became the first congregation of women religious founded in the United States to send their women to a foreign mission.[21] A young congregation founded twenty years earlier through the influence of Pamfilo da Magliano, OSF (OFM), it sent the Sisters after a request from a Franciscan congregation in Scotland for assistance in teaching in the British colony. Their own numbers were small, and they feared their ministry with both the affluent and the poor would be hampered without further recruits to religious life. After a period of adjustment, the two groups of Franciscans formally affiliated, and Jamaican women entered the Franciscan community. By 1897 the women had opened the first government-chartered Catholic teachers college on the island.

Franciscans in Hawaii: Mother Marianne Cope

Undoubtedly, one of the best-known missionaries of the era was Marianne Cope (1838–1918), a Franciscan Sister of Syracuse, New York.[22] Born in Heppenheim in the grand duchy of Hesse-Darmstadt, she immigrated to the United States with her family in 1840 and entered the Sisters of St. Francis in Syracuse after several years as a factory worker in Utica. Her first assignment as a professed Sister was teaching; eventually, she was chosen as the major superior for her congregation.

In June 1883, Cope received a letter from a missionary in Hawaii, Father

Leonor Fouesnel, a priest of the Sacred Hearts of Jesus and Mary who was canvassing the United States looking for help for the mission. He had recruited the Brothers of Mary from Dayton, Ohio, to teach in one of the schools.[23] He was authorized by the local bishop and the local government, he said, to procure Sister-nurses to work in a hospital in Honolulu, but had been unsuccessful in finding French Sisters and in obtaining positive responses to letters he sent to fifty other North American communities. He proposed a number of reasons for her community to come to Hawaii, not the least of which was that "a protestant government has sent me. If I should not succeed, very probably the same government would apply for Sisters at an Anglican Sisterhood and then our case would become almost hopeless."[24] This incentive, however, did not seem particularly compelling to Cope and she knew nothing about Hawaii, but when she read his letter, Marianne's "interest [was] awakened and I [felt] an irresistible force drawing me to follow this call."[25] Yet it was only after Fouesnel visited Syracuse and made known that the immediate need was for service to a hospital filled with unattended leprosy patients that Marianne felt free to consider accepting the mission.

Along with the provincial minister of the Conventual Franciscan Friars (who was the community's superior), Cope called a meeting of the Sisters to determine whether they should undertake the mission. The vote was eight to one in favor, even though Cope had received very little information from Fouesnel about the specifics of the mission. She did write back to him with some stipulations of her own: that the Sisters would be in charge of the hospital, controlling its management and direction, and that they would have a right to open schools. With misgivings from the friar provincial minister, Marianne at the age of forty-five left Syracuse with six Sisters on 22 October 1883, after a farewell Mass at the motherhouse. They traveled for six days by train to San Francisco and then seven days by steamship to Honolulu. Cope was not sure whether she would stay a few months or for several years, as she was still the major superior and needed to be responsible for the overall development of the congregation in Syracuse.

The emissary had promised the Sisters much, but nothing was ready on their arrival, including their convent, so they stayed first with the Sisters of the Sacred Hearts and then in rented quarters. In 1865, the Hawaiian legislature had passed the Act to Prevent the Spread of Leprosy, a law which segregated lepers from other islanders. The lepers would be located on the island of Molokai. In 1873, Bishop Louis Maigret of Hawaii called his priests together to discuss how best to minister to the lepers. Consequent to this discussion, the Belgian, Father Damien de Veuster, left for Molokai and spent his life with the lepers. In 1886, a convert from Protestantism and veteran of the Civil War, Ira Barnes, known as "Brother" Joseph Dutton (1843–1931), joined Father Damien.[26]

A few days after their arrival, a carriage took the Sisters for their first look at Kakaako Hospital, a holding place for those suspected of having leprosy. The Sisters did not appear daunted, however, when they walked through the

Franciscan Sisters in Hawaii: A picture taken in 1899 shows five Franciscan Sisters of Syracuse, New York, who helped administer the leprosarium in Molokai that would later become famous through its popular association with Blessed Damien of Molokai (d. 1899). (Left to right: Srs. Crescentia Eilers, Leopoldina Burns, Mother Marianne Cope, Elizabeth Gomez, Vincent McCormick. Courtesy, Franciscan Sisters Archives)

hospital compound. But it soon became clear that the resident steward, both cruel to the lepers and antagonistic toward the Sisters, and the hospital physician, who diagnosed the patients from afar, impeded the direction the Sisters wished to take at the hospital. They assessed the problems as unsanitary conditions, a lack of care for the residents, and immorality. On the latter point, a sense of anarchy ruled among the outcasts, who felt no hope for themselves. In the evenings after the Sisters returned to their convent, the hospital became a kind of brothel. Quiet, cheerful, and efficient, the Franciscans nevertheless were determined and persistent in bringing to the attention of the authorities the problems they encountered. After many struggles with the steward and with certain persons in the government, the Sisters were given full charge of the hospital on 2 April 1884.

The work was difficult and often frustrating. The women faced circumstances they had not anticipated before arriving in Honolulu. The same year the Sisters were given charge of the Kakaako Hospital, they were also asked to set up the first hospital on Maui, in Wailuku. Four more Sisters joined them in 1885, and they established a school in Wailuku, where the community taught until 1929.

Sister Antonella Murphy had contracted tuberculosis in Syracuse, though she was unaware of the disease at the time, and died in Hawaii by the end of the Sisters' first year. She was twenty-eight years old. Sister Rosalia McLaughlin, due to a combination of several events, eventually lost her mind.

The Sisters' mission mindset moved fluidly between their work and spirituality. They expressed that relationship in the image of the body of Christ, directing their attention at times to the eucharistic body in their small chapel, regarded as a "commencing of the mission," and at other times to the bodies of the lepers.

Once the Sisters were in charge, their first act was a "grand purification" of the hospital. Buckets, mops, hot water, disinfectant, and elbow grease made the area look clean and pleasant. Eventually the residences of the patients were painted, and flowers and trees were planted in the packed earth. In addition to providing what they could of the treatment of leprosy known at that point, the Sisters' care, along with the purification and cleansing of the hospital dwellings, resulted in psychological healing for the patients. The hospital existed no longer as a prison with walls in which the residents thought of themselves as inmates; the patients thought of themselves as family in a home, where self-worth gradually grew.

A few years later, after the initial beautification, the Sisters further removed a low retaining wall from around the convent property and used the components to redefine the boundaries of the settlement, creating a wall to separate the men's and women's buildings. The Sisters' area was now on the same side of the wall as the women lepers. "Redrawing" the lines of the leper hospital to include the convent building signified the Sisters' willingness to identify with the lepers, and particularly with the least of the lepers, the women.

The Franciscan women were often referred to by the government and by the people of the island as the Sisters of Charity. Though members of a minority religion in Hawaii, the relative newcomers practiced an ecumenism of good works. Marianne frequently remarked to the Sisters, "The charity of the good knows no creed, and is confined to no one place."[27] Such an ecumenicity of good works made the Catholic circle quite acceptable to the variety of cultures and religions on the island.

Jesuits and Sisters of the Holy Family in British Honduras (Belize)

American Jesuit priests also went overseas before the twentieth century. Michigan-born Maurice Sullivan, SJ, died in the East Indies before 1900. Charles Gresselin, SJ, of the Canadian-New York Province, spent a brief time in the Bahamas in the latter part of the nineteenth century. The Jesuit superior general transferred the mission of Jamaica from the English Province to the Maryland Province in 1893.[28] When this transfer occurred, nineteen Franciscan Sisters from Syracuse and nine Mercy Sisters from New Orleans were already teaching children, primarily black, in Jamaica.

Also in 1893 the Missouri Province of the Jesuits was asked by the superior general to send men to British Honduras. He noted that since the province no longer had a mission among the Native Americans, the Missouri Jesuits should "undertake some or other foreign mission as a means of fostering the apostolic spirit among its members."[29] Milwaukee-born William Wallace, SJ, was already serving in British Honduras, which had a relatively stable government and a mixed population of Europeans, Chinese, Mayan Indians, Caribs, Spaniards, Creoles, and some blacks. English was spoken mainly in the capital of Belize, but Spanish, Carib, Maya, and Creole were the languages outside the city. In 1893 the names of ten Jesuit priests and two Jesuit Brothers were on the mission list.[30]

The work of the Jesuits consisted of teaching in a Catholic select school for Spanish-speaking residents in the capital, reinstating a boarding school (St. John's), and establishing four mission stations outside Belize. In these outlying areas, the missionary divided his time between the hometown, such as Stann Creek, and periodic visitation (monthly, biweekly, or weekly) of the dependent villages scattered over rough terrain. A Jesuit noted that in the villages

> the League of the Sacred Heart flourishes; every visit is fruitful in confessions and Communions, in couples reclaimed from an evil life. The work is very hard and demands not merely great physical endurance and the ability to live upon beans and maize, but also patience and more endurance of a very high order.[31]

When the Jesuits invoked the Sacred Heart they were not merely promoting a devotion prominent in Catholic life in the United States or even in the mission. They appealed to the image as a source for love relationships — in this context, the proper love between man and woman, sanctified in marriage. The priests spent much of their time convincing the men to marry the women by whom they had children. Devotion to the Sacred Heart was used to firmly implant values of family life and to rid future marriages of "the irrevocable curse of miscegenation."[32] While we don't know if the same was done in British Honduras, American Jesuits in Jamaica had established an association of men who wore white silk capes with red hoods (the red, of course, representing the heart's blood) when they processed into the church for their trimonthly communion in common. Emphasizing collective male identification under the aegis of the Sacred Heart intended to promote a moral family life and a responsible male role in that family. While Europeans and Americans tended to use devotion to the Sacred Heart to affirm the papacy and infallibility, especially after Vatican Council I, such acts of piety in Belize were meant to lay the cornerstone for a more regularized family life.[33]

In addition to establishing the League of the Sacred Heart, one of the missionaries, Father Newell, preached yearly "novenas," which were annual missions similar to those the Jesuits practiced in the United States. Over the next ten years Newell noticed a growth in the number of confessions and communions as a result of these "revivals." The priests also taught catechism regularly in the Catholic public schools in a country where all public schools were denominational.

One of the missions, Corozal, experienced a turnover of pastors because of ill health. This created difficulties over the next ten years of the mission.

> In this country, to a greater extent than elsewhere, the influence of the priest is a matter of slow growth; the people take a long time in making his acquaintance, and often repel his advances for years, until his patient kindness has won a hold upon their affections. Hence a frequent succession of pastors in a place sets the work back considerably.[34]

In the next few years the Jesuits reinstated the boarding school at St. John's College, a school for Spanish-speaking students, in order to attract young men from other Central American countries. At that point the Jesuits felt that "the black people generally are not fitted for any higher education than that afforded by the public schools."[35]

The Jesuits thus employed three methods of mission praxis, each associated with some aspect of their spirituality: education, mission "novenas," and Sacred Heart devotion. Through education of a select group, in this case the Spanish-speaking young men, the Jesuits hoped to form leaders for British Honduras and for all of Central America. They followed the principle of their founder, Ignatius Loyola, who emphasized the formation of an "elite" corps, who, in turn, would command and lead others. Mission "novenas" acted to dispel religious apathy, reordered the Catholic liturgical community, and stabilized the parish community. Sacred Heart devotion provided a religious and social identity, especially for men, and encouraged the male to be the head of family life.

The Jesuits sought a congregation of women religious to carry on the work of the mission schools. The spirituality of the congregation that responded to this invitation reinforced some of the values the Jesuits emphasized. In 1898, Mother Austin, the major superior of the Sisters of the Holy Family, New Orleans, received a letter from the Jesuit Sicilian bishop of British Honduras to open a school for the black Indian children in Stann Creek. This congregation, founded in 1842 by two African American women of French and Cuban backgrounds, Henriette Delille (1813–62) and Juliette Gaudin (1808–87), had from its beginnings intended to extend its mission to other countries. The name of their congregation — the Holy Family — their Rule of St. Augustine, and their devotion to the Sacred Heart all stressed love as the source of mutual charity and traditional family values.

Many Sisters volunteered for the mission, and in March 1898 Mother Austin Jones, three Sisters, and a lay woman traveled to Belize, where they were welcomed by the Sisters of Mercy from New Orleans. At Stann Creek, the Jesuits Leib and Antillach and the people welcomed the Sisters at the dock on Palm Sunday with singing and waving branches. The pastor had prepared a frame house with a zinc roof, one of the few nonthatched buildings in the village. This act would typify the support, both financial and spiritual, which the Jesuits provided the Sisters over the years. The parishioners shared their provisions with the Sisters. The school at Stann Creek, opened by a Jesuit Brother, was staffed by four men and one woman before the Sisters' arrival. Eventually the Sisters maintained several primary schools and an ecumenical high school. The Carib spoke little English and the Sisters spoke no Carib, so it took a while for both to adjust to the other. In 1908 a Carib woman, Guadeloupe Ogaldez, entered the novitiate of the Sisters of the Holy Family and after her profession returned to work in British Honduras. Sixteen months later, she became ill and died. By 1948, however, as the Sisters' work extended to the capital, at least nineteen women had entered the congregation from British Honduras. By the same year, there was only one ordained Carib priest, who had been a student at the Sisters' school, Sacred Heart.[36]

European Congregations with American Missionaries

In addition to the response of U.S. religious congregations, several individuals took missions with congregations in European provinces. Some Americans became well known in the early twentieth century to readers of *The Field Afar* and *Catholic Missions*. Mother Suzanne Boudreaux, a religious of the Sacred Heart and native of Louisiana, and Mother Bauday Gareshé left St. Louis on 12 December 1879 to begin a foundation in Timaru, New Zealand. Two American Sisters of Charity, Joanna O'Connell and Catherine Bushman, were the first U.S. Catholic women missionaries to China in 1896 and 1898, respectively, when they went as part of the French Province of that congregation.[37] German-born Father Remy Goette, OFM, was sent from the United States to China (Hupeh Province) in 1881. His younger brother, Father Athanasius Goette, OFM (1857–1908), became an American citizen, studied for the priesthood at Quincy, Illinois, and St. Louis, and was ordained in 1881. He served in Shensi (central China) and was appointed the first American missionary bishop in China when he became vicar apostolic of northern Shensi in 1905.[38]

New directions for U.S. Catholic missions overseas had appeared on the horizon by 1893. The World Parliament of Religions, a Chicago conference organized by Protestants with a cross-cultural background, brought to North America some of the "exotic" religions of the East. The Catholics who participated in this conference formed part of a group that would soon be labeled "Americanists." Their ideas and the Spanish-American War provided fresh reasons for U.S. Catholic missions abroad.

Focus and Characteristics of Mission

What, then, can be said about the characteristics and focus of missions abroad during a time when the U.S. Catholic Church was growing, mainly through

Irish and German immigration? First, the nineteenth century does not provide as bleak a picture in terms of overseas mission as is popularly believed. One of the arguments given for the foundation of Maryknoll in 1911 was that there virtually were no congregations where one could go in order to be a "foreign missionary." While not nearly as much effort went toward missions overseas as toward pastoral work in the United States, individuals and groups nevertheless did respond to the call to spread the gospel, if not to the ends of the earth, at least a good distance from home shores. A move beyond one's borders and familiar surroundings immediately made one a "missionary." "Foreign" mission work in this period was mainly to Native and black Americans, European colonists or dignitaries, and to people of mixed race, but primarily to those who were or had been Catholic. Conversion of others appeared to be a secondary aim of mission, especially for clergy.

Second, several of those who went overseas were themselves immigrants to the United States and had already experienced the process of adjustment to a new land and people. Marianne Cope, German by birth, entered a community of German and Irish women at a time when cultural differences were still marked in language, food, and religious devotions. In her administrative responsibilities, she dealt with an Italian friar provincial. Her first group of Sisters to Hawaii were Irish and German. The Holy Family Sisters in British Honduras were of French, Creole, or Cuban heritage and met a racially mixed group of students in Stann Creek. A number of the missionaries, such as Kent Stone and Joseph Dutton, were spiritual immigrants, converts to Catholicism. The few lay missionaries had worked previously with the particular congregation with whom they labored on the mission.

Third, we note that there are both external and internal dimensions of the call to mission overseas. The external promptings for American Catholics came from the Propaganda Fide office in Rome. This office had a global view of the mission world, and the director was able to shift groups to new mission areas pending outcomes of war or political machinations of countries, whatever their predilection for Christianity. Requests were made to the U.S. Bishops and to major superiors of international orders or congregations. Major superiors performed the same function as Propaganda Fide and were able to shift missions and personnel from one province to another, depending on the political climate or nationalist impulses.

Internal motivating factors provided the personal, spiritual energy for missions overseas. The orders and congregations, which had European provinces, provided an outlet for American men and women to respond to this interior call, especially if their local group did not engage in missions overseas. Such was the case, for example, with Catherine Bushman and Joanne O'Connell. No formal "mission preparation" was provided; the primary formation for mission was community spirituality or charism, the members' personal life of faith, trust in Divine Providence, and avocational experience. Such resources enabled missionaries to work on the problems of adjustment, to gain strength in their difficulties, and to relate to people whose customs were often different from their own. For women missionaries, "housing" the Blessed Sacrament in their chapel and corresponding prayer in the presence of the Eucharist provided security and affirmation of their mission call. Redemptorists, Jesuits, and the Sisters of the Holy Family brought along the devotions for which their groups were known, but they developed varying mission strategies based on that spirituality.

Fourth, there were differences, as well as similarities, in the way the women and men approached mission. Women had strength of numbers because they lived and worked in community. Any sense of loneliness and isolation in a new land was less acute because of daily companionship. Women tended to be in regular contact with a variety of socioeconomic classes and especially with persons of another color or race, who were in the majority. The Sisters identified with indigenous people almost at once. Because of this sustained association, people were inclined to place their confidence in the Sisters more readily than the clergy. The Sisters' generally positive appreciation for indigenous potential was allied with the belief that the people had a role to play in the development of social and intellectual culture.

On the practical side, people could see more immediately what the Sisters were doing in "mission": dirt gave way to cleanliness, illness gave way to health, illiteracy gave way to a new kind of knowledge. Sewing and cleaning not only made their convent feel like a "home," but these skills helped domesticate the hospital and classroom, extending the ecclesial environment to a more civic domain. The civic environment consequently became the locus of ecumenicity, the place where people of varied religions and cultures interacted with each other and with Roman Catholics. Further, domestic skills taught to indigenous girls enabled them to create an income, thus making them self-sustaining.

Missionary clergy saw their primary task as establishing, or reestablishing, the Church, and emphasized sacramental practice. Often this meant physically building a church, the sacramental home for Catholics. In many cases in the Caribbean, "regularizing" marriages was the first step priests attempted in the "rehabilitation" of those who had been baptized Catholic. Salvation and eternal life, which the clergy preached and offered through the sacraments, were more illusive concepts. The apparent remoteness of such theological ideas was sometimes reflected in the distance clergy felt between themselves and the people, at least initially. Because a traditional source of income was needed for spiritual ministration, the clergy returned to the United States more frequently than women in order to raise funds. Select schools also provided a source of income for some male religious congregations. While several men might arrive together from the United States, once in the mission land they spent much of their time traveling alone from station to station. There was thus little solace for loneliness and isolation. The necessity of clergy for the mission's chief liturgical action made the parishes dependent on clergy presence. In their absence either the community faltered and had to be rebuilt, or Sisters and laity stepped in to be liturgical leaders, especially in devotional prayer.

Priests tended to raise the specter of Protestant mission activity as motivation more than women. Outward recognition for clergy appeared as a bishopric for one of the first priests to work in the area, a pattern which would continue into the twentieth century. Acquisition of ecclesiastical authority frequently involved travel from the mission either to the United States or, sometimes, to Rome. A good deal of clerical time was spent establishing ecclesial jurisdiction in the early years of a mission.

For both men and women the activities of the mission were diverse, simultaneously involving full-time work as teacher or pastor and other tasks such as visitation of the sick and building churches; their work filled the entire day. Mission was a twenty-four-hour profession. Because the men and women recognized that they were the "foreigners," both sought opportunities for support. Mission fatalities, which came from ill adjustment physically or psychologically to climate and circumstances, occurred among both sexes.

Sisters and clergy occasionally appropriated tasks which had traditionally belonged to each other. The needed flexibility in mission situations called for women to perform liturgical functions at times and for men to prepare their own meals, for example. Often a shared spirituality (the liturgy in the Bahamas, devotion to the Sacred Heart in Belize) between the men's and women's groups created a further bond. While devotional life among immigrants in the United States during this period often emphasized asceticism, the purgative way, and the corresponding virtues of obedience and loyalty to authority,[39] devotional practice in the mission areas highlighted traditional family values. The Jesuit use of Sacred Heart devotions further underscored a masculine identity, which affirmed relationship and affectivity as the basis of love.

Fifth, mission methodology was an unselfconscious response to immediate conditions in the mission. In addition to spirituality, which was the primary foundation for mission praxis, women and men viewed the schools as a nucleus for conversions. If missionaries engaged the children they could attract the parents to Catholicism. More women than men discharged this apostolate. Women opened their schools almost immediately to "natives," whereas the men generally favored "select" schools for the English (British) or Spanish-speaking families or other more well-to-do families. Such was the case with the Brothers of Mary in Hawaii and the Jesuits at St. John's College in British Honduras. The "free" schools generally provided an education for more girls than boys. The Sisters tended to include persons from mixed ethnic or African origin in the circle of higher education, whereas the Jesuits tended, at least in these years, to limit learning opportunities. To some extent, mission practice was affected by assumptions missionaries held about the strength and limits of various populations.

Finally, in the last decades of the nineteenth century the missionaries, living among people of contrasting cultural practices, standards of living, and educational levels, served as a goad to U.S. Catholics to reevaluate their American lifestyle. Mother Mary Rose, ruminating over her visit to her Sisters of Charity in the Bahamas, penned a letter on the train on her way back to New York:

> Amid all [the Sisters'] privations (and they are many) — they are bright and happy and sunny — pious and zealous — sowing for others to reap.... My eyes fill when I look upon them, and think how easily some of us grumble up north. These are among the "ten good men" who save the city.[40]

Chapter 4

The Spanish-American War, the Americanist Period, and a National Focus for Missions Overseas, 1898–1919

The mission of America abroad took on new meaning after the Spanish-American War. Theodore Roosevelt, in a talk published subsequently, noted: "If we stand idly by, if we seek merely swollen ease and ignoble peace, if we shrink from the hard contest...then the bolder and stronger peoples will pass us by, and win for themselves the domination of the world."[1] The tone of this statement, which reflected some of the themes of Progressivism, sounded in the international transactions of the U.S. government, in the Student Volunteer Movement for Foreign Missions, and in a new consciousness about overseas missions among American Catholics. Several churches, including those in the United States and Australia, were removed from their "mission" status by the reorganization of the curial offices in Rome in 1908. Ecclesially this meant that churches were self-sustaining both financially and in vocations from among their citizens. This change of status occurred within the context of other international events in which the United States was squarely placed.

Political Context of the Spanish-American War

In 1895, Great Britain rebuffed President Cleveland after he had offered to arbitrate the long-standing border dispute England had between Venezuela and British Guiana. That same year Cubans, financed by American sugar planters interested in American control of the island, revolted against Spanish rule. Cruel subjection of General Valerian Weyler, who led the insurrection, other arguments between the United States and Spain over Cuba, the yellow journalism of the Hearst and Pulitzer newspapers, and the sinking of the U.S. battleship *Maine* in the Havana harbor eventually erupted in a war between the United States and Spain in April 1898. At the request of Pope Leo XIII, an optimistic archbishop, John Ireland, had been sent to mediate between the U.S. and Spain in order to avert the war, but he failed and returned home disappointed. The United States was psychologically and physically prepared for war, having strengthened the navy and increased the congressional budget for national defense. By August, Spanish forces in Manila had surrendered and the "splendid little war" was over. Negotiations started in October, and the Treaty of Paris was signed on 10 December 1898. Under the treaty's terms the United States annexed the Hawaiian Islands, occupied Cuba, and acquired the Philippine Islands and Guam. Puerto Rico was confirmed as an unconsolidated territory. The United States had become a world power.

Additional territorial acquisition continued after the war for "liberation." Secretary of State John Hay aggressively argued for an Open Door Policy in China in 1899; the following year the Hay-Pauncefote Treaty opened Central America to American influence. In 1903, the United States stepped in to create the country of Panama to secure the area for an Isthmian canal, and U.S. business enterprise expanded to the south. The Monroe Doctrine continued to be invoked in America's favor. Flexing of the country's international muscle coincided with an increasingly optimistic spirit throughout the land.

Catholic Reaction to Protestant Mission Efforts

Increased influence of the United States as a world power and the enthusiasm of the Progressive Era found another outlet in the growing numbers of college students who went overseas through the work of the Student Volunteer Movement for Foreign Missions, identified with John R. Mott.[2] The words of the evangelical Josiah Strong, who a decade earlier had apostrophized the Saxon in America, could now be applied to the whole world: "The Saxon in America [the American Protestant] holds in his hands the destinies of mankind."[3]

Not only did Protestants have an invigorated group of young missionaries to send to China and to many countries which had been or were English colonies, but after the war of 1898 they had new places to evangelize: areas which had been traditionally Catholic and Spanish. As Mott remarked, "For the first time in the history of the Church practically the whole world is open...."[4] Protestants had engaged in missionary work in the Caribbean since the late 1700s, German Protestants had immigrated to Brazil in the nineteenth century, and Latin America had received Protestant groups who had served small missions to Native Americans since the 1880s.[5] But the presence of these Protestant groups in southern Catholic countries had not seemed a threat to the mainly Spanish or Portuguese Catholic leadership.

However, after the 1898 war Catholic missionaries took note, often with dismay, at the influx of Protestants. While the Redemptorists had been in the Caribbean for several decades, they came to Puerto Rico in 1902, after the departure of Spanish Redemptorists, fearing what they thought to be a Protestant government coming from the United States. The U.S. Redemptorists changed their style of preaching subsequent to the Treaty of Paris. With many evangelically minded Protestants flooding the area, clergy concentrated on fundamental teachings of the Catholic Church and apologetics in an effort to untangle what they saw as religious confusion among their parishioners. The Redemptorists were asked by the governing agent to tend to the prisons, but when the missionaries arrived they found that Protestants had already taken leadership in that domain. In the early 1900s, noting that Protestants were rounding up the youth of Mayaguez, Father Charles Sigl (1853–1921), who had been holding catechetical classes for the youth of the city, decided that the only way to combat the influence of Presbyterians who were filling their schools and institutions with Puerto Ricans was to open parish schools for the children.[6]

Protestant efforts to learn the dialects of the people for effective evangelization were also noted by a young U.S. Jesuit, who remarked on his arrival in the Philippines in 1905:

> Here (shall we not blush to admit it?) the protestant minister leads the way. My last visit to Bilibid prison in Manila was saddened by the sight of a protestant minister, who has made a special study of Taglo [*sic*], the Manila native dialect, in order to preach in that tongue, and one of the first things I heard on my arrival here was that another American protestant minister was preaching in Ilocano to the natives of this place. Unless this section of the Islands be soon supplied with priests speaking the native dialect, hundreds, nay thousands, will be lost to the church.[7]

Consequences of War for U.S. Catholics

Catholics in the United States, emerging from periodic bouts with nativism, stood toward the end of the nineteenth century affirming the compatibility of Catholicism and American liberties. Lest there be doubt about this in anyone's mind, once the Spanish-American War began, the U.S. Bishops forthrightly stated: "Whatever may have been the individual opinions of Americans prior to the declaration of war, there can now be no two opinions as to the duty of every loyal citizen.... We, the members of the Catholic Church are true Americans, and as such are loyal to our country and our flag and obedient to the highest decrees and the supreme authority of the nation."[8]

Relations with Puerto Rico, Cuba, and the Philippines

A large number of Catholics fought in the war. Priests volunteered to be chaplains and several congregations of women religious nursed the wounded soldiers.[9] At war's end, a Catholic was invited to be on the Peace Commission in Paris, but he declined. The Vatican sent Archbishop Placide Chapelle of New Orleans, who was in Rome at the time, to be its representative as an observer at the peace treaty meetings. He was appointed apostolic delegate to Cuba and Puerto Rico (and to the Philippines the next year). While representing the interests of the Catholic Church, he had to be sensitive to the American experience of Church independence from the state.[10]

American Catholics had several concerns subsequent to the Treaty of Paris. In general, they feared that any enactment with respect to the separation of Church and state, especially in traditionally Catholic areas of Puerto Rico, Cuba, and the Philippines, might affect legislation in the United States, heightening anti-Catholic bias. The consequences of possible state withdrawal of funds from the Catholic Church after several hundred years of support posed a daunting prospect in those countries. The Catholic Church held vast tracts of land (for cemeteries and institutions) and buildings (for education, hospitals, and other humanitarian services). Tremendous adjustments would need to be made in education and the running of hospitals and other social institutions.[11] Stories, real and imagined, of the immoral behavior of clergy compounded the issue of reimbursement to the Church for these lands. This was a particularly volatile subject in the Philippines, where the newspapers carried anti-friar articles. In 1903, four American clergy, three from Philadelphia, were appointed by Rome to head Filipino dioceses. Archbishop John Ireland was able for a few months to recommend U.S. lay teachers for positions in the Philippines. He particularly sought men for these appointments.

> It is now arranged that I can have application confirmed without delay in Washington and have the appointees at once sent forward to Manila. As a matter of fact, all who are to be appointed through me must be prepared to leave San Francisco by the first of July. Later on all appointments will be made under the rules of the Civil Services and there will be no longer any opportunity to have Catholics appointed as Catholics.[12]

In Cuba, the U.S.-appointed governor endeavored to promulgate laws declaring the religious ceremony of marriage invalid. This was an effort to eliminate concubinage, because pastors charged for these religious ceremonies as a means of income and, as many were too poor to pay the fees, the man and woman simply lived together. Because Puerto Rico would be permanently annexed to the United States, the Church would be responsible overnight for an additional million Catholics.[13] Marist Father James H. Blenk, SM, succeeded the Spanish bishop of San Juan, followed in this office by Augustinian Father William A. Jones, OSA.

Several religious congregations of men and women sent missionaries to teach or to take over institutions in these countries, though not all of these people were successful.[14] Three Jesuits were sent from the New York Province to Manila, invited by Archbishop Jeremiah Harty. The Spanish Jesuits had an observatory and the Ateneo de Manila, but the young American Jesuits were needed to teach English to Filipinos and for sacramental ministration to the American troops on the islands.[15]

Americanist Controversy and Missions to Protestants

Political concerns and an internal Church issue also intertwined, exemplified by a group eventually identified as the Americanists. Among these persons were Archbishop John Ireland, Archbishop John J. Keane, Monsignor Denis J. O'Connell, Paulist Father Walter Elliott, and the French Abbé Félix Klein. They were arguing with "Romanists" in the United States and in Europe over a number of issues, among them the American republic's experiment with the separation of Church and state. At this time, the Catholic Church held that the ideal was the union of Church and state, with the Church, of course, being the Roman Catholic Church. Conservatives felt the Americanists were arguing for the American experience of democracy as the norm for Catholicism around the world. Some of these same issues erupted among Protestants as well, involving the distrust European Protestants felt for liberal Protestants in the United States, later coming to a head at the Stockholm Conference on Life and Work in 1920.[16]

Walter Elliott's publication in French of a life of the Paulist Fathers' founder, Isaac Hecker (1819–88), brought Hecker's ideas to the attention of Father Charles Maignen and the Jesuits in Rome. The French translation was poor, and certain persons in Rome were looking for an excuse to condemn the Americanists' ideas. Earlier suspicions of Cardinal Rampolla, the Vatican secretary of state, that American Catholic societies had been involved in attempts to overthrow Spanish-backed Cuban leadership now compounded with insinuations about heterodoxy. In January 1899, a month after the Treaty of Paris was signed, an ailing Pope Leo XIII issued a condemnation of Americanism. By Americanism he referred to teachings purportedly held by Hecker and others which attempted to "modernize" the Church. These teachings included a supposed rejection of the need for outside direction in spiritual matters, preference for active rather than passive virtues, and repudiation of religious vows as incompatible with Christian freedom.[17] These points, in some respects, distorted what Hecker believed. Though the ideas were denounced by Rome, the Paulist's approach to evangelization was not. The pope wrote:

> If among the different methods of preaching the word of God, that sometimes seems preferable by which those who dissent from us are spoken to, not in the church but in any private and proper place, not in disputation but in amicable conference, such method is not to be reprehended....[18]

This positive, even somewhat ecumenical, approach to Protestants had been a key factor in Isaac Hecker's methodology. While supporting the authority of the pontiff, the Paulist founder believed that at this point in history it was important to pay attention to the work of the Holy Spirit, who speaks in all persons and is the source of the aspirations within the individual human heart. Through the power of persuasion, any earnest individual seeking God would be convinced of the truth of Christianity in the Catholic Church and, hence, be converted. His approach provided a sharp contrast to the polemical apologetic of the period. His disciple, Walter Elliott (1842–1928), reintroduced this persuasive approach in the missions to non-Catholics, which he renewed in 1892.[19]

Elliott and a younger Paulist from California, Father Alexander Doyle (1857–1912), had at least tangential ties to the war. Doyle was consulted by Theodore Roosevelt in the appointment of Catholic military chaplains. From May 1898 through 1901, Doyle published thirty articles and editorials in the *Catholic World* on the notion of American expansionism consequent to the treaty. Elliott, a veteran of the Civil War, organized and presided at a memorial service at St. Paul's, New York City, for those who had died aboard the *Maine*. Two years before the war, the two Paulists organized the Catholic Missionary Union, whose purposes were to engage priests and laity as missionaries to non-Catholics in the United States, to provide for their maintenance, to distribute Catholic literature, and to assist bishops in carrying on home missions. Publication of reports from these missionaries appeared in the *Missionary*, a magazine devoted to the conversion of America.[20]

Mission Congresses

Catholic Missionary Union

Doyle and Elliott periodically brought together the missionaries who preached to non-Catholics around the country. The first of the congresses was held in Winchester, Tennessee, in 1901. Four subsequent gatherings took place through 1909. As one participant observed, the meetings awakened a dormant mission interest among Catholics. Doyle and Elliott enunciated the principles of the missionary movement in America: the mission vocation as the primary vocation of Christians, clergy responsibility for all persons in the parish area, whether or not they were Catholics, and a persuasive rather than a controversial method of apologetics. Missions to non-Catholics were not to be the work of a religious congregation but part of the regular ministry of diocesan clergy. Laity were the "junior partners" in mission work.[21] Protestants took note of these conferences and were surprised at the ameliorating spirit they saw. Said one editor of the *Churchman* (Episcopalian), "How these missionaries reconcile their spirit with the spirit of the Syllabus of 1864 or the *Pastor Aeternus* of 1870 we do not know. Perhaps the love of souls constrains them not to think about it."[22] By 1909, twenty-three dioceses had a missionary band, with a total of fifty-four priests.

To train missionary priests for the conversion of America and with some mention of those who would go to other countries, Elliott and Doyle opened the Apostolic Mission House in 1902 on the grounds of the Catholic University of America in Washington, D.C. After holding classes in Catholic University buildings for a year, a permanent facility was built on the Michigan Avenue side of campus and dedicated in April 1904. In the dedicatory sermon, John J. Keane, the rector of the university, noted that the proximity of the university to the Mission House was a reminder that though love of learning for its own sake was praiseworthy, "scholarship needs to be infused with zeal." He spoke of students at the Mission House as "chosen Knights of the Round Table of the Prince of Peace,...[t]rained to the noblest development intellectual, moral, and spiritual, hampered by no limitation of parochial obligations..., men of valor and of power who can be called on, and depended on, for every hardest and highest achievement."[23]

The architecture of the Mission House was patterned after Spanish colonial buildings with red brick covered with stucco, tile roofs, a loggia on the second floor, and an austere interior, the latter furnished through the assistance of the Georgetown Visitation Nuns. "It was in the *loggias* of the old missions that the priests spent hours in meditation, walking backward and forward. All the student priests who will come to the Mission House will be expected to spend certain hours each day in meditation and silent study and prayer."[24] Elliott had in mind the correlation of contemplation and mission as the foundation for the missionary's formation.

The need for such a mission formation program seemed even more of a necessity after the Spanish-American War.

> There is a bitter complaint among the Southern bishops that they cannot secure the kind of apostolic missionaries which the impoverished and necessitous condition of their dioceses demand. Moreover, it has been given out that the settlement in the Philippines may necessitate the withdrawal of some of the Spanish friars as soon as their places can be filled with American or native priests. There is, therefore, an urgent demand for priests who will devote themselves to the missionary life in our new colonies, and consequently a seminary in which they may be educated for the work.[25]

The first diocesan priest in the Catholic Missionary Union, Cleveland's William Stephen Kress (1863–1936), remarked to his fellow participants at the 1901 missionary congress:

> The United States may or may not become a great world power. Some are wishing for this, others dreading it; but whatever their diversity of views on this point, it cannot be doubted that the Catholic Church must ever be true to her name. She is not for those alone who can boast of a Catholic ancestry; but belongs to all. In proportion as American influence extends, the opportunity for the American missionary broadens. We have evidently a part of our own to perform in the final triumph of Christianity.[26]

In spite of the original plan to train priests for missions overseas, the Apostolic Mission House concentrated on missions to non-Catholics and Catholics and trained some of the Josephite Fathers to evangelize among African Americans. However, it was at the 1904 congress sponsored by the Catholic Missionary Union that Father Thomas F. Price (who attended several of the conferences) and Father James A. Walsh were to meet for the first time to share their vision for a seminary for overseas missionaries. Before this project came to light, however, Francis Clement Kelley (1870–1948), with leadership from the Midwest and with a mission theology quite different than that of the Catholic Missionary Union, organized two mission congresses under the auspices of the Catholic Church Extension Society, a mission-funding organization which he founded in 1906.

The Catholic Church Extension Society and Its Missionary Congresses

As a pastor in the small town of Lapeer, Michigan, where Catholics were a minority, Kelley delivered a paper at the Catholic Missionary Union Congress in 1904 on the "missionary wedge." By this he meant that a priest would speak first on secular subjects such as history or ethics on the lyceum circuit, a "distinctly American institution." Non-Catholics in small towns would thereby obtain a favorable image of Catholicism because of the knowledgeable priest. The speaker would thus be a "wedge" for the missionary coming later, a secular word preceding the sacred word. Kelley himself had done this in order to obtain additional income for his mission congregation.[27]

Kelley was impressed with the large Protestant churches in the small towns where Protestantism was the majority religion. He felt these buildings induced pride and respect among the people. He would spend much of his life collecting funds to construct equally impressive structures for poor and country parishes. Splendid buildings, "no matter how small, are the surest guarantee of the stability of the Church."[28] "Without a church there would soon be no Faith, for the Christian pride would surely die."[29]

Starting first with an office in Lapeer, then Detroit, and finally Chicago, the Catholic Church Extension Society was inaugurated after nineteen men gathered with Kelley at the home of Chicago Archbishop James E. Quigley. Kelley wanted to draw the attention of American Catholics to people in the vast geographic areas away from the centers of population, where Catholics tended to cluster. The image and direction of the society came from Kelley's visit to the office of one of the men gathered at Archbishop Quigley's home, Ambrose Petry, an advertising agent. Kelley henceforth would appeal to good and efficient business practices to run a successful society. Petry, who earned a seat on the board of the society, advised Kelley in setting up the extension office in Chicago:

> Put the best foot forward. It is always a good thing to smile even if it kills you, and in business to think and to look like a millionaire. People may criticize, but they will come across with the money just the same; and, now and then, you will meet a man who would give you five dollars in a poor office but five hundred in a good one. You'll find before you are long at this work that it is a business proposition as well as a religious one.[30]

A secular business would provide the model that Kelley would follow. To promote the importance of home missions, Kelley began a popular magazine, *Extension,* the first issue of which appeared in 1906. Its purpose was to raise funds for priests in home missions, particularly in the South and West, and to build churches, the catalysts for conversions. The masthead on the magazine in the initial months was "Advocate of the Missionary Spirit." Over the years, the appellation changed to "A Catholic National Monthly" and finally to "The World's Greatest." When Kelley settled the Extension Society in Chicago, he opened the office in the impressive Rookery Building.

Unlike the Society for the Propagation of the Faith, the Extension Society director was unable to gain official recognition in the parishes, particularly in the East.[31] Kelley hoped to unify these mission efforts springing up around the country, as he felt these were competing with each other. To achieve this end and to draw attention to the work of the missions, he organized the First American Catholic Missionary Congress, held in Chicago from 16 to 18 November 1909. Some eastern clerics thought it presumptuous of Chicago to accommodate such a gathering. But earlier well-publicized national events in the Windy City — the World's Fair (1892–93), the World's Parliament of Religions (1893), and the World's Columbian Exposition (1893) — signified that the Midwest was an area to be reckoned with. Archbishop Quigley's inspiration for the congress came from having witnessed Protestant mission gatherings while rector of the cathedral in Buffalo. Kelley, a good organizer, put together the event.

The congress was attended by laity, clergy, religious, and the hierarchy, and included speakers from various mission agencies: home missions in the city (including settlement programs for homeless men), immigrant-assistance organizations, and Catholic Indian and Negro missions. Kelley spoke on the Catholic Church Extension Society, and Doyle addressed the group on the apostolic mission activity of diocesan priests. Two Army personnel in the Philippines, the Reverend Joseph Casey and Major E. J. Vattmann, spoke mainly of the work with U.S. military on the islands and in defense of the friars.[32] The conference was successful financially ($35,000 was raised for the missions) and in terms of enthusiasm and in numbers attending, especially from the laity. However, Kelley did not achieve his goal to unite the mission fund-raising groups, though he continued this quest.

By the time the Catholic Extension Society director organized the Second American Catholic Missionary Congress in Boston from 19 to 22 October 1913, missions overseas were represented by "real live missionaries,"[33] Americans Denis J. Dougherty, bishop of Jaro, Philippines; James F. McDermott, SJ, from Jamaica; and Redemptorist John Lynch from Puerto Rico. The mission picture in Africa was presented by the Reverend L. J. Van Den Bergh, and Divine Word missionary Joseph Koesters spoke on missions in Manchuria. The apostolic delegate, Giovanni Vincenzo Bonzano (1867–1927), a former missionary to China and, later, president of the Missionary College of Propaganda Fide, was the papal representative. The conference took place in the city where two years earlier an immense, month-long mission congress, "The World in Boston," had been held, sponsored by seventeen Protestant mission boards on the East Coast.[34] Kelley continued to have difficulty gaining the confidence of eastern bishops, but the archbishop of Boston, William O'Connell, was amenable to hosting the conference in his archdiocese.

When the mission congress convened, Holy Cross Cathedral in Boston was festooned with cardinal-red swags draped around the pillars. Knights of Columbus and ecclesial dignitaries in full regalia processed into the church for the Mass, accompanied by a hymn, "O Sacred Cross," composed by the archbishop. Other songs included the "Hymn of the Martyrs in the Colosseum," and the "Congress Hymn," which emphasized the light of truth and freedom in contrast to the darkness of the world, which "quaffed the sin-cup." In addition to talks given at Symphony Hall in Boston, speakers fanned out throughout the area each evening to speak on mission themes at parish churches.

At the conference, Kelley again addressed the need to unify the fund-raising efforts growing around the country. Finances were under control of individual agencies, which often produced magazines to solicit funds. Mission funds were also collected by priests or bishops (both from Europe and mission areas), and at the congress one speaker noted that the United States was a "well-worked field" by 1913. When the special committee appointed by the Extension Society board met at the 1913 conference, it noted that the time had come "when collections for missions should be thoroughly organized and put rather upon an official basis than a purely sentimental one."[35] Again, nothing came of Kelley's efforts.

American Branch of the Society for the Propagation of the Faith

During the first years of the Catholic Church Extension Society, Kelley felt competition from the papally endorsed Society for the Propagation of the Faith, one of several European mission-funding societies started in the nineteenth century during the reinvigoration of European missions. The Leopoldine Foundation and the Ludwig Verein, for example, sought to aid German overseas missionaries. The Catholic Church in America, especially in the Midwest, benefited greatly from these groups. The Holy Childhood Association, founded in France in 1843 by an aristocrat, Bishop Charles de Forbin-Janson, in 1866 already had a director in the United States, Theodore Thery, a New York Jesuit. At the time of his death in 1889, the association had been established in thirty-seven dioceses and the children had amassed $162,000. The founder had thought of the association not simply as a fund-raising organization but as an apologetic argument for Catholics who sought to save the lives of children other groups had left to die. The *Annals of the Association of the Holy Childhood* eventually were published in Europe in several languages.

The Holy Spirit Fathers, though unsuccessful in receiving aid from this association for missions to African Americans in the United States, assumed responsibility for a national office, and a Holy Spirit Father was appointed in

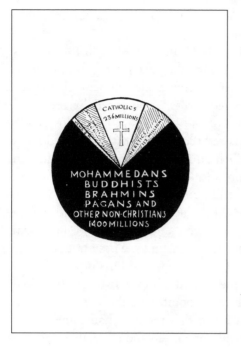

THE RELIGIOUS WORLD
TODAY

Send forth, O God,
Thy Light and Thy Truth.
"And the land that was desolate
and impassable shall be glad
and the wilderness shall rejoice
and flourish like the lily...
They shall see the glory of the Lord
and the beauty of our God."
Psalm xlii; Is. xxxv

Society for the Propagation
of the Faith
Boston, Mass.

Propagation Animation Efforts: An example of "popular piety" in a less ecumenical age, the front of this holy card circulated in 1910 by the Boston Society of the Propagation of the Faith on one side gave statistics on the numbers of Catholics, "heretics" [Protestants], "schismatics" [Orthodox], Jews, and members of the major world religions; and on the other gave a prayer for Catholics to say for the spread of their faith. (Courtesy, Archives, Archdiocese of Boston)

1892. Five years later, Father John B. Willms, CSSp, became director and served until his death in 1914. During his term, the association raised about $418,000. The association was particularly successful in German parishes in the United States. The idea of the society was to have children helping children around the world, though by the early 1920s the funds were used to educate Chinese seminarians. Much of the success of this operation in these years was due to the unpaid labor of Charles Jaegle, the founder and editor of the *Pittsburgh Observer,* who ran the office on a day-to-day basis from 1890 to 1904. While the association raised fairly substantial funds, after Willms's death a priest with financial and business experience was sought for the directorship.[36]

In 1822, Pauline Jaricot responded to the poverty she saw at the Sulpician House of Foreign Missions, where her brother was a student, by establishing a group of friends to contribute to the support of future missionaries.[37] The mission-funding society was founded in Lyons, France. The U.S. Bishops had approved the foundation of the SPF in the United States in 1884, but the organization was not incorporated until 1897, with its center at the Sulpician seminary in Baltimore. The rector, Alphonse Magnien, decided to appoint a director who would correspond with American clergy and write articles about foreign missions. The clergy would introduce the society into their parishes,

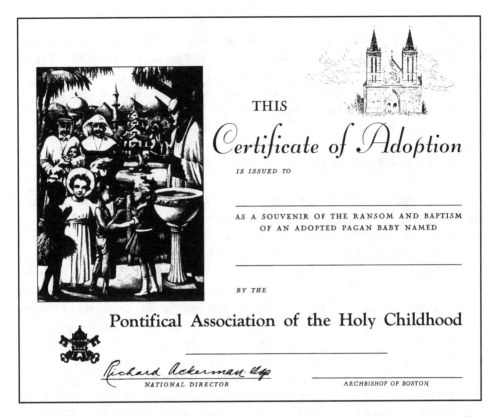

THIS

Certificate of Adoption

IS ISSUED TO

_____

AS A SOUVENIR OF THE RANSOM AND BAPTISM
OF AN ADOPTED PAGAN BABY NAMED

_____

BY THE

Pontifical Association of the Holy Childhood

Richard Ackerman &c.

NATIONAL DIRECTOR   ARCHBISHOP OF BOSTON

Adopting and Ransoming Pagan Babies: As orphanages and child care institutions were staffed by Catholic overseas missionaries, one of the favored ways of personalizing requests to the laity to support them was the appeal to ransom pagan babies. This "Certificate" was issued to benefactors of the Pontifical Association for the Holy Childhood (see pages 134–37). (Courtesy, Archives, Archdiocese of Boston)

rather than have missionaries leave their people for extended periods. First, Henry Regis Granjon (1863–1922) assisted Magnien, and after Granjon's appointment as bishop of the Arizona Territory in 1900, the Reverend Joseph Freri (1864–1927) took on this work.[38] Freri remained the national director of the SPF until 1924. A Sulpician-trained missionary in the Arizona vicariate from 1888 to 1896, Freri then taught canon law at St. John's Seminary, Brighton, Massachusetts, until his appointment as SPF director. The national SPF office moved to New York City in 1903. Through his book, *Native Clergy for Mission Countries,* and many articles in his national magazine, *Catholic Missions,* Freri kept before his audience the need for native clergy and featured the wide variety of men and women missionaries throughout the world.[39]

A second area of emphasis in the SPF material was the importance of the laity for missions. The widely read Charles Montalembert's *Monks of the West* divided the epochs of mission history into the apostolic age, the "national" period of monks like Patrick, Cyril, Methodius, and Boniface, and the time of sixteenth-century missionaries who moved beyond Europe to the New World and elsewhere. Freri portrayed mission history after the apostolic age as an era of union and protectorship, when "the temporal powers of the world united to establish the Kingdom of Jesus Christ." In the third, present time, "Providence substituted the people for the kings."[40] This was the age of the laity, and in Lyons this was especially true, as the mostly lay SPF board made decisions about financial allocations for missions.

Catholic Foreign Mission Society of America (Maryknoll)

In the meantime, new developments for mission abroad had come in the intersecting lives of the founders of the Catholic Foreign Mission Society of America, the first group founded in the United States to focus specifically on missions overseas.[41] As many European countries each had a "national" foreign mission society, so this group, as its title indicated, was intended to be the official missionary society in the United States for missions overseas. As James A. Walsh noted in an editorial in *The Field Afar*: "We rejoice in the fact that we belong to and represent the Church in the United States, and we pray that the time may come when Catholics ... will be glad to point to the Seminary at Maryknoll as one of the great national results of American Catholic activities."[42]

Since before the turn of the century, Bishop Henry Vaughan (1852–1903), founder of the Mill Hill missionaries in England, had urged that the Americans, so generous with their mission funds, begin a seminary for foreign missionaries. He had traversed the country seeking money to start his society and had even tried his hand prospecting for gold. He admired the Americans' energy, sense of high adventure, and ability to risk everything for a good cause. In 1889, he addressed the U.S. Catholic Bishops on the centennial of the establishment of the Catholic Church in the United States and encouraged them to sponsor a foreign mission seminary.[43] The expertise at the Apostolic Mission House rested with missions to Catholics and non-Catholics, so Elliott had suggested that the Society for the Propagation of the Faith councils in Lyons and Paris set aside funding for a seminary in the United States for missions overseas. John Cardinal Farley, known for his love for the missions,[44] had considered opening such a seminary. The Divine Word Missionaries, founded specifically for missions abroad in 1875 by the German priest Arnold Janssen in Steyl, Holland, had established an American province by 1895 and opened their mission house, St. Mary's Seminary, in 1908 in Shermerville, twenty miles northwest of Chicago. Their work at this point was mainly to blacks in the southern United States. The sister congregation also founded by Janssen, the Missionary Sisters, Servants of the Holy Spirit, arrived in the United States in 1901, led by Mother Mary Leonarda Lentrup (1874–1937). In the next five years, forty Sisters arrived from Steyl to help the Divine Word Missionaries by teaching in Mississippi and Arkansas.[45] These two mission congregations sent missionaries from the United States in 1918 (men) and 1920 (women).

The three persons whose energy, insight, and work created the Catholic Foreign Mission Society were Thomas Frederick Price (1860–1919), James A. Walsh (1867–1936), and Mary Josephine Rogers (1882–1955).[46] Thomas Price, who grew up in Wilmington, North Carolina, had been an altar boy for James Gibbons when the latter was a missionary there. Sunday worship was held in the homes of Catholics, a minority in the area, and the priest traveled from place to place. In 1886, Price became the first North Carolinian to be ordained a priest, and he also became a missionary to North Carolina. Intrepid in his mission work, he walked hundreds of miles speaking with people in the mainly Protestant South. From his experience he defined three mission urgencies: a literary journal to inform people of Catholic truths, a missionary apostolate for priests outside the state to develop Catholic life in North Carolina, and a home for children whose parents were too poor to provide for them. To meet the first need he founded *Truth,* a magazine intended to portray Catholic belief and practice. To fill the second need he founded a seminary in 1897, Regina Apostolorum, outside of Raleigh, North Carolina. The same year he opened Nazareth Orphanage, situated on the grounds of the seminary and staffed by the Sisters of Mercy from Belmont, North Carolina. It began to occur to him that the success of the local apostolate might be contingent on a wider concern for missions overseas, an idea which he wrote about in *Truth.* While engaged in these activities Price also preached missions in other parts of the country and was well known to many priests and bishops.[47]

As a young boy, James A. Walsh heard the *Annals of the Propagation of the Faith* read around the kitchen table in Cambridge, Massachusetts. He grew up in a city which had a rich tradition of Protestant missionary agencies, among which was the American Board of Christian Foreign Missions. Most of these groups published mission information and programs to promote missions. Catholics in the area had benefited from the Society for the Propagation of the Faith offices in France. In gratitude for such assistance, Bishop John J. Williams (1822–1907) established one of the first U.S. diocesan branches of the SPF. Further, he invited the Sulpician priests to teach at St. John's Seminary, Brighton, where Walsh attended after a few years at Boston College. Though the courses comprised the standard seminary curriculum of the time, the interaction between the priests and seminarians brought out the missionary dimensions of Sulpician life.[48] Rector of the seminary, Father John Baptist Hogan, presented talks on various aspects of mission life and from him Walsh learned about Theophane Vénard, Hogan's classmate and Paris foreign missionary martyred in Tonkin. A classmate of Walsh, Charles F. Aiken (1864–1924), who would later chair the theology department at Catholic University of America, wrote in his diary of the impression one of the professors, Francis Gigot (1859–1920), made on him:

Last night I called on Fr. Gigot as usual to help him in his study of English. He had just received a letter from a young friend who had set out last year on a perilous mission to China; a beautiful soul, Fr. Gigot said, one of the most distinguished and wealthy families of Paris. He chose, for the love of God, to renounce the brilliant prospect that tempted him to a life of ease and luxury in Paris,...to wear out his young life, perhaps spill his blood, in apostolic service among the heathen. He was sent to one of the most dangerous districts of China, where fierce persecution has been going on for some months. Churches and schools had been leveled to the ground, and his own life was in jeopardy. Oh! what a living example of heroic self-sacrifice! What an elegant reproach to us Seminarians who find it hard to deny ourselves a few petty worldly pleasures and honors and who, living in peace and comfort, find it irksome at times to maintain that ardor of zeal which ought always to stir every fibre of a young ecclesiastic's heart.[49]

Walsh was ordained in 1892, and after a few years as a curate at St. Patrick's Parish, Roxbury, he was invited to replace Father Joseph Tracy as director of the Boston SPF in 1903.[50] Walsh's interest in missions continued to develop through reading Protestant mission literature, and he decried the absence of similar information in English for Catholics. He learned about the Paulist methods of evangelization through the pages of Elliott's the *Missionary*.

Sitting in his cramped office on Malden Street, he pored over letters from missionaries around the world who sought aid for their work. One of these missionaries, Sister Xavier Berkeley (1861–1944), was an English Daughter of Charity who would not only receive his monetary help during her forty years of service in China, but who would become a friend, visit at Maryknoll, and provide a model for the Maryknoll Sisters in how to identify with the Chinese people.[51] Along with Fathers Joseph Tracy and Joseph Freri, Walsh went to Europe in 1905 to press the case for a distinctly "American" version of the *Annals of the Society for the Propagation of the Faith*. He wrote weekly mission articles for the *Pilot* and corresponded with many missionaries. With a desire to awaken the mission spirit among American Catholics and with hopes for eventually beginning a seminary for American foreign missionaries, the zealous director invited one of his former professors, Sulpician priest Joseph Bruneau, along with Fathers John I. Lane and James F. Stanton to form the Catholic Foreign Mission Bureau. To meet these goals, Walsh wrote and published several books and pamphlets on European mission martyrs and started a mission review, *The Field Afar*. The first issue appeared in 1907, a few months after Francis Clement Kelley's *Extension*.

Mary Josephine (Mollie) Rogers had first approached Walsh in December of 1906, when, as a demonstrator/instructor in the zoology department at Smith College, she sought information about Catholic overseas missions. The women's college responded favorably to the reinvigorated Student Volunteer Movement for Foreign Missions, and a faculty advisor had encouraged Rogers to start a mission-study club for Catholics. Rogers contacted the SPF director for materials and assistance in forming a mission group. A few months later, Walsh published Rogers's mission-study outline in *The Field Afar*, though without mention of her name.[52]

Rogers, who attended public schools in Jamaica Plain, Massachusetts, had an interest in missions from childhood. After graduating from Smith College in 1905 and teaching there for two years, she returned to Boston in 1908, having given up her plan to work on a master's degree. She taught in two public schools and in her free time assisted with clerical work in the SPF office in Boston, translating some of the French materials, organizing the photograph collection, and writing several articles for *The Field Afar*.[53] She proved an invaluable leader in spiritual formation, in practical organization, and as a coworker with Walsh in the development of Maryknoll.

In the meantime, Walsh had attended the Catholic Missionary Union Congress, where he met Thomas F. Price of North Carolina. After further letters and subsequent discussion at the Montreal Eucharistic Congress in September 1910, they agreed to start a foreign mission seminary. With the support of Cardinal Gibbons, they presented the idea to the archbishops when they assembled in Washington, D.C., for their annual meeting. The bishops approved the Catholic Foreign Mission Society of America on 25 March 1911.[54]

By this date the Catholic Foreign Mission Bureau had ceased, after William O'Connell had become the archbishop of Boston in 1907 and began to centralize the diocese. It was rumored that he wanted to merge Walsh's magazine with the *Pilot* and to substitute *Extension* magazine for *The Field Afar*. Archbishop John Farley warmly welcomed Walsh to New York, as did the Reverend (and later Bishop) John J. Dunn (1867–1933), the SPF director for the New York Archdiocese, who became a lifelong friend and supporter of the Catholic Foreign Mission Society.[55]

Before going to Hawthorne, New York, with Price and Walsh in January 1912, Mary Louise Wholean, Mary Augustine Dwyer, and Sara Teresa Sullivan, who had contacted Walsh and expressed a desire to work for foreign missions, met at the Cenacle retreat house in order to discern their future. "We were strangers to each other and differed in age, training and disposition, but we had been brought together and were henceforth to be united by the common desire of serving the cause of foreign missions."[56] Walsh wanted Rogers to lead the women's group, but she had to wait a few months until a generous person took care of her family financial obligations. When the Maryknoll group moved from Hawthorne to a hill overlooking the Hudson River near Ossining, New York, in September 1912, Rogers had arrived, and under Walsh's direction, assumed leadership of the women, whose numbers had grown to seven. Others joined the "Teresians" (after Teresa of Avila), named by Walsh, who saw her as their model. The group was recognized by Rome as a Pious Society without vows in 1917 and, after much difficulty and patience in obtaining ecclesiastical approval as a religious congregation, the Foreign Mission Sisters of St. Dominic received Roman authorization in 1920. Their first mission was among Japanese immigrants in Los Angeles and Seattle in 1920. They sent Sisters to Hong Kong in 1921.

At Maryknoll the women spent most of their day organizing material for *The Field Afar,* preparing the annual budget for the Catholic Foreign Mission Society, doing clerical and translation work, cleaning, and occasionally cooking for the Maryknoll seminarians, who had trouble keeping cooks in the early days. Rogers was an assistant editor of *The Field Afar* and wrote articles for the magazine.

Americanist Overtones and the Missionary Thrust

Within fifteen years of the Spanish-American War, a new slant was taken on American Catholic missions. The war left the United States as an international player with responsibility for quasi-colonial areas. The ecclesial consequences charged the U.S. Catholic Church with specific pastoral obligations in mainly Spanish-speaking areas with significant numbers of indigenous people. While Pope Leo XIII denounced "Americanism," an important "uncondemned" principle of the Americanists lay behind the foundation of the mission conferences convened by Walter Elliott and Alexander Doyle. These gatherings inherited the Orestes Brownson/Isaac Hecker evangelical tradition, slightly altered, of the mission to America. At such gatherings the cofounders of Maryknoll met, and identification of "American" values moved into at least one group of American overseas missionaries.

James A. Walsh and Mary Josephine Rogers both advocated the "American" virtues of adaptability, generosity, the retention of one's individuality, and charity.[57] Adaptability implied a respect for the person and culture the missionary encountered. Rogers included an allied virtue, the "power of gentle persuasiveness." Zeal impelled the missionary to seek out others, rather than waiting for people to come to the missionary.

The years subsequent to the Spanish-American War saw the nationalization of missions for Catholics in the United States through the establishment of national offices of the Society for the Propagation of the Faith and the Catholic Church Extension Society, through the founding of the Catholic Foreign Mission Society of America, and through the American Catholic Missionary Congresses. This occurred at the same time as other Catholic groups, such as the Catholic Education Association and the Catholic Philosophical Association, began to nationalize as well.

Mission promoters began to gain prominence, having the ability to spotlight for U.S. Catholics particular mission themes, images, and persons. Conflict among the various mission groups, purportedly over the importance of geographical centers in the East or Midwest, pointed to differences in the understanding of mission and in the desire of each group to control the funds it raised. At the same time, the traditional European theme of "civilization" and its relationship to missions was being nuanced with American themes.

Mission promoters began to think in terms of "American" responses to mission by reflecting on the positive and negative values they found in their culture. They focused on two areas: the suggestion that missions were an antidote to the ennui experienced because of the excess of material goods, and the passing on of "civilization" to "young America" — no longer "old Europe" — with its tradition of democracy and various uses of capitalism.

The financial muscle of America and the power to buy material objects, thanks to mass production of goods, left Europeans with a view of Americans as "soft." As Walsh observed in *The Field Afar*, "We know...that to be an *American* is, in the minds of many Europeans, to be a *money-maker*, but this is because the average European has had little or no opportunity to observe the American in any other surroundings than those that border on the extremely comfortable."[58] In the minds of European churchmen, this "softness" made Americans unfit to be missionaries. In stark contrast, the missionary was to them a "living martyr," one who has given up every mode of comfort, who has eschewed the commercial spirit of America.

As the Catholic Foreign Mission Society of America had no spiritual predecessor in the country, the cofounders of Maryknoll set about to self-consciously construct a missionary image. They developed a spirituality of martyrdom, though differently from the Europeans. Both had been educated by mission-minded Sulpicians. Price, in his mystical, prayerful way, made a private offering of martyrdom. Walsh, who had visited the mission seminaries in Europe, was particularly taken with the Paris Foreign Mission Society, patterning a number of Maryknoll rituals after theirs.[59] In 1900 several of the Paris missionaries, who were martyred near the Gulf of Tonkin, were beatified. Of them Walsh remarked, "These were heroes; men strong with the strength of the diamond, but gentle as the woman; courageous as the most valiant soldier, but sparing their enemy always. Their warfare was not against kings of earth but against the Prince of Darkness."[60] Walsh published several books on the missionaries, including *In the Homes of Martyrs* (1922), written after he visited the places where they grew up. The hero-martyr image was often found on the pages of *Field Afar* and shaped the perspective of the Catholic Foreign Mission Society, even before the seminary came into being. Unlike Montalembert, whose missionary monks brought civilization, Walsh suggested to U.S. Catholics that missions were a "restraining idea in the light of present day comfort."[61] The missionary possessed "character," developed a hardiness and ruggedness toward life, and faced danger and risk. Some of the mission literature Walsh produced proposed a startling contrast to the sentimentalized Victorian literature already on the wane in the United States. Mary Joseph Rogers also was imbued with the martyr theme, having visited Europe in July 1913 with Julia Ward. Rogers was particularly impressed with the Roman Colosseum and San Stefano Rotundo, which the women visited three times. The church was renowned for its "heroic-sized pictures of the ten great persecutions of the church."[62]

Other Americans also decried the "modern" values. They had a suspicion of urban luxury, reacted to feelings of helplessness they saw in the culture, and rejected static systems and a dependence on republican moralism while preferring the delights of rustic nature. In the early part of the twentieth century, camping outdoors, for example, as well as the arts and crafts movement represented this "antimodern" impulse.[63] These trends were reactions to a disengagement with nature and expressed resentment toward the growing influence of technology in life.

Changing Shape of "Civilization" Discussion

Echoing through both mission congresses organized by Kelley and through literature published by the Catholic Foreign Mission Society and the New York SPF offices was the thought that America's "mission moment" was at hand. Catholic America was now the new standard-bearer for civilization. Use of the word *American,* along with its various nuances, began to be associated with the European (and particularly the French) notion of civilization. Mission literature and promotional talks linked these ideas, but adapted them to include the experience of democracy as one of the fundamentals of civilization. This was reflected, for example, in Bishop Patrick J. Donahue's speech to the 1909 American Catholic Mission Congress audience: "We have heard through able advocates the cry of the pagan child, begging for its life, for its liberty and for the pursuit of happiness."[64] These ideas reflected the themes of Hecker and Elliott. John Dunn, the New York SPF director, quoted for his audience a letter from a French missionary: "Personally I think that five American priests will do more to win the people than twenty of any other nationality, for the people are becoming obsessed with the idea that your country contains the best in civilization." A link between these principles and care for women and children was also found frequently in the pages of *Catholic Missions.* As a later writer would note, "Through its missions, the Christian religion has shielded the life of the child, championed the dignity and rights of woman, broken the bonds of slavery, ennobled labor, and proclaimed the social principles of personal liberty, equality, and private property."[65]

At the Second American Catholic Missionary Congress (1913), James Joseph Walsh (1865–1942), a neurophysician, delivered a paper titled "Missionary Work and Civilization."[66] His topic was certainly not new to the audience. Against the background of the Enlightenment's severance of religion from reason, the Catholic Church in Europe had argued that "civilization" had advanced because of the work of the faith through the ages. Walsh indicated that European explorers, who risked everything for the sake of science, were persons interested in the spread of religion as well. Indeed, the risks involved in the scientific venture were dictated by the missionary spirit, anxious to spread the faith. The doctor enumerated various mission excursions from the fourth century onward and noted, "Wherever missionary influence was lacking, the savage learned the vices of civilization before he learned to practice its virtues and the result was [his] destruction."[67] The physician thus aligned science and faith, painting the missionary as the link for such bridge building.

The word *civilization* did not develop until the mid-1770s, following the French Encyclopedists. By the late 1800s the word had become important as a backdrop for understanding the missionary. The term derived from *civis* (the city), the presumed source of culture, and was set against *pagani* (pagans), those from the countryside, where presumably there was little or no culture. The French perceived the world in a hierarchical, three-tiered universe with the *sauvages* at the bottom, the *barbares* (i.e., those with beards) next, and, on the top, the *civilisés,* those who were *urbain,* from which issues the English word *urban.*[68] Mission literature from France and from Germany presumed this quasi-philosophic foundation.

The second part of the "civilization" discussion, the relationship between religion and science, was advanced by *Catholic Missions* and, later, the American Province of the Divine Word Missionaries. While the world travelers of the late eighteenth and early nineteenth centuries contributed "facts" about peoples and their customs to the Encyclopedists, missionaries, too, were contributing "facts" to what were to become the sciences of anthropology, linguistics, and ethnography. This was particularly the Catholic German contribution in such notable journals as the *Anthropos International Review of Ethnology and Linguistics,* inaugurated by Wilhelm Schmidt, SVD (1868–1954), which was already on the shelves of the Boston Public Library shortly after its first issue in 1906. These groups emphasized missionaries who studied the culture and customs of the people to whom they were sent. One of the models presented to American audiences was the work and words of Bishop LeRoy, CSSp, the great missionary to Africa and founder of the Congregation of the Holy Ghost:

> "To raise in the midst of a pagan people this beacon of light and moral salubrity, called the Catholic Church, it is necessary that the missionaries shall set before themselves as a plan of campaign the customs, the laws, religion, and language of the people. And if, in order to become better missionaries, they devote some time to various studies, why should they not share the information acquired by their discoveries with the world at large?" To help the cause of the missionaries, therefore, is to extend the scientific and literary domain of mankind.[69]

The mission press at Techny later published, in English, German materials from this perspective, including Joseph Schmidlin's *Catholic Mission History* (1931) and *Catholic Mission Theory* (1933), both translated by Father Matthias Braun, SVD.

Catholic Missions almost always presented a positive view of the "natives" under study, even though the term *savages* might have been used. The assumption at the base of this scientific investigation was a positive anthropology of the person, which presumed a relationship between nature and grace and the belief that all persons had the potential for conversion, though their outer appearance and customs appeared to be quite different from those in the United States. Maryknoll literature sought to make the "heathen" friendly to U.S. Catholic audiences by making other cultures appear less "foreign." Such was the case, for example, with a 1909 cover portraying a young Japanese couple, dressed in kimonos, reading a copy of *The Field Afar* to each other in their Tokyo "living room." As an American, one could not help but identify with this Victorian snapshot of a typical Sunday afternoon in a middle-class family. These cover photos were made into postcards and sent to donors as a thank-you for contributions. While these favorable images attempted to offset the stereotypic views of Asians which issued in the "Gentlemen's Agreement" between Japan and the United States, restricting Japanese immigration after 1907, ironically the Victorian values assumed in the magazine covers represented the antithesis of Walsh's spirituality of martyrdom and risk.

American Capitalism and Modern Means of Evangelization

Extension Society President Francis Kelley, who inherited business sense from his father, was convinced that good business practice would assure a stable financial footing for mission funding. One made money by spending money. Modern means of persuasion, including the "democracy of congresses," advertising, and the press, were put to good use to prompt Catholics toward zeal and charity for the missions. Kelley assessed the mission problem as a lack of coordination and systematization. As he sought to remedy the situation, the Extension president exemplified the trends in business toward increasing bureaucracy.[70] The culmination of his efforts to unify mission funding came in 1919, when the American Board of Catholic Missions was approved in principle by the U.S. Bishops, though its formal inauguration did not take place until 1925. The Holy Childhood Association sought a financier-priest as its director in 1922.

While still Boston director for the SPF, James A. Walsh had begun to set up an international exchange of goods and capital by offering to sell products made at the Chinese missions. One group who benefited from such exchange was that of Sister Xavier Berkeley. Later, the Maryknoll Sisters did the same thing. Some mission magazines offered spiritual gifts in return for material ones. One could buy "land slips" to help build the Maryknoll seminary and, in return, would be remembered in the prayers of the Fathers and Brothers. One could send an offering for a Mass intention to a mission organization, which in turn would pass the offering to missionaries, who had no source of income. One mission bishop, in thanking William Cardinal O'Connell for sending the stipends, wrote: "More than I can express, I appreciate that donation of Your Eminence, for by doing so you contributed to the salvation of my mission. Mass intentions have become more scarce than diamonds...."[71] The goods of modern life were exchanged for the goods of the spirit and, in so doing, the missionaries profited. Mission magazines began to realize by 1913 that a considerable number of women were sending small, but steady, amounts of money to support the missions. In the absence of large "Carnegie" donors, mission magazines, such as *Extension,* made an explicit financial appeal to women in columns devoted to making clothes, running a household, and raising children. The SPF suggested bequests and the Divine Word Missionaries prepared annuities to finance mission operations.

In some respects, the mission response related broadly to the modernist theological agenda, which revolved around a problem relatable to evangelization: to what extent were various aspects of "modern life" compatible with Church teaching? Intellectually and philosophically, European theologians such as Alfred Loissy, Maurice Blondel, and Baron von Hügel sought to bring Catholic doctrine, along with emphasizing a return to religious experience, in tune with realities in their time. In the United States, missionaries William S. Sullivan and John R. Slattery, and Sulpicians John B. Hogan and the Dunwoodie Circle of the *New York Review,* attempted a similar theological task. In contrast to the Romanists who viewed tradition as immutable and supernaturally bestowed, regarded the Church as ahistorical, and highlighted the authority of the papacy, the modernists reacted against the "system" of Manual theology, viewed the Church as an organic, living body, spoke of the need for the experiential and the transcendent, and attempted to deal with historical-critical scholarship.[72] The modernists were condemned in 1908 and by 1910 Pope Pius X required seminarians and clergy to take the modernist oath. But the modernist issues pervaded every area of life, not just philosophy and theology.

Walsh and Price certainly never saw themselves as modernists in a theological sense. Yet Walsh in particular sought to update the notion of sainthood by publishing lives of "modern" martyrs and reacted to the increasing bureaucracy in the Church. Before his assignment as Boston SPF director, he was one of five curates at a parish where the work had become divided among the priests, and each was responsible for a segment of activity much like the modern assembly lines in nearby Massachusetts factories. While Romanists placed a singular emphasis on the papacy's authority, the Catholic Foreign Mission Society (or the Maryknoll Society, as it was known) chose 29 June as their foundation day, the feast of Peter and Paul, traditional models who linked Church authority and evangelization. The development of the martyr/hero image allowed the Maryknoll cofounder to shape a contemporary self which drew on the nineteenth-century Romantic attraction for nature and placed the missionary "in the wilderness," at the edges of civilization — a theme familiar to the antimodernists. Such asceticism of self-denial was not to be an isolating experience, for later, as missionaries were sent around the world, they were reminded of their connection to the living vine of "the Knoll."

Ecclesially, modernism was interested in the relationship of the Church to the social and political order, which included the role of women. As the men of Maryknoll sought to construct their identity, so the women of Maryknoll, directed by the charismatic Mary Josephine Rogers, drew on some of the same sources as Walsh and Price, but employed other images as well. They referred to themselves as the Teresians, after the Carmelite reformer and contemplative of the sixteenth century, Teresa of Avila. This model provided a mission spirituality which stressed both the "active" virtues and contemplation as mutually important foundations for mission. Teresa, in a proposal offered by Walter Elliott as well, further suggested that women had both a reforming and evangelical role in the Church. The Maryknoll women chronicled their life together in a journal titled *Distaff*, named after the spindle on which flax or other material is wound in spinning. The Maryknoll women all longed to go overseas to mission, but in the meantime they viewed their work "at home" as essential to the mission endeavor because they freed the priest and Brother for mission life. Though the prevailing ecclesiology presumed the indispensability of the mission priest for church planting and attendance at sacraments, Walsh left open the possibility that women would need to "step in" to that place:

> A priest is a precious individual. Almighty God works through him in a special manner, as he would not work through an ordinary layman. As you think of your work, it would be a good thing for you to keep in mind the thought that where you can take the place of a priest, you will do it. You will be the *ancillae* — the handmaids of the priestly service. This is the apostolate, and as far as you can, you should exercise it.
>
> That is more or less of a modern idea. If we look back into the history of the world Orders, we find there was a period when the Orders of women were largely cloistered.... We have come to the period when Sisters are in Universities, establishing colleges, and working along other lines. They are coming into their own.[73]

As we have seen in the previous chapter, women were more or less easily taking the ecclesial place of men when the need arose. But an ambiguity about women's role in missions overseas existed alongside the SPF's promotion of the importance of women missionaries.

Toward the Next Decades of Mission

Approximately six congregations of men and women religious, among them the Redemptorists, did send missionaries to Cuba, Puerto Rico, and the Philippines, the countries most affected by the Spanish-American War. A few army chaplains stayed to work in the area, such as Father Gerest in Cuba. But American presence in these colonies and protectorates did not surge forward until 1921, when the Aragon Province of Jesuits in the Philippines was transferred to the Maryland/New York Province and a contingent of twenty American Jesuits was sent to teach at the Colegio de San Jose and at the University of the Ateneo. Though the Americans had sent four clergy who became prelates in the Philippines, the shortage of priests which Jesuit William A. Stanton had noted eleven years earlier still held true in 1913:

> There is not a single American priest in the whole archipelago, outside of three or four chaplains who are of course "hiking" with their soldier boys. English-speaking priests for the ministry are sadly needed here at present, whilst unfortunately there are some dozens of "preachers" trying to pervert the natives.[74]

Unfortunately, another war provided the next impetus for U.S. Catholic missionaries overseas, and China, with its millions of people, would receive much attention from the mission promoters, mission societies, and from many congregations who up to this point had not sent any women or men overseas.

Chapter 5

"America's Hour" for Missions Overseas, 1918–35

World War I created tremendous upheaval for Roman Catholic world missions. Seminaries were closed and the young men sent into the army. Missionaries were recalled to Europe to become chaplains for French, Belgian, and German armies, countries which had sent the most missionaries abroad. It was estimated that at least one-third of the French seminarians or missionaries were killed in the war. Shipping channels to send supplies to the missions had been disrupted. The treaty signed after the war cited a spirit of nationalism in the missions as a reason for the expulsion of European, and particularly German, missionaries. Colonial countries sought English-speaking missionaries.[1] Profiting from the efforts of Secretary of State John Hay early in the century, the United States had full scope to conduct business in China, a country which gained new prominence as an American business venture after the war.

American Catholics, who desired to rally support for missions overseas, cited these international developments as the "golden opportunity" for U.S. Catholics to

> scatter pagan darkness by the "Light of the World." The Catholic Church must not allow the pall of death to spread over its missions to heathen lands. Those missions are its glory, the evidence of its divinely given universality. Catholics in large-hearted America will be the saviors of the church in its missionary work.[2]

In the next decade and a half, this sense of "America's hour" pushed the mission enterprise in four directions, leading toward the creation of a student organization for mission education and promotion; the nationalization and coordination of mission agencies through the hierarchy; an outreach to Catholics in Latin America; and the convergence on China of U.S. Catholic missionaries. The latter phenomenon, which resulted in a major concentration of interest, money, and personnel on the part of American Catholics, will be treated in the following chapter.

Catholic Students Mission Crusade

While several seminaries and convents had been sending their members overseas by war's end, virtually no specific training for mission was offered in their educational program. The curriculum for the men remained the standard seminary courses. While seminarians and novices absorbed the "feel" for missions from missionary letters sent home or from returned missionaries, two seminarians sought to study more carefully the mission situation and to aid those abroad by establishing a nationwide student mission organization.[3] Aware of the success of John Mott's Student Volunteer Movement for Foreign Missions and hearing articles from *The Field Afar* read in the dining room at St. Mary's Mission House, Techny, Illinois, in 1914, Clifford J. King (1888–1969) and Robert B. Clark, two Society of the Divine Word seminarians, resolved to start a similar organization. Encouraged by the mission promoter at the time, the Reverend Bruno Hagspiel, SVD, who had studied the Catholic students' mission movement in Europe, King and his friends issued a circular, "The Coming Crusade," in May 1917, inviting seminarians and college students to join. From 27 to 30 July 1918, one hundred clergy, laity, and a few bishops assembled at Techny, outside Chicago, for the conference which launched the Catholic Students Mission Crusade.[4]

King was invited to be on the executive board, but declined because he had received a call as a seminarian to leave for one of the German Society of the Divine Word missions in China, which was in danger of closing due to possible repatriation of the missionaries. He sailed for Shantung in October 1918 and was ordained there in 1920. He and classmate Robert B. Clark became the first Americans ordained in China.[5]

With offices at Mount St. Mary's Seminary of the West until 5 September 1920 and then at the Catholic Welfare Building of the Cincinnati Archdiocese until 1923, the CSMC soon coalesced the energy and leadership of thousands of college-age students. The executive officers were seminarians John J. Considine, MM, Edward A. Freking and Frank A. Thill (1893–1957), Catherine McCarthy, and J. Paul Spaeth.[6] Monsignor Thomas J. Shahan, rector of the Catholic University of America, was president, and Monsignor Francis J. Beckman, rector of Mount St. Mary's Seminary of the West, was chairman of the executive board. Much of the correspondence and the day-to-day activities were handled by the field secretary, Floyd Keeler, whose salary was provided by the Paulist Fathers through Peter J. O'Callaghan. A convert from the Episcopal Church, Keeler had been an archdeacon in Kansas and held similar mission responsibilities for that church.[7]

The movement grew rapidly, with units springing up all across the country in men's and women's colleges, seminaries, and high schools. Support was provided by many bishops and magazine editorials, including several in *America*.[8] Professors and rectors were alerted to the movement's importance through

Catholic Students Mission Crusade: The CMSC, founded in 1917 by Clifford King, SVD, and friends, by 1923 had held conventions in Techny, Illinois (when it had 16 units), in Washington, D.C. (158 units), and Dayton, Ohio (317 units). This 1923 photo shows the CMSC at its then largest meeting at the University of Notre Dame when it was comprised of between 630 and 640 units. (The photo is the frontispiece of *To Defend the Cross: The Story of the Fourth General Convention* [Cincinnati: CSMC, 1924]).

the 1919 Catholic Education Association conference, when Peter Janser, SVD, spoke on its origins. Within the first five years, 1,800 seminaries and schools had affiliated with the organization and, by the early 1930s, a half-million students were members. Government directives forbade publication of new magazines during World War I, so early CSMC information was channeled through a column in the *Missionary.* After this ban was lifted, the movement published a quarterly magazine, *Spread,* from which grew the *Shield.* Thill organized a mission-study program for the movement, "Round Table Discussions." Starting in the 1930s, the staff compiled statistics of U.S. Catholic missionaries overseas and published the first national directory in 1940.[9] Almost from its foundation, CSMC saw two parts to the movement: the support and promotion of home and foreign missions through prayer and study, and the development of leadership skills for young Catholics in America.

Until the organization's demise in 1971, twenty-four biannual conventions attracted up to four thousand students and religious leaders to hear mission speakers, to attend seminars, and to interact with students from other countries. Key mission leaders and heads of missionary congregations in the United States provided young Catholics with current mission understandings, practice, and motivation. The CSMC produced plays, radio broadcasts — especially in the Cincinnati area — audio-visual resources, and mission kits, in addition to various newsletters to keep local mission units abreast of activities.

From its onset the group picked up the militarism and idealism of the First World War, but thrust these attributes back in history to the medieval Crusades:

> Catholic Students, young men and young women! To each of you, no matter how humble, how retiring, is offered an opportunity to do great things for God and souls. The spirit of Peter the Hermit and of St. Bernard is urging a 20th century Crusade, as noble and chivalrous as that which prompted Christian armies to traverse a continent for the purpose of saving from desecration the sepulchre of the Lord.... Catholic Students! The work has been started and its object is too noble, too holy, too necessary, not to succeed. "God wills it!"[10]

In 1923, a year after the Yale historian of missions, Kenneth Scott Latourette, noted a missionary awakening among U.S. Roman Catholics,[11] the students met for their fourth conference, held at the University of Notre Dame. Under the theme "To Defend the Cross," CSMC representatives heard stories from leaders of the major missionary religious orders and societies in the United States, learned about mission problems, and wandered through colorful mission exhibits. Conference participants lacked neither enthusiasm nor zeal. The format for the meeting was an opening prayer, songs, or musical pieces performed by the college choruses and orchestras, a mission talk, discussion, and sometimes a further song. Joseph McGlinchey, director of the Propagation of the Faith office in Boston, spoke on "The Foreign Missions of the Catholic Church" after an opening prayer by John Forbes, coadjutor vicar apostolic in Uganda. The

St. Joseph College orchestra concluded the session with the musical selections, "In China" and "In Arabia."

Monsignor Francis Beckman, chairman of the CSMC board, made clear to the participants that this was not a mission convention but a Crusade convention. But there was some ambiguity in this statement, because in the same address to the fifteen hundred college students and seminarians he also noted that the aim of the Crusade was to "make us full-fledged Catholics because to be a full-fledged Catholic means to be a missionary. A Catholic must be another Christ, and Christ was essentially a missionary."[12] While the 1923 conference proceedings devoted a smaller amount of time to the Crusade leadership idea, increasingly missions became almost subsumed within the Crusade symbol. The medieval symbolism could be observed in the Crusade Castle, where the national staff worked,[13] the CSMC hymn, the title of the magazine, the *Shield*, the development of orders, ranks, and insignia for the members, and in the rhetoric used by several of the movement leaders.

One of the highlights of the 1923 conference was the enactment of the first ordinal of admission into the Crusade. In this pageant-drama and procession across the Notre Dame campus, blue-, gold-, and crimson-costumed medieval pages bearing silver trays preceded the participants to the church door, as the university bells pealed in the summer air. When the doors were thrown open the call was sounded, "Crusaders, follow me." Inside, each candidate's place bore a white tunic with an embroidered crimson cross, the Crusade's insignia, on its front. At the end of the procession came the red-robed Hermit,[14] who scrutinized the young men and women as to their readiness to take on this new crusade. After prayers, recitation of the confiteor, and the donning of the tunic, the group proceeded to the Lourdes Grotto on the campus with their candles flickering in the darkness and the strains of "Awake, Set Forth for Jerusalem" echoing in the background.

Frank Thill's many addresses to CSMC units around the country often referred to a fourteenth-century legend about two crusaders. The dying wish of one of them, Robert Bruce, was that his heart be carried to the Holy Land by his fellow knights. On the way, his friend's unit was attacked by a large force of Muslims. When defeat of the Crusaders seemed imminent, Sir James Douglas hurled into the Muslim army the silver casket, wherein Bruce's heart had been placed. "Follow the heart of Bruce," the rallying cry, provided the impetus for the Christian soldiers to defeat the Muslims.[15] So, too, were the missionary crusaders to give their heart to the cause of the "Crusade."

The use of medieval symbolism reflected the desires of Americans who sought an alternative to the effects of mass production and capitalist and bureaucratic tendencies in the United States.[16] The medieval motif appeared in two emphases of the Crusade. First, the conventions, magazine, dramas, and induction into the various ranks of the Order of the Paladin drew on "sentiment" and a romantic view of the past to motivate young Catholics to develop a personal responsibility for the defense and spread of their faith, and to develop leadership skills which would carry over into parish involvement after they graduated from school.

> Without sentiment and emotion this Crusade would go to pieces the next hour. It is precisely sentiment and emotion we have to appeal to in order to get where we want to get, and it is precisely under that head that *The Shield* does make its appeal.[17]

This perspective had intersected by the late 1930s with the development of lay leadership under the aegis of Catholic Action.[18]

Second, the organization also reflected the view of some medieval revivalists that missionaries forwarded the cause of science in their development of such fields as anthropology, linguistics, and comparative religion. The "romantic aesthetic" in the rhetoric and dramas of the CSMC combined with the apologetic use of the Crusades to highlight the medieval notion of Christendom as the source of light and culture. In this respect, they inherited the nineteenth-century resurrection in Europe of the medieval tradition. In the ongoing argument about the role of science and religion, Charles Montalembert had written a multivolume work crediting missionary monks and nuns with creating centers of learning, culture, health, and science.[19] Reflecting this perspective, many noteworthy publications came from the CSMC office over the years. Their mission-education efforts drew the attention of Dr. Joseph Schmidlin at the University of Münster. After CSMC publication of books on leadership in the 1930s and missionary statistics throughout the 1940s, James A. Magner, in collaboration with Louise F. Spaeth and James T. Hurley from the national office of the CSMC, published *Latin American Patterns,* one of the early attempts of U.S. Catholics to analyze the social, political, and religious situation in that part of the world. As the CSMC leadership grew to maturity, the organization produced *Fundamentals of Missiology* and *Perspectives in Religion and Culture* in the 1950s. In the 1960s, they made Catholics aware of cultures around the world in books such as *Southeast Asia in Five Hours* and *College Readings on Africa.*[20]

Beginning in the early 1930s, CSMC references to a medieval past provided a sustained criticism of the political forces at play in socialism and communism, a third use of the medieval theme. Thill clearly sketched the social dimensions of the missionary vocation by noting that the apostolic spirit inspired any effective attempts to reach other persons, either through conversions or through "setting the whole of the world's social system in order."[21] American missionaries, whose lives had been touched by communism either through imprisonment or through torture and harassment, spoke before the CSMC audiences at their conventions and were the living embodiment of the *Shield*'s anticommunist philosophy.

The medieval elements entwined with an "American and Catholic" theme. In addition to the red, white, and blue Crusade flag with the motto *cognoscetis veritatem* ("you shall know the truth") emblazoned in the center, individual units displayed a service flag, similar to those found in homes of families with young men serving in World War I. CSMC units mounted a cross on their flags' white background for every unit member who became a missionary.

Post–World War I restrictions on immigration had allowed gradual assimilation of Catholics into the economic fabric of American society. The patriotism of the student crusaders was expressed through a variety of pledges pronounced at the start of the local unit meetings. The first of these pledges was to the "Flag of Our Country":

> Flag of our Country, beneath whose generous folds our Land has grown rich and our Church strong, we pledge ourselves to share the blessings we have so abundantly received with those who sit in darkness and in want. Our wealth shall relieve their poverty; our Faith shall banish their spiritual night. Great-hearted Americans shall bring to the pagan lands the blessings they have enjoyed beneath the radiant banner of the Stars and Stripes.[22]

The CSMC from its inception until at least the early 1960s provided a major vehicle for the mission education of seminarians, college, and high school students throughout the country. The organization drew on the wealth of Protestant mission literature and experience, as well as on the wisdom of more and more American Catholic missionaries. The conferences and publications provided a consistent opportunity for mission superiors and mission educators to present to laity and seminarians a vision of the missionary vocation, the needs of missionaries, and the premise that to be Catholic is to be missionary. While a fair number of student crusaders did become missionaries, the organization differed from the Student Volunteer Movement in that CSMC mainly promoted mission study and prayer rather than recruitment.

American Board of Catholic Missions

The U.S. Bishops' pastoral in 1919 had made a specific plea to Catholics to engage them in mission at home and abroad. The letter appealed to young men to consider a missionary vocation and to the laity to garner financial support for "the devoted men who already are bearing the heat of the day and the burden."[23] The organization of mission funds, new mission societies, and burgeoning mission magazines, a project which Francis C. Kelley had been advocating since his missionary congresses, gained new impetus and coincided with the establishment of a national organization of bishops. Having worked together successfully after World War I as the National Catholic War Council, the U.S. Bishops established the National Catholic Welfare Council, a permanent, official, though voluntary, agency of the bishops of the United States, through which discussion and concerted action could be taken on issues which affected Catholics in America.[24]

James Cardinal Gibbons, the president of the Catholic War Council, invited representatives from missions, hospitals, charities, educational institutions, and the press to a meeting from 22 to 24 July 1919 at Notre Dame. The outcome of this gathering was the permanent secretariat of the National Catholic Welfare Council. The missions committee at this meeting was composed of seventeen mission directors, who represented superiors of male mission societies, the Extension Society, the Holy Childhood Society, the Catholic Students Mission Crusade, the newly established Irish Chinese Mission Society (The Society of St. Columban), and other key mission groups. Joseph Freri, the national director of the SPF, was absent due to illness.

The zealous and bright bishop of Toledo, Joseph Schrembs, who was a member of the NCWC planning commission, chaired the meeting of the mission representatives. Among the agenda items were the organization of mission funds, the promotion of missions, and the relationship of the home and foreign mission agencies in the United States. Conflicting mission perspectives, still unresolved after the 1913 mission congress in Boston, were no closer to solution. Kelley suggested that a subcommittee meet to work on a plan; what emerged for the group's consideration was basically his own blueprint for an American Board of Catholic Missions. The main points included severance of ties with the SPF offices in France, the establishment of an American society for this purpose, and an appointment of a bishop to be president of the board. The board was to "coordinate and unify all our missionary activity, which is the first work of the Church, so that they may be in close union with the Holy See, directed and controlled under the auspices of the American Hierarchy, and reach into every diocese and parish."[25] Mission agencies would have to report collections and disbursements to this board.

The prelates accepted the plan for the ABCM when they met on 24 September 1919, making some modifications. The bishops appointed five bishops to the standing committee and nine priests to the advisory group to the board.[26] Three of the five appointees had mission experience or great interest in missions: Archbishops Patrick Hayes (New York), Jeremiah J. Harty (Omaha, formerly archbishop of Manila), and Bishop J. F. Regis Canevin (Pittsburgh). The work of the ABCM was hampered over the next years due partly to the disapproval of William O'Connell (Boston), who thought the plan had not been submitted to Rome, and to the simultaneous submission to Rome of the plans for the organization of the NCWC. The latter, "quietly suppressed" by the Vatican, did not receive approval until 1922.[27] The ABCM was approved the same year, though it did not have a constitution and did not officially begin its work until 1 January 1926.

The centralization issue — placing control of all mission funds in the hands of the hierarchy — raised issues which touched all mission groups, each of whom saw itself struggling to gain the attention and monies of U.S. Catholics. The Extension Society desired entry into each diocese but had no authorization to do so. The society slipped into ecclesiastical trouble for soliciting funds with-

out permission in New York.[28] With no percentages addressed in the plan —
the percentage of monies for home and foreign missions — home missions
could make a strong case for greater financial support than they were presently
receiving. Kelley also thought that a national board could control the mush-
rooming number of mission magazines and mission collection agencies because
the plan called for all authorization to come from the ABCM.[29] James A. Walsh,
who had visited the French SPF offices many years earlier and saw the mission society as an "old fashioned" lay group, hoped to obtain more financial
support for his fledgling society. He supported the idea of a bishop in charge
"for the greater prestige that will give."[30] The board would regulate all mission collecting agencies and have a department in each for home and foreign
missions.

The international organization of the Society for the Propagation of the
Faith was undergoing radical changes at the time of the Notre Dame meeting.
The Americans were not the only ones interested in reshaping the lay-founded
mission-funding society, which, some Americans said, favored French missionaries. In 1922, one hundred years after its founding, the headquarters moved
from France to Rome and was placed under the more immediate control of
the Vatican offices. This was one of the efforts made by the cardinal prefect of
Propaganda Fide, Willem Van Rossum (1854–1932), to coordinate all mission
activity from his office. The changes were in accord with William O'Connell's
sentiments that such a move "will stimulate more than ever proper unity and
relations with Rome, now the real and active centre of missionary activity."[31]
Joseph Freri, the national SPF director, had suggested such an action himself.
He also had serious reservations about the ABCM Plan, which put control of
SPF funds in the hands of the U.S. Bishops. After consultation with the diocesan
SPF directors, Freri wrote to Kelley that the directors

> refuse to yield "the organization and machinery of the American Society
> for the Propagation of the Faith to the Foreign Mission Section of the
> American Board of Catholic Missions," and they object to "the changing
> of its regulations, directors and name." They advise me that, unless or-
> dered to the contrary positively and directly by the Holy See, we continue
> our work as in the past with certain modifications and reforms which I,
> myself, suggested not long ago to the Church authorities at Rome.[32]

For Freri, the issue was denationalization. For O'Connell, the issue was Ro-
manization. For all mission groups, the concern was to keep control of their
own funds for missions, yet somehow to work together.

Freri requested that his name be withdrawn from the ABCM Committee on
Foreign Missions. He feared that bishops would have control of the money and
properties of mission societies and that clergy members of the board would
vote only for allocations to keep their colleges and seminaries running, and
disregard the total mission picture. "Is it not better to continue to let apostolic schools and seminaries struggle for themselves? It will force their directors

to practice a wholesome economy and to be very prudent in the admission of candidates."[33] Freri resigned his national position in 1924, was made a titular bishop of Constantia, and left the United States. The Reverend William Quinn was appointed in his place. That same year the U.S. Bishops voted to authorize a national mission Sunday in all dioceses and to accept the ABCM's recommendation on mission funds, allotting 60 percent for foreign missions and 40 percent for home missions. Technically, all mission-funding groups, including the SPF and Catholic Extension Society, fell under the authority of the ABCM in order to systematize the U.S. Catholic mission effort. However, Van Rossum's disagreement with the plan eventually delivered a blow to such coordination.

In the end, Propaganda Fide changed the course of the ABCM. The office noted that each bishop had the right to set up mission programs independent of the ABCM. Territorial dependencies of the United States (the Philippines, Alaska, and Puerto Rico) were to be treated as foreign missions by Propaganda, but were to receive home mission funds from the United States.[34] Discouraged after years of effort to coordinate mission funding, Francis Kelley in the meantime had become bishop of Oklahoma.

Bishops' Committees and Latin America

While internal structural details were being worked out for cooperative financial support of missions, a more direct involvement with people beyond U.S. borders occurred as a result of the hierarchy's national meetings during the 1920s and 1930s. Liberal thinking of politically elite Latin Americans had effected a profound shift in the religious and political patterns of the hemisphere since the latter part of the nineteenth century. The centuries-old pattern of church-state relationships changed perceptibly as many of these countries moved to a constitution which separated church and state. While this provided an opening for Protestant missionaries, the ferment also brought expressions of anti-clericalism, religious persecution, and government appropriation of church properties. It was in this context that the U.S. Bishops issued a "Resolution on Guatemala" on 25 September 1924, declaring themselves in solidarity with the Guatemalan Catholics experiencing religious persecution under the presidency of Jorge Ubico.

That same year, the Houston Council of Catholic Women, under the leadership of Josephine Irons, a social worker, opened a free clinic for Mexican women escaping religious persecution and unjust social conditions and seeking a more stable economic environment. Two years later, a U.S. Bishops' pastoral, aimed against increased persecution of Catholics in Mexico, paired with action by the National Catholic Welfare Council, which actively worked with the State Department and the Mexican Consulate to negotiate for religious tolerance in Mexico.[35]

The Mexican problem remained on the agenda of the annual meeting of the

National Catholic Welfare Council through the 1920s and 1930s. To deal with the growing numbers of Mexicans coming north of the Rio Grande River, the NCWC Bureau of Immigration in 1931 added two offices at El Paso and Juárez, Mexico, in addition to an office in the port of New York and a central office of administration in the District of Columbia. With three exiled Mexican hierarchy having arrived in the United States by the fall of 1932 — one of them the apostolic delegate — the NCWC through its general secretary, the Reverend John J. Burke, pursued diplomatic channels and visits with President Roosevelt to pressure the Mexican government to permit the practice of religion for American nationals and to restore religious freedom.[36] Though Catholics and the country were divided on whether to intervene in Mexico, in 1934 the U.S. Bishops issued the document "Tyranny in Mexico" in an attempt to persuade American Catholics to pressure the American government to address the situation. At the same time, the NCWC produced eight booklets for the Catholic population on various aspects of the topic. The Knights of Columbus distributed one million copies of the bishops' pastoral and donated $150,000 for relief work among Mexican clergy and nuns.

The U.S. hierarchy responded to their Mexican confreres with practical help to follow up their public statement. The Mexican Bishops had appealed to them to help fund a seminary in the United States for exiled Mexican seminarians, because the Mexican government permitted no seminary to operate. Though the United States was feeling the effects of the Depression, the bishops at their annual meeting in 1935 voted for the project and, in 1936, a large tract of land and suitable buildings were purchased in Las Vegas, New Mexico, for the Montezuma Seminary.[37] By 1955, one-fifth of the diocesan clergy of Mexico had been educated at this seminary.[38]

In the late twenties, thirties, and early forties, the National Council of Catholic Women was corresponding with their South American counterparts on matters relating to Catholic colleges and the experience of the North American Church.[39] The U.S. women's group also passed a 1931 resolution to "cooperate with American institutions interested in the exchange of teachers and students with Latin America and assist in establishing friendly relations between the Catholic women of the United States and the Catholic women of Latin America through the mediums of correspondence and travel."[40] By the early 1940s, the women's Inter-American Committee was providing Spanish translations of books, articles, and ideas from their study circles for promulgation in Latin American publications. While American Catholics in the 1930s were defending Catholic doctrine against the attacks of communists, especially during the Spanish Civil War, by and large that discussion did not appear to be uppermost in this work of the National Council of Catholic Women.[41] The Foreign Visitors Desk, associated with the National Council of Catholic Men, hosted Catholics from abroad after their arrival in Washington, D.C. A steady stream of Catholic Latin Americans, mainly in governmental or socially prestigious positions, came through this office.

A significant step in hemispheric relations occurred at Rio de Janeiro on 10 October 1933, when representatives from North and South American countries met to sign a Treaty of Non-aggression and Conciliation. The U.S. Senate ratified the treaty on 15 June 1934. Subsequently, articles about Latin America increased in North American papers. Universities such as Harvard, Wisconsin, California, and Duke offered courses on the culture and history of the region. The NCWC urged Catholic colleges to do likewise, particularly because the foundations of modern-day Latin American culture were Catholic in origin.

A formal structure to gather the work of laity and hierarchy and to inaugurate new initiatives for mutual understanding of the people of Latin America came through the assistant director of the Social Action Department of the NCWC, the Reverend Raymond A. McGowan.[42] The formation of a Latin American Bureau was assisted by a three-year gift of fifteen thousand dollars from New York Judge Morgan J. O'Brien, who had interested others in the project. Initially thought of as an "experiment"[43] in January 1931, the bureau had started its life less formally in 1929. Elizabeth B. Sweeney, secretary for civic education at NCWC, wrote to various American universities seeking a director who was to be a Spanish-speaking, practicing lay Catholic, though not a Latin American. The search was extensive and included correspondence with Carlos Castaneda, the librarian of the Latin American Library and faculty member at the University of Texas, Austin, who, though a Latin American, came highly recommended for the position. While several lay and clerical candidates were interested and willing to take the position, McGowan remained the director in the 1930s in addition to his other responsibilities with the Social Action Department.

The bureau's purpose was "to help Catholics of Latin America and the United States to know one another and to become acquainted with one another's accomplishments and experiences particularly in Catholic action."[44] Toward this end, over two hundred articles and press releases, translated into Spanish, were sent to five hundred persons and groups in Latin America in 1932. The bureau sought to increase knowledge of Latin America, particularly in Catholic colleges in the United States, and worked with the Latin American Committee of the Catholic Association for International Peace.

While the actual numbers of converts to Protestantism in Latin America were relatively small in the early 1930s, Catholics became concerned that Protestant missionaries were becoming interpreters of Latin American religious culture to the North American public. One such example was John A. Mackay, well-known secretary for the Board of Foreign Missions of the Presbyterian Church in the United States, who was asked to speak on "The Spiritual Spectrum of Hispanic Americans" at the Institute of Public Affairs in 1932. Such incidents started to pose a threat to U.S. Catholics, who considered the social and intellectual elite of Latin America as their spiritual peers and as their provenance.

Anna Dill Gamble, convert to Catholicism and a member of several committees of the National Council of Catholic Women, reported in *Catholic Action* on the activities of Protestant mission organizations and of private and public groups working in Latin America. She urged U.S. Catholics to become knowledgeable about the situation in the Latin American republics, which were experiencing radical change, and to study the history of the Spanish roots of Catholic experience in Latin America. The apologetic of the NCCW and Social Action Department leadership attempted to respond to the permeation of communist ideas and other widely circulated political, social, and religious values.

Without specifically alluding to communism, North American Catholics called for a general social reform of all Latin America through principles of Catholic social action. Their analysis of the situation pointed to lethargy among North Americans in learning about the rich Catholic culture of the southern countries. Their apologetic was directed toward strengthening Catholicism in a political and social milieu which permitted the free exercise of Protestantism. As Dr. Samuel Guy Inman, longtime executive secretary for the Committee on Cooperation in Latin America (American and Canadian boards in Latin America), remarked to McGowan, whom he knew personally:

> Whether it is desirable or not, these lands have ceased to protect officially any one faith and their citizens are determined to discuss all types of religion and philosophy. Under such conditions, I feel that Protestantism will appeal to some people who are no longer Catholics, because of certain situations, or satisfied with Catholic attitudes toward life.... If there was ever a time when any religious organization had a monopoly on any part of the world, it seems to me that such time has passed — just as every extreme of political and social philosophy has invaded the last corner of the globe. But this does not mean that we are to act hostile toward each other, calling each other names, regarding each other as enemies. But rather, while maintaining our peculiar beliefs, to act brotherly, as far as our humanity will allow us, toward all who believe in God.[45]

To ascertain what information was to be conveyed about Latin America to Catholics and the general American public, the Latin American Committee of the NCWC wrote to the bishops there. Summing up these responses, McGowan wrote to John J. Burke, the general secretary for the NCWC:

> Most of the replies stressed the necessity of putting before the American public that *Latin America was not a field for missionary work* and that such incursions do not tend to increase good feeling between the Americas. If the true Latin America, with its rich and colorful history, its folk-lore and legends, its abiding Catholicity, could be faithfully presented to the American people by means of the Press, magazine articles and the Radio, perhaps the erroneous opinions held by many people who have

been influenced by the articles and writings of returned missionaries and badly informed lecturers and who have the Latin American countries represented to them as countries with a nondescript conglomeration of races, as countries which are primitive and superstitious, lacking in spirituality and where the clergy...are for the most part inactive and backward and the people themselves indifferent, might be corrected.[46]

The southern hemisphere was, therefore, not to be seen as a "mission" country but as an extension of Spanish Catholicism in an American setting. *Catholic Missions* took this view, as well. In the first fifteen years of its publication (1907–22), about eighteen articles were published on the Caribbean and South America. With the exception of one article, all told stories about indigenous tribes in the region. Few, if any, U.S. Catholic missionaries worked with those tribes in the 1930s.

McGowan offered several critiques of prevailing hemispheric realities after his trip to Latin America in the summer of 1931. Having in mind Catholic social principles enunciated by Pope Leo XIII, McGowan, the Social Action Department officer, noted three points. First, U.S. policy was one-sided and failed to respect Latin American dignity and rights, having led to interventions in Caribbean countries under terms of the Monroe Doctrine. Second, Latin Americans had themselves become nationalistic, as evidenced in wars between Paraguay and Bolivia and between Colombia and Peru. Both northern and southern hemispheres had fallen prey to the "false gods of secularism, nationalism and business individualism," all of which oppressed people. Latin America's increasing secularism promoted religious indifference and a consequent disregard for its spiritual heritage. Third, with the mutual struggle to build a Christian civilization in both hemispheres, it was imperative that U.S. and Latin American Catholics cooperate with each other, especially in the work of schools and Catholic Action.[47]

Though McGowan's critique presupposed that values attributed to the Catholic Spanish colonial background still held value for present-day Latin America, his analysis addressed specific economic realities and problems. His department also provided one of the few analyses from U.S. Catholics criticizing the existing political and social structures in Spanish-speaking countries. In contrast, "The Church and Reconstruction in Puerto Rico," a report prepared for the Administrative Committee of the NCWC and the Puerto Rican Bishops, hinted that perhaps the very foundations of Catholic culture in Latin America were the source of many problems.[48]

The NCWC Latin American Committee became defunct in 1933 when initial funds were terminated and the committee did not receive any money from the executive board. The bishops' attention in this area remained mainly on the problem of religious freedom in Mexico, but the Social Action Department sponsored several important seminars and conferences on Latin American issues through the 1930s and 40s.[49] By 1940, the United States had only 154 missionaries in all of South America, sixty-eight in Central America, and none in Mexico.

Both the lay involvement in Latin America through the NCWC and the Catholic Students Mission Crusade came to be impelled by the principles of Catholic Action. What relationship existed between this kind of evangelization and the impulse for missions overseas? The increase in lay involvement in these two groups was not lost on the Propaganda Fide office in Rome. Carlo Salotti, its secretary, encouraged cooperation among all such groups, and between them and the mission-funding organizations:

> *Cordial relations of cooperation must be built up between Catholic Action and Missionary Action.* Therefore, should the Directors of the Propagation of the Faith, working in concert with the Directors of Catholic Action, make use of these precious organized forces, they will find them to be of most effective assistance for the diffusion of the missionary idea in the ranks of society.... [50]

While the missionary emphasis always remained a part of the CSMC, later Catholic Action groups, which were more specialized, tended to emphasize an obediential relationship with bishops. That perspective sometimes tended to shore up a notion of "Catholic," which somewhat contained the Catholic Action groups' social efforts.[51]

Medical Missions

While Montalembert's *Monks of the West* and James J. Walsh's *These Splendid Priests* had commended the work of past missionaries in science and medicine, in reality, missionaries in the twentieth century, especially women, struggled long and hard to achieve recognition for medical missions. The professionalization and standardization desired in the Catholic health-care field in the first decades of the twentieth century sought expression in medical missions, as well. At the same time, persons such as Anna Dengel sought a mission theology attuned to such professionalization. Three trends related to medical missions emerged through the 1920s and early 1930s: the value of centralization for the deployment of medical supplies, the global distribution of birth-control information, and the struggle of women religious to become surgical or gynecological physicians. These areas were especially the concern of the Catholic Medical Mission Board, Dr. Agnes McLaren, Dr. Anna Dengel, and the Society for Catholic Medical Missions. At issue in a very specific way was the practical expression of the theological relationship between body and spirit — the incarnational principle.[52]

Many congregations of religious treated disease and sickness among people in their missions, even though that was not the group's primary focus. As noted in chapter 3, the Franciscan Sisters treated lepers in Hawaii in the nineteenth century; early in the twentieth century, Catholics were reading of the plight of the lepers of Molokai in books and mission magazines. American Protestant missionaries had supported medical missions since the nineteenth century, and when Catholic missionaries overseas became ill they were often attended by local Protestant medical missionaries. However, it took some time for the medical field to be recognized by Catholic America as an important focus for mission work.

Most mission stations through the 1920s and 1930s had a small dispensary with a Sister in charge, though the main work of the group was teaching. For villagers too sick to come to the missions, a Sister traveled to them

> along the hot but shady path or sometimes along the seashore, praying fervently for the souls of those whose bodies she has come to treat. The tropical foliage, the blue seas, the quiet — all these things seem to call aloud to the Missionary to worship the One who made her.[53]

Dual concern for the spirit and the body would characterize Catholic medical missions.

Catholic Medical Mission Board[54]

Less than a decade after its foundation, the Catholic Hospital Association sponsored a conference, "Medical Missions in Pagan Lands," in conjunction with the annual meeting 21–23 June 1922. Subsequently, Dr. Paluel Flagg[55] of New York and Father Joseph McGlinchey, director of the Boston SPF, organized what became in 1925 the Catholic Medical Mission Board.[56] Their purpose was to ascertain the medical needs of missionaries and to collect and distribute medical supplies and medicines to them. In 1927, the Reverend Edward F. Garesché, SJ (1876–1960), editor of *Hospital Progress*, joined the staff of the CMMB and remained director from 1929 until his death.[57]

The clearinghouse for medicines and medical supplies was located at the CMMB headquarters on West Seventeenth Street in New York. Supplies from the western United States were sent to the Hearst Building in San Francisco for sorting and distribution to countries nearer the Pacific Ocean. The CMMB collected medicine samples from doctors and bought other medicine with funds collected from Catholics for this purpose. After seeking advice from missionaries and U.S. Army and Navy doctors, the CMMB staff and volunteers also prepared medical mission kits for missionaries who visited the sick. By 1934, the CMMB had shipped 23,000 surgical instruments to almost nine hundred mission stations and had assisted ninety-five religious congregations worldwide. A program for lay volunteers with medical training started in 1928, when two doctors and seven nurses spent several weeks in Puerto Rico after a hurricane had swept through the area. In time, the board formed medical schools to teach natives.

While Garesché tended toward the devotional in much of his writing, his work with the CMMB brought out his appreciation for the logic of business and economics. He noted, for example, the bargaining power of medical supplies. A missionary who provided surgical instruments to medical personnel in poor areas could expect the doctors to "cooperate actively with his work for souls."[58] The director's experience showed him the power of buying wholesale. Centralizing the collecting at headquarters permitted the CMMB to send medical kits for thirty dollars rather than the two hundred dollars they would have cost if purchased in the United States.[59] As Garesché observed the growth of the Catholic hospitals in the United States, he observed that missionaries also represented a "vast potential purchasing power," once the dispensaries grew into large-scale institutions.[60]

Presenting little by way of a theological premise, the director perceived CMMB's work as one of "relief and apostolate," especially for "those unoccupied and unattached potential workers, who, though unable to do anything considerable, would find a program like this just what they need in the way of Catholic Action."[61] While his suggestion misinterpreted the emphasis of Catholic Action, within a theological frame of reference of "corporal works of mercy"[62] many lay medical personnel and millions of pounds of medical supplies nevertheless found their way overseas to alleviate suffering and to prevent disease.

Medical Missions and Women

In the United States, literature written or promoted from the national or diocesan SPF offices presented a consistent view of "pagan woman." Joseph McGlinchey's translation and adaptation of the popular *Conversion of the Pagan World* devoted an entire chapter to the subject of missionary Sisters, whose "chief apostolic work" was to "elevate the condition of women."[63] Especially in Asian and African countries, women were viewed as persons with little or no intellect, as servants to men, and as persons leading generally despicable lives. "Only in the Christian religion is woman considered equal to man in her proper sphere of action."[64] Stereotypes about women contributed toward infanticide, the suicide of widows, and, less dramatically, toward poor self-esteem.

Several medical issues particularly affected women. In the 1920s, as women gained both the vote in the United States and more national prominence, the National Council of Catholic Women was active in the campaign surrounding birth control. For the most part, the council supported the traditional position of the Catholic Church that birth control (except for the "rhythm" method) was not permitted. Representatives from the NCCW attended the hearings on the Cummins-Valle Birth Control Bill.[65] While a number of Catholics perceived birth control as a threat to family stability, others saw the issue as a "race suicide" problem, as a way for Protestants to control immigrant populations.

The bishop of Corpus Christi, Texas, formerly associated with the Catholic Extension Society, remarked:

> I have just returned from a confirmation tour along the Mexican border. ...No birth controll [*sic*] and race suicide, as yet, among my Mexicans; but the protestants are exceedingly active amongst them; and, I am sorry to admit, are gradually making serious inroads amongst them. Subsidized men and women propagandists who have cars to drive out into the ranches and to stay amongst them for extended periods are succeeding in causing defections. I am hoping to be able to offset this propaganda, by and by, by trying to organize groups of catechists who may go out into the ranches, too, to counteract the Protestant propaganda; but it will be a very hard task, because of the lack of necessary funds to procure a few cars, and to support the catechists.[66]

Missionaries in populous countries also noted that birth control was being urged. Obstetrical practices produced abortions and, sometimes, maimed women. But cultural practices also affected the health and life of women, as noted in the story "Paganism in the Solomons," printed in *Alofa Malia,* a Marist mission magazine. The magazine placed before readers the tale of a deceased king's son who kills the king's wife for companionship in the afterlife, to prevent his spirit from haunting the village or the animals:

> Murisivo [the king] now had his companion to serve him. Sleep peacefully, warriors of Gairiri and everyone in the district! Nothing to fear for your yams, coconuts, pigs, nor for yourselves. Even [the king's son] breathed a sigh of relief, happy over his accomplished duty. His belly reproached him nothing.[67]

Similarly, the author drew attention to the inequities between the work of men and women on the islands, a factor which, along with disease and difficulties in childbirth, led to high rates of infant mortality.

> Coming from the plantations, mama will carry the following items: baby, slung in a cloth around her neck and resting firmly on her hip; a fifty-pound load of taros and sweet potatoes on her head in a basket of her own making, and a native *ato* leaf umbrella which protects baby from the burning sun. Hubby walks behind, smoking his pipe, swinging his arms and enjoying the scenery.[68]

Women missionaries and literature from the Society for the Propagation of the Faith were unanimous in the need for women missionaries to work with women. It became a truism among missionary men that if the women were not converted it would be impossible to establish Christianity.[69] But "cute" stories, such as the tale from the Solomon Islands, also raised shrewd questions about the inequities women faced. Greater education for women would alleviate some of these problems, but women also needed good health care and health education.

Anna Dengel: The Society of Catholic Medical Missionaries

The most compelling speaker for medical missions was Dr. Anna Dengel (1892–1980), who made her case in light of the deficiencies in health care for women around the world.[70] Dengel was born in Steeg, Austria, and after reading a pamphlet published by the Franciscan Missionaries of Mary matriculated at a missionary nursing school in Lyons, France. The city provided an important context for her developing mission and awareness of women's problems. Lyons had been a center for lay mission movements and for religious and social resistance during the mid-nineteenth century. Pauline Jaricot began the SPF headquarters there in 1822, and Marie Françoise Perroton, followed by ten more lay women (the beginnings of the Marist Missionary Sisters), embarked from there for Oceania in the 1850s.[71]

Anna Dengel wrote to Dr. Agnes McLaren, a medical-missions promoter, who encouraged her to study medicine at Cork University, where she graduated with honors in 1919. The following year, Dengel began work at St. Catherine's, a small hospital staffed by the Franciscan Missionaries of Mary in Rawalpindi, India. Women there did not receive adequate health care because both the Hindu caste system and the Muslim purdah prohibited male doctors from examining and treating women. In 1924, Dengel returned to Europe exhausted from her work and made a retreat under the direction of the Jesuit, Rochus Rimml. During this time of prayer and reflection, she resolved to establish a religious congregation devoted to medical missions. The young doctor toured the United States to obtain financial help for this work and to interest other women in medical missions. She aimed to professionalize the health-care service in mission countries, which could also benefit the missionaries themselves.

After she and Pauline Willis visited several ecclesiastical dignitaries in the United States,[72] Dengel met with the Reverend Michael Mathis, CSC, who had traveled to India in 1922–23 to visit the mission of the Holy Cross Fathers and Brothers.[73] Mathis, founder of the Holy Cross Foreign Missions Seminary in Washington, D.C., and editor of the *Bengalese,* assisted Dengel in writing a constitution for her community; on 30 September 1925, with the approval of Archbishop Michael Curley of Baltimore, Dengel, Dr. Joanna Lyons, and two registered nurses founded a "Pious Society" of Catholic Medical Missionaries, whose purpose was to provide professional medical help where it was most needed.

Many of the medical problems the society faced affected women. In many countries the infant mortality rate was high, difficult childbirths often claimed the lives of mothers, and, as mentioned, unsafe obstetrical practices sometimes resulted in abortions and serious injury to women. However, the Vatican did not permit women religious to act as obstetricians. For many years Agnes

McLaren and Dengel had lobbied at various offices at the Vatican to obtain such permission, but approval was not obtained until 11 February 1936, when Propaganda Fide published *Constans et Sedula,* which lifted the centuries-old ban on religious Sisters performing surgical and obstetrical work. The women's insistence and the intervention of Denis J. Dougherty and other American bishops finally bore fruit. Also in 1936 the Society of Catholic Medical Missionaries became a religious congregation, the first Roman Catholic congregation of women to work as surgeons, obstetricians, and physicians. Sister Alma (Helen) Lalinsky became the first woman religious to receive a degree as a medical doctor. She graduated from Woman's Medical College of Pennsylvania in 1935 and was missioned to Rawalpindi, where she remained until 1952, to return in 1978.

Dengel defined medical missions as "that branch of missionary work through which skilled medical care is given to the sick and poor of mission countries, as a means of relieving their physical suffering and of bringing to them a knowledge and appreciation of our Faith."[74] She read widely and with depth and possessed a broad range of information about Protestant missions worldwide and about the needs of missions. The Sisters in her pioneering community supervised government hospitals and city health centers and educated native women as midwives and nurses. Anna Dengel remained the superior general of the society from 1925 to 1967 as the group grew to over seven hundred Sisters working in forty countries.

Besides the medical expertise she brought to her task, Dengel also sketched a theology of mission commensurate with the modernization of the field. First, medical missions, rooted in Christ's charity, offered a practical expression of one's love for God and an imitation of Christ, who "prov[ed] the invisible spiritual miracle of forgiving sins by a visible physical miracle of healing disease."[75] These works of mercy were to be performed, even though conversions would not result. "The people must never get the idea that conversion and baptism are necessary to reward your devoted care...."[76] Such missionaries were good Samaritans who ministered to victims of disease and of superstition. But Dengel was well aware that simple oil would no longer suffice to heal or prevent the kinds of diseases she had come across in India. The good Samaritan needed to provide *expert* medical care. A favorite passage she quoted from Pope Pius XI underscored that "unenlightened heroism" was not enough in the missions. Intelligence and science were essential to address the problems of disease and poverty throughout the world.

Second, Dengel saw medical missions as an act of restitution by the "white race," who owed a debt "to peoples subjected and exploited by our forefathers." These persons had sometimes by introducing particular diseases (measles in the South Sea Islands, for example) unwittingly depopulated an area. But in a materialistic culture, practices which were harmful to the spiritual and physical well-being of the global population also needed to be addressed.[77]

Medical missions had shifted emphasis from healing through miracles to healing through skilled care, using technological advances while maintaining a religious identity — an emphasis also promoted by the Catholic Hospital Association.[78] An incarnational theology based on imitation of Christ combined with professionalization in mission to heal the body of Christ. These works of charity served as an apologetic for medicine, which also began to address the social causes of illness. Paul the preacher and Luke the physician rode tandem on the mission circuit.[79]

Conclusions

Circumstances after World War I coalesced with U.S. Catholic money and interest in responding to global mission needs. The bishops' pastoral letter of 1919 preceded the formation of the American Board of Catholic Missions, an effort promoted for years by Francis C. Kelley, though, ironically, the board did not achieve his goal of coordinating all mission agencies. The bishops responded to the pleas of the Mexican bishops to provide a facility for the Mexican seminarians during a period of hostility toward Catholicism in that country. Under the sponsorship of the Social Action Department and the National Council of Catholic Women, laity took leadership in acquainting themselves with the changing situation of Latin American Catholicism. While not thinking of themselves as missionaries who would go overseas, the laity attempted an apologetic in both hemispheres on social principles enunciated by Leo XIII, to respond to changing political/social systems. For their part, Latin Americans did not consider themselves as missionary territory. The confident Catholic Students Mission Crusade built on similar Catholic Action ideals, educating thousands of young persons on the importance of missionary action in the Church. Still unclear, however, was any major correlation between the principles of Catholic Action and the missionary impulse.

A tendency toward centralization throughout the United States and in the Catholic Church since the beginning of the century found expression in the formation of the American Catholic Board of Missions and in the Catholic Medical Mission Board. Though Catholics felt the pinch of the Depression as other Americans did, monies still came in to the various diocesan SPF offices and to missionary societies. Mission magazines continued to proliferate, in spite of Kelley and the ABCM's efforts to control them. Over forty-five Catholic magazines printed in the United States were in circulation by 1930. Mission seminaries, however, had a hard time making ends meet financially.

The image of the missionary as a hero or heroine remained strong, but the professionalization Anna Dengel required gave another impetus to this vocation. "Unenlightened heroism" was giving way, ever so slowly, to the issue of proper missiological formation for those responding to the mission call. The ideal woman, "naturally more sympathetic and pious than men, born to love and sacrifice,"[80] with the missionary Sister as exemplar, acted in a practical and businesslike way in her day-to-day activities. Catholic medical missions, along with the myriad mission societies which had developed during the 1920s and 1930s, all had their venue at the biannual Catholic Students Mission Crusade conferences. The CSMC provided for Catholics a major source of knowledge and education about the mission world for the next several decades.

Other world developments also shaped the U.S. Catholic mission response in the 1920s and 1930s, not the least of which was the leadership of Propaganda Fide and the pontiffs. Two significant mission encyclicals — Benedict XV's *Maximum illud* (1919) and Pius XI's *Rerum ecclesiae* (1926) — promoted missions, native clergy, and local churches. Pius XI followed up his statement with the ordination of the first six Chinese bishops in modern times, some of whom visited the United States on their return to China. He had already hosted a mission exposition in the Vatican Gardens, an exhibition which inaugurated the Vatican Missions Library and Missionary-Ethnological Museum. The United States was well represented at the exposition, with booths and information from many organizations and societies which provided funds or personnel for home missions and missions overseas. American Catholics would interpret all of this mission activity and interest as reason to engage in China as the primary focus of mission outreach.

Chapter 6

"Light to the Darkness":
Mission to Asia, 1918–53

Mission activity among U.S. Catholics picked up considerably after World War I. The suggestion that it was "America's Hour" provided a psychological and sociological foundation for mission education and the promotion of mission vocations. The prestige of the United States, the growth of English as the language of commerce, and the challenge represented by the large number of Protestant missionaries abroad coincided with the increased "homogenization" of religious congregations, who were aligning their constitutions with the newly passed Canon Law of 1918. The opportunity to pioneer overseas missions proved felicitous for many congregations, though the contrast between the mission experience and regulations at home would frequently become a source of conflict for missionaries. Pius XI called for a reform of the Church in "mission territories" in 1924, expressing a desire to turn over leadership to local clergy. But this reorganization also opened areas to American clergy, especially in China.[1] By 1937, U.S. Catholics were working in twelve mission fields around the world.[2] Two countries featured most frequently in SPF's *Catholic Missions* in the 1920s were China and India, but China would become the major focus of money, personnel, and interest for American Catholics. The "reawakening" of the country to outsiders allowed for new accessibility to a vast population of "pagans." The China experience would give an American shape to missions and provide a vision for a mission ethos. A look at China, though, indicates that mission to Asians began on America's doorstep.

Catholic Missions to Chinese in the United States

In the 1850s and 1860s, Chinese were recruited to work in the mines of the western United States and in the construction of the western end of the transcontinental railroad. The Chinese communities in the West consisted mainly of men who worked diligently and sent home most of their earnings. Many Chinese intended to return to their country to be buried with their ancestors. After the bank panic of 1873, these Asians became scapegoats for the depression which followed. The "yellow peril" evoked fear in the country. Chinese were beaten, robbed, killed, or driven from their workplaces, sometimes through arson. Thomas Nast, well-known cartoonist for *Harper's,* frequently displayed the public's abhorrence of "foreigners" and included stereotypes of the Chinese in his drawings. By 1882, the U.S. Congress had created the Chinese Exclusion Act, restricting entry into the country and legitimizing racism. Over the next years, additional laws solidified this policy.

The reversal in U.S. attitudes toward Asian immigrants provided an example of what John King Fairbank called a "disillusioned view," particularly of China, which Americans held. Fairbank outlined two other attitudes toward China: a vogue for "Chinesey" things as a kind of cultural "oddity," and a respect for the ancient heritage of Chinese wisdom which overlooked some of the despotic elements of China's history and culture.[3] Missions to Asians in the United States would modify the last two attitudes and attempt to turn back the first by reaching out, though somewhat tentatively, to the Asian communities.

West Coast

Not surprisingly, the West Coast, with its proximity to Asia, is the first place where missions developed among Asians and Chinese Catholics. Often keeping to themselves and not attempting to mingle with their neighbors, the Chinese were viewed stereotypically. At the request of San Francisco's archbishop Joseph Alemany, the first Chinese priest to work among Chinese immigrants was twenty-nine-year-old Thomas Cian, who arrived in San Francisco on 20 June 1854. He worked there and in Northern California, but was only moderately successful because he spoke Mandarin, while most of the Chinese spoke a Cantonese dialect. His petition to the Society for the Propagation of the Faith in Paris, for funds to build a church for the Chinese, was denied.[4] Several other priests who spoke either Mandarin or Cantonese also attempted missions to the Chinese in San Francisco, but their efforts were largely unsuccessful. In 1894, Archbishop Patrick Riordan invited the Paulist Fathers to assume the administration of Old St. Mary's Parish in San Francisco. Pastor Henry Harrison Wyman, CSP (1849–1929), had alerted the archbishop to the needs of the Chinese, and the Paulists began their ministry with them. In 1904, Archbishop Patrick Riordan requested the Sisters of the Helpers of the Holy Souls (now known as the Society of Helpers), a community which had met some success in Shanghai, to work among the Chinese. The Sisters worked at the mission for forty years. Between 1917 and 1919, Pius L. Moore, SJ (1881–1950), did pastoral work at St. Francis Xavier Japanese Parish in San Francisco and became one of the first five California Jesuits to leave for China in 1928 at the age of forty-eight.[5]

In 1913, Charles Bradley, CSP, the director of the Chinese mission, rented a Chinatown store for use as a classroom, and the Sisters of the Society of Helpers began classes in sewing, English, and catechetics. The store further served as a gathering place for the older Chinese. A gift from Mrs. Bertha Welsh secured a building for the school and mission at 902 Stockton Street in 1920, and the St. Mary's Day and Chinese Language Schools opened on 1 August 1921. The Sisters of St. Joseph of Orange administered the day school and Dr. Chu Chew Shong was appointed the language school director.[6]

Joseph P. McQuaide (1867–1924), priest of the San Francisco Archdiocese and former chaplain in the Philippines during the Spanish-American War, wrote a book in defense of the Chinese. As one who had grown up with negative images of the people, he changed his perception after a trip to China.[7] McQuaide also promoted Maryknoll's work and provided them with the money he received for his priestly silver jubilee.

New York

Some Chinese from the West Coast, attempting to escape hostility and discrimination, moved to New York and Boston. They worked in laundries, restaurants, or small businesses where they would not be in competition with other workers. The New York archdiocesan SPF Office supported the Chinese Mission, which was located on Park Street. In 1910, Father V. Hilarius Montanar had purchased a house for use as a center for the area's Chinese Catholics. In 1909 he had twenty converts, and in 1913 thirty Chinese were baptized — most were men who had wives and children in China. The mission found a home at Transfiguration Parish on Mott Street, a parish which by that time was composed of Irish and Italian immigrants.[8] The Chinese Catholics were prominent on the annual Mission Day, sponsored by Monsignor John Dunn of the New York SPF Office. The event, held at St. Patrick's Cathedral on the weekend closest to 7 December, the feast of Francis Xavier, drew over six thousand people each year. The Chinese often wore their native dress and took up the collection. In 1911 fifteen Japanese Catholics were also present.[9]

The New York Chinese Mission closed down temporarily in 1920 at the onset of the Tong Wars in Chinatown. But there were enough Chinese Catholics in the city to warrant the translation for them of Cardinal Hayes's pastoral on Catholic Charities in 1924. In 1940, a Salesian priest who spoke Chinese worked at the mission, which was visited in 1946 by China's first cardinal, Thomas Tien, SVD. The Maryknoll Sisters replaced the Salesian Sisters at the parish school in 1945, and four years later, James F. Smith, a Maryknoll missionary returned from China, arrived to administer the parish.[10]

Boston

Because of the energy of its directors and support of the archbishops over the years, the SPF office in Boston was well organized and provided significant leadership for missions both locally and nationally.[11] The Boston area itself was a "mission-minded" city, home to at least five Protestant mission societies, including the American Board of Commissioners for Foreign Missions, the Baptist Mission Union, and the Universalist Church Foreign Mission Society. These groups had combined their efforts in a month-long mission exhibition and conference in 1911, "The World in Boston," which concluded with a spectacular "Pageant of Darkness and Light."[12] Both Catholics and Protestants walked through the exhibit areas and attended the pageant.

Joseph Fie Ark seems to have been the first Chinese convert to Catholicism in Boston, and when Archbishop John Williams died, twenty-six Chinese Catholics sent a floral tribute.[13] So when Francis C. Kelley organized the Second American Catholic Missionary Congress (1913) in the Boston Archdiocese, the Chinese theme was somewhat familiar to the city's Catholics. At the mission congress the clergy delegates were treated to a Chinese dinner and a speech by a missionary from Manchuria, Joseph Koesters, SVD, who interpreted the birth of the Chinese Republic as an auspicious time for Americans to send missionaries. The young republic seemed favorable toward Catholicism, and some Catholics held government positions. Koesters further encouraged the audience to adopt Chinese seminarians.[14]

National

The numbers of Chinese in the United States had fallen drastically, dropping from 106,488 in 1890 to 61,639 in 1920. Bishops generally sought individual missionaries or mission congregations to work with Chinese Americans in their dioceses. New York and Boston attempted to integrate Chinese Americans into archdiocesan events on occasions when "foreign missions" were referenced. The use of "Chinesey" trappings at the 1913 mission congress and at New York SPF Mission Days, and the beginning of a Boston Shen Fu mission club for women in 1928, were meant to remind American Catholics of the universality of the Church.[15] While outward costume and custom differed, Christ's message was destined for all. *The Far East* pointed to the more than two thousand Chinese students studying at American universities by 1923 as an important focus for the evangelization of China,[16] but little was done to attract the group to Catholicism, especially since the students maintained minimal contact with Americans. Somehow the Chinese, or Asians in general, seemed more appealing as a U.S. mission focus when they lived in their country of origin.

The SPF had published an equal number of articles about India/Ceylon and China during the 1920s, but China increased in popularity among American Catholics because of several factors: the emphasis mission publications gave to China, the foundation of the Maynooth Mission to China (soon called the Society of St. Columban), and the developing image of the "non-Christian." A new phenomenon arose when other religious congregations with little or no previous experience in overseas missions began sending personnel to China.

The Call to Asia

India and the Philippines

India was the first destination for American Catholic missionaries to Asia. Priests and Brothers of the Holy Cross congregations in Indiana went to the eastern Bengal/western Burma area in 1853. The place was a kind of "holding field" for the community, since there were inadequate personnel to meet the needs of Catholics in the area, much less to reach out to those of other religions.[17] Twenty years later, under financial stress, the Holy Cross community withdrew, but resumed responsibility for the area again in 1888. By 1917, the Holy Cross priests operated a preparatory seminary for Indian boys in Dacca and later started the Little Flower Seminary in Bandura. Michael A. Mathis, CSC, was instrumental in founding the Holy Cross Foreign Mission Seminary at the Catholic University of America, Washington, D.C., for the purpose of supplying Holy Cross priests for the India mission. He visited India in 1923 and subsequently wrote a book about the Holy Cross missions in the area, placing their work in the context of the religious environment of Bengal, without which "our mission field will be an inexplicable riddle to the reader."[18]

The Holy Cross Sisters made an unsuccessful venture to Bengal in 1853 when two American Sisters and two French Holy Cross Sisters went to work with the Holy Cross Fathers and Brothers. All the missionaries had been recalled by 1871. Not having enough Sisters prepared as teachers to send to Dacca, Edward Sorin, superior of the Holy Cross men, said that ten Sisters, who were housekeepers, should be sent. The women left Saint Mary's, Notre Dame, Indiana, in 1879, but their inadequacy for the task made for much unhappiness all around. Mother Augusta had them all return to St. Mary's. She explained to the bishop in India: "I was sorry to see those poor Sisters sent to India; I knew it was a mistake but I could do nothing at the time."[19] A third attempt of the American Province of the Holy Cross Sisters began in 1927. Three years earlier, a wing of the Holy Cross Foreign Mission Seminary had been designated as a formation house for women's vocations to the India missions. At the seminary, several Holy Cross Sisters assisted with the publication of *Bengalese*. Such work, of course, interfered with the preparation the women were supposed to be making to study medicine, Bengali, and "religion." Finally, after several setbacks, four Sisters departed on 6 October 1927 for Dacca, where they taught at the Toomiliah Catholic Mission School.[20]

Anna Dengel's Medical Missionary Sisters by the late 1920s were working at the Holy Family Hospital, successor to St. Catherine's Hospital in Rawalpindi, and were educating their congregation to work in other areas of need. They were informing Catholics in America of their mission in the *Medical Mission-*

ary, a publication which also raised money for these missions. The Catholic Students Mission Crusade promoted India's missions through publication of *Mission Study Tours: India* and through *India and Its Missions.*[21]

Again, because of the removal of European groups from the missions during or after World War I, many missions were depleted of personnel. Requests for assistance went either to Propaganda Fide in Rome or to members of other provinces, if the mission groups belonged to an international order. Such was the case of the Jesuits in India, where German missionaries were repatriated and the Jesuit superior general moved in English-speaking Jesuits from other parts of the world. Two of these men were Henry McGlinchey, SJ (1888–1918), and Henry Westropp, SJ (1872–1952). McGlinchey was a younger brother of Joseph McGlinchey, the active and effective head of the Boston archdiocesan SPF office at the time. Henry was born in Cambridge, Massachusetts, where his father was superintendent of the Sunday School at St. Paul's Church. After college at Cambridge Latin School and Boston College, Henry entered the Jesuit novitiate in 1908 and spent two years at Woodstock. In September 1913 he was studying philosophy at Innsbruck; the following year his brother Joseph took him on a tour of the mission centers of Europe. After war broke out, the younger McGlinchey was stranded in Europe. In March 1916, he was sent to Bombay and took the long way there to avoid contact with German U-boats during the voyage. He was prefect of discipline at the international St. Mary's High School in Bombay and then taught at St. Patrick High School in Karachi. Quite quickly he learned Hindustani, but his missionary life was cut short when he died during an influenza epidemic.[22]

Westropp, originally from Cleveland, went to India in 1916 as part of a mission in Patna and began a "cottage industry" among poor residents of the area. He was missioned to an aboriginal tribe, the Santals, in 1932. Ten years later he founded a Catholic Book Crusade and died in Patna. In 1922 the Patna mission was assigned to the Jesuits of the St. Louis Province.[23]

The American Jesuits also had a new presence in the Philippines. The section of the Philippines previously attended by the Aragon Province of the Society of Jesus was transferred to the Maryland-New York Province when the latter was refused entry into India.[24] The first two representatives, Jeremiah M. Prendergast, SJ, and Edward J. Duffy, SJ, left the United States in 1921, followed later by twenty more of their confreres.[25] International communities like the Jesuits had the flexibility to respond to political or national problems by moving their members from place to place, which maximized the evangelization possibilities and kept their congregations active in the mission field. The goals of the community could still be accomplished, though with personnel from a different country. They could build on what had preceded them, rather than having to "pioneer." At the same time, these international communities were often receiving new members native to their mission territories, adding to the multinational and multicultural character of the group.

American Women in China: A 1926 picture of Mother Mary Joseph, MM (right), and Sister Mary Paul, MM, visiting mission projects in China at a time when American women religious from various congregations were going to China in increasing numbers. (Courtesy, Maryknoll Photo Archives)

China: Impulse and Organization

Readers of *The Field Afar* and *Catholic Missions* in the late nineteenth and early twentieth centuries learned of the work of several U.S. missionaries in China. American Franciscan Francis Xavier Engbring, OFM (1857–95), the first native-born American priest in China, was rector of a seminary for Chinese vocations in Tsaitung, Hunan Province, dean in two districts, and procurator apostolic for twenty-one vicariates in Hupeh Province. The bicycle trips of Angelus Blesser, OFM, across parts of the China mission field were avidly followed by the readers of *Catholic Missions*.[26]

Two Daughters of Charity, Virginia-born Catherine Bushman (1868–1926)[27] and Joanne O'Connell (1862–1921), a South Carolinian, went to China in 1896 and 1898, respectively, under the auspices of the community's French province. Bushman was the first American missionary Sister sent to China. O'Connell was a sister of Denis J. O'Connell, an Americanist and rector of the Catholic University of America. Two American provinces of the Daughters of Charity subsequently left for China in 1922, trained in Shanghai, and established missions in Shansi Province in June 1924. The Sisters of Providence, St. Mary-of-the-Woods, Indiana, in 1920 became the first U.S. congregation to send a group of Sisters to China.

American Protestant missionaries had come to China in great numbers in the nineteenth century. By the turn of the century many of these missionaries were women, a fact noted by several Catholic missionaries who traveled on the same ships with them. The Student Volunteer Movement for Foreign Missions, which had provided thousands of missionaries, was on the decline by 1927, though their accomplishments in China remained considerable.[28] As U.S. Catholic missionaries entered China in larger numbers from 1918 to 1949, the country was experiencing great turmoil, grinding poverty, and desperation. Floods, famine, cholera, and earthquakes taxed the physical capabilities of the people. Anti-foreign sentiment and nationalism colored political activities. From 1918 to 1937, the post–World War I era, missionaries and the Chinese felt the effects of banditry and warlords. Between 1937 and 1945, the Japanese occupied China and the country experienced the effects of World War II. Protestants and Catholics were either placed under house arrest by the Japanese or interned together in larger buildings. Between 1945 and 1953, China experienced a civil war, the Communist Revolution, and the defeat of the Nationalist Party of Chiang Kai-shek, who fled with many of his supporters to Formosa (Taiwan). These again were stressful times for the Chinese, and some missionaries were imprisoned by the Communists. Foreigners were expelled and most Catholic missionaries were repatriated by 1953, except for Passionist Harold Rigney, SVD, and James E. Walsh, MM, the last American to be expelled in the mid-1970s.[29]

In the first quarter of the twentieth century, the Chinese Catholic Church was beginning to see growth in the number of native vocations to religious life and the priesthood, and in the development of lay catechists among men and women.[30] A few native sisterhoods had begun by the 1920s. The important First Council of the Church in China was held in Shanghai in 1924;[31] two years later, the first six Chinese bishops in modern times were ordained in Rome.

Around 1915, mission funds, originating from the active SPF and Holy Childhood offices, were plentiful. More than other Asian countries, China held a special mystique for American Catholics. Walsh and Price specifically expressed a preference for missions to China.[32] China's cause was advanced through mission magazines and other materials, the foundation of an American region of the Columban Fathers, and the developing theme of the Chinese darkness, of the country as a heathendom in need of the light of Christianity.[33]

Promotion of China. James A. Walsh, in his position as Boston SPF director, published biographies of French missionary martyrs in Vietnam and China. But after his trip to Asia in 1922 to gather information for decisions about Maryknoll missions, he published *Observations in the Orient,* whereby Americans could "follow the acts of these American apostles."[34] Communications from China missionaries were compiled in *Maryknoll Mission Letters.* In the early 1930s, Robert Sheridan, MM, published a number of pamphlets related to mission life in China.[35] Slides depicting the early days in the China missions and a 1923 movie, *Maryknoll on the Hudson and Maryknoll in China,* rounded out the varied mass media Maryknoll used to inform American Catholics about the sizable mission field.[36]

Far from being isolationist, like much of America, Maryknoll viewed the modernization wrought by global trade as offering the precise moment for America to go to China.

> The acceptable time to convert the world has come. This is the day, the age of salvation! The marvelous development of practical science and inventions has multiplied the individual missioner's efficiency many times over.... The heathen, too, are more favorably disposed than ever before. International trade with its consequent interchange of ideas has broadened their minds. The massive walls of superstition and prejudice are perceptibly crumbling, a process which will continue with increasing speed. As a result the missioner is less feared, his doctrine is given a fairer hearing, and the road is open to numerous conversions.[37]

It seemed as if technology and economics could break down superstition and make ready the way of the Lord.

The correlation between the coming of the gospel and the potential prosperity of China, a country whose population lived much of its life in stretched economic circumstances, caused one preacher to exclaim at a departure ceremony:

> Now is the auspicious time to send missionaries to China, and this for several reasons: the Chinese are rapidly advancing in modern civilization. In a few years hence they will be less inclined to accept our doctrines; for it goes without saying, that the more prosperous a man is, and the better he gets on materially, the less will he be inclined to turn to God.[38]

The economy of salvation and the potential prosperity of mission lands seemed inextricably linked.

The primary emphasis on China, however, did not go unchallenged. Several articles in *Catholic Missions* during 1918 and 1919 complained that U.S. Catholics had only the evangelization of China in view and recommended that they look to other countries as well, a point a missionary to Africa also made in a letter to the editor in the *Ecclesiastical Review*. He argued that if English-speaking missionaries were needed in China, they were also needed in Africa, especially in countries under English colonial rule. He then chided his audience: "Is it not passing strange that the American Church should have missionaries for China, and none, or hardly any...for the Philippines, Porto Rico [sic], Hawaii, Guam, and other mission districts?"[39]

Society of St. Columban.   Another group with a focus on China was also establishing a U.S. presence. Irish-born Edward J. Galvin (1882–1956), a curate at Holy Rosary Parish, Brooklyn, was ordained at Maynooth Seminary, Ireland, and had hoped to work as a missionary among non-Christians. He set up an appointment to discuss his interests with New York SPF Director John Dunn. The young priest was unable to meet with Dunn because of sick calls on the appointed day, but found to his surprise that John M. Fraser, a missionary to China, was a dinner guest at the rectory. This austere and intense man was in New York collecting money for the Asian missions and looking for another priest to join him in China. By the end of the day, Galvin had decided to obtain the necessary permission to accompany Fraser.

The pair left in 1912. Galvin worked in western Chekiang Province and found few English-speaking priests in the area. The days were long and lonely, as he spoke little Chinese and no French. While Fraser was intending to found his own society for missions to the Chinese, Galvin wrote to Ireland and the United States seeking priests interested in serving the people of China. In 1915, two Irish priests who had read his letters in Irish newspapers came to Shanghai and encouraged Galvin to start a mission society for China. On his return to Maynooth, Galvin met twenty-six-year-old John Blowick, a canonist and professor of theology, who was interested in going to China. He, too, had heard John Fraser speak while the latter spent a few days at Maynooth.

After further discussion, Galvin and Blowick received the approval of the Irish bishops and Roman authorities to build a seminary to prepare missionaries for China. Papal authorization came 18 June 1917. The society was named after the missionary St. Columban, whom Galvin had read about in Montalembert's *Monks of the West.* Galvin sailed through the war-darkened Atlantic to the United States and met with several archbishops to find a location for an American headquarters. On St. Patrick's Day, 1918, Galvin was welcomed to Omaha by Archbishop Jeremiah J. Harty.[40] The archbishop had returned to the United States two years earlier after serving as the first American archbishop of Manila. While in China, Galvin had heard of Harty's work in the Philippines and, at one point, Harty came to China to assist in the consecration of a missionary bishop. On 25 March, the archbishop gave his approval and the Irish Mission to China opened a one-room rented office as the center of operations for their mission magazine, *The Far East.*

In 1918, twenty priests in Ireland took an oath of membership in the society. Eleven of the men left for their mission in Hanyang (Hunan Province) on 17 March 1920, first traveling across the United States soliciting funds, then leaving from San Francisco. One of them, Richard Ranaghan (1889–1937), having worked in the Los Angeles area, saw the value of movies for mission promotion and took along a movie camera and film, creating probably the first mission film directed toward U.S. Catholics. *The Cross and the Dragon* featured Bing Crosby singing "Silent Night" before he recorded it for the music industry.[41]

The men became known as the Chinese Mission Society (and still later as the Columbans) in the United States. One of the first members of the society, a cousin of Galvin's, Edward John McCarthy (1890–1957), ordained at Maynooth in 1915, left Ireland for the United States in 1918 to work on promotion and publication of *The Far East*.[42] Until 1934, when he left for the Philippines, he was the American superior and became the spokesperson for the society at mission meetings and conferences, including the conference of mission superiors at Notre Dame in 1919 for the planning of the American Board of Catholic Missions.[43] The first American Columban student sent to China, Patrick Gately (1904–86) of Brooklyn, traveled to Shanghai after ordination in 1930 and later became seminary rector at Nancheng, where he was expelled in 1950.[44] On his return to the United States, he engaged in mission promotion around the country.

Galvin envisioned the society as an international organization from the beginning. Having been in China prior to its foundation, he had seen the effects of nationalism on the missions.

> We go to China under no flag but the Cross and we feel that under that banner of Redemption we will be safe. From the outset, we set ourselves to establishing an international organization because we feel that we must be prepared to draw our resources from every field if we are to cope with such things as international wars. They will come and there will be a time when the purely national missionaries will be cut away from every field. Take for instance if there were a war between America and Japan with no possibility of sailing the Pacific, where would the Maryknoll mission in China be? It would be completely cut off and her missionaries would starve unless some other organization in China or elsewhere would come to their assistance. With us it would be different; if the Pacific is cut off, Europe is in touch with China, and if Europe is cut off, Australia, perhaps, can help. This is one of our considerations that has decided us to become international.[45]

In actuality, the society remained heavily Irish in culture but international through its regional foundations in English-speaking countries. In the 1980s, candidates for priesthood were accepted from Korea, the Philippines, and other countries where the Columbans served.

James A. Walsh had expressed some resentment toward the Columban Fathers, especially toward the publication of their magazine. He felt that the two groups were competing for the same clientele: Americans of Irish extraction. Aware of the tension, Francis C. Kelley proposed at the 1919 meeting at Notre Dame, which inaugurated what became the American Board of Catholic Missions, that the U.S. Bishops recognize the Maryknoll Society as the official American society and that the "Irish" society be excluded from participation in the proposed mission board.[46] Through the foresight of Joseph McGlinchey, this exclusion did not come to pass and the Columbans became part of the ABCM. However, for about ten years the Columbans were denied permission to collect funds in most dioceses where the Society for the Propagation of the Faith was organized.[47]

In the first years of the society, five priests from Ireland promoted the magazine mainly in Brooklyn, St. Louis, Sioux City, Kansas City, and Pittsburgh. Their stenographer and bookkeeper in Omaha, Margaret Bolan, entered the newly formed Columban Sisters in Ireland as Sister Mary Therese in 1929.[48]

In 1921, benefactors of the society numbered 15,000, and 82 percent sent donations that year. With the mission promoters having left for China, the society depended on the magazine to bring in a steady income; the men were not disappointed. In spite of the postwar economic slump and stolen mail, within three years of its arrival in Omaha the Columban Society was considered a good security by local bankers. A small preparatory seminary was built in Bellevue, a few miles south of Omaha, and was dedicated on 29 June 1922. By that time there were five young men enrolled at St. Columban's and several applicants for a brotherhood and sisterhood. Unlike the Maryknoll Society, however, the Columban Fathers in the United States did not have a large group of women working at the magazine because in the early years most of the copy was done in Ireland.

The Columban Society represented two growing phenomena in the U.S. Catholic mission movement: lay persons as missionaries in their own right and the sending of groups of missionaries from religious congregations that had little or no experience of missions overseas. Between 1908 and 1912, *Catholic Missions* had encouraged women to enter the missions, without distinguishing between lay and religious. In her speech at the Fourth CSMC Convention, Mother Mary Joseph Rogers, MM, indicated that lay women were needed in China. An even stronger article in 1920 suggested the formation of a society of lay missionaries in America. George Stenz, SVD, saw the laity as a "modern" means of mission, more in touch with material things than the clergy. Laity could interact more knowledgeably on a business or professional level with merchants, officers, and others the missionary didn't normally meet, presenting Christianity to secular officials "in a practical way, relieving them of the fear of being persuaded by a missionary who by his very office is not in touch with worldly affairs."[49] Further, laity could provide an example of a "regulated" Catholic family life, that in the context of China there should be no concubines, for example.

Among the inquiries sent to the Columbans, three men made a commitment to work with the society in its founding years. Daniel Sullivan (b. 1891), an office worker from upstate New York, had listened to a Columban preach about the China missions. He offered his services to the society and joined the first Columbans in Hanyang in 1920, organizing the mission office in that area. Sullivan was well liked among the missionaries, efficient, and enthusiastic about his work. After four years of service, he returned home.[50]

Two more men traveled to China with the next group of Columbans in 1921, Otto Scheuerman (1891–1973) and Dr. Robert F. Francis. Scheuerman, a bookkeeper and cashier in Rochester, New York, had spent fifteen months in the Army's medical department in World War I and became interested in medical mission work. After his letter of inquiry to McCarthy about assisting Galvin, a Columban visited Scheuerman's home. Arrangements were then made to have the thirty-year-old join the priest sailing for China in November 1921. Joining Scheuerman were an Irish doctor and Francis, a Notre Dame graduate with a medical degree from the American University of Chicago. Together the men began the medical apostolate for the Columban Fathers. Four years later, fatigued from overwork, Francis suffered a nervous breakdown and returned to the United States. Scheuerman continued mission work in China until he was imprisoned by the Japanese and repatriated in 1943.[51]

Other mission groups had lay missionaries working with them in China. Mary Hubrich (1886–1962), a nurse who had received her education at Women's Hospital, Chicago, left in 1924 to assist the Franciscan Friars in the Wuchang area.[52] Dr. Harry Blaber pioneered hospital work in Kongmoon serving under the auspices of the Maryknoll Society from 1930 to 1935 and then with his wife until 1937.[53] An unnamed man and woman worked with the Friars Minor and the Springfield (Illinois) Sisters of St. Francis in Shantung Province. Bertha Buehler aided the Adorers of the Blood of Christ in that same province,[54] and in 1947, Mary Louise Tully, pioneer of interracial work in Louisiana and the first American member of the Grail (an international Christian movement for lay women's leadership), worked alongside Chinese women as a stenographer and secretary in Hong Kong.[55]

Among the many benefactors to the Columban Fathers were the Sisters of Loretto, whose motherhouse was in Nerinx, Kentucky. They had completed a "burse" for the Columbans and had an active CSMC unit at their Loretto Academy. The Sisters represented the second phenomenon of the 1920s and early 1930s: congregations of men and women sending missionaries overseas for the first time. E. J. McCarthy remarked about the Kentucky congregation in his diary:

> Very superior educationalists with many schools all over America. They have been most enthusiastic supporters of our missions and completed a Burse last year and a $1000 fund for church and school in China. If we could get these Sisters, they would very likely finance their work in China.[56]

The community thought a foundation in China would be possible, and Galvin requested a copy of their constitutions. In March 1922, Galvin responded favorably to McCarthy's inquiry about sending American Sisters to China. McCarthy met in April with the superior general of the Sisters of Loretto, Praxedes Carty, as she traveled across the country visiting her community's missions. While in favor of a mission in China, Carty thought that the matter needed discussion at their General Chapter. The Sisters were already engaged in mission work among Native Americans and Mexicans in Texas and the Southwest, a fact McCarthy saw as a valuable asset in starting a China mission.[57] Galvin's visit in early June at the Sisters' motherhouse in Kentucky brought assurance that some Sisters could be available. In July 1922, the General Chapter approved the mission to China, and on 12 September 1923 the first six Sisters of Loretto left for Hanyang. This mixed ethnic group (two of the six were born in the United States) traveled aboard the *President Jefferson* with twenty other U.S. Catholic missionaries.

The trip by the Sisters of Loretto marked the first noticeable increase in mission sending from congregations of women and men who had not worked in missions abroad. Twenty-six more Sisters' groups and at least nine men's groups sailed to China before the United States closed its borders to foreigners.[58] The Brothers of Mary, the Divine Word Missionaries, the Order of Friars Minor,[59] the Passionist Fathers and Brothers, Vincentians, Dominicans, and Jesuits of the California Province were some of the men who sent missionaries to China. The total number from each group ranged from ten to eighty. Many of these missionaries went through similar experiences, whether they taught in the cities, opened dispensaries for the poor of the villages, inaugurated parishes and mission stations, or prepared men and women catechists.

As outsiders, Americans had no immediate "niche" in the heart of Chinese church and society. Propaganda Fide had the authority to permit clerical jurisdiction in mission lands. Arrangements could also be made through superiors general of clerical societies and religious orders for entrance into a given mission locale. The men's congregations found, however, that in spite of their promotion of "America's Hour" for China missions, the European mission societies only grudgingly and reluctantly "ceded" their mission territory to the Americans. Especially for those who arrived first, time and effort were needed to clarify and adjust jurisdictional and ecclesiastical divisions. Several men's congregations who found cross-cultural difficulties with their European confreres in China preferred to have their own American jurisdiction and vicar apostolic. Such was the case, for example, with the Vincentian Fathers who arrived in the eastern part of Kiangsi Province on 5 August 1921, scheduled to work with the French Vincentians.[60] The American Passionists found that they were better able to work among themselves than with the Spanish Augustinians they first encountered in parish work. In thirty years of work in China, eighty American Passionists worked in Hunan Province.[61]

It soon became clear to the clergy that an Asian Church needed women's help because of the custom of dividing the sexes and because the missionary's assessment of religious needs was linked to values related to family and home life. Most often, after an appraisal of the needs of their mission territory, men's societies contacted women's congregations to assist them in the mission work. Most typically, the women's groups were known to the men because of proximity of provincial houses in the United States or because of a similar spirituality. The Passionist Fathers, in Hunan Province since 1922, invited the Sisters of Charity, Convent Station, New Jersey, to come to China because their central houses were relatively close to each other.[62] The 1926 International Eucharistic Congress in Mundelein, Illinois, provided an occasion for Sylvester Espelage, OFM, to interest some communities, including the Franciscan Sisters of Perpetual Adoration in La Crosse, Wisconsin, to join him in Wuchang, Hupeh Province. The Sisters of St. Francis in Milwaukee responded about the same time to an invitation to Shantung from another Franciscan Friar, Alphonse Schnusenburg, who had also attended the congress.[63] The Sisters of St. Francis had also received but did not accept invitations to South Africa and Latin America, as mission personnel had knocked on the doors of many American motherhouses across the country. This broad "net casting" across the United States was another typical pattern in requesting assistance for the missions.

"Light in the Darkness of Heathendom."   Americans interpreted *Maximum illud*'s (1919) mission to non-Christians mainly in terms of the millions of "unenlightened pagans" in China. Later, when *Rerum ecclesiae* (1926) promoted native vocations all over the world, China still held a special fascination because of its "teeming millions... living in darkness." Robert Streit's book containing stark black, white, and red drawings rendered from global mission statistics captured the immediacy of such a mission.[64] The American version of the SPF magazine conveyed a similar urgency:

> To the Catholics of Christian America, the benighted heathen is crying out for enlightenment and truth. What will America do?... We Catholics of America must take the field against the forces of darkness just as we are now grappling with the enemies of truth and justice. We owe it to ourselves as Americans; we owe it to the heathen; we owe it to the Giver of all things.... We must become in deed what we are in name, "the connecting link of the ancient and modern civilization."[65]

Maryknoll and several other congregations, while trying to be "metanational," sensed that the time was right for the virtues underlying American civilization — democracy, liberty, adaptability, regard for the individual, and enthusiasm — to be at the forefront of the mission enterprise. With the birth of the Chinese republic in 1911, the time seemed even more auspicious to a number of Americans to connect these two countries through evangelization. James A. Walsh had written to all the bishops in China in 1917, seeking a field for his men. He asked the bishops which points should influence Maryknoll as an American society in the selection of a mission field: American prestige, the number of Protestant centers in their area, the need for English-speaking clergy, or the relationship with Chinese in the United States.[66]

China: Sustained Zeal for Mission Work

Finances

Missionaries needed to be concerned with finances for education of personnel, transportation to the mission, and sustained livelihood once there. Missionary clergy depended on "burses," Mass stipends, and contributions from the national or local SPF offices. During the Depression and World War II, when "stipends were as scarce as diamonds," as one missionary remarked, clergy needed to be enterprising to locate other sources of income for their missions. Some communities experimented with annuities for a larger, more sustained source of income.

Another source of mission revenue became available toward the end of the 1920s, when returned China missionaries preached in local parishes. Such was the case, for example, with Raymond A. Lane, MM (1894–1974), a native of Lawrence, Massachusetts, who had worked for five years in Manchuria and who spoke to parishioners in the Boston Archdiocese. Contact with missionaries formed part of an effort to connect Catholics with specific persons and to the mission charism of the Church. This personal relationship was also achieved through books and articles about individual missionaries. Attraction to a mission vocation for many of the 2,500 Maryknoll priests, Sisters, and Brothers, for example, arose from the personal inspiration provided by China missionaries.[67]

When men's congregations invited Sisters to work with them, the clergy clearly preferred communities which would be financially self-sustaining — able to build, supply, and maintain their mission life out of their own resources. Misunderstandings frequently occurred between the Sisters and the vicar or bishop over this issue, especially with the women's groups that were not primarily missionary congregations. Subscriptions to women's mission magazines were not nearly as extensive as those to *The Field Afar, Our Missions,* and *The Far East,* which supported men's congregations. Revenue also came from mission bazaars, sometimes sponsored by local units of the Catholic Students Mission Crusade, general donations to motherhouses, or gifts from relatives and friends. The seminarians at Techny, Illinois, wrote mission plays in the 1920s and performed them for thousands of schoolchildren, who then toured the seminary and its farm.

While women's congregations often made financial agreements with vicars apostolic in the mission area, frequent problems arose between the Sisters and the clergy over control of finances and land once the Sisters arrived. Two such instances involved the Sisters of Providence and the Sisters of St. Francis of Assisi. The former group had signed a contract with Bishop Joseph Tacconi before the first six women left Indiana. Tacconi, on the advice of Cardinal Dougherty of Philadelphia, sought a religious congregation known for higher education to provide a similar education for Chinese women. The bishop would provide for their spiritual life, their living quarters and needs, and would purchase property and handle the income and expenses of the school. He painted a fairly optimistic picture of the area and hinted that rich "mandarin daughters" were waiting to receive an education. In return, the congregation would send the Sisters, providing their best teachers for this endeavor. This arrangement, though, led to interference by the bishop in the daily running of the school and other actions which hampered the Sisters. Three American priests from the Philadelphia area, who had been missioned to the area at the same time as the Sisters, remarked to them, "You sisters will never have any privacy or independence while you are under the Bishop's nose. He is telling all over the province that he is supporting the sisters, but we know that if it were not for your Saint Mary of the Woods, all the sisters would be dead."[68] The mandarin daughters, of course, never appeared.

In the second case, Sister Virginia Wegenek, superior of the Franciscan mission in Shantung Province in the 1930s, wrote to the mother general in Milwaukee about the trouble occurring with the German Franciscan priest in charge of the area:

> I cannot send any account yet, because I do not know how much money we have. The [German] Fathers took all the money that I had. Father Jansen gave it to them and they do not give any definite answer to me when I ask them how much we have. They only say: "Sister do not bother about money, we're all Franciscans." But last Saturday I spoke to Father Alfonse and told him that I would not stand for any of such saying any longer, and that I want to know just how we stand.[69]

The American Franciscan Fathers, who ministered with the Sisters, supported them and urged them "to stand on their American feet." Conflicts about finances were often due to missionary desperation at the enormity of the task, a lack of understanding of the situation the Sisters would encounter, or the women's trust that the bishops would be true to their word.

Two other sources for mission funds had a strong educational component: mission circles and mission magazines. By the mid-1920s, myriad mission circles were springing up around the country. Mission "circles," which assisted men and women missionaries, typified a female approach to mission work. Women needed little convincing to become interested in the work and to involve their network of friends. A description of the Cleveland mission circles, organized in the 1940s, appeared in the local newspaper and indicated the understanding these women had of their role as "auxiliaries" in mission:

> First, you get twelve mission-minded women together. Perhaps they don't even know they are mission-minded, but they are Catholic women who go to church, receive the Sacraments and make the best possible effort to rear their children in the Faith and through this process come to the wonderful realization of how important religion is. The result? They are mission-minded. So these twelve women, leagued together as the twelve Apostles were, decide to help in the project of carrying the Faith to the rest of the world by backing the men and women already actively employed in mission work.[70]

When they met at each other's homes, women of the 1920s through the early 1960s saw this time as an opportunity to socialize with other women — a "night out" — while their husbands cared for the children. The end product, that being the funds, seemed almost secondary to the collaborative experience and personal contact with missionaries through letters and cards. Groups sent their monies to the SPF diocesan or national office, or to particular missionaries whom they "adopted." Unlike the bureaucratic business organizations of the 1930s and 1940s, which inclined toward hierarchical management, women's leadership tended to be "circular" in organization, interactive among diverse constituencies (including the national SPF organization, the pastor, other women of the parish, and the missionaries), and creative in their financial plans.

They kept monthly records tabulating the number of altar linens, vestments, rosaries, scapulars, and baby layettes made, the boxes of food, clothing, and medical supplies amassed, and the books, magazines, greeting cards, and canceled stamps collected. Annual gatherings of mission groups to display what they had collected and created (much of it with their domestic skills) provided an opportunity for public acclaim in local newspapers. Mission fund-raising also gave women leadership in church financial activities, usually the domain of males.[71]

By 1940, however, the Maryknoll Society had ceased to rely on such groups as a means of support and counseled the Divine Word Missionaries to do likewise. Maryknoll suggested that missionaries should work through the SPF and through parishes, where clergy had more control of the finances than lay groups.[72] Furthermore, some missionaries had started their own mission circles to respond to the needs of that particular mission. The Columban Fathers continued to promote mission circles into the 1960s.[73]

Mission magazines provided both finances and mission education. U.S. Catholics followed missionaries overseas in the *Sign, Our Missions,* and over forty mission magazines printed in the United States by the 1930s. Maryknoll's mission-education programs of the 1920s through the 1950s significantly influenced the thought of American Catholics about the nature of mission work.[74]

The Divine Word Missionaries had a press at their provincial headquarters, which printed *Our Missions* and the *Little Missionary* and turned out books and pamphlets of both a devotional and mission nature. While little was published on China for U.S. Catholics during the 1920s through 1940s, among the pamphlets which could be found in church magazine racks were *800 Million Lost* and *Brother Eugene, SVD, An American Missionary Brother.*[75] Two significant books that Matthias Braun, SVD, translated from the German, *Catholic Mission History* and *Catholic Mission Theory,* brought to American audiences in the 1930s the fruit of the Divine Word Missionary tradition of science, anthropology, and ethnology as basic mission tools.[76] The books were the undertaking of Joseph Schmidlin (1876–1944), the founder of Catholic missiology, who taught at the University of Münster and served as director of the International Institute for Missiological Research. Divine Word Missionary material publicized mission needs in general and aimed to educate American Catholics on the cultural significance of the groups they sought to evangelize.

Language and Cultural Awareness

Learning the language and customs of the people, as had been strongly advocated in *Maximum illud,* proved a difficult task for those entering China. How could one prepare to learn an ideographic language and to comprehend its underlying thought pattern when one's own language used a series of letters to express words and ideas? Some communities hired a Chinese tutor for several weeks of classes prior to leaving the United States. Franciscan Sister Servatia Berg (1902–68), lacking any experience with Chinese people before she left for Shantung Province in 1929, searched for a Chinese laundry in Chicago in order to meet the family there and to experiment with a few phrases learned from a Shantung graduate student studying at Marquette University. But most missionaries learned the language, with greater or lesser proficiency, from a Chinese tutor who came to the mission house in China and from missionaries who already had some command of the language. In the 1930s, some men and women used time interned in Spanish convents and monasteries in Beijing while under Japanese occupation to sharpen their language skills. While some missionaries had read something about Chinese history and culture before embarking, most missionaries had little knowledge of the current political situation in various parts of China. They certainly had no idea of the possible impact of political developments on their lives once they arrived.

The Maryknoll Society produced language programs for writing Chinese characters and for speaking Mandarin, Hakka, and Cantonese. Programs included classes and reading in Chinese customs and culture. *First Year Cantonese* by Father Thomas O'Melia, MM, was adopted by the Hong Kong government to examine civil-servant candidates.[77] While language courses were recommended for five years, after the first year many of the priests became too involved in pastoral duties to continue with the intensity of the first-year program. Nevertheless, many gained adequate facility. It was thought that the Maryknoll Sisters, who taught at the two Maryknoll schools in Hong Kong and the Maryknoll Academy in Manchuria, or who served as nurses at the Shanghai Mercy Hospital, need not learn Chinese, though they eventually acquired some of the language. The Sisters in rural areas were forced to learn because no English was spoken. By the mid-1930s, Sister Anna Mary Moss, with the help of a Chinese catechist, had written twenty-four booklets in the local Hakka language, combining stories from everyday life and Christian truths.[78]

Professional Formation

As the primary goal of mission work revolved around pastoral and sacramental ministrations in the local church, seminary education was the main method of training men for mission. Even in missionary congregations the curriculum looked virtually the same as that of other seminaries. The "extracurricular" activities and ambience at the seminary created by CSMC units, talks from returned or visiting missionaries, perusal of mission magazines, and letters posted from those in the field provided the school its mission tone. Men's congregations often took a course lasting a few weeks on first aid and general medical assistance, as did the Passionists, who participated in a medical course at St. Elizabeth Hospital in Brighton, Massachusetts. Among the few communities of Brothers who went to China from the United States, the Marianists, sent to Shantung Province in 1933, arrived with their experience as educators and a congregational history of work with Chinese and Japanese students at their St. Louis College in Hawaii.

Women missionaries went to China trained primarily as medical personnel and as educators. Often a community would send, along with their educators, at least one person who had some basic medical training. Once in China, they found that human need often challenged them beyond their professional preparation. Sister M. Edward Pessina (Adorer of the Blood of Christ), who envisioned herself as a country doctor ready for any emergency, ran a dispensary in Shantung Province and had to perform an operation without really knowing how. The patient lived.[79] Especially after the Registration Reform Act in China (1925),[80] U.S. congregations sought certified teachers to send to the missions. Once there, the women responded to many other needs including parish work, catechetics, care for orphans, and other social services.

Vocational and Spiritual Qualities

After deliberating whether their congregation would take on a China mission, major superiors pronounced their decision either by noting the importance of the two recent papal documents on missions (*Maximum illud,* 1919; *Rerum ecclesiae,* 1926) or by indicating that their resolution was a response to a spiritual blessing. The Franciscan Sisters of Perpetual Adoration proclaimed their first mission venture overseas as a thank offering commemorating the golden jubilee of the establishment of perpetual adoration in their congregation, and the Sisters of St. Francis accepted their China mission as an offering of the community to the Eucharistic King during the Jubilee Year, for example. For those communities whose primary ministry was stateside, candidates for mission work in China were often chosen from a list of volunteers. In some cases, as many as one-third of the community offered to go.

Major superiors had various criteria in selecting persons for this work. The Adorers of the Blood of Christ, who arrived in Shantung Province in 1933, sought women who were "enthusiastic volunteers — not too young, not too advanced in years," physically fit, who felt they could adapt themselves to a new language and environment, and who had been reasonably successful in their professions. James E. Walsh, MM (1891–1981), a member of the first group of Maryknoll priests sent to China in 1918 and later bishop of Kongmoon, painted the picture of an American missionary in his *Maryknoll Spiritual Directory* (1947). He listed eleven mission virtues: accessibility, adaptability, affability, charity, confidence, courage, hardness, humility, initiative, frankness, and loyalty. The missionary's "true nature" showed him to be a man of action, a man with a divine message, a person with disregard for conveniences, spiritually generous, possessing an inquiring mind, and a willingness to learn from others.[81] Though obviously assuming that the missionary was a male, his view was gleaned from James A. Walsh and from Mother Mary Joseph Rogers, both of whom emphasized the value of martyrdom to complete the picture. James A. Walsh and Thomas Price had earlier invited the Baltimore Carmelites to be "martyrs" for the missions through their prayers, in an effort to connect contemplation and mission.[82] Rogers further suggested that qualities among those at Maryknoll were the "power of creating anywhere that we may be sent, the feeling of fitting in, and of attempting anything which you are asked to do.... [This is] part of our life, this moving about and adjusting ourselves to conditions."[83] Between 1918 and the dismissal of most of their personnel from China in the 1950s, the Maryknoll Fathers and Brothers sent 252 men and two lay doctors, and the Maryknoll Sisters sent 173 Sisters as educators, social workers, catechists, hospital and medical workers, and leaders of indigenous sisterhoods. The "American missionary" motif was carried to China by the U.S. Catholic society with the greatest number of missionaries there, but other American congregations subscribed to many of these ideals as well.

Ultimately, spiritual resources would provide the major strength for adaptation in the trying times which beset China missionaries. One sweltering evening, beleaguered by mosquitoes as he wrote, Francis X. Ford, MM, penned his thoughts from the rectory in Yeungkong to seminarian John Considine at Maryknoll:

> I hope for your own good that you will get at least five years on the missions, if only to shake your soul to its very roots. Without this mission training I might have been a better man in many ways, but I don't think I would have seen as clearly as I do God's nearness and love....
>
> Excuse my sermonizing but this is mostly addressed to myself — it would sound stupid aloud: I feel like shouting out or rather whispering to you that *porro unum necessarium est* — that you be a saint, whether Bernard or Paul it matters little. We are not going to convert one soul until we are saints (which is not hard at all, after all); perhaps I really mean we can convert only while we are saints, for we are all saints for whole minutes at times, — and whatever conversions we may seem to make are credited in God's eyes to some saint who is helping us. This may sound like poppycock but it's my conviction that someday some one of us will be a saint for more than a half hour and thousands will be converted.[84]

Sister of Providence Maria Gratia Luking (1885–1964) entreated the superior at St. Mary-of-the-Woods, Indiana, that she send the "right kind" of person to China:

To enter into the thought of the people we have to deal with, to feel for and with them, to gain their confidence and sympathy requires not an ordinary talent; God alone can give it. They must be kind, silent, prayerful, earnest at labor, and ready to forget themselves above all, able to control themselves that they can be cheerful under all circumstances.[85]

In the extraordinary times of physical, political, and emotional turmoil the missionaries experienced in more than three decades of major U.S. Catholic mission work, American ingenuity and adaptability and their own spiritual resources enabled the missionaries to handle the adjustments they continually needed to make, though not all weathered life well on the other side of the Pacific Ocean.

Ritual

When trunks were packed and supplies forwarded, those who had been chosen for the mission often participated in a farewell ceremony. This ritual frequently embodied hopes and dreams for success. Many times the ceremony tapped deeply into the Christian tradition to embody mission life in dramatic form. Family, parishioners, benefactors, and reporters from local newspapers sat rapt in attention and awe as the missionaries were presented with a mission cross, symbol of the life on which they embarked. The Sisters of Loretto touched their congregation's early missionary beginnings by attending Mass on their departure day in the log cabin built by their missionary founder, Charles Nerinckx, in Kentucky. Provincial of the Divine Word Missionaries, Father Burgmer, bestowed the cross on his men with the words: "Behold your guide in all your apostolic journeys; your protection in every danger, your consolation in life and in death."[86] John Considine, who attended a Franciscan Missionaries of Mary departure ceremony, found one element of the ritual, the kissing of the missionaries' feet, "a bit awkward in the church, particularly because movie men cluttered space along the altar railing, but the ceremony must impress the public."[87] This practice, which alluded to the scriptural phrase, "How beautiful on the mountains are the feet of the messenger of good news" (Isaiah 52:7), seemed a bit much for him. One of the first women from the United States to enter the Franciscan Missionaries of Mary, Marie Comtois (Mother Mary Lawrence, 1880–1917), had already served in Manchuria and died there the year Considine entered Maryknoll.[88]

While the symbol of the cross suggested a martyr motif, it also evoked identification with suffering people, a reality which all the communities would experience — both their own suffering and the suffering of those to whom they came. Maryknoll's literature and James A. Walsh's writings had clearly placed the martyr's image before the eyes of the Maryknollers, but the Passionists would be the first to suffer death at the hands of robbers on return from their retreat in Hunan Province in 1929. The "black-robed figures of sacrifice," Fathers Walter Coveyou, Godfrey Holbein, and Clement Seybold, "baptized China with their blood."[89] A fourth Passionist, Constantine Leach, was buried with them, having died of typhoid the same week. Ten years later, Maryknoll had its first martyr in Gerard A. Donovan (1904–38), who died at the hands of bandits, having been kidnapped from the sanctuary of his church.[90] All of these men had been preceded in death by Iowa native Mary Elise Renauldt (b. 1859), a Sister of Providence dispensary nurse, who, after treating the people of her mission for smallpox, succumbed to the disease on 20 April 1921. While martyrdom was technically defined as going to one's death rather than renouncing of the faith, the Passionists interpreted death at the hands of bandits as "martyrdom in the eyes of God."

The mission departure ceremony provided a formal farewell to the missionaries, but private feelings of loss and homesickness were often expressed only to close friends. Thomas Megan, SVD (1899–1951), wrote to a friend:

> As our boat glided beneath the Golden Gate, with the good old USA vanishing from sight, my heart sank. For the first time in my life, I felt violently torn from my moorings and absolutely on my own. Believe me, Eddie, only a Divine Commission from our Lord Himself could have made me leave home and country, relatives and friends, and everything dear to me! I know God will not allow such a sacrifice to go unrewarded. I am looking forward to a happy career in Christ's vineyard in China.[91]

Mission Issues: How to Approach the People?

U.S. Catholic missionaries, working especially in territories where the Paris Foreign Mission Society had been the Chinese people's only experience of "Catholic," soon found that in addition to working for the conversion of China another evangelization needed to happen. U.S. missionaries first tried to convince Chinese citizens and European missionaries alike that America was not a Protestant country. Back in the United States, Catholics were playing a variation of the same theme, trying to convince other Americans that Catholics were not "foreign" but American, that Catholics made good citizens, and that women had a role to play in society.[92] Second, U.S. missionaries wanted to change the prevailing opinion among Chinese that all Catholics were French.[93]

The question of which social or economic strata should be the target for evangelization had been asked and answered in various ways since the time of the apostles. The response to this question generally indicated some assumptions about theories and practice. The Americans' spiritual predecessors in China in the sixteenth century, Matteo Ricci and his Jesuit colleagues, had responded by approaching the educated class and the high courts of governmental power. Patrick Gilgan (1875–1936), an American Franciscan from Brockton, Massachusetts, arrived in 1913 in the Hangyang district of Shansi Province and lived a simple life with an impoverished Chinese family. By identifying with the people in this manner, he attempted to affect the lives of the majority of the economically poor in the area.[94]

The issue faced each new group of missionaries. Should they approach the highest or lowest socioeconomic groups? Not surprisingly answers varied, even within the same congregations, sometimes with consequent conflict among missionaries of the same community. Responses also expressed the groups' missiological assumptions about "planting the church" or "saving souls." On a more mundane level, solutions to this mission problem implicitly affected the financial well-being of the congregations themselves, for if they worked with impoverished groups other sources of income would need to be sought for their livelihood. Therefore, one way to approach the people would be through education, hospital and dispensary work, seminary education, the formation of catechists, and direct evangelization. Another response would require work with the poor, women, and children. Some missionaries favored evangelization among the cultured and educated persons in China. Once converted, these persons would convert others who looked to them as socially superior. All groups presumed that their approach would have its impact on Chinese society and make it more amenable for conversion.

When Edward Galvin sought a mission territory for the newly founded Columbans, he desired a section in the Wuhan cities along the Yangtze River. The founder "felt that this had always been a cultural centre and that schools and other religious developments which he hoped would come through the society's efforts there, would be more likely to have a wider influence than elsewhere in China."[95] Sister of Providence Maria Gratia Luking, superior of the mission band of the first American women's congregation in China, emphasized to her major superior in Indiana that there was "no better way of attracting the Chinese than by high ideals of education. They have the greatest appreciation for learning and it is the most powerful means of gaining souls for the Sacred Heart."[96]

All groups soon learned that an important element in approaching people of high economic or cultural status was the issue of "face."

> Face counts everything in China and I have not that, and never can acquire it. The Sisters suggested that ... if Sister Maximilla [a well-known community artist] would come to China for three or four years, or as long as she would like or care to stay, and take charge of the art and embroidery, she certainly would make face for our Sisters. You see, a few pictures of art, and a few embroidery pieces would suffice to keep up the face for the rest of [our] stay in China.[97]

Fu Jen University

Another effort to reach the upper classes of Chinese society was begun by the American Benedictines, who were invited by Pope Benedict XV to establish a Catholic college in Kaifeng, Honan Province. Preceding the Vatican's interest, though, Vincent Ying (Ying Lien Chih), fearful that Western influence was overshadowing Chinese culture, had opened Fu Jen She, a school for Chinese studies. Inaction on the part of Chinese officials forced the school to close. An American priest, Professor Barry O'Toole, a Benedictine oblate impressed with Mr. Ying's educational effort, stopped in Rome to encourage the Propaganda Fide office to appeal to the American Cassinese Benedictines to start such a school. The Benedictines of Latrobe, Pennsylvania, were invited to take responsibility for this higher-education project. After a visit to the area by the archabbot of Latrobe, it was decided to open the school in Peking rather than Kaifeng. In contrast to the many well-endowed Protestant colleges, the school would be the one Catholic university in all of China. In 1925, Fu Jen Academy was established as a single college in Peking. Four years later the institution had grown to include colleges of liberal arts, natural sciences, and education, and the school was renamed Fu Jen University. Dr. Chen Yuan was named president and O'Toole became rector.

By 1931, fourteen Benedictines from several American priories, priests Carl Hensler of Pittsburgh and William O'Donnell of Canton, Ohio, and four European laymen collaborated with forty-seven Chinese teachers at the university. In late summer 1929, Francis Clougherty, one of three clergy who had accompanied the Sisters of Providence to China and who was now a Benedictine, arrived at St. Benedict's Convent in Minnesota. As a faculty member and chancellor at the Catholic University of Peking, he sought Sisters to inaugurate classes for women in an allied college with Fu Jen. In 1930, six Benedictine Sisters arrived to staff Catholic Women's College, which affiliated with Fu Jen University. During their first year in China, the Sisters concentrated on learning the language. The second year they taught English to some private students, who paid a small tuition. In their third year, the Sisters moved to a larger building and accepted thirty students from the upper class, who had the equivalent of a second-year high school education. The Sisters hoped to advance the students and to develop a college curriculum.

On the heels of the Depression, funds from the United States were meager for both the men's and women's colleges. University officials insisted that the Sisters finance the construction of the women's college, an undertaking for which they were not prepared. These economic factors and an apparent lack of interest from members of the American Cassinese Benedictine abbeys led to the departure of the Benedictine priests from Fu Jen University in 1933. The Sisters left Peking for Kaifeng, Honan Province, in 1935. In 1940, the Missionary Sisters, Servants of the Holy Spirit, were sent to teach at Fu Jen Middle School in Peking.[98] An important Benedictine contribution, however, was the inauguration of the science department, which contributed to the discussion of the question of evolution[99] and emphasized a Chinese style as a basis for Christian expression in art. Noteworthy in this respect was Dom Adelbert Gresnigt, OSB, who helped the architecture of Fu Jen University accord with principles of

Men and Women Collaborating: Passionist Fathers (two in Chinese garb) and Sisters from New Jersey and Sisters of St. Joseph from Boden, Pennsylvania, in Hunan Province; an example of American men and women religious collaborating in response to a variety of needs in China after the Japanese occupation in 1937.

Emphasis on "Native" Clergy: As twentieth-century missions developed, there was increasing emphasis on "native" clergy training in China and elsewhere. In this undated photo, Fr. John J.Considine, MM, visits with an American and a Chinese Jesuit seminarian at a river crossing. Maryknoll itself did not recruit "native" vocations but assisted the development of national diocesan clergy. (Courtesy, Maryknoll Photo Archives)

Chinese design. Gresnigt's perspective reflected the view of the apostolic delegate in China, demonstrated in the delegate's open letter on Sino-Christian
architecture to James A. Walsh, MM, and Edward J. Galvin, SSC.[100]

The Divine Word Missionaries were asked to assume responsibility for the
university. Respected for its pioneering work in the sciences, particularly in
anthropology, the society sent Edgar Oehler, SVD (1907–74), and Harold
Rigney, SVD (1900–1980), to join the faculty in the science department, thereby
enhancing the earlier scientific work of Dr. Barry O'Toole. Oehler was a member of several geological expeditions in Suiyuan and inner Mongolia, important
sites from the 1920s through the 1940s in the search for the first persons on
earth. Rigney received his doctorate in paleontology from the University of Chicago in 1937. Two years later he was in Accra, Ghana, West Africa, and served
as an Air Force chaplain in Africa during World War II. He left Africa for China,
where, besides being rector, he continued his work in paleontology.[101]

Ralph Thyken, SVD, mission procurator at provincial headquarters at
Techny, Illinois, enthusiastically put promotion machinery in place to obtain
funds for the university. Dollar University Clubs, mass stipends, annuities, and
a special appeal to the CSMC units produced successful results.

During the Japanese occupation, the university was allowed to remain open
because of having been declared an international institution. In 1941, American
faculty members were forced to leave the college and German nationals took
their place. After the war, in August 1946, Harold Rigney, SVD, became rector. Inflation of Chinese currency, growing Chinese nationalism, war between
the Nationalists and Communists, and encroaching government regulations affected the university and all schools operated by foreigners. Chinese authorities
imposed restrictions on Fu Jen in 1949, calling for greater responsibility for
Chinese administration, for all finances of the university to be placed in Chinese
hands, and for poor students to be educated at the school's expense.[102] Strictures on the university increased and by June 1952, Rigney was a prisoner of
the Communists. Through his memoirs, *Four Years in a Red Hell,* he would
become a key figure in the publicity surrounding the capture of missionaries in
China after the Communist Revolution in 1949.[103] In addition to the education which the Chinese students received, Fu Jen left another legacy. Since 1935
the university has published *Monumenta Serica,* a leading journal in the field of
Chinese studies. In 1956, Fu Jen alumni expressed an interest in reestablishing
the university in Taiwan. In 1959 Pope John XXIII invited Archbishop Yu Pin
of Taipei to be its first director. Fu Jen continues today under the sponsorship
of the Divine Word Missionaries, the Jesuits, and diocesan clergy.[104]

Women and "Pagan Babies"

Another approach to evangelization concentrated on working with the poor,
women, and children. While these persons were most often the focus of congregations of Sisters, both men and women missionaries operated from a particular

theological and social perspective. Women were seen as the foundation of the family. Without their education and conversion, there was little hope for Catholic life in China. This was made clear, for example, in a letter from Sister Gertrude Hanley, a Sister of Charity in Kiangsi Province, to William Cardinal O'Connell of Boston:

> We are commencing to build a school, where we can keep the little ones as interns, so as to prevent them from being contaminated by home influences, which in many cases leave much to be desired. Now is the time to start with youthful China and if we wish to have Catholic homes, we must have the means to give solid instruction to our Chinese womanhood, so deplorably neglected in the past.[105]

This was also the perspective of Bishop Joseph Tacconi when he spoke with Archbishop Denis Dougherty in Philadelphia in hopes of finding a religious congregation to assist him in Kaifeng, Honan Province. Tacconi's goal was the development of strong family life and the raising of women's status. Dougherty suggested the Sisters of Providence in Indiana, and arrangements were made for their arrival. On the first day in China, after a visit to two refugee hospices for boys in Shanghai, Maria Gratia Luking wrote, "We asked what had become of the girls. The sisters said the women and girls are among the greatest sufferers...but I am too full of the suffering of our people to write more."[106] Mother Mary Joseph Rogers of Maryknoll echoed the idea that the conversion of women was the cornerstone for Catholic Chinese family life. In her address to the fourth CSMC convention, she responded to the question, "Is it true that the majority of women in the non-Christian world can be reached only by women?" by saying:

> We are told one of the methods [Maryknoll priests] have been following in bringing people into the Church is to try to bring in whole families, because there is much danger of interference if only one or two members of the family are Christians. They like to get the whole family at once. Suppose you take a case where all the family would come in but the mother. You might think that would be a small thing, that women would not have much influence. But the influence of women in the Orient is great, and our missionaries will not receive a family until the mother has been baptized....It is the women who teach [their families] how to live a Christian life....The missionary priests can get the conversions. Of course, they perform all the rites and instructions at the end, but to teach the people how to live Christian lives, to apply the doctrines they have learned, in this the help of the sisters is incalculable.[107]

Chinese women were, for the most part, hidden from public view, according to mission literature. Ironically, the Sisters, who over the years in the United States had been acquiring the customs of cloistered nuns, attempted to emancipate Chinese women from their "cloister." Part of this liberation meant addressing the social status of women. Orphanages for babies, mainly girls who were not wanted by their parents and who were found exposed to the elements or at the Sisters' doorstep, provided one response to the low social estimation of women. The Sisters gave names and faces to these "throwaway" persons. The Sisters of Charity introduced readers of *Sign* to the girls in their orphanage, "each unique in her own way and each with a breath-taking history. But this much should suffice to elicit your interest and enlist your prayers for these mended bits of China."[108]

Catholics in the United States were introduced to "pagan babies" through the Holy Childhood Society, through the pages of mission magazines, and through presentations by returned missionaries. The principle behind the Pontifical Society of the Holy Childhood was to have children care about other children around the world. American children saved their pennies in mite boxes, a practice also used by Protestant mission agencies. The society was a "missionary union of children for the purpose of assisting in the rescue and baptism of the abandoned infants of China and other pagan countries."[109] When an American child sent a certain amount of money the "pagan baby" was "saved" (the funds were used to provide food and shelter), and the American received a "certificate of adoption" (see page 73). Part of the strong relationship which bound the child to his or her counterpart in China was that the American could provide a baptismal name for the child. *Catholic Missions* published occasional articles on the abandoned babies as did other mission magazines. The social reality behind "pagan babies" was explained to thousands of high school and college students at a slide presentation at one of the annual CSMC conventions. The viewing had been arranged to commemorate the work of one of the founders of CSMC, Clifford King, SVD, who had been a missionary in China for many years; under siege, he had fled to the Philippines prior to World War II. While watching the slide of "foundlings at breakfast," the narrator explained:

> The care of orphans and abandoned children is one of the most widely known missionary works in China.... The stories of how girl babies have been abandoned by their parents are well known to all of us. Many of these children, however, are brought to the Sisters' orphanages because their parents are unable to provide them with food and clothing. It is a Chinese custom that when such children grow up they may be reclaimed by their parents and, if their parents are pagans, this constitutes considerable difficulty in the matter of the Christian education. Sometimes the Sisters adopt such children by legal methods and in doing so, it is necessary for them to pay the parents something. This is what is meant by "ransoming a pagan baby."[110]

Thousands of these infants were baptized by the Sisters or by the priests over the years. While many died, those who survived grew up in the family environment the Sisters created.

Not everyone agreed, however, that these babies should be the primary focus of mission work. The Columban Fathers' mission magazine never carried advertisements for the babies, because Galvin held that education would remove the need for such work. *The Far East* placed the phenomenon of abandoned babies in the context of various levels of poverty in China and the difficult though important task of addressing the causes of the conditions.[111] This approach, too, was advocated by Maria Gratia Luking:

> One might gather in abandoned babies and old people for centuries, and the more such places multiply, the more there will be to fill them.... [A]t present, it is undoubtedly not the best way to teach Christian ideals of living. [We need] to instruct the coming generation that these practices are evil. It may be hoped that there will gradually be less need for this curing process, and with the funds that are being consumed thus, schools can be maintained and increased.[112]

The Marianist Brothers thought that such rescue work, which meant that a majority of Chinese converts would come from the very poor, was a factor keeping well-to-do Chinese from entering the Church. Further, the Brothers believed that education of young boys, the future heads of households, should be the target of evangelization.[113]

Missionaries who came to China to establish primary and middle schools had to decide, after the Registration Reform Act of 1925, whether to register their facility with the Chinese government. The government was reacting to the effect mission schools had on the Chinese identity of the students as they learned from a system based on Western values. To register would allow for more Chinese governmental control and, in some respects, less autonomy for the mission community, but compliance would give the school value in the minds of the Chinese.[114] If mission schools were not registered they ran the danger of having their materials confiscated. While the act took a few years to take effect in various provinces, at least one city in 1935 still had a Western-oriented curriculum which was apparently appreciated by the Chinese. The Sisters of St. Francis, Milwaukee, teaching primary grades in Shantung Province, remarked, "We are in the city and the Chinese are following the American methods pretty well, so it means for us to be up to date."[115] Many religious communities viewed education of children as a way to convert their parents.

Hospitals and dispensaries provided the places for other mission work. Protestant groups had pioneered medical missions in China and had come to the assistance of many Catholic missionaries in need of their services. Sister Gertrude Hanley of the Daughters of Charity viewed hospitals as "one of the best means to arouse the sympathy of the Chinese."[116] The Sisters of Charity, Convent Station, New Jersey, working in villages in Hunan Province, had several goals for their work in the dispensaries: to have people see that the Catholic Church was behind the undertaking, to make contacts with the people, to learn about various diseases they encountered, and to master the idioms of the language.[117] Mercy and compassion for the sick were viewed as ways to serve the Chinese people, a perspective which became more important to the Chinese themselves as the spirit of nationalism gained strength.

Adaptation

When missionaries left for China, most of them expected difficult adjustments to language and food. As one missionary Sister remarked, "Each day brings varied and startling situations and impressions, so much so in fact, that one scarcely recovers from a constant condition of shock."[118] Many missionaries found themselves in situations where multiple languages were required. The problem of attaining at least minimal language skill was compounded in some missions where American missionaries also needed to interact with missionaries from Europe. In one case, for example, Franciscan Sisters, whose native language was English, were learning Chinese and praying in Latin while having to communicate on an almost daily basis with clergy who spoke German.[119]

Unanticipated stresses called for ways to reconcile missionaries' expectations with the real situations they found in lifestyle and ministry. Within a short time of their arrival, missionaries had to think in terms of adapting to the outer symbols of religious life (clothing and the "order of the day," for example) and facing Chinese customs and regulations. While clergy often felt free to adopt Chinese attire, Sisters gave no thought to this possibility. Modifications came only in the color or type of fabric for their habits, or the shape of the veil, and these changes were made on the basis of comfort and cost.

Not infrequently, communities of men and women experienced internal conflict over the methods to be used for ministry, disagreements compounded because of their distance from administration in the United States. Maria Gratia Luking thought that Sisters needed to adopt a "Chinese style" along with the language in order to understand the Chinese worldview. Sister Joseph Henry Boyle, who followed her as superior of the China mission, emphasized a strict adherence to the schedule and customs as practiced in Indiana. The Passionists experienced friction when they tried to establish an order of the day modeled after the monastery life of their Brothers in the United States, because in the villages of Hunan Province the men were dispersed, rather than living as a group as in the American monasteries.[120]

Superior of a group of Franciscan Sisters in Shantung Province, Sister Reginald Hary (1895–1948), wrote to the Milwaukee mother general requesting a change of community custom to permit the Sisters to visit the homes of their students.

These little pagans are so dear as they can be — if we could only bring them all into the true fold. They love to listen to Sr. Susanna [Chang,

OSF] explain the catechism and tell them Bible stories — all want to become Catholics — but then their parents are in the way. We must gain the
parents through the children. If we could only come in contact with them,
I think we could do much good.... This would not be merely to satisfy
curiosity but to acquire a necessary knowledge which would help us in
dealing with the children. Chinese characters are so vastly different from
ours but it is really a necessity in China to know conditions.... True, it
is not our custom [to visit homes], but working in a missionary country
necessitates some mitigation.[121]

For missionaries engaged in education, the Registration Reform Act forced
modification of curriculum or forfeiture of mission schools. Sisters who observed the practices of Chinese pedagogy, even in areas where public officials
favored an "American" school, requested new mission personnel to come
equipped with artistic and gymnastic skills. One Sister requested that someone from the United States be sent to teach folk dancing, an activity she had
observed in the local Chinese school.

But there were other reasons for adaptation in a country where Americans and non-Chinese were considered "the foreign devil." Missionaries saw
that attendance at marriages performed with Chinese customs and other kinds
of "ecumenism" "helped break down religious barriers,"[122] so that the Chinese would view Catholicism with less suspicion. Experience with customs,
languages, and worldviews so different from their own raised the possibility for these missionaries that *catholic* or *universal* couldn't possibly mean
"sameness."

Another adaptation occurred not because of culture and language, but because of political life in China. Unsettled conditions due to civil war, the
Japanese invasion and occupation, the effects of World War II, and the impact of Mao Tse-tung's Communist forces largely created the mission agenda
between 1920 and 1949. In many cases, the buildings the communities had
constructed were either demolished or in poor condition during any or all
of the political disturbances. Some mission compounds became overcrowded
when thousands of Chinese sought protection. Church leaders frequently became directors of relief services, examples being Bishop Edward Galvin, SSC,
and Father Frederick McGuire, CM. Sometimes their parishioners fled to other
sections of the country to escape the Japanese. At various times the American embassy warned the missionaries to leave the country because the embassy
could no longer protect them. Some missionaries departed for Korea, Formosa
(Taiwan), or the Philippines, or returned home. But the vast majority of missionaries stayed with their people until the Chinese government expelled them
after 1949. The Philippines, Taiwan, and Rome then became a "China mission
in exile" where Chinese seminarians could be educated until their hoped-for
swift return once communism had been defeated.

Problems and Accomplishments in China

The problems missionaries faced in China came from many directions. Not everyone became an accomplished speaker of Chinese. Struggles over approaches to evangelization complicated the mission response for several communities. All missionaries were not up to the stresses of cultural interaction. Some returned home, broken in physical or mental health. Mission goals were not always clear, especially when missionaries arrived. Levels of missionaries' cultural and political awareness were uneven. The political turbulence proved not only frustrating but dangerous. Mistakes were made by identifying too closely with the Nationalist government of the Christian Chiang Kai-shek. Yet in spite of these problems, several important developments took place as a result of the missionaries' work. The missionaries tried experimental approaches to evangelization, nurtured and developed the indigenous Church, and presented the Chinese social system with alternatives to long-held values.

The traditional pastoral pattern of the European missionaries, whom the Americans frequently replaced or worked alongside, generally consisted of a mission compound with outlying stations. Catechumens came to the mission for a four- or five-week course in Christian teaching and living. The priest spent much of his time, however, as a kind of circuit rider, traveling from station to station to visit parishioners, to administer the sacraments, and to make new contacts. While the mission compound remained a staple for American missionaries, other approaches to evangelization were also tried.

Several Maryknoll priests developed new directions in mission work and altered some of the methods promoted by their French predecessors.[123] Bishop Francis X. Ford, MM (1892–1952), advocated the direct apostolate of evangelization for the Maryknoll women, an approach called the Kaying method. Using this strategy, the Sisters traveled in pairs and stayed for days at a time in Chinese houses, made contact with the women, and provided an entrée for questions about the Sisters' religious beliefs. After gaining the women's interest, the Sisters provided instruction in the Catholic faith. New Catholics received follow-up instruction. Sisters visited all Catholics, conducted Sunday School classes, and trained catechists through class and field work.[124]

Bernard Meyer, MM (1891–1975), promoted lay catechists (the Wuchow method), who were instructed in their own surroundings rather than coming from a long distance to the mission compound. After his expulsion from China in 1950, two publications in the United States presented his program for lay leadership based on the image of the Mystical Body of Christ, his theological foundation in China: *Lend Me Your Hands* (1955) and *The Whole World Is My Neighbor* (1962).[125] These Maryknoll contributions bore fruit not only in China but among American Catholics as well.

Several of the twenty-seven communities of women religious who served in China witnessed the profession of Chinese women into their communities, a situation which immensely aided the work of the those congregations. The Maryknoll Sisters, who arrived in Hong Kong in 1921, accepted their first Chinese postulant (Sister Maria Teresa Yeung) from that city six years later.[126] Within a year of the arrival in Yeungkong of the second group of Maryknoll Sisters in 1922, the first Chinese Maryknoll postulant, Aurea Xavier (Sister Chanel), returned with Mother Mary Joseph to the United States for her spiritual and educational formation.

Several U.S. missionaries were instrumental in the formation of native vocations to priesthood and religious life, a value promoted throughout the papal mission encyclicals of the twentieth century. Since almost his first days in Kongmoon, Francis X. Ford had been preparing for a seminary by teaching Latin to some of the parishioners he thought would make good priests.[127] In fall 1926, the Little Flower Preparatory Seminary opened at Pakkai. He was responsible for the formation of a native sisterhood, the Sister Catechists of Our Lady, who soon took charge of an area of his diocese. Bishop James Edward Walsh, MM (1891–1981), began a similar process, educating young boys in the rectory in his Yeungkong parish. Other preparatory seminaries opened in the Maryknoll mission areas of Kaying and Fushun. Between 1927 and 1939 five Chinese sisterhoods were established by Maryknoll priests and trained by Maryknoll Sisters in Kongmoon, Wuchow, Kweilin, Kaying, and Fushun. All five groups of Sisters, after fifty years of Communist harassment and dispersion, have again been united in apostolic communities.[128] Advancing native vocations was also important to Vincentian priests, who taught various levels of seminary in China. Encouragement of native leadership was often in opposition to the attitude of some European missionaries, who retained jurisdictional control of their dioceses and viewed native clergy as "assistants" rather than as leaders in their own right.

In areas of social work, missionaries promoted a leadership role for the Chinese in cooperatives and in health care. The development of Maryknoll cooperative rice, pig, and cow banks, especially in the late 1930s and 1940s, coincided with the efforts of the Chinese government to make their people self-sufficient. Maryknoll was able to shepherd funds from the American Advisory Committee for such projects. Sister Finan Griffin, SC, remained in the background once she had taught a young Chinese man and woman some elementary health principles at the Sisters' dispensary. The Chinese medical team then offered basic health care and distributed medicines based on their diagnoses. Congregations with Chinese members put the local establishments in charge when the "foreigners" either were under house arrest or incarcerated during the Japanese occupation of China.

The educational, social, and medical programs the missionaries offered not only met the immediate needs of people, but the cumulative effect of the work presented alternatives to prevailing social and economic systems. Those who had "rescued" the abandoned infants raised them and taught them skills to become self-sufficient. Whether through carpentry, agricultural cooperatives, sewing, cloth production, or other occupations, young Chinese men and women were able to support themselves once they left the orphanages. Young women from the orphanages were especially sought for marriage. Through education of many Chinese, especially poor children, men, and women, and through the influence of women in schools and dispensaries, the Chinese were presented with new forms of leadership, especially where they saw priests and Sisters working together. Mission at the fringes of society demonstrated that these people were of equal worth as human beings with those who had social status and "face."

Effects of China Missions on U.S. Catholics

Vast numbers of mainly middle-class Catholics began to see the United States and Catholicism in global terms, especially through the energetic work of the Catholic Students Mission Crusade, through numerous mission publications, and through talks by returned China missionaries. A kind of metamorphosis occurred in American presentations about Chinese people and the Chinese Church, roughly parallel with three periods in U.S. Catholic mission: 1918–37, 1937–45, and 1945–53.

In the first period (1918–37), writers and preachers presented China in a positive light, showing appreciation of its great civilization. The millions of unbaptized persons on the other side of the globe presented an almost mystical attraction to Americans. Such was the case in a departure sermon preached in 1928 at the Franciscan motherhouse in La Crosse, Wisconsin.

> It is right and just that we come to the assistance of our Chinese brethren, millions of whom are still groping in the darkness of heathenism. We owe it to them as brethren. We also owe China a debt of gratitude for what the Chinese have done for us in the past in the way of ancient civilization, arts, and sciences. Let us not forget that many of the comforts and conveniences which we are enjoying every day...owe their existence to Chinese ingenuity, Chinese untiring labor: — our teas, silks, chinaware, Chinese manufacturers without number. On the other hand, there remains much for us to learn from our Chinese brethren: their marvellous and paralleled self-control and self-possession, their patient endurance of hardship,...their contentedness in the absence of the very necessaries of life.[129]

Mission literature and sermons also emphasized the image of the warm rays of Christianity shining on the darkness and cold of pagan religions. Maryknoll publications kept from their readers unfavorable aspects of the culture.[130]

Other periodicals indicated ambivalence about certain aspects of the country, pointing out both the glory and the horror of "demon" religions. While expressing an appreciation for Chinese culture and art, including art found in Buddhist and Taoist temples, these publications still held the assumption that these religions must be overcome and replaced by Catholicism. *Catholic Missions* and *Our Missions,* which tended to offer the reader more of a world-religions perspective, featured fairly objective articles describing religious practices in China. Occasional articles in *The Far East* throughout the twenties and thirties portrayed Chinese religions as "bankrupt" in their ability to affect the life and needs of modern China.[131] Both *The Field Afar* and *The Far East,* which, with the exception of *Catholic Missions,* collectively had the largest circulation of mission magazines, underscored the "naturalness" of the Asian conversion process. The Maryknoll magazine portrayed this idea through cover photographs of Asian couples reading *The Field Afar* in their living rooms, which except for Asian artifacts and furniture looked like a living room in America. The Columban magazine frequently wrote about Chinese Catholic parishes and lay catechists, praising the small groups for their courage in "a vast sea of paganism."[132] Some magazines, such as *Franciscan Missions,* provided readers with a sobering view when they published lists of missionaries captured by Chinese bandits.

In the second period of American Catholic presence in China (1937–45), Japanese occupation was no longer the "nuisance" which local bandits had been. Japanese presence threatened the very existence of the mission. Some communities sent their China missionaries elsewhere in the Pacific region to ride out the occupation. Many missionaries, though, stayed in China and adjusted their original ministry to meet the needs of the people, whether Catholic or not, in tumultuous times. A page from the Loretto Sisters' diary provides a feel for their response during the several months of the Japanese invasion of Hanyang, Hunan Province.

March 15, 1937. Han Yang has martial law every day; airplanes every night; bombs; batteries shooting at the planes from the hills.

August 11, 1938. Worst bombing so far. 50 killed . . . behind the Cathedral. We went out after the all-clear and baptized thirty or so. The wounded were taken to the Columban Hospital until there was no more room. . . . Many bled to death.

October 24, 1938. Desolation on all sides; hundreds of people sitting at the door of the Convent asking to be taken in. . . . Warning given that some of the buildings might be dynamited. The Mayor is leaving Hankow and handing over the city to Father Jacquinot, SJ [who created safe zones for refugees outside Shanghai and Nanjing].

November 1, 1938. The hardest day yet evacuating the Refugees. We left home at 7:30 a.m. Gave them some food and tried to get them up. They would not go unless we went with them. Men and women fell on their knees begging us to care for them. What misery. A woman with Sister [Justa] tried to commit suicide. . . . Sister Clementia remained look-

ing after the left-overs — babies left behind as the people said they could
not take them; so they just left them and went.... Many were sick and
could not go. Sisters of Loretto are acting as traffic cops and directing the
refugees;... All are asking us to live in the [refugee] Zone with them, they
are that afraid.[133]

The mission compound, overburdened and itself a target of attack, seemed a
sea of stability in an otherwise chaotic land, but that sense was short-lived. The
Sisters wrote after the Pearl Harbor bombing: *"December 26, 1941.* Dismissed
the Han Yang girls. They cried; we did too."[134]

In the early part of the third period of American Catholic involvement in
China (1945–53), in the first months after the victory of Mao Tse-tung, missionaries disagreed with each other about the compatibility of communism
and the Catholic mission effort. Fu Jen University attempted to comply with
orders from the Communist government, but eventually its rector, Harold
Rigney, SVD, was incarcerated. Other missionaries met the same end. By 1950,
U.S. Catholics viewed Christianity as the light confronting the darkness of godless communism. "The Reds" now seemed more fearful than the "demons"
of Chinese religions. Missionaries embodied the struggle against communism
as mission literature in the late 1940s and early 1950s sought to shape U.S.
Catholic opinion with respect to the global communist movement. This trend
would hold especially true when the plight of incarcerated missionaries, such as
Rigney, Joan Marie Ryan, MM, and Francis X. Ford, MM, became the subject
of books or the focus of CSMC conventions.

By the end of the third period, the image of a "Cold War Missionary" had developed, a living icon of the struggle between Christianity and communism. In
some cases, the "Cold War Missionary" would come into conflict with the mission thrust of Vatican II, especially as global politics changed the relationship
of communist countries to the rest of the world.[135] Information about China
in mission material thus changed over three decades from highlighting Chinese culture to accenting internal Chinese politics to depicting global economic
and political struggles.[136] While missionaries went to China with conversions
as their goal, the mission agenda in China, perforce, became largely influenced
by political events.

Of the Asian countries, China received the lion's share of attention from U.S.
Catholics. The experience of China missionaries affected Catholics in their perception of their American identity, their approach to economics and politics,
and their understanding of ecclesial life vis-à-vis a global Christianity. The post–
World War I disillusionment with progress and decreased optimism, reflecting
the "end of American innocence," which had characterized the literati after
the Gilded Age, did not find its way into American Catholic mission motifs.[137]
Rather, many of the elements these literary men tried to emphasize with a romantic strain in their writings — eternal moral values and belief in progress —
were perpetuated in mission literature, especially from the 1920s through the

mid-1930s. Confidence in progress and "uplift," which were associated with technology and modern ways both in the United States and in China, were supported by a positive theology of the human person rather than a blind belief in progress itself. While the Catholic Students Mission Crusade had expressed confidence and optimism about the Catholics' role in America through images from medieval times, missionaries favored bringing supernatural ideals to bear on very practical problems of illness, famine, and refugees. A Catholic China needed to be built in an environment which favored health, education, and human dignity as essential elements in the formation of the Church.

Missionaries between the 1920s and 1950s went to China as U.S. Catholics were creating a separate culture based on synthesizing tendencies of neo-Thomism and expressed in the nationalization of many "Catholic" organizations. Catholicism as a "civilizing force" of the twenties and thirties was characterized by the correct use of reason and discipline and integrity of thought and effort. Thomistic ideology, which attempted to reconcile disparate elements in society through first principles, sought to guard these values through "integral humanism" and, in Catholic colleges, through "curricular integration" in the late 1940s and 1950s. Missionary clergy had been educated largely in seminary curricula reflecting the condemnation of modernism. Missionary Sisters generally came from backgrounds in liberal arts or humanistic studies, or from increasingly professional medical or teacher training that gave less emphasis to philosophy. Both groups, however, when confronted with the mission experience, discovered that the "civilizing forces" needed in China were much more simple: cleanliness to circumvent disease, order to regulate the chaos of classroom disruption, and cooperatives and simple business endeavors to increase China's self-sufficiency.

Conclusions

Between 1920 and 1953, China became the focal point for the greatly wakened consciousness of U.S. Catholic mission. Prior to 1920, evangelization had been directed primarily to Chinese in the United States, not in China. Whether through reading mission magazines or through participation in the Catholic Students Mission Crusade, mission circles, or other forms of mission education, being "Catholic" meant involvement with "missions." In addition to the aforementioned effects on U.S. Catholics, China missions between 1920 and 1953 had a fourfold impact: linking the spiritual world with the material world of goods and services; modeling social roles and family values through teaching, nursing, and parish work; enlisting new forms of devotional spirituality; and, ultimately, straining the structural resources of the Catholic Church.

Affected by the immediate economic slump after the First World War and later by the Depression, Catholics gave more sparingly to mission causes but still made contributions during these difficult times. Approaching 1950, Catholics became increasingly prosperous — and more middle class — and were able to provide still more money.

Though finances were often a source of conflict, the mission enterprise frequently employed economic imagery to refer to spiritual concepts and physical realities. "Saving souls," "ransoming pagan babies," and "buying back" missionaries from bandits were all joined in the "economy of salvation." The religious world of redemption intersected with the world of finance. Missionaries linked U.S. and Chinese markets, acting as "middlemen," albeit on a small scale, for the manufacture and sale of cloth, vestments, and other objects made at missions in China. Women's domestic work frequently forged limited economic links between the two countries. Goods flowed to and from China and America as mission circles sewed church linens for God's houses in China, and Chinese women at the embroidery school in Hanyang sold items through Benziger Brothers in the United States.

But there was also opposition to such fiscal responsibilities. While Columban Bishop Edward Galvin wanted the Sisters of Loretto to assume full responsibility for the finances at the embroidery factory, the Sisters resisted; they thought such work consumed too much of the young women's day and diverted time from education, the task for which the Sisters had initially come to Hanyang. There was also a discrepancy between the myth and glory of the China missions as they were portrayed and competition among mission societies and organizations for finances and support.

A second conclusion underscores that missionaries, through their work, demonstrated reigning assumptions about social roles and family values. As had been true in the U.S. Catholic mission movement in the nineteenth century, women tended to work collectively. Men, though often sent together, most frequently worked alone. Unlike Protestants in China during these decades, men continued to outnumber women Catholic missionaries. Individual men tended to author books which associated their name with a geographic area or method of evangelism, while much of the day-to-day evangelical activity was carried on either by native catechists or by Sisters. The China mission had not simply the formation of the local church as its goal, but the development of the Catholic family as the foundation for that church. American Catholic missionaries sought to "stabilize" the Chinese family by eliminating concubines and by liberating women from some of the social strictures which prevented an "ideal" family life.[138] At the same time, in the United States, struggle over Catholic family life was reflected in the crusade for birth control, increased numbers of divorces, and a more public role for women.

Third, missions captured the religious imagination of U.S. Catholic devotion. A mission spirituality fashioned on the value of sacrifice counterbalanced the individualism, "New Paganism" — as *Commonweal* editor Michael Williams described it — and narcissism of the 1920s. Much of Catholic personal piety often revolved around ethnically related devotions, which served to bond members of the immigrant parishes, to reinforce a sense of belonging to the community, and to provide reassurance about the saving of one's soul. Such devotions, when performed with a mission consciousness, often expanded thoughts about one's own salvation to a fruitful awareness of a larger Christianity. Such was the case, for example, in the life of Capuchin Solanus Casey (1870–1957). Casey, who spent his life as porter at the Capuchin friary in Detroit, soon became well known, sought by poor, troubled, or ill people for his advice and assistance. Casey exhorted them to develop a life of prayer, to show gratitude to God ahead of time for the favor which God would bestow, and to give toward the missions. The Capuchin Mission Unit was greatly enhanced and sustained through such contributions.[139] A similar perspective wedding mission and prayer is found in two pamphlets published by Robert Sheridan, MM, in the 1930s: "Novena for Mission Vocations" and "Novena to St. Francis Xavier." The great popularity of Therese of Lisieux, "The Little Flower," among missionaries throughout this period pointed to the need to keep prayer and mission together. Such piety joined the American Catholic with those who, at least potentially, would shed their blood for their beliefs. It further united them with Catholics halfway around the world, a people whose "sing-song" chanted prayers reached heaven as surely as their own.

The mission ethos, which had been built on the hero/martyr image, especially in some men's mission magazines,[140] was nuanced a bit when the image of a suffering people became more prominent, especially in the 1940s. Self-sacrifice at home for the missions linked U.S. Catholics to the self-sacrifice of the martyr. The image of the hero surfaced again after 1949 when released missionaries, who represented the drama and trauma of Christian witness, wrote books about their experience and spoke at CSMC conventions. The Church now had American martyrs, interpreted as a sign of effective evangelization but increasingly related to political realities.

Though with less short-term impact on the U.S. Catholic Church, a few gains were made in ecumenism and in the lay mission vocation. Catholics were well aware of the success of Protestant missions in China and alluded often to their considerable accomplishments, especially in the medical field and higher education. Protestants remained very much of a competitive reality for American Catholics, but modest occasions for ecumenism resulted through shared imprisonment and other circumstances of war. Brief encounters with Chinese ceremonies, which offered a way to break down the hostility toward foreigners, provided a glimpse into practices many missionaries had only read about. A number of lay missionaries had been sent overseas by 1953, but general acceptance of their role did not come until the end of the decade. Those interested in evangelization could become part of a small but important movement of lay preachers in the United States or could respond to the inspiration of the Spirit through local involvement in Catholic Action.[141] They need not go halfway around the world.

Finally, the U.S. Bishops' involvement in Asia came slowly over these decades. In 1920, a nonsectarian group, the American Committee for China Famine

Fund, had been set up to provide aid to famine victims. A caveat warning U.S. Catholic bishops not to become part of this effort was issued by Joseph Freri, national SPF director, who mentioned that the committee's substantial overhead, salaries, and advertising costs were claiming much of the collected funds. Freri suggested that the bishops send their contributions directly to the affected provinces.[142] China missions were assisted financially through the SPF and the ABCM, the latter after its rocky start in the 1920s. By the 1940s, the U.S. Bishops were providing institutional support to meet the needs of those displaced in the Second World War. Catholic Relief Services, begun in 1943 to aid famine sufferers, was the first example of sustained hierarchical support for overseas concerns. Throughout these years, however, the National Catholic Welfare Conference acted as a clearinghouse for problems which arose with regard to China missionaries. After the Second World War, matters of indemnity, release of prisoners, new commercial treaties with China, lost and destroyed property deeds — issues often involving the U.S. State Department — required more attention than the bishops were able to provide. These were some of the factors which led to the formation of the Mission Secretariat in 1949. A Vincentian missionary to China since 1932 and director of Catholic Relief Services in his district, Frederick A. McGuire, CM, was chosen to head the agency.

For the most part, American Catholic missionaries worked with the poorer classes in China. The great equalizing doctrine of communism, which had appeal to the poor, had centers ready to organize people when Chinese Communists gained control of mission compounds and institutions. Preceding them had been the missionaries, who had also seen the great poverty and worked with less impact for similar social goals. The expulsion of foreigners from China and the Korean cease-fire of 27 July 1953 heightened the conflict between the "godless communists" and the Christian West, a struggle for the "soul of the world." However, emphasis in the 1950s on the Iron Curtain and "wall" of communism shielded the small group of local Chinese churches from the outside world. After more than thirty years of intense concentration on missions to mainland China, by 1960 the country and the Chinese Catholic Church had dropped dramatically from the consciousness and interest of most U.S. Catholics.[143]

Chapter 7

The Struggle for World Order, 1946–59

In the fifteen years between the end of World War II and Pope John XXIII's call for an Ecumenical Council, the U.S. Catholic mission picture was redrawn in significant ways. The country's Catholics were again called on to repair the damages to international missions because of the impact of the war. A national organization, the Mission Secretariat, was formed in 1949 to handle mission problems subsequent to both World War II and the Korean War. The key national figures at the hub of mission promotion over the next twenty years emerged and remained influential up to the Second Vatican Council. Missionary experience formed the foundation for a theological formulation of world Christianity in the context of an emerging world order struggling with the presence of communism. And, finally, encouraged by the papal encyclical *Fidei donum*, which focused on missions to Africa, more lay mission groups emerged, though the prevailing notion lingered, especially among clergy, that "real" missionary activity was the work of priests.

World War II and Mission Work

The Second World War brought devastation to an even larger part of the world than the First World War. Mission life was once again dramatically altered; even more U.S. Catholic missionaries were affected than in 1919. Some mission clergy took on new tasks, serving as chaplains for the U.S. armed forces.[1] Following his release in a prisoner exchange with the Japanese, Harold Henry (1909–76), pioneer Columban Father in Korea, became a chaplain for a group of combat engineers in Africa and then returned to Korea in 1947. Missionaries . lost their lives with civilians and soldiers when the Pacific islands were overrun by Japanese and U.S. forces. The Divine Word missions in New Guinea were so devastated by the deaths of missionaries and destruction of property that they had to be completely restaffed. American missionaries were serving in countries affected by both sides in the war. Twelve Sisters of Notre Dame de Namur, who in 1924 became the first unit of American Sisters to go to Japan, were imprisoned and then expelled during the war.[2] When Japan invaded the Philippines, CSMC founder Clifford King, SVD, having already fled China, was forced to hide out in the Philippine mountains to avoid being taken prisoner. Unsafe

Building for the Future: World War II wreaked havoc in lands where missioners worked and devastated Europe, whence came most Catholic missioners. Meanwhile the United States remained untouched. This March 1941 photograph shows two seminarians watching a new wing under construction at Maryknoll, New York. American missionary groups recruited members and built for the future in relative tranquility, while the world was at war. (Courtesy, Maryknoll Photo Archives)

shipping lanes in the Pacific and Atlantic prevented travel from the United States to Asian missions. Unable to send new recruits to their Pacific missions, the Marist Missionary Sisters, having worked in the Solomon Islands since 1936, opened a leprosarium in Spanish Town, Jamaica, in 1941.[3] Missionaries were repatriated from China and Japan during and after the war, many of them returning to the United States aboard the ship *Gripsholm*. At home, the Catholic Students Mission Crusade in 1941 suspended their biannual conferences until 1948.

Edward Cardinal Mooney of Detroit established the Missionary Sisters of St. Francis Xavier to work in the rural areas of postwar Japan and India.[4] European missionary societies, which previously had no American foundations, opened houses in the United States to obtain vocations and funds.[5] Among these groups were the Xaverian Fathers and Brothers, the Mill Hill Fathers, and the Medical Missionaries of Mary. In 1943 the newly formed Bishops' Relief Committee was asked to provide some assistance for missionaries in China.

Following the postwar settlement, Japan and the Pacific islands were occupied by the U.S. armed forces. The government of occupation preferred to have American missionaries in charge of the missions in these territories, which resulted in the arrival of more U.S. Catholic missionaries. In Oceania, for example, there were 329 U.S. Catholic missionaries at the start of the war. By 1949, that number had increased to 617. Vincent Kennally, SJ, was called to serve as apostolic administrator in the Caroline and Marshall Islands in 1946, replacing a Spanish Jesuit. The New York Province of Jesuits was appointed to work there the following year and sent Hugh Costigan, SJ, to the island of Pohnpei in September 1947. He was joined by fellow Jesuits Thomas Feeney and Thomas Donahue the next month. After months of adjustment and review of needs, Costigan began a cacao plantation, a model farm, and an agricultural institute for the people of the islands.[6] Richard and Kay Finn arrived in Pohnpei in 1948 to teach and work as lay volunteers and stayed for thirteen years.[7] Jesuit Brother John Walter worked as a master builder in Micronesia from 1949 to 1984, and Paul Acer served there from 1951 to 1980. The first three of twenty-nine Maryknoll Sisters arrived to teach in the Marshall Islands in September 1950.

The African missions were also affected by the war, especially those served by Italian, German, or Belgian mission societies. The Italian Servites, who had been in Swaziland since 1913, were in need of new personnel, having lost both men and property as a result of the war. In October 1946, their general superior arrived in Chicago to press for American men to continue the work in Africa. After minimal preparation, including learning first-aid procedures and elementary dentistry, three U.S. Servites, Edwin Kinch, Michael Delahanty, and Timothy Culhane, sailed for South Africa in May 1947 to assist the Italian Servites. Very soon, however, the American Province had its own district of Ingwavuma and Tongaland.[8]

Eight American Divine Word Missionary priests and two Brothers were sent to Accra, Ghana, in 1941, because the war prevented their European confreres from serving in the mission. The society was entrusted with the Accra Diocese in 1947. With the advent of the Americans, Ghanaians observed both black and Anglo SVDs working together at the mission. Harold Rigney, SVD, who later went to China, was first missioned to Ghana, where he was chaplain to the American armed forces until after the war. In 1946, the Holy Spirit Missionary Sisters from Techny, Illinois, arrived at the mission.[9] The 1950s were a "boom time" for vocations, and young recruits were being educated in newly expanded seminary buildings to take on new and old missions.

Formation of the Mission Secretariat

During and after World War II, more and more communications about overseas missions, particularly with respect to China, Japan, and the Pacific islands, came to the attention of the National Catholic Welfare Conference in Washington, D.C. Correspondence in 1944 between the NCWC, the SPF, and the State Department dealt with a range of topics, including the internment of missionaries, missing or murdered missionaries, and the reappropriation of mission property usurped during the war. William F. Montovan, legal counsel for NCWC, and Bruce Mohler, specialist in procuring passports and visas, were especially called on to provide their services for missionaries, the number of which almost doubled from 2,222 in 1940 to 4,123 by 1949.[10] Not only were greater numbers of missionaries going abroad through traditional missionary societies such as the Jesuits, Maryknoll men and women, and the Franciscan Missionaries of Mary, but congregations who were sending their members overseas for the first time contributed to that number.

In the summer of 1944, John Considine, MM, now on the General Council for Maryknoll, and Calvert Alexander, SJ, editor of *Jesuit Missions,* realized that an office would be required to coordinate the complex activities which affected missionaries. Considine had outlined a job description that year and had pressed Francis Cardinal Spellman, head of the Episcopal Committee of the Propagation of the Faith and Commander of the Military Ordinate, to bring the matter before the U.S. Bishops. Spellman delayed doing so until after the war ended.[11] By this time, Bishops John O'Hara (Buffalo) and Michael J. Ready (Columbus, Ohio) had visited Japan at the request of that apostolic delegate and assessed the situation, especially as it related to American missionaries and institutions of American missionary congregations. The prelate noted that a delegation of American Protestants had arrived in Japan several months earlier and had met with General MacArthur as well. "Considerable publicity was given their meetings with Christian leaders in the large cities of Japan. Of course, the impression [the Protestants] aimed at creating was that democracy, Christianity and Protestantism were one name for the same thing."[12]

NCWC staff member Catherine Schaefer attended meetings on global concerns on behalf of the bishops' organization. On 9 April 1948, she represented the NCWC at a meeting of the Princeton Club. Present were the chairman of the English-speaking section of the Board of Foreign Missions, an executive officer of the National City Bank of New York, an official of the National Association of Manufacturers, a business advisor to the U.S. delegation at the Havana International Trade Organization meeting, and a Foreign Trade Council official. At issue was how American overseas missionaries and businessmen could understand each other's purposes, "so that the two groups would not be undercutting each other vis-à-vis the natives of the country." In her report on this gathering, Schaefer commented:

> It seems to me that business would certainly benefit from a knowledge of the Church's mission abroad, and certainly the mission seminary groups ought to have a knowledge of economics in terms of Catholic social doctrine, as a criterion for familiarity with the operation of American enterprise, but I should think it would be wrong and dangerous to the Church for it to become in any way identified either here or abroad, in the public mind, with American business interests. It strikes me that the plan discussed presents such a danger....If the project were for mutual exchange on the basis of the Christian teaching on economic life, I think the opportunities would be greater. My impression, however, is that the project envisages mutual "conversion," i.e., to free enterprise as a protector and stabilizer for the missions, and to the missions as a means of helping free enterprise.[13]

The process for adopting an overseas office to attend to these issues proceeded slowly. John Considine and Calvert Alexander continued to work behind the scenes to promote the plan. Active involvement of Protestant mission groups in public discussions of American business interests overseas led Considine to suggest the title, "Overseas Desk," for the proposed position. The Maryknoller wrote:

> It would seem better for such a Desk at NCWC to avoid any public connection with the term "missionary," and that for the following reasons: (1) Protestant missionary organizations have a tradition of annoying government and commercial agents and enjoy general disesteem; hence in non-Catholic circles the word "missionary" carries a heavy handicap; (2) In Latin America, many Catholic circles resent the idea that they receive missionaries, even Catholic missionaries.[14]

Because much of the work would entail contact with government, some suggested that the Secretariat should be located in Washington, D.C. Others thought that the office should be under the direction of the national director for the Society for the Propagation of the Faith in New York. SPF director Thomas McDonnell's correspondence with the Vatican Propaganda Fide office in 1948 made the stipulation that the proposed organization come under the jurisdiction of the Society for the Propagation of the Faith in the United States and be subject to the Episcopal Committee for Missions. "The Episcopal Committee admitted that some control must be inaugurated in these matters."[15]

In their annual meeting in November 1949, the bishops disregarded the title, "Overseas Desk," but approved the opening of a Mission Secretariat, once the Bishops' Mission Committee, chaired by Spellman, had forwarded its basic approval. The Secretariat was to be "a center for mission information, a representative of the Foreign Mission Sending and the Mission Aid societies, and a central clearing office for all matters pertaining to the missions."[16] More particularly, the office was to provide a means of contact among mission-sending groups and mission-funding agencies and a place where their representatives could handle interactions with governmental and non-governmental offices having a bearing on mission work. It would further provide a means of contact between Catholic agencies in the United States and Catholic missionaries.[17]

A provisional plan for the "Secretariat of the Catholic Societies of the United States Engaged in Foreign Mission Activities" was drawn up on 30 November 1949, and on 11 April 1950 the Secretariat began to function. John Considine, Calvert Alexander, Robert Hunter, SVD, Mary Augustine Kerby, SMSM, and Frederick McGuire, CM (1905–83), were appointed advisory board members.[18] Several persons were suggested for the position of director for the Secretariat, including Francis Clougherty, who had returned to the United States from China without an assignment. The bishops' choice for the organization's executive secretary was Frederick McGuire, a missionary in China since 1932 and former executive secretary of the Catholic Welfare Committee of China. Thomas McDonnell, by virtue of his office as national SPF director, was appointed the director of the Mission Secretariat.[19] Financial support for the office was to come from contributions of the mission-sending societies, with a donation from the national SPF office. However, the national office did not provide any monies, at least for the first seventeen years of the Secretariat.[20]

The Mission Secretariat communicated with its members by means of a newsletter, *Washington Service,* and an annual conference. After the first few conferences, workshops were organized for various subgroups in attendance: clergy, religious, editors, lay missions, medical personnel, procurators, promoters, and vocation directors. Attendance at annual conferences grew to over a thousand.[21] The Secretariat continued, however, to have several unresolved problems. The first was the indefinite function and position of the Secretariat in relation to the national structure of the Church. Lines of authority were crossed or were unclear. This led to further areas of conflict, especially between Frederick McGuire, the executive secretary, and Fulton J. Sheen, who became the national SPF director in 1950. The original intention of the mission-sending societies had been "not to place this Secretariat in any way under the hierarchy, but rather to have their own executive board control the organization."[22] In effect, this structure put the mission-sending groups under the authority of a mission-funding group. Second, the mission-aid societies (such as SPF and the Holy Childhood) were not making use of the Secretariat's services, especially in drawing on the expertise of missionaries. Finally, while the Secretariat attempted to give all mission-sending groups an equal footing in the solicitation of mission funds, parishioners continued to be bombarded from many mission groups, and women's mission communities ended up being slighted.[23]

The Mission Secretariat was significant, however, for several reasons. The annual conferences provided the first shared gathering of major superiors of women's and men's congregations to discuss common problems and to seek appropriate solutions.[24] The meetings provided shared mission expertise and an arena for identifying problems of returned missionaries. The annual conferences served as a forum for the development of the lay mission vocation (Association for International Development) and as a meeting place to address the identity and vocation of the Brother religious.

Association for International Development

In 1957, the Association for International Development was founded in Paterson, New Jersey, by Gerald F. Mische and John S. Connor to "inform and form mature Catholics for assuming Christian responsibility and leadership through service at home or abroad." AID had been inaugurated under the auspices of the men's major superiors during the Mission Secretariat annual meeting. The association was supported by a board which included several prominent businessmen.[25] Mische, its director, had worked in Bacalar, Mexico, with Father Donald Hessler, MM, as part of an experimental group of American lay missionaries.

Stateside training for missions overseas consisted of an eight-month evening and weekend session, which examined the mission of the Church in the modern world, lay spirituality, Christian social teaching, the Church in international society, leadership, and the value of intercultural exchange. The group also sponsored three-week institutes for the formation of Catholic laymen, to provide them with the skills and insight to work toward the "establishment of a social order fully human and truly Christian."[26] On weekends, the members worked among the Puerto Ricans in the New Jersey area. Women soon became part of the program, especially in their role as wives. Several persons expressed a desire to have women on the board:

> Do not forget to consider having a woman on the [AID] Council.... We would just make the point that a woman, preferably one who is a mother with children, could give AID the motherly, loving touch that is required if we are not to develop into a hard-hearted, all business organization of male leaders.[27]

Given the composition of the board, this point was intended to balance the emphasis on finances with the spiritual dimensions of the mission task.

AID emphasized laity's role of going into areas where clergy could not go, particularly "in the marketplace"; for this reason, AID members did not become catechists. The missionaries came at the request of particular Latin American bishops and were under contract with them for a three-year period.

The organization was beset by problems in trying to establish a solid financial base (as was true of most mission groups), confusion about the role of laity in particular situations, and communication difficulties between those in the field and those at headquarters. Nevertheless, one hundred persons were active in the organization within its first five years.

The Brother's Vocation

The Mission Secretariat conferences provided the avenue for Brothers to discuss their discomfort with the public perception of their vocation. Some Brothers, such as the Christian Brothers, were engaged in teaching. Their preparation for mission consisted in coursework toward that end, as well as the spiritual preparation involved in their religious life. But there was other work the Brothers did. When new missions opened they performed an important function in creating the physical spaces of mission buildings. The Brothers' farm and animal husbandry, nursing, carpentry, bookbinding, and printing skills allowed missionaries to establish themselves with less cost in a new land. The Brothers constructed buildings which made the mission more comfortable and convenient for those not yet accustomed to life in a new environment. Often Brothers supervised local laborers at the mission and had the most day-to-day contact with the men.

The life of a non-teaching, missionary Brother was variously depicted. The Divine Word Missionary Brothers were to be what St. Joseph was for the Holy Family. As priests were "other Christs," so their counterparts, the Brothers, were "other Josephs."[28] Robert Streit, OMI, editor of *Bibliotheca Missionum*, described them as "Christian Labor cooperating with the mission. His many-sided activity may be called the engineer's service in the great missionary army."[29] The Brother's vocation was frequently contrasted with the responsibility and high profile of the priest, described as a vocation "happy and carefree, fraught with less danger . . . and [with] fewer disappointments than the priesthood."[30] In the minds of many, the Brothers' work relieved the clergy so the latter could do the "real" mission work. One Divine Word Missionary, who sought more Brothers for his mission in China, wrote to his provincial in the United States:

> Regarding Brothers, I might say right here, that one ought to be [sent] that can do office work, accounting and answering correspondence, etc. If we have a fairly capable Brother of this kind, then all our Fathers can be free to do important and immediate mission work. The other Brother (or Brothers) can be just ordinary common-sense men, able to lend a hand in supervising all sorts of work, building, farming, etc.[31]

In 1943, the Society of the Divine Word printed a pamphlet, *Brother Eugene, SVD, An American Missionary Brother,* and in 1951 the society produced a film, *Religious in Overalls,* to promote vocations to the brotherhood.[32] But for other persons, the hiddenness of the vocation did not detract from the Brother's call:

> Just as the early monks civilized and converted the barbarians by teaching them trades and agricultural pursuits, so does the brother of today bring the neglected pagan into the fold and raise him even to the culture of our own land.[33]

This two-tiered brotherhood, the teachers and those in overalls, reflected a division in education in the United States at the time, consisting of a smaller, though growing, group of citizens who were receiving an education beyond high school and those who went immediately into a trade after a general education.

At the annual meetings of the Mission Secretariat, the Brothers' mission vocation and identity came to the fore among the Brothers themselves, who sensed that the kind of "hiddenness" they had experienced was not helping them personally, nor was it attracting vocations to that way of life. A *Brothers' Newsletter* for the non-teaching Brother was printed at Techny, Illinois, beginning in 1958, though the publication was not exclusively devoted to missionary Brothers. The bulletin was an outgrowth of the Brothers' panel at the Mission Secretariat conferences. The Brothers began to speak for themselves, gaining self-confidence and identifying the strength they had provided the Church. These sentiments were found in the early issues of the newsletter:

> It is important to explain to externs just why our work and lives are important, how we are following Christ (St. Joseph is our model whose life we imitate, but it is Christ whom we follow). It is Christ Who counseled us to come, follow Me, not St. Joseph or anyone's favorite saint. Might not this be a reason for the common opinion that we have taken a second-rate choice: emphasis on the imitation of someone other than Christ? ...[34]
>
> Without the Brothers bishops couldn't fill their seminaries; pastors couldn't open or maintain their schools; missionary orders couldn't establish or run their foreign or home missions.... They can be called on to do anything that it takes to make a monastery or a mission run smoothly and successfully.[35]

The shift in the perception of their vocation was reflected in the newsletter's quarterly portraits, which highlighted the work of particular Brothers. By the end of the 1950s, this self-consciousness had reshaped the role of the Brother from mission helper, albeit a skillful one, to a missionary whose primary goal was to convert people. One of their own, Brother Bede (Charles) Horgan, MM (b. 1909), addressed them at the 1959 Mission Secretariat Conference and noted that the Brother sometimes tended "to forget that he is a missioner first and a worker second. He may let his physical labors suffice for conversions he could be making. His very efficiency at work may repel souls rather than attract."[36] By 1961, Bruce Malina, OFM, had developed "An Outline for a Theology of the Brotherhood."[37]

These several advantages of the Mission Secretariat notwithstanding, ambivalence about the relationship between the Secretariat and the SPF director lingered into the 1960s, when the Secretariat was dissolved and the United States Catholic Mission Council was formed in 1967.

Fulton J. Sheen and the SPF

On 12 September 1950, Bishop Fulton J. Sheen (1895–1979) replaced Bishop Thomas McDonnell as national director of the Society for the Propagation of the Faith. Sheen remained in this position until 1966, just after the Second Vatican Council. This executive change produced considerable consequences for the society. By the time he walked into the SPF offices on Fifth Avenue, the handsome Sheen had already gained a vast following among Catholics and many other Christians as a result of his radio and television programs and his impressive number of books. While in office as national SPF director, he received an Emmy Award and the Look Television Award for his *Life Is Worth Living* television and radio shows. Though a recipient of many honorary degrees, early in his career he had decided that he would focus on public preaching and making converts, rather than on an academic career.[38] He had seen the reach of his preaching when, while traveling with Cardinal Spellman to Australia during World War II, Sheen discovered that missionaries were using material from his programs and books for their own sermons.

The bishop theologized on the positive values he saw in the electronic age. "Radio is like the Old Testament, for it is hearing of the Word without the seeing. Television is like the New Testament, for the Word is seen as it becomes flesh and dwells among us."[39] In his view, he had two approaches to evangelization: directly, by means of radio, where he presented Christian doctrine in easy-to-understand language, and indirectly, on television, where he said he depended more on the grace of God. He envisioned a third approach for a future audience formed by the electronic age. This approach he called anthropological:

> The presentation of religion had been principally from God to man, but now it will be from man to God. . . . It will start with the disorder inside of man himself. It will take all the findings of our psychological age and use them as a springboard for the presentation of Divine Truth.[40]

It seemed that one who had this understanding of the power of modern communications would be the ideal person to draw the attention of all Catholics to mission. Over the course of his directorship of the SPF, contributions multiplied as did funds Sheen received from royalties and from his talks.

The national SPF office made a significant contribution to mission literature

Bishop Sheen in Africa: Bishop Fulton J. Sheen became head of the National Society for the Propagation of the Faith in 1950. He personified both American Catholicism's post–World War II anticommunism and its interest in overseas missions. In this 1957 photo, Bishop Sheen is with then-Bishop, later Cardinal Otunga, Kenya's first local bishop. (Courtesy, Society for the Propagation of the Faith; photo by W. Tourigny, MAfr)

in *Worldmission,* though a dispute seems to have arisen over control of the publication and over who would fund it: the SPF or the Mission Secretariat.[41]

From its first issue in 1950 through its last in 1981, the magazine featured contemporary thinking about missions from European and American Catholics. *Worldmission* succeeded another excellent though more scholarly publication, the *Missionary Academia,* which throughout the 1940s presented lengthier articles for study by seminarians and clerics.[42] After completion of the *Academia*'s six-year study program, SPF's Thomas McDonnell thought there was an effective knowledge base for a mission publication to sustain and deepen that foundation. The *Worldmission* editorial board, in addition to Sheen, Considine, and McGuire, consisted of Gordon Fournier, a Missionary of Africa with experience in Africa and local superior of his community in Washington, D.C., Marion A. Habig, OFM (1901–84), specialist in Latin American history, and Edward L. Murphy, SJ (1904–73), one of three American Catholics with a doctorate in missiology in the early 1950s and renowned for his preaching to working-class men in the Boston area.[43] Among the authors represented in *Worldmission* through the 1950s were Jacques Maritain, Joseph J. Tennant, Francis X. Ford, MM, Andrew Suemois, OMI, Johannes Hofinger, SJ, and Yves Congar. Sheen's editorials were reprinted later in his *Missions and the World Crisis.*

World Christianity and World Order

American Missionaries and Communism

In the wake of the Second World War, major philosophical and political problems remained for the Western world. People had experienced both a growth in world consciousness and the seeming collapse of civilization. How was the postwar world to be ordered? Would communism, racism, socialism, or nationalism be the major forces which would weld the globe in the wake of international collapse? Could world Christianity provide a viable international system for healing the disintegration among groups around the world? Competing world philosophies presented serious alternatives to Christianity. Among these political and ideological positions, Catholics spent the most time refuting communism.

Catholic involvement in the attack against communism had been sustained and vocal, especially since the 1930s. *America* had printed a series of pamphlets elaborating on Pope Pius XI's encyclical on atheistic communism, *Divini Redemptoris.* A symposium written for Our Sunday Visitor, *The Modern Social and Economic Order,* featured a chapter on communism in the context of social principles and economic orders.[44] While condemning communism as atheistic, the two American publications highlighted the contrasting economic philosophies of communism and capitalism, favoring the Catholic regard for individuals, the right to private property, and current approaches to the economically impoverished. The encyclical had laid the framework for the battle between the two world cultures seeking prominence around the globe: Christianity (i.e., "civilization") and communism. The latter was heralded as a godless and secularist philosophy, built on dialectical materialism. Proponents of communism were criticized for advocating socialist principles which seemed to demote the family and to deny the right of individuals to hold property.

By the 1950s, the "Red Scare" had produced paranoia among some Americans and certainly alarm in many others. By this time, communism had control of one-fourth of the world's people and land mass. The person who undertook the most extreme and most publicized response to communism was Joseph McCarthy, a Catholic senator from Wisconsin.[45] His ferreting out of citizens who appeared even to be "pink" (those he claimed had even a tinge of the "red" communist in their ideas) eventually led to his downfall and defeat. While no mission group or missionary had the notoriety McCarthy did in the 1950s, incarcerated missionaries were provided as living symbols of the impact of "godless communism." American Catholic missionaries had personal experience with communism in China and Korea. Imprisonment, forced marches, and torture clashed with the image of the refined, long-enduring culture of the Orient, which missionaries had written about in the 1920s. Stories of incarcerated missionaries flooded the United States during the 1950s. But American Catholics were also concerned about communism closer to home in Latin America.

Geographical differences but, more important, diverse ideas about mission brought varied responses to the threat of communism. American Catholic approaches to mission emphasized communism's effects on the missionary, who was portrayed as a Suffering Servant; Harold Rigney, SVD, represented one such case. Douglas Hyde adapted communist leadership techniques in order to spread Christianity. Fulton Sheen, and, to a lesser extent, Francis Spellman, endeavored to counter the philosophical and ideological basis of communism. Other approaches related Russian and Chinese communism to events in Latin America (Richard Cushing) and provided an American base for leadership training for exiled Cubans (The Miami Plan).

Catholic media frequently emphasized the "godlessness" of communists, who tortured and imprisoned missionaries and destroyed faith and religion, thus creating a "silent Church." Antipathy toward communism became personalized and popularized through published stories of missionaries imprisoned in China. Former superior of the Wuchow, China, mission, Maryknoll Father Bernard Meyer published a magazine of cartoons in 1962 expressing the horrors of communism. His book was also translated into Spanish for distribution in Latin America.[46] Two of the most celebrated examples of this antipathy were *Nun in Red China*,[47] a fictionalized account of an imprisoned Maryknoll Sister, eventually produced on screen with Jane Wyman as the nun, and Divine Word missionary Harold Rigney's *Four Years in a Red Hell*.

As rector of Fu Jen University, Rigney (1900–1980) had attempted to deal with Chinese Nationalists as best he could after 1949. However, on 25 July 1951 he was imprisoned and was then transferred among prisons until his release on 11 September 1955. Rigney's return to the United States was carefully orchestrated. Several publishers vied for his story, including the *Chicago Sun-Times* and Colliers. The Chicago newspaper, the Society of the Divine Word, Rigney's mother and family, a vigorous letter-writing campaign in Chicago, and eventually the efforts of U.S. House Speaker John W. McCormack secured Rigney's release under the Geneva Convention. Rigney wrote to the *Chicago Sun-Times* thanking them for the "truly great help you rendered me in publishing my case and in contacting both the American government and the People's Government of China on my behalf."[48]

Both the Society of the Divine Word and journalists saw the publicity value of the missionary's release. SVDs hoped for more vocations and for a more accurate perception of the intellectual capabilities of missionaries. On the latter point, Ralph Wiltgen, SVD, wrote to Provincial Lawrence Mack, SVD, "Very many of the government officials in Washington are Harvard and Princeton men who regard missionaries as spiritualistic individuals of low intellectual ability. F[ather] Rigney could change their opinion of the Catholic missionaries."[49] Frank Robertson, a journalist who had covered the war in the Pacific, also remarked to Mack:

> As a newspaperman, I feel very strongly that Father Rigney's story is, in a sense, public property; Collier's [*sic*] I'm sure would welcome the chance to bid competitively for it. And as a Catholic, I think it deserves far wider circulation than the Sun-times [*sic*] can hope to give it. *The Reader's Digest* undoubtedly would pick it up from Collier's [*sic*] ... and publish it in their many different language editions.[50]

Newspapers bought the story from the *Sun-Times* for a cumulative circulation of 5,180,000. Some of the released missionary's story appeared in the *Congressional Record* as an extension of the comments of Senator Paul H. Douglas of Illinois.[51] Rigney and Thomas Tien, exiled cardinal of Peiping (Peking) and member of the Society of the Divine Word, appeared at a meeting of the Catholic Students Mission Crusade, and their stories were carried in the organization's publication, the *Shield*.[52]

The public representation of Rigney's incarceration emphasized the missionary as a modern suffering Christ who had endured the afflictions of communism: isolation, pain, torment, incarceration, false accusations, and endless questioning before communist officials. The German and Chinese Missionary Sisters of the Holy Spirit, who brought packages of soap and toilet paper to the prisoner every three weeks, followed the model of Veronica, who had responded so remarkably to Jesus' plight as he walked toward Calvary. Rigney's story was compelling and ended with a short discussion that he had with one of his captors. Rigney explained to him that the People's government had no cause to fear Catholics, who "were willing to labor under any form of government, including the communist government. They only ask the government to grant them religious freedom."[53] Rigney and other missionaries personalized the effects of godless communism, "the struggle against [which] must not be allowed to die."[54]

One of the most notable persons in the American Catholic fight against communism was an Englishman, Douglas Hyde (b. 1911), "converted" communist and former editor of the London *Daily Worker*. Shortly after the Korean War, Hyde visited Asia to learn something of the nature of the "battle for the hearts and minds of people." The journalist traveled to Hong Kong and Japan, with brief stops in other Asian countries, but he spent most of his time talking with the Columbans and Maryknollers in Korea. He published his experiences in *One Front Across the World,* wherein he portrayed missionaries as the "elites of the Church" and bearers of civilization, as those who were "the front line fighters in the decisive fight of our time."[55] While the book was meant to highlight the pervasiveness of world communism, most of Hyde's story narrated the impressive work of the few U.S. Catholic missionary groups in Korea.[56] Columban seminarians heard the book read to them during their mealtimes, and Maryknoll featured Hyde's volume as a selection of their book club.[57] He was constantly on the circuit giving workshops and talks all over the world, encouraging the use of "cell" techniques he learned as a communist, which he now put to a new purpose. He spoke at Maryknoll, at the CSMC convention at Notre Dame, at a Mission Secretariat conference, and at St. Bernard Seminary after Sheen became bishop of Rochester, New York. Hyde's methodology acknowledged that communism used certain nonideological approaches which Catholics could readily use for evangelization.

Fulton J. Sheen countered the threat of world communism through a philosophical platform. He had written and spoken extensively about communism since the 1930s.[58] His philosophical method of refuting communism reflected his advanced degree from the University of Louvain, where Désiré Cardinal Mercier had inaugurated a revival of Thomistic theology. Sheen shaped his methodology in two steps: first, one should ask what the modern world was thinking about. Then, one should delve into the medieval systematic philosopher and theologian, Thomas Aquinas, to find the answer to the errors of modern philosophy. Sheen's oratorical skills and his well-turned phrases played up the two conflicting forces, "demonic" communism and Christian civilization. Speaking with almost apocalyptic imagery, Sheen announced that the communist persecution of the Church was prophesied in the Scriptures. Unclean animals occupied the ark along with clean animals. Cockle grew with wheat. Evil was "forming a 'mystical' body all its own. It has its Peter and Paul in Marx and Lenin; its bible in *Das Kapital* of Karl Marx; its twelve apostles in the Soviet Presidium...." Missionaries stood in the breach, so to speak, "going to the Communists, not to hold dialogue with them, but to be persecuted as witnesses of Christ."[59] Sheen became the national director of the Society for the Propagation of the Faith in 1950, just at the height of the Cold War.

Another person whose animosity toward communism became legendary was Francis Cardinal Spellman, chairman of the Bishops' Committee on Missions during the 1940s. He had a diplomatic office and was a friend of Eugenio Pacelli, who later became Pope Pius XII. Rather than delving into the realm of ideas, an arena that Sheen believed to be central to the "religion" of materialism, Spellman drew on his political interests to combat communism. From the time of Franklin Roosevelt's presidency through Lyndon B. Johnson (with the notable exception of the presidency of John F. Kennedy), he had acted, in effect, as an "American emissary," often advocating measures in Latin America (and elsewhere) suggested by the U.S. government. He did so because his personal views many times paralleled those of the government.[60] He was perplexed by Roosevelt's "discussions" with the communists and feared what other liberal politicians might do. In addition to his popular visits with military personnel in his capacity as military vicar of the U.S. armed forces, he frequently called on the leaders of the Latin American countries. A supporter of Joseph McCarthy, Spellman ignored the subtleties of Latin American politics, as well as a report sent by his advisor after a fact-finding trip. At one point, Spellman even painted the Guatemalan rebel forces as communists, preferring to back an intransigent dictatorial regime. The New York cardinal also supported the anticommunist position of Cardinal Mimmi of the Pontifical Committee for Latin America. Spellman further demonstrated his anticommunist feelings as he rallied the Catholics of New York in protest of the shameful treatment of the imprisoned Cardinal Mindszenty.[61]

While many of the American arguments against communism in the 1950s were directed against Soviet Russia, other Catholics connected communism in Russia with the mission experience in China. Popular mission magazines suggested this link, as did Richard Cushing. Well known for his anticommunist stance, the future cardinal published *Questions and Answers on Communism,* one hundred thousand copies of which he distributed in Latin America. One chapter on China and communism made this connection explicit:

Question: Is the Communist conquest of China due principally to Soviet influence?

Answer: Yes, to Soviet influence and trickery, accompanied eventually by American betrayal of the Chinese people into Soviet hands. As early as July 1912, five years before the Bolshevik *coup d'état* in Russia, Lenin had published articles on Dr. Sun Yat-sen's agitation for democracy in China, and had concerned himself with how to turn the coming "democratic revolution" there finally into a "proletarian revolution."

Immediately after the "Bolshevik Revolution" in Russia, Moscow began to interfere in the internal affairs of China, as Chiang Kai-Shek states in the opening of his remarkable book, *Soviet Russia in China:* "Moscow's

China policy was a double-faced one. On the one hand, the Soviet Foreign Office carried on diplomatic negotiations with the Chinese Government. On the other, the Communist International proceeded to set up a Chinese Communist Party."[62]

The threat of a ubiquitous communism infiltrating not only half a world away but near the southern shores of the United States was one of the motivations for Cushing, who, as we will see in the next chapter, figured prominently in the policy of the U.S. Catholic Church toward Latin America.

Still another approach to mission at this time lay in the pastoral and practical realms. Cuban refugees, a number of them well educated, and the Catholic Actionists of the 1950s began to stream to Miami after Fidel Castro took power in Cuba. Under the leadership of Bishop Coleman Carroll, the Miami Archdiocese responded in 1961 by opening the Institute of Social Action to enable the exiles to reconstruct Cuban society after what they thought would be communism's imminent defeat in their country. Carroll's interest in the program came from his earlier engagement in the 1930s with Pittsburgh labor schools, which sought to combat communism in the labor unions. Several former faculty of the Villanova University in Havana conducted evening classes for the Institute of Social Action. After it became clear that the exiles' immediate return to Cuba was not possible, the faculty moved to positions in other universities and the institute disbanded.

In 1964, the Miami Diocese, under the chairmanship of Monsignor Bryan O. Walsh, created another program, the Inter-American Institute of Social Formation, to educate and train young men from Latin America "in those spiritual and human values that would enable them to build a new society in Latin America based on the dignity of man under God."[63] Mauro Barrenechea, SJ, a renowned expert in trade union organization and leadership training, was named director. The organizers identified two social realities which they intended to address: (1) insufficient leadership among members of the lower socioeconomic levels of Latin America; and (2) "the grass-roots level as a battleground between the forces of Christian social justice and atheistic Communism."[64] Community development as part of the urban-planning process was emphasized during the month-long programs in order to address problems of economic marginality in the southern hemisphere.

Initially Latin Americans considered the program too "right wing" in its response to Cuban communism, but eventually the institute won the confidence of many Catholic leaders. In the year or so of its existence, the Inter-American Institute of Social Formation trained 218 leaders from nine Latin American countries. Plans were set in motion for a sixth training session for Latin American clergy when the Miami Diocese became inundated with still more Cuban refugees, and the diocese diverted its funds from the institute to meet immediate needs.

Thus, while these mission-related groups and persons, in the twenty years after the Second World War, detested communism, their responses reflected different tactics and rejoinders to that threat. Missionaries themselves, especially those who lived closely with the people, began to recognize that communism addressed socioeconomic factors keeping the people impoverished. At a 1954 Maryknoll meeting in Lima, Peru, assessing the mission to Latin America, Bernard Meyer, a critic of communism, noted some of the positive characteristics of communists supplying the needs of those the Maryknollers served.[65] Columban Bishop Harold Henry in Kwangju, Korea, was impressed with zeal manifested by any group, including communists (and, he hastened to add, Presbyterians).[66] The Jesuits, reflecting the policies of their superior general in the 1950s, realized that fear tactics did not subvert communism. A "steady flow of accurate knowledge" and "the whole weight of Christian social teaching and method [are needed] to bear upon the grave social, racial, and economic abuses that are Communism's hunting or breeding grounds."[67] The voice of the missionaries on this point would become increasingly more strident in the 1960s, especially in relation to Latin America.

Fulton Sheen and John Considine

In his 1951 mission encyclical, *Evangelii praecones,* Pope Pius XII had noted the global impact of all areas of life, including science, business, medical care, and food growth and distribution. "To teach all nations" now held a new social and political meaning. Discussion of world religions and ideologies had a fresh context. Fulton Sheen and John J. Considine, MM, who figured prominently in American Catholic mission promotion in the 1950s and who sat side by side for many years on the editorial board of *Worldmission,* both abhorred the growth of world communism, but drew from the experience of missionaries' differing perspectives on world Christianity as a viable response to these new realities. They differed in their understanding of global Christianity, their methodology, and their perception of the role of missions.

Fulton Sheen, the national SPF director, trained in Thomist philosophy at Louvain, had been a brilliant student and had received the Cardinal Mercier award for his dissertation. Adroitly using scholastic principles and methodology, Sheen pursued knowledge about communism, Marxism, and world religions, slicing through their deficiencies with his quick, often witty, quasi-apocalyptic speech and swirled red cape. His neo-Thomist methodology assumed an ideal, unified social order. The nature of this philosophy, which was to divide and categorize in order to see the location of each part, in Sheen's hands became a kind of binary system, pitting two world orders against each other: "demonic" communism and civilization/Christianity. Sheen noted that politics had ignored the influence of missions in world affairs and had gained ascendancy over mission education in alerting citizens to world problems.[68]

By "World Christianity" Sheen meant that Catholic missionaries were to be found on every continent. The sooner that they were able to move to all parts

Telling the Mission Story: This 1950s Divine Word Missionaries (SVD) exhibit is typical of displays used by American missionary groups at Catholic meetings, where they attempted to tell the mission story, to recruit men and women to join them, and to raise money to support their work. (Courtesy Society of the Divine Word Archives, Techny, Illinois)

of the world, the greater the possibility for global Christianity. An increase in funds for the missions, which Sheen so readily reaped from his appearances and book sales, would permit this phenomenon to occur. The missionaries were at the heart of this battle, having experienced the worst of communism and the best of civilization. The famous evangelist understood mission funding and particularly the role of the Society for the Propagation of the Faith as an act of charity, a kind of supernatural philanthropy which could defeat communism in this world. In the spiritual world, prayer provided the energy for this battle. Customarily, the staff prayed the rosary daily in the SPF Fifth Avenue office.[69]

From Maryknoll's cofounder, James A. Walsh, John Considine gained a view of mission as "world-wide apostolate." Work done with a "universal outlook" was his favorite concept.[70] Through years of contact with missionaries from all over the world, while at Propaganda Fide in Rome, Considine developed a careful theology of world Christianity, crystallized almost in digest form in a 1945 book of that title.[71] He analyzed four "Universalisms" or "Worlds": communism, Nazism, modern "power politics" — such as that suggested by the failed League of Nations — and Christianity.

The Maryknoller defined world Christianity as systematically cultivating

- regard, love for, and knowledge of all persons and cultures;

- promotion of the welfare of all;

- justice according to Christian ideals; and

- the transmission of Christ's teaching to non-Catholics and non-Christians.[72]

Missionaries, in contact with cultures of various histories, worldviews, and customs, were in a prime position to provide knowledge about diverse peoples as well as insight on how to live with racial differences within the United States.[73]

The two leaders' anthropological foundations differed considerably. Sheen, with a talent for modern means of persuasion and communication, saw humans as basically disordered, with no possibility for dialogue with a philosophy he viewed as satanic. Considine's view of the human person recognized the good and aspirations of the human heart. The striking difference in their understandings was also the often unnamed source of friction between the national SPF director and other mission leaders and missionaries themselves.[74] In the much-later U.S. Bishops' pastoral, "To the Ends of the Earth" (1986), Considine's view gained recognition.

The Sheen and Considine conversations were part of a larger discussion in the 1940s and 1950s among those who sought a new global order and who employed the mission experience as a foundation for their thought. James Keller, MM, in *The Priest and a World Vision* (1946), and James E. Walsh, MM, in *The Church's World Wide Mission* (1948), each attempted to lay theoretical and practical foundations for the new awareness of a world family. The Columbans' *The Far East,* normally reticent when it came to commenting on political or philosophical issues, ran a lengthy article on the topic. The discussants were the editor, two Army colonels, and the Jesuit chairperson of the economics department at Creighton University.[75]

The topic would be nuanced differently in the 1960s, but in the 1940s "world Christianity," especially as developed by Considine, also led to an examination of life in the United States. Two areas where this global dimension affected those at home were racial discrimination and world Christianity's potential impact on the Catholic school curriculum.

World Christianity and Racial Problems

Nationalism was a situation unacceptable to many missionaries and some mission promoters. One missiological resource which addressed the resulting racism in the United States appeared in the 1940s in the outline presented in the *Missionary Academia.* Week thirty-six of the outline was devoted to the topic of interracial justice. After an introduction to the "philosophy and theology of equality," the outline noted the strengths and weaknesses in the actual practice of missionaries and concluded by addressing the error of superiority on the part of missionaries and the effects that had on native peoples. Because the outline was addressed to future priests, they were also being reminded that the principles applied to parishes in urban America.

During the height of World War II, John Considine worked closely with the National Catholic Education Association Mission Committee to establish school programs which would overcome "the present sad ignorance of and disdain for so many people who live beyond our nation's confines, [which] is contrary to true Catholic principles."[76] In the process of working with these educators, he forged his outline of the missiological implications of the Mystical Body:

> Mission education and Catholic tenets on race relationships are both but single phases of fundamental Christian teachings. We develop these teachings in their world proportions and we call the result world Christianity — the systematic cultivation in children, young folks and adults of (1) a knowledge of and regard for the peoples of the earth, our brothers in Christ, and appreciation of our responsibility to promote the welfare of all mankind according to Christian ideal; (2) devotion to the Church's task of carrying to all non-Catholics and non-Christians Christ's teachings and life of charity.[77]

Considine wrote several articles on the topic and spoke from the twin themes at many commencements and teacher-education gatherings around New England and New York. As was his custom, he experimented with his ideas when, as chaplain, he visited the Sisters at the Maryknoll Cloister. Though he was not an original thinker, Considine was able to organize ideas in new ways, drawing heavily on his experience with missionaries and his voracious reading of both Catholic and Protestant mission literature.[78] In brief, his position to counteract racism was built on several pillars found in his theology of world Christianity:

- Trinitarian love, expressed in Jesus, was to be effected in love for all, especially in the social ideal of justice;

- The essential unity of the human race was signified in the doctrine of the Mystical Body, wherein all persons were one in Christ; and,

- The peoples of each culture presented a strength and value of their own.

While some persons argued that certain groups were condemned to remain in ignorance or suffering and that others were meant by nature to suffer indignation, the Maryknoller recalled the actual experience of missionaries who worked with diverse cultural groups around the world to counteract that assertion. In his outline on "missiography," Considine discussed at length that, while persons might be unequal by circumstances of their birth, they had an equal right to justice and deserved universal respect. As he asserted:

> God does not require each individual to feel equal affection for the Americans, the Japanese, the Uzbeks, the Jews, but he does require each to show these and all other peoples equal respect. Devotion to missions is not Catholic unless it represents devotion to all men; a gift for the peoples of a far land is void if our hearts cherish at the same time racial antagonism toward any group on earth, at home or overseas.[79]

World Christianity and the Curriculum

Those with racist attitudes in the 1940s had no desire to understand the African continent from whence so many African Americans had come, but Considine specifically chose that part of the globe to illustrate how textbooks often were slanting information because of the Anglo-American experience. Insufficient knowledge of people, he argued, abetted racist attitudes. Course materials presented a Western and capitalist view of these countries and stereotypes of the culture. Referring to a popular series of geography texts used in the Catholic schools, Considine pointed out that few pages, in proportion to the rest, were devoted to the African continent. The image of the inhabitants reflected the economic realities in the United States:

> In speaking of the African highlands, [the text says] "it may be that white people will live in these highlands and direct the work of the natives in the lowlands." Thus we have a picture of a continent of blacks which is to be dominated by the whites.[80]

Considine pointed out that students did not receive from Africans the worldview, perceptions, or image of the people. Rather, the text presented the political divisions in Africa that were created by European governments, highlighted the products which supplied European and American markets, and in discussing some of the folk customs implied that the people were "backward" in their ways. Also missing from the book was any reference to African Christianity.

Considine believed that, in a rapidly shrinking world, education played a significant role in appreciating rather than denigrating other cultures. One way to obtain this larger understanding of the human race was to influence the curriculum. Rather than add more content, Considine argued, educators must change the focus of the subjects presented. Maryknoll again contributed its considerable talents toward a critique of the Catholic School curriculum. Throughout 1943 and 1944, Considine, in charge of the Maryknoll Mission Education Bureau, also directed the Mission Education Committee of the Catholic Education Association with this goal in mind.[81] Sister Rosalia Walsh of the Missionary Helpers of the Holy Souls, James E. Walsh's sister and an accomplished catechist, developed course outlines for grade schools.

Sister Mary Just David, MM (1891–1959), a native of Greenville, South Carolina, became the best spokesperson for a positive appreciation of world cultures and of the people themselves. She had been an instructor in French at Wellesley and Smith Colleges before entering Maryknoll in 1921. The convert from the Episcopalian Church was a staff member of *The Field Afar* and taught in the Maryknoll Japanese School in Los Angeles for six years. On her return to New York, she wrote biographies of missionaries and worked diligently in preparing mission books for children, each book starting with the title, *Our Neighbors*. Her last work was *The Digest of Catholic Mission History*, a publication intended for the study of missions in Catholic schools.[82]

Fidei Donum and Africa

Africa was also on the mind of the Propaganda Fide Congregation in Rome. A Marian Congress had been held in Lagos, Nigeria, in 1954. In 1957, Pius XII issued an encyclical, *Fidei donum,* to draw attention to the sub-Saharan section of that continent, an area which seemed to many U.S. Catholics an even more distant corner of the world than China. The pontiff recognized the rapidly changing face of African countries brought about by rapid introduction of technology. He stressed the perennial theme of indigenous church leadership and noted that

> it is not enough merely to preach the Gospel as if this were the whole of the missionary's task. The present situation in Africa, both social and political, requires that a carefully trained Catholic elite be formed at once from the multitudes already converted. How urgent it is then to increase the number of missionaries able to give a more adequate training to these native leaders.[83]

After World War II, U.S. Catholic missionaries in African countries numbered 197. That figure had increased to 781 by 1960.[84]

The American group with the most missionaries in Africa at the time of the 1957 encyclical was the Congregation of the Holy Ghost (also known as the Spiritans), who were already deeply committed to African American missions. Five U.S. Spiritans had joined their European confreres in 1923: three men went to Tanganyika, one to Nigeria, and one to Sierra Leone. Dispersing the Americans to separate countries was viewed unfavorably by the Spiritan Provincial Council in the United States. Recalling World War I, the U.S. provincial wrote to the superior general:

> Using [the men] in five or six different countries is absolutely against the American mentality, and frankly speaking, no one here wants it. The generalate will remember that during the war the commander in chief of the Allies had wanted to bolster the American soldiers by surrounding them with British and French regiments. But our General Pershing refused that arrangement and demanded a sector to be defended by the American soldiers under American officers. It was granted and the results, as you know, were splendid.[85]

In 1932, the U.S. Spiritan Province received what they wanted: their own vicariate covering Kilimanjaro (later called the Moshi Diocese) and Tanganyika (Tanzania).

The Spiritans were interested in teaching Americans about the African experience and in engaging them for service on that continent. For these purposes the missionaries opened the Institute of African Studies at Duquesne University, Pittsburgh, in 1957. Almost from the start the U.S. federal government provided grants to support the institute, especially in the institute's production of a morphology and syntax of Swahili, the common language in British East Africa. Eventually, Duquesne compiled study materials for over one hundred languages in Africa. Other courses ranged from politics to anthropology. The teaching staff went to Africa every two years to keep current with developments. Undergraduate and graduate degrees were offered in African studies. In 1972, President Nixon abolished most of the scholarships, and the institute closed in 1978.[86]

Six Sisters of the Holy Names, Albany, New York, assisted by women from their other provinces, had been working in a school and clinic in Basutoland (Lesotho) since 1931. To date, twenty-one American Sisters have been missioned there. In 1942, this congregation had the greatest number of Catholic women missionaries serving in Africa; thirty of the 132 were American, though that number included some from Canadian provinces. That same year, twenty-nine Holy Ghost Fathers, thirteen Oblates of Mary Immaculate (from the province in Lowell, Massachusetts), and ten Brothers of the Sacred Heart were serving in sub-Saharan Africa. Taking responsibility for mission area previously held by the White Fathers, the Maryknoll Fathers and Brothers opened large new missions in 1946 in Tanganyika (Tanzania), and four Maryknoll Sisters arrived there as teachers, nurse, and pastoral worker.[87]

In 1938, two Divine Word Missionaries, Father Alphonse Elsbernd from the United States and Father August Gehring from Germany, were sent to Ghana. Father Harold Rigney arrived six months later, because Gehring had returned to Germany for health reasons. The mission society was engaged in parish ministry in Accra and Koforidua and in education at the Achimota School near Accra. Elsbernd, who became the general manager of Catholic schools in the eastern region, prevented the government from abolishing private education. In 1947, several Divine Word Missionaries were on the staff of the recently founded Catholic Teacher Training College. The men also provided leadership in developing and staffing the St. Paul's Technical School in Kukurantumi and a similar school at Saboba in northern Ghana. Priests in mission stations were also administrators of primary schools. Brother James Heeb, SVD, was instrumental in the Brothers' formation program for Ghanaians. The Divine Word Missionaries taught and were rectors at several of the seminaries for the education of diocesan clergy and also began to work among people in unreached areas of the country. Later, Ronald Lange, SVD, established the Divine Word Language Center in Abetifi. The Tamale Institute of Cross Cultural Studies, founded by Father Jon Kirby, SVD, introduced new missionaries to the language and culture of Ghana.[88]

The Catholic Students Mission Crusade sponsored a study session subsequent to their 1941 CSMC Conference resolutions on "The Negro." John T. Gillard, SSJ, began a study of the modern African American with a chapter on their ancestral home in Africa. He explained that the continent was called "dark" by Europeans and Americans because "the light of truth and fairness has not illuminated men's minds concerning it." Africans and blacks in America had been given little or no credit for any contributions to civilization.[89] The study-club book was written to enlighten the minds of Catholic Americans about the history and culture of African Americans on the premise that accurate knowledge about people would dissipate the darkness of racism.

Among the groups responding to the papal call to come to Africa were the Salvatorian Sisters, who joined their European Sisters in Tanzania, as well as two men's communities, the Society of Mary and the Jesuits, both of whom went to Nigeria. The superior of the Cincinnati Province of the Society of Mary journeyed to Africa's west coast in 1957 and returned enthusiastic about the possibilities for a mission there. The Marianists responded to an invitation from the priests of the Society of African Missions in Benin City, Nigeria, to teach at the College of Asaba. After his visitation, Provincial Joseph Hoffer, SM, preached retreats for the Brothers, bringing with him maps of Africa to encourage the members to volunteer. Three men left Dayton, Ohio, on 24 September 1957 and sailed to Africa on the *African Glen*. Following the intent of *Fidei donum*, one of these men, William T. Anderson, SM, had begun organizing college students for leadership in Africa by the early 1960s.[90] Their work was seriously impeded, however, by the political upheaval on the African continent in the 1960s.

The New York Province of Jesuits was asked by the superior general to open a new university center in Lagos, Nigeria. Joseph Schuh, SJ, chairperson of the biology department at St. Peter's College, Jersey City, left New York to begin the work of building up the university in August 1962. In 1968, the Jesuits made a small beginning in Ghana. Within a few years their work expanded to include retreat direction, teaching in various secondary schools, and the formation of Nigerian and Ghanaian Jesuit seminarians.[91]

Lay Missionaries of the 1950s

Women Volunteers for Africa

Profiting since the 1930s from a strong emphasis on Catholic Action's lay leadership model and the emphasis of the Mystical Body theology on social action, and encouraged by the two papal encyclicals of the 1950s, several lay groups in the United States were preparing for overseas mission work by the 1950s.[92] Two of these groups were started specifically in response to the needs of Africa: the Women Volunteers for Africa (later called the Women's Volunteer Association) and the Lay Mission Helpers of Los Angeles. The Grail had reached maturity by the 1950s and provided significant lay mission formation and leadership. The Grail and the Lay Mission Helpers continue to the present.

In 1950, after a fall down her apartment stairs, twenty-one-year-old Elizabeth Behrend spent months in a St. Louis hospital recovering from back surgery. The accident left her physically disabled. She was impressed with her first contact with the nursing Sisters at the hospital, and later entered the Catholic Church. She began the Women Volunteers for Africa, an organization of mainly medical and teaching personnel who worked under the direction of the White Sisters of Africa. Five Baltimore nurses, after several months of training, worked in Uganda hospitals in 1959. The next year four nurses from the United States and Canada did similar work in Nyasaland.[93]

Lay Mission Helpers of Los Angeles

Having traveled throughout Africa for three months, Monsignor Anthony J. Brouwers, a diocesan priest from Los Angeles, saw the need for skilled lay persons to "elevate the masses in body and soul."[94] In 1955, Cardinal McIntyre approved a constitution, rule of life, contract, and schedule of classes for the Archdiocesan Lay Mission Helpers. The young adults, who excelled well enough in a specific trade, skill, or profession to teach it to others, spent eight months in preparation for mission, studying several evenings a week and on weekends. By the early 1960s, candidates ages twenty-two to forty were taking the Minnesota Multiphasic Personality Inventory as part of their admission requirement.

The first class of five women and one man consisted of nurses, teachers, and a photojournalist who were sent to the Sudan, Tanganyika, and Nigeria. Members committed themselves to mission work for three years. Several Mission Helpers renewed their commitment for up to nine years. By 1960, the group had sent a total of eighty-nine missionaries mainly to African countries, but in 1960 women and men were also sent to Ecuador, Mexico, New Guinea, and Pakistan. By 1970, one-sixth of the long-term U.S. Catholic lay missionaries were trained and financially supported by this archdiocese. The missionaries included an African American woman, Anita Liddell (1962), and several Hispanics.

The group stressed personal holiness and a strong sacramental life as a foundation for mission. While their original constitution noted that the laity with specific competencies were *aiding* the often overtaxed Brothers, Sisters, and priests, it was clear that these laity were *"God's* helpers" and truly missionaries themselves. Areas of involvement for these women and men included agriculture, medicine, education, skilled trades, accounting, and secretarial work.[95] On the day of their enrollment as missionaries they received a ring as a reminder of their calling.

As the missionaries assessed their task, they noted a world "split between the affluent society of the north, with abundance and technology, and the hungry land below the 30th parallel," many of the people there being in a "despairing abyss of ignorance, disease, empty stomachs, and futility. Daily their anguish cries out, pleads for human compassion." For missionaries to "manifest the divine compassion of the gospel" in such a divided world, lay involvement was absolutely necessary. Missionary work was seen as the outcome of a normal, healthy life of faith.[96]

The Grail

The Grail, an international association founded in Holland in 1921, had a base in the United States by 1940 and eventually located its headquarters near Cincinnati. Under the leadership of Dr. Lydwine van Kersbergen, one of the cofoundresses, the group emphasized the spiritual formation of women of all races and professions in order to bring spiritual values to modern society. The group consisted of a nucleus of permanent members and those with freer association.

The organization was to some extent an elite group of self-confident women who intended an active apostolate built on a strong liturgical and contemplative foundation. Kersbergen spoke for a broader, stronger role for women beyond the domestic domain. The formation of the "New Eve" or the "Valiant Woman" needed to take into account her intelligence and intuition, her bent toward contemplation and inwardness, and her sense of total dedication and selfless love.[97] Preparation for mission brought out the individual talents of each member to fit her for the apostolate.[98]

The Grail had a two-pronged effort in world mission. In 1950, they opened both a School of Missiology, which emphasized the education of American Catholic women for the lay apostolate abroad, and an Oriental Institute, which prepared women from other countries for leadership roles to aid conversion in their native lands. The institute was formed after several Chinese women from Hong Kong arrived at the Grail in 1947. The Grail concentrated on educating women who in turn would prepare other women around the globe for a broader role for women in society. Both aspects of mission reflected the idea that the women, as leaven in the dough, were to be agents of change. The first Grail missionaries to South Africa and Basutoland went as nurses in 1952 and 1953. In the discussion around what international developments might shape the future, women of the Grail clearly saw lay leadership in the Church as a significant element in the conversion of the nations.[99]

In spite of a tremendous increase in the numbers of U.S. missionaries to the African continent from 1946 to 1959 — from almost 200 to almost 800 persons — there was still little national publicity for their work with the exception of Thomas Calkins's books *Umfundisi* and *Kisimusi* about missionary life and the people and places in Zululand and Swaziland.[100] The Catholic Students Mission Crusade provided a collection of readings about cultural, economic, political, and religious dimensions in modern Africa, just as the Civil Rights era was coming to flower in the United States.[101]

Conclusions

The strength of America's global role after World War II was recognized by international orders such as the Jesuits and Servites as well as by the Roman Propaganda Fide office, who expected and prompted American provinces to undertake new missions overseas, especially in colonies affected by World War II. These responses brought a substantial rise in the number of U.S. Catholic missionaries abroad. By the close of 1958, 109 groups had sent missionaries abroad. Fifteen of those groups represented forty-seven provinces of American religious communities, which sent almost 82 percent of U.S. Catholic missionaries. Ninety-six lay missionaries served overseas that year.

Mission experience contributed to and initiated American discussions about politics, ideology, and society after World War II. Regarding communism, few mission representatives favored the scare tactics of Joseph McCarthy, though, ideologically, Cardinal Spellman came closest to this side of the spectrum. Tendencies to divide the world into the two camps of communism and Christianity often divorced Christianity from its concern for social justice. John Considine and the Miami archdiocesan program attempted to express principles of social action in their response to the threat of communism. In spite of the larger numbers of missionaries who went to Africa in this period, and in spite of efforts of mission educators to present a fuller picture of African culture and civilization, with the hope that such knowledge would alleviate racism, little appreciable difference in attitudes toward blacks emerged.[102]

Mission experience enhanced theological theory and practice for some Catholics in the United States. Out of the discussion on world order, a predominant theme in the wake of World War II, Considine's proposition for a world Christianity used traditional Christian themes such as the Trinity, but employed them to make mission a primary reality of the Church rather than a secondary or even charitable venture. Though more laity were missioned overseas by 1959, a shift of focus had occurred from earlier Catholic Action leadership of the 1930s and early 1940s. In those decades, the relationship between North and South American women and men, using the Catholic Action pattern, was built on "like to like," educated to educated, in order to develop public Catholic leadership. A redirected focus for North American involvement, especially in post–World War II Latin America, was a response to the social shifts in many of those countries. Cities were being inundated with people who came from the villages to work in new industries. Population was increasing and "the People" were joining mass parties and labor federations. The resulting socioeconomic effects of this displacement, which included poverty and illiteracy, called for a different pattern of lay involvement. North Americans who had education or skills went directly to those who (or so they thought) were not educated or skilled. Attention was aimed more toward the "masses," at least in Latin America, rather than toward those who might attain leadership positions.

With more groups involved in missions, the close of the China missions, and the challenges created by the world war, leadership in some missionary communities sought to resolve common problems by forming the Mission Secretariat. They also sought to influence the direction of mission-funding groups, whom they hoped would call on missionaries for information, vision, and expertise. The spotlight fell on mission funding with the luminous arrival of Fulton J. Sheen on the national stage. Under the SPF's direction, *Worldmission*, successor to the *Missionary Academia*, became the first collective effort by U.S. Catholics to create a mission journal aimed at world mission theology and practice rather than fund-raising.

Encouraged by the papal documents in the 1950s supportive of lay mission vocations, numerous lay groups arose throughout the United States. The first national conference on lay mission work was hosted at the Loyola University Law School in Chicago from 27 to 29 November 1959, with 541 persons present. Its theme was "World Mission of the Church — A Challenge to the Laity." Participants heard John Considine, Elizabeth Reid from the Grail, and Dr. Tom Dooley, who spoke on the jungle hospitals of Laos. The lay groups provided workshops about their spiritual gifts and emphasis in mission. The conference served as the threshold for national and international recognition of a distinctive lay mission vocation.

Great rumblings began to occur in the understanding of the mission vocation itself, as we have seen in the discussions among missionary Brothers. Priests particularly had often thought of "real" mission work as a clergyman's vocation. However, papal support for lay missionaries in both the 1951 and 1957 encyclicals and almost three decades of Mystical Body theology and Catholic Action experience provided the groundwork for a renewed understanding of the mission vocation as central to the life of the Church and for all Christians. This would be seen quite clearly in the next area to experience an increase in publicity, interest, and numbers of missionaries: Latin America.

Chapter 8

From "Rehabilitation" to "Development": Latin America, 1959–71

U.S. Catholic Presence before 1959

As the struggle for world order gave way to a Cold War between Russia and the United States, another upheaval occurred in the life of Catholics around the world: Pope John XXIII's announcement in 1959 of a reform council. The event triggered a tremendous amount of energy as well as personal contact between bishops from all the continents. At the same time, an intensive focus by the Vatican on the "rehabilitation" or renovation of the Latin American Church and the need for interaction among the churches of the northern and southern hemispheres brought about the next surge in overseas missionary activity for U.S. Catholics. Over the next twelve years, while the Jesuits, Franciscans, the Divine Word Missionaries, and Maryknoll men and women remained the largest mission-sending groups, other religious congregations, groups of laity and clergy, and dioceses began to train their members for work in Central and South America. This same period, which would catapult Catholics into new liturgical experiences and result in changes in religious practice and emphasis, also brought about major changes in finances and structure in the U.S. Catholic Church and a transformation in theology partially due to its mission focus on Latin America.

As noted in chapter 3, U.S. Catholics had sent missionaries to Central and South America and the Caribbean since the nineteenth century. In 1892, the Laredo and San Antonio Ursulines founded a school in Mexico at the invitation of the bishop in Puebla. Some of those earlier groups, including the Sisters of the Immaculate Heart of Mary (Philadelphia), the first women's congregation to establish a mission in South America (1922, Miraflores, Lima, Peru),[1] and the Redemptorists (1930, Guarani Indians, Campo Grande, Brazil),[2] would offer hospitality and advice for newer American arrivals in the area. In the 1930s, the Milvale Franciscans from Pittsburgh went to San Antonio Parish, Rio Piedras, Puerto Rico (1931), the Sisters of Mercy (Rhode Island) were in Central America (1932), and the St. Louis Province of the Brothers of Mary began teaching in Lima schools (1938). Between 1937 and 1942, forty Bernardine Sisters left their motherhouse in King of Prussia, Pennsylvania, to work in Brazil among people of mixed races south of the Guaíba River. The Sisters began to educate this group overlooked by the government. Soon, native women joined the Bernardines.[3]

During World War II, European communities were cut off from their missions in Latin America, and the United States was again requested to assist in pastoral and mission work. In 1944, the Friars Minor (Immaculate Conception Province, New York) began their ministry in Honduras, in response to an appeal from Central American Bishops the previous year for "help in preserving the faith of their people."[4] The Redemptorists in the Amazon jungle of Brazil invited the Adorers of the Precious Blood from Wichita, Kansas, to work among the indigenous people of Coari; four Sisters left their motherhouse in November 1947. As they began to learn the language soon after their arrival, the Sisters visited people in their homes, comforted the sick, and spoke with the women doing the family laundry along the riverbank.[5] The Sisters subsequently began a system of education among the people, something which their Brazilian overlords had denied.

Interest in sending Catholic missionaries to Latin America gained momentum when John Considine's *Call for Forty Thousand* was published in 1946. The book appeared three years after the Central American Bishops had invited the U.S. Bishops to send priests to assist them in renewing the Church. Combining in masterly fashion personal stories, statistics, and excerpts from missionaries' diaries and letters, Considine painted a picture of the Latin America he had come to know through his earlier travels throughout that part of the world as a staff member at the Propaganda Fide office in Rome. Each chapter, which explored a different country in Latin America and the Caribbean, provided the reader with the region's history, geography, demographics, economy, social, religious, and cultural life. The book was sold across the country and found its way into convents, rectories, seminaries, high schools, and colleges. Considine calculated that if the spiritual needs of Latin Americans were to be met, the continent would require forty thousand new priests to provide a ratio of one cleric to two thousand persons. While still recognizing a place for the lay missionary, Considine based the mission to Latin America on the presence of clergy. This book became a classic reference for those inquiring about the needs of Latin America in the late 1940s and 1950s.

Call for Forty Thousand went to print after Maryknoll had decided to send missionaries to Latin America. Maryknollers were in Bolivia in 1942, and the Maryknoll Sisters arrived there the following year. Societies such as Maryknoll and the Columbans, who were founded to serve China in particular, needed to review where to send growing numbers of seminarians. The Columbans, the title of whose magazine, *The Far East,* allowed for locations beyond China, had started missions in Korea (1933), Burma (1936), and Fiji (1952). In 1958, they sent some of the Irish Columbans to Chile and Peru.

In a reassessment in the midst of World War II, Maryknoll found that over half of their 369 members were in war zones. With probable disruption in the

East for years to come, veteran China missionary and superior general James E. Walsh decided with his council to send members to Latin America. The mission area was not chosen by default, but represented a definite commitment. Considine, one of the councilors, remarked in his diary that he had a "good talk" with Walsh about the subject:

> [Walsh] admits that our policy of entering S. America not merely to convert the pagans but to influence the Catholic life of the two continents is an enlargement on the original purpose of MK [Maryknoll]. On my part I feel it to be a thoroughly legitimate enlargement....[6]

In their first departure ceremony for that part of the world, Bishop James E. Walsh, successor to Maryknoll founder James A. Walsh, explained to the men:

> We go to South America — not as exponents of any North American civilization — but to preach the Catholic Faith in areas where priests are scarce and mission work is needed. As far as the elements of true civilization are concerned, we expect to receive as much as we give.[7]

When Pope John XXIII urged religious congregations and societies in 1961 to pledge 10 percent of their personnel to Latin America, Maryknoll already had 25 percent of its members working in eight countries in Central and South America. The men and women of Maryknoll would play a formative role for North American missionaries arriving after 1959.

Among those leaving the United States in the 1950s were the Sacred Heart Province of the Friars Minor from St. Louis (Brazil, 1958),[8] and the Cistercians from Spencer Abbey, Massachusetts, who sent several of their men to found a house in Azul, Argentina (1958), and one near Santiago, Chile (1960). Vincent Dwyer was one of the young monks who went to Chile (1961–64) and who later developed a renewal program of videotapes and faith-sharing groups (*Genesis,* 1975) in the United States. The Maryland Province sent the first American Jesuits to South America in October 1959, to replace the Society of the Divine Word in Osorno, Chile.[9] For the most part, however, the attention of U.S. Catholics and their compatriots had drifted away from Central and South America, with the exception of businessmen, who often aligned themselves with the military and dictatorships.[10]

The U.S. government had long been active in the region, especially through the Central Intelligence Agency and through transactions related to the Panama Canal. By the 1950s, the southern hemisphere was broiling in political unrest and instability. "Yankee go home!" was the cry of many, who saw U.S. policy aiding in the oppression of the poor. Vice President Richard Nixon was pelted with rocks as his motorcade drove through the streets in Lima and Caracas. Extremist groups on the right and the left claimed to speak for the country. Populists in Latin America, who combined personal charm with support of nationalism, social reform, and participation by "the masses," sought to stem the growth of communist parties through various mass movements. Communists

Aid for Latin America: In the years after World War II the "priest-poor" situation of the Church in Latin America led various orders to give greater priority to that continent. Cardinal Cushing of Boston was especially active in that cause. This 1960 photo shows Cushing at the San Ricardo Social Center in Lima, Peru, on one of his many trips to Latin America. (Courtesy, Archdiocese of Boston Archives)

aimed at social and agrarian reform. This combination of factors provided some of the energy for the antipathy toward Yankees. Marxist communism did seem to offer the majority poor a better economic chance in life.

In 1959 Fidel Castro took over Cuba and planted the first communist regime in the hemisphere, much to the shock of religious leaders. Communism was now more than an ideological threat. President John F. Kennedy focused new interest and U.S. foreign policy on the southern hemisphere through the Alliance for Progress (1961), which intended to do for Latin America what the Marshall Plan had done for Europe after World War II. The failed Bay of Pigs invasion and the presence of Russian missiles in Cuba made the Spanish-speaking south imminently close.

President Kennedy visited Colombia, Puerto Rico, Venezuela, and Mexico between 1961 and 1962. The following year, as Soviet expansion appeared to threaten the western hemisphere, the United States signed an agreement with seven Central American countries to unite against this aggression. In 1964, the U.S. Marines landed in the Dominican Republic to protect Americans during civil war. The U.S. government was interested in the stabilization of Latin America, as were U.S. businesses, who could profit from the labor of those on their *haciendas.* It would be the U.S. Catholic missionaries who would, often unintentionally, upset the balance by working with large numbers of the laborers and the poor.

Diocesan Clergy in Latin America: The St. James Society

John XXIII had created many new dioceses in Latin America. John Considine noted in 1963 that one out of every three of the bishops and prelates in Latin America that year governed ecclesial territories which were less than eight years old. There were 160 of these new ordinaries taking part in this colossal program of renewal for the Church in the Latin American world.[11] With such vast pastoral needs, the area seemed a fertile field for North American clergy. Several U.S. diocesan clergy had gone to Latin America prior to 1959. When Joseph Walijewski was ordained in 1950, he petitioned his La Crosse, Wisconsin, bishop for an overseas mission assignment. Bishop John P. Treacy suggested some pastoral work in the diocese first. In 1956, when Maryknoller Charles Brown, auxiliary bishop of Santa Cruz, Bolivia, preached at the parish where Walijewski was working, the two spoke at length about the needs of Latin America. Walijewski joined Brown shortly thereafter to start a parish among the people of a poor and expanding area near the Bolivian jungle. Almost immediately another La Crosse priest, Aloysius Wozniak, joined him. That same year, three priests from the St. Louis Diocese served in La Paz, Bolivia, and were joined the following year by two more from the same diocese.[12]

The great push for diocesan priests in Latin America, however, came through the efforts of Richard Cardinal Cushing. Until his death in 1970, he also pumped millions of dollars into Latin American projects.[13] His personal charism and his confidence in God opened (or forced open) the pockets of many. John Considine remarked in a letter to the Boston prelate, "I have watched the way you have operated for years and recognize that you have counted on Divine Providence to come through with these gifts, and Divine Providence has a way of being rather quixotic, sometimes sending the man with the cash very quickly and sometimes leaving you hanging on a hook for a long period."[14] One of Cushing's biographers has remarked that in the poverty and illiteracy of the majority of Latin Americans, the Boston cardinal "saw qualities that made the Church so vital to the Irish immigrants of South Boston in their bitter conflict with Protestant Yankees."[15]

But Cushing gave more than his money. In 1958, he founded an organization of diocesan clergy to serve in Peru, Bolivia, and Ecuador. Early thoughts about such a program stemmed from an *ad limina* visit to Rome in 1948. Cushing told Pope Pius XII about his "lend-lease" program, whereby the "surplus" priests of the Boston Archdiocese served dioceses in the West. The pontiff suggested sending some of those priests "south." Cushing, never very able with Latin, assumed he meant the southern part of the United States. After they left the pope's chambers, the interpreter said to him, "Do you realize that 'south' meant South America?" Meanwhile, a Portland, Oregon, priest, Francis Kennard, had been working among the very poor in the archdiocese of Lima in the late 1940s and 1950s. The archbishop, Peruvian Franciscan Juan Landázuri Ricketts, asked him to write to the bishops of the United States to see if any other priests would be willing to serve in the area. The only person who responded was the Boston cardinal. He invited Kennard to address the younger clergy in his diocese to see if anyone was interested.

On his way to Boston in 1957, Kennard stopped in Milwaukee to visit some of the Brothers of Mary whom he knew from their schools in Peru. He paid a visit to the Cardijn Center, the headquarters in Milwaukee for the Young Christian Students movement. While there, he met a newly ordained priest, John Maurice, and invited him to come to Latin America. Kennard and Maurice became the first two members of the Society of St. James the Apostle.[16] Maurice had his social consciousness awakened at St. Francis Minor Seminary, where John Beix, the founder of the Milwaukee Cardijn Center, taught sociology. The young priest joined Kennard in August 1958 in Hurachiri, Peru, where he had been working among the Quechua Indians. Within a few months, Spanish Opus Dei priests forced them out of the parish, much to the dismay of the Quechuans. From there the two priests went to Abancay in the diocese of Cuzco, Peru. There were misunderstandings with Cushing, and Maurice remarked that

> Fr. K[ennard] got a real raw deal. He was told that we have nothing to do with the Society of St. James, it is now a group for Boston priests alone. The Cardinal went back on his word in this a great deal, especially when you think of all the work that Fr. K. did for him.[17]

In effect, the two founding clergy were thrown out of the society, though shortly thereafter priests from other U.S. and English-speaking areas were able to join.

Cushing deputed Edward F. Sweeney, the archdiocesan director for the Propagation of the Faith, to represent him on a visit to the Lima area in 1958. In Peru, Sweeney met with Charles McCarthy, MM, a childhood friend who would become influential in the Society of St. James. Maryknoll had experience in Peru and was willing to share that experience with the new group. Sweeney felt that the men would not be able to bear the harsh conditions under which Kennard lived, and suggested parishes which would allow a somewhat easier adjustment for the new missionaries. The issue of location created conflict between Sweeney and the early members, who preferred work with the very poor. The society's first mission was San Ricardo Parish in Lima, an area experiencing burgeoning population growth, with many poor people arriving in the city from villages to look for work.[18] San Ricardo, named after Cushing, was adjacent to Maryknoll's Our Lady of Guadalupe mission.

The Society of St. James requested that the Sisters of St. Joseph, Brighton, Massachusetts, assist in the work of the mission, and their first four missionaries left for Peru in September 1965.[19] They described San Ricardo to the Sisters back home:

There are over 40,000 people living in our parish, the majority are *obreros* or blue-collar workers and there are some white-collar workers, also. Most of these live in a government apartment project named "Matute." There are also thousands living in a *barriada,* Mendocita, two blocks from the convent. Actually, the parish constitutes a sociologist's nightmare! Our problem is how to give these three groups of people, with such varied backgrounds, an idea of the Mystical Body.[20]

While some society members created a "little Boston" (i.e., a facsimile of what they knew at home), others, such as Cushing's nephew, William Francis, offered the people something else. He confided to his uncle:

By our choice to live here with the people in the same circumstances and with the same privations, we have been able to make a terrific impact on them. When we first came down here as a Society some of the rectories we built [on Sweeney's recommendation] gave the people the "ugly American" impression; we want to avoid this as long as possible.[21]

In the first twenty-five years of its existence, the society sent 270 priests to the three chosen countries. Initial contracts were signed for five-year periods of service, but many stayed well beyond that time and some planned to retire at their mission station. A number of clergy discovered that the religious and social warmth of their people added a missing dimension to their own seminary training. They found the self-sacrifice of their people a challenge to their priestly ministry. Some of the clergy viewed their work to defend the rights of the poor as an extension of "works of mercy" from their Catechism, even though this work brought the wrath of those who stood to profit from unjust labor situations.[22] At the time of the founding of the St. James Society, Cushing had hoped he might resign from his diocese to be a missionary himself, though this did not happen.

Because of having founded this society, his twenty-three years as director of the Propagation of the Faith office in Boston, his fund-raising, and his presence on the Latin American Bureau board and numerous other mission organizations, Cushing became a nationally and internationally recognized advocate for missions. In a letter to a friend, Cushing remarked, "All my priestly years have been spent in elevating the position of missionaries from second class members of the Mystical Body of Christ to the prominent place that they have at the present time."[23]

Cushing also provided large sums of money for religious congregations in his diocese who sent missionaries around the world. He supported the Sons of Mary Missionary Society, which became his responsibility after the death of its founder, Edward F. Garesché, SJ. The Sons of Mary specialized in bringing medical and catechetical aid to the sick poor and in training the native population to give medical help to their villages. They used Cushing's episcopal motto, *Ut cognoscant Te* ("That they might know You"), as the direction for their mission work.[24]

Pontifical Commission for Latin America: Beginnings and Platform

The numbers of American priests, Brothers, and Sisters missioned to Latin America rose slowly. By 1958, 33 percent of all American Catholic missionaries were in the southern hemisphere: 807 in South America and 392 in Central America. This was a great increase from the 1940 figures, though not significant enough to meet the apparent pastoral and social needs. The U.S. Bishops continued to support the Montezuma Seminary through the 1960s, and in 1961 Cardinal Cushing gave $125,000 as a first allotment to a Regional Minor Seminary in Lima, Peru.

After their meeting at the Eucharistic Congress in Rio de Janeiro in 1955, the Latin American Bishops formed a regional conference (CELAM) to deal with the religious situation and growing unrest in their dioceses. Bishop Manuel Larraín of Talca, Chile, noted after the conference that

> We must pass from a plane of national isolation to one of inter-American cooperation. Goals must be determined in terms of human need; Latin America is on the threshold of imminent and radical reforms. Shocking social inequality, the existence of immense proletarian and sub-proletarian masses living in inhuman conditions, and the monopoly of land ownership all show how urgent it is for us to take a definite stand in this regard. With us or without us, social reform is going to take place.[25]

A significant boost in funds, interest, and personnel for Latin America came through Pope John XXIII, elected pontiff in November 1958. This former national director of the Society for the Propagation of the Faith in Italy wrote an encyclical on missions (*Princeps pastorum*, 1959) and took a special interest in Latin America, redirecting to those countries funds scheduled initially for Asia, Africa, and other missions. A Pontifical Commission for Latin America was established in Rome in 1959 to study the fundamental problems of Catholic life in Latin America and to coordinate efforts for a renewal and revitalization of Catholic life in the southern hemisphere. CAL and CELAM as the national gatherings of Latin American Bishops would greatly affect the future of missionaries to those countries.

Marcello Cardinal Mimmi, a conservative and an avowed anticommunist, presided over CAL. The approach of CAL to Latin America essentially indicated that Catholicism needed to be defended from two "menaces": Protestants, who had been vigorous in their mission work now that church-state separation was a reality in some Latin American countries, and communism. The success of Protestantism, CAL maintained, was due to the religious ignorance of the majority of Latin Americans, the lack of clergy to instruct them, and the attractiveness of Protestant teaching offered to "ignorant people." The more dangerous reality — communism — was a threat to the very foundation of faith and Christian morals. Communists had infiltrated the universities, offering a vision of a new world crowned with a socialist economy. The poor, especially indigenous people, were attracted to communism, which seemed to offer hope to starving and ignorant persons. The regions in most need of help were listed in order as Brazil, Chile, Bolivia, Cuba and Haiti,[26] Nicaragua, Honduras, and Guatemala.[27] CAL called on the Catholic Church throughout the world, but especially the United States, to "rehabilitate" the Church in the southern regions.[28] Anticommunism would provide a renewed Catholicism in Central and South America.

Development of the Latin American Bureau

Foundations

In addition to the presence of the Maryknoll men and women, the most influential work performed by U.S. Catholics in Latin America, specifically as a rejoinder to CAL's initiatives, occurred at the Latin American Bureau. On 16 November 1959, the U.S. Bishops voted to set up a more structured NCWC committee for Latin American affairs with Richard Cardinal Cushing as chairman. This decision came subsequent to a papal-promulgated meeting earlier in the month in Washington, D.C., between representatives of the North and South American bishops. The Church leaders sought solutions to pastoral problems and coordinated action plans for Pan-American pastoral collaboration. The U.S. Bishops summarized their discussions by noting the need in Latin America for

- more priests and seminaries;

- more teachers, schools, and better social institutions; and

- missionary programs unhampered by communists and by Protestant activity.

This, or course, was also the Pontifical Commission's agenda.

When the NCWC decided to reinstitute a Latin American Bureau that year, a person of vision, with experience with the Latin American Church and with good management skills, was required to give the office more visibility than its forerunner in the 1930s. Cushing, already nationally known for his fund-raising ability for missions, requested that John J. Considine (1897–1982) be released from his responsibilities with the Maryknoll Fathers to become director of the bureau. A year later, Dr. Carlos A. Siri, on leave from El Salvador's Ministry of Foreign Affairs, was appointed assistant director. Cushing personally supplied

$25,000 to launch the bureau, which in 1961 was incorporated to coordinate U.S. response to papal appeals for aid to Latin America. Cushing and Considine became key influences in the concentration of American personnel and funds to Latin America in the 1960s.

Considine, the director of the Latin American Bureau from 1959 to 1968, came with a wealth of experience and knowledge of missions around the world. After his ordination in 1923, he had worked at the Propaganda Fide office in Rome, visiting missionaries and gaining firsthand information about all aspects of their work, including the geography, culture, statistics, needs, and particular problems confronting each mission. Eventually Considine published several books based on this information. As the founder of Vatican Fides News Service, he made available in five languages information to the general public about Catholic missions all over the world. Missionaries were impressed with his broad vision and understanding of their mission situations. When appointed to the LAB, Considine had served for thirteen years on the Maryknoll General Council and had just published *New Horizons in Latin America*. In addition to his wisdom and experience, Considine had a knack for efficiency. His secretary at the LAB remarked that the department seemed to run on ball bearings. Personally, he was thorough, diplomatic, and congenial. Such a person was needed to deal with the various constituencies of the Latin American Bureau.

In addition to addressing the pastoral concerns mentioned at the 1959 Bishops' meeting, the Latin American Bureau also concerned itself with other elements of the "Papal Program for Latin America":

- recruitment and training of lay personnel;

- effective religious instruction across the southern countries;

- stronger Catholic school systems in Latin America;

- strengthened social-action programs; and

- mass communications.

Considine spent about half his time corresponding about details for personnel for Latin America. His office offered a documentation service as one way to educate North American Catholics about the possibilities and problems of the Church in the southern hemisphere. In 1960 he traveled through Latin America, as his assistant Carlo Siri did the following year, to examine the situations where bishops were seeking personnel from North America.

By 1960, the U.S. Bishops were contributing one million dollars a year to the Pontifical Commission for Latin America for assignment to those countries as CAL saw best. This budget then returned to the U.S. Bishops for approval. There was some dissension, however, as some bishops noted that the German Bishops, who were raising over six million dollars for Latin America, could make decisions about money without CAL's intervention. These monies were in addition to a 5 percent appropriation CAL received from the Society for the Propagation of the Faith in the United States. This was an unusual move because, technically, most of Latin America did not qualify for SPF funds.

The perspective on Latin America the bureau provided differed from the perspective of lay persons who had worked mainly with middle- and upper-class Catholics through NCWC in the 1930s and 1940s. The source for much of the material published or disseminated from the Latin American Bureau in the 1960s came from missionaries who worked, not with social elites, but with the masses of people affected by the rule and perspective of the government and the military. Though founded partially on the premise that communism needed to be assailed in Latin America, the bureau remained amazingly free of diatribe and of the fiery anticommunist rhetoric of the period.

Within its first four years, the bureau under Considine's direction had become the national hub of organization and consultation for the Papal Volunteers for Latin America, the Center for Intercultural Formation, the Catholic Inter-American Cooperation Program, and the meeting at Notre Dame of major superiors of women and men religious. Each of these efforts focused the energy and interest of the American Catholic community and expanded the numbers of missionaries to Latin America. By January 1967, 56 percent of the 9,500 U.S. Catholic missionaries abroad were in Latin America, compared to 33 percent during the 1950s. Indeed, there was so much interest from Catholics in the Church below the Rio Grande River that Cardinal Cushing remarked within three years of the push in this direction, "My thinking is that there are all together too many organizations springing up to help the Church in Latin America and there is no uniformity of programs or action. From Italy and other parts of Europe, from everywhere, it seems somebody is calling day by day with a new plan to save Latin America."[29]

Papal Volunteers for Latin America (PAVLA)[30]

The focus of the NCWC in the 1930s had rested on the foundations of Catholic Action, through which educated laity had addressed the social problems of Latin America. The method used the principle of "like to like," one social group working with their social counterparts, and formed part of a larger thrust by U.S. Catholics in the 1930s and 1940s toward social action and toward a Catholic revival in the United States and abroad. Pius XI's encyclical on Catholic Action (1931) and Pius XII's encyclical on the Mystical Body (1943) furthered the theoretical basis for lay action by advocating

- lay formation through study, action, and prayer, helping to create social consequences from personal piety;

- the specific role of laity in building a "civilization" built on Christian principles;

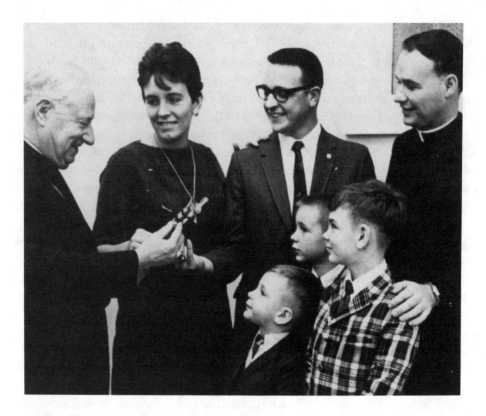

Papal Volunteers: Before Vatican Council II, most American overseas missioners were members of religious orders. In the early 1960s, in a process immensely augmented by the Council, lay persons began to seek ways to serve. This 1968 photo shows Archbishop William Cousins of Milwaukee with Brenda and Jim Nelson and their children, who spent two three-year terms in Guaiuba, Brazil. Fr. Russell Tikalsky, Milwaukee director of the Papal Volunteers for Latin America, is on the right. (Courtesy, Russell Tikalsky)

- a self-confident laity; and
- the belief that the reconstruction of social structures could be effected through Catholic social principles.

By the 1950s, the approach was also being used in several Latin American countries by the Young Christian Students and the Young Christian Workers. Joint meetings of Inter-American Catholic Action groups responded to the changing social and political tempo of the time by seeking to unmask traditionally Catholic cultures through evangelical agendas, including renewal in pastoral practice, attention to indigenous groups, and challenges to the collusion of church and state.[31] The mission focus adopted by the Papal Volunteers in Latin America targeted groups traditionally disregarded by the upper class or groups which had been victims of oppressive governments.

Origins. The announcement by the Pontifical Commission for Latin America in May 1960 of a Vatican-endorsed program for lay missionaries was a logical outcome of the stress on Catholic Action in papal encyclicals over the past thirty years. In July, Monsignor Paul Tanner, general secretary for the NCWC, sent a letter to the U.S. Catholic Bishops announcing the project and asking that the Papal Volunteers for Latin America program be established in their dioceses. In January 1961, Cardinal Cushing, on behalf of PAVLA, and Chicago's Albert Cardinal Meyer for the Catholic Extension Society invited the bishops to name directors in their dioceses for candidates interested in either mission group. Within the year, ninety-six dioceses had done so. A complete PAVLA program was considered to include an organized plan of promotion, a system for financial support, and a plan for the candidates' formation at home before they began a field placement abroad. PAVLA was intended to embrace all lay apostolic effort providing personnel for Latin America. Latin American bishops were to work with U.S. bishops to identify pastoral and technical projects. PAVLA representatives were to collaborate with established sending societies, to encourage enlistment in the societies where practical, and to seek sponsors for their members who were to serve. Volunteers would be assigned to teams according to the specific needs of ecclesiastical authorities in Latin America.

Father Michael Lies, instrumental in coordinating the efforts of the four Kansas dioceses, was named national PAVLA director for the first year.[32] He worked part-time for the program afterward, and Victor Fernandez became the national director. A Panamanian by birth and member of the Jesuit Province of California, Fernandez had volunteered his time to the Latin American Bureau while studying at Georgetown University. He resigned as director in 1964 to work in South America, and Raymond Kevane, a priest from the Sioux City, Iowa, Diocese, who had worked in lay missionary formation, became the national PAVLA director from 1964 to 1969.

During the first year, 112 out of 1,500 applicants completed their training and traveled to Latin America, mainly to Brazil, Peru, and British Honduras. Laity came from forty dioceses and, over the years, assisted in teaching, educational development, rural education, nursing and medical practice, social service, youth work, catechetical organization, agricultural development, social research, community development, and the organization of credit unions.

The national PAVLA office initially had designated four categories of volunteers, those under the direction of

- the diocesan director,

- the director in a Catholic college or university,

- religious congregations, or

- lay mission societies.

The national PAVLA office thus could serve as an umbrella organization, encouraging friendly and helpful relationships among the groups.

Phases of PAVLA. From 1960 to 1962, a fledgling period, John Considine and national PAVLA Director Victor Fernandez, who worked in cramped head-quarters in Chicago, sought to sell the program to the U.S. Catholic Church, to coordinate the Church's Latin America programs, and to examine requests from those countries. Traditionally Catholic areas of New York[33] — Rockville Centre and Brooklyn — had no PAVLA volunteers. Washington, D.C., had one, Philadelphia and Boston each had four, Chicago had sixteen, St. Louis had ten, and Milwaukee had nine volunteers.

Fernandez reasoned that if the program were well promoted, the U.S. Bishops would provide the necessary funds and would recruit candidates. During a visit to Latin America in 1962, he found that Church leaders there saw PAVLA as powerless, due especially to an inadequate financial base. That money collected in the United States first had to go to CAL, which then decided how the funds would be used, was considered useless and impractical by the Latin American Bishops.

The task of coordination was more complicated. With so much apparent "goodwill" surfacing and with so many agencies involved, PAVLA soon felt the headaches of systematization. In December 1961, Considine filed a confidential report, "Toward Improved Procedure in U.S. Assistance to the Church in Latin America," in order to clarify the role of CAL, CELAM, LAB, and other national groups.[34] His summary called for a world field director who would act on behalf of Archbishop Samore of CAL to coordinate requests from Latin America for funds and personnel. The report also mentioned the need for language institutes and cultural orientation for all those planning to serve in Latin America.

The next phase of the PAVLA movement, nationalization, lasted from 1963 to 1968, a period when there were both greater numbers of Papal Volunteers and more mission formation programs. On the advice of long-term missionaries in Latin America, particularly the Maryknoll Society, a regional representative was designated in the countries where PAVLA served, improving communication and support among the members.

Calling for better training programs, the Ponce Institute at the Catholic University in Ponce, Puerto Rico, opened its doors to PAVLA missionaries in 1963. An official relationship was established among the Latin American Bureau, NCWC, and the Ponce Institute, which had been teaching priests, Sisters, and Brothers for several years. Other programs, such as those at Marian College, Fond du Lac, Wisconsin, and the Catholic University of America, attempted to provide a better theological, pastoral, and anthropological foundation for the Volunteers. By 1965, more money was available for Latin American programs because of a newly established annual collection for the Latin American Church. In the first year, a net of more than one million dollars was collected to strengthen the pastoral life and religious activities which CELAM promoted. Some of this money went into PAVLA programs.

Volunteers and diocesan directors desired greater representation and decision making in the areas affecting their work. In November 1963, PAVLA reorganized to include a board of directors with five lay persons and ten clergy. This was in addition to an executive committee and a three-hundred-member PAVLA National Council which held annual conferences to examine various aspects of the movement. The national office had further recommended centralizing the training and assigning of Papal Volunteers, meaning that Latin American bishops could deal with the national office to meet their volunteer needs. However, those with strong diocesan programs, especially dioceses in the Midwest, resisted nationalization. For one thing, they felt they would have little or no voice in PAVLA issues and regretted the shift from PAVLA's original emphasis on bishop-to-bishop contact.

The last phase of PAVLA (1968–70) encompassed the reassessment and demise of the movement. In 1968, upon John Considine's resignation, Louis Michael Colonnese became the director for the Latin American Bureau. The Iowa priest had opened the nation's first Office of the Lay Apostolate in 1961 in Davenport and was a national chaplain for the Young Christian Student movement. Both Cushing and Considine were interested in the young priest and had recruited him in 1965 to help at the LAB. He consented, provided he could work from his Davenport office.[35]

While lay missionaries had contributed to a 45 percent increase in personnel in Latin America between 1960 and 1966, formation for the lay apostolate was again an issue at the Inter-American Bishops Conference in June 1968. CELAM proposed, and the group agreed on, a three-phase training program for all lay persons, religious, and clergy coming to Latin American countries. The program included the same areas as previous formation efforts: screening and orientation, intensive language training, and general acculturation. What was new for PAVLA volunteers was specific training for integration into the pastoral plan in the region they would serve.[36]

There were signs, however, that the Papal Volunteer movement was on the decline. In 1967, the number of PAVLA volunteers declined to 251 from 400 in 1965. Colonnese was never sold on the PAVLA initiative. The bishops of Latin America continued to voice the problems they experienced with the volunteers. By this time, too, other dynamics in the LAB and the volatile political and social environment in many Latin American countries were causing confusion and disruption, which, in turn, affected the volunteers.

Problems in PAVLA. Some difficulties in the Papal Volunteer Program were eventually solved. Better screening more readily identified immature candidates and those with psychological troubles. More professional training programs, such as the Center for Intercultural Formation (see below) and the Language and Acculturation Training program in Mexico City, directed by Wilbert Wagner, SVD, gave the candidates a more realistic picture of what they would encounter and thus minimized early terminations. The Grail, which in 1961 had organized a four-month residential training program for PAVLA, complained that the recruits lacked a deep spiritual and theological life and tended to be more devotional, which, to the Grail leadership, did not support the values of self-sacrifice, discipline, and teamwork.[37]

Other problems identified included attitudes of superiority on the part of some volunteers and the desire to be a "main impulse" rather than a catalyst in service. In addition, local churches needed to propose programs and projects "realistically and carefully delineated to insure success."[38] Various trips to Latin America by PAVLA national leadership had revealed a lack of acceptable sites and projects for the volunteers, and eventually PAVLA relied heavily on projects supervised by the Maryknollers, the St. James Society, and American congregations already at work in the southern hemisphere. Kevin Dwyer, a married man from Boston, became the on-site coordinator in Lima for the Papal Volunteers in Peru, Chile, Bolivia, and Ecuador. Archbishop Coleman Carroll, Bishop Humberto Medeiros, and Colonnese met with CAL to examine how to make PAVLA more responsive to Latin American needs as perceived by Latin Americans themselves.

From the beginning, however, PAVLA had chronic problems which contributed to its demise. Two major problems were clerical leadership of a lay group and the decision to nationalize. In 1963, when Fernandez resigned as director, he recommended that David O'Shea, the national secretary, take his place. The suggestion was not taken, and Considine telephoned the Jesuit to convince him to stay. While the rhetoric was in place for the development of lay mission vocations, many clergy on a practical level did not think the laity had a long-term commitment to missions like the clergy and religious. They contended that short-term lay involvement of one to three years was not effective for missionary work. This same argument did not seem to apply to the five-year commitments of those from the St. James Society, nor to missionaries from religious congregations who spent only a few years overseas.

For at least half the life of the program, while Considine was the Latin American Bureau director, most of the finances and energies promoted the sending of priests and religious rather than laity. This was true also for Cardinal Cushing, the other important figure in the Latin American effort. On a more theoretical level, both men believed that the core of the mission effort lay with the clergy and the sacramental life to effect change. In his *Call for Forty Thousand,* Considine had issued a clarion call:

> Meeting the needs of the Puerto Rican countryside is a problem in mathematics; it is the counting of priestly heads. There is no substitute for the priest in Catholic life; there is little use in learned inquiries on bad customs when the principal cause for them is obviously the long absence of the spiritual leader.[39]

Though Considine had spoken of the need for lay cooperation in "works of religion and social action" at the Lima Methods Conference in 1954, the bureau director did not appear to change his mind about the centrality of clergy for mission.[40] Louis Michael Colonnese, who became the LAB director in 1968, came from a rich background in lay leadership training and, in this regard, was different than Considine and Cushing. However, Colonnese did not believe in the program and felt that the national office used papal endorsement as a "crutch" to promote PAVLA. Latin American bishops themselves held divergent attitudes about what some saw to be interference of the papacy in local jurisdiction.

The second endemic problem was the nationalizing of PAVLA. On the one hand, the national director felt that while the NCWC had given the office responsibility to develop and administer the papal program, PAVLA had little authority to assign volunteers and insufficient finances for effective administration. It was also difficult to keep up with and to guarantee quality in the many lay formation programs springing up around the country. On the other hand, by nationalizing and assigning lay persons to Latin America from the central office, PAVLA brought about the resistance of diocesan directors, mainly in the Midwest, who had been the backbone of the movement. Midwest PAVLA directors feared that centralization would hamper the creativity of local churches and would diminish their ability to address issues affecting their candidates. Kevane, named PAVLA director in 1964, found himself in a difficult position because he himself was from the Midwest.

Ultimately, PAVLA also participated in the larger problems of the Latin American Bureau, problems which hinged on the evolving role of missionaries in a changing socioeconomic context and the policy of the Church with regard to violence and guerrilla warfare.

Legacy of PAVLA. Many Papal Volunteers engaged in projects which had lasting effects. Such is the case, for example, of Mary McCormick. She was an unlikely PAVLA candidate, a widow and a mother of seven children who knew no Spanish when she applied in Milwaukee to be a Papal Volunteer. Ultimately, her home, not the parish rectory, was where the poor found assistance and a listening ear. In 1968, she left for Bogotá, Colombia, with three teenage daughters for a one-year commitment. She stayed for twenty years, working in Barrio Juan XXIII in the mountains in northeast Bogotá. As was true for many Papal Volunteers, she did diverse work. She organized a nutrition and milk program for young mothers, began a day-care center, and developed a loan program for those who wanted to improve their dwellings. She made medical appointments for those unable to do so and aided persons seeking jobs. In later years, she also organized a four-week program of "Conscientization" for North Americans, in which students lived with local families in Bogotá and followed Mary in her work in the barrio.[41]

Married Papal Volunteers offered a model of family life, which religious and clergy could not provide. This offering was not always appreciated by the clergy. Cushing had remarked to Considine, "As for myself, I cannot understand this program of sending parents with five or six small children to foreign lands. It doesn't make sense to me. As far as I can make out wherever they are going they will only be saving the saved."[42] Nevertheless, a number of PAVLA couples with children worked as effective missionaries. James and Brenda Nelson of Fond du Lac, Wisconsin, provide one example. Parents of three boys, one of whom was born during their mission years, Jim, a mechanical engineer, and Brenda, a teacher, worked in a small village outside of Fortaleza, Brazil, for six years (1962–68). Jim taught math and opened a vocational woodworking school and pottery shop to enable the men to start a local industry. Jim and Brenda worked with the local diocesan priest in the parish catechetical program and provided marriage instruction for people of the parish.

The experience in Latin America also had lasting effects on Papal Volunteers. Many were struck with the generosity and warmth of the poor indigenous peoples. Volunteers began to "think beyond boundaries" and realized that "they are part of the Body of Christ."[43] Their spiritual growth resulted from a practical experience of social action, mission, and prayer. Some Volunteers entered the priesthood or religious life. For example, James Hasker, a PAVLA worker from the combined Kansas programs, was ordained a priest for the archdiocese of Belém, Brazil. Sally Hanlon, who had worked with the Maryknoll Sisters in Lima, entered that community in 1963.[44] PAVLA also provided an important outlet for young women to use their gifts in the service of the Church. Of the 150 volunteers in 1962, 109 of these were single women. While definitive statistics are unavailable, it does appear that about two-thirds of the Papal Volunteers were women.

The Church in the United States benefited from the experience of its Papal Volunteers, who brought back to their home parishes the social and global dimensions of Catholicism. While the formal PAVLA program ended in 1970–71, a number of dioceses continued a lay missionary program. Some dioceses "adopted" a Latin American parish and regularly sent laity and diocesan clergy there to assist the local Church. Such was the case in Rochester, New York; Erie, Pennsylvania;[45] Cleveland; Milwaukee; and Bridgeport, Connecticut, for example.[46]

Center for Intercultural Formation

In addition to formation programs for laity which took place in the United States, some of which included the study of language, a number of other missionary preparations were in place by the early 1960s. While Fordham University did not have enough faculty to sustain a mission center on its campus at Rose Hill in the Bronx, Jesuit anthropologist J. Franklin Ewing drew together missionaries and social scientists in several important conferences from 1953 to 1962 at the Mission Institute at Fordham (see chapter 10). Well-known Fordham sociologist Joseph Fitzpatrick, SJ, specialist on the pastoral care of Puerto

Ricans in New York, was called on to interpret their needs to pastoral personnel in the archdiocese.[47]

To prepare missionaries for Brazil, the Franciscans had opened an Institute of Intercultural Studies at Petrópolis. For those preparing for missions in Spanish-speaking areas, a language training institute had opened at the Catholic University in Ponce, Puerto Rico. The university was begun in 1948 by James Edward McManus, CSSR (1900–1976), bishop of Ponce. McManus saw the university — intended to provide higher education for those who could not afford it — primarily as a "means of defending the faith of the people of Puerto Rico, to give the Church an image on the Island [i.e., education was a sign of effective Church leadership], and to give glory to God."[48] The institute director was James S. Stefaniak, MM, of Milwaukee. Ivan Illich, a priest of the New York Archdiocese and former research associate at Fordham University, was the assistant director. Since the mid-1950s, Francis Cardinal Spellman had been sending his New York priests there to study Spanish so they could communicate and work with the large numbers of Puerto Ricans in his diocese. Several Fordham faculty provided lectures for the language students at Ponce. The Maryknoll Society ran a language school at Cochabamba, Peru, for clergy, religious, and laity who planned to work in Latin America. Unhappy with the program at the time,[49] the Society of St. James began its own school in 1962 at Cieneguilla, twenty minutes outside of Lima, with Frederick Cameron as director.

The Center for Intercultural Formation in Cuernavaca, Mexico, was initiated in 1961 by John Considine, Frederick McGuire of the Mission Secretariat, and Fordham University, and cosponsored by the Bishops Committee on Latin America. The Pontifical Commission for Latin America allocated forty thousand dollars to inaugurate the work. In 1965, the CIF became independent from Fordham. Initially, the CIF rented an old hotel in Cuernavaca, about forty miles southwest of Mexico City, to house the four-month training program. The first students entered the program on 19 June 1961. The center offered an intensive program based on principles delineated by its controversial, colorful, and impassioned director, Ivan Illich. Born in Yugoslavia, he had spent some time in Austria before coming to the United States, where, from 1951 to 1956, he resided at Incarnation rectory, which was located in a predominantly Puerto Rican area of New York City. Illich opened job placement centers for the Puerto Ricans and invited New York social workers to live among their clients.[50] Identification with the people would become a hallmark of the Cuernavaca program. He became assistant director of the language institute at Ponce, Puerto Rico, but fell into disfavor with McManus, the university founder who suspended Illich from his diocese.[51] McManus felt that Illich's ideological leanings and his relationship with the governor of Puerto Rico jeopardized what McManus saw as the beleaguered position of Catholics on the island. Illich was then available to assume responsibility for the new language institute.

The CIF director complained about the lack of psychological and spiritual maturity of many persons who came to Latin America thinking that "goodwill" alone would carry the day. Illich and his staff[52] attempted to "inculturate" the North Americans (and later those from other countries) with a realistic and comprehensive formation. With a ratio of five or six students to one instructor, participants had ample opportunity to acquire facility with the spoken language. The center also offered competencies in intercultural communication, an understanding of the nature of culture and of cultural differences between North and South Americans, and spiritual formation. The center was envisioned, at least by some, as the "Harvard" among training institutes.[53]

The students regularly ate meals prepared with ingredients found in Latin American homes. Visits to families and local parishes introduced the participants to the "real" world they would encounter if they chose to go to Latin America. Native speakers from the countries where they would be sent addressed them on the current political and economic situations in Latin America. Joseph Fitzpatrick was among those who presented the principles of the social sciences, introduced so students might "understand the moral relativity of many customs and ways of behavior" they had appropriated and "understand from a Christian point of view the moral problems involved in economic development."[54] Louis Luzbetak, SVD, presented classes on anthropology for missionaries. Seminars were offered on a variety of topics ranging from community organizing and the transformation of the concept of the parish to the development of popular Latin American music. Students visited parishes, which exemplified various aspects of the institute's perspectives. Among these parishes was that of Chicago priest Leo Mahon in Panama. Mahon also presented lectures at the center.

As Mexico did not permit persons to wear signs of religious commitment, the women religious in particular found Cuernavaca an adventure. Short hair and "secular" clothing were more noticeable for the women than for men religious; the men often exchanged their habits for slacks and shirts and their hair was never covered by a veil.[55] One of the participants, Anne Jude Van Lanen, CSA, who in 1964 was preparing to go to Nicaragua, wrote to her major superiors:

> [Cuernavaca] gives a more complete preparation for missionaries who have not had missiology courses, for the students receive in addition to language study, church history of Lat. Amer., and Lat. Amer. cultural and sociological studies. But above all this, the spirit of the Lat. Am. Church is present in all phases of life at Cuernavaca.... One is not taught how to be a missionary, but rather how a missionary should think, and then he [sic] will know how to act in any given situation.[56]

Participants had the opportunity to examine realistically their call to serve in Latin America. Late-night discussions and invited speakers evoked heated and intense arguments about all aspects of mission life. Formation at Cuernavaca required persons to confront, sometimes painfully, their North American biases. The staff warned those from the United States that the Latins' estimation of close family relationships could often be at odds with northern business sense and efficiency, for example. Latin American Catholic group identity might clash with North American "religion of individual practice." Students were also presented with the diversity of Latin American Catholic cultures.

Illich stressed the importance of emotional and spiritual maturity, partly because lay persons would be pioneers, facing unmarked paths in the apostolate. Often laity would have to explain what they were doing not only to the people they served but to the priests and religious who might not be used to lay persons working side by side with them. Twelve PAVLA members, seven AID members, ten Sisters, seven priests, one Brother, and one seminarian completed the first four-month course at Cuernavaca. By the end of 1962, CIF had trained 68 of the 177 lay volunteers at work in Latin America that year. Illich also initiated *conversaciones*, bringing together small groups of North and South Americans to converse with each other and with the CIF staff. He amassed a substantial library with funds from U.S. Catholics.

The program, or, rather, Illich, ran into controversy several times. While Illich was charismatic, he did not possess strong managerial skills and seemed to spend money without accountability, a source of friction with Considine, who addressed him on the latter issue several times. An October 1961 article in *Time* and an editorial Illich wrote in *CIF Reports* in December 1962 drew the ire of Cushing and the bishops. For a while, the bishops revoked their support of the CIF.[57]

Among the mission formation programs for Latin American personnel, the CIF was the most radical. It challenged common assumptions about mission formation in three areas: "foreign missions" and geography, the nature of language acquisition, and the purpose of missions. Illich clearly outlined his principles in a paper, "Basic Policies for Courses of Missionary Formation." First, to be a missionary was not necessarily a matter of geography, of moving American Christianity across a border, of transplanting a South Boston parish to a South American barrio. Rather, it was the "capacity to leave...home at least spiritually and to talk to strangers."

Second, this kind of exposure to the worldview of the Latin hemisphere broadened the foundation of what it meant to learn a language. To speak in a new tongue required more than mastery of tenses and correct usage. Language was communication, a willingness to embrace a culture, an expression of the desire to become one with the missioner's new people. The student was meant to "enter into a universe of concepts distinctly different from that in which he was brought up."[58] This inner disposition required great detachment, "missionary poverty,"[59] the exemplar being the prototypical missionary, Jesus Christ, who became one with us.

Third, as Illich assessed the situation, pouring "men and money" into Latin America had only made the Church there more "foreign" and "priest-ridden." Latin bishops became beggars and more mired in the colonial system, which kept masses of people poor, uneducated, and oppressed. The question, he asserted, is why do we send missionaries at all?[60] Considering that the number of U.S. missionaries present in Latin America would peak the following year in 1968, this radical query threw self-doubt into some of those preparing for mission to Latin America. Others dismissed his question as they dismissed Illich's perspective in general.

Catholic Inter-American Cooperation Program

The Latin American Bureau was not only busy, but under Considine it had become authoritative in the minds of many North and South Americans. The director was asked to be on the boards of several groups who focused on Latin America, including the Peace Corps, the U.S. government organization founded at the same time as PAVLA to provide humanitarian assistance to developing countries. Because of his leadership, Considine was appointed by the Vatican in 1963 as a consultor to the Pontifical Propagation of the Faith Commission. As Cushing remarked to him, "You are God's gift to the Church of the United States' contribution to the church of Latin America."[61] For his part, Considine felt that his work for Latin America gave him "a sense of deep purposefulness."[62] The services of the LAB office were drawn on by other groups in and beyond the NCWC, as well.

The U.S. Bishops' Subcommittee for Inter-American Cooperation and LAB were the sponsoring agencies for the Catholic Inter-American Cooperation Program. The organizing secretary for the CICOP conferences was Louis Michael Colonnese, at this point the assistant director for the Latin American Bureau. Plans for the first meeting were launched in 1962. The purpose of the CICOP conferences was to provide U.S. Catholics with a knowledge of the real situation in Latin American countries and to have personal contact across the hemispheres.

To lay the groundwork for the conference, informal luncheon meetings between North and South American bishops, organized by Bishop William J. Quinn of NCWC, took place in the piazzas of Rome while the bishops were participating at the Vatican Council. The meetings were held especially to interest U.S. bishops in the plight of the southern churches and to gain some rapport with Latin American bishops, who were largely unfriendly to the U.S. bishops at the council.[63]

The first CICOP conference, chaired by cardinals from both hemispheres, was held in January 1964 at the Edgewater Beach Hotel in Chicago. A few months before the conference was to begin, Antonio Samore of CAL wrote Considine to congratulate the planning group on the inauguration of the conference, noting "that it is of capital importance to make known with precision, also to non-Catholics, the place held by the Church in Latin America, the driving force she represents for the progress of those nations and its effective interest in the betterment of their economic and social conditions."[64]

The invited guests included Cushing, other U.S. archbishops and bishops, and

South American archbishops known for their progressive leadership. François Houtart[65] spoke of the need to establish a Latin American master plan, which took inventory of human resources and attempted a more effective use of mission personnel due to the priest shortage. Aristides Calvani of Caracas, Venezuela, spoke on the importance of laity in evangelization. A summary of social and religious data for each of the twenty Latin American nations was provided to the participants. Senator Hubert Humphrey of Minnesota also gave a presentation, mainly affirming the importance of CICOP to further a better understanding between North and South America and praising Chile for its progressive developments.[66] Chilean José Cardinal Silva used this meeting as an opportunity to speak afterwards with the Foreign Relations Committee of the Senate and with officials of the Alliance for Progress.

At the second CICOP meeting in Chicago in 1965, Houtart described the social confrontation between Latin America and the United States. South American prelates Marcos McGrath (Panama), Juan Landázuri Ricketts (Peru), and Manuel Larraín (Chile, president of the Latin American Bishops' Council) described the religio-social conditions in their part of the world. For many in attendance, this was their first exposure to a social-scientific analysis of the Latin American world and certainly presented a different picture than the "abiding Catholicity" presumed to exist in the southern countries. The meetings produced interest, concern, and alarm about the situation in the southern hemisphere. Participants were hearing for the first time, uncensored, the role of the United States in Latin America. Along with several hundred church members, U.S. State Department personnel were in attendance. Some of the latter attempted to intimidate the bishops.[67] This was not the first time the U.S. government became interested in the work of missionaries.

The goals for CICOP echoed similar Catholic Action themes of the 1930s and 1940s: to direct public opinion about the religious and social problems of Latin America and to form among Catholics a knowledge of actual situations there. The first meeting attempted to assist the U.S. hierarchy in comprehending the role of the Church in the new Latin America. By the next conference, thought was given to pairing North and South American lay educators, lawyers, and other professional persons to provide leadership in planning the new social reforms in Latin America, especially along the lines of Joseph Cardinal Cardijn's "Observe, Judge, Act" movement of Young Christian Students and Young Christian Workers. The results of such efforts would lead to quite different consequences in the 1960s and 1970s.

In all, five CICOP conferences were held. After the mid-1960s, the Latin American Bureau had become controversial for the bishops. Senators and congressmen were using the bureau for their research. The bureau was in correspondence and personal contact with many key Latin American leaders, some of them revolutionary and insurrectionist. Colonnese, director of the LAB, felt a need to protect his sources, lest they experience retaliation from the United States or their own government. He published several statements about Latin

America without clearing his remarks with the U.S. Bishops, for he considered the statements they passed ineffective and watered-down. Bishop Joseph Bernardin fired Colonnese in 1971 and Colonnese left for South America, eventually founding an orphanage for young boys, Hogar Juvenil Divino Salvador, in Sonsonate, El Salvador.[68] Nevertheless, Colonnese's leadership and that of the NCWC (after 1969 known as the U.S. Catholic Conference) created conditions for important interhemispheric dialogue. CICOP ended in 1972.

CICOP, as well as CIF at Cuernavaca, the Sister Formation Conference, the Inter-American Conferences of Major Superiors, and the Sister Formation Movement became significant vehicles for North American familiarity with progressive Latin American bishops, especially Larraín (Chile), Helder Camara (Brazil), Landázuri Ricketts (Peru), and McGrath (Panama), and with a strong socioeconomic approach to the Church in that hemisphere. Particular U.S. missionaries were heard from less through these channels while the needs of the Latin American Church came more to the front. Clearly social justice and disclosure of socioeconomic inequalities were on the front burner of what CICOP saw to be the missionary agenda.

Meetings of Major Superiors

Rome, 1959

In a gathering of major superiors of religious congregations held in Rome on 29 May 1959, Archbishop Antonio Samore of CAL and his committee[69] disclosed their analysis of the two dangers to the Latin American Church: the success of Protestantism, and communism. While a high value had been placed on the work of clergy in Latin America, Sisters also had a role "in the defense of the faith." Involvement of women's communities would enable the local church to "take soldiers from certain less dangerous posts to send them where the enemy is penetrating without meeting with any resistance. We must fill the breach before it is too late."[70]

Women and men religious were urged to send 10 percent of their members to Latin America as soon as possible, even at great sacrifice to the congregation. They were to prepare to fight against Protestant influence and communism. For the former "battle," Sisters needed to know the slogans Protestants used against Catholic dogma, sacraments, indulgences, and the clergy. The women were urged to study Scripture, doctrine, and Church history, especially those topics which Protestants tended to attack. To fight communism, Sisters would need to be associated with the poor, workers, and students, who needed to become knowledgeable about communist propaganda and the social teachings of the Church.

Sisters in Latin America were advised to take seriously the duty to catechize all age groups by every possible means:

Without neglecting any of the duties of their state, the Sisters of Latin America cannot content themselves with teaching their pupils according to the State curriculum, or with nursing the sick in their hospitals. They must be apostles, they must help the priests in their mission of teaching, and where there are no priests, the Sisters must take their place and teach Catholic Doctrine "opportune, importune," to the fullest extent of their capacity.[71]

The papal delegate noted that the Church existed in Latin America, in spite of its difficulties, due mainly "to the deep piety of South American women. The Protestants admit that one of the great obstacles they meet with in these Republics is the 'fanaticism of the women' who maintain Catholicism in their families."[72] Teachers needed to modernize their methods (otherwise students would turn to the Protestants) and reach the children of the poor, as well as of the upper classes. More schools and colleges were imperative to combat the secularism of state schools.

With this announcement, some congregations began immediately to plan and prepare their members to respond to this call. The Sinsinawa Dominicans in Wisconsin were one such case. In addition to CAL's commendation, they had received a request from the Dominican master general, who supported CAL member Paul Philipe, OP. The Sisters decided on the location of their mission after the La Crosse priest, Joseph Walijewski, wrote to their major superior with a request for teachers and catechists in his parish in Santa Cruz, Bolivia. Four Sisters left the Dominican motherhouse in Sinsinawa on 2 October 1960 after receiving their mission crosses from Mother Coleman, MM. This was a fitting ceremony, as this Dominican congregation had provided the initial formation of the Maryknoll Sisters in their early years.[73]

Notre Dame, Indiana, 1961

Not content with the official Vatican statement on the need to send people to Latin America, Archbishop Samore intervened to put the topic on the agenda for the August 1961 meeting of major superiors, though the agenda had already been established. The work and content of the session devolved on John Considine. CAL informed the leadership of the conference that the meeting should appeal for religious for Latin America and should suggest a practical plan of action to send them. Only one session on the topic was worked into the schedule when the group met from 16 to 18 August 1961. Samore was to be the speaker, but the death of Marcello Cardinal Mimmi prevented him from attending. Agostino Casaroli, a member of the Sacred Congregation of Extraordinary Affairs, spoke on his behalf.

Addressing the religious leaders whose congregations would be neophytes in Latin America, Casaroli suggested nine areas for practical consideration:

1. The Latin American Church needed to be rebuilt by the people there. Religious personnel from outside should not move into public leadership positions but should cooperate with the "vigorous, inspired leadership" of the southern republics.

2. While there might be an attraction to the most abandoned areas, U.S. missionaries should work with local authorities in locations where rapid improvement for the local church and an increase in native vocations were possible. When these areas had a stronger faith, then the more abandoned areas could be targeted for mission.

3. Because the national and provincial capitals were of such importance for influencing the rest of the country, parochial life should be strengthened there first.

4. For those involved in education, low-fee schools should be available for the middle-class population. Catholic schools should emphasize an apostolic spirit among the upper class.

5. A plan with pastoral, educational, and social goals should be adopted to mesh with the goals of the Latin American Church. Religious should not be sent to Latin America simply to "plug holes."

6. Sufficient numbers from a congregation should be sent to guarantee "vigor of action" and religious strength for the members themselves.

7. Missionaries should participate in a cultural and language orientation strong enough to guarantee a respect for local cultures and customs.

8. Each local community should be strengthened to provide its own vocations to priesthood and religious life, which meant that U.S. congregations should consider establishing Latin American provinces.

9. Religious congregations should consider ways to work with PAVLA men and women.[74]

The goal proposed was to send two hundred priests, Brothers, and Sisters to Latin America each year for ten years. The response of religious congregations, especially of women, many of whom had not previously sent their members abroad, was swift and vigorous, though the hoped-for 10 percent of community membership was not achieved. Women religious, experiencing the burdens of the institutionalization of their successful work in teaching and nursing, sought places in Latin America where they could work with "the poor" rather than teach in American-type schools or perform hospital work as the South American Bishops frequently requested and as CAL had proposed.[75]

Sister Formation Conference in Peru, 1964

The collective response of U.S. Catholics to the call to Latin America coincided with a time of tremendous transformation in religious life. Significant leadership for women came through the influence of the Sister Formation Movement.[76] A growing Catholic population had created numerous schools and other institutions to meet its needs since the 1940s. Pastors and bishops called for more Sisters to staff these places. Consequently, women were often sent to teach with little professional preparation beyond their first one or two years in the congregation. In 1941, Sister Bertrande Meyers, DC, called for better professional and spiritual preparation for their ministry. At the 1954 meeting of the National Catholic Education Association, several persons discussed the issue at length. From this group was born the Sister Formation Conference, a movement intended to provide an integrated four-year college program, encompassing spiritual, intellectual, cultural, and religious life formation. The Everett Curriculum was developed to meet these goals. Sisters attended regional conferences and workshops on topics related to an "integrated" formation. Bishops and clergy, intent on immediate diocesan and parochial needs, often had to be persuaded of the plan, which postponed for four years the entrance of the young women into education, nursing, and social work.

U.S. women religious began to work and plan together across congregational lines, as some of them had started to do through the Mission Secretariat meetings. This increased their communal resources and taught thousands of Sisters to league together for solutions to common problems. These dynamics plus the previously established Overseas Project, the presence of missionaries on their board, and an invitation from the apostolic delegate in Peru, Archbishop Romolo Carboni, came together to have the Sister Formation Conference consider a possible program in Latin America.

Early in their work, the interests of the Sister Formation moved beyond U.S. borders with invitations to Sisters in Uganda, India, and South America to attend colleges in the United States. The Overseas Project grew from work initiated by the Sisters of Mercy in 1960 and was organized by a person with experience with this program, Josetta Butler, RSM, president of Saint Xavier College in Chicago. Within the first year, thirty colleges hosted eighty-three Sisters from twenty-eight foreign communities.[77] The intent of this educational endeavor was to have women religious assume leadership positions in their churches back home. The experience of the student Sisters from around the world uncovered a number of problems: lack of solid spiritual and intellectual preparation for college work, problems of adaptation, lack of communication in the United States with Sisters from their own country, and problems of adjustment on returning to their native countries. Butler made a seven-week trip around the world to discuss these issues with the congregations who sent women to the United States.

At the same time as the Overseas Project, the leadership of the Sister

Formation Conference was attending the CICOP meetings and the annual Mission Secretariat meetings. The presence of Anna Dengel (1955–59), Frederick McGuire (1960–66), and Celsus Wheeler, OFM (1962–63),[78] on either the National Consultative Committee or on its own board made the Sister Formation Conference aware of specific needs of the Church in other countries. Through these board connections, Ivan Illich gave conference members a "thinking" workshop in 1962 and François Houtart provided a series of conferences in 1963 on the mission of the Church in an era of global technology.[79]

The work of the conference captured the interest of persons overseas. At the invitation of one of the Peruvian religious superiors and of Carboni, Annette Walters, CSJ, executive secretary for the conference, and Ritamary Bradley, CHM, editor of the *Sister Formation Bulletin,* went to Latin America to examine the formation needs of women religious. After consultation with Considine to set their itinerary for several South American countries, Walters and Bradley left for a three-week trip in January and February of 1962 to meet the women religious and appropriate ecclesiastical officials. Their trip was made possible by Cushing's two thousand-dollar gift. The spring 1962 issue of the *Sister Formation Bulletin* carried their itinerary, letters from the notables, stories of their meetings, and two articles on missionary Sisters: "The Missionary Sister after Three Centuries of Waiting," by Vincenzo Cardillo, SJ, and "Latin America and the Sister Formation Program," by John J. Considine, MM.[80]

The Sisters wrote a confidential report to Carboni, wherein they noted several difficulties they encountered in meetings with women religious in the several countries they visited. Annette Walters remarked that some Sisters in leadership positions were complacent and did not admit to a need for improvement in Sisters' education. Further, training for Sister-teachers in these countries did not encompass the total vocation of the women. Their report stated:

> Peruvian Sisters have seen the vigorous activity of Protestant groups and have been led to take on new schools staffed by inadequately prepared Sisters in order to keep the schools from being opened by Protestants. We have tried to point out that the real strength in Protestant activity in Latin America is the attraction of a genuine spiritual bond among its members and the persons being reached in Protestant schools and social work projects. Hence, it is imprudent to rush unprepared Sisters into the mere external control of the works in question, neglecting the apostolic and professional formation that can effectively make the Catholic Church attractive to the masses.[81]

Few knew how unprepared many Sisters were for teaching. Walters further observed that the Peruvian Sisters were not accustomed to working together, which left them isolated and unable to handle the growing social and educational problems in Latin America.

The trip resulted in the formation of a counterpart to the U.S. Sister Formation Conference, the Comité para la formación de las Religiosas in Lima. Peru was chosen for two reasons: the strong possibility of obtaining State Department funds for education through the Alliance for Progress, which was targeting Peru at the time, and the conference's belief that what happened ecclesially in Peru would set the pattern for all of Latin America.

Gretchen Berg, a Franciscan from Rochester, Minnesota, with a recent doctorate in literature and language, was sent to Lima in March 1963 to open a university center, Regina Mundi, for the educational and spiritual formation of Peruvian women. In addition to the Catholic University in Lima, with which Regina Mundi became affiliated, Lima had two other schools for teacher preparation. Peruvian Sisters, many of whom had not completed high school, were often unable to pass the entrance exams to get into these institutions.

When Berg arrived in Lima, Carboni invited her and seven young Peruvian Sisters for dinner at his residence. He said to the new director of Regina Mundi, "Accept every Sister the communities here will give you. At the end of the first semester, we will cancel the admission test to the University for all who pass the first-semester courses." Berg put together a first-rate library and procured the latest instruments for science classes. The faculty consisted of professors from the Catholic University, from San Marcos University, and five American Sisters. Six of the seven women who were enrolled the first semester passed their courses at the university center. In the four years Regina Mundi remained open, twenty-four women finished the two-year program to gain entrance into the university.

Perhaps a more important development which occurred in conjunction with Regina Mundi was the weekly seminars it sponsored on liturgy, ecclesiology, Scripture, and the church in the modern world. This pastoral program for fifty-three major superiors and novice directresses in the Lima area carried the impetus of Vatican II as it was occurring, providing Sisters with the latest theology. A subject was introduced one week and the following week questions and applications to religious life in Peru fleshed out the practical ramifications of what the women had heard the previous week. Nine of the eleven contemplative communities were also provided with conferences. Juan Cardinal Landázuri Ricketts, the progressive archbishop of Lima, had urged the major superiors to consider attendance at these conferences a "moral responsibility."

In addition to content, a significant factor in the gatherings was that rich and poor congregations were meeting and speaking with each other for the first time. In the end, rich communities felt this consciousness raising was destabilizing them. Poor communities were realizing they were just as important as the rich communities. Further, the communities who ran the normal schools felt competition from Regina Mundi. In August 1967 Gretchen Berg and the American Sisters left Peru. Years later, several clergy who had worked with Regina Mundi told Berg that it was only in retrospect that they could see Regina Mundi as a "bright light" of the Peruvian Church.[82]

From "Rehabilitation" to "Development"

Mission as Development

The Catholic Church in the United States understood the goal of mission to be the establishment of the visible Church (under the direction of native hierarchy), a concept which had been explicit from Benedict XV's *Maximum illud* (1919) through Pope Pius XII's *Evangelii Praecones* (1951). It was assumed that the visible Church would continue with the priest as the pivotal point. Few missionaries from the United States had any formation specifically for mission in the early 1950s (see chapter 10), and those relatively familiar with mission theology relied on European thinkers, especially the work of Joseph Schmidlin and Pierre Charles, SJ. With the exception of *Is France a Mission Country?* (1943), which made little distinction between mission to those who had not heard God's word and the evangelization of those in a secularized country, the definitional "norm" was well in place into the 1950s. Maryknoll employed this definition of mission in their 1957 constitutions.[83]

The Catholic Students Mission Crusade in 1961 noted, "The apostolate is the mission of Christ as teacher, king and priest, delegated to the apostles, and continued in the Church for the salvation of all men."[84] Assuming Christ's priesthood as the theological foundation for mission, the CSMC divided the mission apostolate into its strict sense of establishing a visible Church and its wide sense as a penetration of Christian values into other cultures and institutions. The CSMC further distinguished mission activity from the pastoral apostolate, the latter understood as a "strengthening, preserving and defending the faith of believers."[85]

But the experience of missionaries in Latin America (and elsewhere), the continuing background encouragement from Vatican II documents, the United Nations' declaration of the 1960s as a "decade of development," and the information that U.S. Catholics were receiving from the Latin American Bureau, CICOP, the *National Catholic Reporter,* and other publications brought an increased socioeconomic emphasis to the understanding of mission. This would eventually cause conflict and a reexamination of the nature and meaning of *mission,* as well as *church.*

On a more theoretical level, *development* initially was aligned with the earlier missionary goal of *civilization.* However, when missionaries actually went to various parts of the world and saw the extent and depth of people's poverty, they began to realize that the values of "civilization" about which missionaries spoke could not be transmitted in situations in which the majority of the people had all they could do to keep body and soul together. Further, "civilization" presumed some literacy and a certain amount of economic security.[86]

John Considine in 1943 described the work of the missionary monks, the traditional builders of "civilization":

[The monks of the West] did not merely teach the Creed and establish the Mass. They examined the entire social condition of the people. They sought to preserve what was good, and gave the assurance that they came to build on whatever of loveliness was already present, aiming to crown the local culture with Christianity. They relieved the physical ills by works of mercy, and lifted the pall of ignorance by education. According as the people needed it, and in order that their assistance would not consist of mere profitless kindness described today as playing Santa Claus, they sought to train the people to better living in the field of economics and to better government in the field of politics.[87]

As we have seen in previous chapters, work with poverty-stricken people or those afflicted by natural disasters or by disease had been an important part of mission outreach, especially for women missionaries. For example, the first dispensaries begun by Dr. Mercy Hirschboeck, MM, in Korea in 1936 grew into well-equipped hospitals after the Korean War, with provision made for the training of local people in medical skills. Male missionaries had frequently engaged in road building, construction of wells, and the introduction of better farming methods, especially as a way to find their "niche" within a new community unaccustomed to outside visitors. However, the prevailing view U.S. Catholics had of Latin America tended to heighten a Catholic "civilization," which had been its presumed glorious heritage. North American outreach through Catholic Social Action of the 1930s and 1940s had worked to restore the brilliance of Spanish Catholicism as it had supposedly once been.

Considine began to emphasize a different approach in the early 1940s, when he wrote and spoke about what he first called "socioeconomic betterment" in 1943 (then "development" in 1960), just as the Maryknollers were shifting their sights from China and engaging in work in Latin America. In his realistic assessment of many of the countries of the southern hemisphere, Considine noted that, though there were exceptions, the majority of the people were poor and illiterate. The chaplain to the cloistered Maryknoll Sisters remarked in a monthly talk, "Any sombre picture of the bulk of men condemned to ignorance, to poverty, to sufferings and indignities is not God's picture."[88]

To explore the subject more deeply, the Maryknoll Fathers and Brothers sponsored a four-day conference at Ossining, New York, during Easter Week in 1958. The gathering was cosponsored by the Fordham Institute of Mission Studies and the Catholic International Rural Life Movement. A group of experts in community development, urban problems, credit unions, and other social concerns met with sixteen field missionaries knowledgeable about these areas. The assumption of this all-male conference was that the missionary was to be a catalyst for better living in urban and rural areas, not a technician. The talks were published and disseminated both across the United States and to missionaries abroad.[89]

One of the presentations had been on the importance of cooperatives and other economic unions as a way to "build character" and the economy. Catholic men and women missionaries from the United States already had been in the forefront of such developments in several countries. Orphaned Chinese boys and girls had been taught skills and crafts which would enable them to become financially sufficient as they grew older. Education itself was seen as a way to a job with enough income to raise a family in comfortable surroundings. But cooperatives also developed economic power within the groups of poor persons themselves. The cooperatives were not dependent on prevailing economic systems in order to function and to develop leadership among the people.

Perhaps the best known of the cooperative unions was initiated by Sister Gabriella Mulherin, MM (1900–1993), who served in Korea from 1926 to 1942 and from 1952 to 1967.[90] Returning to war-torn Korea in 1952, Mulherin worked with young, displaced war widows and other women to teach them skills which would provide their livelihood. Realizing that the postwar voluntary agencies would eventually leave the country, she spent some months in Nova Scotia learning about the Antigonish Movement, a program of adult education which used leadership training in credit-union organization to promote democratic values and to build group trust and responsibility for their own lives. In early 1960, the Credit Union Movement began with twenty-eight members in Pusan, on the Maryknoll Sisters' compound. After serving as managing director for the Korea Credit Union League for a year, she turned the organization over to Korean leadership. By 1988, over one million people belonged to the credit union.

Her work was acknowledged by the Korean government in 1988 with the erection of a commemorative stone. The credit unions had assisted the country in moving from postwar deprivation to a relatively healthy economy.[91] Mulherin's view of the credit unions was that "my work was motivated by a religious vocation first: my desire to help the people know the true meaning of love of neighbor as we see it in the Gospel. It was not merely the spreading of a particular socio-economic system — it was an expression of God's love for us and our response to it."[92]

The first two CICOP conferences continued these social and economic themes, taking a social-scientific, "expert" approach to identifying the problems of the "new" Latin America. The missionaries themselves, as we will see in the next chapter, were providing community-building skills and economic resourcefulness, especially for indigenous and poor persons, as a way to develop trust among these groups and as a means of economic self-sufficiency.

Pope Paul VI's *Populorum progressio,* frequently translated as "On the Development of Peoples" (1967), addressed the issue of economic development specifically. Having traveled to Latin America, Africa, and India, the pope had witnessed firsthand the positive and negative effects of the globalization of industry. His encyclical was addressed to all believers, to those of goodwill, government authorities, and promoters of development. The document promoted the positive aspects of development that enabled all people to have a better standard of living but warned against those who had no social conscience and who created wealth for themselves at the expense of the poor. The underlying value of the dignity and worth of the human person could not be sacrificed to runaway capitalism. Economic structures needed to be at the service of the complete human being, including people's spiritual development.

Both the Vatican II documents, especially *Gaudium et Spes* ("The Church in the Modern World"), and the 1970 Bishops' Synod gave impetus to this direction in mission. A line from that synod, "Action on behalf of justice is a constitutive element of the gospel," would become an oft-quoted reference by Catholics intent on justice and social development. Some persons raised the question whether "development" was, indeed, the new name for mission.[93]

The significance of promoting socioeconomic interests in countries where missionaries were sent was the slow development of a new understanding of mission, which relied more heavily on a response to human needs. This emphasis in practice was a far cry from a "rehabilitation" or "renovation" of the Latin American Church, especially in places where reformers urged swift and complete structural change, a condition Roman authorities feared would serve Soviet political interests. There would be no return to a supposed golden past of Catholic civilization. Shifting economic boundaries in Latin America affected all other aspects of life, including the ecclesial and religious, especially in countries with strong historic ties between church and government. U.S. Catholic missionaries, appalled by the poverty and even more by the attitude that such conditions were "normal" and not to be challenged, would, along with the Central and South American people themselves, work to change the systems which kept people poor. As Considine had noted even in 1943, such conditions were not "part of God's plan."

Bishops' 1971 Pastoral on Mission Activity

Always a part of the Catholic approach to mission, the social and economic life of communities seemed to be taking predominance at the expense of the "religious" or spiritual, at least according to some. In December 1971, the National Conference of Catholic Bishops issued a statement on missions which spoke to the importance of the missionary vocation but then posed what seemed to be a problem with respect to the issue of development:

> Salvation for some today means meeting people's needs in the temporal order. For others it cannot be found this side of eternity. The meeting of these two points of view constitutes the alleged conflict as to which is primary in the missionary effort, the development or the evangelization of people.[94]

Alluding to *Populorum progressio*, the bishops reiterated the importance of paying attention to spiritual as well as economic needs. They suggested that those who held that science and technology were the "only avenues to liberation" were misled. The production of goods should serve the values of justice and the recognition of the dignity of all human persons. After recommending that Catholics give actively to the missions through the Society for the Propagation of the Faith and the Holy Childhood Society, the bishops urged U.S. Catholics to pray, make sacrifices, and

> become personally involved in ministering to the needs of our less fortunate neighbors, wherever in this world they may live, whatever might be their need. In what other way can wars, racism, exaggerated nationalism, violence, and injustice, as well as the hunger, disease, ignorance, and misery they engender, be conquered?[95]

The bishops' statement thus encouraged not only a financial response but a personal involvement in social issues. However, this understanding of mission still carried the idea that missions were a kind of charity, the view held by outgoing SPF director Fulton Sheen. If enough sacrifices were made and finances provided to missionaries they would have the necessary resources to rectify some of the economic inequities at the base of the social evils the bishops mentioned. Having lived through a tumultuous national experience in the 1960s and having heard of the political turbulence in Latin America, some of the U.S. Bishops realized that social structures would not be changed by sending more money to missionaries. Further, the economic disparity in countries was often due to an entrenched government set on preserving the wealth of a few families and foreign businesspeople. There was no unanimity among either bishops or U.S. Catholics about the strong emphasis on social development of the 1960s and early 1970s, especially with respect to Latin America. Further, missionaries themselves were not of the same mind on the subject, as we will see in the next chapter.

Conclusions

In 1959, CAL's agenda for Latin America noted two factors impeding a renovation of the Latin American Church: the increased presence and activity of Protestant missionaries and the threat of communism. What happened to that agenda over the next ten years? Male missionaries tended to mention the "Protestant threat" more than women. But the "threat" of Protestantism was not an overriding concern in the development of the Latin American Bureau and associated groups, such as CICOP and PAVLA, which along with Maryknoll were the major associations advising U.S. personnel about Latin America. The rhetoric of anticommunism could be found in the SPF, especially during Sheen's term as national director, and in the visit of Douglas Hyde to mission organizations, but was not the dominating motif among those sent to Latin America. CAL had encouraged Sisters particularly to be associated with the poor. Exposure to the actual conditions of people often induced missionaries to do something about the people's plight, with little time left for ideological battles.

Missionaries from the United States did not have a strong "civilization" sensitivity like many of the German, French, and Belgian missionaries. Maryknoll claimed that it did not want to take an "American" civilization to South America in 1942.[96] U.S. missionaries paid more attention to the actual social and cultural realities they found. Thus, the second point of the CAL agenda, the "rehabilitation" of the Church, tended to take on strong socioeconomic nuances rather than ecclesial perspectives. In the end, as we will see in the next chapter, ecclesiology would be reshaped because of this emphasis.

The 1931 report from the Latin American Bishops to the NCWC had stressed that "Latin America was not a field for missionary work." Fifteen years later, Maryknoll's Chapter Committee concluded that "even had the war not precluded increasing our personnel in the Far East, the field in Latin America is essentially missionary in character."[97] The realization was growing that despite a history of Catholic presence and culture in a country, the daily life of its people would not necessarily be touched by Catholicism in all its inner vigor. Catholic culture did not guarantee "faith."

Latin America became the focus of extensive institutional support from the U.S. Bishops, laity, and religious, and the subject of intense national publicity. In 1968, when U.S. Catholic missions overseas reached their peak, 1,026 missionaries served in Oceania, 2,471 in Asian countries, and 1,157 in Africa; there were 2,455 men and women missionaries in South America and 936 in Central America. The physical linkage and accessibility of the northern and southern hemispheres along with the large number of missionaries sent to Latin America focused national attention on this area. Large sums of money went to open seminaries, schools, and mission projects, and many congregations of women and men religious learned about this area firsthand. Maryknoll, which sent a considerable number of missionaries to the southern hemisphere in the 1960s, also had influence through its personnel and promotional capabilities to provide focus and direction for the mission needs of Central and South America. Articulate and sometimes controversial figures — Ivan Illich, Joseph Fitzpatrick, John Considine, and Richard Cushing — represented the Latin American experience to the nation. The experience of missionaries in Latin America, more than any other region, shaped a new theological vision for missionaries and U.S. Catholics in the 1960s, 1970s, and early 1980s.

The presence of lay missionaries increased significantly during the 1960s, supported by papal exhortation, lay initiative, and by articles and publications supporting lay mission. The number of lay missionaries rose to a high of 529 in 1973, but had fallen to 221 by 1980.[98] But their numbers never reached the same proportion among Catholics as they did in many Protestant groups. At least two reasons for the disproportion could be cited for the period 1959–71. Several lay groups, such as AID and PAVLA, had difficulty securing recognition of authoritative lay leadership because a priest often served as the "official"

Church representative. Consequently, lay leaders were "middle management." The majority of lay missionaries were women. Second, even well-meaning clergy still assumed that mission centered on priestly tasks, in spite of expansion in the area of "development" and papal encouragement for lay missions. Clergy often felt the responsibility of mission rested on their shoulders and saw the task of the laity in the "lay" field, that is, in the financial support of missionaries. In the eyes of some bishops and clergy, lay missionaries, who often were married, had a family, and, thus, a short-term commitment to a mission area, were less significant than religious orders and congregations with "long-term" commitments.

Conflicting understandings of the mission task came to light sporadically, and chiefly in the context of Latin America. What was the correct balance between transcendence and immanence, between the human and divine in the missionary message? As the 1971 Bishops' pastoral phrased the problem, should the choice for missionaries be "revolution and violence" or liberation as a "peaceful evolution under the guidance of the gospel"?[99] Not all missionaries came up with the same answers.

The outcome of the Vatican Council meetings and the documents published throughout this period pointed to a new ecclesiology, which had surfaced partially from the work of missionaries. North and South American bishops, often wary of each other at first, came to know each other at the council, through meetings arranged through CICOP, and through other mission meetings, some of which were held in the United States.

Signs of a stronger and renewed Latin American Church began to appear after the 1968 meeting of CELAM bishops in Medellín. A kind of mission in reverse occurred when Maryknoll published the CELAM proceedings and distributed them to Latin Americanists in the United States, while the Latin American documents it printed could not be published in that region for fear of government reprisal.[100] By the 1970s, Maryknoll's Orbis Books had become the leading U.S. Catholic publisher of books in English presenting the experience and thought of churches from Latin America. The *National Catholic Reporter* presented story after story about the political and religious situations in Central and South America. This reverse mission became even stronger once missionaries returned to the United States and began to speak both privately and publicly about their experience.

In the following chapter we will examine more closely the mission of several groups and individuals in Central America and their interactions with the United States. Their experience led in the 1970s to a reexamination of the goal and meaning of mission.

Chapter 9

A Time for Reassessment: Liberation Theology and the "Option for the Poor," 1965–80

Lessons from Two Case Studies

Growth in numbers of U.S. Catholic missionaries continued through the 1960s and peaked in 1968. The largest concentration of U.S. missionaries and the greatest increase over that decade in South America occurred in Brazil, Peru, and Bolivia. The total number of U.S. missionaries in Chile nearly tripled in less than ten years, but this number had fallen almost to previous levels four years later.[1] The Sister Formation Conference, CICOP, the USCMC, the Latin American Bureau, and meetings of major superiors became the vehicles for U.S. Catholic familiarity with progressive bishops from Latin America.[2] Lay missionaries and diocesan clergy who returned from Latin America further bridged the experience of the southern and northern Church. Missionary action in this part of the world provided the focus of a major theological shift. While missionaries had frequently targeted people on the economic and social fringes of a country, change in mission emphasis came with a new perception of the structural reasons for poverty. An "option for the poor" grew to mean a commitment to long-range changes, both ecclesially and in society. In the process, mission methodology in Latin America — with an emphasis on experience, especially that of the poor — provided an alternative communal and collaborative approach to prevailing theological strands. This, in turn, led to more political awareness on the part of missionaries, who found themselves, along with progressive South American religious leaders, more prophetic and analytic. Ultimately, mission to Latin America pointed toward a changed ecclesiological emphasis noted in Vatican II.

The most dramatic stories of U.S. Catholic missionaries arose in Central America, where numbers of missionaries expanded from 392 in 1958 to 936 ten years later.[3] Two case studies of U.S. Catholic missionaries in Panama and Nicaragua will illustrate the intersection of the pastoral needs of Central America with Catholic Action principles, experimentation with new ecclesial models, and the increased political consciousness of missionaries and the subsequent conflicts this created. Once again, the theme of martyrdom surfaced with the deaths of a number of North Americans between 1965 and 1990.

215

Panama

Three persons, despite having grown up in different areas, brought backgrounds in Catholic Action and social justice to bear on their pastoral concerns in Panama and would interact closely during their missionary service. The first, Marcos McGrath, was born in Panama in 1924. His father, John Thomas Mc-Grath, was from Trenton, New Jersey, and his mother, Louise Renauld, was born in Costa Rica to a French family which had emigrated from Louisiana. McGrath's father was captain of a dredging team for the Panama Canal and died as the result of a work-related accident when his son was four years old. Marcos received his early education in Panama and on Long Island, the latter in the Christian Brothers high school. After a year studying economics at the Catholic University of Chile (1939–40), he transferred to Notre Dame. The step proved highly formative; he was introduced to Catholic Action from its well-known proponent, Louis Putz, CSC,[4] and associated with William Cunningham, CSC, a Latin American scholar.

McGrath entered the Congregation of the Holy Cross in late summer, 1942. After further studies at Notre Dame and Holy Cross College, Washington, D.C., he was ordained a priest on 11 June 1949. After graduating *magna cum laude* from the Angelicum in Rome, a Dominican school, he requested an assignment in Latin America. Of his experience in graduate education, McGrath remarked:

> I learned the techniques of research, but more importantly, I developed a method and rigor for theological reflection, which would later be a precious gift for me....I had the opportunity to come in contact with the great thinkers and theological currents of Europe (Congar, De Lubac, Rahner, Guardini, the biblical and liturgical movements), as well as with the philosophical movements (personalism, Christian humanism) which were stirring at the time and which laid the groundwork for the Second Vatican Council.[5]

In 1953 McGrath was sent to teach theology at the Catholic University of Chile, where he earlier had met the Jesuit Gustave Weigel, who was chair of dogma.[6] McGrath worked vigorously to upgrade the theological training offered at the university. While in Chile, at the time a forward-looking Church in Latin America, he was influenced by Bishop Manuel Larraín and Cardinal Raúl Silva Henríquez, who later became known to U.S. Catholics through the CICOP meetings.[7] For eight years, McGrath directed formation groups for students and adults, called the St. George Social Action, as a way of shaping a social conscience among those attending the university and the high school. On weekends he took the young people to meet the poor in their own neighborhoods, to raise an awareness among those whose careers and summer homes precluded any contact or concern for the majority of Chile's population. His Catholic Action background served him well.

On 8 October 1961, he received an episcopal appointment as auxiliary bishop to the archbishop of Panama; while in this position, he became a member of the Vatican II Doctrinal Commission, which prepared the pastoral constitution, "The Church in the Modern World."[8] From 1964 to 1969 he was the bishop of the diocese of Santiago de Veraguas, Panama, and was made archbishop of Panama, assuming full responsibilities on 11 February 1969. In the 1960s, he became president of CICOP, which attempted to introduce the North American Church to the key progressive leaders of the Latin American Church. His strong voice was also heard at various mission conferences in the United States.[9] He assumed a position of leadership among the Latin American Bishops, serving as Second and then First Vice President of CELAM and one of the five speakers at the Medellín, Colombia, conference in 1968. With the exception of three years as vice president, he remained president of the Panamanian Bishops Conference from 1969 to 1994.

Respected as a theologian, McGrath was also an eminently pastoral man who supported lay leadership, the development of a social conscience among all his people, and a presence and action among poor persons and indigenous groups. As archbishop of Panama, he promoted native vocations to priesthood and religious life. He worked to improve dialogue between opposing political parties, no small task in a country which had experienced a military coup in 1968.

Another prominent missionary in Panama was Ellen McDonald, MM, whose Maryknoll community had arrived in 1943 at the request of the Vincentian priests from Germantown, Pennsylvania, working there. Two Maryknoll Sisters directed the Vincentian school in Santiago de Veraguas, when Marcos McGrath became the first bishop of the newly created Santiago de Veraguas Diocese. McDonald, who had been assigned to Panama, went first to the Coady International Institute at St. Francis Xavier University in Antigonish, Nova Scotia, where she took courses and did field work in teaching group economic action to adults. At a meeting in the United States for women religious, McGrath approached Mother Mary Coleman, MM, with a request for McDonald to be his secretary after she took language courses at Cuernavaca. Coleman acquiesced, provided a companion could also attend the center. McDonald worked in Panama for close to twenty-seven years, both as McGrath's secretary and then as a catalyst to effect a shared vision of the Church. She did this through the pastoral and theological formation of women's groups in the 1970s, and in the 1980s through consolidation of an archdiocesan office for lay ministry and the diaconate.[10]

The third person whose path intersected Panama was Leo Mahon (b. 1926). During his formation at Mundelein Seminary outside Chicago, Mahon became captivated with the teachings of Reynold Hillenbrand (1904–79), rector at St. Mary of the Lake Seminary in Mundelein in the 1930s and 1940s and a force for social and liturgical renewal in the Chicago Archdiocese. Hillenbrand was a proponent of Joseph Cardinal Cardijn's method of "observe, judge, act," which formed small groups of workers or students who attempted with their peers to re-Christianize society. With this impetus toward integrating faith and social-justice principles, Mahon had volunteered to work with African Americans and, after his ordination on 3 May 1951, he was sent to the Woodlawn section of Chicago.[11]

At the same time, some Chicago Catholics desired to learn more about the background of the large number of Spanish-speaking people moving into the city. In his first assignment, Mahon was approached by Puerto Ricans who moved into his neighborhood, saying to him, "You have to help us." The young priest knew no Spanish and never intended to work with Hispanics, but he told the group he would help as best he could. He began to meet with people from the University of Chicago to gain insight about the Mexican, Cuban, and Puerto Rican groups in the archdiocese, and he traveled to Puerto Rico to learn more about the situation. Samuel Cardinal Stritch placed him in charge of the Archdiocesan Committee for the Spanish-Speaking, which brought him into conversation with national figures such as Robert Fox of New York and sociologist Joseph Fitzpatrick, SJ.

In collaboration with Mary Xavier O'Donnell, MM, who had worked for a year at CIF in Cuernavaca, Mahon experimented with new approaches to evangelization of Hispanic-speaking groups in Chicago. In 1965, the two of them published a *Catechism of the Family of God,* a plan of religious instruction for Spanish-speaking families, which brought together traditional family values of Hispanic people and the theological language emerging out of the Second Vatican Council. The text, which grew out of successful experimentation in the Woodlawn area, was targeted for lay catechists who had little or no background in teaching or discussion techniques. Their approach emphasized what people already knew and, through affirmation of that experience, drew them to new awareness and understanding of God's Word for their lives.

In the late 1950s, the Chicago Archdiocese was ordaining the largest classes of seminarians in their history. This seemed an ideal time to present the new Chicago cardinal, Albert G. Meyer, with a memorandum about possible missionary action on the part of the archdiocese. Mahon wrote to Meyer that Chicago should be interested in going to Latin America because of the papal call and because of the numbers of Hispanics in the archdiocese with few clergy who understood their language and needs. Furthermore, with so many new priests available, those who wished an overseas mission experience should be allowed to respond to that call. Mahon suggested four options for the cardinal to consider:

1. Have the clergy join something like the St. James Society.

2. Find a Latin American bishop to work with in this endeavor.

3. Start a Chicago mission in Latin America.

4. Form an experimental parish where the Word of God comes before an emphasis on the sacraments and where priests work with the laity, for

there would never be enough priests to meet pastoral needs of the southern hemisphere.

Meyer's first response was negative. Later, however, as he served on a Vatican Council committee, he had the opportunity to meet many of the Latin American bishops, an experience which changed his mind. The Chicago cardinal agreed that some kind of "experiment" would be started.

In the meantime, Leo Mahon met Marcos McGrath at a CICOP planning meeting in Chicago in 1962. The bishop invited him to tour Latin America to determine the location for a possible parish. After visiting Panama, Peru, and Chile, Mahon decided that the critical area would be the barrios surrounding cities like Panama City, where those who sought work set up shanty huts and lived at a subsistence level. An agreement was reached between Archbishop Beckmann of Panama and Cardinal Meyer of the Chicago Archdiocese, and the San Miguelito Project, as it came to be known, began in 1963 outside of Panama City. McGrath initially wanted the Chicago Archdiocese to begin a parochial school and a high school, but Meyer and Mahon both wanted the "experiment." Mahon remained in Panama until 1975, having been made vicar of the San Miguelito area ten years earlier. The Panama and Chicago Archdioceses reached an agreement to end the latter's involvement in the mission in 1984.[12]

The San Miguelito Project was significant for its emphasis on experience and community and for its foundation in the principles of Catholic Action and social justice, serving as one of the first loci of what came to be called liberation theology. At the same time, however, the vortex of antagonistic voices in Panama brought Mahon to trial twice (1968, 1973) for heresy.[13]

Mahon's background in the Cardijn method of "observe, judge, act" and his association with Hillenbrand formed the foundation of his approach to the people in San Miguelito. Working in small groups, "little churches" as he called them, parishioners used this method to interweave faith and action. This approach de-emphasized the traditional "numbers count" for various sacraments as a measure of the success of a mission, and accented the use of Scripture for communal reflection on the people's many social and economic problems and harsh realities.

Teams of priests, Sisters, and laity, who reflected on the meaning of the Word of God for themselves, went among the people and developed within the small groups the same capacity to observe their daily lives, to listen to the Word, and then to take action which reflected the values of the reign of God. The method called for strong communication skills with team members and with the people. Team ministry also required the development of lay leaders, who, in turn, became an important part of the process of evangelization.[14] Such formative communities were part of *liberation theology,* a concept which became known to North American audiences in 1970 through Peruvian Gustavo Gutiérrez's book of that name.

Mahon identified for the CICOP participants in 1964 the foundational principles behind the San Miguelito Project:

- creation of community (family) rather than an organization

- building "church" rather than schools

- formation of *social* consciences

- formation of a saintly *people*, which stressed holiness in the context of the group

- formation of a committed people, rather than an emphasis on imparting information

- sacraments as encounters with Christ, rather than tally marks for the supposed faithfulness of a group

- an emphasis on love rather than on legalism

- formation of Christians in their social milieu, rather than creation of Christian societies

- seeking the truth, rather than claiming it[15]

Mahon's approach represented a new direction away from some of the points highlighted by the Council on Latin America and even by some Latin American bishops. His emphasis marked an antithesis to some of the effects of little pastoral action or of church practice which simply reinforced ecclesial structures.

Mahon also spoke about these pastoral values at Cuernavaca and at the Ponce Institute, Puerto Rico. An attendant at the latter, Emily Schug, CSA, who eventually spent twenty-five years in Nicaragua, wrote to her major superior from Ponce, summarizing some of Mahon's points:

> The conferences this past week were the most thought provoking of all, given by Fr. Leo Mahon....He is what many consider to be a radical, especially concerning the sacraments. (Don't worry, we won't become radicals.) Nevertheless, he still has some valuable ideas. Just to mention one thing — in bringing out the idea of community, he teaches justice, which can be considered something like charity in action. The Liturgy comes from the community, not the community from the Liturgy.[16]

New ways of evangelization meant different patterns of association among the missionaries. The relationships of members with each other and with their people, in the face of a difficult mission task, were characterized by informality and intensity. The highly structured socio-ecclesial roles many had experienced, especially in some eastern U.S. dioceses, gave way before this unceremonious, less-structured, and in many cases, physically threatening, existence. These factors led to the formation of lasting friendships, and in a number of cases, to marriage between those who had worked as missionary Sisters, Brothers, or clergy.

In practice, the San Miguelito experience brought about some intense confrontations, both with the government and with the Church. Mahon remarked after his return to Chicago:

> We felt — to be consistent and integrated — social consciousness ought to come out of the word of God that the people have. Much of the church in Latin America advocates a strong social position but retains old theological positions. But we were concerned with the word of God as being primary, and if putting that philosophy into action meant standing up against the military government, that's what we did. Our expulsion order was signed three times, but the people protested against it. Then the government asked Cardinal Cody to remove us, but he refused. [General Omar] Torrijos, Panama's Chief-of-State, said that if he lost control of the country, it would be because of the priests of San Miguelito.[17]

The influence of San Miguelito extended beyond the area's borders. Ivan Illich sent his students from the Center for Intercultural Formation in Cuernavaca to observe. Other missionaries on their way to serve Latin America made their way to San Miguelito to note Mahon's team approach in an urbanized area. In the 1950s and 1960s, three sources intertwined for what would be called liberation theology: the intellectual and academic resources of some of the universities, the educational approach of Paulo Freire, and the pastoral method of Christian base communities. The San Miguelito Project was the forerunner of the latter in the early 1960s, thus contributing, along with the efforts of the Latin American people, a notable foundation for a new theological emphasis.[18]

Nicaragua

A second case study in Central America incorporates two groups who worked together in several areas of Nicaragua. The Detroit Province of Capuchins arrived in eastern Nicaragua in 1939. The Sisters of St. Agnes, from Fond du Lac, Wisconsin, a community noted for teaching and nursing, departed for Nicaragua six years later. The work of these men and women demonstrates patterns of development in mission thinking and practice as well as some problems that many U.S. Catholic mission groups faced in Central America. Their responses also affected the U.S. government and the U.S. Catholic Church. The work of these two groups from their arrival to the present can be divided roughly into three periods.

Initial mission work for both communities centered on traditional works: responsibility for a mission vicariate, parish work, mission stations for the men, and teaching and clinics for the women. This pattern had changed by the mid-1960s, with women spending more time in pastoral and catechetical work and less in formal schools or other institutions. The men became more involved in building Christian communities and in humanization efforts. Both men and women emphasized lay formation and team ministry. By this time, native women and men had joined the North Americans as members of their respective communities. That, and the later response to the 1979 Sandinista revolution, raised misunderstandings between the members of the congregation in the United States, between the U.S. members and the native members, and among the native members themselves. Finally, from about 1982 to the present, native diocesan priests and Sisters, especially in the Managua area, have returned to the earlier role separation, with priests doing pastoral work and Sisters teaching. A closer look at this pattern will help trace the development of the Agnesian and Capuchin missions in Central America and its effects on the U.S. Catholic Church.

During the Spanish Civil War in 1936–39, many clergy were murdered and seminaries were closed. Spanish clergy in Nicaragua were either killed or had to flee the country. The Propaganda Fide office in Rome asked the Detroit Province of the Order of Friars Minor Capuchins to send some of their members to the Bluefields Vicariate in eastern Nicaragua in 1939.[19] This area was located along the Atlantic coast and comprised about half the country. Honduras bordered to the north across the Rio Coco. The vicariate was on the opposite side of the country from the capital, Managua, and the Somoza government frequently did not pay much attention to the needs of the people in the Bluefields area, especially those outside of the port cities. Some parts of Puerto Cabezas held enclaves of Americans who worked for the United Fruit Company and other U.S. businesses, but most of the diocese consisted of indigenous people, Chinese, Creoles, Hispanics, or people from the Caribbean islands and from Africa.

Four Capuchin priests were sent to the new mission, supported partially by their Detroit Province and partially from monies received through the Seraphic Mass Association.[20] This order made a commitment to send two of their men annually to Nicaragua. In 1943, Matthew Niedhammer (1901–70) was appointed vicar apostolic of Bluefields and assumed formal possession of his cathedral on 21 September 1943.[21] A seminary for the Bluefields Vicariate opened in 1953, with Salvador Schlaefer as its first rector. Schlaefer would succeed Niedhammer as bishop of Bluefields on the latter's death in 1970.

Niedhammer had been educated by the Sisters of St. Agnes at Our Lady Queen of Angels School in Manhattan. When Mother Angeline Kamp, CSA, who had been principal of his grade school, became the major superior of the Agnesian Sisters, the Capuchin invited that congregation to serve in the Bluefields Vicariate. The first invitation to the Sisters was issued in 1941. Several requests later, after World War II, four Sisters chosen from among ninety-six volunteers embarked for the Central American mission in September 1945.[22] Nurse and dietician Mary Agnes Dickof (1895–1961) from Marshfield, Wisconsin, teacher and organist Francis Borgia Dreiling (b. 1907) from Victoria, Kansas, German-born teacher and counselor Pauletta Scheck (1895–1992), and homemaker Agnes Rita Fisette (b. 1916) from Marquette, Michigan, stopped in

New Orleans for ten days on their way to their mission to learn about tropical diseases under the tutelage of the Daughters of Charity.

The Agnesians first staffed a school, including kindergarten through sixth grade, for children of mixed ethnic population in the town of Waspam. Mary Agnes Dickof opened a clinic on the day of their arrival when the Sisters found people gathered in large numbers on the steps of their convent. Word of this service traveled among the area residents:

> When people heard that a Mrs. Doctor, as I was called in the beginning, was in Waspam, they came for care, sometimes travelling days on the river with their sick to reach the clinic.... All my experience in hospital work in the States seemed to have left me void; I never saw humanity in such a miserable state as I witnessed it now. It was a revelation of an abject poverty in its worst form. I had no supply of medicine to speak of — a little supply of quinine, a small bottle of atabrine, a little of this and a little of that was nothing to handle this crowd of festering humanity until further supplies came in from friends at home.[23]

On one occasion, a small boy who had swallowed kerosene was brought to Dickof for treatment. She "prayed first to the Divine Physician, then called on her departed mother, and opened the Merck Manual to find a remedy for the case at hand. Yes, MILK was given which saved the boy's life."[24]

In 1967, the Sisters inaugurated a maternity center, Clínica Santa Inés, to train midwives and to develop health leaders for the Miskito communities along the Rio Coco.[25] Not only did this program multiply the medical efforts of the Sisters, it provided another area for lay leadership. The Sisters described the women's program at Waspam:

> Each Thursday morning 40–50 women from neighboring villages come for a morning of special attention just for them. Those who are expecting [babies] receive physical and laboratory exams. All receive classes and participate in animated discussions. The local midwives review their knowledge and skills. All receive sewing classes and have a little lunch of fruit and milk before returning to their homes. We hope to be able to help them appreciate more their dignity as women and prepare them to be more responsible wives and mothers.[26]

Niedhammer's emphasis on education led to the arrival of other groups to teach in the area, including the Maryknoll Sisters, who had arrived in Siuna in 1944, some Managuan Sisters, and the Christian Brothers. The Agnesian schools expanded to include the upper grades and a high school on the eastern coast. They also staffed a grade and high school in Managua, along with the Christian Brothers.

While engaged in teaching, the Sisters also joined with the Capuchins to provide medical, catechetical, and pastoral visits to the Miskito Indian communities. The Sisters and Capuchins visited the surrounding barrios of Managua and the people in the leprosaria, and celebrated the Sunday Eucharist with those who lived around the city dump. The Sisters' work included the formation of native women; the first candidates went to Fond du Lac, Wisconsin. After the formal establishment of a house for this purpose in Nicaragua in 1962, they held the profession of the first novices there in 1967.

By 1960, President John F. Kennedy's Alliance for Progress and Catholic Relief Services had started to provide surplus U.S. food commodities for the people of Nicaragua. The Capuchin houses began to act as distribution centers to the people of their vicariate. After a year or two, the missionaries began to reconsider the value of this practice. For one thing, they noticed that such programs were creating a dependent and passive people, who were abandoning their own farms. Florian Ruskamp, OFM (b. 1918), pastor at Puerto Cabezas, wrote to the Latin American Bureau about the situation:

> We are trying to do something about our social problems. Yes, we are studying Fr. Considine's wonderful book on the missionary's role in this matter. In March of next year all the missioners will get together and discuss the same theme. . . .
>
> But I would like to know if Fr. Considine could influence the Alliance in Washington to start something down here soon. Right now the Catholic Relief Services are given [sic] us food. But we would much rather have a work program, rather than a dole system.[27]

The Sisters who arrived in Nicaragua in the 1960s received their mission formation at the language institute at the Catholic University of Ponce, Puerto Rico, and at the Center for Intercultural Formation at Cuernavaca, Mexico. For those Agnesians and Capuchins who had been in the country for some time, Ruskamp provided talks on Scripture and spirituality and an annual Bible Week for religious in the area. During the 1960s, the Capuchins and the Agnesians were implementing the liturgical changes for people in the diocese. Capuchin Berard (Philip) Casper worked with the Moravian missionaries in the vicinity to translate the Bible into the Miskito language.

Periodically, questions arose among the Sisters about the locus of their mission efforts. The congregation had Sisters in Ecuador (1963–72) and in Honduras (1968–69), as well as in Nicaragua. The delegates to the 1965–66 Agnesian General Chapter in the United States heard about the changing perceptions of their Sisters in South America. Their "Chronicles" for that year indicated that "the Sisters working at Cardinal Spellman School (Quito, Ecuador) felt that teaching English at this school was not satisfying their deep-down desires of being out in the barrios working with the destitute who needed them so desperately."[28] Discussion about their mission focus carried into the next years, and some Agnesians argued for teaching the wealthier classes. They noted that some of their students did come from poorer classes and that the "observe, judge, act" method of Cardinal Cardijn was used in the high school in Managua. Further, a house in a more congenial climate and with some amenities could provide missionaries respite from inclement weather or difficult living conditions.[29] Emily Schug, who served in Quito at the time, summarized for her U.S. superior the conversations with missionaries who directed schools for the affluent. These directors thought

> that education work is a must with the upperclass because they are to be the leaders, etc. They gave fabulous examples of how their graduates spend at least a year working for the less fortunate of their countrymen. Another is working under a situation that I think is much more profitable. They gave their school over to a group of laymen but work in connection with them. It is more difficult — there is less chance of Americanizing the natives.

She then added:

> I'm wondering if being a [school] director gives an opportunity of "witnessing Christ." I'm sure one who actually teaches the children can help form them. One who just handles money is usually not the favorite of the people anyway, much less when she is a "rich American." Last night I talked to one who was several years in Nicaragua. Her idea is that where there is no opportunity for the natives to go to school we should supply it — like in poor towns, in Siuna, Puerto Cabezas, etc. — but in large cities, no. Where possible, work with the natives. The natives resent being told what to do by Americans. Besides being resented as directors they don't know the organizational systems of other countries.[30]

But almost from the beginning of their work in Managua, the Sisters taught not only the well-to-do but the poor; this produced a collision of attitudes with their clientele at Colegio Asunción Managua, a school directed by the Asunción Sisters:

> In the morning we taught the academy girls but in a more natural and acceptable situation, in a specific classroom. Good grief! Each girl recites aloud individually. We tried to introduce the American method...but to no avail, although the girls seemed to like it better. They responded quite agreeably. These students, however, resented the fact that we also taught the poor children. It is certainly a traditional aristocratic nation which has a very deplorable disadvantage in not educating all, and of course, we did not approve. The same class distinction prevailed in chapel, wearing different veil and dress and uniforms....[31]

By the mid-1960s, the Sisters were spiritual guides for the Legion of Mary, Bible circles, and the Luisa de Marillac, groups of women who attended to the needs of poor persons. Trained by Maryknoll women, the Agnesians participated in women's renewal groups called *cursillos*. They implemented the Cardijn method of "observe, judge, act," as part of their Bible-circle evenings and as part of the classes given to the wealthy in the school in Managua.

Bible instruction for those on the eastern coast was provided by a Nicaraguan Scripture scholar, Uriel Molina, OFM. The Sisters described these meetings in 1966:

> [Molina's] classes are worth a million dollars.... A group of about twenty-five — mostly men — maybe three or five women, gather in a humble dirt-floor home, one wall all plastered with magazine advertisements of all kinds — soap, beer, whiskey, perfume, etc., — all intermingled with pictures of favorite saints. The crowd is motley; some come without shoes but with Bible under their arms. The purchasing of the Bible is edifying. It costs only twenty *cordobas,* but this is almost equivalent to two days' salary, so you can see their financial difficulties.[32]

The Sisters and priests who worked among the Rio Coco people set about to "form a true Christian community, aiming to make individuals aware of their own personal worth and the worth of their neighbor," and in Puerto Cabezas, the missionaries focused on sharing "with the poor people things that will make them feel more a part of the people of God in bringing to them some of the learning of which they have been deprived."[33] But it was also clear in the process that, while the missionaries had come with enthusiasm to "bring Christianity," they were also edified by the simple, struggling faith of the people.

In the late 1960s, the Capuchins began work in remote rural areas. These pastors kept in touch with each other through daily talk-ins on their ham radios and enhanced this communication network through twice-yearly meetings for input, reflection, and recreation. During these gatherings, the friars created a document on the Jewish and Christian Scriptures written in Spanish understandable to the farmers. The men wrote a history of the Nicaraguan Church in the form of a novel and opened the story for dialogue with the people's questions. In the 1970s, to continue their efforts to put the Bible into the hands of lay persons, the Capuchins produced a Bible calendar, which became so popular it was used in Costa Rica, Panama, and Honduras. It was the only calendar printed in all of Nicaragua during the year after the Sandinista takeover.

The Capuchins revised for their rural population the program which Leo Mahon had developed in more urban San Miguelito for the formation of *delegados* of the Word. By the time of the Sandinista revolution in 1979, there were 2,500 *delegados,* who had been formed in social consciousness, leadership training, and Scripture, which had been infused into their daily life.

The Agnesians and Capuchins witnessed the growth of self-confidence and group cohesion among indigenous groups by the early 1970s:

> The Miskito people themselves have organized into an Alliance for the progress of the Miskitos and Sumos. The thrill for us is that now they themselves are beginning to realize that they can help themselves and that they have among their own many prepared leaders. Their initial efforts have been simple and praiseworthy. If only they don't become intimidated

Reassessing American Involvement in Latin America: This 1986 photo shows Agnesian Sisters Maureen Courtney, Jean Steffes, and Rhea Emmer in Rosita, Nicaragua, in a light moment doing their laundry, during a period when rapid social change and revolution caused many American missioners in Latin America to reassess what shape their involvement should take. (Courtesy, Sisters of St. Agnes Archives)

by the opposition they are receiving. Their making themselves seen and heard at election time is giving rise to them and all of us connected with them being suspected of communist activities. They are so far from being ready to take care of themselves but have at least ventured out to take their first steps alone.[34]

This community development would not necessarily show up on the annual statistical report to Propaganda Fide which listed the number of baptisms, communions, and confirmations taking place in the missions.

Reassessment of the locus and meaning of mission had been occurring continuously for both the Capuchins and the Agnesians throughout the 1960s and into the 1970s, hastened by the changes suggested by the Vatican Council and by several internal and external tensions among community members. One source of external stress was earthquakes, one in 1968 and one still more devastating in Managua in 1972, which destroyed the buildings where the two communities worked. The destruction helped to hurry along the evaluation process.

Since their beginnings in Nicaragua, the Sisters had constantly been involved in many other activities expanding on their original work. The Sisters had noted in 1977–78 that much of their work in the towns and areas where they ministered actually took place outside of the formal, traditional structures of education. Bible studies, basic courses in Christian family life, catechetics, human development skills — including midwifery, agriculture, homemaking, parish cooperatives, and youth work — and formation of Christian communities were becoming priorities. Further, teamwork, with an emphasis on a presence among the people, especially in the Managua barrio,[35] echoed the approach which the Maryknoll Sisters had taken in China in the 1930s and 1940s.

Other congregations of women religious in Latin America were experiencing the same kind of close involvement with the people while moving away from institutions. From Peru in 1971, the St. James Society superior wrote to the superior of the Sisters of St. Joseph in Brighton, Massachusetts:

> We hope also to institute another apostolate that we have been anxious to try — apartment living as a presence in one of the neighborhoods that has little contact with the parish complex. As you remember the parish is quite heterogeneous. More and more the local church is re-examining the approaches to the preaching of the gospel and we are having second thoughts about the huge complexes that we have built....[36]

A political earthquake occurred on 19 July 1979, when the revolutionary Sandinistas overthrew the fifty-year reign of the Somoza family. The Agnesian chronicles noted:

> With the long years of oppression and deprivation, it was not surprising that the revolution finally broke out in full force this past year. Fighting increased steadily from day to day in June, particularly in Managua and the surrounding area. The bombing and shooting continued day and night. Our Sisters reported shortages of food and the influx of many people coming to the convent for safety. At one point Sister Bertha Bumann said that she had placed a loaf of bread before the tabernacle, after which food began to trickle in so that they could take care of all.[37]

Several younger U.S. Capuchins expressed some euphoria over the turn of events, while the older men remained skeptical. In their early years in Nicaragua, life under the Somoza family had been relatively benign. The first group of Agnesians and Capuchins had noted that the family provided various perquisites for their work. By the mid-1970s, however, the Capuchins wrote to the Somozas to inform them of the "disappearance" of their parishioners. Hundreds of copies of the letter were also circulated by students at bus stops. While the people congratulated the friars for drawing attention to their plight, some of the friars found that the military were present thereafter in the churches on Sunday, taking notes on all that was said.

Tensions also arose between the native and the U.S. Sisters and between all the Agnesians in Nicaragua and the Sisters at their motherhouse. Agnesian

Maureen Courtney (1944–90), who had arrived in Nicaragua in January 1978, expressed some of her discomfort in a letter to her general superior:

> Sometimes I feel so "pulled" to one side or the other, that I begin wondering if it's possible to remain open to both. I think there's a real tendency in human nature to want to categorize and we'd all be "happy" if we could get each other into little boxes with labels on them. . . . I must admit it, too, it was very hard for me at times at the motherhouse to see how much polarization has taken place regarding Nicaragua . . . that each of us must be either 100 percent Sandinista or 100 percent anti-Sandinista. The reality is so much more complex. And I believe we must be faithful — not to one political group or the other, but to the gospel, and that gospel can lead us to see good and bad in both extremes.[38]

In November 1979, the Agnesians gathered for a week to respond to the unsettling experiences of the revolution. The theme of their meeting was "Contemplation of God's Word through Our Lives as Women Religious." The women reflected on four questions: What have I experienced personally with the revolution? Do I think God was in all of this? What have my experiences done to me? How have I dealt with what it has done to me inside? At the end of their assembly, though they still had differences of opinion, they constructed a credo which expressed their commonly held values: the special presence of God, especially among those in need of liberation, the need for personal conversion of the missionary, prayer and contemplation as essential aspects of mission, and a participation in "the rising of a new dawn for the Nicaraguan woman." With respect to the revolution itself, the document stated: "We Believe: That it is the moment for giving our support to the historical process that is in the making, and that the christian principles that are present will triumph in the revolutionary process."[39]

The case studies of missionaries in Panama and Nicaragua illustrate the increased use of social-action principles as a pastoral response to the needs of people and the experimentation with a new ecclesial model in order to invigorate Catholic life and to make Catholicism responsive to people in their ordinary lives. These examples also indicate that U.S. Catholics carried with them presuppositions about human rights, justice, and respect for the dignity of all, values which ultimately entailed a reassessment of their relationship with their home government and the government of the country where they served.

To what extent should the missionaries have involved themselves in local politics? The answer depended in part on how the secular and sacred realms meshed and included the reality that missionaries were political outsiders, not nationals. Some, like the Capuchins, protested the civil and human rights violations they witnessed through letters to government officials. Other missionaries, seeing the complexity of the political situation, encouraged shared Bible study and reflection, letting the people work out their own political destinies. The

U.S. Bishops produced a document in 1974 in support of human rights in Chile and Brazil.[40]

Missionaries and the CIA, 1974–76

By the mid-1970s, younger "social activist" missionaries had become unsympathetic to the earlier rhetoric of anticommunism and were drawing attention to the results of U.S. government intervention in their countries, especially by the Central Intelligence Agency. Though other areas experienced intervention, South America drew the most immediate public attention to U.S. activities. President Gerald Ford was quoted in 1974 as saying, "It is a recognized fact that historically, as well as presently, such actions are taken in the best interests of the countries involved."[41] It was alleged that the CIA had used U.S. missionaries to gain access to information about people and "subversive" movements. Further, missionaries themselves noted that CIA intervention had caused fear, oppression, hatred, and, in some cases, death, among their people.

Among the missionaries who reportedly had obtained substantial remuneration from the CIA was Belgian Roger Vekemans, SJ, who worked at the Centro Bellarmino in Santiago, Chile; he was an occasional speaker at conferences sponsored by mission groups in the United States, as well as a colleague of Miguel D'Escoto, MM. Vekemans had supposedly used the money to support anticommunist labor unions, as well as the presidential campaign of Eduardo Frei. In the anticommunist climate of the early 1960s, some missionaries had received CIA aid to run radio stations, which were intended to increase literacy but which were also used to broadcast anticommunist propaganda.

In October 1974, chief officers of major U.S. national Protestant mission agencies met in New York with directors of U.S. Catholic mission-sending groups to protest President Ford's position and the CIA interventions. Their protest was published in the *Congressional Record,* within the statement of Representative Robert Drinan, though their remarks received little public attention at the time.[42] The issue came to the fore with the publication the following year of *Inside the Company: CIA Diary* by Philip Agee, a CIA agent in Latin America, and John D. Mark and Victor Marchetti's controversial *The CIA and the Cult of Intelligence.*[43] The CIA was linked in particular to the Association for International Development, which provided food and funding to various groups through established agencies in the countries it served. Catholic Relief Services, which had eighty-seven staff members around the world in 1974, was a major distributor of surplus foodstuffs and other assistance from various sources. Catholic and Protestant mission agencies often sought such aid for the projects they were developing, and it was alleged that the process of procuring supplies had unwittingly provided information to the CIA. Other organizations influenced by the CIA, the authors claimed, were the International Catholic Student and Catholic Action groups.

The U.S. Catholic Mission Council published press releases on the CIA and missionaries and also sent letters to William Colby, director of the CIA. On 29 July 1975, Donald Ehr, SVD, chairman of the Conference of Major Superiors of Men's Mission Committee of the U.S. Catholic Mission Council, wrote to Colby:

> It is a widely held belief, both among indigenous church personnel in the Third World and among many U.S. missionaries, that the CIA has, over a long period of time and in many countries, routinely sought the cooperation of missionaries in tasks that are wholly inconsistent with the evangelizing and pastoral mission of the church.
>
> It appears that in some instances the cooperation was sought — and sometimes regrettably granted — with full knowledge that the CIA was involved. In the majority of cases, however, the source of the request was evidently less overt, appearing to come simply from someone attached to a local U.S. embassy or consulate....
>
> We wish to register with you our deep shame and disappointment that such actions could have taken place and we urge ... that you take whatever action is necessary to ensure that never again will the Central Intelligence Agency seek to enlist the support or cooperation of religious missionaries or church personnel for any of its activities.[44]

Colby later told Senator Mark Hatfield of Oregon that the CIA had used missionaries in the past for political and intelligence-gathering reasons and would continue to do so.[45] Hatfield pushed for federal legislation (S.R. 2784) to prohibit the CIA or other U.S. government agencies from employing missionaries for the purpose of collecting intelligence. In the same month when H. R. Haldeman, Robert C. Mardian, John Mitchell, and John Ehrlichman were being convicted for their part in Watergate, a Rockefeller Commission was set up to investigate the practices of the CIA in general and its history of employing missionaries as conduits for information. For American citizens, the issue was the separation of church and state, because it appeared that the CIA was funding religious groups. For missionaries, the issue was the effect of the CIA's action on their mission and on their credibility as missionaries.

In May 1976, the new director of the CIA, George Bush, issued a revised regulation affecting the CIA and missionaries:

> In light of the special constitutional concern with church-state relationships, CIA shall establish no secret, paid or unpaid contractual relationship with any American clergyman or missionary. This restriction applies to any person whether or not ordained, who is sent out by a mission or church organization to preach, teach, heal, or proselytize. In addition, American church groups will not be funded nor used as funding cutouts for CIA purposes. The CIA will, however, continue to welcome information volunteered by American clergymen or missionaries. If, in the

determination of a senior Agency official, such individuals might possess important foreign intelligence information, the Agency might initiate contact so as to afford an opportunity for channeling this information to the Government. Such initiation, however, shall not be taken abroad.[46]

Senator Hatfield withdrew his legislation.[47] As a result of the Rockefeller Commission investigation, President Ford in February 1976 declared substantial changes in U.S. agencies which gathered intelligence, including the establishment of an independent "oversight board." But the federal government, especially the FBI and the CIA, remained interested in the work of missionaries, particularly because they frequently worked with groups of poor or indigenous persons and were in touch with people the government considered destabilizing to U.S. interests abroad. The issue was not dead by any means. Federal government interference with missionaries arose again as an issue in 1980,[48] and in 1996 the CIA was still using a loophole in its regulations to obtain information from missionaries.[49]

Problems of Missionaries at Home and Abroad

Specific needs that missionaries had on their return to the United States began to be identified by 1959. Some sought theological renewal, especially during and after the Second Vatican Council. Others were traumatized by the violence they had experienced, either in their person or among their people. A number of missionaries became more vocal about the adverse effects of global companies and of U.S. intervention; some had returned from their mission assignments because they were expelled by governments. Many felt uncomfortable in an American culture they no longer recognized.

At its annual meeting in 1958, the Mission Secretariat featured a panel on the problems of returned missionaries and, three years later, Maryknoll organized its first seminar for returned missionaries with the idea of updating them in theology.[50] Beginning in 1968, Philip Hoelle, SM, started a six-week summer institute at the University of Dayton for missionaries from religious congregations. While providing courses on renewal theology and mission, the institute also enabled participants to bond as a community and to begin to rethink what it meant to be a missionary in the post–Vatican II Church. This program continued over several years. Less formal assessments of the needs of returned missionaries also took place. For the six years he directed the World Mission Program at the Catholic Theological Union, Chicago, Lawrence Nemer, SVD, interviewed each returned missionary and summarized that information for faculty members so they could understand the background and needs of these men and women.[51]

In 1974, the year the Synod of Bishops took evangelization as its topic,[52] the U.S. Catholic Mission Council, in collaboration with other groups, provided a seminar in Boston for returned missioners, "Evangelizing the Evangelizers," and continued these workshops over the next few years. The USCMC conducted a survey of the needs of returned missionaries in 1980 and categorized the problems they experienced as cultural, emotional, and ministerial. Missionaries were dismayed at the amount of waste and affluence in American culture compared with the poverty from which many had come. They felt alienated from an American culture they did not know. Being uprooted from the people they had grown to love, from friends and significant work, the missionaries felt lonely and fearful that they did not "fit in" with life in the United States. Many had witnessed the violent deaths of their parishioners, had themselves been attacked, and had seen so much suffering that the contrast between what they had known and what they saw in the United States left them discomfited, guilty, and rootless. Some missionaries needed to deal with alcoholism or other destructive responses to life in the missions, or had to come to terms with the discrepancies between their dreams and the reality.[53]

In addition to the adjustment problems, however, missionaries also possessed a wealth of experience, a depth of understanding about the global Church, and particular knowledge about local politics and the local church in other countries. Communication between missionaries abroad and their base constituencies in the United States frequently pointed out the problems working in Third World countries. One group which drew attention to these issues met in Archbishop Helder Camara's diocese of Recife, Brazil, in September 1968. They drafted a letter to protest U.S. foreign policy, American paternalism, and American corporations. These corporations kept the best of the dividends for themselves while inhabitants who worked for them often did not have the basic necessities of life. Acerbically, these missionaries wrote:

> Progress in the Northeast of Brazil has bejeweled the fingers and perfumed the armpits of a small number of people already bejeweled and perfumed. The wealth of one small class has been technically modernized and the "royal" position more firmly entrenched. But for the majority of the people, mostly peasants and industrial workers, "progress" is associated with better living conditions for all.... For the majority of the people, "progress" is a spectator sport. Their participation in economic growth is to look on as "progress" parades by, clear their throats and spit on the newly paved parade routes. Underneath the growing mounds of spittle lies the North American people. For the spittle of anti-Americanism is the gratitude which the basic policy of United States economic assistance, United States aid, United States dollars has earned for the American people.[54]

Three months later, two of the signers, Darrell Rupiper, OMI, from Carroll, Iowa, and Peter Grams of St. Louis, along with two of their parishioners were imprisoned in Recife.

A similar protest against the policy that made other countries dependent on the United States was carried out by William T. Wood, SJ, who appeared before the Trust Committee of the United Nations in the 1970s and early 1980s to protest, along with Lutherans, the Baptists, the United Church of Christ, and various Catholic religious congregations, the "dole" system perpetrated after World War II. The United States, through the United Nations, had set up the system of dependency that, as a consequence, depreciated the cultures of these areas.[55]

Another consequence of the U.S. government's involvement in other countries was that some of the indigenous people sought asylum, especially in the United States. Returned missionaries provided the point of contact for oppressed or hunted people to seek asylum and to find U.S. families and organizations who could provide for their needs on arrival in the United States. The mission experience in Mexico and Central America also helped lay the groundwork for the Sanctuary Movement of the 1980s. Anthony Bellagamba from the United States Catholic Mission Council was one of the signers of the open letter affirming the Sanctuary Movement in June 1985.[56]

Renewal of Martyr Theme

Language acquisition and acculturation created tensions, as expected, for missionaries, but these stresses were compounded during periods of revolution or civil war, as seen in China and Latin America. One example was the "disappearance" of many Nicaraguans, especially the indigenous groups and *campesinos* in opposition to the government. Personal harm was a possibility for missionaries as it was for the people they served.[57]

Among the innumerable stories is the story of Patricia Hayes, CSA, a nurse who went to Nicaragua in 1983, arriving during a time of hostilities between the Sandinistas and the Contras. On a mission trip during Holy Week, Hayes, Sisters Jomarie Zielke, CSA, and Raymond Grieble, CSA, Father Wendelin Schaefer, and Deacon Isidoro Alvarado were caught in an early-morning ambush led by the Contras. Bombing, mortar fire, and gunfire continued for about three hours. The Sisters took refuge on the floor of their elevated, wooden house until the fighting stopped. After the Contras had fled, when they had received permission, Hayes and Zielke, who was also a nurse, began attending the wounded Sandinista soldiers. Patricia Hayes examined an injured sixteen-year-old soldier who had been shot in the stomach. The treatment required medication, intravenous fluids, and, ultimately, a surgical procedure — none of which she was equipped to administer. She covered the protruding intestines with sterile gauze and gave him aspirin to control the pain. She offered sips of water, even though that was inadvisable due to the nature of his wounds. She and her companions were afraid that the Sandinistas would shoot them in their frustration, fear, and rage with the U.S.-sponsored Contra war and its toll on their comrades — but they did not. When Sandinista reinforcements arrived, the North Americans were loaded, with their patients, onto the back of pickup trucks and evacuated to the *Tronquera*. The injured soldier was ultimately transported to the hospital in Puerto Cabezas. Patricia worked at the hospital and was able to visit him daily until his discharge.[58]

Between 1959 and 1990, eleven Catholic missionaries sent from the United States were killed, all of them, with a few exceptions, in Central America.[59] The list included a lay woman (Jean Donovan, El Salvador, 1980), a male religious (James Miller, FSC, Guatemala, 1982), women religious (Maura Clarke, MM, Ita Ford, MM, Dorothy Kazel, OSU, El Salvador, 1980; Maureen Courtney, CSA, Nicaragua, 1990), and clergy (William C. Kruegler, MM, Bolivia, 1962; Raymond Herman, Bolivia, 1975; Conventual Franciscan Casmir Cypher, Honduras, 1975; William H. Wood, MM, Guatemala, 1976; Stanley Rother, Guatemala, 1981).

The deaths that received the most publicity and which galvanized many people in the United States were those of the four women murdered in El Salvador. Vigils in their honor were held all around the United States.[60] As the circumstances of their death came to light, U.S. groups, many of them ecumenical, called for an investigation and arrest of those responsible.

The Agnesian Sisters also experienced the death of one of their missionaries, Maureen Courtney. Her days were spent in myriad ordinary activities in addition to her main work in catechetics, community development, and leadership training. Her death, and the death of one of their native Sisters, was described by Emily Schug, with whom she lived:

> Throughout her life Maureen's outstanding quality was her concern for others. She always seemed to know what their needs were and how to respond, however demanding that would be on her time and energy. She gave every ounce of strength even when it was almost non-existent. Examples could be multiplied in just about every imaginable field — lugging bolts of material for the sewing cooperatives; tramping through knee-deep mud to put boards or stone or "whatever" under the tires to get out of the mudholes and be able to continue her trip of merciful, loving service; studying Miskito in her room when everybody thought she was getting a much needed rest.... These are just some of the examples that I personally witnessed in my few years of living with Sister Maureen.
>
> Her last act of charity was for me. I was alone at Rosita for New Year's Day. She wanted me to have the company of my Sisters for at least part of the feast day. That is why she left Siuna in the evening and didn't want to wait until morning.... The Sisters were on retreat and were returning home, in caravan with Bishops Paul Schmitz and Schlaefer. They were to stay overnight in Siuna and return 2 January to the mission. Maureen wanted to continue to drive to Rosita and remain there overnight with me.... She managed to get the permission of the police who ordinarily didn't allow people to travel outside the towns at night. When the bishops

saw that she was determined, Bishop Paul offered to accompany them, not wanting the women to be traveling alone.

Everybody knows what happened about an hour later, around 6:30 p.m. January 1, 1990. An ambush violently and instantly took the beautiful life of Maureen Courtney who was completing 25 years as a religious. Bishop Paul, seated next to Maureen, had his arm almost severed from his body, probably from raising it to protect himself from the rocket that killed Maureen. The two Sisters in the back seat were wondering how to protect themselves from the bullets. Teresa de Jesus, 25 years old, and just one year professed, fell over Francisca Maria, seemingly to protect her. Moments later Francisca, herself riddled with shrapnel, realized that her dearest friend was dead. Bishop Paul commended them to the Lord.[61]

When newspapers and magazines had earlier depicted U.S. missionary killings in China and Korea, they did so by painting the men, hero-martyrs, as solitary figures against the backdrop of "paganism." Their deaths were seen as a *modern* assurance of the validity of the gospel message. The portrayal of murders of later U.S. missionaries in Central and South America highlighted their relationship with a people, their inextricable ties to a community. Mission meant being *with* a people even to the point of death, as had been true of Jesus, the protomartyr. Harold Rigney's imprisonment in China had raised sentiments that affirmed the righteousness of Western values and that resulted in the employment of U.S. influence to secure his release. The deaths of missionaries in Latin America, however, raised skepticism about the purity of U.S. foreign policy. In both periods, the imaginative vehicle used to connect an oppressed people with the lives of missionaries was the theme of suffering; in Latin America, the suffering of the masses was related to the suffering of a lesser number of U.S. mission martyrs.

Experience Leads to Reevaluation

Simultaneous evaluation of mission experience by various groups began to occur in the early 1960s. Reflection on their previous experience led to new emphases in their understanding of mission and to tension created by differences in ecclesiology as well as in mission. The Grail was one of the first lay mission-sending organizations to begin this assessment. By 1960, the Grail had trained thirty-five women from the United States who were working with teams from Europe and from local areas in Africa, Vietnam, Indonesia, Singapore, and Brazil.[62] After almost twenty years of lay formation, Grail leaders had begun to question whether *mission,* as the term was understood at the time, had value. They suggested that *international cooperation* might be a more fitting term to express the reality of how their members were involved around the world.[63] At their annual meeting in 1965, the women's group consciously changed their sustaining theological image from Mystical Body to communion, which "conveyed a concept of unity which was interpersonal rather than ideological or organizational."[64] In so doing, they were moving decidedly from what had become a separate Catholic culture.

A second group where reassessment was taking place was the Mission Secretariat. The Secretariat's original purpose was to emphasize missionary initiative and mutual assistance to solve common problems. Toward the end of the 1960s, the Secretariat, which had grown in numbers over the years, felt a need for more effective communication between mission-sending and mission-funding organizations. Some rethinking on this matter had been taking place at the Mission Secretariat and elsewhere as early as 1962.[65]

The successful national conferences of the Mission Secretariat included lay missionaries and bishops, as well as men and women religious. Though the outer appearance of the conferences tended to be "high church" with a strong physical presence of bishops and clergy, the workshops provided a wealth of information and sharing among all missionaries and mission executives. At the 1963 Mission Secretariat conference, for example, Marcos McGrath and Joseph Fitzpatrick were among those who addressed more than a thousand participants.[66] But a still more inclusive national organization was sought.

A national mission council had been encouraged by Pope Paul VI's *Ecclesiae Sanctae* (no. 11) and the Vatican II document *Ad Gentes* (no. 38). In September 1967, the National Council of Catholic Bishops formed their first Committee on Missions and encouraged superiors of women's and men's religious congregations to do likewise. In 1968, the Mission Secretariat was disbanded by the bishops in favor of a more comprehensive agency. By 1969, a new national mission organization emerged, the United States Catholic Mission Council, which hosted its first general assembly in November of that year. In June 1970 a second assembly was held at Maryknoll; it was decided that Washington, D.C., should be the location for the USCMC office. Joseph Connors, SVD, was elected the executive secretary, and on 1 September 1970 the USCMC office opened.[67] One of its first acts was to publish a document, "The Whole Missionary Church," which summarized Vatican II teaching on mission and urged all U.S. Catholics to appropriate a mission perspective. The essential missionary nature of the Church, an understanding expressed as early as 1957 by members of the Grail, now found national expression and exposure.[68]

The council was composed of representatives of mission committees of the bishops, the men's and women's religious congregations, lay mission organizations, and the mission-funding agencies. But the question of self-identity and purpose and the nature of the council's authority initially kept the group from having influence as a national entity. Problems left over from the Mission Secretariat — competing special interests and the duplication of mission efforts — remained. The demise of the Catholic Students Mission Crusade in 1972, an organization which for over fifty years had involved thousands of young people in mission education, seemed to underscore the lack of national Catholic interest in missions and the need for new leadership.

First, for a year under Brother Thomas More Page, CFX, in 1973, and then under the directorship of Anthony Bellagamba, IMC, a more team-centered approach and ecumenical outreach provided the council greater visibility and cohesiveness of purpose. The council published an annual *Mission Handbook*, which provided statistics on the numbers of U.S. Catholic personnel in overseas missions and sponsored a study of the understanding of mission among seminarians and seminary professors. Channels of communication among mission groups continued to be strengthened. Ann Gormly, SND, Joseph Nangle, OFM, and Anthony Bellagamba traveled throughout the country providing talks and programs to reanimate mission and global awareness among U.S. Catholics.

In 1976, the USCMC cosponsored a meeting which transformed International Liaison, a New Jersey–based organization, into a national clearinghouse for lay mission groups. That same year the USCMC provided a panel on mission and global awareness at the Eucharistic Congress and prepared a paper on global aspects of mission and "reverse mission." The USCMC worked in collaboration with those who began to plan for the "*Convivencia,* Convergence, Solidarity" meetings. In 1978 topics for national planning included cross-cultural ministry and mission from the Third World to the United States. A liaison office was established at the United Nations, staffed by Lawrence Zorza, IMC, a member of the Office of the Permanent Observer of the Holy See. This development sought to bring missionary concerns to the United Nations and to make available appropriate U.N. resources to missionaries. In 1979, efforts were made to have mission congregations with overseas experience interact with those which targeted domestic issues.

By 1980, the bishops seemed to have drawn farther away from the USCMC, which felt that it had reached a turning point. It saw itself in the image of a servant and closed its first ten years of existence by analyzing that symbol:

> A servant must have a genuine, warm and respectfully affectionate relationship with the one served. The one served cannot be only master without compromising the integrity of the servant, nor can the one who serves be only a dependent without draining the life of the master. The early Church understood the remarkable paradox of the Servant Jesus, without ever perfectly attaining its own servant role. This reflection is not meant to be critical in a negative way, but hopefully to offer a challenge the staff feels is inescapably present to the Church of the Gospel and of Vatican II.[69]

This ecclesiology implicitly called for more shared authority in the USCMC, a position the bishops did not appear to share with the rest of the council members. The bishops withdrew from the organization and continued to work through their Committee on Missions, which had been established in 1967.[70]

The USCMC was responsible for gathering religious superiors, enhancing their global consciousness through meetings with colleagues and with bishops from North and South America. Such encounters would also lead to further questions about the nature and purpose of mission activity.

Contacts between Northern and Southern Major Superiors[71]

In 1970, 72 institutes of men religious, 188 institutes of women religious, 11 lay mission organizations, and 373 diocesan priests served in missions around the world. That year the United States Catholic Conference's Division for Latin America (the former Latin American Bureau) sent a confidential questionnaire to the bishops of Latin America and to missionaries to assess the presence of North American missionaries in their dioceses over the last ten years. Six areas were appraised: language training, the missionary's socioreligious role, personal satisfaction, cultural adaptability, and contribution to the pastoral plan in local churches in Latin America. Though several fine formation programs were in place designed specifically for Latin America, many missionaries still complained of inadequate training, especially in sociology, economics, and culture.

With the responses to these questions as the backdrop, eighty-two delegates from congregations of religious from North and South America assembled in Mexico City in 1971 to reflect on the missionary experience of the past decade. Segundo Galilea presented a picture of the pastoral situation in Latin America.[72] Two persons gave an overview of the contributions of foreign missionaries, and Edgar Beltrán spoke on the integration of missionary religious into the local church. The conference reached several conclusions. On the negative side, in the enthusiasm of the time, persons were chosen too hastily to serve in Latin America, without proper screening or adequate formation. Many religious were sent without a suitable understanding of the needs of the local Church. The consequence was that missionaries applied familiar strategies or improvised approaches to situations. Quantity rather than quality of personnel sometimes reinforced ecclesial structures which were not life-giving. The concentration of personnel and U.S. Church money in some locations made the local churches dependent and slowed the process of their "liberation." This centralization of North American missionaries created a ghetto mentality and fostered attitudes of superiority. The result was not enculturation into the area but the transplantation of American-style parish structural patterns.

With all these glaring faults, were missionaries from North America still needed? The new Latin American Church, more self-confident after their bishops' 1968 meeting at Medellín, promoted the formation of a Christian laity, native vocations, a new role for Latin American women religious, and an ecclesial structure, which, while not disregarding the parish, looked to reevaluate its relationship with workers and university students. Smaller groups of base communities enabled the Church to identify more closely with poor and oppressed persons.

In light of this new Latin American identity, better-trained U.S. religious were needed to integrate plans for pastoral priorities and programs, often evangelizing outside traditional structures. Women and men religious needed to identify with the poor, while leaving direct involvement in politics to the Latin Americans. Religious from both hemispheres were to assume a prophetic role for the Church through openness to new forms and structures of religious life. North Americans examined how their congregational charism could be appropriately related to local churches. The conference stressed the importance of acculturation for missionaries. No one was to come to Latin America without having been prepared to appreciate the feelings, mentality, and culture of Latin Americans and to understand the differences between the hemispheres. The critiques were not new, having been voiced many times by others throughout the decade.[73] The critiques also expressed the changing pastoral agenda of the Latin American Bishops, who in the '30s, '40s, and '50s had requested educators for upper-class schools, though U.S. missionaries often sought to work in poorer areas.

Inter-American Conferences of Religious Superiors were held again in 1974 (Bogotá), 1977 (Montreal), 1980 (Santiago), 1985 (Marriottsville, Maryland), and 1994 (Santo Domingo).[74] The meetings treated themes of identification of religious with the poor, more mutuality in interaction between the hemispheres, and the type of missionary needed in Latin America. These occasional gatherings also kept U.S. major superiors aware of global issues and the need to set domestic agendas in their own congregations reflective of these connections.

"Convivencia, Convergence, Solidarity," 1976–78

Following the 1977 Inter-American Conference of Religious Superiors, the pleas of two Holy Cross priests, Martin Garate and Philip Devlin, ousted from Chile, resulted in meetings of U.S. major superiors around a three-year theme: *"convivencia,* convergence, solidarity." The first step of this plan, cosponsored by USCMC and the major superiors, was to have a small group of superiors meet (*convivencia*) as a kind of pilot group in 1977, with a greater number of superiors gathering the following year (convergence). The third-year meetings (solidarity) were to be held regionally. The intention of these gatherings was to develop a corporate response to specific problems of world injustice, especially as observed by missionaries and others who had noted these problems firsthand. The United States Catholic Mission Council, the leadership of the men's and women's communities, and the Center of Concern in Washington, D.C., prepared the processes and agenda.[75]

Many religious congregations had been responding individually to specific situations of injustice which they encountered in their mission areas. The planning group for the *convivencia* meeting hoped for a coordinated effort "to respond more evangelically to our Christian commitment to create a peaceful and just world."[76] Missionaries brought home to their superiors the importance of educating their North American constituents on "Third World reality and U.S. foreign policy." Returned missionaries also questioned the values promoted by the American way of life and began to form intentional communities committed to a simple lifestyle.[77] They had discovered firsthand that a comfortable life for U.S. citizens often came at the cost of the lives of the poor persons they knew. The political and the economic worlds were connected to the spiritual world and mission.

As a process and agenda were being constructed for the first meeting of the men and women, one person remarked that many women superiors were already aware of the inequities but needed direction about solutions. The committee was also mindful that it would probably be difficult to get the communities of male religious on board.[78] The participants were to meet for five days to pray, reflect, share, and listen. The presence of six native religious from around the world would keep the group focused beyond the United States.

The general format for the gathering, led by Joseph Holland and Peter Henriot from the Center of Concern, used a version of the "observe, judge, act" process, which they termed social analysis. Over the five days the participants went through three steps:

1. Analysis of Experience
   a. personal sharing
   b. group reflection
   c. structural analysis

2. Theological Reflection
   a. private meditation
   b. common themes
   c. framework

3. Planning Response
   a. examples
   b. structural implications
   c. discernment and commitment[79]

The new factor in this approach, which made it more "scientific" than Cardijn's method, was a greater knowledge and understanding of economics and social structures. The process came to be known as the "pastoral circle."

Joseph Holland and Peter Henriot presented a significant analysis of past missionary policies by placing them in economic categories: capitalization, distribution, and transformation. By this the men meant that missionaries tended in the 1950s and early 1960s to look at mission areas as underdeveloped, as deficient in clergy (capital). The solution was that the "clerical capital" of other countries needed to be shared with poor people. If the clergy did not go to the poor, the communists and Protestants would. The pastoral shift to identification with the poor brought changes but also great frustration for missionaries when faced with the immensity of the situation. The problem had been considered in terms of greater distribution of clergy. What missionaries needed now, the two presenters proposed, was a transformation of the role of religious professionals and of ministry itself. Holland and Henriot suggested social analysis as a tool for that transformation, a response that would deal with systemic change.[80]

At this point, encouragement for such direction had come through the 1971 Bishops' Synod on Justice, Pope Paul VI's encyclical *Evangelii nuntiandi* (1975), recommendations to the major superiors by the "Call to Action" meeting in Detroit, and, during the year of "convergence," the inter-American meeting of women and men religious, which had asked religious to "take a stance with and for the poor of the world." Social analysis would enable groups to identify the fundamental causes of poverty and oppression and could enable all persons to engage in the transformation of systems of injustice wherever they might be found.

"Solidarity" regional meetings in 1978 followed this national gathering, making use of local resources and providing opportunities for still more men and women religious to be involved in the process of social analysis.

These mid-1970s gatherings were significant because the mission agenda infiltrated the domestic agenda of many religious congregations. An explicit connection was made between the focus of mission overseas and the emphasis on social justice among North Americans. The pastoral circle of social analysis returned to the northern hemisphere in a more scientific and systemic mode, a process which linked experience, the Word of God, and action.

Conclusions

In the post–Vatican II period, change was the order of the day for many local churches. Transformation happened not only as a result of the conciliar documents, but prior years of missionary experience had contributed to and augmented the changes. Between 1965 and 1980, developments were particularly noticeable in the theological and pastoral/ecclesial realms of both North and South America.

First, in the theological area, while the number of U.S. Catholics in Latin America never achieved the 10 percent target, greater numbers of laity and religious in the area set the tone and themes of U.S. Catholic mission theology for the 1960s, 1970s, and early 1980s. The "rehabilitation" of Latin America in 1959, which had become "development" in the 1960s, moved to "option for the poor." Thematically, evangelization, justice, and presence among the poor became the touchstones of authenticity, a kind of measuring rod for missionaries. While many U.S. missionaries focused all along on serving the lower socioeconomic groups and indigenous people, "option for the poor" specifically connoted a transformation of systems as part of the infusion of the values of the reign of God.

Second, this theology provided an alternative in the 1960s and 1970s to the prevailing neo-Thomism. The latter approach was partially characterized by the assumption of an ordered universe of ideas, the application of universal concepts to particular experience, the implementation of philosophy as the thought structure for theology, and the practice of theology, usually, by a select small group of men. The methodology of what came to be called liberation theology began with experience, notably that of the poor, continued with reflection on Scripture, and moved to action to bring one's individual, communal, and political life in line with the gospel. Community-oriented theology moved from the university to the barrios, the *favelas*, and the *campo*, from a scientific method based on philosophy to a rudimentary scientific method of Cardijn's "observe, judge, act," which Peter Henriot, SJ, Joseph Holland of the Center of Concern, and others refined later as the "pastoral circle."

Third, the task of theology widened to include the political as well as the socioeconomic world. While some missionaries tended to emphasize this aspect more than others, global connections were such that one could not ignore pastorally what was happening politically. When missionaries saw their parishioners disappear — either imprisoned or murdered — become dependent on outside help for life's necessities, and lose a feeling of dignity and worth as a result of either U.S. government intervention or policy sanctioned by the United Nations, the patriotism of the missionaries of the 1940s and 1950s frequently gave way to critical analysis and prophetic speech.

A fourth significant change occurred in the pastoral/ecclesial realm. A number of Latin Americans participated in pre–Vatican II progressive movements in Europe and worked to renew local churches. The Church in Peru, for example, which had a high number of U.S. Catholic missionaries in the 1960s and 1970s, had a key group of reform-minded persons "who through their experience among the poor...led the way for missionaries to recognize new roles for pastoral agents in the post Vatican Church."[81] It was from Peruvian Church leaders, for example, that a number of U.S. missionaries learned of Vatican II reforms.

Other Latin American clergy took for granted the poverty and illiteracy of the majority of their people, many of whom were indigenous. North American missionaries were appalled at what they saw. As outsiders, they perceived that an experimental pastoral approach was needed in Latin America and proceeded to change the way things had been done for several hundred years.[82] For women religious, the move from educational institutions to pastoral work, and for clergy, the move from administration of the sacraments as a primary emphasis to formation of a community of the Word, flowed from a different conception of church than the prevailing sacramental-clerical model. Maura Clarke, MM, the last Maryknoll superior at the Capuchin parish school in Siuna, left the parish to work with the poor in Managua for twelve years and then went to El

Salvador. Ironically, while Clarke would be murdered in that country, Maureen Courtney, CSA, engaged in catechetical work among the indigenous in Nicaragua, would be killed very near Siuna, where Clarke had worked. Team ministry, life among the people — particularly among the poor — and a priority on lay leadership demonstrated less of an emphasis on "doing for others" and more on people doing for themselves. This "horizontal" communitarian ecclesiology did not find favor among all people, however, as evidenced in the dissatisfaction of some local clergy with U.S. mission personnel, in CIA interest, and in the deaths of missionaries. Tensions in the USCMC also reflected discomfort with a more egalitarian type of ecclesial leadership.

Adoption of an ecclesial model which emphasized the sacramentality of human beings, promoted cohesiveness and collective experiential knowledge, and brought the Word of God to bear on daily life was a reversal of the passivity, silence, and dependency which had been the experience of the majority of the people in Latin America. Listening to people tell their stories induced a spirit of humility among pastoral ministers. Niles Kauffman, pastor in several parishes during his seventeen years in Nicaragua, reflected:

> I went to Nicaragua thinking I was going to teach these people what Christianity is. I don't know who learned more. One day I was in a chapel on the Prinzapolka River to teach the people something about Christianity. The children of one of the men were making a disturbance so I couldn't be heard. When I complained, the man said to me, "All I have is my house of bamboo and furniture, which I have made with my own hands, and two machetes, my wife, and my children. I am happy when I hear them play or cry or talk. They are my treasure."[83]

While those who used Catholic Action principles had attempted to re-Christianize society in the 1930s and 1940s, the practice of this method resulted in a prophetic stance in the 1960s and 1970s. An observable change in ecclesiology appeared when pastoral personnel, bishops, and laity themselves acted on behalf of the poor in order for all persons to have equal access to education, work, and economic benefits. The reassessment of mission by the women of the Grail, Maryknoll, the Capuchins, Jesuits, and the Agnesians, among others, had moved them practically and theoretically as early as 1961 from "planting the church" to serving the people of God, often under local Church leaders.[84] That God had a special presence among the poor came to be an overriding emphasis in ecclesiology and theology, even though many missionaries sought to be open to people on all sides of the political spectrum, difficult as that was at times.

With Third World theologians and bishops addressing mission congresses and writing in U.S. publications, a sense of "reverse mission" began to be recognized. Not only were missionaries bringing something (so they thought) to people elsewhere, other Christian communities were bringing something to missionaries and to the North American Church. One area where this was particularly evident was the influence of the Latin American experience on Hispanic ministries in the United States.[85] In a trend that started with Cardinal Spellman's seminarians in Puerto Rico in the 1950s, diocesan clergy would return from several years' experience in Central or South America in later years to work with Spanish-speaking people in their home dioceses. The opening of the Mexican American Cultural Center in San Antonio, the U.S. Catholic Bishops' document on pastoral care of Hispanics, and three National Hispanic Pastoral Meetings (*Encuentros*) are just a few examples of the effect of the U.S. Catholic Church's involvement in Latin America at home.

People who went to Latin America for even a brief time were deeply affected. Helena Steffens-Meier, SSSF, a well-known Wisconsin artist who specialized in wood and sculpture, began to create works which reflected a visit to her congregation's Guatemala mission. In the mid-1960s, Thomas Merton, who had lived with Nicaraguan Ernesto Cardenal in the Trappist monastery in Gethsemane, Kentucky, had considered transferring to Latin America.[86] Henri Nouwen's (1932–96) recollection of his time in Bolivia and in Peru, *Gracias: A Latin American Journal,* became popular reading for U.S. Catholics. Daniel Berrigan, SJ, credited his Latin American "exile" with his personal "radicalizing."[87] Those returning from overseas often faced lifestyle issues which centered around the choice of living more simply in the face of North American consumerism. Others, who had visited Latin America for anywhere from a few weeks to a few months, sometimes returned to the United States as self-styled "experts" on the church and politics in that part of the world.[88]

Even though significant mission developments were taking place, there were signs of a decreased interest in the overseas mission thrust in general. By 1968, volatile social problems in the United States had begun to claim the attention of citizens. The divisive and explosive racial riots that year, the problems of urban decay, and the war in Vietnam diverted the attention of U.S. Catholics from Latin America and from the mission picture in general. The revitalization of the U.S. Catholic Church after Vatican II through liturgical renewal, changes in religious congregations, and the development of parish councils and lay leadership energized U.S. Catholics and seemed to result in a loss in emphasis on overseas mission. Many mission magazines either ceased or appeared in reduced format. Religious congregations, many of whom had been in Central and South America for fifteen years or more, were not replacing their members. In some cases, their territories were now served by native clergy, religious, and active laity. Congregations lost members not only in the United States but also abroad. The number of lay missionaries grew slightly, however, a number of them affiliating with missionary societies such as Maryknoll and the Jesuit Volunteer Corps.

The Sisters of St. Joseph in Peru, writing in 1970, lamented to their Sisters in the Boston Archdiocese:

What has happened? There has been a steady decrease in interest and enthusiasm for work away from home. Is it because many Sisters who did consider the mission apostolate previously are now content with increased involvement at home? Has there been too little and very poor communication between Peru and Boston? Have we lost the vision of the Universal Church? Are we looking "in" most of the time? Are we working to satisfy our personal needs instead of the needs of the Church? Nobody knows just what has happened, but the fact remains — Latin America is mission territory and we are a very far cry from having 10 percent of our community here.[89]

The number of U.S. Catholic missionaries to Peru peaked the year after this letter. Five years later the number of missionaries had plummeted from 693 to 492, a substantial decrease for such a short period. Nevertheless, the mutual encounter of the Churches of the two hemispheres had summoned both groups to examine themselves and to act more critically from a gospel and pastoral perspective. The experience set theology for the whole Church in a fresh direction.

In the 1980s, two mission themes emerged for U.S. Catholics as a result of missionary work, especially in Asia in the wake of American involvement in the Vietnam War. Large numbers of Asian immigrants made U.S. Catholics aware of the world religions which formed the cultural and spiritual background of that part of the world. Catholics were now working and living side by side with Asian peoples, with growing numbers of African Americans, and with Spanish-speaking people arriving from all over Central and South America. World religions and multiculturalism became the mission watchwords of the 1980s and 1990s.

Chapter 10

U.S. Catholic Mission History: Themes and Threads, 1850–1980

Several factual and statistical matters can be cited at the outset in an overview of the American Catholic overseas mission movement, a phenomenon which began in the mid-nineteenth century. Cumulatively, men's religious congregations, societies, or religious orders which have sent the most American personnel are the Jesuits, Maryknollers, Franciscans, Redemptorists, Divine Word Missionaries, Marianists, Oblates of Mary Immaculate, and Capuchins. The women's religious congregations which have sent the most personnel are the Maryknoll Sisters, Marist Missionaries, Medical Mission Sisters, School Sisters of Notre Dame, and Sisters of Mercy. While these groups were the mainstay of the mission venture, hundreds of other missionaries were sent in smaller numbers by dioceses, lay mission societies, and religious congregations not necessarily founded specifically for overseas mission. Over the years, organizations such as PAVLA, the Volunteer Missionary Movement, the Catholic Medical Mission Board, the Jesuit International Volunteers, and lay men and women associated with Maryknoll, the Columban Fathers, and with other mission groups have responded to the mission call. Diocesan clergy served as missionaries through their own dioceses or through groups like the St. James Society or Maryknoll. In 1980, the year which closes our study, 72 institutes of men, 211 institutes of women, 17 organizations, and 10 dioceses had missionaries outside of the United States. (See statistics in appendix.)

The countries which have received the largest numbers of U.S. Catholic missionaries have been China (1919–50), the West Indies and Pacific islands (1954–70), and Peru, Brazil, and the Philippines (1962–85). The number of U.S. Catholic missionaries in sub-Saharan Africa reached a high of 1184 in 1966, during the tremendous upheaval brought about by African independence movements. The total number of missionaries overseas peaked in 1968, at 9,655.

It is impossible to calculate the numbers of mission circles and mission-funding organizations which sprang up, especially after World War I. These groups provided finances, education about mission, and opportunities for female leadership. Institutionally, the Roman Catholic Church in the United States formed a strong national office of the Society for the Propagation of the Faith, an American Board of Catholic Missions (1925), a Latin American Bureau (1959), and a bishops' national committee on missions (1968). When the U.S. Catholic bishops wrote their pastoral on mission, "To the Ends of the Earth" (1986), they summarized the history of extensive U.S. Catholic mission experience, as well as a theology of mission.

The promotion of the American Catholic mission movement depended to a large extent on a strong, organized base of mission programs in Catholic grade schools, high schools, and colleges. The number attending Catholic schools has diminished since the 1970s, but the Columban Mission Education Program has continued to promote mission to the Catholic school population, to religious education programs in parishes, and to participants in the Rite of Christian Initiation formation by providing visual and printed materials in Spanish and English.

The most obvious reality of the American Catholic mission movement has been that people of diverse ethnic backgrounds, having learned to live with each other on American soil, were sent to diverse peoples overseas. Multicultural contacts often moved in several directions simultaneously. English-speaking missionaries (some born in Europe who had moved later to the United States) worked with European missionaries and learned native languages, though Americans were notorious in many cases for not mastering these well. Missionaries all along have been the bridges between people they served and those "back home." An added dimension to that bridge building today involves missionaries who present talks for multicultural or global awareness programs in the United States and thereby assist American understanding of the continuously evolving world cultures in its own hemisphere.[1]

These particular points represent the tip of the iceberg, underneath which lies the complex, fascinating, and variegated patterns of the U.S. Catholic missionary movement. The Second Vatican Council has often been cited as a "watershed" for tremendous changes in Catholic life. Certainly one of the major theological shifts was in ecclesiology: a conscious choice of the image of "People of God" over the "Perfect Society." Both ecclesial symbols reflected the political and spiritual circumstances in which they arose. True as this may be, many of the theological and pastoral modifications that occurred after the Second Vatican Council had actually developed beforehand, providing the experiential base for theological changes. As we have seen, missionaries themselves pioneered "People of God" theology, enculturation, and base Christian communities before the ideas found their way into official Church documents. To examine the themes and threads of change over the 140 years of U.S. Catholic mission outreach, we return to the questions raised in our introduction:

- What were the social, political, cultural, and religious factors which gave rise to mission efforts toward particular areas of the world at various times in U.S. history?

- What presuppositions lay at the foundation of American Catholic thought and practice of world evangelization?

- What were similarities and differences between genders in the perception of the nature and practice of world evangelization?

- To what extent did U.S. Catholic missionaries contribute to the shift in mission theory and practice?

These questions divide into the following areas of discussion: external and internal influences prompting missionaries to leave the United States, changes in mission formation, and differences and similarities between genders, all of which aided in the configuration of American Catholic contributions to mission theology.[2]

External and Internal Factors Promoting Mission

Wars, Politics, and Economics

From the founding of the United States of America to the twentieth century, the mission focus of U.S. Catholics lay with the evangelization of European immigrants. That endeavor consumed much of the energy of the bishops, European and American clergy, and the various religious congregations which served immigrant populations. To a lesser extent, mission energies were directed toward and came from within groups of Native Americans, African Americans, and Asian Americans. Nevertheless, Propaganda Fide in Rome did not hesitate to call on a young country to respond to evangelization needs in geographic areas which came under its political sway. This was true already with Leonard Neale, the first "foreign" missionary born in the United States, who went to British Guiana in 1779–80, during the Revolutionary War. International politics further provided openings for Americans to go to the Philippines and Cuba after the Spanish-American War, to China after World War I, to Oceania, Africa, and Latin America after World War II, and to Korea after 1953. International religious congregations dealt with the same political and colonial realities. The Redemptorists took parishes in the Virgin Islands in 1918, the year after the U.S. government took control from the Danes, the American Province of the Divine Word Missionaries "held" their German-founded Chinese missions, and the Spanish Jesuits transferred their Philippine mission to the American Jesuits.

Another political factor in mission activity was the assumption of many missionaries that democratic values, with a concomitant emphasis on the individual, were important to the mission task. An American flag might not have flown over their mission station or their dispensary, but many missionaries espoused freedom and the rights of the individual and presupposed them to be part of how they went about their work. Missionaries always had to deal with the politics of their local situation, even though, as in China, they frequently understood little of the larger sweep of politics. Opening schools, negotiating for property, and importing machinery and supplies all called for governmental interaction and acquaintance with local forms of "economic and political persuasion." By the 1960s, missionaries had acquired various degrees of political sophistication and critical skills to judge both American political involvement in their countries and the causes of poverty and oppression. Governments continue to monitor missionary activity.

Throughout the entire span of time when mission theology moved from "saving souls" to "bringing the Good News into all strata of humanity for its transformation" and to a broader appreciation of the religions of the world, American Catholic missionaries viewed the economic realities of people's lives as somehow bound up with the mission task. While missionaries' expressed purpose was the conversion of people and the formation of the local church, they also realized that poverty, oppression, and injustice were not "of God," and needed to be remedied. In the 1940s, correction of larger social issues began to be associated with the need to address structural economic and social problems. In 1945, Anna Dengel noted:

> The roots of the conditions we have just examined lie far deeper than in a mere lack of medical care. They are grounded in the social and economic indigence of missions...all over the world. All endeavor can avail but little unless it is accompanied throughout by a great effort, a striving toward the realization of a Christian ideal in our basic social and economic structures.[3]

To redress these maladies, missionaries promoted both capitalism and cooperatives. Sister Maria Teresa Yeung, who in 1927 became the first Chinese woman to enter the Maryknoll Sisters, was instrumental in beginning the successful self-supporting industrial department in Hong Kong. In the 1940s, Jesuit John P. Sullivan, a leading figure at the St. Louis Mission Institute, promoted cooperatives in the Jesuit Jamaican mission. In the 1960s, Sister Gabriella Mulherin, MM, spearheaded the cooperative movement in South Korea, and in the 1970s, Ellen McDonald, MM, studied the adult-education methods of Monsignor Moses M. Coady to better understand the cooperatives and economic developments in Panama.

Economic support for missions was provided in various ways. With the exception of Richard Cardinal Cushing and Bishop Fulton J. Sheen, who were able to amass great sums, American missionaries had no substantial single benefactors. The Society for the Propagation of the Faith and the Society of the Holy Childhood provided income for a number of missions. Those who gave to the SPF often gave money to other mission groups. Hundreds of thousands of dollars were raised, small amounts at a time, through mission circles, mission clubs at grade schools and high schools, and through wills and annuities. Mission clergy received Mass stipends from various dioceses and organizations in the United States. Because many priests' major functions were liturgical, it took some time for any appreciable financial support to come from a local church, especially in territories with few Catholics. Supplements to income included chaplaincies in the U.S. armed services or at an already established parish near mission stations. Dependence on outside finances, especially at the onset, caused clergy to return to the United States or sometimes to Europe for financial contributions from bishops and parishes.

Women's mission communities were expected to be economically self-sufficient. They brought marketable skills with them: teaching, sewing, music, art, nursing, and domestic skills. In addition, they often enabled their students to become financially self-sufficient by helping them work collectively and by teaching individual skills. Groups "back home," such as relatives, religious congregations, or the grade schools and high schools where Sisters taught, provided the necessary funds until the mission community had achieved some stability. Both men and women acted as intermediaries in the buying and selling of goods across the seas — indigenous handmade creations sent to the United States and altar linens, books, supplies, and medicines shipped to missionaries abroad.

Advances in technology brought mass-produced goods to more Americans, corresponding to a rise in the business and efficiency culture. Not insignificantly, the first large-scale movement of men and women overseas to China from congregations not traditionally engaged in missionary work came when the membership had moved from a diversification of roles to specialization in church and society. The heroic image of missionary (rarely noted in the literature as a heroine) and the appeal of the adventure of missionary life emerged when bureaucratization had become part of American society in general and of religious congregations in particular.

Propaganda Fide and Papal Documents

The "Roman factor," through Propaganda Fide and twentieth-century papal encyclicals and mission promotion, was a second influence in encouraging American mission activity. Authorization to begin a mission ultimately derived from Propaganda Fide. Six significant mission encyclicals and many related smaller documents were issued between 1919 and *Evangelii nuntiandi* (1975). Roman initiatives enabled American Catholics to invest in the universal mission of the Church and provided the rationale to go beyond the shores of the United States at a time when naysayers sought to have home mission needs filled first. Incentives for better mission formation programs, for native clergy, for religious architecture in keeping with the culture of the country, and for thinking beyond one's local church were papal values which challenged American mission leaders. Official Church communications, such as the call to Latin America and Africa, helped induce American action. In other cases, certain theories and practices appeared in American Catholic missions before the ideas found confirmation in official Church documents. This was true, for example, regarding theological considerations about development and a trinitarian foundation of mission.

Attitudes toward Protestant Mission Activity

A third external factor which precipitated mission activity was Protestant mission achievement. Whether expressed in letters sent home or in the creation of the papal program for Latin American evangelization, the effective work of Protestant missionaries acted both as a threat and goad to American Catholics. The competition in some cases led Catholic missionaries to have separate "Catholic" facilities, as in the United States. A pioneer missionary in Nicaragua in the late 1940s, Mary Agnes Dickof, CSA, said of their work:

> One more important plea still needs to be fulfilled. In all Nicaragua, there is not a Catholic hospital. The Moravians, the Baptists, the Adventists function in various parts of the country. We ask: "Why cannot the members of the Mystical Body of Christ do likewise?" Father Charles, the present pastor of Waspam, is directing his energies to that end, collecting funds for the erection of the hospital. Maybe in God's good time we will see our Catholic Indians cared for in a Catholic atmosphere and prepared to enter eternity with the consolations of Holy Mother Church.[4]

Converts to Catholicism frequently invigorated mission awareness. James Kent Stone, who led the Passionists' work in Argentina and Chile; Floyd Keeler, who played a significant role in the Catholic Students Mission Crusade; and Paul Wattson and Laurana White, founders of the Graymoor Institute,[5] which continues to promote ecumenical dialogue, are just some of the important American Catholic mission leaders who were converts. Well known also is the story of Maryknoll's Mother Mary Joseph, who, as a student at Smith College, witnessed the impressive Student Volunteer Movement ceremony. A number of Catholic mission leaders read Protestant missionary literature well before Vatican II. Catholics joined Protestants in the formation of the Chicago Cluster of Theological Schools in 1970 to combine the strength of missionary faculty in a mission program.[6] Protestants (conciliar and independent) and Roman Catholics formed the American Society of Missiology in 1972. Catholic mission faculty joined the professional society of American Professors of Mission.[7] Some ecumenical mission efforts were seen in missionary gatherings in the 1960s, and Gerald H. Anderson and Paulist Father Thomas F. Stransky coedited an ecumenical series of mission "trends" books between 1974 and 1984. The number of American Catholic missionaries did not reach that of conciliar Protestant missionaries, but by 1970 both groups were on the decline numerically and were being superseded by missionaries of mainly Pentecostal and charismatic groups.

American Protestant and Catholic Mission Characteristics

European mission activity generally followed the routes of respective colonial empires. The British Empire's heavy involvement in India and Africa meant that missionaries from religions of the North Atlantic countries could be found on those two continents. After the mid-nineteenth century, American mainline Protestant denominations were often found in the colonies of the British Empire. With some exceptions, American Lutheran missionaries generally had an affinity for German colonial countries. As a nation, the United States had little geographical "colonial" territory in the way of the Europeans. "Colonization" came in the form of U.S. political and economic influence and the corresponding interest in learning English.

Andrew Walls has named six characteristics to describe the American nuances of the world Christianity movement: vigorous expansionism, ready innovation, full use of technology, maximized organizational and business strategies, democratic values and church-state separation, and a "commonsense," practical theology.[8] American Catholics demonstrated some of the same characteristics. Catholics and Protestants shared an optimism and enthusiasm borne from the sense of an American "can-do" attitude and Progressive Era values, which lasted well beyond that period for missionaries. Catholics generally carried a similar sense of the "American experiment," and found a crisis of conscience in their ministry when they saw local governments, some of whom were supported by the U.S. government, trample on values missionaries thought America stood for.

Unlike the pattern for conciliar Protestant missionaries, the total number of Catholic women missionaries (about 45 percent) never exceeded the number of men (about 55 percent).[9] That so many single and married Protestant women missionaries were in the field (about 66 percent) was interpreted as an indicator that Protestant men had lost interest in overseas missions. While Protestant and Catholic women postulated differing theological premises, especially prior to the mid-1960s, they shared some approaches to mission. As a vocation, mission life at some points provided an option besides marriage for single Protestant women. Roman Catholics looked on the single vocation of religious life, either male or female, as an acceptable alternative to matrimony.[10] "Women's work for women" was a common theme for both religious groups. Women in mission-funding groups generally equated food and funds: literary "entertainments," refreshments, sewing, and crafts made use of personal talents as sources of income for a missionary's monthly "maintenance" and provided occasion for much-anticipated social interaction with other women. However, there were some differences between Protestant and Catholics in the characteristics indicated by Walls, apart from theological distinctions.

As noted earlier in the chapter, mission funding never reached the proportion for Catholics that it did for Protestants. Catholics had no Rockefellers or Luces for major financing of mission work, and even the vast sums raised by Cushing and Sheen did not all find their way into mission.[11] For the most part, contributions were more broadly based and, more often than not, came from women, children, and clergy.

Mission Vocation and Images

The call of the mission vocation to "Go [to the ends of the earth] and teach all nations" was an internal factor in the mission movement. As early as the mid-nineteenth century, when the Holy Cross men and women went to India, one of the primary responses to that mission call was seen in religious life. The life of prayer, Eucharist, and other community exercises provided motivation for mission. The lay mission call was often expressed through a spirituality of the Mystical Body of Christ, especially from the 1920s to the 1960s, and was engaged by the dynamics of Catholic Action.

Mission magazines portrayed certain assumptions about the mission vocation. The call was frequently presented as a "modern" vocation, filled with spirit, adventure, and hardiness, an opportunity to "bring God" to those who had not heard the Good News. Beginning with the 1923 Catholic Students Mission Crusade convention, the missionary vocation was displayed in literature, dioramas, slides, and films about mission work. If one could not go abroad, Catholics could identify with particular missionaries and vicariously adopt the vocation through such plans as the Co-Missionary Program, begun by Bruno Hagspiel, SVD, "to adopt the missionary himself as a brother-priest, thus aiding him directly in his work for God and souls."[12] Membership cards contained a photograph of "their missionary" on one side and a prayer for him on the other side. Books which featured the work of individual missionaries provided implicit and explicit assumptions about the mission vocation. The "modern" vocation of the Sister missionary was depicted in Maria del Rey, MM, *Bernie Becomes a Nun*, a book with crisp text and large "real life" photographs.[13]

The symbols surrounding the mission vocation went through transformation over the time we have studied, but many virtues remained the same. Sulpician Alphonse L. Magnien, the first SPF director, was eulogized in 1902, not only for his intellectual leadership at St. Mary's Seminary, Baltimore, but for the characteristics which made him a "true missionary." Magnien was proclaimed as

> a man of resource and adaptability, an untiring worker, a priest of perfect self-sacrifice and absolute disinterestedness,...having only one object in view, the salvation of souls,...able to adapt himself to the spirit of the country and become like those among whom he lived (to the extent that that is possible).[14]

Many of these characteristics remained as imitable virtues through the next decades for both men and women missionaries.

Generally, the qualifications for a missionary vocation tended to be identified in three areas: physical, intellectual, and spiritual.[15] Physical characteristics of the missionary vocation were physical stamina and strength, with a correlative disregard for one's comfort or convenience. A 1916 *Catholic Missions* article, which described the vocation of a missionary, captured the optimism prevalent in mission consciousness well into the 1960s. "Before the push and pluck, the dare and do of apostolic zeal, all barriers have been thrown down.... Nothing can balk their persistence."[16] These physical attributes not only gave one a better chance of a healthy adaptation to new climates and circumstances, but were also needed when male missionaries, especially, crossed rugged terrains and forged new territories for the Church. Associated with these corporeal attributes were the virtues of initiative, courage, and confidence,[17] which tended to carry forward the "muscular Christianity" of early twentieth-century America.

Among the intellectual characteristics thought necessary for missionaries were an inquiring mind, a willingness to learn from others, the ability to acquire a language, and adaptability. In 1933, Michael Mathis, CSC, mission promoter for the Holy Cross Fathers and Brothers, suggested that missionaries needed above-average intelligence because they "must have the ability to fathom the mental processes of some keenly intellectual representatives of often an ancient and alien culture, as well as the ability to appreciate the limitations of sometimes vicious and ignorant barbarians."[18] He further identified the need for a "constant study of the ethnology of the people" where missionaries were sent. This, in turn, meant that missionaries needed to adjust and accommodate themselves to all sorts of circumstances. Or, as one of the first Servite Fathers in South Africa in the mid-1950s noted, "All missionary work is a kind of improvising to a certain extent."[19] Mathis's plea for ethnologic knowledge was heard by few except the Divine Word Missionaries, who were major proponents of this approach.

Missionary spirituality included "proven virtue," generosity, self-sacrifice, a life of prayer, and zeal. Bishop James E. Walsh summed it up by noting: "The missioner, inasmuch as he is the sole representative of God in his locality, the quintessence of Christianity, the Universal Church in one man, requires every virtue in one form or another."[20] This certainly seemed both a Sisyphean and captivating ideal! The relationship between prayer and action was a theme which continued to be explored throughout the years. Many missionaries sought contemplative counterparts for support in their work. Paulist missionary Walter Elliott frequently corresponded with Carmelite nuns around the country and was instrumental in the publication of the spiritual writings of John Tauler and Teresa of Avila.[21] The Maryknoll Sisters had a contemplative branch of their community for women who had served for some years on mission. The immense popularity of Therese of Lisieux (1873–97), a French contemplative, who had also desired to be a missionary, was evidenced in the numbers of mission circles, overseas parishes, and seminaries graced with her name and in frequent references by missionaries to her life.

The depth of one's spirituality also grounded one for the possibility of martyrdom, an image which remained consistent throughout the entire history of U.S. Catholic mission experience. One of the significant aspects of the use of this motif is the change in theological interpretation from early Christianity. In the Church's "age of the martyrs," martyrdom was viewed as a witness to the resurrection of the body. One's physical death, especially in the horrible circumstances of martyrdom, and the accompanying decay and putrefaction of the flesh held a special value in the attacks on Christianity by those who disputed the value of the body, such as the Gnostics and Docetists, as well as by disbelievers in bodily resurrection. In the case of twentieth-century American martyrs, the martyrs' bodies were not emphasized so much as their blood, which was both the "seed" of the church and a guarantee of a future local church. Theologically, the image highlighted the resurrection of the local church body, not the individual body.[22] The interpretation of martyrdom in the case of those killed in Central and Latin America beginning in the 1960s further stressed identification with the death and pain of oppressed people, as if in the form of a modern-day collective, suffering Jesus.

Figurative language used to describe missionaries during and after the First and Second World Wars and the Korean War tended toward military images, especially for men. By the end of the 1950s through the 1980s, these military images had ceased, as did almost every other image, except that of martyr. The image of women missionaries tended to be presented in domestic and invitational language. Sister Ellen Brunda, an Adorer of the Blood of Christ, Ruma, Illinois, "tried to make her dispensary attractive [in China] in order to overcome the patients' fears and bring them to Christ."[23] This community also attracted Chinese girls through music, play, and games. The ordinary events of life — washing and making clothes, feeding families, mending bodies, conversing about children — provided initial contact with these missionaries and images for women's evangelization of women.

Letters and magazines, which from the 1920s to the 1950s highlighted mission in China, often discussed poverty, floods, bandits, and disease among the people in somewhat generic terms. Catholics learned more about the difficulty of the missionary's life than about the people. In the 1960s and 1970s, particular images of the missionary receded from the literature but were replaced with an emphasis on the people the missionary served. Missionaries described the socioeconomic activities of the natives, and they appeared incredibly busy!

As the process of identifying missionary qualities evolved, the idea was advanced that mission life was a distinct and special vocation which prescribed accommodation to the geographic and social circumstances of a cross-cultural setting.[24] One needed to "go away" to be a missionary. While men generally authored such descriptions, women subscribed to the same perspective. The signs of a mission vocation were obvious. The mission images were clear. The mission task was unambiguous.

However, as we have seen in the 1950s and early 1960s, missionaries were beginning to realize that some of the assumptions from which they worked were actually antithetical to the formation of a Christian community. "Saving souls" and tabulations of convert and communicant numbers could not guarantee a vibrant parish community. Mission was larger than church implantation. Traditional institutional works, such as schools and large hospitals, and attempts to reach parents through children tended to divert men and women from other pressing social and religious needs. Formation of Christian communities through the Word of God took on greater priority for many clergy, laity, and religious. One result was decreased social division between the institutional Church and the people of God, but the new priority also created conflict between the missionary and either the host government or the U.S. government. A new approach required new ministerial skills. Those who did well in their mission as a "lone ranger" did not necessarily have the ability for team ministry. Those who maintained that the priest was the most important factor in the mission sometimes could not support training for local lay leadership. Divergent mission practices had also exacerbated division among community members by the early 1960s. To add to the confusion, theological differences in the missions were frequently demonstrated in the context of volatile political environments.

On a theoretical level, confusion for missionaries resulted because some of the statements from the Second Vatican Council appeared paradoxical toward missionary activity. *Lumen Gentium* ("The Constitution on the Church"), which proclaimed the necessity of baptism for salvation (par. 14), also acknowledged a positive recognition of those persons who lead a moral life without knowing the Christian God. The Vatican decree on missionary activity indicated a "secret presence of God" among people of other religious traditions. Conversion language appeared to be replaced with dialogue and respect for other religions. A 1957 CSMC publication, *Perspectives in Religion and Culture,* was a step in the direction of respect with chapters devoted to the major world religions and the importance of understanding their values.[25] Additional questioning of the mission vocation came with Ivan Illich's article, "The Seamy Side of Charity," and through ideas such as Karl Rahner's "anonymous Christian." Could one be "Christian" without acknowledging Christ? If so, of what use was the missionary? These emphases deflected the spotlight from the missionary and placed it on the work of God among peoples, the "manifestation or epiphany of God's will, and the fulfillment of that will in the world and in world history."[26] Such emphases also had missionaries looking at a variety of indigenous and Eastern spiritualities to determine what might be of value for a Christian spirituality.

Since the late 1950s, religious congregational meetings, symposia, books, and articles had addressed the diversity and complexity of the changing mission picture. Several articles in the 1968 *Worldmission* suggested that missionaries themselves needed to be the subjects of conversion, that the witness of life was often more powerful than spoken words. Such a disposition required a tremendous amount of humility and the ability to listen to others, to God, and to self. Mission zeal, so often concentrated on action, work, and the salvation of "souls," now seemed misplaced. Mission standards began to emphasize "incarnating" rather than "implanting," "being with" rather than "doing for," a "reign of God" rather than "church" discourse. Mission magazine subscribers after 1965 were more likely to read articles which identified with the people and their suffering than with the missionary and hardships of mission life, as had been the case earlier.

Bishop James E. Walsh's *Spiritual Directory* (1952) appears to be the first full treatise on mission spirituality by a U.S. Catholic. In 1974, New York Jesuit Michael Collins Reilly, SJ, whose mission experience included many years in the Philippines, formulated *Spirituality for Mission*.[27] The author, who completed his studies at Union Theological Seminary, New York, acknowledged his intellectual debt to Lesslie Newbigin, R. Pierce Beaver, and other Protestant missiologists. Reilly suggested that missionaries' spirituality might not have kept pace with actual realities of "mission to six continents." His work reflected Vatican II values of dialogue and openness as new spiritual skills needed to address a secular, diverse, and fragmented world.

Struggle for Cooperation

A fourth factor in the development of mission was both cooperation and competition among various groups in the mission enterprise. We have noted this phenomenon in the problem Francis Clement Kelley, the Catholic Church Extension Society founder, saw in the proliferation of mission magazines, which, in his mind, represented a diminution of financial resources for mission. Each mission group wanted to attract Catholics to its cause and projects. A kind of "territorial imperative" reinforced assurance of financial support for mission projects of particular congregations. Fear prevailed that common efforts would dilute assistance to these projects or places. Individual congregations would have little or no control over collective financial resources. Struggles on a national level between some of the mission-funding organizations and mission-sending groups arose over opposing conceptions of mission and strategies of operation.

For almost fifty years, the Catholic Students Mission Crusade provided a common forum for missionary personnel and organizations to attract young people to mission. Their conferences demonstrated to young Catholics the collective strength of American missions. Though there were great drawbacks to the Latin American Program of the 1960s and 1970s, the collaboration of laity, clergy, religious, and bishops has been, thus far, the most sustained collective undertaking for missions overseas by the U.S. Catholic Church. In 1965, Louis Luzbetak, SVD, of the Center for Applied Research in the Apostolate, directed a feasibility study for a combined program for missionaries. Cooperative ventures in mission formation among religious congregations did not work out, however, until 1970 with the establishment of the global mission program at the Catholic Theological Union. The coordination of mission needs and response to common problems continued through the Mission Secretariat (1950–69), the United States Catholic Mission Council (1969–81), and the United States Catholic Mission Association (1982–present). Bishops and mission leadership, though, did not always work from the same democratic style — a point of underlying tension.

Another aspect of cooperation included the sending of lay missionaries abroad. While papal encyclicals had encouraged lay mission work, several national organizations such as PAVLA allowed for little direct lay leadership in the organization. Priests were often the "intermediaries" or "liaisons" with the bishops. Many clergy in the United States and abroad doubted that laymen and lay women could be effective evangelizers in their own right. The Mystical Body theology of the 1920s through the 1950s was used both to involve laity in mission and at the same time to view them as "auxiliaries." This meant that laity did "secular" work, such as secretarial duties, medical work, or teaching secular subjects rather than being involved in direct evangelization. While today some mission congregations have a form of lay association for mission, the Grail and the Volunteer Missionary Movement are examples of groups which believe that laity do not need to be affiliated with the charism of a particular mission-sending religious congregation, because the call to mission proceeds from one's baptismal call. It is perhaps significant that in a time of fewer priests and religious serving abroad the number of lay missionaries continues to increase.

Formation for Mission

Just as the image of the missionary changed over time, so, too, did the missionary's formation. By and large, mission seminarians pursued the same academic program as their diocesan counterparts. This consisted of Manual theology, the philosophic premises of scholasticism, and the prevailing spirituality at the seminary. Formation for mission occurred informally through CSMC units, talks by returned missionaries, and through mission literature in seminary libraries. In 1904, a formal missionary formation program was suggested by the Paulists at the Apostolic Mission House. But as emphasis on non-Catholic and Catholic missions predominated in the Apostolic Mission House curriculum, preparation of overseas missionaries was discontinued. Michael Mathis, CSC, authored an article on an "Ideal Foreign Mission Seminary" in 1933, and in 1941 he proposed a graduate school of missions for the Holy Cross Fathers and Brothers. He argued for a spiritual formation proper to missionaries and an academic program which "provided adequate knowledge and practical ability to win disciples for Christ."[28] The goal was the formation of a missionary "saint and scholar," a "combination of the contemplative and the man of action."[29]

Others offered ideas and plans for mission formation for seminarians, though not all of the plans were effected. John Considine, MM, prepared a weekly study program in his "Outline of Missiography" in 1944.[30] Formation for mission was the subject of the 1946 educational conference of the Franciscan Friars of the United States.[31] A heavy emphasis on the sciences, including mathematics, the social sciences, and the natural sciences, in addition to linguistics,

Latin, Greek, German, and French, were part of the Divine Word Missionary curriculum in the United States.[32]

Two programs before 1960 attempted to use anthropology as a significant tool for missionaries. The earliest was started by John Montgomery Cooper (1883–1949), an apologetics professor at the Catholic University of America, founder of the department of anthropology, and cofounder, along with consultant Leopold Tibesar, MM (1898–1970), of the Catholic Anthropological Conference (later "Association"). The conference, formed in 1926, had two purposes: to increase understanding about diverse people and cultures through promotion of research and publication by missionaries and anthropologists and to encourage anthropological training of missionary candidates. The association ceased in 1969, in light of increased ecumenical efforts in the mission sciences, but its journal, *Primitive Man,* inaugurated in 1928, continues to the present as *Anthropological Studies.*[33]

The Society of the Divine Word, through Louis J. Luzbetak, SVD, and the Mission Secretariat, through Frederick McGuire, CM, prevailed on the Catholic University of America in the 1950s to establish a program in mission studies, which would lead to a master's degree.[34] Conventual Franciscan Ronan Hoffman became professor of missiology at the Catholic University from 1958 to 1970 and sought to include missiology in everyone's formation, not just the formation of missionary seminarians.[35] The anthropological direction in mission also continued at the university through Luzbetak (b. 1918), who introduced an anthropology course tailored specifically to missionary needs. Luzbetak had been a student of Wilhelm Schmidt and had done field work in New Guinea from 1952 to 1956, an experience which led him to examine the relationship between faith and culture. His 1958 article, "Toward an Applied Missionary Anthropology," was the first on the subject of culture and faith.[36] These reflections and his teaching experience culminated in *The Church and Cultures: Applied Anthropology for the Church Worker* (1963), which became a classic in its field.[37] Widely received by Catholics and Protestants, the work was translated into several languages, including Spanish, Polish, and Indonesian.

A second program with an anthropological emphasis began in 1951 at Fordham University, fresh on the heels of Pius XII's encyclical, *Evangelii praecones.* Six months after its publication, John Considine, MM, at an October 1951 meeting of the Mission Secretariat, proposed that a group of mission specialists explore a more satisfactory formation program. The result was the World-mission Institute, formed with Fulton J. Sheen as its ecclesiastical director. The work of the specialists was channeled by Considine and by J. Franklin Ewing, SJ, head of the anthropology department at Fordham University.[38] Ewing was a Harvard-trained anthropologist with missionary experience in the Philippines. Noting both the attention to cultures and the need for more adequate mission formation emphasized in the papal encyclical, Ewing developed the Fordham Mission Institute in 1953. He worked closely with Considine and sought advice from Edward L. Murphy, SJ,[39] a staff member of *Jesuit Missions.*

There were two parts to the institute: annual gatherings of mission experts, which took place from 1953 to 1962, and an academic summer program for those preparing for mission or for returned missionaries.

Ewing had inaugurated a "Practical Course for Prospective Missionaries," held from 10 to 15 April 1950 and attended by eight laity and members from twenty-two religious congregations. Subsequently, he constructed a master's degree program in sociology-anthropology, with a curriculum based on "what the papal writings so strongly recommend, a solid foundation in missiology and a thorough exposition of sociological principles."[40]

The Fordham program presumed a formation in Catholic doctrine and practice, a prayer life according to the spirit of a particular religious institute, and an avocation, such as teaching or medicine. Those to be missioned would come to the institute for "specialization" in mission: i.e., in anthropology and an area course, which would examine the particular part of the world to which the missionary would be sent.[41] General principles learned in an anthropology course were to be applied in the area studies. An experienced missionary and a "scientist" teamed together to present the course. Summer courses were taught by Considine, Murphy, and experts in non-Christian religions, health, intercultural communications, and contemporary missions. However, by 1960, the program had closed for want of students. Ewing cited the cause as a "lack of willingness to learn" on the part of missionaries and a lack of cooperation among mission groups.[42]

The Fordham Mission Institute also sponsored the annual meetings of mission experts from 1953 to 1962 and published their proceedings for six of those years. Topics included the training of converts, indigenous leadership, social action, communication arts, and the global mission of the Church.[43] Another program which incorporated anthropology as part of a larger emphasis on mission was developed by a former missionary in China, Joseph A. McCoy, SM. He tabulated questionnaire responses from 259 American missionaries around the world and discovered that they had not been well prepared in language or in knowledge of local religious and social culture. Many missionaries reported they had been taught by persons who themselves had no mission experience.[44] Fifty-two persons surveyed had no command of the native language. *Advice from the Field* mainly reported McCoy's findings but also sketched a comprehensive mission formation program.

Other university-sponsored mission institutes included summer courses for missionaries at St. Louis University in the 1940s. In the early 1960s, the University of Dayton's Philip Hoelle, SM, organized eight-month formation programs ("Front Line") for lay persons responding to a mission call either in the United States or overseas,[45] and by the late 1960s, Hoelle had begun Summer Mission Institutes for men and women religious. Among the faculty in the latter program was Lawrence Nemer, SVD. Returned and new missionaries quickly learned a community spirit in this environment. Diocesan- or institute-sponsored formation programs for laity began in 1950 with the Grailville School of Missiology/

Oriental Institute and the Lay Mission Helpers of Los Angeles. Americans were also influential in language programs for mission formation in Puerto Rico; Cuernavaca, Mexico; Petrópolis, Brazil; and Peru.

Congregations and societies with an international membership, such as the Society of the Divine Word,[46] the Jesuits, the Dominicans, and the Franciscan Missionaries of Mary did not necessarily highlight their "Americanness," either in their formation or in their spirituality. Some groups sent members from various ethnic backgrounds to work together in a mission. Nevertheless, that international groups had U.S. provinces often proved helpful in sending their members to countries where some other nationalities might not be welcome.[47]

Gender, Role, and Mission

Gender frameworks for mission were affected by related issues in American society and by Catholic philosophical premises about men and women. The segregated gender spheres of nineteenth-century America were supported by capitalism and by the "cult of domesticity." Post–Civil War, gender-specific topics included temperance and women's suffrage, though few American Catholics espoused the latter. Rather, educated nineteenth-century Catholic women tended to promote literature, the arts, and the intellectual framework of "genteel" women and men. Twentieth-century gender issues revolved around family, the passage of women's suffrage, birth control, and women in the labor force. American Catholic women were more active in labor unions and assumed leadership in these organizations. American Catholic missionaries both drew on the values of their culture and amended them, as well.

Role of Men Missionaries

For much of the period we have examined, the role for mission clergy was indisputable and unambiguous. When the goal of mission was implantation of the church, the priest's role was primarily sacramental and liturgical. In 1912, Joseph McGlinchey translated and adapted Paulo Manna's classic on the missionary vocation, *The Workers Are Few.* In 1954, Nicholas Maestrini, PIME, adapted McGlinchey's work but discussed only the clergy's vocation as missionary. While Manna and McGlinchey had also presumed a key position for clergy in the scheme of things, they had promoted the role of women and Brother missionaries, as well, topics missing in Maestrini's book.

A report on the mission exhibit at the national conference of the Catholic Students Mission Crusade in 1933 captured both the ideal of the priest and missionary and the goal of mission:

> Although interest was provided by the description of a life different from
> American ways, there was never lost to view the motif of the exhibit,

shown in a triptych painted with much feeling. The title was "A Missioner's Dream" and the picture showed a missionary seated astride his horse, looking down from a mountain on a typical village, while in the clouds there hovered the church he ambitioned to erect in every such village. The whole painting symbolized the reason for the missionary's presence in that country, and his glorious task in bringing God to souls.[48]

Though this was an idyllic representation, it is significant that the priest stands (or in this case sits) apart from the village and is placed between the people and the church "in the clouds," as the theology of priesthood suggested at the time. The priest was one "set apart" in order to perform on behalf of the people the rituals which united them to God. Further, the missionary priest often did spend much of his time on his horse or its equivalent. One man thought that out of his twenty years in China, he had spent ten of them "in the saddle." This image furthered the idea of the solitariness of the vocation, literally, the "lone ranger," like the man pictured in the mural noted above. This man also ably demonstrated the "muscular Christianity" which Theodore Roosevelt had exemplified in an earlier period.

The life of a circuit-rider priest described by the Jesuits working in Belize included "regular care of their home towns," periodic visitation of villages connected to the main mission, sick calls, "confessions and Communions, and couples reclaimed from an evil life."[49] Once a parish had gained a foothold, Jesuits often came around to preach a mission to renew the fervor of the Catholics and to keep them regular in their attendance of the sacraments. But until at least a small congregation could be established, the missionary priest was intent on many other things: constructing roads, digging wells, erecting buildings, and applying first-aid remedies for small medical problems of the people. These tasks were for some priests a prelude to the "real work" of mission. Noted one missionary among the Zulus in 1959:

> Sunday, however, is pay-off day. That may be an undignified name but it is a very accurate one for God's Day on the missions. It's the time for gauging progress, Sunday morning. It's the day when people give back; the day on which their turn comes to respond to grace and all the secondary means you have been using on them during the week. While visiting the huts the people might treat you as a king; when they come around for medicine and favors they could not be more respectful. But this means little in the long run if they don't attend church on Sunday. Because there is where we get our heavy blows in, the Mass, catechism, sermon, benediction. There, in church, is our golden opportunity to pass on all this Good News we have for them.[50]

The work of mending bodies, so to speak, became a secondary task, required in order to attract persons to "something better" rather than being something significant in itself. Such statements were not uncommon within an ecclesiology which highlighted the priest as the pinnacle of God's work. To move from this ecclesial perception to a "People of God" framework would require not only a great degree of humility but a major intellectual and attitudinal shift.

Men came to be the recognized scientists of the culture, ethnographers, linguists, and "experts" in mission study, though initially, before the advent of more-developed language training programs in the 1950s and 1960s, the men had frequently relied on native women and native young men, who performed household tasks for the clergy, to act as their interpreters, translators, and general liaison with the host culture, especially at the onset of the missionary's arrival.[51]

However, not all male missionaries were clergy. Religious Brothers formed a second classification of men. The same missionary virtues of initiative, courage, and confidence were directed inward, so that Brothers' "auxiliary" positions made it easier for the clergy to perform their ministry. Those in the brotherhood, which was described at one point as a "haven of peace and a harbor of safety," were to demonstrate "a willingness to work, to suffer and to be forgotten."[52] But through their construction activities, printeries, and technology, and through education and teaching trade skills to the local people, the Brothers had access to the lives of the people in some of the same ways as the women.

Several factors were emerging which led to new images of mission. Experimentation in catechetical adaptation, accent on promoting native vocations for a native church, Francis X. Ford's emphasis on the "direct apostolate" of Maryknoll women in China, and Leo Mahon's promotion of a community gathered around the Word of God all represented a change in the role of the missionary, whereby the spotlight shone not on the missionary as a "hero" but on the people for whom he had come. Other mission traits — being a presence among the people, listening to people's stories, and ritualizing the space of ordinary life — began to be publicly emphasized by the 1960s and offered areas in which women had felt at home.

Role of Women Missionaries

Several conflicting messages about women in general, and missionary life for women in particular, were reflected in the American Catholic Church as the twentieth century opened and moved forward. The nineteenth-century American "cult of domesticity," its virtues of humility, cleanliness, purity, order, and harmony, emphasized women as homemakers, consumers, and as keepers of the family shrine. Their nurturing home life was to be a "safe" place from the dangers of the public sphere of finance, law, and industry, an environment where young men could be attracted so as not to wander either toward other women or alcohol. This domestic theme fit the pattern of the woman as the civilizing agent in society. The American Catholic woman's role in the missions was considered an extension of her domestic role in that she was to be a helpmate, an "auxiliary" to missionary clergy who were in the public or "real" world of saving souls. However, women also had access to the missionary virtues of initiative and "ruggedness," which they combined as they saw fit. Therefore, two other options were also found in the theory and practice of women missionaries: women as leaders in their own right, capable of direct mission and necessary for its fruition, and, especially after 1965, team leadership with men. In no case were women taken for granted.

Bishop Fulton J. Sheen probably best summed up the "separate and distinct spheres" for men and women, a prevailing perception for Catholics and a view that some hold to this day:

> Man was made by God; woman was made by God from man. Man coming directly from God, has initiative, power, and immediacy of authority. Woman coming from God through the ecstasy of man has intuition, response, acceptance, submission and cooperation. Man's mission is to rule over the external world and subject it; woman's mission is to prolong life in the world and rule it in the home.[53]

Such separation made it imperative for women to be the civilizing agents of society, because it was from the home that young men would go into the world of business and politics. This seemed ironic and paradoxical, that the "weaker sex" should be the foundation of "civilization." Sheen attributed these distinctions in role to differences in "psychology" between the two sexes. "Once it is granted that the psychology of a woman is different from a man, it follows that the missions must utilize both the one who is closest to the body and its ills, and the one who as a priest is closest by Divine appointment to the soul and its ills."[54]

While these "distinct spheres" might appear to constrict the work of women in mission, in fact, many women missionaries viewed their efforts almost as a global extension of domesticity. The world was being made "safe" for living as part of the growth of the Church and the reign of God. Women missionaries frequently performed on a religious level what women at home did for their families. They set the table, whether at an orphanage or at the eucharistic liturgy, clothed the family, either literally or through enterprises which taught women to do so for themselves, and healed the sick. Many times, it was these domestic "chores" performed toward all persons which impressed indigenous people and made them interested in Catholicism.

The boundary between the masculine and feminine, as it related to Church activity, was often quite permeable, either because the clergy believed that women could be direct evangelizers (as in the case of Bishop Francis X. Ford in China) or because there were too few priests to conduct the work. Such was the case reported by Sister Bernardina Maria, SSpS, in her article, "Where Priests Are Scarce — A Nun Takes Over."[55] This woman, who spoke several languages, wrote about her experience as an itinerant mission preacher in Pôrto Alegre, Brazil. Catechetics was another area which crossed the boundary from official Church doctrine or theological concepts to the world of everyday life. While men tended to be the "recognized" mission theologians and theoreticians, at least until the 1970s, women took theological ideas and adapted them quite readily to local situations. To do so, they sometimes called on native women to help them because the indigenous people knew appropriate examples, images, and stories to convey religious ideas. The popularization of the Maryknoll men's ideas about world Christianity, for example, occurred through the work of the Maryknoll women educators, who constructed the textbooks which were used by Catholic schools.

Another gender-related mission premise held that women "redeemed" other women. To accomplish this work, the missionary women were often painted with idealized features. Robert Streit's *Catholic Missions in Figures and Symbols* spoke of her as "the messenger of glad tidings, announcing redemption and salvation to oppressed womankind in pagan lands. She is the bright angel of purity, passing through the night and the marshes of paganism elevating and saving wherever she passes."[56] To "pass through the marshes of paganism" did not require passivity but resourcefulness and initiative. In such descriptions, the Catholic woman closely resembled her Protestant counterpart.

The first American Catholic *apologia* for an active leadership role for women in mission came from the pen of an unknown "American Woman," who wrote a lengthy tour de force on the subject in the *Catholic World* in 1875.[57] Marshaling examples from Greek and Roman mythology and from Jewish history, she presented evidence for the strength and feats of women in propagating religion. She concluded the first section of her argument by saying that "no greater thing can man do than these." She then proceeded in the main portion of her paper to answer the question, "What have women done to propagate Christian faith?" Beginning with the martyrs, the ascetics, and great Christian leaders, such as Catherine of Alexandria and Helen of Sweden, she reiterated that women had sacrificed everything for the faith. She listed a roll call of women who formed religious orders which significantly influenced the social order and which included prominent Christian lay women in the secular world. She noted women as teachers and as scholars, and, on this latter point, mentioned women at the University of Bologna, whom, she noted, even Thomas Aquinas admired. Her final point in her declaration was the "subtle power of mother and wife.... She has been taught that [her husband and children] must be saved with her, or she must perish with them."

Few Catholics read her words, as the *Catholic World,* which mainly reached clergy and the upper middle class, had a subscription of about 2,200 readers at the time. Much of her view about women's importance in mission was reflected, however, in *Children of Providence,* published from 1894 to 1923 by the Sisters of Charity, Mount St. Vincent on Hudson, Bronx, New York (chapter 2). Descriptions of decisive women leaders in all fields and articles about African American issues assumed that women had a role to play in addressing the problems of racism; the object of the League of Divine Providence was described as the "conversion of the Colored People of the Bahamas." The leaders pictured by the "American Woman" and the *Children of Providence* seemed to be in almost immediate sympathy with the people of the culture.

James A. Walsh selectively used the record of women's leadership in mission and evangelization, in order to have the women as "ancillae" to the priests in mission work. As seen in chapter 4, while the Maryknoll cofounder noted that women were only recently, in "modern" times, coming out of their cloisters, he made no mention of the record of women's leadership in the evangelization of women in general.

Common Characteristics of Missionaries

Salvation in the hereafter did not lessen attention to improvement of the present. Even in the 1970s, when the U.S. Bishops expressed the fear that the transcendent aspects of the Christian vocation were being neglected in an emphasis on development, the question of social works being unimportant to mission never arose. American missionaries frequently sought to improve the lives of those who had been placed on the edges of society: the lepers, women, children, the infirm, and aged. In cases where the first mission work took place in an institution, a school or parish church, for example, American women and men frequently sought other ways to have contact with people who otherwise would not have contact with the institutional Church.

Both men and women missionaries saw the virtue of self-sacrifice, which had been so important to the nineteenth-century cult of true womanhood, as invaluable for accomplishment of the mission task. Unlike the Victorian ideal, mission self-sacrifice provided positive energy for action and improvisation. Men and women had to "make do" with what was available. This mission virtue became the source of flexibility and innovation in choice of location for witness (moving from large convents or rectories located on parish property to a simple house closer to people in slum areas, for example), catechetics, medical services, education, and liturgy. Self-sacrifice was twinned with prayer, the sine qua non for mission. The shape of the prayer varied, from devotional activities to contemplative perspectives. Adaptability, prayer, friends, and a sense of humor were sometimes the only resources which enabled missionaries to move through pastoral and personal tensions. Not all experienced success or even a small satisfaction as missionaries. Men and women bore scars equally from the inability to acculturate. Martyrdom did not discriminate between the sexes.

Both men and women contributed to the discussion starting in the late 1950s of the need for converted attitudes in the missionary. Mutual exchange of ideas and the willingness to minister together in teams of laity and clergy — men and women — "working to so meld the differences among us as to make an effective team for the work of the Church,"[58] provided more support for the entire mission process even as mission called for the development of new interpersonal and analytical skills.

Theological Shifts in Mission

The theological changes in mission perspective in the twentieth century were global and complex and were related to significant developments in economic, political, and social realities.[59] Mission thought before Vatican II employed Aristotelian and neo-Thomist language, which tended to stress "missions" as a geographic territory, church implantation or extension as the work of mission specialists, and a one-way movement from Europe and North America toward other countries. Once the church was "planted," mission ceased. When the first Vatican Council was held in 1870, the "world church," for all practical purposes, was mainly thought of as European; the "universal" was a theoretical construct. Almost one hundred years later, using more biblical language and recognizing that the Church was "in a new situation," the Vatican II document on mission, *Ad Gentes,* declared that "The Church on earth is by its very nature missionary, since according to the Plan of the Father, it has its origin in the mission of the Son and the Holy Spirit."[60] When the bishops gathered in Rome for the Second Vatican Council, the composition of their group reflected diversity of cultures much more than Vatican I. The Vatican documents highlighted the reign of God and the importance of the local church. The use of new theological vocabulary and biblical symbols often provided a more adequate framework for interpreting what missionaries were actually doing. *Ad Gentes* presented a positive evaluation of other religions, acknowledging the "seeds of the word" present beyond the Catholic Church and present before the missionary's arrival. Mission theology then began to take a new look at the role of Jesus with respect to world religions. The recognition of pluralism in the church and in the world led to a reexamination of the meaning of a "universal" church, so that by 1980, mission theology had turned a new corner with discourse on the uniqueness and role of Jesus in light of the recognition of God's work in all religions.

How did the paradigm shift? Again, the answers are complex, but traditional theological premises, while ingrained in theory prior to Vatican II, were often malleable in practice, especially in areas where missionaries were faced with immediate, practical decisions in their daily interaction with people. This had occurred to some extent in the colonial and European immigrant missions in the United States, as well as among mission to the First Nations and African Americans. Missionaries themselves contributed toward the transformation of mission.

In the narrative of the mission movement of the U.S. Catholic Church, we have seen a change in understanding of mission from primarily a territorial and administrative category to a profound theological classification. The words *apostolate* and *missions* were dropped in favor of *mission.* The former terms tended toward a practice of charity on the part of selected and magnanimous individuals. The lay missionary section of the 1958 Mission Secretariat meeting addressed the more comprehensive theme when it spoke on the need to foster a world vision in American Catholics. One of the disagreements John Considine and Fulton Sheen had in the 1950s revolved around this point. Considine wrote to a superior of a religious congregation:

> The term "missions" is sacred to me, but living with it now for some forty-five years, I find in it a problem of semantics. Too often it connotes a divisory factor in the thinking of a community. In the popular mind the idea can lodge that we have main line activities for the Church as such and then we have works of supererogation that may include the missions. I would like to aid in eliminating this type of thinking by making it evident that all members labor equally in an integrated program for the whole church.... The world expansionist program of the Church is not a work of supererogatory zeal; it is of the essence.[61]

In 1963, Columban Harold Henry, archbishop of Kwangju, Korea, responded in a similar fashion with respect to the idea that stateside parishes and those abroad "adopt" each other. In a letter to Sheen, the national SPF director, Henry remarked, "With this system, I do believe the Missions could be taken out of the 'charity' bracket, and made an integral part of every diocese and parish, thus giving our Catholics a true consciousness of their obligations as members of Christ's Mystical Body."[62]

Another theological shift reflected the movement from church implantation to development to liberation to the option for the poor, with less emphasis on the institutional Church and more prominence to the reign of God. The supporting ecclesiology advanced from triumphalism to a more humble stance toward the grace of God, whether present in the individual or in a people and their culture. While still encouraging individual conversions, emphasis on the communal nature of conversion called for teamwork and cooperation among all mission groups. As we have seen, U.S. Catholic missionaries were active in the development of base ecclesial communities, cooperatives, and local churches.

A final theological shift we will highlight is the growth in the American Catholic understanding of itself as a world Church, and, correspondingly, in the value of lay leadership. For almost one hundred years, lay persons, representatives of religious congregations, and clergy have accompanied each other in the work of mission. Besides the traditional financial support that laity provided to missions, their teaching of "secular subjects," clerical work, medical assistance, and willingness to learn about a new culture were just some of the reasons lay missionaries began to become more noticeable by 1930. Though fewer in number than clergy and religious, laity claimed their place in the mission of the Church, supported first through a theology of the Mystical Body, the growth of the Cardijn movement, Catholic Action, and, by the 1950s, through the encouragement of papal encyclicals. Former missionary to China Joseph A. McCoy, SM, discussed the "Right of the Laity to Teach All Nations" during the 1963 Mission Secretariat meeting of mission-sending societies. By that time, the Church had experienced an explosion of mainly women candidates for mission work in such groups as the Grail, the Lay Mission Helpers, and the Papal Volunteers for Latin America. The number of lay missionaries peaked in 1966; since 1986, the number again has been on the increase. With a theology of mission rooted in a baptismal call and work clearly essential to the life of the Church, lay mission has a bright future, provided all members of the Church trust laity to be as dedicated as were (and are) many priests, Brothers, and Sisters.

U.S. Contributions to Mission

Much of twentieth-century mission theology, which U.S. Catholics either taught or read, tended to come from European sources. The translations by Matthias Braun, SVD, of Joseph Schmidlin's classic works of mission history and mission theory, published by the Mission Press at Techny, Illinois, were some of the well-worn volumes Americans had used since the 1930s. Through translations, the work of the Belgian missiologist Pierre Charles, SJ, became available to English-speaking audiences. Beginning in the 1940s, translations of the theology of Jean Danielou, Yves Congar, OP, and Karl Rahner, SJ, provided Americans with important ideas related to the construction of mission theology.

However, even within the scholastic (and particularly neo-Thomist) framework, which prevailed in mission theology at least into the mid-1960s, U.S. Catholics explored important theological nuances. We have seen that John Considine outlined in the 1940s a theology of world Christianity based on a trinitarian foundation. John F. Clarkson, SJ (1952), and Ronan Hoffman, OFMConv (1962), in the search for a new theology for mission, constructed a missiology using Aristotelian categories.[63] But William B. Frazier, MM (1967), broke from the scholastic framework through his reflection on images of the Church found in the Vatican Council document, *Lumen Gentium*.[64] That same year, the editor of *Jesuit Missions*, Calvert Alexander, used an approach similar to Frazier in a theological commentary on the missionary document of Vatican II.[65]

Prior to 1980, an American missionary to the Masai of Tanzania had made a sustained contribution to mission theology, starting in 1965 with *The Church as Mission*. Eugene Hillman, CSSp, was born in Boston in 1924 and ordained in 1950. After attending the Fordham Mission Institute, he continued to correspond with its director, J. Franklin Ewing, who gathered friends together in New York for a fund-raiser for the Spiritan missionary. Hillman eventually became an assistant to the secretary of the East African Bishops in their discussion of preparatory documents for the Vatican Council and had the opportunity to observe the final debate on the document on missions. In correspondence and in person, Hillman interested Karl Rahner in mission issues by indicating that European theologians needed to broaden their experiential base to consider mission realities and questions.[66]

Hillman contributed the only U.S. Catholic article to the 1966 Concilium volume, *Rethinking the Church's Mission*. While his *Polygamy Reconsidered: African Plural Marriage and the Christian Churches* raised some ecclesial eyebrows,[67] the missionary stood by his position that the Church needed to reexamine its policy on polygamy. He saw it "as a problem of the monogamy rule which came from Roman law, not from scripture. [The rules on this] came at a time when the church was expanding throughout the Roman Empire."[68] While Hillman spent many years of his life in Africa, his work was also known in the United States through numerous publications and through his teaching at various universities. Hillman's call for serious ecclesial thought about indigenous religion and its significance for Christianity paved the way ten years later for an equally controversial publication of a new generation, Paul Knitter's *No Other Name*, which suggested new ways to probe the depths of classic world religions for dialogue in a world newly sensitive to global ecological and economic problems.

Other contributions to mission in a variety of categories need to be recognized. U.S. mission groups have somewhat facilitated the gathering and work of theologians from North and South America and from the Third World. The participation of U.S. and Latin American Catholics in the NCWC in the 1930s and 1940s, the Fordham Mission Institute of the 1950s and 1960s, the CICOP conferences of the 1960s and 1970s, and the "conscientization" meetings of the congregations of religious in the 1970s offer a few examples of the theologians' interaction, not only with North Americans but with each other as well.

Under the direction of Frederick McGuire, CM, the Mission Secretariat brought together men and women missionaries in annual conferences, which brought mission "experts" to discuss contemporary mission theory and also allowed shared experience and collaboration.[69] Sponsored by the Mission Secretariat, the Center for Applied Research in the Apostolate was founded and brought together over thirty professional researchers who worked to develop mission strategies for congregations, the laity, and for dioceses. Its director from 1965 to 1973 was Louis J. Luzbetak, SVD, known around the world for integrating cultural anthropology into mission studies.

In the field of publication, *Worldmission*, edited through the national office of the Society for the Propagation of the Faith, represented an important effort to share and stimulate mission thought in the United States. The Mission Press of the Divine Word Missionaries made available European mission theorists in the 1930s and 1940s and published other mission literature. Orbis Books, launched by Maryknoll in 1970 in recognition of new understandings of globalization, has become a major venue for writers in non-Western theological disciplines. The books have been used extensively in mission-related and world cultures courses around the globe.

We end this narrative of 140 years with two contemporary stories. Recently a New Jersey parish gathered for Sunday worship with their pastor. A missionary spoke at all the eucharistic liturgies. The congregation was composed mainly of elderly persons of European backgrounds, the pastor was an African American, and the missionary was Nigerian. In a southern Texas parish, four lay persons from Colombia work as missionaries among mainly Hispanic parishes. The world Christianity John J. Considine had articulated in the 1940s has now been realized on the shores of his country in a way he might not have envisioned. And yet the cross-cultural mission picture of the United States in the mid-nineteenth century has endured as we move toward the twentieth-first century.

Field Distribution of U.S. Catholic Missionaries Overseas, 1960–96

Year	Africa	Near East	Far East	Oceania	Europe	North America	Carib-bean	Central America	South America	TOTAL
1960	781	111	1959	986	203	337	991	433	981	6782
1962[1]	901	75	2110	992	93	224	967	537	1274	7146
1964	1025	122	2332	846	69	220	1056	660	1796	8126
1966	1184	142	2453	953	38	211	1079	857	2386	9303
1968	1157	128	2470	1027	33	251	1198	936	2455	9655
1970	1141	39	2137	900	38	233	1067	738	2080	8373
1972	1107	59	1955	826	39	234	819	728	1889	7656
1973	1229	54	1962	811	40	253	796	763	1783	7691
1974	1121	60	1845	883	43	241	757	752	1716	7418
1975	1065	71	1814	808	37	252	698	734	1669	7148
1976	1042	68	1757	795	34	313	671	712	1618	7010
1977	1003	62	1659	784	34	296	629	702	1591	6760
1978	966	57	1601	769	34	339	593	705	1537	6601
1979	923	65	1562	743	37	332	562	686	1545	6455
1980	909	65	1576	711	35	294	548	699	1556	6393
1981	946	70	1529	696	36	315	511	686	1535	6324
1982	956	62	1501	673	32	319	522	669	1511	6245
1983[1]	990	68	1468	640	34	346	517	650	1533	6246
1984	967	84	1420	644	29	329	513	650	1498	6134
1985	986	78	1366	650	31	312	500	692	1441	6056
1986	944	73	1356	631	28	306	495	743	1461	6037
1987	971	76	1335	635	27	283	499	762	1485	6073
1988	984	72	1332	584	27	289	466	818	1491	6063
1989	968	65	1299	595	28	267	472	832	1475	6001
1990	945	64	1253	560	–	264	449	796	1413	5744
1991	933	65	1198	546	–	265	453	785	1350	5595
1992[1]	949	59	1163	512	–	105	431	810	1286	5467
1994			Survey results inconclusive for exact distribution by area.							4875
1996[2]	799		965	213	172	82	360		1573	4164

[1]Total number of missionaries for these years is accurate. Due to errors in accounting by region, however, figures do not add up to the total indicated.

[2]Figures for Near East and Far East are combined; figures for Central and South America are combined.

Source: U.S. Catholic Mission Association

Appendix II

U.S. Catholic Missionaries Overseas, 1960–96

Year	Diocesan Priests	Religious Priests	Religious Brothers	Religious Sisters	Seminar-ians	Lay Persons	TOTAL
1960	14	3018	575	2827	170	178	6872
1962	31	3172	720	2764	152	307	7146
1964	80	3438	782	3137	157	532	8126
1966	215	3731	901	3706	201	549	9303
1968	282	3727	869	4150	208	419	9655
1970	373	3117	666	3824	90	303	8373
1972[1]	246	3182	634	3121	97	376	7656
1973	237	3913[2]		3012		529	7691
1974	220	3048	639	2916	101	458	7418
1975	197	3023	669	2850	65	344	7148
1976	193	2961	691	2840	68	257	7010
1977	182	2882	630	2781	42	243	6760
1978	166	2830	610	2673	43	279	6601
1979	187	2800	592	2568	50	258	6455
1980	188	2750	592	2592	50	221	6393
1981	187	2702	584	2574	43	234	6324
1982	178	2668	578	2560	44	217	6245
1983	174	2668	569	2450	48	247	6346
1984	187	2603	549	2492	40	263	6134
1985	171	2500	558	2505	30	292	6056
1986	204	2473	532	2481	30	317	6037
1987	200	2394	570	2505	53	351	6073
1988	200	2420	504	2495	50	394	6063
1989	209	2364	494	2473	51	410	6001
1990	200	2257	477	2347	42	421	5744
1991	187	2200	468	2264	30	446	5595
1992	181	2183	449	2222	26	406	5467
1994	177	2007	408	1887	22	374	4875[3]
1996	173	1770	347	1513	18	343	4164[4]

[1]A corrected total for 1972 should read 7937, indicating losses of 436 from 1970 to 1972, and 246 from 1972 to 1973.
[2]Includes Religious Brothers and seminarians.
[3]Totals estimated due to inconclusive survey results.
[4]Alaska and Hawaii are no longer included as overseas missions.

Source: U.S. Catholic Mission Association

Notes

Introduction /
The Missionary Movement of the United States Catholic Church, 1841–1980

1. Marion Habig, OFM, a historian specializing in Latin America, identified some of the "first" American Catholic missionaries overseas in "The First American Foreign Mission-ers," *Illinois Catholic Historical Review* 11 (January 1929): 239–50, 364–69. See also his "Who Was First?" *Worldmission* 5 (Spring 1954): 55–78; Edward L. Murphy, SJ, *Teach Ye All Nations: The Principles of Catholic Missionary Work* (New York: Benziger, 1958); and Francis X. Curran, SJ, "Some Reflections on American Mission History," in J. Franklin Ewing, ed., *The Global Mission of the Church*, vol. 1 (New York: Fordham University Press, 1962), 1–7.

2. See, for example, R. Pung, SVD, *SVD Word in the World 1995/1996* (Steyl, Holland: Steyler Verlag, 1995), 9–120.

3. In the United States, Francis Markert, SVD, founder of the Mission Press at Techny, Illinois, originated the idea of Catholic Press Month. In addition to the society's mission magazines, the press produced large numbers of devotional pamphlets and other Catholic literature and provided apprenticeships for the technological aspects of journalism. The press building burned to the ground in 1960 and was not restored. Most of the twenty-six Brothers who had been working at the press used their skills in other Divine Word missions.

4. Joseph F. MacDonnell, SJ, *Jesuits by the Tigris: Men for Others in Baghdad* (Boston: Jesuit Mission Press, 1994). The Jesuits were invited by the Iraq government to open a high school and college (al-Hikma University) for Muslim young men. Simon Smith, SJ, a faculty member, identified Iraq as a "faith mission, where you must *be* because you can't proselytize.... Baghdad forced us out of the traditional mode of thinking about missions." Smith remarked about the strong bonds created between students and faculty. Over the course of the Jesuits' service, about half of the Catholic alumni left Iraq and came to live in the United States (interview by author).

Chapter 1 /
Mission in the Colonial Period, 1492–1775

1. John Gilmary Shea, *History of the Catholic Missions among the Indian Tribes of the United States, 1529–1854* (New York: Edward Dunigan & Brother, 1855). For an analysis of Shea's motifs and approach to history, see Henry Warner Bowden, "John Gilmary Shea: A Study of Methods and Goals in Historiography," *Catholic Historical Review* 54 (1968): 235–60.

2. For an overview of major historians of the American Catholic experience through John Tracy Ellis, see J. Douglas Thomas, "A Century of American Catholic Historiography," *U.S. Catholic Historian* 6 (Winter 1987): 25–49.

China historian John King Fairbank argued for an examination of the missionary, the "in-visible figure" in American history, to understand U.S. expansion after the Spanish-American War. The argument appeared in his presidential address to the American Historical Association, "Assignment for the '70s," *American Historical Review* 74 (February 1969): 861–79. It could be further argued that the missionary (as well as the mission movement) has been the "invisible figure" in American Catholic historiography over the past thirty years.

3. Document in John Tracy Ellis, *Documents of American Catholic History,* vol. 1 (Wilmington, Del.: Michael Glazier, 1987), 1–2.

4. Secular power frequently interfaced with the ecclesial realm. In addition to Philip II's concern for orthodoxy in religion, for example, he also desired to have the Franciscans and Cistercians freed from French control and to have Jesuits in Spain released from French authority. Reports from the missionaries back to the Crown provide insight on mission problems and approaches. See, for example, *Friar Bringas Reports to the King: Methods of Indoctrination on the Frontier of New Spain, 1796–97* (Tucson: University of Arizona Press, 1977). Bringas, a *criollo,* was born in Sonora in 1762 and attended the Franciscan mission college at Querétaro, where he eventually became procurator and official visitator to the Pimería Alta missions. Later he was a chaplain to the Royal Army and became involved in various plots against Mexican independence.

5. For the history of its foundation, see Josef Metzler, ed., *Sacrae Congregationis de Propaganda Fide memoria rerum, 1622–1772* (Rome: Herder, 1973); Henry Outram Evennett, *The Spirit of the Counter-Reformation* (London: Cambridge University Press, 1968); and Karl Müller, SVD, "The Main Principles of Centralized Government for the Missions," in *Rethinking the Church's Mission,* Concilium Series, vol. 13 (New York: Paulist, 1966), 11–33.

6. The seventeenth century saw the formation of several mission seminaries, including the Carmelites (Rome, 1613), the Vincentians (Paris, 1625), and the Paris Foreign Mission Society (1658, 1663).

7. For an overview of European Catholic presence in colonial times, see John Tracy Ellis, *Catholics in Colonial America* (Baltimore: Helicon, 1965); James Hennesey, SJ, *American Catholics: A History of the Roman Catholic Community in the United States* (New York: Oxford University Press, 1981); Jay Dolan, *The American Catholic Experience: A History from Colonial Times to the Present* (Garden City, N.J.: Doubleday, 1985); and Charles H. Lippy, Robert Choquette, and Stafford Poole, *Christianity Comes to the Americas, 1492–1776* (New York: Paragon House, 1992). For the perspective of the conquered people, see Miguel León-Portillo, *The Broken Spears: The Aztec Account of the Conquest of Mexico* (Boston: Beacon Press, 1962). For an analysis of the religious dimensions of cultural interaction, providing insight as to why religious interaction did or did not produce lasting results among the First Nations, see Henry Warner Bowden, *American Indians and Christian Missions: Studies in Cultural Conflict* (Chicago: University of Chicago Press, 1981); James Axtell, *The Invasion Within: The Contest of Cultures in Colonial North America* (New York: Oxford University Press, 1986); Belden C. Lane, *Landscapes of the Sacred: Geography and Narrative in American Spirituality* (New York: Paulist Press, 1988); Catherine Albanese, *America: Religions and Religion,* 2d ed. (Santa Barbara: University of California Press, 1992), 37–43; and Gary H. Gossen, ed., *South and Meso-American Native Spirituality: From the Cult of the Feathered Serpent to the Theology of Liberation* (New York: Crossroad, 1995).

For an understanding of the Franciscan approaches to mission, see Francisco Morales, ed., *Franciscan Presence in the Americas, 1492–1900* (Potomac, Md.: Academy of Franciscan History, 1983); John Leddy Phelan, *The Millennial Kingdom of the Franciscans in the New World,* 2d ed. (Berkeley: University of California Press, 1970); Edwin Edward Sylvest, Jr., *Motifs of Franciscan Mission Theory in Sixteenth Century New Spain* (Washington, D.C.: Academy of American Franciscan History, 1975); Robert Ricard, *The Spiritual Conquest of Mexico: An Essay on the Apostolate and the Evangelizing Methods of the Mendicant Orders in New Spain, 1523–1572* (Berkeley: University of California Press, 1966); Rosalind B. Brooke, *The Coming of the Friars* (New York: Barnes & Noble, 1975); Juan Alfonso, "Spirit of the First Franciscan Missionaries to Texas," *U.S. Catholic Historian* 9 (1990): 49–66;

and Moises Sandoval, *Fronteras: A History of the Latin American Church in the U.S.A.* (San Antonio: Mexican American Cultural Center, 1983).

8. For an overview of the Dominican's life and for translations of his work, see Bartolomé de Las Casas, *The Only Way,* ed. Helen Rand Parish, trans. Francis Patrick Sullivan (New York: Paulist Press, 1992); Las Casas, *Tears of the Indians,* ed. Arthur Helps (Williamstown, Mass.: J. Lilburne, 1970); George Sanderlin, *Witness: Writings of Bartolomé de Las Casas* (Maryknoll, N.Y.: Orbis Books, 1992); Francis P. Sullivan, notes and translations, *Indian Freedom: The Cause of Bartolomé de Las Casas* (Kansas City, Mo.: Sheed & Ward, 1995); Gustavo Gutiérrez, *Las Casas: In Search of the Poor of Jesus Christ* (Maryknoll, N.Y.: Orbis Books, 1993).

9. Pope Paul III, *Sublimis Deus,* in Ellis, ed., *Documents of American Catholic History,* 1:7–8.

10. Figures cited in Ricard, *Spiritual Conquest of Mexico,* 23. For a map locating the establishments of the three mendicant groups (c. 1570), see ibid., 62–63.

11. Ibid., 38.

12. George Kubler, "Two Modes of Franciscan Architecture: New Mexico and California," in Morales, ed., *Franciscan Presence in the Americas,* 369–75.

13. The periodization is from Phelan, *Millennial Kingdom of the Franciscans.* For the thirteenth-century Franciscan approach to mission, see E. Randolph Daniel, *The Franciscan Concept of Mission in the High Middle Ages* (n.p.: University Press of Kentucky, 1975).

14. Sahagún, quoted in Sylvest, *Motifs of Franciscan Mission Theory,* 45.

15. Sahagún, quoted in ibid., 51.

16. Phelan, *Millennial Kingdom of the Franciscans,* 49.

17. Sahagún, quoted in Ricard, *Spiritual Conquest of Mexico,* 40.

18. Sylvest, *Motifs of Franciscan Mission Theory,* 64. Dominicans and Augustinians also produced some linguistic books. For a description of the development of ethnography and linguistics among the mendicant orders in Mexico, see Ricard, *Spiritual Conquest of Mexico,* 39–60.

19. Ricard, *Spiritual Conquest of Mexico,* 58.

20. A list of the fifty-one Jesuits who served over the years in lower California, along with an indication of their city of origin, appears in Zephyrin Engelhardt, OFM, *Missions and Missionaries of California,* vol. 1 (San Francisco: James H. Barry Company, 1908), 285. The lot of the Jesuits expelled from New Spain was difficult. Many languished and died in the port cities because no vessel would return them to Spain.

The Spanish viceroy assigned the Jesuit missions to the Franciscans. The Dominicans requested from the friars some of these missions. See the concordat between the Franciscan and Dominican friars dividing the California missions in Ellis, ed., *Documents of American Catholic History,* 1:31–33.

21. Mission colleges were founded in Mexico to form men specifically for work with indigenous groups. The first missionary college in the Americas, Santa Cruz, was located in Querétaro and was founded on 8 May 1682. A second apostolic college was founded at Guadalupe, Zacatecas, by a former missionary in Texas, Antonio Margil. The third Franciscan college of San Fernando, Mexico City, was founded on 15 October 1734. The official decree which authorized the monasteries indicated that these apostolic colleges were to be characterized by self-denial and spirituality. Prescriptions about poverty, fasting, and going barefoot were to be meticulously observed. Mental prayer was to be practiced for an hour each morning and evening. The description is similar to the points of the Franciscan Capuchin reform, which had occurred between 1529 and 1536 in Europe. In the apostolic college, lectures were given on the language of the First Nations and on the manner of converting, teaching catechism, and instructing converts. The men went on mission in pairs. For a description of the colleges and selections from their charter, see Engelhardt, *Missions and Missionaries of California,* 1:614–17. The colleges remained active until 1908, when they were suppressed by the Franciscan minister general.

22. *Diary of Fra Juniper Serra, Being an Account of His Journey from Loreto to San Diego, March 28 to June 30, 1769* (North Providence, R.I.: Franciscan Missionaries of Mary, n.d.), 26–27. Mary of Agreda (1602–65), a Poor Clare mystic in Spain, was said to have bilocated and instructed the Jermano tribe in Christianity before 1629. The tribe is located in modern-day San Angelo, Texas.

23. Ibid., 25.

24. Charles W. Polzer, *Rules and Precepts of the Jesuit Missions of Northwestern New Spain* (Tucson: University of Arizona Press, 1976), discusses Jesuit mission methodology and includes translations of source material from official visits of Jesuit missions in the Sonora area.

25. Eusebio Francisco Kino, *Historical Memoir of the Pimería Alta*, trans. Herbert Bolton, 2 vols. (Cleveland: Arthur Clark Co., 1919; Berkeley: University of California Press, 1948); Kino, *Kino Reports to Headquarters*, trans. Ernest Burrus, SJ (Rome: Institutum Historicum Societatis Jesu, 1954); Thomas J. Campbell, "Eusebio Kino (1644–1711)," *Catholic Historical Review* 5 (January 1920): 353–76; Herbert E. Bolton, *The Rim of Christendom: A Biography of Eusebio Francisco Kino* (New York: Macmillan, 1936).

26. *Reductions* was a term for the " 'leading back' of peoples from uncivilized, rustic living conditions to more highly organized communities as a mission" (Polzer, *Rules and Precepts of the Jesuit Missions*, 61).

27. For examination of the concept of *frontier* as it relates to continued Catholic life in the Southwest and in Texas, see *U.S. Catholic Historian* 12 (Fall 1994), which is devoted to the topic. Several articles point out that the end of the "mission" period was not necessarily the end of the "Church" in the Southwest and Texas.

28. For documents relating to the French missions, see Shea, *History of the Catholic Missions*, and Shea, *Jesuit Relations and Allied Documents*, 10 vols. (Cleveland: Burrows Brothers Publishers, 1896–1901; New York: Pageant Book Company, 1959).

For the work of French missionaries in the New World, see David O'Brien, *Faith and Friendship: Catholicism in the Diocese of Syracuse, 1886–1986* (Syracuse, N.Y.: Catholic Diocese of Syracuse, 1987), chap. 1; Thomas Hughes, SJ, *History of the Society of Jesus in the United States,* vol. 1, 1580–1645, vol. 2, 1645–1773 (New York: Longmans, Green & Company, 1908, 1916); Louis Hennepin, *A Description of Louisiana,* trans. John Gilmary Shea (French ed., 1683; facsimile, Ann Arbor, Mich.: University Microfilms, 1966); Hennepin, *A New Discovery of a Vast Country in America,* ed. Reuben Gold Thwaites, 2 vols. (1698; facsimile, Chicago: A. C. McClurg & Co.); Claude L. Vogel, *The Capuchins in French Louisiana, 1722–1766* (New York: Joseph F. Wagner, 1928); and Léandre Poirier, OFM, "Franciscan Recollects en Nouvelle-France, 1615–1849," in Morales, ed., *Franciscan Presence in the Americas,* 162–94.

Narratives of French missionary women in North America appear in Marguerite Bourgeoys, *The Writings of Marguerite Bourgeoys: Autobiography and Spiritual Testament,* trans. Mary Virginia Cotter, CND (Montreal: Congregation of Notre Dame, 1976); Maryann Foley, CND, "Uncloistered Life for Women: Marguerite Bourgeoys' Experiment in Ville-Marie," *U.S. Catholic Historian* 10, nos. 1, 2 (1992): 37–44; and Mary of St. Augustine Tranchepain, *Account of the Voyage of the Ursulines to New Orleans in 1727* (n.p., n.d.), translated by John Gilmary Shea from the edition of the original manuscript printed in Shea's Cramoisy series, 1859. *The Ursulines in New Orleans and Our Lady of Prompt Succor* (New York: P. J. Kenedy, 1925) contains several letters and other documents, including the treaty between the Ursulines and the Dutch West India Company, 1727.

29. An excellent summary of seventeenth-century ecclesial, spiritual, and political life appears in Christopher J. Kauffman, *Tradition and Transformation in Catholic Culture: The Priests of Saint Sulpice in the United States from 1791 to the Present* (New York: Macmillan, 1988). See also Dominique Julia and Willem Frijhoff, "The French Priest in Modern Times," *Concilium* 47 (1969): 147–59.

30. P. de Bérulle, *Oeuvres complètes,* ed. J.-P. Migne, 630, quoted in Julia and Frijhoff, "The French Priest in Modern Times," 149.

31. For the interaction of missionaries with First Nations in Canada, see John Webster Grant, *Moon of Wintertime: Missionaries and Indians of Canada in Encounter Since 1534* (Toronto: University of Toronto Press, 1984).

32. Joyce Marshall, ed. and trans., *Word from New France: The Selected Letters of Marie de L'Incarnation* (Toronto: Oxford University Press, 1967); *The Autobiography of Venerable Marie of the Incarnation: Mystic and Missionary,* trans. John J. Sullivan (Chicago: Loyola University Press, 1964).

33. Hennesey, *American Catholics,* 25.

34. The date of this letter is 1 June 1649. Edna Kenton, ed., *The Indians of North America,* vol. 2 (New York: Harcourt, Brace & Company, 1927), 17. These books are selections from *Jesuit Relations and Allied Documents.*

35. Kenton, ed., *The Indians of North America,* 2:15 (date of letter is 1649). See also Shea, *Jesuit Relations and Allied Documents,* chap. 6, document no. 203.

36. Ellis, ed., *Documents of American Catholic History,* 1:49–51 (from Shea, *Jesuit Relations and Allied Documents,* 12:17–123). The reference to the crucified Christ might also be an echo of the missions in France in the seventeenth century. In one mission exercise, the priest took the part of Christ in the passion procession. At the end of this living drama, which included the "crowds" who came to the mission, the parishioners were led to tears and repentance, having been moved to the heart by this "living passion."

37. "Documents: A Bishop for the Indians in 1790," *Catholic Historical Review* 3 (1917): 79–89.

38. Joseph P. Donnelly, SJ, *Jacques Marquette, 1637–1675* (Chicago: Loyola University Press, 1989), interweaves Marquette's missionary call with his practical and technical skills.

39. Hennepin, *A Description of Louisiana,* 335–39; Hennepin, *New Discovery of a Vast Country in America.*

40. Hennesey, *American Catholics,* 31–32.

41. See the excerpt from *Jesuit Relations and Allied Documents* in Ellis, ed., *Documents of American Catholic History,* 1:86–93. A list of the names of French missionaries, most of them Jesuit, appears in the appendix to Shea, *History of the Catholic Missions.*

42. The first Ursuline congregation was established by Angela Merici in 1538, two years before the Jesuits were founded. Merici wanted a "workable relationship between prayer and the apostolate," an opportunity not provided for women religious of the time. See Lynn Jarrell, OSU, JCD, "The Development of Legal Structures for Women Religious Between 1500 and 1900: A Study of Selected Institutes of Religious Life for Women," *U.S. Catholic Historian* 10, nos. 1, 2 (1989): 25–36. Quotations taken from Tranchepain, *Account of the Voyage of the Ursulines to New Orleans in 1727.*

43. Sister Marie Magdeleine Hachard de St. Stanislas to her father in France, 24 April 1728, in *The Ursulines in New Orleans and Our Lady of Prompt Succor,* 230.

44. Ibid., 231.

45. See Kauffman, *Tradition and Transformation in Catholic Culture,* for the history of the Sulpicians. An earlier history of the society devoted a chapter to Sulpician Missionary bishops and missionaries. See Charles Herbermann, *Sulpicians in the United States* (New York: Encyclopedia Press, 1916), 140–93.

46. Hennesey, *American Catholics,* 30.

47. Andrew White's account of the establishment of the church appears in Ellis, ed., *Documents of American Catholic History,* 1:100–108. For the work of Jesuit missionaries in the English colonies, see Peter Guilday, "An Account of the Catholic Religion in the English Colonies of America," *Catholic Historical Review* 6 (January 1921): 517–24, which is an overview report sent to Propaganda Fide; Thomas Hughes, SJ, *History of the Society of Jesus in North America: Colonial and Federal Period,* vol. 1; and Edwin W. Beitzell, *The Jesuit Missions of St. Mary's County, Maryland* (Abell, Md.: privately printed, 1977).

48. Hennesey, *American Catholics,* 43. A few secular clergy traveled in the area, visiting small groups of Catholics, instructing them, hearing confessions, and celebrating Eucharist. One of these priests was Joseph Moseley. The first German clergy arrived in Pennsylvania in July 1741.

49. Maryland historian J. Thomas Scharf, noted in Beitzell, *Jesuit Missions of St. Mary's County, Maryland,* 4.

50. Ellis, ed., *Documents of American Catholic History,* 1:103–10, here 108.

51. Beitzell, *Jesuit Missions of St. Mary's County, Maryland,* 5.

52. Ibid., 7; Dolan, *American Catholic Experience,* 77–78.

53. Dolan, *American Catholic Experience,* 88.

54. For Carroll's biography, see Peter Guilday, *The Life and Times of John Carroll, Archbishop of Baltimore, 1735–1815* (New York: Encyclopedic Press, 1922), and Anabelle Melville, *John Carroll of Baltimore, Founder of the American Catholic Hierarchy* (New York: Scribner, 1955). For an analysis of his approach to leadership, see James Hennesey, SJ, "An Eighteenth-Century Bishop: John Carroll of Baltimore," in Gerald P. Fogarty, ed., *Patterns of Episcopal Leadership* (New York: Macmillan, 1989), 5–34.

55. Carroll to Farmer (n.p., n.d.), *John Carroll Papers,* 1:156–57, quoted in Hennesey, "An Eighteenth-Century Bishop," 16. Another letter on this subject is Carroll to Charles Plowden, Rock Creek, 18 September 1784, *John Carroll Papers,* 1:151, quoted in ibid.

56. The Jesuits were disbanded from 1773 to 1814 (and earlier in other European countries), so technically Neale was not a Jesuit at the time of his mission work. For documents on Neale's authorization, see Leonard Neale Papers, 12 A-U-1, pp. 2–20, Archives, Archdiocese of Baltimore. Finbar Kenneally in *United States Documents in the Propaganda Fide Archives* notes Neale in vol. 1, nos. 28, 29, 30; vol. 3, no. 1259. Neale received his first Propaganda Fide assignment to Demerara in 1789, but surrendered his papers to Propaganda Fide because this agency had decided not to employ him on that mission. He received his assignment again on 11 July 1780. Information obtained from the Reverend Paul K. Thomas, archivist, archdiocese of Baltimore, 24 April 1995. See also Sister M. Bernetta Brislen, OSF, "The Episcopacy of Leonard Neale," *Historical Records and Studies* 34 (1945): 24–25.

57. Thomas Jefferson's response of 15 May 1804 appears in Ellis, ed., *Documents of American Catholic History,* 1:184–85.

58. This story is told in Henry J. Koren, *The Serpent and the Dove: A History of the Congregation of the Holy Ghost in the United States, 1745–1984* (Pittsburgh: Spiritus Press, 1985), 4–19.

59. Bowden, *American Indians and Christian Missions,* 67–69.

60. Ibid., 54–56.

61. The Jesuits did have at least one "reduction" outside of Québec started by Paul Le Jeune. See Donnelly, *Jacques Marquette, 1637-1675,* 84.

62. This explanation is developed at length in Walter Ong, *Orality and Literacy* (London: Methuen & Co., 1982).

63. J. B. Harley, "The Map as Mission: Jesuit Cartography as an Art of Persuasion," in Jane ten Brink Goldsmith et al., eds., *Jesuit Art in North American Collections* (Dobbs Ferry, N.Y.: Morgan Press, Inc., 1991), 28–31, here 31.

64. Jacques Bruyas came to Canada with Marquette. For information on Garacontié, see O'Brien, chap. 1; on Ganneaktena, see Shea, *History of the Catholic Missions,* 261–62; on Tekakwitha, see Ellis, ed., *Documents of American Catholic History,* 1:63–71; *The Positio of the Historical Section of the Sacred Congregation of Rites on the Introduction of the Cause for the Beatification and Canonization and on the Virtues of Katharine Tekakwitha: The Lily of the Mohawks* (New York: Fordham University Press, 1940); and *The Kateri Movement: First Nations Spiritual Traditions Coming Alive in the Roman Catholic Church* (Toronto: Villagers Communications, 1992). Kateri's cause for beatification was initially proposed at the Third Plenary Council of Baltimore (1883), and she was declared "blessed" by Catholic Church authorities in 1980.

Chapter 2 /
Mission within the United States, 1820–1920

1. Louise Callan, *Philippine Duchesne: Frontier Missionary of the Sacred Heart* (Westminster, Md.: Newman Press, 1957); Catherine Mooney, *Philippine Duchesne: A Woman with the Poor* (New York: Paulist Press, 1990).

2. Maria Michele Armato, OP, and Mary Jeremy Finnegan, eds., *The Memoirs of Father Samuel Mazzuchelli, OP* (Chicago: Priory Press, 1967).

3. Philip Gleason, ed., *Documentary Reports on Early American Catholicism* (New York: Arno, 1978), presents the missionary side of Bishop Flaget, 1815; Archbishop Maréchal, 1818; Stephen Badin, 1821; and Bishop Bruté, 1836, in that the documents provided the Propaganda Fide with an idea of the needs of their respective dioceses, and in so doing indicated the men's perspective on mission and evangelization.

4. Peter Clarke, "John England, Missionary to America, Then and Now," in Gerald P. Fogarty, *Patterns of Episcopal Leadership* (New York: Macmillan, 1989), 68–84. See also Clarke, *A Free Church in a Free Society: The Ecclesiology of John England, Bishop of Charleston, 1820–1842, A Nineteenth Century Bishop in the Southern United States* (Hartsville, S.C.: Center for John England Studies, 1982).

5. Clarke, "John England, Missionary to America," 71–72.

6. *Lay trusteeism* is the term used to describe lay management and administration of church property apart from ecclesiastical supervision and control.

7. Clarke, "John England, Missionary to America," 71–72. England had also been given a diplomatic mission to Haiti by the Vatican.

8. Some representative immigration figures in the nineteenth century would include:

Country	1830	1860	1880	1890
Germany	6,761	951,667	718,182	1,452,970
Ireland	50,724	914,119	436,871	655,482
Italy	408	9,231	55,759	307,309
Total of all immigrants	143,439	2,598,214	2,812,191	5,246,613

Source: Gerald Shaughnessy, *Has the Immigrant Kept the Faith?* (New York: Macmillan, 1925), 274–75.

9. James Hennesey, SJ, *American Catholics: A History of the Roman Catholic Community in the United States* (New York: Oxford University Press, 1981), and Jay P. Dolan, *The American Catholic Experience: A History from Colonial Times to the Present* (Garden City, N.Y.: Doubleday, 1985).

10. Extensive research has been done on immigrant groups in the United States. Among the books which treat nineteenth-century Catholics are Shaughnessy, *Has the Immigrant Kept the Faith?*; Carl Wittke, *We Who Built America: The Saga of the Immigrant* (New York: Prentice-Hall, 1939); Milton M. Gordon, *Assimilation in American Life: The Role of Race, Religion, and National Origins* (New York: Oxford University Press, 1964); Cecyle S. Neidle, *America's Immigrant Women* (Boston: Twayne Publishing, 1975); Randall M. Miller and Thomas D. Marzik, eds., *Immigrants and Religion in Urban America* (Philadelphia: Temple University Press, 1977); Stephen Thernstrom, Ann Orlov, and Oscar Handlin, eds., *Harvard Encyclopedia of American Ethnic Groups* (Cambridge: Harvard University Press, 1980); and Dolores Liptak, RSM, *Immigrants and Their Church* (New York: Macmillan, 1989).

For a selected overview of Irish, German, Italian, and Polish Catholic immigrant experience, see Dolores Liptak, RSM, ed., *A Church of Many Cultures: Selected Historical Essays on Ethnic American Catholicism* (New York: Garland Publishing Company, 1988).

11. First Provincial Council of Baltimore, "Pastoral Letter to Clergy," 17 October 1829, in Hugh J. Nolan, ed., *Pastoral Letters of the United States Catholic Bishops*, vol. 1 (Washington, D.C.: U.S. Catholic Conference, 1983), 50–65, here 56. The writing of this pastoral is attributed to John England.

12. For this archbishop's biography, see Peter Leo Johnson, *Crosier on the Frontier: The Life of John Martin Henni* (Madison: The State Historical Society of Wisconsin, 1959).

13. Ibid., 27–28.

14. The Ludwig Mission Society was established in 1838 in Munich by King Ludwig of Bavaria as a German counterpart to the SPF of Lyons and Paris. Some nativists in Henni's diocese viewed the society as a political front for subversive foreign activities in Milwaukee.

15. Suellen Hoy, "Late in the Field: Catholic Sisters in Twentieth Century Ireland and the New Religious History," *Journal of Women's History* 6, no. 4 (1995): 64–98, presents one reason for the increase in the numbers of Irish women entering religious congregations in the United States. Sister Eustace, a Sister of Mercy, ran a women's "seminary" and was responsible for over seven hundred women going abroad, four hundred of whom entered religious congregations in the United States. Hoy notes that of the two "waves" of women who came, the first, mainly older women recruited by bishops and clergy, were innovators, while the second, younger "wave" recruited by American Sisters were consolidators in the congregations where they assumed leadership.

16. For a specific example of the Sisters' understanding of "women's role," see Maureen Fitzgerald, "The Perils of 'Passion and Poverty': Women Religious and the Care of Single Women in New York City, 1845–1900," *U.S. Catholic Historian* 10, nos. 1, 2 (1989): 45–58.

17. Mary Carol Conroy, SCL, "Sister Joanna Bruner, Catalyst of the Health Care Ministry of the Sisters of Charity of Leavenworth, 1858–1984," *U.S. Catholic Historian* 10, nos. 1, 2 (1989): 107–12.

18. *The Travels of Mother Frances Xavier Cabrini: Foundress of the Missionary Sisters of the Sacred Heart of Jesus* (Strentham Hall, Exeter: Giovanni Serpentelli, 1925); Mary Louise Sullivan, MSC, *Mother Cabrini, "Italian Immigrant of the Century"* (New York: Center for Migration Studies, 1992).

19. *Concilii Plenarii Baltimorensis II, Acta et Decreta* (Baltimore: John Murphy, 1868), 237–38. The bishops also appended to this document the 1745 decree of Pope Benedict XIV on the usefulness of missions. Ibid., 328–32.

20. Joseph Wissel (1830–1912), *The Redemptorist on the American Missions* (New York: Arno Press, 1920), 3. For the relevance of these missions, see Jay Dolan, *Catholic Revivalism: The American Experience, 1830–1900* (Notre Dame, Ind.: University of Notre Dame Press, 1978).

21. Dolan, *American Catholic Experience*, 245–46.

22. Albert Raboteau, "A Progress Report on 'Afro-American Religious History: A Documentary History Project,'" *The Council of Societies for the Study of Religion Bulletin* 20 (September 1991): 57–61.

23. Overviews of the history of African American Catholics appear in John Thomas Gillard, SSJ, *The Negro American: A Mission Investigation* (Cincinnati: Catholic Students Mission Crusade, 1935); Gillard, *The Catholic Church and the American Negro* (Baltimore: St. Joseph's Society Press, 1929; New York: Johnson Reprint, 1968); Gillard, *Colored Catholics in the United States* (Baltimore: Josephite Press, 1941); Cyprian Davis, OSB, *The History of Black Catholics in the United States* (New York: Crossroad, 1990); and Stephen Ochs, *Desegregating the Altar: The Josephites and the Struggle for Black Priests, 1871–1960* (Baton Rouge: Louisiana State University Press, 1990). See also *U.S. Catholic Historian* 5, no. 1 (1986), the theme of which is "Black Experience," and *U.S. Catholic Historian* 7, nos. 2, 3 (1988), whose theme is "The Black Catholic Community, 1880–1987."

24. "Chronology of Black Presence in Catholic Maryland, 1633–1989," a helpful outline, can be found at the Archdiocese of Washington Office of Black Catholics, Neville R. Waters, Jr., coordinator.

25. The other two communities of women religious were founded by free women of color. Most of the eight communities taught some black children. See Barbara Misner, SCSC, *"Highly Respectable and Accomplished Ladies": Catholic Women Religious in America, 1789–1850* (New York: Garland Publishing, 1988), 75, 203–6.

26. Maria M. Lannon, *Response to Love: The Story of Mother Mary Elizabeth Lange, OSP* (Washington, D.C.: Josephite Pastoral Center, 1992); Sister M. Reginald Gerdes, OSP, "To Educate and Evangelize: Black Catholic Schools of the Oblate Sisters of Providence, 1828–1880," *U.S. Catholic Historian* 7, nos. 2, 3 (1988): 183–200.

27. Sister Mary Francis Borgia Hart, SSF, *Violets in the King's Garden: A History of the Sisters of the Holy Family of New Orleans* (New Orleans: privately printed, 1976); Vincent J. Giese, "The Sisters of the Holy Family: Dedicated to the Needy," *Our Sunday Visitor,* 9 April 1989, 10–11.

28. Guilday, *National Pastorals of the American Hierarchy,* 221. See also the decree *De nigrorius salute procuranda,* in *Concilii Plenarii Baltimorensis II, Acta et Decreta,* 243–47.

29. Cyprian Davis, OSB, "Black Catholics in Nineteenth Century America," *U.S. Catholic Historian* 5, no. 1 (1986): 1–17, here 11. Augustine Tolton (1854–97) was the first recognized African American priest. He was ordained in 1886 at the Lateran Basilica in Rome and worked principally in the Chicago Archdiocese.

30. Ibid., 1. The 1829 Provincial Council of Baltimore passed a decree putting the Indian and Negro missions under the charge of the Jesuits. For an overview of Catholic parish life in the South, see Michael J. McNally, "A Peculiar Institution: Catholic Parish Life and the Pastoral Mission to the Blacks in the Southeast, 1850–1980," *U.S. Catholic Historian* 5, no. 1 (1986): 67–80.

31. W. H. Gross, "The Missions for the Colored People," in *Memorial Volume: Sermons of the Third Plenary Council* (Baltimore: John Murphy, 1884), 71–74, here 72.

32. For an understanding of Slattery's life, his methods of evangelization of black Americans, and his intellectual position vis-à-vis modernism, see the analysis of William L. Portier, "Modernism in the United States: The Case of John R. Slattery (1851–1926)," in Ronald Burke, Gary Lease, and George Gilmore, eds., *Varieties of Modernism* (Mobile, Ala.: Spring Hill College, 1986), 77–97; Portier, "John R. Slattery's Vision for the Evangelization of American Blacks," *U.S. Catholic Historian* 5, no. 1 (1986): 19–44; and Sister Jamie T. Phelps, OP, "John R. Slattery's Missionary Strategies," *U.S. Catholic Historian* 7, no. 3 (1988): 201–14. For the Josephite's speech at the Columbian Catholic Congress, see John R. Slattery, "The Negro Race: Their Condition, Present and Future," *Catholic World* 58 (November 1893): 219–31.

33. Portier, "John R. Slattery's Vision for the Evangelization of American Blacks," 41.

34. J. J. Mueller, SJ, Ann Rule, and Sister Carol Stoecklin, RSM, *Valuing Our Difference: The History of African-American Catholics in the United States* (n.p.: Roa-Brown, 1993), 88.

35. *Three Afro-American Catholic Congresses* (reprint, New York: Arno Press, 1978).

36. Almost a century later, the black bishops of the United States issued a pastoral, "Black Bishops' Pastoral on Evangelization," *Origins* 14 (18 October 1984): 273–87.

A remarkable set of documents is in the Secret Vatican Archives, telling the story of early twentieth-century black American Catholics. One item, written by Joseph Anciaux, a Belgian missionary to Native Americans, provided a frank portrayal of the social, political, legal, and civil status of blacks in the United States, identified examples of discrimination of blacks in the American Catholic Church, including their exclusion from attendance at the Catholic University of America, and at Benedictine, Jesuit, and Dominican colleges, and their refusal as candidates for the diocesan priesthood. See Joseph Anciaux, *De miserabili conditione Catholicum negrorum in America* (Nammurei: E. Typis Jac Godenne, 1903). This report was sent to the apostolic delegate and is located in Titolo II, fasc. 160b/1, Apostolic Delegation, Stati Uniti, Vatican Archives. For information on Anciaux and the work of Katharine Drexel among blacks and Indians, see Joseph Martino, *Canonizationis Ser-*

vae Dei Catharinae Mariae Drexel, Positio Super Virtutibus, vol. 1, *Expositio Historica et Documenta* (Rome: Guerra, 1986).

Thomas Wyatt Turner, the chairperson of the Committee for the Advancement of Colored Catholics, an organization formed in 1916, wrote to Cardinal Gibbons, the leading prelate of the American Catholic Church, and to the apostolic delegate about the condition of black Catholics in the United States. For the Turner correspondence, see Titolo II, fasc. 160b/2, Apostolic Delegation, Stati Uniti, Vatican Archives. For a history of the organization, see Marilyn Wenzke Nickels, *Black Catholic Protests and the Federated Catholics, 1917–1933* (New York: Garland Publishing, 1988).

37. For their story in the southern United States, see Henry Koren, CSSp, *To the Ends of the Earth: A General History of the Congregation of the Holy Ghost* (Pittsburgh: Duquesne University Press, 1983).

38. The story of the Sisters' work appears in Mary E. Best, *Seventy Septembers* (privately printed, Holy Spirit Missionary Sisters, 1988).

39. "Katharine Drexel Crafts Constitution of Her Congregation, May 25, 1907," in John Tracy Ellis, ed. *Documents of American Catholic History,* vol. 2 (Wilmington, Del.: Michael Glazier, 1987), 574–76, here 575.

40. For observations about the first members of this congregation, see Patricia Lynch, SBS, "Collective Biography: Founding Women of the Sisters of the Blessed Sacrament," *U.S. Catholic Historian* 10, nos. 1, 2 (1989): 101–6. For Drexel's biography, see Consuela Marie Duffy, SBS, *Katharine Drexel: A Biography* (Philadelphia: Peter Reilly, 1965). On 20 November 1988, Drexel was declared "blessed" by the Roman Catholic Church, a step in official Church recognition of a person's sanctity. The documents assembled for this process appear in Martino, *Canonizationis Servae Dei Catharinae Mariae Drexel.*

41. For the life of the foundress, see Sister Mary Tonra, *Led by the Spirit: A Biography of Mother Boniface Keasey, MSBT* (New York: Gardner Press, 1984).

42. For the role of religion in frontier times, see Ferenc M. Szasz, ed., *Religion in the West* (Manhattan, Kans.: Sunflower University Press, 1984); on the images and place of frontier women, see Sandra L. Myres, *Westering Women and the Frontier Experience, 1800–1915* (Albuquerque: University of New Mexico Press, 1982).

43. Blandina Segal, *At the End of the Santa Fe Trail* (Milwaukee: Bruce, 1948).

44. Granjon to Cardinal Gibbons, 22 July 1900, A-17, Henry R. Granjon Papers, Archives of the Tucson Diocese. The bishop had worked at the restoration of this mission and had earlier labored with Joseph Freri in northern Arizona. Granjon was in charge of the national Society for the Propagation of the Faith in 1897, and Freri became national director from 1903 to 1922. For Granjon's perceptions of the settlers and indigenous people in his diocese, see Henry Granjon, *Along the Rio Grande: A Pastoral Visit to Southwest New Mexico in 1902,* edited and annotated by Michael Romero Taylor (Albuquerque: University of New Mexico Press, 1986).

45. For primary documents, see Frederic Baraga, *The Diary of Bishop Frederic Baraga: First Bishop of Marquette, Michigan,* edited and annotated by Regis M. Walling and N. Daniel Rupp, trans. Joseph Gregorich and Paul Prud'homme (Detroit: Wayne State University Press, 1990). Maksimilijan Jezernik, *Frederick Baraga: A Portrait of the First Bishop of Marquette, Based on the Archives of the Congregatio de Propaganda Fide* (New York: Studia Slovenica, 1968), contains information from the Baraga documents at Propaganda but is also hagiographical. Charles A. Ceglar, *The Works of Bishop Baraga,* vol. 1 (Hamilton, Ontario, Canada, 1991), contains facsimile pages and overviews of Baraga's devotional, catechetical, and doctrinal works, which he translated into Indian languages, and a catalog of correspondence and works written in Slovenian. For Baraga's biography, see Joseph Gregorich, *The Apostle of the Chippewas: The Life Story of the Most Rev. Frederick Baraga, the First Bishop of Marquette* (Chicago: The Bishop Baraga Association; Lamont, Ill.: Franciscan Fathers, 1932).

46. The last French Jesuit, Du Jaunay, left the Indians of Arbre Croche in 1773. No

priest was among them until Pierre Dejean arrived in 1829 and Baraga in 1831. When Baraga was compiling his Otchipwe dictionary, he was unaware of Du Jaunay's Ottawa dictionary (Ceglar, *Works of Bishop Baraga*, vol. 1, 160).

47. Baraga to Leopoldine Foundation, Detroit, 13 March 1835, quoted in ibid., 27. While in Detroit, Baraga stayed with Gabriel Richard, pioneer missionary and statesman in Michigan. Detroit resident and historian Richard Elliott, brother of Paulist missionary Walter Elliott (see chap. 4), wrote several articles about the work of Baraga for the *American Catholic Quarterly Review.*

48. For this missionary's notes on the Church in the Northwest, see Francis Norbert Blanchet, *Historical Sketches of the Catholic Church in Oregon,* ed. Edward J. Kowrach (Fairfield, Wash.: Ye Galleon Press, 1983). On Blanchet's approach to evangelization, see Philip M. Hanley, *History of the Catholic Ladder,* ed. Edward J. Kowrach (Fairfield, Wash.: Ye Galleon Press, 1993). Photographs of the Catholic Ladder and drawings illustrating its use among Indians are also found in Jacqueline Peterson, *Sacred Encounters: Father de Smet and the Indians of the Rocky Mountain West* (Norman: University of Oklahoma Press, 1993), 110–11.

49. "The protestant ministers... have put together an imitation of our historical ladder and they have not hesitated to put on it a mark at the sixteenth century to designate the birth of their religion" (Blanchet, quoted in Hanley, *History of the Catholic Ladder,* 92).

Two years before Blanchet's death, however, the Second Provincial Council of Oregon made the decision to adopt Butler's *Catechism,* published in English and approved by the Irish Bishops, for English-speaking Catholics. The move was made for the sake of uniformity. This meant that if the Indians knew English, they forfeited the color and visual impressions of their Catholic Ladder for the black-and-white words of the catechism. The year after Blanchet's death, the Baltimore Council published its own catechism for even greater uniformity in the vast United States.

50. P. J. De Smet, SJ, *Western Missions and Missionaries* (1859; Shannon, Ireland: Irish University Press, 1972); De Smet, *Origin, Progress, and Prospects of the Catholic Mission to the Rocky Mountains* (Philadelphia: M. Fithian, 1843; facsimile reprint, Fairfield, Wash.: Ye Galleon Press, 1972); John J. Killoren, SJ, *"Come, Blackrobe": De Smet and the Indian Tragedy* (Norman: University of Oklahoma Press, 1994); Robert C. Carriker, *Father Peter John De Smet, Jesuit in the West* (Norman: University of Oklahoma Press, 1995); Jacqueline Peterson with Laura Peers, *Sacred Encounters: Father De Smet and the Indians of the Rocky Mountain West* (Norman: University of Oklahoma Press, 1993).

The biography of De Smet's sometimes companion, Nicolaus Point, whose paintings and sketches of life among the Indians captured the imagination of Europeans, appears in Cornelius M. Buckley, *Nicolaus Point, SJ: His Life and Northwest Indian Chronicles* (Chicago: Loyola University Press, 1989). For documents on the Jesuit initiatives in the Northwest, see *The Oregon Province Archives of the Society of Jesus Alaska Mission Collection* (Spokane, Wash.: Gonzaga University, 1980), microform. For examples of Jesuit presence among Indians over several decades, see Ross Enochs, *The Jesuit Mission to the Lakota Sioux: A Study of Pastoral Ministry, 1886–1945* (Kansas City, Mo.: Sheed & Ward, 1996).

51. The significance of the visit might be noted from the perspective of Marie and the Ursulines. While technically under "cloister," the women had a strong mission focus which included teaching native tribes in the area. For insight on this work, see Leslie Choquette, "*Ces Amazones du Grand Dieu:* Women and Mission in Seventeenth-Century Canada," *French Historical Studies* (Spring 1992): 627–55.

52. For a description of her mission experience, see Sister Saint Angela Louise Abair, "Mustard Seed in Montana," *Montana, the Magazine of Western History* 34 (Spring 1984): 17–31; Florence Gilmore, "Sarah Dunne: An American Missionary in Alaska," *Sign* (July 1923): 489–92; [Mother Angela Lincoln], *Life of the Reverend Mother Amadeus of the Heart of Jesus: Foundress of the Ursuline Missions of Montana and Alaska* [c. 1919]; and Mother Clotilde Angela McBride, OSU, *Ursulines of the West* (1935). For Jesuit methodol-

ogy, see Gerald McKevitt, SJ, "The Art of Conversion: Jesuits and Flatheads in Nineteenth Century Montana," *U.S. Catholic Historian* 12, no. 4 (1994): 49–64.

The Mission High School begun by the Ursulines at St. Paul, Chinook, Montana, was staffed until 1936, when the School Sisters of St. Francis, Milwaukee, were invited to take the mission. The Ursuline superior of that time wanted from three to five Sisters present for full liturgical celebration, and the number of Ursulines was not adequate for this, so the Ursulines withdrew. The action was also consequent to a devastating fire which destroyed the church and Sisters' convent. The school then became a day school, rather than a boarding school. On the history of the mission, see Sister M. Clare Hartmann, OSF, *As It Was: History of the Mission High School* (Chinook, Mont.: The Chinook Opinion, 1984).

53. The Sisters of St. Anne were founded near Montreal in 1850 and opened a house in the United States in 1866. They began a hospital in Juneau, Alaska, in September 1886 and the following year opened St. Ann Academy, the first of seventeen missions among Eskimos, a work the Sisters continue to the present. Sister Marie Jean de Pathmos, *A History of the Sisters of St. Anne* (New York: Vantage Press, 1961).

A twentieth-century Jesuit's experience in Alaska appears in Louis L. Renner, *The KNOM/ Father Jim Poole Story* (Portland, Ore.: Binford and Mort Publishers, 1985). Poole (b. 1923) specialized in radio ministry.

54. *Address of the Catholic Clergy of the Province of Oregon to the Catholics of the United States: President Grant's Indian Policy, in Its Bearings upon Catholic Interests at Large* (Portland, Ore.: The Catholic Sentinel Publication Company, 1874).

55. Ibid., 16.

56. *Manual of Catholic Indian Missionary Associations* (1875), microfilm. Original in the Ryan Memorial Library Archives and Historical Collections, St. Charles Seminary, Overbrook, Philadelphia. The document contains a synopsis of the status of Catholic Indians and workings of the Bureau of Indian Missions. The women raised money through mission circles of fifteen members each.

57. C. J. Seghers, "Indian Missions," in *Memorial Volume: Sermons of the Third Plenary Council*, 114–19, here 115, 116.

Later, laity founded the Marquette League for Catholic Indian Missions in 1904 to establish schools and other institutions which might improve the condition of the Native Americans and to ameliorate the adverse conditions which surrounded them. The organization continues to this day, though members are fewer (letter from the Reverend Thomas A. Modugno, director of the Marquette League, to author, 23 June 1987).

58. Information on the Catholic Indian Congresses obtained from conversation 31 December 1996 with Mark Thiel, archivist of the Bureau of Catholic Indian Mission Records, Marquette University, Milwaukee; Mark Thiel, "Catholic Sodalities and the Sioux," 1989, excerpts of which were published in *West River Catholic*, December 1990, p. 14, and January 1991, p. 11; and Sister Mary Ellen Quality, SBS, "An Historical Narrative of the Catholic Sioux Indian Congress, 1890–1978," Bureau of Catholic Indian Missions, 6 June 1979. The latter work, which contains many photographs from the congresses, is largely a collection of notices about the congresses published in the *Indian Sentinel*. Thiel's paper provides a list of congress sites and approximate attendance for 1890–1910, though the congress continues to this day (the Kateri Tekakwitha Conference) and includes more tribes.

For the relationship of the Benedictines, Native Americans, and white people over a century, see Terrence Kardong, OSB, *Catholic Life at Fort Berthold, 1889–1989* (n.p.: Assumption Abbey Press, 1989).

59. For Marty's life and perspective, see Robert F. Karolevitz, *Bishop Martin Marty: "The Black Robe Lean Chief"* (Yankton, S.D.: Benedictine Sisters of Sacred Heart Convent, 1980). Marty, a linguist by training, took up ministry in 1876 among the Native Americans in the place where De Smet had worked about six years earlier. Marty was a friend of fellow countryman John Martin Henni and vacationed at the archbishop's house in Milwaukee.

60. Thiel, "Catholic Sodalities and the Sioux," 8.

61. Hecker's first biographer was his friend and fellow Paulist, Walter Elliott, *Life of Father Hecker* (New York: Columbus Press, 1891). For an analysis of Hecker's spiritual journey as embodied in his diary, see John Farina, ed., *Isaac Hecker: The Diary* (New York: Paulist Press, 1983). For discussion around key issues related to Hecker, see John Farina, ed., *Hecker Studies* (New York: Paulist Press, 1983).

62. Representative speeches among the Americanists, who particularly embody this concept, are Isaac T. Hecker, "The Future Triumph of the Church," in *Sermons Delivered During the Second Plenary Council of Baltimore* (Baltimore: Kelly and Piet, 1866); Hecker, "The Church, in View of the Needs of the Age," *The Church and the Age* (New York: Office of the Catholic World, 1887), 7–63; Orestes Brownson, "Mission of America," in Henry F. Brownson, ed., *The Works of Orestes Brownson,* vol. 11 (Detroit: Thordike Norse, 1884), 551–84; John J. Keane, "The Providential Mission of Leo XIII," sermon given at the Baltimore Cathedral, 1878, John J. Keane Papers, ACUA; John Ireland, "The Mission of Catholics in America" [1889] and "The Church and the Age" [1893], *The Church and Modern Society* (St. Paul: Pioneer Press, 1904); Denis J. O'Connell, "A New Idea in the Life of Father Hecker" [1897], in Gerald Fogarty, *The Vatican and the Americanist Crisis: Denis J. O'Connell, American Agent in Rome, 1885–1903* (Rome: Gregorian University, 1974).

63. These ideas appear, for example, in Brownson, "Mission of America," 551–84.

64. Harry F. Brownson, "Lay Action in the Church," *The Catholic Congress* (Baltimore: John Murphy, 1889), 25–32.

65. Walter Elliott, "On Catholic Missionary Work," in *The World's Columbian Catholic Congresses* (Chicago: J. S. Hyland, 1893), 55.

66. For an overview of lay leadership from this period to the 1980s, especially in terms of social issues, see Patrick Carey, "Lay Catholic Leadership in the United States," *U.S. Catholic Historian* 9, no. 3 (1990): 223–47.

67. Joseph Freri, *The Society for the Propagation of the Faith* (Baltimore: Society for the Propagation of the Faith, 1902), 3, 4.

68. For the history of the organization, see Alfred J. Ede, "The Lay Crusade for a Christian America: A Study of the American Federation of Catholic Societies, 1900–1919" (Ph.D. diss., Graduate Theological Union, Berkeley, Calif., 1979).

69. Christopher Kauffman, *Mission to Rural America: The Story of W. Howard Bishop, Founder of Glenmary* (New York: Paulist Press, 1991).

Chapter 3 /
Missions Overseas, 1820–93

1. In addition to those persons who came to the United States as slaves, some of the Catholic African American population arrived in 1793 in Baltimore as refugees from the revolution in Santo Domingo (Haiti). The Jesuits had considered the establishment of a mission in Liberia as early as 1830. The Provincial Council of Baltimore (1833) requested the Jesuits to send missionaries to aid the Catholics in Liberia. Information was obtained from correspondence with Emmett Curran, SJ, who made available records from the Roman Archives of the Society of Jesus.

The first appeal to the U.S. hierarchy to take responsibility for an area outside of its boundaries came to Bishop John Carroll, when he was asked by Propaganda Fide to take the Virgin Islands under his jurisdiction. On Carroll's behalf, two French priests from the Congregation of the Holy Ghost were sent: Henry Kendal and Matthew Hérard, who were named prefect and vice prefect, respectively.

2. M. J. Bane, *The Catholic Story of Liberia* (New York: The Declan X. McMullen Company, 1950), 34. See also Kelly's diary in *U.S. Catholic Historical Society Records* (1910); and Richard K. MacMaster, "Bishop Barron and the West African Missions, 1841–

1845," *Historical Records and Studies of the United States Catholic Historical Society* 50 (1964): 83–129.

3. Barron, quoted in Bane, *Catholic Story of Liberia,* 42.

4. For the history of the Benedictines in the Bahamas, see Colman Barry, *Upon These Rocks: Catholics in the Bahamas* (Collegeville, Minn.: St. John's University Press, 1973), which contains a large amount of primary source material. Schreiner continued his academic interest while he remained in the Bahamas. He wrote the "Bahamas" entry for *The Catholic Encyclopedia* and was instrumental in having the name of Watling Island changed to San Salvador, in keeping with the title chosen by Christopher Columbus for his landing. The New Orleans Jesuit provincial had suggested to Archbishop Corrigan that the Benedictines would likely do well in the Bahamas, as it was widely thought that this group could cultivate the land and thus maintain the mission financially. St. Francis Xavier Church was built largely through funds supplied by Lady Georgiana Ayde-Curran and by New York priest Charles O'Keefe. The latter is buried at West Point and had intervened to obtain a Catholic chapel for the military school.

5. Mother Mary Ambrosia Sweeney, unpublished account of her life, typescript, p. 208, Sisters of Charity, Bronx, Archives.

6. Ibid., 210.

7. For the narrative of the early years of this mission, see Marie de Lourdes Walsh, *The Sisters of Charity of New York, 1909–1959,* vol. 3 (New York: Fordham University Press, 1960). The work of the Sisters in this part of the world might have been presaged by a visit to their motherhouse in the Bronx in 1879 of some Carmelite Sisters from Spain who had been ousted from Guatemala. In gratitude for hospitality, the Carmelites gave a statue of the Child Jesus to the Charity Sisters, who placed it in a niche over the entrance to their dining room.

8. Quoted in ibid., 260.

9. Father John McGoey, Scarboro Fathers, pastor of Blessed Sacrament Church, quoted in ibid., 286.

10. Sweeney, unpublished account of her life, 203.

11. Marie, "Nassau Papers," *The Children of Providence* (1921–22): 7. The "queen" might have been either a spokesperson for an African god or a spirit medium.

12. Barry, *Upon These Rocks,* 187.

13. Schreiner to Abbot Bernard, Nassau, 24 March 1891, quoted in ibid., 116.

14. Sister Felicitas to Mother M. Rose, Nassau, 3 January 1897, 523 Nassau Mission folder, Early Correspondence, 1892–1900, Sisters of Charity, Bronx, Archives.

15. "Pastoral Letter, Third Baltimore Council, 1883," in Hugh J. Nolan, ed., *Pastoral Letters of the United States Catholic Bishops,* vol. 1 (Washington, D.C.: U.S. Catholic Conference, 1983), 238.

16. Ibid.

17. Magnien was the personal secretary to Cardinal Gibbons and confidant of Archbishop James J. Keane. Other Sulpicians whose mission awareness affected the development of the U.S Catholic missionary impulse included Edward Dyer, who was on the Catholic Missionary Union Board and treasurer of the Indian and Negro Mission Fund, James Hogan, Francis Gigot, Gabriel André, and Joseph Bruneau. Among the clergy affected by the Sulpician missionary ideals during the period from about 1885 to 1905 were Thomas F. Price, Joseph Tracy (a secular priest who taught at St. John's Seminary, Brighton, Massachusetts, and the Boston Archdiocese's first SPF director), James A. Walsh, Charles Aiken, Austin Dowling, John Dunn, James Cardinal Farley, Joseph Freri, Bishop Henry Granjon, Cardinal Hayes, and Abbé Felix Klein (a student of Hogan's in France). Many of these clergy were identified with attitudes reflected in Americanism (chap. 4).

For the details on the foundation of the SPF in the United States, see Angelyn Dries, " 'The Whole Way into the Wilderness': The Foreign Mission Impulse of the American Catholic Church, 1893–1925" (Ph.D. diss., Graduate Theological Union, Berkeley, Calif., 1990), 68–78.

18. On the early foundations, see R. P. Juan Gauci, CSSR, *Redemptorist Apostolates in the Caribbean of the Nineteenth Century* (Santo Domingo, Dominican Republic: privately printed, 1989). In February 1918, the Redemptorist communities on St. Thomas and St. Croix were placed under the jurisdiction of the Baltimore Province. For background on the spiritual condition which led to the potential for schism in these islands, see Henry J. Koren, *The Serpent and the Dove: A History of the Congregation of the Holy Ghost in the United States, 1745–1984* (Pittsburgh: Spiritus Press, 1985), 44–47.

19. John Gauci, CSSR, "Redemptorist Apostolates in the Caribbean Part II: 1900–1980," p. 7, unpublished manuscript, RFBA.

20. Morgan Hanlon, CP, "The First Passionist in America," *The Passionists' Compassion* (Fall 1990): 10–15.

21. Sister Veronica Inez Rodrigues, OSF, "The Franciscan Sisters of Allegany, New York," *The Provincial Annals 1985* (Holy Name Province of OFMs): 135–54.

22. Sister Mary Laurence Hanley, OSF, and O. A. Bushnell, *A Song of Pilgrimage and Exile: The Life and Spirit of Mother Marianne of Molokai* (Chicago: Franciscan Herald Press, 1980).

23. For the work of these Brothers, see *Marianist Missions: Japan, China, North Africa, Hawaiian Islands, Puerto Rico* (Dayton, Ohio: Mount St. John, 1935), and Eugene Paulin and Joseph A. Becker, *New Wars: The History of the Brothers of Mary (Marianists) in Hawaii, 1883–1958* (Milwaukee: Bruce Press, 1958).

24. Leonor Fouesnel quoted in Hanley and Bushnell, *Song of Pilgrimage and Exile,* 47.

25. Cope quoted in ibid., 45.

26. Howard D. Case, ed., *Joseph Dutton [Memoirs]: The Story of Forty-four Years of Service among the Lepers of Molokai, Hawaii* (Honolulu: Honolulu Star-Bulletin, 1931).

27. Cope quoted in Hanley, 152. Mother Marianne died in 1918 at Kalaupapa, Molokai, where she had spent most of her time in the islands. Her cause for beatification in the Catholic Church is being considered.

28. Francis J. Osborne, SJ, *A History of the Church in Jamaica* (Chicago: Loyola University Press, 1988).

29. Gilbert J. Garraghan, SJ, *The Jesuits of the Middle United States,* vol. 3 (New York: America Press, 1938), 517. The Mercy Sisters from Louisiana had preceded the Jesuits in British Honduras, arriving 20 January 1883. Within the first week after their arrival, they staffed the Spanish school (later called Holy Redeemer) and the English school (St. Catherine). They also were visiting the sick in their homes and began visitation of the prison, barracks, and hospital. In their home visits, they observed statues of Christ dressed in the clothing of an Indian chief. See Mary Hermenia Muldrey, RSM, *Abounding in Mercy: The Life of Mother Austin Carroll, RSM* (New Orleans: Habersham, 1988), 209–10, 219.

30. For a biography of an early U.S. Jesuit in British Honduras, see William T. Kane, SJ, *A Memoir of William A. Stanton, S.J.* (St. Louis: B. Herder Book Co., 1927). Stanton (1870–1910) went to teach in the new Jesuit college in Belize in 1896 and remained there, except for further training at the Jesuit observatory in Manila, until his death from cancer. He attempted to construct a Maya/English vocabulary list in order to learn that language.

31. "Lengthy Account of the Mission," *Woodstock Letters* 23 (1910): 335.

32. Ibid., 332.

33. For the history of the popular magazine, the *Messenger of the Sacred Heart,* and its changing character, see Robert Emmett Curran, ed., *American Jesuit Spirituality* (New York: Paulist Press, 1988), 334–37. On the political foundations which gave rise to this devotion, see Jacques LeBrun, "Politics and Spirituality: The Devotion to the Sacred Heart," in Christian Duqouc, ed., *The Concrete Christian Life,* Concilium Series (New York: Herder and Herder, 1971), 29–43.

34. "Lengthy Account of the Mission," 337.

35. Ibid., 345.

36. The Sisters of the Holy Family story in Belize is told in *Golden Rays Through*

Clouded Years, 1898–1948 (Belize: The Commercial Press, 1948), and Sister Mary Francis Borgia Hart, SSF, *Violets in the King's Garden: A History of the Sisters of the Holy Family of New Orleans* (New Orleans: privately printed, 1976). Additional information obtained from letters between author and the archivist, Sister M. Boniface Adams, SSF, 6 March, 29 March, and 6 June 1995.

37. For Catherine Bushman's biography, see Elizabeth J. Weber, *Celestial Honeymoon: The Story of Sister Catherine Bushman, S.C.* (New York: Benziger Brothers, 1950).

38. On the Goette brothers, see Marion A. Habig, OFM, *In Journeyings Often: Franciscan Pioneers in the Orient* (St. Bonaventure, N.Y.: Franciscan Institute, 1953). For a listing of some of the early missionaries sent from the United States, see Marion Habig, "The First American Foreign Missioners," *Illinois Catholic Historical Review* 11 (January 1929): 239–50, 364–69; and Habig, "Who Was First?" *Worldmission* 5 (Spring 1954): 55–78.

39. For a perceptive analysis of immigrant spirituality, see Joseph P. Chinnici, OFM, *Living Stones: The History and Structure of Catholic Spiritual Life in the United States* (New York: Macmillan, 1989).

40. Mother Mary Rose to Sister Geronimo, 1 March 1900, 523 Nassau Mission folder, Early Correspondence, 1892–1900, Sisters of Charity, Bronx, Archives.

Chapter 4 /
The Spanish-American War, the Americanist Period, and a National Focus for Missions Overseas, 1898–1919

1. Theodore Roosevelt, *The Strenuous Life* (New York: Century Company, 1905), 20.

2. See his classic text, John R. Mott, *The Evangelization of the World in This Generation* (New York: Student Volunteer Movement for Foreign Mission, 1900).

3. Josiah Strong, *Our Country* (New York: Baker and Taylor, 1885), 179.

4. Mott, *Evangelization of the World*, 15. For an overview of the U.S. basis for Protestant missionary activity, see William Hutchison, *Errand to the World: American Protestant Thought and Foreign Missions* (Chicago: University of Chicago Press, 1987); Patricia Hill, *The World Their Household: The American Woman's Foreign Mission Movement and Cultural Transformation, 1870–1920* (Ann Arbor: University of Michigan Press, 1985); and Joel A. Carpenter and Wilbert R. Shenk, eds., *Earthen Vessels, American Evangelicals, and Foreign Missions, 1880–1980* (Grand Rapids, Mich.: Eerdmans, 1990).

5. For a sample of Protestant and Roman Catholic documents which provide firsthand impressions of one another, of indigenous people, and of missionary life from the 1600s to the present, see H. McKennie Goodpasture, *Cross and Sword: An Eyewitness History of Christianity in Latin America* (Maryknoll, N.Y.: Orbis Books, 1989).

6. John Gauci, CSSR, "Redemptorist Apostolates in the Caribbean Part II: 1900–1980," p. 30, unpublished manuscript, RFBA.

7. John J. Thompkins, SJ, "Our Missionaries," *Woodstock Letters* 34 (1905): 398.

8. *New York Freeman's Journal*, 14 May 1898, quoted in Frank T. Reuter, *Catholic Influence on American Colonial Policies, 1898–1904* (Austin: University of Texas Press, 1967), 11–12.

9. Mary Magdalen Wirmel, OSF, "Sisterhoods in the Spanish-American War," *Historical Records and Studies of the United States Catholic Historical Society* 32 (1941): 7–69; Judith Metz, SC, "In Times of War," in Ursula Stepsis, CSA, and Dolores Liptak, RSM, eds., *Pioneer Healers: The History of Women Religious in American Health Care* (New York: Crossroad, 1989), 57–65.

10. On internal Church events relating to this concern, see John Tracy Ellis, *The Life of James Cardinal Gibbons, Archbishop of Baltimore, 1834–1921*, vol. 2 (Milwaukee: Bruce Publishing Company, 1952), chap. 16.

11. For an account of these matters as they related to education, see Thomas C. Middleton, OSA, "The Philippine Commissions: Reports on Religious and Educational Matters," *American Ecclesiastical Review* 28 (1903): 262–302.

12. Ireland to Farley, 4 May 1903, box I 6 A-B (1903), roll 2, Cardinal Farley Papers, microfilm, AANY.

13. For an overview of the history of this relationship, see Jaime R. Vidal, "The American Church and the Puerto Rican People," *U.S. Catholic Historian* 9, nos. 1, 2 (1990): 119–35. For details on the immediate problems in the transition to American principles of church-state separation in one of these areas, see Edward J. Berbusse, SJ, *The United States in Puerto Rico* (Chapel Hill: University of North Carolina Press, 1966).

14. One such case was Mother Agnes at Sancti Spiritus School in Cuba. In an effort to staff the school and to economize, community postulants replaced apparently competent teachers. This resulted in loss of students, and the Sisters of Mercy were advised by Cardinal Farley to return to New York. See Archbishop Farley to Mother Agnes (Cuba), 18 March 1911, box I 14 (1911), roll 3, Cardinal Farley Correspondence, AANY.

15. John J. Thompkins, SJ, *Woodstock Letters* 34 (1905): 247–73; 35 (1906): 186–209; 36 (1907): 322-31, contains the narrative of their trip. On the way, the three men visited the Brothers of Mary in Hawaii (chap. 3). The Jesuit missions in the Philippines were transferred from the Aragon Province to the New York Province in 1920, and U.S. Jesuits arrived the following year.

16. On this point, see William Hutchison, "American Missionary Ideologies: 'Activism' as Theory, Practice, and Stereotype," in F. Forrester Church and Timothy George, eds., *Continuity and Discontinuity in Church History* (Leiden: Brill, 1979), 351–62.

17. For the complete document which condemned Americanism, see "Pope Leo XIII's Encyclical, *Testem Benevolentiae* on Americanism, January 22, 1899," in John Tracy Ellis, ed., *Documents of American Catholic History,* vol. 2 (Wilmington, Del.: Michael Glazier, 1987), 576–79. For the vast literature about this internal Church matter, see Gerald Fogarty, *The Vatican and the Americanist Crisis: Denis J. O'Connell, American Agent in Rome* (Rome: Gregorian University, 1974). For an understanding of the conservative position, see Robert Emmett Curran, *Michael Corrigan and the Shaping of Conservative Catholicism in the United States* (New York: Arno, 1978).

John Tracy Ellis in his *Life of James Cardinal Gibbons* remarked that no relationship existed between the outcome of the war and the condemnation of Americanism. However, the opposite seems to be the case. See Angelyn Dries, " 'The Whole Way into the Wilderness': The Foreign Mission Impulse of the American Catholic Church, 1893–1925" (Ph.D. diss., Graduate Theological Union, Berkeley, Calif., 1990), 17–20.

18. *Testem Benevolentiae*, in Ellis, *Documents of American Catholic History,* 2:546.

19. For more on this issue, see Lawrence V. McDonnell, CSP, "Walter Elliott and the Hecker Tradition in the Americanist Era," *U.S. Catholic Historian* 3, no. 2 (1983): 129–44. For a recent analysis of the interpretations of Hecker's spiritual passages, see Patrick Allitt, "The Meanings of Isaac Hecker's Conversions," *Journal of Paulist Studies* 3, no. 1 (1994): 9–30. For a biographical sketch of Elliott and Alexander Doyle, CSP, see James McVann, CSP, *The Paulists, 1858–1970,* vol. 1, privately printed (1983), Paulist Archives.

20. Missionary bands focused both on Catholics and Protestants. Elliott claimed that by 1908, 25,000 converts had been received into the Catholic Church. For an analysis of the Missions to Non-Catholics Movement, see Thomas J. Jonas, *The Divided Mind: American Catholic Evangelists in the 1890s* (New York: Garland Press, 1988).

21. Reports from these various conferences appear in *The Winchester Convention: Papers by the Missionaries to Non-Catholics on the Work of Making Converts* (New York: Office of the Missionary, 1901); *The Missionary* 6 (October 1901); William E. Stang, "First National Congress of Missionaries to Non-Catholics," *American Ecclesiastical Review* 25 (October 1901): 331–39; *The Washington Conference* (Washington, D.C.: Apostolic Mission House, 1904); William L. Sullivan, CSP, and Walter Elliott, CSP, "The Winchester Conference

of Missionaries to Non-Catholics," *Catholic World* (October 1901): 90–106; *The Mission Movement in America, Being the Mind of the Missionaries Assembled in the Third Washington Conference at the Apostolic Mission House* (Washington, D.C.: Apostolic Mission House, 1906); *The Missionary* 11 (July 1906); and *The Missionary* 14 (July 1909): 3–6.

22. *The Churchman,* 3 November 1906. Modernism was condemned by the Vatican in 1907 with the decree *Lamentabili* and the encyclical *Pascendi.*

23. Keane's address appears in *The Missionary* 9 (April 1904): 9–11, here 10. Elliott's *A Manual of Missions* (Washington, D.C.: Apostolic Mission House, 1922) synopsized notes from his classes at the Mission House.

24. *The Catholic University of America Bulletin* 10 (July 1904): 389.

25. "A Seminary for Home and Foreign Missions," *The Missionary* 6 (October 1901): 68. The goals for this seminary are presented in *The Apostolic Mission House for the Training of Missionaries to Non-Catholics* (1902), Ryan Memorial Library Archives and Historical Collections, St. Charles Seminary, Overbrook, Philadelphia. The probable author of this work is Alexander Doyle.

26. Stephen Kress, "The Growth of a Movement," *The Missionary* 6 (October 1901): 79–80. Kress met Elliott while a student at Catholic University. St. Edward's Parish, Cleveland, became the diocesan headquarters for the Apostolic Missionary Band after 1899, when Kress was pastor. Kress lectured and wrote on socialism and joined Maryknoll in 1920.

27. *Washington Conference,* 79.

28. *Mission Movement in America,* 58.

29. Francis Clement Kelley, *The Story of Extension* (Chicago: Extension Press, 1922), 16. For the details of Kelley's life, see James Gaffey, *Francis Clement Kelley and the American Catholic Dream* (Bensenville, Ill.: The Heritage Foundation, 1980).

30. Kelley, *The Story of Extension,* 78. In addition to his business sense, which he saw modeled in his father, Kelley is described with other characteristics, which influenced his leadership at the Extension Society and later as bishop of Oklahoma City (1924–48). According to Gaffey, these characteristics are "intelligence and a will to expand it; an enormous sense of responsibility; energy and flair, as well as the nerve to face public life and controversy; strong habits of work; and a willingness to follow anywhere the pastoral mission of the church" (*Francis Clement Kelley,* 70).

31. Kelley did experience aloofness from some bishops, often because he did not follow proper ecclesiastical protocol. On Gibbons' reserved attitude, see Ellis, *The Life of James Cardinal Gibbons,* 2:404–7.

32. For these speeches, see Francis C. Kelley, ed., *First American Catholic Missionary Congress* (Chicago: J. S. Hyland, 1909).

33. Francis C. Kelley, ed., *Second American Catholic Missionary Congress* (Chicago: J. S. Hyland, 1913), 69.

34. See *Handbook and Guide of the World in Boston* (Boston: World in Boston, 1911). The congress was inspired by the successful "Orient in London" congress, sponsored by the London Missionary Society in 1908.

35. "Report of the Special Committee, Appointed by the Board of Governors of the Catholic Church Extension Society of the United States at Their Meeting Held 13 November 1912, to Consider Ways and Means of Promoting the Cause of Home Missions," p. 3, box P4, I-75 (1906–49), Historical Letters and Documents of Extension Society, The Catholic Church Extension Society Papers, Loyola University of Chicago Archives. Kelley complained that the proliferation of mission magazines was ruining the cause of the home missions. See Kelley to Monsignor J. P. Dineen [chancellor for Archbishop Hayes of New York], 3 January 1921, V-6 (1922), roll 10, Patrick Cardinal Hayes Papers: Correspondence Submitted to Counsellors, AANY.

Among the laity present at the conference were Martha Moore Avery, Paul Hanley Furfey (later a well-known sociologist at Catholic University), and David Goldstein, convert to

Catholicism and lay preacher. *The International Review of Missions* 4 (1915): 60 made note of this second congress.

36. For an overview of the persons involved in the U.S. chapter of the Association of the Holy Childhood in its early years, see William F. Stadelman, CSSp, *The Association of the Holy Childhood, History of the American Branch, 1846–1922* (Pittsburgh: The Colonial Press, 1922), and Henry J. Koren, *The Serpent and the Dove* (Pittsburgh: Spiritus Press, 1985), 148–50.

37. For the history of the society in France, see Edward J. Hickey, *The Society for the Propagation of the Faith: Its Foundation, Organization, and Success* (Washington, D.C.: Catholic University of America Press, 1942; New York: AMS, 1974). The most recent book on the foundress of the SPF is George Naidenoff, *Pauline Jaricot: Heroic Lay Missionary* (Dublin: Pontifical Missionary Aid Societies, 1988). The SPF started by raising funds for the work of the bishop of New Orleans, Louis W. Dubourg.

38. For background on Granjon and Freri, see Dries, " 'The Whole Way into the Wilderness,' " 116. It has been difficult to uncover the history of the SPF's national office due to the unavailability of resources at the national office in New York. The author has constructed the story from correspondence in many other archives.

39. Joseph Freri, *Native Clergy for Mission Countries* (New York: Society for the Propagation of the Faith, 1917); Freri, "Native Clergy for Mission Countries," *American Ecclesiastical Review* 57 (1917): 113–28. The Society for the Propagation of the Faith offices moved to Rome from France in 1922, and the group became a pontifical organization, as did the Holy Childhood Association. In the former case, administration moved from lay decision making to ecclesiastical management.

40. Joseph Freri, *The Society for the Propagation of the Faith* (Baltimore: Society for the Propagation of the Faith, 1902), 4.

41. The answer to "who was first" depends on whether one includes U.S. provinces originally founded from Europe that were called on to send missionaries abroad (the Redemptorists in chap. 3, for example).

42. *FA* 9 (January 1915): 3.

43. Vaughan to Cullen, 6 January 1903, Letters on the Foundation of Maryknoll, MMA. For a copy of this letter, see "Documents," *Catholic Historical Review* 30 (October 1944): 290–98. For the relationship between Vaughan and James A. Walsh, see Jean-Paul Wiest, *Maryknoll in China: A History, 1918–1955* (Armonk, N.Y.: M. E. Sharpe, 1988; Maryknoll, N.Y.: Orbis Books, 1997), 14–18.

44. On this point, see Florence Cohalan, *A Popular History of the Archdiocese of New York* (Yonkers, N.Y.: United States Catholic Historical Society, 1983), 209–11. Under Farley's leadership, New York also had an active mission band.

45. For their story in the southern United States, see Mary E. Best, *Seventy Septembers* (privately printed, Holy Spirit Missionary Sisters, 1988). For the early history of the congregation, see Ann Gier, *This Fire Ever Burning: A Biography of Mother Leonarda Lentrup, SSpS* (Missionary Sisters of the Holy Spirit: Privately printed, 1985), and Herman Fischer, SVD, *The Life of Arnold Janssen* (Techny, Ill.: Mission Press, 1925), Part 5.

46. Narratives of the beginnings of the Catholic Foreign Mission Society of America appear in George C. Powers, *The Maryknoll Movement* (Maryknoll, N.Y.: Catholic Foreign Mission Society, 1922); James G. Keller and Meyer Berger, *Men of Maryknoll* (New York: Charles Scribner's Sons, 1943); Robert E. Sheridan, MM, *The Founders of Maryknoll* (New York: Catholic Foreign Mission Society of America, 1980); John C. Murrett, MM, *Tar Heel Apostle: Thomas Frederick Price, Co-founder of Maryknoll* (New York: Longmans, 1944); Sister Jeanne Marie Lyons, MM, *Maryknoll's First Lady: The Life of Mother Mary Joseph, Foundress of the Maryknoll Sisters* (New York: Dodd, Mead, and Company, 1964); and Camilla Kennedy, MM, *To the Uttermost Parts of the Earth: The Spirit and Charism of Mary Josephine Rogers* (Maryknoll, N.Y.: Maryknoll Sisters, 1987).

By the time of Maryknoll's establishment, Farley had received at least four requests from

Europeans to found a mission seminary in his diocese. Requests had come from the Divine Word Missionaries and John Fraser, a missionary to China and later a founder of the Scarboro Fathers in Canada. The friendship between John Dunn and James A. Walsh was a deciding factor for Farley.

47. On Price, see Murrett, *Tar Heel Apostle*, and Sheridan, *Founders of Maryknoll*.

48. For an excellent portrayal of the history and spirit of this group, see Christopher Kauffman, *Tradition and Transformation in Catholic Culture: The Priests of Saint Sulpice in the United States from 1791 to the Present* (New York: Macmillan, 1988). On the Sulpician influence on Walsh, see Angelyn Dries, OSF, "The Sulpician Mission Legacy and the Foundation of Maryknoll," *Bulletin de St. Sulpice* 17 (1991): 167–76.

49. Charles F. Aiken, Diary, 1886–88, p. 50, no. 46, Charles F. Aiken Papers, Large Collections, ACUA. Aiken became an Orientalist and taught at the Catholic University of America (1897–1924). His best-known work was *The Dahmma of Gotama the Buddha and the Gospel of Jesus Christ*, which was his 1900 dissertation. He provided entries on various world religions for *The Catholic Encyclopedia* (1906–12) and was one of the translators of *Sacred Books and Sacred Literature of the East* (New York: Parke, Austin, and Lipscomb, 1917), a multi-volume work.

50. Joseph Tracy (1860–1947), a diocesan priest who taught New Testament exegesis at St. John's Seminary, was appointed the first diocesan SPF director in the country in 1899. He established the Mission Academia among the seminarians in 1901. During these monthly meetings, papers on mission topics were presented, thereby providing an informal course in missiology. Tracy found himself at odds frequently with William Cardinal O'Connell, with respect to highlighting the role of parish life and "minimiz[ing] the importance and authority of the diocese and the bishop, and abet[ting] 'Sulpician intrigue' " (Robert E. Sullivan, "Beneficial Relations: Toward a Social History of the Diocesan Priests of Boston, 1875–1944," in James M. O'Toole and Robert E. Sullivan, eds., *Catholic Boston: Studies in Religion and Community, 1870–1970* [Boston: n.p., 1985], 231).

51. Berkeley continued to be financed from the Boston office under subsequent SPF directors Joseph McGlinchey (1911–28) and Richard Cushing (1928–44). Berkeley's work with abandoned Chinese babies, the sick, and the poor led her to establish a House of Mercy on Chusan Island, which faced the island containing Kwan Yin's (a bodhisattva of mercy) shrine, a famous Buddhist pilgrimage site. James A. Walsh viewed the Daughter of Charity as a "cofounder" of Maryknoll, because her manner of living and working with the poor was a model he envisioned for the Maryknoll Sisters. Her story appears in Mary Louise Hinton, *Sister Xavier Berkeley, Sister of Charity of St. Vincent de Paul* (London: Burns Oates, 1949), and Sister Mary Just and Mark Leo Kent, *The Glory of Christ: A Pageant of Two Hundred Missionary Lives from Apostolic Times to the Present Age* (Milwaukee: Bruce Publishing Company, 1955).

52. *FA* 2 (1907): 2.

53. For details on Rogers's life, see Lyons, *Maryknoll's First Lady*. For a synopsis of her life and important primary documents related to the women's group, see Kennedy, *To the Uttermost Parts of the Earth*.

54. For Gibbons's letter in support of Maryknoll, see "The Launching of the Catholic Foreign Mission Society of America (Maryknoll), March 25, 1911," in Ellis, ed., *Documents of American Catholic History*, 2:576–79; see also Sheridan, *Founders of Maryknoll*, 103–4. For Price and Walsh's letter to Gibbons and Farley after they went to Rome to secure authorization for the seminary, see Walsh and Price to Dear Archbishop, 15 October 1911, I-14 (1911), roll 3, Cardinal Farley Papers, AANY.

55. Starting in 1903, Dunn wrote a weekly mission column in the diocesan *Catholic News* and inaugurated a mission publication, *Good Work,* in 1907. New York Catholics that year were second in the world in their contributions to the SPF ($56,600.96) and were first three years later ($100,737.27).

56. *Teresian Diary,* 1 January 1912, MMA. Wholean was a teacher and graduate of

Wellesley College, Dwyer had her own business in Boston, and Sullivan was secretary to the dean of Harvard Medical School. The last of the seven founding women, Sister Mary Gemma Shea (b. 1894), died in 1992.

57. These qualities are mentioned in Kennedy, *To the Uttermost Parts of the Earth*, in documents 38, 211, and 207, 208. The attributes are mentioned, however, during many of Walsh and Rogers's conferences for the women and men of Maryknoll.

58. *FA* 19 (July 1916): 100.

59. The Paris Foreign Mission Society, the first congregation formed exclusively for missions overseas, started in the early 1660s to extend the mission field to laity and those not in religious congregations. They particularly sought development of native clergy in the Far East. Walsh, always attracted to music, was impressed by their mission-sending hymn, which stressed the ideal of martyrdom.

60. *FA* 1 (March 1907): 7. Other examples from *The Field Afar* linking martyrdom and heroism can be seen in "All the World Loves a Hero...," *FA* 2 (May 1908); "Blood of Pioneer Apostles," *FA* 7 (May 1913); and "Extraordinary Heroism," *FA* 13 (December 1919): 255. See also John F. McConnell, MM, "The Whole Way: Frs. Walsh and Price and the Mystique of Martyrdom," *Channel* 20 (Fall 1977): 6–11; and McConnell, "Father Price and Sister Regina Holmes, 1917–1919," *Missionary Spirituality* 5 (Winter 1981–82): 5-7, on "the pact of martyrdom." Walsh published several books about the Paris Foreign Missionary martyrs. For the "Maryknoll Spirit," see Wiest, *Maryknoll in China*, 37–42.

61. *FA* 7 (July 1913): 3. On the construction of the modern "self," see Charles Taylor, *Sources of the Self: The Making of the Modern Identity* (Cambridge: Harvard University Press, 1989), and William Connolly, "Taylor, Foucault, and Otherness," *Political Theory* 13 (August 1985): 365–76.

62. Descriptions of these pictures and more about the development of the martyrdom theme for Rogers appear in Angelyn Dries, OSF, " 'The Whole Way into the Wilderness,' " 222. See also Wiest, *Maryknoll in China*, 42, and, for more on the martyrdom mystique at Maryknoll, see pp. 37–39 of Wiest's volume.

63. On this point, see T. J. Jackson Lears, "From Salvation to Self-Realization: Advertising and the Therapeutic Roots of Consumer Culture, 1880–1930," in T. J. Jackson Lears and Richard Wightman Fox, eds., *The Culture of Consumption* (New York: Pantheon, 1983), 7–12. These thoughts are developed more extensively in T. J. Jackson Lears, *No Place of Grace* (New York: Pantheon, 1981).

64. Patrick James Donahue, "The Possibilities of the Future," in Kelley, ed., *The First American Catholic Missionary Congress*, 304–19, here 308.

65. Robert Streit, OMI, "Missions and Civilization," in National Office of the Society for the Propagation of the Faith, comp., *The Mission Apostolate* (New York: Society for the Propagation of the Faith, 1942), 25–30, here 26. At the time, Streit was the director of the Vatican Mission Library. The same theme was found earlier in James Gibbons, *Our Christian Heritage* (Baltimore: James Murphy Company, 1889), introduction.

66. Pennsylvania-born Walsh was probably best known in Catholic circles for his oft-printed *The Thirteenth Century, the Greatest of Centuries* (1907) and for *The Popes and Science* (1908). His writings emphasized that most of the great scientists of the past were devout Catholics and that many were firm believers in Christianity. He received his medical training at the University of Pennsylvania (M.D., 1895) and conducted further neurological research at the Universities of Paris, Vienna, and Berlin, just as the science of psychology was seeing the light of day. He was dean of the Fordham University School of Medicine and a consulting physician for several clinics and hospitals which treated physio-psychological disorders. Walsh gave up his Fordham post when the faculty did not support the departmental reforms he suggested. See Harry W. Kirwin, "James J. Walsh — Medical Historian and Pathfinder," *Catholic Historical Review* 40 (January 1960): 409–35.

67. James J. Walsh, "Missionary Work and Civilization," 265–70, here 267. This is the argument of the classic nineteenth-century work of Charles Montalembert, *Monks of the*

West (London: W. Blackwood & Sons, 1861–79). Alexander Doyle, CSP, used this same argument in the lengthy pamphlet he wrote to solicit funds for the building of the Apostolic Mission House in Washington, D.C. Monsignor Denis J. O'Connell, in his famous Fribourg speech, relied on the Montalembert work and urged Catholics to Christianize democracy. Other examples of the theme of the Church as the bearer of civilization appear in Rev. John Walsh, "Roman Catholics and Civilization," *The American Catholic Quarterly Review* 10 (1885): 193–217. Henry Woods, SJ, "What Is Civilization?" *The Catholic Mind* 13 (1915): 101-5, attempts to define civilization and to distinguish it from culture.

68. For an analysis of French material regarding the term, see Lucien Febvre, "Civilisation: Evolution of a Word and a Group of Ideas," in Peter Burke, ed., *A New Kind of History* (New York: Harper & Row, 1973), 219–57.

69. LeRoy quoted in *CM* 1 (1909): 136.

70. For an overview of business developments during the Progressive Era, see Alfred D. Chandler, *The Visible Hand: The Managerial Revolution in American Business* (Cambridge: Belknap Press, 1977).

71. Peter Rossillon, bishop of Bizol, to O'Connell, 29 November 1930, box 3, folder 9, Record Group III.D16, Society for the Propagation of the Faith, AABoston.

72. For a careful analysis of both the Europeans and Americans, see R. Scott Appleby, *Church and Age Unite: The Modernist Impulse in American Catholicism* (Notre Dame, Ind.: University of Notre Dame Press, 1992); Appleby, "Modernism as the Final Phase of Americanism: William L. Sullivan, American Catholic Apologist, 1899–1910," *Harvard Theological Review* 81, no. 2 (1988): 171–92; and Margaret Mary Reher, "Americanism and Modernism: Continuity or Discontinuity?" *U.S. Catholic Historian* 1 (1981): 87–103. These authors indicate a connection between modernism and Americanism.

73. Robert G. Sheridan, comp., *Discourses of James A. Walsh* (Maryknoll, N.Y.: Orbis Books, 1981), 143, from his talk to the Sisters in the *FA* office, 5 April 1924, commending them for their work. For an overview of the development of American Catholic domesticity and related issues, see Colleen McDannell, "Catholic Domesticity, 1860–1960," in Karen Kennelly, ed., *American Catholic Women: A Historical Exploration* (New York: Macmillan, 1989), 48–80.

74. Letter of Stanton to a scholastic, 3 March 1902, quoted in William T. Kane, SM, *A Memoir of William A. Stanton, S.J.* (St. Louis: B. Herder Book Co., 1927), 110–11.

Chapter 5 /
"America's Hour" for Missions Overseas, 1918–35

1. The conference of German missionary congregations met on 23 July 1919 to discuss the problem of nationalism in German missions. They published a series of declarations, which aimed to respect the rights of both the government and missionaries. See "Principles and Declarations Regarding the Mission Question," *FA* 13 (October 1919): 227–28.

2. John Ireland quoted in an obituary article by Joseph Freri, *CM* 12 (November 1918): 262. For an example of gratitude toward American intervention in saving a German mission area from missionary repatriation, see A. Hennighaus, SVD, "The Other Side of the Story," *CM* 13 (August 1919): 178–80. American Catholics had strongly supported this area of South Shantung, China, financially. At issue in this case was the presence of Japanese troops in the area. See John King Fairbank, *The United States and China,* 4th ed. (Cambridge: Harvard University Press, 1983), 233.

3. A few seminaries, not educating men for missions overseas, had earlier established mission organizations for students. Some drew from the nineteenth-century German revival of missions. One of these was the St. Philip Neri Mission Society at St. Francis Seminary, Milwaukee, organized by the seminarians in 1912. The group's annual Mission Sunday began

with a Pontifical High Mass and mission sermon and was followed by mission addresses, entertainment, and a play. The event was modeled on the German Mission Feast popular in the late nineteenth century. See Anthony Freytag, SVD, *The Catholic Mission Feast: A Manual for the Arrangement of Mission Celebrations,* adapted for America by Cornelius Pekari, OFMCap, and Bruno Hagspiel, SVD (Techny, Ill.: Mission Press, 1914). Students also provided mission books and magazines for the library and interested seminary alumni.

4. Narratives about the origins of the CSMC appear in Clifford J. King, SVD, *I Remember* (Techny, Ill.: Divine Word Publications, 1968), 48–57; *God Wills It!* (Cincinnati: CSMC, 1919); *The Sacred Heart for the World, The World for the Sacred Heart,* CSMC Bulletin, no. 3 (1918): 44–46; "Young Man Named King," *Golden Jubilee Booklet of the Catholic Students Mission Crusade* (Notre Dame, Ind., 1968), 9, 11–12; and Edward A. Freking, "The Catholic Students' Mission Crusade," chap. 28 in *The Mission Apostolate: A Study of Mission Activity of the Roman Catholic Church and the Story of Mission Aid Organizations* (New York: National Office of the Society for the Propagation of the Faith, 1942).

To highlight the importance of seminary involvement in missions, Peter Janser, SVD, Francis Clement Kelley, and James A. Walsh presented the major papers in the seminary section of the annual Catholic Education Association Conference in 1919. See the Seminary Section, "Report of the Proceedings and Addresses of the Sixteenth Annual Meeting," *The Catholic Educational Association Bulletin* 16 (November 1919).

5. In the departure ceremony and sermon, Chicago's archbishop George W. Mundelein told the Divine Word Missionaries to "give the Maryknolls a run for their money" (William J. Bonner, SVD, to author, 12 August 1993). Clark died in China soon after his ordination. King kept the CSMC informed about developments in China over the years and was a speaker at several conventions when he was in the United States.

6. More will be heard about Considine in later chapters. Frank A. Thill was in his second year of theology at Mount St. Mary's of the West, Cincinnati, in 1918. He received permission throughout his student years and after his ordination to continue full time with CSMC work, serving as secretary-treasurer until 1935. A dynamic speaker, he traversed the country attending local rallies of CSMC units and organizing educational programs on missionary problems. He became bishop of Concordia in 1938 and bishop of Salina, Kansas, in 1944. J. Paul Spaeth worked with CSMC for almost fifty years. Later he was active in the missionary movement in Latin America in the 1950s; Louise, his wife, also remained active in both areas for much of this time.

By 1921, CSMC had an advisory board which included Joseph McGlinchey, Boston director of the SPF; James A. Walsh; mission promoter Bruno Hagspiel, SVD; and J. M. Fraser, founder of the Scarboro Fathers in Canada and former missionary to China.

7. Keeler had been converted through the influence of Paulist Father John Handly in 1918. He studied for the priesthood while he was in his seventies — his wife had died when three children were at home — and was ordained by the bishop of Richmond, Virginia. An article he wrote before his reception into the Catholic Church is "Simple Gospel Not Enough," *Truth* 21 (January 1917): 5–6.

8. See for example the editorials by Joseph Husslein, SJ, in *America,* 2 June 1917 and 22 June 1918.

9. *A Missionary Index of Catholic Americans* (Cincinnati: Crusade Castle, 1942). Subsequent editions were published in 1944, 1946, and 1949. The Reverend Michael Mathis, CSC, had also compiled information about religious congregations who sent missionaries overseas from 1936 to 1940; the report was compiled for well-known Catholic missiologist Joseph Schmidlin.

10. *God Wills It!,* 15.

11. Kenneth Scott Latourette, "The Missionary Awakening among Roman Catholics in the United States," *International Review of Missions* 11 (1922): 439–44.

12. Francis J. Beckman, "Why We Met at Notre Dame," in *To Defend the Cross: The Story of the Fourth General Convention of the Catholic Students' Mission Crusade,* ed. Con-

vention Secretary (Cincinnati: Catholic Students Mission Crusade, 1924), 15, 20. By the 1930s, these conferences had provided for a gathering of major superiors through formation of a Catholic Conference of Clerics and Religious, which affiliated with CSMC. On this point, see C. Joseph Nuesse, *The Catholic University of America* (Washington, D.C.: Catholic University of America Press, 1990), 326.

13. In 1923, the Reverend Peter Dietz, who had established the first U.S. Catholic school for social service in Hot Springs, North Carolina, gave the CSMC the house he had used for his American Academy of Christian Democracy. The building, known as the Crusade Castle because of its fortress-like architecture, was an appropriate symbol for the philosophy of the CSMC movement.

14. The person represented Peter the Hermit, who led the Crusades.

15. *Golden Jubilee Booklet of the Catholic Students Mission Crusade*, 13.

16. Two important works to understand these ideas are Philip Gleason, *Keeping the Faith* (Notre Dame, Ind.: University of Notre Dame Press, 1987), and T. Jackson Lears, *No Place of Grace: Antimodernism and the Transformation of American Culture, 1880–1920* (New York: Pantheon, 1981). Gleason identifies three main areas in which Catholics used medievalism: in apologetics, in a "romantic aesthetic," which was "a quietly evocative glow suffusing this view" (20), and in social critique (often along the lines of German solidarism). His detailed footnotes provide abundant sources tracing the theme.

17. These are the comments of the Reverend Leo Sponar, CPPS, at the Fourth General Convention of the CSMC (*To Defend the Cross*, 178).

18. See an outline of this CSMC plan in Sister Rosaria, PBVM, "Student Crusaders for Catholic Action," *Catholic Action* 23 (May 1941): 13–14.

19. James J. Walsh, *These Splendid Priests* (1926; reprint, Freeport, N.Y.: Books for Libraries Press, 1968), also carried the motif.

20. The chapters of *Fundamentals of Missiology* (Cincinnati: Catholic Students Mission Crusade, 1957) were written by various Crusade units in seminaries around the country. J. Paul Spaeth edited and wrote the introduction, "Areas of Ideological Study," for *Perspectives on Religion and Culture* (Cincinnati: Catholic Students Mission Crusade, Paladin Press, 1957). The book presented chapters illustrating the spectrum of world religion as well as the perspectives of communism and secularism; the latter was provided by the pastoral of the U.S. Catholic Bishops on the topic in 1947.

21. Frank A. Thill, "1933–1934 Program of the Student Crusaders," *CA* 15 (October 1933): 21.

22. *Leader Book of the Catholic Students Mission Crusade* (Cincinnati: Catholic Students Mission Crusade, 1930), appendix, unnumbered pages.

23. "Pastoral Letter of 1919," in Hugh J. Nolan, ed., *Pastoral Letters of the U.S. Catholic Bishops*, vol. 1 (Washington, D.C.: U.S. Catholic Conference, 1983), 291.

24. The archbishops customarily met once a year. The NCWC included all bishops for an annual meeting. For a general overview of the formation of the NCWC, see Thomas T. McAvoy, CSC, *A History of the Catholic Church in the United States* (Notre Dame, Ind.: University of Notre Dame Press, 1969), 378–83. For a detailed picture of the importance of the Catholic War Council and its development into the National Catholic Welfare Council, see Elizabeth McKeown, *War and Welfare: American Catholics and World War I* (New York: Garland, 1988). Gerald Fogarty, SJ, *The Vatican and the American Hierarchy, 1870–1965* (Stuttgart: Anton Hiersemann, 1982), 214–28, provides background on the initial condemnation of the NCWC.

25. "Meeting Attended by McGlinchey at Notre Dame," 1919–20 folder, Record Group III.D16, Society for the Propagation of the Faith, AABoston. This document is Kelley's plan submitted from the subcommittee. For a helpful narrative on the various meetings which led to the approval of the ABCM, see Gaffey, *Francis Clement Kelley*, 307–29. For a candid appraisal of James A. Walsh and Francis Kelley, see Edward J. McCarthy, SSC, "Reminiscences of the Early Days of St. Columban Society in the United States, Reverend Edward J.

McCarthy," written in the 1950s, 8.c.4, CFA. For Walsh's remembrance of the 1919 meeting, see Sheridan, *Discourses of James A. Walsh*, pp. 73-76, MMA.

26. The clergy were John J. Burke (Catholic Board for Mission Work among the Colored People), Edward J. Knaebel, CSSp (Association of the Holy Childhood), Peter T. Janser, SVD, Edward J. McCarthy, James A. Walsh, William H. Ketcham (Bureau of Catholic Indian Missions), Joseph Freri, Peter J. O'Callaghan, CSP (Catholic Missionary Union), and Francis C. Kelley.

27. For developments in the structure and plans of the ABCM after 1922, see "Suggestions and Constitutions of the ABCM Committee of January 1, 1926, Annual Meetings of the Hierarchy," 124:1926, ACUA. The minutes of the 1924 and 1925 annual meetings contain suggestions for changes in the ABCM plan. Gaffey points out that "since the authorization of this board preceded the formation of the permanent secretariat, the ABCM was from its beginning 'superior' to the new National Catholic Welfare Council" (*Francis Clement Kelley*, 308). For a presentation of the ABCM's work to Catholics who subscribed to mission magazines, see "The American Board of Catholic Missions," *Our Missions* 1 (1921): 18–19.

28. See, for example, Diomede Falconio to Farley, 10 November 1909, I-13 (1910) to I-14 (1911), roll 3, Cardinal Farley Papers. AANY.

29. Kelley wanted to hold the number of magazines to five and wanted to abolish mission collecting agents, many of whom were not bonded. He thought that the greater the number of mission agencies, the more diluted the impact of the funds collected.

30. Sheridan, *Discourses of James A. Walsh*, 74.

31. O'Connell to Pietro Fumasoni-Biondi (copy), 21 March 1923, box 2, folder 8, Record Group III.D16, Society for the Propagation of the Faith, AABoston. Amandus Reuter, "De Nova et novissima S. Congregationis de Propaganda Fide ordinatione a Summis Pontificibus S. Pio X et Paul VI," in *Sacrae Congregationis de Propaganda Fide, Memoria Rerum*, vol. 3 (Rome: Herder, 1975), 354–81, presents a synopsis of the reforms in the Propaganda Fide office from 1908 to the 1970s. For developments during the Redemptorist Van Rossum's administration, see Joseph Metzler, "*Praefekten und Sekretaere der Kongregation in der neuesten Missionsaera (1918–1972)*," in ibid., 303–53. Prior to his service in this office, Van Rossum had been president of the Vatican Biblical Commission in 1914 and prepared the papal statement *Spiritus Paracletus*. After World War I, he began a school for mission service at Propaganda Fide University similar to the school at the University of Münster and emphasized the formation of native clergy around the world.

32. Freri to Kelley (copy), 30 October 1919, V-2 (1919), roll 10, Correspondence Submitted to Diocesan Consultors, Patrick Cardinal Hayes Papers, AANY. Freri had his own plan for the reform of the SPF: see Freri letters to Cardinal O'Connell, 19 August 1919, 22 September 1919, and 6 July 1920, box 2, 1919–20 folder, Records of Institutions, Record Group III.D16, Society for the Propagation of the Faith, AABoston.

33. Freri's comments on the 1919 plan are given in "Some Remarks on the Plan and Methods of the American Board of Catholic Missions," n.d. [probably late 1919 or early 1920], box 5, III. Record Group 10, Sulpician Archives, Baltimore.

34. More currently, the ABCM defines itself as a support for home missions. It distributes 40 percent of Mission Sunday monies to home missions, 51 percent to the SPF, and 9 percent to the Catholic Near East Welfare Association. Information from the ABCM office, 10 June 1987.

35. "Pastoral Letter on Mexico" (1926), in Nolan, ed., *Pastoral Letters of the U.S. Catholic Bishops*, vol. 1; Douglas J. Slawson, "The National Catholic Welfare Conference and the Church-State Conflict in Mexico, 1925–1929," *Americas* 47 (July 1990): 55–93. Francis C. Kelley, Catholic Extension Society founder and bishop of Oklahoma by 1924, was one of those who went to the State Department on this issue. His concern for Mexico remained, and he wrote about his visit there in *Blood Drenched Altars: Mexican Study and Comment* (Milwaukee: Bruce Publishing Company, 1935). He considered the Mexican "adventure" as the "most interesting event" in the Catholic Extension Society's life. See Francis C. Kel-

ley, *The Story of Extension* (Chicago: Extension Press, 1922). For a description of Kelley's involvement, see Gaffey, *Francis Clement Kelley,* vol. 2, chaps. 11 and 12.

The U.S. Bishops had expressed their concern about the Mexican problem in 1921 because certain dioceses were experiencing an influx of Mexicans. This same year the bishops noted that Filipino and Native American boys were being proselytized by Protestants. See "Report" made to the U.S. hierarchy at the gathering of the National Catholic Welfare Council, 21, 22 September 1921, Annual Meetings of the American Hierarchy Collection 124, ACUA.

36. For the bishops' 1932 statement, see *CA* 15 (February 1933): 5. For the "Statement on Tyranny in Mexico," see Nolan, ed., *Pastoral Letters of the U.S. Catholic Bishops,* vol. 1. For a narrative of the NCWC's involvement, see "The National Catholic Welfare Conference and the Mexican Church-State Conflict of the Mid-1930s: A Case of Deja Vu," *Catholic Historical Review* 80 (January 1994): 58–96. Throughout 1933, William F. Montovan, legal advisor to the NCWC, wrote several articles on the Mexican problem in *CA;* he was made a Knight of St. Gregory for his work. Because they were banned, the number of U.S. Catholic missionaries to Mexico was listed as zero until 1944, when five missionaries are identified.

John J. Burke (1875–1936) filled the post of general secretary for the NCWC for seventeen years. He was also cofounder of the National Catholic School of Social Service at Catholic University. See John B. Sheerin, *Never Look Back: The Career and Concerns of John J. Burke* (New York: Paulist Press, 1975), for biographical details.

37. Minutes, Annual Meeting of the Hierarchy, 1935, 1936. "Bishops Propose to Provide in the U.S. a Seminary for the Training of Mexican Priests," *CA* 18 (October 1936): 14; "U.S. Bishops Plan Seminary to Train Mexicans for Priesthood," *CA* 19 (April 1937): 11, 14. Another seminary for the same purpose had been set up in the 1920s in Castroville, Texas. Using a building provided by the Sisters of Divine Providence, St. Philip Seminary lasted for three years.

Officially named the national Pontifical Seminary of Our Lady of Guadalupe, the Montezuma Seminary opened on 23 September 1937 and was administered by the Jesuits of the Mexican Province in cooperation with the U.S. Catholic hierarchy. After 1972, the seminary relocated to Tula, Hidalgo, Mexico, and is known today as Seminario Interregional Mexicano (correspondence with Marina Ochoa, director, Office of Historic-Artistic Patrimony and Archives, archdiocese of Santa Fe, New Mexico, 23 May 1995).

38. Over the years, the bishops increased their annual support to $60,000 (1947) and $100,000 (1954). In 1957, 64 percent of the income for the Montezuma Seminary came from the U.S. Bishops, 25 percent from Mexico, and 8.5 percent from other donations. Because of lack of space in 1962, eighty students were not allowed into the seminary. Information is from the NCWC Annual Reports for those years. "[I]t seemed to be the opinion of many that the foundation and maintenance of Montezuma was the outstanding contribution of the church in the United States to Latin America" (NCWC Annual Report, 1962, 40).

39. In 1931, at least four schools offered scholarships for Latin American students: College of Saint Catherine, St. Paul, Minnesota; College of Saint Teresa, Winona, Minnesota; Creighton University, Omaha, Nebraska; Georgetown University, Washington, D.C.

40. NCWC press release, 1931, LAB Files, ACUA.

41. On the U.S. Catholic discussion of communism in the 1930s, see Robert L. Frank, "Prelude to Cold War: American Catholics and Communism," *Journal of Church and State:* 34 (Winter 1992): 39–56. By and large, women's organizations responded more readily to the programs and were more active than the men (see McKeown, *War and Welfare,* 183). A predecessor to the National Council of Catholic Women was the national League of Catholic Women, which grew out of the Women's Catholic Congress at the 1893 Columbian Exposition and which espoused evangelistic, philanthropic, and social goals. See Aaron Abell, *American Catholicism and Social Action: A Search for Social Justice, 1865–1950* (Garden City, N.Y.: Hanover Press, 1963), 122–23.

42. Information on McGowan's work at the NCWC is available throughout Gerald M.

Costello, *Without Fear or Favor: George Higgins on the Record* (Mystic, Conn.: Twenty-third Publications, 1984).

43. R. A. McGowan to Joseph Apodoca, 6 May 1932, 10/1 folder, Apodoca, Joseph, LAB, ACUA.

44. NCWC press release, 1931, LAB, ACUA.

45. Inman to McGowan, 18 December 1931, box 10/2, "I" file, LAB, ACUA.

46. Memorandum to Father Burke [probably from McGowan], 9 December 1931, p. 1, box 10/1, Burke folder, Inter-Office 1930–33, LAB, ACUA, emphasis mine. In this same memo, Bishop Sieffert of La Paz, Bolivia, recommended that the U.S. Catholic Church set up schools to teach English and use the Protestants' methods with dispensaries, schools, missions among the Indians, and the establishment of secondary and commercial colleges. He recommended the "teaching of English especially, since this is certain (through the experience of some Irish nuns in Cochabamba) that if a Catholic American mission comes to establish institutions in which English is taught the same as in the Protestant colleges, the latter will finally disappear" (ibid., 2). Comments from this summary were published in Elizabeth K. Sheridan, "Latin American Catholics Welcome NCWC Cooperation," *CA* 14 (January 1932): 18.

47. Unsigned article, "Inter-American Cooperation," box 10/3, McGowan, Personal Letters, 1931–33, LAB, ACUA. This article appeared in *CA* 15 (March 1933): 13, 31. McGowan saw an opposition between capitalism and a Catholic philosophy of life, though he did not see a clash between the Church and industry with its new machines and methods. For his thoughts on the matter as it related to the problems Catholic countries were experiencing politically, economically, and socially, see McGowan to Montavon, 3 September 1931, box 10/3, McGowan, Personal Letters, LAB, ACUA.

48. "The Church and Reconstruction in Puerto Rico," *CA* 18 (January 1936): 15, 23. The Latin American Bureau also promoted Pan-American Day each year.

49. In December 1938, an Inter-American Commission of Women was established at the Pan-American Conference in Lima, Peru. The NCWC realized the importance of representation by U.S. Catholic women on that commission in order to influence its thinking. The National Council of Catholic Women was particularly interested in having Latin American women see the social role of the Church in the United States and its influence on national life. A second focus of this women's group was to obtain scholarships for Latin Americans. By 1940, sixty-seven new scholarships were offered to women and forty-two to men.

50. Emphasis mine. Carlo Salotti, secretary of Propaganda Fide, to "Very Reverend Sir," Rome, 3 June 1932, box 4, folder 3, Record Group III.D16, Society for the Propagation of the Faith, AABoston.

51. By 1920, the Mystical Body had come to be the controlling metaphor for Catholic Action. For a bibliography of some of the significant Catholic Action literature of the 1920s and 1930s, see *Fundamentals of Missiology* (Cincinnati: Catholic Students Mission Crusade, 1957), 27–31; Burton Confrey, *Catholic Action: A Textbook for Colleges and Study Clubs* (New York: Benziger Brothers, 1935); John J. Harbrect, *The Lay Apostolate* (St. Louis: B. Herder Book Co., 1929); W. Joyce Russell, "Catholic Action," *Sign* 13, no. 12 (1933): 757–58; and Charles A. McMahon, "The Meaning of Catholic Action," *CA* (January 1932): 7–8. For a reminiscence about Catholic Action and the way it followed the model of Cardinal Cardijn, see Louis Putz, CSC, "Reflections on Specialized Catholic Action," *U.S. Catholic Historian* 9 (Fall 1990): 433–39.

52. For a medical-anthropological approach to this issue, see Leder Drew, ed., *The Body in Medical Thought and Practice* (Boston: Kluwer Academic Publishers, 1992), which also provides a cultural, historical, and theoretical overview of the body from a medical perspective.

53. *Marist Missions* 1 (September 1936): 1.

54. Floyd Keeler, *Catholic Medical Missions* (New York: Macmillan, 1925). For the lay missionary aspects of the CMMB, see "Laymen Meet the Medical Need," *Worldmission* 21, no. 3 (1970): 50–52.

55. Flagg provided a "Doctor's Column" in *The Field Afar* beginning in 1914, and by the early 1920s provided medical courses for Maryknoll seminarians. Flagg's daughter, Sister Virginia Flagg, joined the Maryknoll Sisters in 1930 and worked in China and Hong Kong. On Flagg, see Jean-Paul Wiest, *Maryknoll in China: A History, 1918–1955* (Armonk, N.Y.: M. E. Sharpe, 1988), 132–38.

For an overview of health services provided by U.S. women religious, see Ursula Stepsis, CSA, and Dolores Liptak, RSM, *Pioneer Healers: The History of Women Religious in American Health Care* (New York: Crossroad, 1989).

56. A Catholic Medical Mission Society seems to have been in existence since at least 1916. See the pamphlet, "The Catholic Medical Mission Bureau," 1916.

57. For an overview of Catholic health care, see Christopher J. Kauffman, *Ministry and Meaning: A Religious History of Catholic Health Care in the United States* (New York: Crossroad, 1995); for some of Garesché's ideas about medical missions, see Edward F. Garesché, SJ, "The Medical Mission Board," *CA* (September 1934): 11, 14, 17. Garesché's articles on the Catholic Medical Mission Board appeared in *Woodstock Letters* 58 (1929): 248; 69 (1940): 29–39; 70 (1941): 156–57; and 72 (1943): 105–15.

Garesché belonged to a well-known family from St. Louis. After a short time practicing law, he entered the Society of Jesus and founded the *Queen's Work,* a national publication of the Sodality of Mary. He established and directed the International Guild of Catholic Nurses. In 1935 the Jesuit founded a religious congregation, Daughters of Mary, Health of the Sick, and in 1952 was responsible for beginning a similar congregation for men, Sons of Mary, Health of the Sick, which had its headquarters in Framingham, Massachusetts. For Garesché's work with the Catholic Hospital Association and with the CMMB, see Kauffman, *Ministry and Meaning,* 214–17.

58. Garesché, "The Medical Mission Board," 11.

59. Ibid., 14.

60. Ibid., 11.

61. Ibid., 17.

62. Wiest, *Maryknoll in China,* 200.

63. Paulo Manna, *The Conversion of the Pagan World* (Boston: Society for the Propagation of the Faith, 1921), 158. The work was translated and adapted for the United States by the Reverend Joseph McGlinchey, the SPF director in Boston.

64. Ibid.

65. Gertrude Hill Gavin, president, NCCW, to His Eminence Patrick Cardinal Hayes, 17 September 1924, roll 4 Q 9 (1924), "National" folder, Correspondence of Cardinal Hayes, AANY. This same year two women were elected governors: Miriam Ferguson in Texas and Nellie Ross in Wyoming.

66. Ledvina to Cardinal William O'Connell, 24 May 1932, box 4, folder 6, Record Group III.D16, Society for the Propagation of the Faith, AABoston.

67. "Paganism in the Solomons," *Alofa Malia* (Summer 1936): no page number. The magazine was the forerunner of *Marist Missions.*

68. *Marist Missions* 1 (September 1936): 5. The editor of this magazine for many years was Sister Augustine Kerby, SMSM (1909–95).

69. This is alluded to in Manna, *Conversion of the Pagan World,* 162.

70. For background on Dengel's life and her part in medical missions, see Katherine Burton, *According to the Pattern: The Story of Dr. Agnes McLaren and the Society of Catholic Medical Missionaries* (New York: Longmans Green & Company, 1946); and M. M. McGinley, "Mother Anna Dengel, M.D. — A Pioneer Medical Missionary," *Worldmission* 31 (1980): 26–31.

For the history of Dengel's congregation, see Mother Anna Dengel, SCMM, "The Society of Catholic Medical Missionaries," in The National Office of the Society for the Propagation of the Faith, comp., *The Mission Apostolate* (New York: Society for the Propagation of the Faith, 1942), 179–86; Aloysius Roche, *In the Track of the Gospel: An Outline of the*

Christian Apostolate from Pentecost to the Present (New York: P. J. Kenedy, 1953), 181–86; and M. Bonaventure Beck, "The Society of Catholic Medical Missionaries: Origin and Development" (M.S. thesis, Catholic University of America, 1955). *If It Matters* (Philadelphia: Medical Mission Sisters, 1967) provides a mainly pictorial representation of the works of the Sisters during the 1960s. Richard F. Long, *Nowhere a Stranger* (New York: Vantage Press, 1968), is a popularly written work which presents a brief history of ten missions of the Medical Mission Sisters.

Gerard Jansen, "Christian Ministry of Healing on Its Way to the Year 2000: An Archaeology of Medical Missions," *Missiology* 23 (July 1995): 295–307, provides a quick overview of the history of Christian healing as it relates to missions. See also Pia Maria Plachl, *Kreuz und Askulap* (Vienna: Herold, 1967); and Wiest, *Maryknoll in China*, 132–38, 154–62.

For an early assessment of the role of women in missions, see Frederick Schwager, SVD, *Woman's Misery and Woman's Aid in Foreign Missions* (Techny, Ill.: Mission Press, [c. 1917]). Schwager (1876–1929) came to the United States in 1924 and spoke to various groups at Catholic University. He left the Church shortly thereafter.

71. See Marie Cecile de Mijolla, SMSM, *Origins in Oceania: Missionary Sisters of the Society of Mary, 1845–1931* (Rome: n.p., 1984), 25. Information about the lay women's work in Oceania is in "Missionary Sisters of the Society of Mary: Unfolding Our History, 1845–1881," 1994, typescript, p. 1, Archives of the Marist Missionary Sisters, Waltham, Massachusetts.

72. See, for example, Pauline Willis to Cardinal Hayes, November 1924, roll Q 9 (1924), Correspondence to Hayes, AANY. Cardinal Dougherty, former archbishop in the Philippines, displayed a particular interest in her work, coached her on how to present her case in Rome, provided the congregation she founded with financial support, and welcomed them to his archdiocese in 1928. For this side of Dougherty, see Margaret Mary Reher, "Denis J. Dougherty and Anna M. Dengel: The Missionary Alliance," *Records of the American Catholic Historical Society of Philadelphia* 101 (1990): 21–33. The two women also met with John Considine and Dr. Flagg. They were guests of National Catholic Social Services through the invitation of John J. Burke and Agnes Regan, executive secretary for the National Council of Catholic Women.

73. Willis was secretary for Dr. McLaren's St. Catherine's Hospital project. The same year Dengel met with Mathis the latter published *With the Holy Cross in Bengal* (Washington, D.C.: n.p., 1924), which explains through photographs and text the work of the Holy Cross mission in India. The book provides a fairly objective view of the beliefs and practices of various kinds of Hinduism.

74. Anna Dengel, M.D., *Mission for Samaritans: A Survey of Achievements and Opportunities in the Field of Catholic Medical Missions* (Milwaukee: Bruce Publishing Company, 1945), 1.

75. Ibid., 5. While living in the vicinity of the Catholic University of America, she drew on the thought of two of its professors, William Kerby, especially his *The Social Mission of Charity* (New York: Macmillan, 1924), and anthropologist James M. Cooper, who wrote the foreword to *Mission for Samaritans*. See also Anna Dengel, "First Aid for the Missions," *Catholic Missions* (1926), and the Medical Mission Sisters Archives, Record Groups 1–4, which provide talks and other materials illuminating the spiritual underpinnings of medical work.

76. *Osservatore Romano*, 9 August 1935, quoted in Dengel, *Mission for Samaritans*, 3–4.

77. Dengel, *Mission For Samaritans*, 5. It was from the Medical Mission Sisters that Mother Teresa of Calcutta learned how to deal with poor and sick persons.

78. Kauffman, *Ministry and Meaning*, chap. 8, discusses this development in the Catholic Hospital Association.

79. This image appeared in the New York archdiocesan SPF newspaper, *Catholic Mission News*, 3 October 1927, 3.

80. Manna, *Conversion of the Pagan World*, 214.

Chapter 6 /
"Light to the Darkness": Mission to Asia, 1918–53

1. The following chart indicates missions turned over to American men's groups after 1924:

Mission	Year	Group in Charge
Kongmoon	1924	Maryknoll Fathers
Yuangling [*sic*]	1925	Passionists
Kaying	1929	Maryknoll Fathers
Chowtsun	1929	Friars Minor
Yukiang	1929	Congregation of the Mission
Wuchow	1930	Maryknoll Fathers
Kanchow	1931	Congregation of the Mission
Kienow	1931	Dominican Fathers
Fushun	1932	Maryknoll Fathers
Sinsiang	1936	Society of the Divine Word
Shasi	1936	Friars Minor
Kweilin	1938	Maryknoll Fathers
Yaowan	1939	Friars Minor

Chart taken from Joseph P. Ryan, "American Contributions to the Catholic Missionary Effort in China in the Twentieth Century," *Catholic Historical Review* 31 (July 1945): 171–80, here 179.

2. *America* 56 (May 1937): 588. The Catholic Students Mission Crusade, which began to publish compilations in the 1940s, indicated the following distribution of American Catholic personnel for 1942:

Africa	130	Oceania	329
China	651	East Indies	7
Korea	52	Philippines	262
India	206	Alaska	61
Japan	42	Canada	65
Manchukuo	69	Central America	112
Western Asia	34	South America	227
Thailand	6	West Indies	486

These figures are taken from Catholic Students Mission Crusade, *A Missionary Index of Catholic Americans* (Cincinnati: Crusade Castle, 1942), and are also found in *Missionary Academia* 3, no. 6 (1944).

3. John King Fairbank, *The United States and China*, 4th ed. (Cambridge: Harvard University Press, 1983), 317–19.

4. *St. Mary's Chinese Schools, 65th Jubilee, 1921–1986* (San Francisco: privately printed, 1986), 13. This book has a helpful chronology of the mission to the Chinese in the San Francisco Bay area. St. Mary's Chinese Day School began teaching Chinese to its students in the late 1950s. The school became known, among other things, for its Chinese Girls Drum and Bugle Corps. The National Catholic Chinese Conference started at the mission in 1960. In addition to the two congregations of women religious mentioned, the Missionary Sisters of the Immaculate Conception and the Sisters of the Precious Blood (a Chinese community from Hong Kong) have worked in the parish. See also John B. McGloin, SJ, "Thomas Cian, Pioneer Priest in California," *California Historical Quarterly* 18 (March 1969): 45–58.

5. Peter Joseph Fleming, "Chosen for China: The California Province Jesuits in China, 1928–1957: A Case Study in Mission and Culture" (Ph.D. diss., Graduate Theological Union, Berkeley, Calif., 1987), provides a vitae for Moore, 671–72. He founded Gonzaga

High School, Shanghai, in 1931 and stayed in China until 1937, when he returned to the United States to raise funds for the mission.

6. Bradley was also called on to aid Chinese going through the immigration process in San Francisco. See, for example, E. J. McCarthy, "Diary of Progress at St. Columban's, Omaha, Neb.," 6 July 1922, CFA. For a description of St. Mary's during the time of Charles Bradley, CSP, see *FA* 9 (February 1915): cover photo and 19.

Chinese converts are also mentioned in Spokane, Washington, in Pius L. Moore, SJ, "Our Japanese Mission in San Francisco," *Our Missions* (1926): 10. In St. Paul, Minnesota, an eastern hub of the transcontinental railroad, several Chinese converts had been baptized at St. Vincent Church in 1903. In the early 1920s, the Jesuits at Creighton were tending to the education of several Chinese students.

7. McQuaide was rector of Sacred Heart Parish, San Francisco, when he wrote *With Christ in China* (San Francisco: The O'Connor Co., 1916). He dedicated the book to the Maryknoll Society and encouraged Americans to go as missionaries overseas. McQuaide became chaplain of the Knights of Columbus in San Francisco in 1902 and their first state chaplain in 1904. This kind and public-spirited man was active in relief efforts after the San Francisco earthquake in 1906 and served as chaplain in World War I. Information about McQuaide comes from correspondence with Dr. Jeffrey Burns, archivist, archdiocese of San Francisco, and from obituary articles he provided.

8. *Transfiguration Church, a Church of Immigrants, 1827–1977* (New York: Park Publishing Company, [1977]), 20–21; *FA* 3, no. 4 (1909): 7, 8. In 1908, Ernest Coppo, the first Salesian pastor of Transfiguration Parish, had requested that the bishop of Canton send a priest to work among the Chinese in the New York area. Father V. H. Montanar, a Paris Foreign Mission Society priest, arrived several months later. The perceived interference of returned China missionary John W. Fraser (1877–1962) in the parish led Montanar to write to the archbishop about the problem. About the same time, Fraser was attempting to get into the New York Archdiocese to begin a mission seminary, just as J. A. Walsh was beginning the Maryknoll seminary. Fraser later cofounded the Scarboro Mission Society (V. H. Montanar to Most Rev. and Dear Sir, 29 January 1911, I-14 [1911], roll 3, Catholic Mission folder, Cardinal Farley Papers, AANY). Additional documents in this folder indicate that Archbishop Farley queried the appropriate French missionaries in China regarding Fraser's background and character. Fraser was not recommended by his superiors to begin the seminary in New York.

9. Dunn wrote a regular column on missions in *Catholic News*, the New York archdiocesan newspaper. The description of these mission days appears around 7 December each year. The story of a prominent Chinese Catholic family, Laurence Woo, is told in *FA* 9 (August 1915): 117.

10. *Transfiguration Church*, 47. The parish returned to diocesan administration in 1976, and Mark Cheung became the first Chinese administrator. See also John Voghera, SSFS, to Patrick Cardinal Hayes, 6 May 1924, roll 4 Q8 (1924), Correspondence of Cardinal Hayes, AANY.

11. The first four directors of the Boston SPF office were Joseph V. Tracy (1898–1903), James A. Walsh (1903–11), Joseph F. McGlinchey (1911–28), and Richard J. Cushing (1928–44), all of whom significantly influenced mission promotion nationally. As archbishop and cardinal, Cushing would continue to provide tremendous support and finances to mission work.

12. For a description of this event, see *Handbook and Guide of the World in Boston: The First Great Exposition in America of Home and Foreign Missions Held in Mechanics Hall, April 22–May 20, 1911* (Boston: World in Boston, 1911). In 1946, Archbishop Richard Cushing requested the Maryknoll Sisters to work with the Asian community in Boston. Several of the women had experience in Guangdong Province.

13. Ark is pictured in *FA* 1, no. 3 (1907): 11. The Reverend Walter J. Browne worked

with the Boston-area Chinese, conducting a Sunday School and mission, as early as 1905 (*FA* 1, no. 2 [1907]: 4).

14. Francis C. Kelley to William Cardinal O'Connell, 10 October 1913, M-1021, American Catholic Missionary Congress folder, AABoston. Joseph Koesters's speech appears in Francis C. Kelley, ed., *The Second American Catholic Missionary Congress* (Chicago: J. S. Hyland, 1913), 69–73.

15. Its three thousand members were taught "missiology," ideas they then spread to their homes, social organizations, and places of work.

16. "Chinese Students Meet in Conference," *FE* (November 1923): 171–72; "Wither Will China Turn?" *FE* (January 1924): 5–6.

17. In order to receive papal approval, this community, founded in Le Mans, France, in 1837 by The Reverend Basil Moreau, was required to take responsibility for this area (James T. Connelly, CSC, archivist, to author, 7 April 1988). For the work of the Holy Cross Fathers and Brothers, see Raymond Clancy, CSC, *The Congregation of Holy Cross in East Bengal, 1853–1953* (Washington, D.C.: Holy Cross Foreign Mission Seminary, 1953), and Edmund Goedert, CSC, *Holy Cross Priests in the Diocese of Dacca, 1853–1981* (Notre Dame, Ind.: Province Archives Center, 1983).

18. Michael A. Mathis, CSC, *With the Holy Cross in Bengal* (Washington, D.C.: n.p., 1924), 11.

19. Copy of a letter in Council Archives, 19 December 1893, Holy Cross in India 1852–76, correspondence re Saint Anne's Convent and School, Akyab, quoted in Charlotte Bayhouse, CSC, "The Holy Cross Foreign Mission Convent: An Early Experience in Collaboration," unpublished paper, 1988, provided to author by Charlotte Bayhouse, CSC. A brief description of the three periods of the Sisters' mission foundations appears in Sister Mary Eleanore, *On the King's Highway* (New York: D. Appleton and Company, 1931), 426–28.

20. Michael Mathis, CSC, got the idea of having a group of women work with the priests on the magazine from his visit to Maryknoll, where he saw seventy-five women producing *The Field Afar.* For his reorganization of the magazine operation, see Bayhouse, "The Holy Cross Foreign Mission Convent."

21. Joseph F. McGlinchey, *Mission Tours: India* (Boston: Society for the Propagation of the Faith, 1925), narrates his trip to many of the missions to which the Boston SPF had responded financially through the years; see also Capuchin Mission Unit, *India and Its Missions* (New York: Macmillan, 1923). Students worked on the latter book for four years. Using statistics taken from *Die Katolischen Missionen,* they wrote a history of contemporary Catholic and Protestant missions in India.

22. Information about Henry McGlinchey's life appears in Neil Boyton, *Yankee Xavier* (New York: Macmillan, 1937), and in McGlinchey, *Mission Tours: India,* 178–87.

23. Information about Westropp's life from R. E. Wilkinson, "A Short History of Fr. Henry I. Westropp, SJ," 1953. This booklet is in the Lillian and Clara Westropp Collection, MC 215 Schlesinger Library, Radcliffe-Harvard University, Schlesinger Women and History Manuscript Collection. Westropp participated in the Second American Catholic Missionary Congress in Boston. His photograph appears opposite p. 135 in Kelley, ed., *Second American Catholic Missionary Congress.* For a short history of the midwestern province's work in this part of India, see John Francis Bannon, SJ, *The Missouri Province of Jesuits: A Mini-History* (St. Louis: The Missouri Province, 1977), 18–20. After 1928, the Patna mission became the mission of the newly formed Chicago Province.

24. *Woodstock Letters* 49 (1920): 391.

25. Their departure and reception in the Philippines is told by one of their members, Henry L. Irwin, in *Woodstock Letters* 50 (1921): 319–31; 51 (1922): 386–400; and 52 (1923): 41, 353. Ten years later an account of these missions appeared in *Woodstock Letters* 62 (1932): 164. The Jesuit community was composed of Americans from the Maryland/New York and New England provinces and Filipino men. Another example of such "shifting" is provided by the American Vincentians, impelled by their French superior general to

assume some of the depleted missions in China in 1920. For the work of the American provinces of Vincentians in China, see Edward R. Udovic, CM, " 'Go Out to All the Nations!' The Foreign Mission Apostolate: 1914–1987," in John E. Rybolt, CM, ed., *The American Vincentians: A Popular History of the Congregation of the Mission in the United States, 1815–1987* (Brooklyn: New City Press, 1988), 367–96.

26. On Engbring, see Marion A. Habig, OFM, *Pioneering in China: The Story of Francis Xavier Engbring, OFM* (Chicago: Franciscan Herald Press, 1930), which also provides a short summary about several other Franciscans who went to China in the early twentieth century. See also Marion A. Habig, OFM, *In Journeyings Often: Franciscan Pioneers in the Orient* (St. Bonaventure, N.Y.: Franciscan Institute, 1953). Angelus Blesser, OFM, was joined by Juniper W. Doolin, OFM, from the California Province of OFMs. Blesser tells his story in *CM* 1 (1907): 129, 193; 2 (1908): 29, 97–102, 151–55; and 3 (1909): 40–41, 71–72.

27. Elizabeth J. Weber, *Celestial Honeymoon: The Story of Sister Catherine Bushman, S.C.* (New York: Benziger Brothers, 1950). The foreword was written by Mother Mary Joseph Rogers. Bushman's niece, Sister Alma Virginia Weber, joined the Maryknoll Sisters. The story of another American Daughter of Charity, one of the first sent by the American Province of the society, is that of Sister Clare Groell, *White Wings in Bamboo Land* (Emmitsburg, Md.: St. Joseph's Provincial House Press, 1973).

28. The SVM was founded in 1886. Gerald H. Anderson summarized reasons for the loss of SVM-sponsored missionaries: the Depression, secularism in college education, the development of the Social Gospel, and religious differences expressed in fundamentalism and modernism ("American Protestants in Pursuit of Mission: 1886–1986," *International Bulletin of Missionary Research* [July 1988]: 106).

Key books for examining American Protestant missions are R. Pierce Beaver, *All Loves Excelling: American Protestant Women in World Mission* (Grand Rapids, Mich.: Eerdmans, 1968); Patricia Hill, *The World Their Household: The American Woman's Foreign Mission Movement and Cultural Transformation, 1870–1920* (Ann Arbor: University of Michigan Press, 1985); Jessie G. Lutz, *Chinese Politics and Christian Missions* (Notre Dame, Ind.: Crossroad, 1988); Suzanne Wilson Barnett and John King Fairbank, eds., *Christianity in China: Early Protestant Missionary Writings* (Cambridge: Harvard University Press, 1985); Jane Hunter, *The Gospel of Gentility: American Women Missionaries in Turn-of-the-Century China* (New Haven: Yale University Press, 1984); Leslie A. Flemming, ed., *Women's Work for Women: Missionaries and Social Change in Asia* (Boulder, Colo.: Westview Press, 1989); James Reed, *The Missionary Mind and American East Asia Policy, 1911–1915* (Cambridge: Council on East Asian Studies, Harvard University, 1983); William Hutchison, *Errand to the World: American Protestant Thought and Foreign Missions* (Chicago: University of Chicago Press, 1987); Valentin H. Rabe, *The Home Base of American China Missions, 1880–1920* (Cambridge: Harvard University Press, 1978); John King Fairbank et al., *The Missionary Enterprise in China and America* (Cambridge: Harvard University Press, 1974); Jessie G. Lutz, *China and the Christian Colleges, 1850–1950* (Ithaca, N.Y.: University of New York Press, 1971); and Kenneth Scott Latourette, *Missions and the American Mind* (Indianapolis: National Foundation Press, 1949).

A look at the development of Chinese Christianity appears in Daniel Bays, *Christianity in China: From the 18th Century to the Present* (Stanford, Calif.: Stanford University Press, 1996).

29. Helpful background reading on the period in China from 1918 to 1960 is Fairbank, *The United States and China,* and Jung Chang, *Wild Swan* (New York: Simon & Schuster, 1991). While the latter is fiction, the author draws heavily on the experience of three generations of women in her family who lived through the same events as U.S. Catholic missionaries in China. On the Chinese warlord period, see Hsi-Sheng Ch'i, *Warlord Politics in China, 1916–1928* (Stanford, Calif.: Stanford University Press, 1976). An overview chronicling major events in the Catholic Church in China from 635 to 1992 appears in Wiest, *Maryknoll in China,* xiii–xvii.

30. On the growth of the Catholic Church in China, see Wiest, *Maryknoll in China,* 203–60.

31. This event was described for American audiences in an article and large photograph in "China's First Plenary Council," *FE* (1924): 176–77. For developments and issues in the Catholic Church in China in the period of heaviest U.S. Catholic involvement, see *Collectanea Commissionis Synodalis* 1 (May 1928) — 7/12 (July–December 1947), microform, and Jean-Paul Wiest, editorial advisor, *Collectanea Commissionis Synodalis: Guide to the Microfiche Collection* (Bethesda, Md.: Academic Editions, 1988).

32. Wiest, *Maryknoll in China,* 25.

33. At the end of 1943, of the 2,896 U.S. Catholic missionaries overseas, the largest number (635) were in China (Ryan, "American Contributions," 174).

34. James A. Walsh, *Observations in the Orient* (Ossining, N.Y.: Catholic Foreign Mission Society, 1919).

35. James A. Walsh, ed., *Maryknoll Mission Letters, China* (New York: Macmillan, 1923), 182; Wiest, *Maryknoll in China,* 414.

36. Wiest, *Maryknoll in China,* 418.

37. *FA* 14 (February 1920): 303.

38. Departure Ceremony, Franciscan Sisters of Perpetual Adoration, 3 September 1928, 1.3.28, box 1/1, China: Plans for and Departure of Sisters to China, 1928, FSPAA.

39. Oswald Waller, prefect apostolic of Eastern Nigeria, *American Ecclesiastical Review* 60 (January 1919): 72–74.

40. On the origins of the Society of St. Columban, see Edward Fischer, *Journeys Not Regretted: The Columban Fathers' Sixty-five Years in the Far East* (New York: Crossroad, 1986), 12–16; E. J. McCarthy, "The Chinese Mission Society," in *Fourth General Council Diocesan Directors, Society for the Propagation of the Faith* (Cleveland: n.p., 1930). The official founding day for the Maynooth mission to China was 29 June 1918. Farley in New York gave the society $250 and O'Connell in Boston gave Galvin $1,000. More important, Galvin became friends with Joseph McGlinchey, the Boston SPF director, who proved a good friend to the society. E. J. McCarthy, "Reminiscences Written in 1950s," 6.8.c.4., CFA. In this typed transcript, the first superior of the American region recounts the beginning of the Columban Society in the United States.

41. McCarthy, "Reminiscences Written in 1950s," 21; *Those Who Journeyed with Us: Deceased Columbans, 1918–1992* (Omaha, Neb.: Missionary Society of St. Columban), 134.

42. In 1934, McCarthy left for the Philippines and inaugurated student Catholic Action groups two years later. Circumventing the masonic orientation of the school system at the time, which did not permit him to work with the students, he became a student himself at the university. Returning to the Philippines from Australia in 1942, he was captured and interned in Burma; he returned to Ireland in 1945. He died of injuries resulting from an automobile accident in Los Angeles in 1957 (Paul Casey, SSC, to author, 25 August 1988; Jim MacDevitt to "Father Paddy," 29 January 1939, CFA). For an insight into McCarthy's spiritual perspective on mission, especially on the relationship between mission and contemplation, see James McCaslin, *The Spirituality of Our Founders: A Study of the Early Columban Fathers* (Society of St. Columban, Maynooth Mission to China, 1986).

43. At the Fourth General Convention of the CSMC, McCarthy spoke about various arguments for mission awareness. The soundest argument, he concluded, was the "value of the human soul" (Catholic Students Mission Crusade, ed., *To Defend the Cross* [Cincinnati: Catholic Students Mission Crusade, 1924]).

44. Of the forty-six Columban men born in the United States and deceased by 1990, almost half of them worked at the home base in promotion, seminary teaching, or internal ministry. Among those who went overseas, eight were missioned to China, nine to the Philippines, five to Korea, one to Fiji, one to Burma. An unknown number of Irish-born Columbans who served in China eventually became U.S. citizens.

45. E. J. McCarthy to Sister Antonella, Sisters of Loretto, 16 September 1921, Han Yang folder, Loretto Sisters, 1920–23, negotiations re going to Han Yang, 1.c.6., CFA.

46. E. J. McCarthy, "Reminiscences Written in 1950s," 30. McCarthy's account of the 1919 meeting at Notre Dame appears on pp. 23–30 and is instructive and candid on the differences between the mission leaders and their perspectives at the meeting.

47. E. J. McCarthy, "The Chinese Mission Society," in *Fourth General Council of Diocesan Directors of the Society for the Propagation of the Faith* (Cincinnati: Society for the Propagation of the Faith, 1930), 170.

48. Her story appears in transcript of taped interview. Sister Therese Bolan, interview by Nick Kill, August 1975, 8.c.2., CFA.

49. George M. Stenz, SVD, "Lay Missionaries in China," *CM* 14 (July 1920): 156.

50. Han Yang — lay helper, Dan Sullivan, 1920–22, 1.c.2., CFA.

51. Han Yang — lay helper, Otto Scheuerman, 1921, 1.c.1., CFA.

52. Hubrich was born in Hoenigsdorf, Silesia, Germany. She came to Milwaukee in 1914 and then worked at St. Margaret's Foundling Home in Chicago for a number of years before she left for China. She opened a dispensary in Huang-shih-kang and founded a small community of native Sisters in the late 1920s. The group dressed in Chinese attire. After the Japanese invasion, the Chinese wished for a native superior. In effect, Hubrich was dismissed from the community. She worked in a Catholic Center in Taiwan for a few years, then went to Jerusalem where she lived the remainder of her life as a quasi-hermit. The Chinese community disbanded in the late 1940s. See Florence Wedge, *Franciscan Nun in China* (Pulaski, Wis.: Franciscan Publishers, 1963). The author noted that in the 1920s many laity were interested in going to China. See also *Franciscan Herald* (April 1924): 160.

53. Wiest, *Maryknoll in China*, 152–54. Several other laymen assisted in Maryknoll's medical mission in China.

54. Information from response to Thomas Stransky's questionnaire, Adorers of the Blood of Christ folder, Stransky Collection, Paulist Fathers Archives.

55. Mary Louise Tully, "I'm a Lay Apostle Overseas," *The Shield* (January 1950): 6–9; Nicholas Maestrini, *My Life with the Chinese: Laughter and Tears, 1931–1951* (Avon, N.J.: Magnificat Press, 1990), 306–9. Tully spent three years in Hong Kong and left because of ill health. Additional information about Tully from letter of Grailville archivist, Janet Kalven, to author, 12 January 1996.

56. McCarthy, "A Diary of Progress at St. Columban's, Omaha, Neb.," 29 December 1921, CFA.

57. Ibid., 2 April 1922.

58. The author obtained this number from a conversation with Xiaoqing Li. Ryan indicates that there were fifty-three groups of American Sisters and priests at fourteen missions in China up until World War II (Ryan, "American Contributions," 174). His number appears too large.

59. Arnulf Camps, OFM, and Patrick McCloskey, OFM, *History of the Order of the Friars Minor in China, 1294–1955* (St. Bonaventure, N.Y.: Franciscan Institute Publications, 1996), features the history of the Franciscan men in China who came from various European and American provinces. The book concentrates on the years 1925–55 and provides an account of the twenty-eight mission territories entrusted to the Friars Minor in China with an indication of the leadership, personnel, founding of local congregations, and apostolic works in each province and individual vicariates/prefectures. The book has many statistics, maps, and an appendix with key correspondence for the administration of the Franciscan missions in China.

60. Letter to author from Edward R. Udovic, CM, 1 March 1995. The French Vincentians, as was true of many European missionaries in general, did not think U.S. Catholics mature enough for the challenge of mission work. There seems to have been, as well, a conflict between French Vincentian ways and values of religious life and those expressed by the American Vincentians. On this point, see Udovic, "Go Out to All the Nations," 369–96.

61. For an analysis of the mission emphasis of the Passionists, see Robert Carbonneau, CP, "Life, Death, and Memory: Three Passionists in Hunan, China, and the Shaping of an American Mission Perspective in the 1920s" (Ph.D. diss., Georgetown University, 1992); Carbonneau, CP, "Passionists in China, 1921–1929: An Essay in Mission Experience," *Catholic Historical Review* 66 (1980): 392–416; Carbonneau, CP, "The Passionists in Twentieth-Century China," in Jeroom Hendryickx, CICM, ed., *Historiography of the Chinese Catholic Church, Nineteenth and Twentieth Centuries* (Louvain: Ferdinand Verbiest Foundation, 1994), 76–85; and Caspar Caulfield, *Only a Beginning: The Passionists in China, 1921–1931* (Union City, N.J.: Passionist Fathers, 1990). The author has also benefited from conversations with Carbonneau and Caulfield.

62. The Sisters of Charity, Convent Station, New Jersey, sent five Sisters to Hunan Province, invited by the Passionist Fathers, who had sent thirteen priests to the interior of China in 1922. Three Sisters were Irish-born, one a nurse (Sr. Mary Finan Griffin), one a housekeeper (Sr. Patricia Rose Hurley), and one an elementary school teacher (Sr. Maria Loretta Halligan). Two were American-born: they were teachers in grade school (Sr. Maria Electa McDermott) and high school (Sr. Marie Devota Ross). The Sisters had two mission-sending ceremonies, one at the Passionist Monastery in Union City, New Jersey, the other at their motherhouse at Convent Station before they departed for Hunan on 22 September 1924. An excellent history of their experience in China and their interaction with the Passionist Fathers is Mary Carita Pendergast, SC, *Havoc in Hunan: The Sisters of Charity in Western Hunan, 1924–1951* (Morristown, N.J.: College of St. Elizabeth Press, 1991).

63. The Eucharistic Congress outside Chicago in 1926 featured a student writing contest jointly sponsored by the CSMC and the Society of the Divine Word. The theme was "The Eucharist as the Center of Missionary Life." Some of the winning entries were published in *Our Missions* 6 (1926): 125-27, 149–51. Nine top contestants received room and lodging at the Divine Word Missionary seminary at Techny while they attended the conference.

64. Robert Streit, OMI, *Catholic Missions in Figures and Symbols, Based on the Vatican Missionary Exhibition* (New York: Society for the Propagation of the Faith, 1927).

65. G. Cramer, "What Will America Do?" *CM* 12 (1918): 232–33. The issue of native clergy runs throughout articles in *Catholic Missions* from 1910 to 1919, and an article on native Sisters appeared in *Catholic Missions* in 1920.

66. Walsh to "Bishop," no date, but located in March 1917 section, "Letters for the Foundation of Maryknoll" folder, MMA.

67. Wiest, *Maryknoll in China,* 423–24.

68. Quoted in Ann Colette Wolf, *Against All Odds: Sisters of Providence Mission to the Chinese* (St. Mary-of-the-Woods, Ind.: Office of Communications, 1990), 43. The three priests who came to China at the same time were F. X. Clougherty, who became one of the first Benedictines in China, J. Kerin, and Howard Paul Lawton (1892–1979). The men opened a school for boys. Lawton was a convert to Catholicism at age eighteen. After ordination by Cardinal Dougherty in 1919 and a year as a parish assistant, Lawton went to China from September 1920 to October 1922. He was diocesan director of the SPF in Philadelphia from 1927 to 1932 and spent most of his life at St. Madeleine Sophie Parish, Philadelphia; he died of cancer (Archdiocese of Philadelphia Record of Priests).

69. Sr. Virginia to Dear Mother, 18 November 1929, box 251, file 11, Correspondence — Sr. Virginia (2) 1929–30, China Files, Sisters of St. Francis, Milwaukee Archives.

70. Newspaper article by Elsie Harrison, undated [1948], in vol. 10, Scrapbook of Patna Mission and Mission Circles, Lillian and Clara Westropp Papers, 1922–68, MC 215, Schlesinger Library, Radcliffe College.

In 1938, the nucleus of mission circles in Cleveland provided help to the Jesuit Mission in Patna, India. Eventually one of its organizers, Clara Westropp (1886–1965), cofounder of the Women's Federal Savings Bank, was influential in the formation of the Cleveland diocesan mission office. The office began sending lay missionaries to Latin America in the 1960s, including Jean Donovan and Ursuline Sister Dorothy Kazel, two of the four women martyred in El Salvador in 1980.

71. Of particular note is the Missionary Association of Catholic Women, an organization run by women for women, which started with a sewing circle in Germany in 1914. The American section was organized in 1916 by Mary Gockel (1874–1925), a secretary in Milwaukee. Annual conventions featured missionary speakers, displays of items that the women had made for the missions, prayer, and social interaction. The units contributed money, handmade linens for mission altars, and clothing for children. The association exhibited some of their items at the 1925 Missionary Exposition at the Vatican. For information on Gockel and the Missionary Association of Catholic Women, see Angelyn Dries, OSF, "Mary Gockel: Proclaimer," *Catholic Evangelization* (March/April 1989): 34–35; and C. M. Thuente, *A Sketch of the Life and Work of Mary Gockel* (Milwaukee: Missionary Association of Catholic Women Publishers, 1926).

72. John J. Considine (assistant general, Maryknoll Society) to Charles Michel, SVD, provincial, 18 March 1941, Institute of Mission Studies folder, SVDA. "Group work independent of the local clergy is regarded as unwise on account of the injudiciousness of such groups in their relations with the clergy, their tendency to rival or to ignore parish activities; on account of the desire of so many groups for publicity, or their feeling that great publicity is necessary to accomplish their ends; an impression is given that a great deal is being done for the Society when, as a matter of fact, the results are relatively small" (ibid.). A Women's Foreign Mission Auxiliary, which had started under the leadership of convert Mrs. Ada Livingston of New York, continued, however, until 1954 ("Fifty-Years A-Growing," *Maryknoll Distaff,* MMA; John M. Hilpert, "Mission Circles," in *Fourth General Conference of the Diocesan Directors of the Society for the Propagation of the Faith* [Cleveland: n.p., 1930]: 91–93; Our Lady of the Angels Fraternity, Third Order of Saint Francis, *History of the Tertiaries' Mission Circle* [Cleveland: privately printed, 1933]). This group started in 1923 to aid the OFM missions in China and the OFM work with Native Americans. One of the early Columban Mission Circles in Brooklyn continues to the present.

73. The Columban mission magazine featured several important mission circles around the country in Robert Brady, "Going Around in Circles," *FE* (September 1963): 14–16.

74. For the influence the Maryknoll Society had on U.S. Catholics, see Wiest, *Maryknoll in China,* chap. 8. It is significant that while the 1942 figures (n. 1) indicate large numbers of American Catholic missionaries in Oceania and the West Indies, for example, no Maryknollers were present in these locations. The missions received little publicity nationally, except through *Catholic Missions,* which attempted to cover all areas of the world and all mission congregations. Most mission magazines tried to raise funds for individual congregations and the particular missions they staffed.

75. Herman J. Fisher, SVD, *800 Million Lost* (Techny, Ill.: Mission Press, 1933); James E. Mertz, SVD, *Brother Eugene, SVD: An American Missionary Brother* (Techny, Ill.: Mission Press, 1943). This latter pamphlet narrates the story of an American Brother who died in New Guinea at age thirty-five. The Maryknoll Society also published an extensive series of pamphlets of "both a devotional and mission nature." See Wiest, *Maryknoll in China,* 413–14.

76. Joseph Schmidlin, *Catholic Mission History,* ed. Matthias Braun, SVD (Techny, Ill.: Mission Press, 1933); Schmidlin, *Catholic Mission Theory* (Techny, Ill.: Mission Press, 1933).

77. For the language preparation of Maryknoll men and women in China and Manchuria, see Wiest, *Maryknoll in China,* 268–81.

78. Ibid., 276.

79. Reported in Sister M. Pauline Grady, ASC, *Ruma: Home and Heritage, the Story of a Convent in Rural Southern Illinois, 1876–1984* (Ruma, Ill.: privately printed, 1984), 142–43.

80. In 1925, Chinese newspapers were filled with articles about reform in education. Educational reform came later in different provinces, but eventually all provinces responded.

At issue was the government's insistence that Chinese educational rights be restored. Mission schools had their own curriculum, which did not necessarily include Chinese history, culture, or language. The government thought Chinese were losing their identity. Mission schools then had to decide whether they should adopt the Chinese material into their programs. This also meant that mission schools had to have high academic standards, adequate materials — including science equipment — and a financial endowment. On these points, the author has benefited from conversation with Xiaoqing. For an overview of Chinese educational developments from 1900 to the 1930s, see John King Fairbank, *The Great Chinese Revolution, 1800–1985* (New York: Harper & Row, 1987), 182–203.

81. James E. Walsh, *Maryknoll Spiritual Directory* (Maryknoll, N.Y.: Field Afar Press, 1947).

82. Conversation with Dolores Liptak, RSM, 29 March 1996. She has organized the archives of the Baltimore Carmelites.

83. "Conference of Mother Mary Joseph on 'The Maryknoll Spirit,' August 4, 1930," document 39 in *Discourses of Mother Mary Joseph,* p. 211, MMA.

84. Francis X. Ford to John Considine, 22 August 1922, subseries 2, Considine Correspondence 2/9, Considine Papers, MMA. Over twenty years later, Considine, in turn, preached the very same idea at the profession and reception ceremonies of the Maryknoll Sisters: "It is true that we as missioners are pictured principally as men of action, who regard life as something to be dashingly used and cheerfully hazarded. But in times of crisis, those prove best for the task who have cultivated a healthy interior life, who have learned to act not on their own impulses, but according to the will of God" (6 January 1941, box 8/3, Considine Writings, MMA).

85. Maria Gratia quoted in Wolf, *Against All Odds,* 76.

86. Edward J. Wojniak, SVD, *Atomic Apostle: The Life Story of Thomas Megan, SVD* (Techny, Ill.: Divine Word Publications, 1957), 26.

87. John J. Considine Diaries, 14 September 1944, 5 (3) 1:1942–44, United States, MMA.

88. Marie Comtois was born in Pierreville, Canada, but moved as a child to Worcester, Massachusetts. She worked in a factory after she completed school and entered the novitiate of the Franciscan Missionaries of Mary in 1904, the year the congregation opened its first house in the United States. After her formation years in Québec, Mother Mary Lawrence, as she was known, was sent to New York, where she frequently visited the Chinese women on Mott Street. She became directress of novices in Rome in 1912 and, about eighteen months later, was chosen to go to China. Joseph McGlinchey, director of the Boston SPF, was present for her departure ceremony. The other American among the fifty-two departees was Mother Lillian, who also went to China. Mother Mary Lawrence arrived at Chang Chung, Manchuria, on 17 July 1914. She directed a boarding school, a home for the aged, and an orphanage. She contracted smallpox and died on 6 April 1917 (D. J. O'Sullivan, *Life Sketch of Mother Mary Lawrence, F.M.M.* [Boston: Society for the Propagation of the Faith, 1919]). The book both lauded her work and goaded Boston Catholics to continue contributing.

89. "More Laborers for the Harvest," *Sign* 1 (January 1922): 28; "Letters from Our Missionaries," *Sign* 9 (August 1929): 54.

90. For Donovan's biography, see John J. Considine, *When the Sorghum Was High* (New York: Longmans Green & Company, 1940).

91. Wojniak, *Atomic Apostle,* 27. Megan (1899–1951), born in Eldora, Iowa, went to Honan Province after his ordination in 1926. After twenty-two years in China, where he was described as an "atomic apostle," he returned to the United States in February 1948 to raise funds for a hospital in Sinsiang, Honan. He was sent in 1949 to Hattiesburg, Mississippi, to begin the Rosary Catholic Mission.

92. These ideas were often specifically addressed by James A. Walsh. See, for example, *Observations in the Orient,* 176–78.

93. This position was noted repeatedly by James A. Walsh and by other groups, as ev-

idenced in Brother L. Charles, "What the Chinese Think of American Catholicism," *Our Missions* 1 (1921): 184–85.

94. Gilgan's story is told in Flavian A. Walsh, OFM, "The Story of Our Family, Part 10," *Friar Lines* 3 (Winter 1991): 17–24. The missions Gilgan eventually opened were later turned over to the Columban Fathers.

In addition to Groell, *White Wings in Bamboo Land,* other books providing the missionaries' view are Mary Rosalia [Kettl], MM, *One Inch of Splendor* (New York: Field Afar Press, 1941); Mary de Paul Cogan, MM, *Sisters of Maryknoll through Troubled Waters* (New York: Charles Scribner's Sons, 1947); Servatia Berg, OSF, *A Cross in China: The Story of My Mission* (Fort Wayne, Ind.: Cuchullain Publications, 1989); and Joseph Henkels, SVD, *My China Memoirs, 1928–51* (Techny, Ill.: n.p., 1988).

95. E. J. McCarthy, "Reminiscences Written in 1950s," 15.

96. Maria Gratia to Mother Mary Cleophas Foley, quoted in Wolf, *Against All Odds,* 19. I have also benefited from correspondence with Wolf.

97. Sr. Virginia to Dear Mother, Tsinanfu, Hungkialou, 8 July 1930, box 251/11, Correspondence — Sr. Virginia (2) 1929-30, China Files, Sisters of St. Francis, Milwaukee Archives.

98. The Benedictine Sisters' story appears in M. Grace McDonald, OSB, *With Lamps Burning* (St. Joseph, Minn.: Saint Benedict's Priory Press, 1957), 267–86. The four Holy Spirit Missionary Sisters who arrived at Fu Jen Middle School were Edna Polt, Marguerite Gales, Pierre Fischette, and Leonardine Huetemann. The community's first American missionaries to Sinyangchow, Honan Province, in 1924 were Lima Wellbrock, Alvina Summers, and Adalrica Wernimut.

99. Significant developments in archaeology and paleontology were taking place in China in the 1920s through the 1940s in the search for "Peking Man." Rector George Barry O'Toole, a "scholastic biologist," attempted to combine scholasticism and modern science, an ongoing concern of neo-Thomism. He authored *The Case Against Evolution* (New York: Macmillan, 1925).

100. On this point, see Thomas F. Ryan, SJ, *China Through Catholic Eyes* (Hong Kong: Catholic Truth Society, 1941), 126–29; Adelbert Gresnigt, OSB, "Reflections on Chinese Architecture," *Bulletin No. 8 of the Catholic University of Peking* (December 1931): 3–23; and Gresnigt, "Chinese Architecture," *Bulletin No. 4 of the Catholic University of Peking* (May 1928): 33–45, Archives, St. Vincent's Archabbey, Latrobe, Pennsylvania. For the open letter of the apostolic delegate, see "The Need of Developing a Sino-Christian Architecture for Our Catholic Missions," *Bulletin No. 3 of the Catholic University of Peking* (September 1927): 7–15. These references contain Gresnigt's drawings. Gresnigt's ideas appear in three articles in the *Digests of the Synodal Commission of the Catholic Church in China, 1928–1947:* 1928, no. 1, 258; 1932, no. 5, 418ff., 438ff.

The Columbans in Korea later referred to Gresnigt's ideas when they were rebuilding churches after the Korean War. Michael Healy commented that trying to make churches "racy of the soil" did not fit current styles on the peninsula. "At the moment in Korean life the emphasis is on *sin-sik* (new style) — and the *kou-sik* (old style), in all departments is apt to be looked down upon. In fact that is one of the big sticks our Protestant brethren use to beat Mother Church with — that the Catholic Church is the 'Old Church,' and that the Protestants are the 'New Church....' Nowadays, all new buildings are built in Western style — constructing a new building in Eastern style might not help the prestige of the Church" (Michael Healy, Kwangju, Korea, 1957 [copy], p. 66, Kwangju folder — Vicar Apostolic 6.A, CFA).

For the Benedictine Sisters' work at the Catholic women's college, see Sister M. Grace McDonald, OSB, *With Lamps Burning.* The Benedictine women opened a dispensary for the sick poor in Kaifeng and provided religious instruction for the children. After the Pearl Harbor attack, two Sisters returned to the United States; six Sisters left China in the spring of 1949 to begin a girls' middle school at T'ainan, Formosa (Taiwan). For the Benedictine men's involvement at Fu Jen, see *The Catholic University of Peking: A Missionary Foundation of the American Benedictines.* For information on the Divine Word Missionary era at Fu Jen while the university was in Peking, see Henkels, *My China Memoirs,* 38–72, and various files related to the university in the Divine Word Missionary Archives, Techny, Illinois. As of this writing, the files are not cataloged.

101. Rigney named the important fossil Oehler found *Morgonucadon oehleri,* a jawbone indicating an important stage in the development of mammals. Information about Oehler from "Obituary," Edgar Oehler, SVDA, and from correspondence with Ernest Brandewie, 19 February 1996.

102. Rigney memo to staff at Fu Jen, 25 March 1949, Catholic University of Peking folder, SVDA.

103. Harold Rigney, SVD, *Four Years in a Red Hell* (Chicago: Henry Regnery Company, 1956).

104. For the history of Fu Jen in Taipei, see *Fu Jen Catholic University, 1986* (Taipei: privately printed, 1986).

105. Sister Gertrude Hanley to Cardinal O'Connell, 16 January 1920, SPF Files 2/2, AABoston.

106. Maria Gratia Luking quoted in Wolf, *Against All Odds,* 8.

107. Mother Mary Joseph, "Reaching the Women," in *To Defend the Cross,* 59.

108. Sisters of Charity, "Mended Bits of China," *Sign* 13 (June 1934): 672.

109. William F. Stadelman, CSSp, *The Association of the Holy Childhood, History of the American Branch, 1846–1922* (Pittsburgh: The Colonial Press, 1922), 5–6.

110. Script for slide 74, Clifford King slide presentation, Catholic Students Mission Crusade Files, Archdiocese of Cincinnati Archives.

111. W. S. McGoldrick, "The Poverty of Poor China," *FE* (June 1925): 126–28.

112. Maria Gratia to Mother Mary Cleophas Foley, quoted in Wolf, *Against All Odds,* 19.

113. *A Brief Pictorial of Marianist Missions in China* [c. 1940], p. 12, Brothers of Mary Archives, Dayton, Ohio. Four Brothers of Mary arrived in 1933 in Hungkialou, Shantung. A second group came to Hankow in 1936 to open Sangtze Middle School. Brother Joseph A. McCoy, in the second group, later wrote one of the first comprehensive U.S. Catholic works on missionary formation, *Advice from the Field* (Baltimore: Helicon, 1962). Fifteen Marianists served in China from 1933 to 1947.

114. Information from Li Xiaoqing's talk at the June 1995 History of Women Religious Conference, Milwaukee.

115. Sr. Reginald to Venerable and dear Mother, 14 December 1935, box 258/5, Sr. Reginald 1929–40, Sisters of St. Francis, Milwaukee Archives.

116. Hanley to O'Connell, 16 January 1920, SPF Files 2/2, AABoston.

117. Sisters of Charity, "Dispensary Experiences," *Sign* 13 (February 1934): 415–18, here 417.

118. Sister Dominica, FSPA, to Members of the Catholic Women's Missionary Association of Carroll, Iowa, from Wuchang, Hupeh, China, 17 February 1929, 1.3.28., box 1/1, China: Plans for and Departure of Sisters to China, 1928, FSPAA.

119. Virtually the same idea is found in the remark of Father Robert Cairns, MM, on 27 June 1924: "I had supper in Chinese, went to confession in French, prayed in Latin, sang in Scotch, and slept in 'American'" (noted in conversation of Jean-Paul Wiest with author, 18 April 1997).

120. Carbonneau, "The Passionists in China," 402–3.

121. Sr. Reginald to Venerable and dear Mother, 14 December 1935. Sister Reginald developed an excellent facility with Chinese and learned several other languages, including Japanese. She died from complications of an appendectomy and was buried in China.

122. Urbany to Members of the Catholic Women's Missionary Association of Carroll, Iowa, 17 February 1929. Sister Dominica had completed her term in congregational leadership and then became superior of the Chinese mission.

123. Maryknoll adapted French missionaries' approach by altering the focus of the French Happy Life and Death Societies. The initiation fee was used to buy land, which then was rented to the Chinese for less than the Chinese landlords charged. Eventually, the Maryknollers put such monies into agricultural cooperatives and home industries. See Wiest, *Maryknoll in China,* 180–85.

124. Jean-Paul Wiest, "The Legacy of Bishop Francis X. Ford," in Gerald H. Anderson et al., eds., *Mission Legacies: Biographical Studies of Leaders of the Modern Missionary Movement* (Maryknoll, N.Y.: Orbis Books, 1994), 232–41. For the Sisters' report on their experience of direct evangelization, see Sister M. Marcelline, *Sisters Carry the Gospel* (Maryknoll, N.Y.: World Horizon Report, no. 15, 1956). Jean-Paul Wiest also summarizes the contributions of Ford, J. E. Walsh, and Meyer in *Maryknoll in China.*

125. See Bernard F. Meyer, MM, *Mission Methods: Pastoral Instructions to the Clergy of the Prefecture of Wuchow, Kwangsi, China* (n.p., 1936), which outlines his essentials of rural evangelization, and *Like to Leaven: Mission Methods in China* (Hong Kong: Catholic Truth Society, 1950). Wiest notes, however, that Maryknoll did not actively promote lay catechists until the 1940s, when China experienced the effects of a worldwide Catholic Action emphasis. See also Bernard F. Meyer, *Lend Me Your Hands* (Chicago: Fides, 1955); and *The World Is My Neighbor* (Notre Dame, Ind.: Fides, 1964). His previous work published in the United States, *The Mystical Body in Action: A Workbook of Parish Catholic Action* (Herman, Pa.: Center for Men of Christ the King, 1947), covered the same theme.

126. Wiest, *Maryknoll in China,* 61, mentions Yeung as a Maryknoll Sister in 1924. In addition to sections in Wiest's book, the work of the Maryknoll Sisters in China is discussed in Kettl, *One Inch of Splendor,* which features the work of the author and Sister St. Paul; Sister Mary de Paul Cogan, *Sisters of Maryknoll Through Troubled Waters* (New York: Charles Scribner's Sons, 1947), which describes the house arrests and other experiences until they departed China in 1949; and Penny Lernoux, *Hearts on Fire: The Story of the Maryknoll Sisters* (Maryknoll, N.Y.: Orbis Books, 1993), 44–77.

127. Wiest, *Maryknoll in China,* 207. Several biographies of Ford have been published: Raymond A. Lane, *Stone in the King's Highway: The Life and Writings of Bishop Francis Xavier Ford* (New York: Macmillan, 1953); John Donovan, *The Pagoda and the Cross: The Life of Bishop Ford of Maryknoll* (New York: Charles Scribner's Sons, 1967); Robert Sheridan, *Compassion: The Spirit of Francis X. Ford, MM* (Ossining, N.Y.: Maryknoll Publications, 1982). See also Wiest, "The Legacy of Bishop Francis X. Ford." Ford died in a Cantonese prison.

128. Wiest, *Maryknoll in China,* 223–41. See also Susan Bradshaw, OSF, "Religious Women in China: An Undertaking of Indigenization," *Catholic Historical Review* 68, no. 1 (1982): 28–45.

129. Departure Sermon, Franciscan Sisters of Perpetual Adoration, 3 September 1928, pp. 1–2.

130. Wiest, *Maryknoll in China,* 448–51; Lernoux, *Hearts on Fire,* 74.

131. See, for example, *FE* 2 (September 1919): 202–6; and *FE* 7 (1924): 123.

132. Patrick Laffan, "Parish Life in China," *FE* 20 (June 1937).

133. Loretto Sisters, Hanyang Diary, 1927–47, copy, typescript, 1.c.5., CFA.

134. Ibid.

135. Point gleaned from conversation with Robert Carbonneau, CP.

136. For an extensive analysis of Maryknoll's political awareness and involvement in China, see Wiest, *Maryknoll in China,* 318–407. For an analysis of American missionary attitudes toward a government regime hostile to Christianity, see Virginia Unsworth, "American Missionaries and Communist China: 1941–1953" (Ph.D. diss., New York University, 1976). Not all Chinese priests stayed at home. In 1954, nine exiled Chinese priests were serving in various parishes in the United States.

137. Conversation on the issue appears in Henry F. May, "The Rebellion of the Intellectuals, 1912–1917," *American Quarterly* 8 (Summer 1956): 114–26; May, *The End of*

American Innocence: A Study of the First Years of Our Own Time, 1912–1917 (New York: Knopf, 1959); and William Halsey, *The Survival of American Innocence* (Notre Dame, Ind.: University of Notre Dame Press, 1980).

138. For the family emphasis provided by Protestant women missionaries, see Marjorie King, "Exporting Femininity, Not Feminism: Nineteenth-Century U.S. Missionary Women's Efforts to Emancipate Chinese Women," in Flemming, ed., *Women's Work for Women,* 117–35; and Dana Robert, *American Women in Mission: A Social History of Their Thought and Practice* (Macon, Ga.: Mercer University Press, 1996), esp. 39–80.

139. For a biography of this Capuchin's life, see Michael F. Crosby, OFMCap, *Thank God Ahead of Time: The Life and Spirituality of Solanus Casey* (Chicago: Franciscan Herald Press, 1984).

140. See, for example, *Sign's* portrayal of the death of the first three American Passionists at the hands of bandits: editorial, 2 (July 1923): p. II; Harold Purcell, CP, "Off for the High Romance!" 3 (August 1923): 12; editorial, 3 (May 1924): unnumbered page; John A. Duffy, "The Call of God," 3 (July 1924): 489–92; and 8 (June 1929): 672 a-d, insert.

141. See, for example, Debra Campbell, *David Goldstein and the Lay Catholic Street Apostolate, 1917–1941* (Ann Arbor, Mich.: University Microfilms International, 1985). Goldstein participated at the Second American Catholic Missionary Congress in 1913.

142. Freri to Cardinal O'Connell, 11 February 1921, box 2/11, Record Group III.D16, SPF, AABoston.

143. In the 1990s, the U.S. Catholic Church still pays little attention to mainland China. Some mission congregations have sent English-language teachers there. One organization that gathers information about the Catholic Church in China is the U.S. Catholic China Bureau, begun in 1987 by Janet Carroll, MM. The USCCB has provided month-long study trips to China, an annual conference, and a newsletter which keeps readers informed about events in China.

Chapter 7 /
The Struggle for World Order, 1946–59

1. The national office of the Society for the Propagation of the Faith published a book of photographs and lists of commissioned Catholic World War II chaplains, *The Priest Goes to War* (New York: Society for the Propagation of the Faith, 1945). Commenting on the work of the chaplain, the text notes, "When the priest goes to war, his object is to save souls, and he is at home wherever there are souls to be saved. Wherever he has gone, he has found the Church there before him, often in the person of young American missionary priests, who have left father and mother and kindred to carry the light of Faith to those who have sat in darkness" (unnumbered page).

During the war, some seminarians were accused of being draft dodgers. One priest ordained in 1947 remarked, "I think the reverse is nearer the truth. We were far from the violence of war, and I think most rather hoped that they would be asked to be chaplains. Some left the seminary so that they could join up" (Edwin Kinch, OSM, "A Short History of Our Lady of Ingwavuma Mission," 1996, typescript, copy from Kinch sent to author).

2. For a history of the work of these Sisters in Japan, see Sister Aimee Julie, SND de Namur, *With Dedicated Hearts* (Ipswich, Mass.: Sisters of Notre Dame de Namur, 1963). The Sisters were invited to replace the French Sisters of the Infant Jesus, who had been in Okayama for thirty years and whose personnel were dwindling. The first superior of the mission, Sister Mary Kostka, had been moderator of the Wekanduit Missionary Society and had taught at Trinity College, Washington, D.C., for fourteen years before going to Japan.

In 1942, 42 American Catholic missionaries were serving in Japan (down from 53 in 1940): in addition to the SND de Namur Sisters, there were 14 Maryknoll men, 8 Marianist Brothers, 4 Maryknoll Sisters, 2 Sisters of St. Ann (Marlboro, Massachusetts), 1 secular priest, and 1 Jesuit (John J. Considine, *Across a World* [New York: Longmans, Green & Company, 1942], appendix). The statistics are derived from information provided by the CSMC. However, two years later only two American missionaries were listed as actually being in Japan.

3. For accounts of their experience in the Pacific, see Sister Mary Consolata, SMSM, *Samoa with Love: Reminiscences of Forty-five Years of Marist Missionary Service* (Waltham, Mass.: privately printed, 1991); and Sister Mary Paulita, SMSM, *Half-Pint on Guadalcanal: A Saga of Heroism, Commitment, and Love, as Told by Sister Mary Evangeline* (Waltham, Mass.: privately printed, 1943). Sister Evangeline was a missionary in the Solomon Islands for over forty-three years. On the work of the Marist Missionary Sisters in Jamaica and especially on the beginnings of the Damien-Dutton Society to assist lepers, see Howard E. Crouch and Sister Mary Augustine, SMSM, *Two Hearts, One Fire: A Glimpse Behind the Mask of Leprosy* (Bellmore, N.Y.: Damien-Dutton Society for Leprosy Aid, 1989).

4. See Louise Tentler, *Seasons of Grace: A History of the Catholic Archdiocese of Detroit* (Detroit: Wayne State University, 1990). In 1943, the community began to publish the *Catholic Mission Digest*. Three Sisters remained in the community in 1994.

5. On this point, see "Suggested Statement for the Bishops," in material for the 1952 Mission Secretariat meeting of mission-sending societies, Annual Meetings of Mission Sending Societies, 1950–68, 4/3, USCMA Archives, MMA.

6. For the history of the Catholic Church in these islands, see Francis Henzel, SJ, *The Catholic Church in Micronesia* (Chicago: Loyola University Press, 1991), which provides a listing of all the Europeans, Americans, and islanders who served as priests, Sisters, or Brothers in Micronesia. The U.S. Navy was under the impression, at first, that all of the Pacific islands were under the jurisdiction of the American Jesuits.

7. Ibid., 99. This couple received the annual Xavier Award of the Jesuit Seminary and Mission Bureau, the first such award given by the Jesuit New York Province to laity: see Mission Secretariat folder, LAB, ACUA.

8. For the internal history, see Thomas Calkins, OSM, "Servites in Zululand," typed manuscript with handwritten marginal comments and corrections by Edwin Kinch, OSM, Servite Fathers Archives, Chicago. Kinch was one of the first three Servites there.

Calkins portrayed the early missionaries as active, enthusiastic Americans, even though one Brother was Irish. Commenting on the various items purchased in the United States for their work, Calkins remarked that one of the men "had in mind that they would be under the same conditions in Swaziland that our Marines had been in recent Guadalcanal, only this would be a 'beachhead for the Lord,' his favorite expression" ("Servites in Zululand," 11). Calkins also noted that "in later years, the press of Africa, along with time itself, rubbed away some of our instinctive brashness" (ibid., 67). Information also gathered from correspondence with Edwin Kinch, OSM, from June 1995 to June 1996, and from Kinch, "A Short History of Our Lady of Ingwavuma Mission."

9. An anecdotal and pictorial history of the Society of the Divine Word Fathers and Brothers is John Boberg, SVD, ed., *The Word in the World: Divine Word Missionaries, 1875–1975* (Techny, Ill.: Divine Word Missionaries, 1975). On their work in Ghana, see Edward Dudink, SVD, ed., *The Word in the World: Ghana* (Techny, Ill.: Divine Word Missionaries, 1972). John Koster, SVD, physics professor at the university in Ghana, was the first to discover the Russian satellite Sputnik. The author has also benefited from correspondence with Ernest Brandewie, who is completing a history of the U.S. Province of the society.

10. For an account of the contacts between the NCWC and the U.S. State Department from 1927 to 1932, see the seven-page report of Julius Schick, CM, and his letter to Monsignor Carroll, 31 July 1951, box 10/20.4, Church: Missions, NCWC Executive Department VIII, Office of General Secretary, ACUA. Among the correspondence detailing the increased responsibilities for SPF and NCWC with respect to problems associated with mission work, see Thomas J. McDonnell to Your Eminence, 23 October 1946 (copy), Samuel

Cardinal Stritch to Archbishop McNicholas, 23 November 1946 (copy), Archbishop McNicholas to Your Eminence, 8 December 1946 (copy), all in box 10/20.3, Church Missions, 1945–49, NCWC Executive Department VIII, Office of General Secretary, ACUA.

11. On these plans, see JK to Father Considine, 20 February 1945; "Note for Monsignor Carroll," 24 March 1945; and Considine to Spellman, 7 April 1945, all in box 10.6.3, Church Missions, 1945–49, NCWC Executive Department VIII, Office of General Secretary, ACUA.

12. Request from apostolic delegate (Bishop Breton) to Japan via Colonel August Gearhard, U.S. Army, box 10/20.10, Church Missions, Japan 1946–48, NCWC Executive Department VIII, Office of General Secretary, ACUA. The bishops' lengthy report, which includes their itinerary, lists of material items and properties lost during the war, names of American missionary agencies in Japan, and so forth, is in box 10/20.10, Church Missions, Japan, LAB, ACUA.

A follow-up letter summed up Bishop Breton's conversation with the American bishops by identifying the needs of his diocese: material renovation; spiritual renovation (the Japanese hierarchy and clergy had cooperated with the "militaristic and racist elements of the country"); relief from the problems of an all-Japanese hierarchy; education; and the work of Sisters (Bishop Albert Breton to O'Hara and Ready, Yokosuka, Japan, 20 July 1946, box 10/20.10, Church Missions, Japan, LAB, ACUA).

In 1947 the apostolic delegate to Japan proposed to the American bishops that they open a seminary in the U.S. for Japanese seminarians. The U.S. Bishops did not respond favorably, chiefly because of the differences in the two cultures. Training in the United States would not prepare Japanese seminarians for life in the Japanese Catholic Church.

13. Catherine Schaefer to Monsignor Carroll, 13 April 1948, box 10/20.3, Church Missions, 1945–49, NCWC Executive Department VIII, Office of General Secretary, ACUA.

14. John Considine, "Note for Monsignor Carroll, Overseas Affairs Desk," 24 March 1945, box 10/6.3, Church Missions, 1945–49, NCWC Executive Department VIII, Office of General Secretary, ACUA. Considine reflected a number of times in his diary on the slow and often disappointing steps taken in the formation of the Mission Secretariat. See August, September, and November 1948 annotations in John Considine Diaries, 5 (4) 6:1948-51, United States, MMA.

15. Minutes of the Annual Meeting of the U.S. Bishops, 1948, quoted in Herman J. D'Souza, "Origins of the Mission Secretariat," *Worldmission* 8, no. 3 (1957): 106.

16. Minutes of the Annual Meeting of the U.S. Bishops, 1949, pp. 29–32, here 29, ACUA.

17. Organizational Matters 1/1, History of Mission Secretariat, 1949–67, MMA. See also *Worldmission* 1, no. 1 (1950): 87–88; and D'Souza, "Origins of the Mission Secretariat," 103–8.

18. The mission-sending groups had wanted an executive board elected by their members. The hierarchy did not approve this.

19. A consultation conference, "The Work of the Missions in Education and Social Action," held at Maryknoll from 6 to 8 September 1949, was arranged by the social action and education departments of the NCWC Committees on Asia, Africa, and Latin America. Catharine Schaefer and Alba Zizzamia from the NCWC office for United Nations Affairs were particularly active in obtaining speakers for the event and in spearheading some of the discussion. The conference was attended by representatives of mission-sending societies in the United States and several others who had special competence (R. A. McGowan to Monsignor Carroll, NCWC interoffice memo, 14 September 1949, box 10/20.11, Mission Secretariat, Origin, LAB, ACUA).

20. "Origins of Mission Secretariat," typescript (no author given, but presumably written by Frederick McGuire), p. 9, Organizational Matters 1/1, History of Mission Secretariat, 1949–67, MMA.

21. An example of the variety of interests at the annual conferences appears in Society for

the Propagation of the Faith, *Proceedings of the Annual Meeting of the Mission Secretariat* (Washington, D.C.: The Secretariat, 1957).

22. Talk by Frederick McGuire, CM, talk to quinquennial meeting of SPF directors, 7 November 1967, Organizational Matters 1/1, USCMA Archives, MMA.

23. The Missionary Cooperation Plan was worked out with the bishops as early as 1953. Nevertheless, individuals were still being contacted by priests after a missionary had spoken at the Masses, thus defeating the purpose of the plan, which was to coordinate all mission-fund collection so that parishioners would not be receiving multiple mission appeals, and, presumably, diluting the funds. See, for example, J. W. Carney to McGuire, 1 August 1959, box 3, folder 1, Missionary Cooperation Program, 1959–68, USCMA Archives, MMA. Mary Augustine Kerby, SMSM, remarked that missionary Sisters did not have the same access to this plan as the priests. Further, Sisters' finances did not allow for their members to travel throughout the United States for this purpose. Kirby spoke on this topic at the ninth annual meeting of the Mission Secretariat, 1958.

24. The first gathering of women religious to share common concerns had occurred earlier at the Sister Formation Conference. These persons were not major superiors but they were responsible for initial formation of Sisters in their congregations.

25. The businessmen included John D. Revene, senior vice president, Chase Manhattan Bank; Joseph G. Smith, vice president, Pittsburgh Steel; and Thomas C. Butler, president, Grand Union Company. The bishop of Paterson, James A. McNulty, and the president of Seton Hall University, Right Rev. Monsignor John J. Dougherty, represented the hierarchy. On the foundation and work of the organization, see "Association for International Development," *Jubilee* 5 (October 1957): 11–13.

26. Brochure for the organization and outline of its program found in box 10/5, AID folder, LAB, ACUA. Speakers at the sessions included Daniel Berrigan, SJ, Bernard Cooke, SJ, Edward L. Murphy, SJ, Dr. Margaret Mead, and James O'Gara of *Commonweal*.

27. George and Jeanne Wolf, box 10/5, AID folder (1963), LAB, ACUA.

28. *Seventy-Fifth Anniversary, Fifty Years in America: Society of the Divine Word* (Techny, Ill.: Mission Press, 1950), unnumbered page.

29. Robert Streit, OMI, *Catholic Missions in Figures and Symbols* (New York: Society for the Propagation of the Faith, 1927), 73.

30. Charles Erb, SVD, "Brothers in the Missions," in Society for the Propagation of the Faith, *The Mission Apostolate* (New York: Paulist Press, 1942), 41–45, here 45. Erb later visited Francis Nkrumah of the Gold Coast while the latter was in prison for sedition in 1948. The African leader agitated for independence from English colonial rule (noted in John J. Considine, *Africa: World of New Men* [New York: Dodd, Mead, 1954], 38–40).

31. Peter Heier, SVD, to Provincial, 22 January 1935, SVD Regions (China), Sinsiang folder, SVDA.

32. James E. Mertz, SVD, *Brother Eugene, SVD: An American Missionary Brother* (Techny, Ill.: Mission Press, 1943). Brother Eugene was born in 1900 and died in New Guinea in January 1935.

33. Brother Florentius, CSC, "Missionary Brothers," in *To Defend the Cross: Proceedings of the 1924 Catholic Students Mission Crusade* (Cincinnati: Catholic Students Mission Crusade), 122–24, here 123.

34. *Brothers' Newsletter* 1 (January 1959): 2, USCMA Archives, MMA.

35. *Brothers' Newsletter* 1 (March 1959): 3, USCMA Archives, MMA.

36. Summary of Horgan's talk in *Brothers' Newsletter* 2 (January 1960). An autobiographical narrative of one of the Maryknoll Brothers, Aloysius (Horace) Moliner (1889–1978), who was born in Cuba and worked as a carpenter and farmer at Maryknoll and at the Venard Seminary, appears in "Brother Aloysius Moliner," privately mimeographed, 1968, Rogers Library, Maryknoll Sisters, New York. Much of this work is in the style of a prayer and spiritual reflection with pieces of early Maryknoll history scattered throughout. Father Robert Sheridan, MM, worked with the Maryknoll Brothers' vocation and forma-

tion program for many years, with the result that more men began to enter the brotherhood. Further development of the Brothers' mission vocation appears in Antonio Baceza, SJ, "A New Age for the Brothers," *Woodstock Letters* 95 (1968): 269–87; Pius Agyemang, SVD, "A Personal Assessment," *Word in the World* (Techny, Ill.: Society of the Divine Word, 1972), 135–37; Peter van de Wiel, SVD, "Brothers in Papua New Guinea," *Word in the World* (1992–93), 148–51; "Pastoral/Theological Reflection in the Maryknoll Brothers' Formation Program," New York, May 1980, Rogers Library, Maryknoll Sisters, New York; and Bernard Spitzley, SVD, "We Walk This Earth as Jesus Did," *Word in the World* (1994–95): 44–46.

Three "in-house" SVD booklets treated the vocation and ministry of the Society's Brothers: "Booklet 1" (January 1978), "Booklet 2" (October 1978), and "Booklet 3" (March 1979), SVDA.

37. Bruce Malina, OFM, "An Outline for a Theology of the Brotherhood," *Brothers' Newsletter* 3 (January 1961); and 3 (March 1961).

38. Fulton J. Sheen, *Treasure in Clay: The Autobiography of Fulton J. Sheen* (Garden City, N.Y.: Doubleday, 1980). See also Kathleen Riley Fields, "Bishop Fulton J. Sheen: An American Catholic Response to the Twentieth Century" (Ph.D. diss., University of Notre Dame, 1988).

39. Sheen, *Treasure in Clay,* 63.

40. Ibid., 73.

41. Considine remarked that Sheen had phoned him asking who was financially responsible for the publication. "My reply, of course, was that *Worldmission* belongs to Mission Secretariat but Cal Alexander, not in on its establishment, disagrees" (John Considine Diaries, 7 May 1951, 5 (4) 6:1948–51, MMA.

42. Mission study was promoted through the Sacred Congregation of Seminaries and through the national office of the SPF. See F. J. Spellman to William O'Connell, 21 April 1942, M-1169, Academias in the Diocesan Seminaries, AABoston. In its seven volumes (1943–49), the *Missionary Academia* published articles from missionaries on Church experience around the world, the history of Protestant and Catholic missions, and missionary accommodation. The outline for the articles followed a six-year course of study for seminarians. The entire course outline may be found in box 1753, Mission Institutes folder, Foreign Missions, Brothers of Mary Archives, Dayton, Ohio.

43. Murphy wrote *Teach Ye All Nations: The Principles of Catholic Missionary Work* (New York: Benziger, 1958). He became noted for his charism and interest in preaching. Murphy, whose family home was in Jamaica Plain, Massachusetts, taught for three years as a Jesuit scholastic at the Ateneo de Manila, Philippines. He studied missiology at the Gregorian University, Rome, and taught ascetical theology and sacred eloquence at Weston School of Theology, Massachusetts. From 1948 to 1955 he organized retreats and days of recollection through one of the Jesuit parishes in Boston, where he became famous for his preaching to the working class. He was on the editorial staff for *Jesuit Missions* after 1955 (John Walsh, SJ, to author, Campion Center, Weston, Massachusetts, 2 September 1994).

44. *Pamphlets on Communism* (New York: America Press, [c. 1936, 1937]); *The Modern Social and Economic Order: A Symposium for Our Sunday Visitor* (Huntington, Ind.: Our Sunday Visitor Press, 1939). For a view of U.S. Catholic anticommunist positions in the 1930s, see Jay P. Carron, "H. A. Reinhold, *America,* and the Catholic Crusade Against Communism," *Records of the American Catholic Historical Society of Philadelphia* 105 (Spring–Summer 1994): 47–69. For the U.S. Catholic Bishops' statement, see "Crisis of Christianity," *CA* 23 (December 1941).

45. Donald F. Crosby, SJ, *God, Church, and Flag: Senator Joseph R. McCarthy and the Catholic Church, 1950–1957* (Chapel Hill: University of North Carolina Press, 1979). Crosby distinguishes between liberal (those who followed Bishop Sheil) and conservative (those who followed Cardinal Spellman) approaches to communism among American Catholics.

46. A duplicated copy of the English version of the book appears in the Bernard Meyer Papers, MMA, without a cover to provide title and publication information.

47. Sister Mary Victoria (Maria del Ray Danforth), *Nun in Red China* (New York: McGraw-Hill, 1953).

48. Rigney to Thomas Reynolds, managing editor, *Chicago Daily Sun-Times,* 21 October 1955, Harold Rigney Papers, SVDA.

49. Ralph Wiltgen to Lawrence Mack, 8 March 1956, Harold Rigney Papers, SVDA.

50. Frank Robertson to Lawrence Mack, 15 October 1955, Harold Rigney Papers, SVDA. The former China missionary wanted to use the money received from his memoirs to pay off the debts incurred by Fu Jen University.

51. *Congressional Record,* 8 February 1956, A1314–A1366.

52. The CSMC moved into a more philosophical discussion of ideologies in J. Paul Spaeth, *Perspectives in Religion and Culture* (Cincinnati: Catholic Students Mission Crusade, Paladin Press, 1957). The initial chapter defined ideology and its role in the world. The chapter on communism came from their earlier publication, *Communism: A Catholic Survey* (Cincinnati: Catholic Students Mission Crusade, n.d.).

53. Harold Rigney, *Four Years in a Red Hell* (Chicago: Henry Regnery Company, 1956), 207.

54. Ibid., frontispiece of book. A comparison might be made with the representation of incarcerated Protestant missionaries in such works as F. Olin Stockwell, *With God in Red China: The Story of Two Years in Chinese Communist Prisons* (New York: Harper & Brothers, 1953).

55. Douglas Hyde, *One Front across the World* (Westminster, Md.: Newman Press, 1956), 39.

56. In 1942, a total of 52 U.S. Catholic missionaries were in Korea (37 Maryknoll men; 12 Maryknoll women; 3 Columban men). By 1962, there were 152 Americans. The largest number of U.S. Catholic missionaries in Korea was 232 in 1970 (USCMA figures, Washington, D.C).

57. The Maryknoll Fathers went to northern Korea in 1923. The Maryknoll Sisters arrived in 1924 and the Columban Fathers in 1933. Among the notable American missionaries in Korea during this period were Mary Mercy Hirschboeck (1903–86), native of Milwaukee and Maryknoll's first medical doctor; Minnesotan Harold Henry (1909–76), who arrived in Korea in 1933 and became bishop of Kwangju; and Patrick J. Byrne (1888–1950) from Washington, D.C., who died on a death march toward Manchuria. Information about these persons appears in Sister Maria Del Rey, *Her Name Is Mercy* (New York: Scribner, 1957); Penny Lernoux, "Mercy," chap. 9 in *Hearts on Fire: The Story of the Maryknoll Sisters* (Maryknoll, N.Y.: Orbis Books, 1993); Edward Fischer, *Light in the Far East: Archbishop Harold Henry's Forty-Two Years in Korea* (New York: The Seabury Press, 1976); and Raymond Lane, *Ambassador in Chains* (New York: P. J. Kenedy, 1957).

58. Among Sheen's books which treat communism at length are *Liberty, Equality, and Fraternity* (New York: Macmillan, 1938); *The Cross and the Crisis* (Milwaukee: Bruce Publishing Company, 1928); and *Freedom under God* (Milwaukee: Bruce Publishing Company, 1940).

59. Fulton J. Sheen, *Missions and the World Crisis* (Milwaukee: Bruce Publishing Company, 1963), 18, 23. This book is a compilation of his editorials in *Worldmission.* Sheen carried his debate on communism into the 1970s with "A New Theology of Missions," *Worldmission* 22, no. 3 (1971): 20–25. I would somewhat disagree with Kathleen Riley Fields's analysis of Sheen in her "Anti-Communism and Social Justice: The Double-Edged Sword of Fulton Sheen," *Records of the American Catholic Historical Society of Philadelphia* 96 (1988): 83–91. She portrays Sheen as a popular interpreter of Catholic social teaching. Because Sheen crusaded for that and against communism, he helped Catholics move into the mainstream of American life and thought (Fields, "Anti-Communism and Social Justice," 84). However, I think that other factors, such as his apocalyptic treatment of communism,

his neo-Thomist methodology, and the implications of his personal love for ecclesial power and pomp, skew his presentations in quite the opposite vein—Catholics are able to be more entrenched in a Catholicism separate from the "mainstream" while displaying some of the outward marks of American success.

60. For some of his dealings with Guatemala and the Dominican Republic, see John Cooney, *The American Pope: The Life and Times of Francis Cardinal Spellman* (New York: Times Books, 1984), 234–38, 296–98. On Spellman's and Sheen's similar positions toward communism, see Crosby, *God, Church, and Flag,* 170.

61. For an interpretation of Spellman as a "superpatriot" and his "thoughtless anticommunism," see Crosby, *God, Church, and Flag,* 15.

62. Richard Cushing, *Questions and Answers on Communism* (Boston: Daughters of St. Paul, [1961]), 114. *Christ to the World,* an international Catholic journal published in Rome, grew from the experience of collaboration and zeal in China before communism and from the experience of the *China Missionary Review. Christ to the World,* first published in 1955 and sponsored by the Propaganda Fide office, had ten aims as a journal, two of which referred to communism.

63. Bryan O. Walsh, "A Training Project for Latin American Grass Roots Leaders in Miami," unpublished manuscript, archdiocese of Miami, n.d., 12. Document provided to author by Walsh. Information on this project was also obtained in letters from Monsignor Bryan O. Walsh to the author, 25 January and 3 February 1995, and in Mauro Barrenechea, SJ, "Training Latin America's Leaders," *America* (3 April 1965): 447.

64. Bryan O. Walsh, "A Training Project for Latin American Grass Roots Leaders in Miami," 11.

65. See *Lima Methods Conference* (Maryknoll, N.Y.: The Maryknoll Fathers, 1954), 285–86.

66. Harold W. Henry, "I Choose the Legion," *The Priest* 16 (September 1960): 766–72, here 766, describes the evangelization approach he found effective in his Korean diocese.

67. John LaFarge, SJ, *A Report on the American Jesuits* (New York: Farrar, Straus, and Cudahy, 1956), 184. Frederick McGuire, CM, had the same idea that intellectual laziness on the part of American Catholics made them oblivious to what happened beyond U.S. borders and, hence, ignorant of the Church's mission (McGuire, "One World in Christ," *CA* [September 1952]: 9-11).

68. Sheen, *Missions and the World Crisis,* 67, 68. In 1964, Sheen received the Order of Lafayette Freedom Award for "distinguished leadership in combating communism."

69. On applying the rosary for this purpose, see Stephen W. Johnson, *Companion to the World Mission Rosary Map* (New York: National Office of the Society for the Propagation of the Faith, [1952]).

70. Sheridan, *Profiles of Twelve Maryknoll Missioners,* 23. Another influential person in Considine's life was his teacher, James E. Walsh, who wrote *The Church's World Wide Mission* (New York: Benziger Brothers, 1948). A fourth person to consider would be Calvert Alexander, SJ, longtime editor of *Jesuit Missions,* and his *The Missionary Dimension: Vatican II and the World Apostolate* (Milwaukee: Bruce Publishing Company, 1967).

71. John J. Considine, *World Christianity* (Milwaukee: Bruce Publishing Company, 1945). Considine's thoughts on world Christianity can also be found in his other works: *Across a World,* written in collaboration with Thomas Kernan (New York: Longmans, Green & Company, 1942), ix–xvi; "The Church's Teaching on the World Apostolate" (1944), John Considine Papers, Considine Writings, MMA; "Education to World Christianity" (Washington, D.C.: National Catholic Education Association, 1944); and "An Outline of Missiography," *The Missionary Academia* 1, no. 8 (1944).

72. Considine, *World Christianity,* xv–xvii. A key conclusion to his ideas on world Christianity is the equality of the races. When he sought supporting ideas for his presentation on a proper response to racism, he came across J. H. Oldham's influential *Christianity and the Race Problem* (London: SCM, 1924), noting in his diary, "I feel now that I have found what

I want" (Considine Diaries, 4 April 1943, 5 [3] 1:1942–44, John Considine Papers, MMA). Anglican J. H. Oldham (1874–1969), ecumenist, organizing secretary for the World Missionary Conference of 1910, and founder of the *International Review of Missions,* a journal Considine began to read in his seminary days, published *Christianity and the Race Problem* to address the racial problems he saw in Africa. For a brief biography, see Kathleen Bliss, "J. H. Oldham, From 'Edinburgh 1910' to the World Council of Churches," in Gerald H. Anderson et al., eds., *Mission Legacies: Biographical Studies of the Leaders of the Modern Missionary Movement* (Maryknoll, N.Y.: Orbis Books, 1994), 570–80.

73. For a lengthier analysis of Considine's position, see Angelyn Dries, OSF, "Toward a U.S. Theology of Global Christianity: John Considine, MM (1897–1982)," *Records of the American Catholic Historical Society of Philadelphia* 103 (Winter 1992): 23–31.

The influence of Considine's ideas about world Christianity is further evidenced in the publication of two works by the CSMC: *Fundamentals of Missiology* (1957) and the re-publication in the *Shield* (November 1962) of Considine's 1962 Fordham Mission Institute presentation on the topic.

74. One might add that their ecclesiologies also differed. Sheen was working particularly with a view toward his place in ecclesiastical structures. Considine turned down a request from representatives in eastern Africa, who had requested of Maryknoll that they release him to become the apostolic delegate there.

Ironically, McGuire, the Secretariat director, who was frequently at odds with Sheen, held a similar view of the problem of communism. The former missionary to China perceived the world conflict as a "tragedy wherein two opposing forces fight for the possession of men." "Unless the Church, offering the only real opposition based on reason to communism, will extend its influence, there will be a world cataclysm in which the Church will find itself once again in the catacombs" (McGuire, "One World in Christ," 9–11, here 10, 9).

Considine wrote in his diary, "Mons. Sheen expressed his first serious difference by lambasting Fred McGuire for getting $6000 from the CPA for the Benzinger plan. Unfortunate, but I have a feeling that Fred has been inviting it by not cultivating the Monsignor sufficiently" (Considine Diaries, 9 March 1951, 5 [4] 6:1948–1951, MMA); "Ed Murphy [SJ] and I spoke briefly of Monsignor [Sheen's] hostility to the Mission Secretariat" (9 April 1951); "Bishop [McDonnell] gave us the story that Sheen has been giving Cardinal [Spellman] against McGuire and the Secretariat" (26 November 1951).

Mary Augustine Kerby, SMSM, who was on the *Worldmission* editorial board from the start of publication, remarked that the advent of Sheen, though he brought in large sums of money for missions, "nullified the missionary effort," because "people had to do a lot of posturing" when dealing with him (interview by author, 4 November 1994).

75. Donal O'Mahony, "The Way We See It," *FE* (July 1959): 4–8, 12–15. This is the lengthiest article the magazine had published to that time.

76. *Catholic News,* 26 August 1944. As early as 1925, while he was in Rome, Considine had spoken with Monsignor Burns, dean of the School of Education at Catholic University of America, about the need to infuse Catholic schools with knowledge of the missions.

77. "The Teacher and World Christianity," 1944, pp. 1–2, box 8/7, Considine Writings, John Considine Papers, MMA.

78. For places where he developed this perspective, see John J. Considine, "An Outline of Missiography"; "Education to World Christianity"; "Teacher and World Christianity"; and *Fundamental Catholic Teaching on the Human Race,* World Horizon Report, no. 27 (Maryknoll, N.Y.: Maryknoll Publications, 1960). All these sources are found in Considine Writings, MMA.

In summarizing his ideas on the topic for the Maryknoll Cloistered Sisters, Considine acknowledged Francis de Sales and Thomas Aquinas as his sources for understanding such an all-embracing love of God. However, Considine's perspective on the Incarnation is more clearly that of John Duns Scotus. This Franciscan perspective can be seen already in Considine's thesis at Catholic University, discussing the missionary methods of a Franciscan layman, Raymond Lull.

79. Considine, "An Outline of Missiography," 8. In 1960 he reiterated his position against racism, especially in view of the discrimination against African Americans. See his *Fundamental Catholic Teaching on the Human Race.* The theme of a proper respect for all cultures was emphasized in Pius XII's encyclical *Evangelii praecones* (1951).

80. Considine, "Teacher and World Christianity," 17.

81. For information on the Maryknoll Mission Education Bureau, which began in 1937, see Wiest, *Maryknoll in China,* 415–16. Many Maryknoll Sisters, including Alma Erhard, Immaculata Brennan, Chaminade Dreisoerner, Louise Trevisan, and Juliana Bedier, wrote, edited, or illustrated much of the mission education materials.

82. Sister Mary Just, *Immortal Fire: A Journey through the Centuries with the Missionary Great* (St. Louis: Herder, 1951); Mark Leo Kent and Sister Mary Just, *The Glory of Christ: A Pageant of Two Hundred Missionary Lives from Apostolic Times to the Present Age* (Milwaukee: Bruce Publishing Company, 1955).

83. Pope Pius XII, *Fidei donum,* 21 April 1957, in Claudia Carlen, IHM, ed., *The Papal Encyclicals, 1939–1958,* vol. 4 (Wilmington, N.C.: McGrath Publishing Company, 1981), 321–32, here 324, document no. 26.

84. In 1955, New York, Massachusetts, and Pennsylvania supplied 40 percent of the Catholic missionaries overseas. The Boston Archdiocese stood out with 447 missionaries, Brooklyn with 223, Philadelphia with 274, and New York with 223. The Baltimore, Chicago, Detroit, Pittsburgh, and St. Louis dioceses each had over one hundred missionaries (*The Priest* 11 [1955]: 802).

85. Correspondence between Generalate and Eugene Phelan from 20 March to 21 June 1927, quoted in Henry Koren, CSSp, *The Serpent and the Dove* (Pittsburgh: Spiritus Press, 1985), 338. This book and Koren's earlier *To the Ends of the Earth: A General History of the Congregation of the Holy Ghost* (Pittsburgh: Duquesne University Press, 1983) provide detailed information about the work of the Spiritans in Africa and an overview of the emphasis on mission spirituality inherited from Francis Liebermann, their founder.

An early missionary from this congregation, Philadelphia-born John Simon, CSSp (1885–1920), worked for nine years in Sierra Leone, where he died of blackwater fever. At the Missionary Congress in Boston in 1913, a European Spiritan had spoken to the delegates about his African experience. See L. J. Van Den Bergh, "Address," in Francis C. Kelley, ed., *The Second American Catholic Missionary Congress* (Chicago: J. S. Hyland, 1913), 83–89, who mainly highlights the missionary's coping strategies on arrival.

86. Correspondence between Henry J. Koren, CSSp, and author, 18 June 1996.

87. For Maryknoll's early years in eastern Africa, see Considine, *Africa: World of New Men,* 302–17. An appendix contains a list of mission-sending groups in Africa in 1953. For an overview of the Sisters' work and their eventual expansion to Kenya in 1969, see Lernoux, *Hearts on Fire,* 209–33.

88. Fred Timp, SVD, "The Ghana Story," *SVD Word in the World, 1994–1995* (Steyl, Holland: Steyl Mission Press, 1995), 183–86.

89. John T. Gillard, SSJ, *The Negro American: A Mission Investigation* (Cincinnati: Catholic Students Mission Crusade, 1941), 3. The publication of this monograph occurred in the same year as Gillard's *Colored Catholics in the United States* (Baltimore: Josephite Press, 1941). See also Gillard, *The Catholic Church and the American Negro* (Baltimore: St. Joseph's Society Press, 1929; New York: Johnson Reprint, 1968).

90. For the history of Marianist work in Asaba and in other areas of Nigeria, see Father Bob Hertwick, SM, ed., "The Marianists in Nigeria," typescript, box 1961, P27, Asaba, Society of Mary Archives, Dayton, Ohio. Also instructive about the intent of the Brothers' work are the letters sent back to the United States in the early 1960s from one of their first missionaries, William T. Anderson, "Footloose in Africa," box 1753, Foreign Missions, Society of Mary Archives, Dayton, Ohio.

91. For their history in the mission, see *From Generation to Generation: The Story of the Nigeria/Ghana Mission of the Society of Jesus* (New York: privately printed, 1993). An appendix lists the indigenous Jesuit members and those from the New York Province and from other provinces serving in these missions. See also William T. Wood, SJ, "Nigeria: A New Challenge," *Woodstock Letters* 92 (1963): 13–25.

92. The value of Catholic lay missionaries in China had already been noted (see George M. Stenz, SVD, "Lay Missionaries in China," *CM* 14 [1920]: 156). Some examples of the articles which appeared in the 1940s and 1950s are Nicholas Maestrini, "Lay Missionaries: Their Role and Goal," *America* 80 (2 April 1949): 715–16; and Douglas Roche, "The New Boom in Lay Missionaries," *Sign* 38 (April 1959): 36–38. *Ave Maria* (16 January 1960): 5–10, listed ten lay mission groups, their geographic emphases, training needed, type of work, and obligations.

A woman from Oakland, California, wrote of her work as secretary to Bishop Harold Henry in the Kwangju Vicariate (see Rita Kreiss, "Lay Apostles in Korea," *FE* [September 1959]: 10-13). She and her husband, Edward, a retired naval officer, assisted the Columbans for three years, the result of Columban contact with American soldiers in the 1950s. The Columban Fathers, working in Korea since 1933, acted as advisors and interpreters for the Americans during and after the Korean War. American soldiers reciprocated, by providing labor and personal donations for various Columban missions.

93. Glen Goellner, "An Accident Germinated Her Career," *St. Louis Review,* 28 October 1960; Patricia McGerr, "The Women Volunteers Association," *The Priest* 20 (October 1964): 850–52. A brochure for the organization is in the USCMA Archives, MMA.

94. During the Marian Year, 1954, Brouwers accompanied Cardinal McIntyre to the Marian Congress in Lagos, Nigeria. After this event, he made his tour of Africa. See also Harold V. Laubacher, "Laymen Go *Ad Gentes:* The View from the Sending End — The Lay Mission Helpers of Los Angeles," *Worldmission* 21, no. 4 (1970–71): 36–39.

95. Information from pamphlets and brochures from the Lay Mission Helpers, Los Angeles, in possession of the author. While these are undated, Lillian Wood of the organization identified the approximate years for each. Within the first six years, the archdiocese sent ninety-two women and forty-two men overseas.

96. Quoted from various Lay Mission Helpers brochures of the 1960s.

97. Lydwine van Kersbergen, *Woman: Some Aspect of Her Role in the Modern World* (Loveland, Ohio: Grailville, 1956). For another key woman's view of the role of the laity, see Elizabeth Reid, *I Belong Where I Am Needed* (Westminster, Md.: Newman Press, 1961), a narrative illustrating the work of Grail members around the world, and Reid, "Lay Apostolate and the World," in William Richardson, ed., *Revolution in Missionary Thinking* (Maryknoll, N.Y.: Maryknoll Publications, 1966).

98. For the history and analysis of the Grail, see Alden V. Brown, *The Grail Movement and American Catholicism, 1940–1975* (Notre Dame, Ind.: University of Notre Dame Press, 1989). For a somewhat different perspective on some aspects of its development, see Mary Jo Weaver, "Still Feisty at Fifty: The Grailville Lay Apostolate for Women," *U.S. Catholic Historian* 11 (Fall 1993): 3–12. See also Leo R. Ward, CSC, "The Grail Movement," *Catholic Life, USA, Contemporary Lay Movements,* 91–106. On the national lay mission congresses held from 1959 to 1967, see box 9, folder 1, Lay Missioner Information, miscellaneous USCMA files, MMA.

99. See *The Laity and the International Scene* (Loveland, Ohio: Grailville, 1957).

100. Thomas M. Calkins, OSM, *Umfundisi, Missioner to the Zulus* (Milwaukee: Bruce Publishing Company, 1959); Calkins, *Kisimusi, the Story of a Zulu Girl* (Milwaukee: Bruce Publishing Company, 1962).

101. Robert S. Payne, ed., *College Readings on Africa: A Collection of Discussions on the Cultural, Economic, Political, and Religious Aspects of Present Day Africa* (Cincinnati: Catholic Students Mission Crusade Press, 1963). Authors of these chapters represented the

experience of those at the United Nations and at Georgetown University's School of Foreign Service. One chapter was written by a young Father Vincent Donovan.

102. On the issue, see Paul E. Czuchlewski, "Liberal Catholicism and American Racism, 1924–1960," in Edward Kantowicz, ed., *Modern American Catholicism, 1900–1965: Selected Historical Essays* (New York: Garland Press, 1988), 148–66.

Chapter 8 /
From "Rehabilitation" to "Development": Latin America, 1959–71

1. For their story, see Margaret Reher, " 'Get Thee to a (Peruvian) Nunnery': Cardinal Dougherty and the Philadelphia IHMs," *Records of the American Catholic Historical Society of Philadelphia* 103 (Winter 1992): 43–52. A helpful overview of the key events and issues in Latin American Church history appears in Enrique Dussel, *A History of the Church in Latin America: Colonialism to Liberalism* (Grand Rapids, Mich.: Eerdmans, 1981).

2. *Silver Jubilee of the Redemptorist Fathers, Vice-Province of Campo Grande, 1930–1955* (privately printed, 1950), RFBA. A promotional booklet was printed for the 1939 CSMC convention, "The American Redemptorists Have Missions in Paraguay, Brazil, Virgin Islands, Puerto Rico with Three Hundred Mission Stations," RFBA.

3. Their story is told in Mother Mary Edmund, CSB, "Twenty-two Years in Camaqua," *Worldmission* (Spring 1960): unnumbered page, and in "Saga das Irmas Bernardinas" (1990), typescript, copy from Bernardine Sisters' archivist to author.

4. The work of this Franciscan province appears in Leonard Bacigalupo, OFM, *The American Franciscan Missions in Central America* (Andover, Mass.: Charisma Press, 1980).

5. For a history of the Adorers of the Precious Blood Sisters' mission and an interpretation of their encounter with native religions and customs, see Sister Mary Loretta, *Amazonia: A Study of People and Progress in the Amazon Jungle* (New York: Pageant Press, 1963).

6. Considine Diaries, 19 October 1942, 5 (3) 1:1942–44, United States, MMA.

7. James E. Walsh, MM, Easter Sunday 1942, First Departure Ceremony for South America, MMA. See also the documentation compiled by William D. McCarthy, MM, in support of the point (correspondence from McCarthy to author, 3 July 1996).

8. Barnabas Dikemper, "The Missions in Brazil," in Marion Habig, ed., *History of the Franciscan Province of the Sacred Heart, 1959–1979* (Chicago: Franciscan Herald Press, 1979), 218–27.

9. Joseph P. O'Neill, SJ, "The Osorno Venture," *Woodstock Letters* 91 (1962): 315–25.

10. Many of the Alliance for Progress files are found in the James Stanford Bradshaw (1921–) papers, the JFK National Security Files, and the JFK President's Office Files at the John Fitzgerald Kennedy Library, Boston.

11. Considine to Archbishop Karl J. Alter, 6 May 1963 (copy), box 10/5 (1963), Alter, LAB, ACUA.

12. Information on La Crosse priests through telephone conversation with La Crosse Mission office, 28 June 1996. Some information on the other clergy appears in Anthony P. Wagener, "To Bridge the Gap," *The Priest* 15 (1959): 400–405.

13. It is difficult to calculate the actual total financial contribution Cushing made toward Latin America. In one instance, Considine inquired of him:

> This April the Pontifical Commission for Latin America will have been in existence five years and a special report to the Holy Father is planned. Among other things, the Commission wants to indicate the financial contributions to Latin America of the Church in the United States. The Archbishop plans a paragraph on your personal activities. He has a financial record of the activities of the Society for St. James the Apostle. He asks if he would be making a proper statement if he made the declaration to His Holiness that during the past three years your Eminence has contributed

[given or promised] approximately four million dollars to Latin America institutions. He would be particularly grateful if you would specify several of the larger gifts which you have made. (Considine to Cushing, 23 March 1963 [copy], box 10/6, Cushing File [1963], LAB, ACUA)

There is no record of Cushing's response.

14. Considine to Cushing, 15 May 1961 (copy), ACUA.

15. John Henry Cutler, *Cardinal Cushing of Boston* (New York: Hawthorne Books, 1970), 191.

16. John Maurice, interview by author.

17. Maurice to "Dear Folks," 3 February 1959, Maurice's personal correspondence. On the mission call for clergy, see Brother Knopp, SM, "The Diocesan Clergy are Missionary, Too," *Worldmission* 9, no. 1 (1958): 76–79, which relates the story of Francis Kennard's work in Peru.

18. For information on the events which led to the founding of the society, I rely on an interview 12 November 1994 with William Milhomme, who is currently researching its history, an interview 18 January 1995 with John Maurice and the latter's personal letters to his family and friends. See also James J. O'Rourke, "Cardinal Cushing's Legacy," *Maryknoll* (July 1983): 21–25. Pius XII had encouraged diocesan priests to go abroad as missionaries in his 1957 encyclical, *Fidei donum*. For the experience of one priest from the society, see A. J. McMahon, "A Diocesan Priest in the Foreign Missions," *The Homiletic and Pastoral Review* 62, no. 10 (1962): 853–58.

19. Sisters St. Timothy (Mary) Cahill, Malmaura Cleary, and Rose Agnes Urban, all experienced teachers, and a nurse, Helen Edward Feeley, were the first of about fifteen women this congregation sent to Lima. The Sisters remained in Peru until 1991, when the last Sister, Carlotta Gilarde, who had been there since 1965, returned to the Boston area.

20. The Sisters in Lima to "Dear Sisters" (in Boston), 5 December 1966, p. 5, folder 662.2, no. 22, Letters to Congregation 1965–67, Sisters of St. Joseph Archives. These letters, sent to the superior in the United States, were intended to be duplicated and sent to all their houses or posted on the Sisters' bulletin boards.

An important work which narrates Peruvian Catholic Church history is Jeffrey Klaiber, SJ, *The Catholic Church in Peru, 1821–1985* (Washington, D.C.: The Catholic University of America Press, 1992). The work was published originally in Spanish.

21. Fr. William Francis to Cushing, 5 November 1963, box 26/11, Cushing Papers, South America, AABoston.

22. See O'Rourke, "Cardinal Cushing's Legacy," 21–25.

23. Cushing to Considine, 11 July 1963, box 10/6, Cushing folder, LAB, ACUA. Ivan Illich makes an interesting observation of Cushing in a letter to his "boss," Considine. "It is still my belief that Cushing is a man with whom one can deal only from great poverty or great strength. He is at the same time the man who does most for Latin America and who allows the worst mistakes in this area of U.S. church enterprise which others will have to pay for dearly after his death.... I have the greatest respect for him but not for everybody around him — he has collaborators in the Latin American deal (as you so well know) who use his goodness and generosity to do serious damage to the Church, who make him look foolish in Latin America" (Illich to Considine, 30 September 1961, box 10/5, CIF-Cuernavaca Correspondence, LAB, ACUA).

24. Information on the society in box 26/7, Record Group I.81, Cushing Papers, "Sons of Mary, 1965," AABoston. Garesché was also the founder of the Catholic Medical Mission Board.

25. Larraín, quoted in Bacigalupo, *American Franciscan Missions in Central America,* 166.

26. The Sisters of St. Anne went to Haiti in 1944 and opened several missions there over the next few years. More recently, the Oblates of Mary Immaculate had over twenty-five of their members in Haiti.

27. Report from Second Meeting of Superior Generals in Rome, 29 May 1959, box 9/14, I-003, Superior Generals 1874–1966, School Sisters of St. Francis Archives.

28. U.S. Bishops used this word in speaking of Latin America. See Minutes of the Annual Meeting of the United States Bishops, 1965, p. 11, ACUA.

29. Cushing to Considine, 29 May 1963. Gerald M. Costello, *Mission to Latin America: The Successes and Failures of a Twentieth Century Crusade* (Maryknoll, N.Y.: Orbis Books, 1979), is a key book to identify the issues and persons in U.S. Catholic missionary work there and includes a chronology of dates significant for the presence of U.S. Catholics in Hispanic America.

30. The English rendering of the Latin title of Marcello Cardinal Mimmi's letter to the bishops announcing the program was actually, "The Papal Volunteers for Apostolic Collaboration in Latin America."

31. See Scott Mainwaring, "The Catholic Youth Workers' Movement (JOC) and the Emergence of the Popular Church in Brazil" (working paper no. 6, Kellogg Institute for International Studies, University of Notre Dame, December 1983), and Mainwaring, *The Catholic Church and Politics in Brazil, 1916–1985* (Stanford, Calif.: Stanford University Press, 1986), 115–41.

32. On the Kansas program for overseas lay missions and the subsequent program after PAVLA, see John Stitz, *A New Pentecost: A Short History of the Kansas Lay Mission Program for Papal Volunteers, 1961–1969* (Kansas City, Kans.: Archdiocese of Kansas City, 1992); and Stitz, *The Kansas Volunteers, Archdiocese of Kansas City in Kansas: A Short History, 1983–1992* (Kansas City, Kans.: Archdiocese of Kansas City, 1993).

Two other books which describe the PAVLA experience in addition to Costello, *Mission to Latin America,* are Dan B. McCarthy, *Mission to Peru: A Story of Papal Volunteers* (Milwaukee: Bruce Publishing Company, 1967), and Joseph Michenfelder, MM, *Gringo Volunteers* (Maryknoll, N.Y.: Maryknoll Publications, 1969). See also "Volunteers for Peace," *Sign* 42 (May 1963): 7–11, 14–17.

33. The dearth of official interest in PAVLA in the New York Archdiocese led Monsignor Michael Dwyer, director for Catholic Charities, to begin a lay program in 1962, Catholics for Latin America. Illich complained that it ignored Papal Volunteer rules, but Cardinal Silva of Santiago and Archbishop Carboni of Lima gave it their approval. The program emphasized presence with the poor (after the manner of Charles de Foucauld) and "aiding the poor directly while working towards the day when they can help themselves" (brochure of the Catholics for Latin America and correspondence, box 10/6, Cushing File, LAB, ACUA; Michael F. Dwyer, interview by author, 3 March 1995).

34. 14 December 1961, box 10/9, Apostolic Delegation File, LAB, ACUA.

35. In May 1968, the Davenport and Chicago offices were coordinated in Washington, D.C.

36. USCC Annual Report, 1968, p. 51, Minutes and Proceedings of the Annual Bishops' Meetings, ACUA.

37. This point is noted in Alden V. Brown, *The Grail Movement and American Catholicism, 1940–1975* (Notre Dame, Ind.: University of Notre Dame Press, 1989), 76–77.

38. Considine to Victor Fernandez (copy), 3 January 1962, box 10/6, Fernandez, LAB, ACUA.

39. John J. Considine, *Call for Forty Thousand* (New York: Longmans, Green & Company, 1946), 227.

40. Considine's remarks appear in the discussion of the Findings Committee, *Lima Methods Conference of the Maryknoll Fathers* (Maryknoll, N.Y.: Maryknoll Fathers, 1954), 287.

41. The Reverend Russell Tikalsky, interview by author; *National Catholic Reporter* 31 (28 October 1994): 3–4; *Catholic Herald Citizen* (10 September 1981): 4.

42. Cushing to Considine, 29 May 1963.

43. Tikalsky interview.

44. Thomas J. Finnegan, Jr., director of vocations, archdiocese of Boston, to Considine, 11 October 1963, box 10/10, LAB, ACUA.

45. *Mission of Friendship, Erie, Pennsylvania, USA, Celebrating 25 Years, 1971–1996, Cooperation and Support* (Erie, Pa.: Diocese of Erie, privately printed in Spanish and English, 1996).

46. Committee for the Church in Latin America, National Conference of Catholic Bishops, *Sharing Faith across the Hemisphere* (Washington, D.C.: U.S. Catholic Conference; Maryknoll, N.Y.: Orbis Books, 1997), presents an overview of inter-American church relations, mainly highlighting ecclesial documents since the founding of the USCC's Secretariat for Latin America (the former Latin American Bureau of 1959). An appendix provides information garnered from a survey of North American diocesan, parochial, and religious congregational involvement in Latin America.

47. Fitzpatrick's introduction to intercultural differences came professionally through his graduate work at Harvard University with Oscar Handlin (noted for his study of immigrants) and Talcott Parsons, a leading sociologist. The Jesuit wrote a paper on Matteo Ricci and the Chinese Rites in the latter's class. When Fitzpatrick started his teaching career at Fordham in 1949, Puerto Rican immigration was on the rise in New York. He was sought as an expert by many social and religious agencies to learn about the background of these immigrants. At Fordham, he initiated courses in cultural assimilation and comparative cultures. See his autobiographical introduction in Joseph P. Fitzpatrick, SJ, *One Church, Many Cultures: Challenge of Diversity* (New York: Sheed & Ward, 1987). Some of Fitzpatrick's works about Puerto Ricans include *The Spiritual Care of Puerto Rican Migrants: Conference on the Spiritual Care of Puerto Rican Migrants, San Juan, Puerto, Rico, 1955* (New York: Arno Press, 1980); *Puerto Rican Americans: The Meaning of Migration to the Mainland* (Englewood Cliffs, N.J.: Prentice-Hall, 1971). The title of Fitzpatrick's memoirs is *The Stranger Is Our Own: Reflections on the Journey of Puerto Rican Migrants*, ed. Madeline Moran (Kansas City, Mo.: Sheed & Ward, 1996).

48. James Edward McManus, *Memoirs* (typed copy), p. 52, RFBA. The University of Notre Dame Archives contain the papers and notes of Sister Miriam Therese O'Brien (1909–92), who wrote a biography of McManus and several other U.S. clergy who became bishops in Puerto Rico. She also narrated the work of her congregation, the Sisters of St. Joseph, who taught in Puerto Rico.

49. The Maryknoll language school in Cochabamba was reorganized and updated in the late 1960s and became a leading institution to which many mission groups have sent their members. The St. James Society returned there in the 1970s (William D. McCarthy, MM, to author, 17 March 1997).

50. For information on Illich's life, see Francine du Plessix Gray, *Divine Disobedience: Profiles in Catholic Radicalism* (New York: Alfred A. Knopf, 1970), 231–322. This engaging narrative provides information on the "inquisition" of Illich in 1968 in Rome and some of the details of the events of the 1960s which relate to the center. Illich left the priesthood in 1969.

51. McManus suspended Illich from his diocese in October 1960. See McManus to Illich, 16 October 1960 (copy), RFBA; Illich to Considine, 27 January 1961, Center for Intercultural Formation folder, LAB, ACUA; and Illich to McManus, Fordham University, 1 February 1961, RFBA.

52. Among the staff members at the start of the program were the Chilean priest Segundo Galilea, William McKeon, MM, and Wilbert Wagner, SVD. Wagner cofounded the Divine Word mission in Mexico in 1962. Illich had requested that Sister Xavier (Mary Rose) O'Donnell, MM, coauthor of *A Catechism of the Family of God* (Maryknoll, N.Y.: Maryknoll Publications, 1965) with Leo Mahon of Chicago, be assigned to the staff. This forward-looking woman had worked with Spanish-speaking people in San Juan Bautista, California, and Chicago, and later worked with Cesar Chavez in the early years of the United Farm Workers. For a brief description of the life and work of O'Donnell, see Penny Lernoux,

Hearts on Fire: The Story of the Maryknoll Sisters (Maryknoll, N.Y.: Orbis Books, 1993), 144–47. O'Donnell spent a year in Cuernavaca, and in 1964 Sister Marcos Marie (Catherine) Carden, MM, was sent to work in the office and to take care of the students and scheduling. Carden's work at the CIF enabled her later to organize a catechetical institute in Colombia under CELAM auspices (Catherine Carden, interview by author, 21 March 1995, and Carden correspondence with author, 30 March 1995).

53. Considine to Laurence J. McGinley, SJ, president of Fordham University, 11 October 1961, box 10/5, CIF-Cuernavaca-Board of Directors and Incorporation folder, LAB, ACUA. On the typical difficulties missionaries encountered with a new language, see Sister M. Cuthbert (Monica) Hellwig, SCMM, "The Language-Learning Problems of the Ordinary Missionary," *Worldmission* 15, no. 3 (1964): 27–32. Hellwig contributed a chapter on the apostolate in medieval and modern history in Edward A. Freking et al., eds., *The Church at Work in the World: Selections for a Readings Course on the Theology, History, and Methods of the Mission Apostolate* (Cincinnati: Catholic Students Mission Crusade, 1961). Hellwig later taught at Georgetown University.

54. For the overview of the CIF program as it was proposed to the U.S. Bishops, see "The Center for Cultural Formation, Cuernavaca, Mexico," 25 January 1961, box 145, CIF Cuernavaca Report folder, LAB, ACUA. (Quotation from p. 2.) For Illich's observations on the center, see Ivan Illich, "The Meaning of Cuernavaca," *Jesuit Missions* 41 (April 1967): 19–25.

55. One Maryknoller remarked, "I felt so awful when I took my habit off.... My legs were bare. I didn't come out of my room for supper the first night, I was so self-conscious" (Catherine Carden, interview by author, 21 March 1995).

56. Sr. Anne Jude, CSA, to "Dear Mother," 15 June 1964, Mexico City folder (1964–75), CSAA.

57. Joseph P. Fitzpatrick, SJ, "Training Center at Cuernavaca," *America* (24 February 1962): 678–80. Considine congratulated Fitzpatrick on this article and noted that this was the first time that anything about CIF written from Cuernavaca contained any reference to its relationship with the bishops. "Heretofore there has been quite a categoric insistence that CIF possesses no connection except with Fordham. True, the connection with the Bishops' Committee at present is quite tenuous since any establishment of a genuine bond has never been pursued" (Considine to Fitzpatrick, 28 February 1962, box 10/5, CIF folder, LAB, ACUA).

58. "The Center for Cultural Formation, Cuernavaca, Mexico," ACUA.

59. Ivan D. Illich, "Basic Policies for Courses of Missionary Formation: Missionary Poverty," box 10/5, CIF-Cuernavaca Report, LAB, ACUA.

60. His views are especially reflected in his reprinted 1967 article, "The Seamy Side of Charity," in Ivan Illich, *Celebration of Awareness* (Garden City, N.Y.: Doubleday, 1970), 53–68.

61. Cushing to Considine, 20 May 1961, box 10/6, Cushing, Cardinal (1961), LAB, ACUA.

62. Considine to Mrs. Bruno Benziger, 4 October 1962, box 10/6, Considine, John J., Personal (1962), LAB, ACUA.

63. Considine to Cushing, 30 September 1963, box 24/21, LAB, ACUA.

64. Antonio Samore to Father Considine, 9 October 1963, box 10/5, LAB, ACUA.

65. Houtart was director of the Centre de Recherches Socio-Religieuses in Louvain, Belgium, and secretary general of the International Federation of Catholic Institutes of Social and Socio-Religious Research. In 1952–53, he studied at Indiana University and the University of Chicago under a U.S. government fellowship. He also directed for a short time a center for religious sociology in Bogotá. He wrote the foreword to Prudencio Damboriena, SJ, *El Protestantismo en América Latina* (Friburgo and Bogotá: Oficina Internacional de Investigaciones, 1962), which used his method to examine Protestant presence and which included charts and lists of Protestant organizations, along with a brief explanation of each group. The book listed the number and locations of hospitals, schools, and other Protestant insti-

tutions throughout Latin America. Houtart became a *peritus* at the Vatican II Council for Archbishop Helder Camara.

Ivan Illich had been invited to the first CICOP meeting, presumably to give a presentation. Illich dictated a hasty note to Joseph Gremillion at NCWC as Illich left New York for Rome, saying that he thought the CICOP meeting "would embarrass the Latin American effort of the U.S. Church, rather than help it" (Illich memo to Considine, 1 September 1963, box 10/5, LAB, ACUA). Gremillion and Illich had differing views on what the U.S. Church should be doing in Latin America. It is difficult to understand why Illich would not have wanted a CICOP meeting, because progressive Latin American bishops, who had an affinity with the oppressed people of their countries, would be presenting their needs and the realities of the southern Church — something Illich thought should happen. However, the embarrassment of which Illich spoke referred to the expense of flying Latin American bishops to the United States and holding meetings at a first-class hotel to discuss "poverty."

66. Senator Humphrey noted the value of the conference in his remarks in Congress, statements entered into the *Congressional Record,* 29 January 1964.

67. Information on CICOP from Louis Michael Colonnese, interview by author, Davenport, Iowa, 16 February 1994. The proceedings for the first conference were published as John J. Considine, ed., *The Church in the New Latin America* (Notre Dame, Ind.: Fides, 1964). The second conference proceedings were published as Considine, ed., *Social Revolution in the New Latin America: A Catholic Appraisal* (Notre Dame, Ind.: Fides, 1965). On the last years of CICOP, see Costello, *Mission to Latin America,* 173–79.

68. Colonnese interview. Friends characterize Colonnese as outspoken and compassionate, but as an angry man as well. When he first went to El Salvador, he advocated the use of violence to effect change. For a description of some key events in his life, see James Dyer, "A Legend Leaves Iowa, Father Michael Colonnese," *Iowa City Mercury* 1 (April 1992): 12–14.

69. Arcadio Larraona, secretary of the Sacred Congregation of Religious; Paul Philippe, OP, commissioner of the Sacred Congregation of the Holy Office; and Dino Staffa, secretary of the Sacred Congregation of Seminaries, were the members of the committee.

70. Report from the Second Meeting of General Superiors of Religious Orders and Congregations of Women, 29 May 1959, p. 4, box 9/14, 1-003, Superior Generals 1874–66, School Sisters of St. Francis Archives.

71. Ibid., 5.

72. Ibid., 8.

73. For an overview of their Bolivian experience until the mid-1960s, see Alice O'Rourke, OP, *Let Us Set Out: Sinsinawa Dominicans, 1949–1985* (Dubuque, Iowa: Union-Hoermann Press, 1986), 77–88.

74. Information about the meeting can be found in box 10/8, Missions, Major Superiors of Men Religious Annual Meetings, LAB, ACUA. These considerations were developed by John Considine following the August meeting ("Some Policy Considerations for Religious Congregations Entering Latin America," 16 October 1961, box 10/7, Major Religious Superiors, Men, File, LAB, ACUA).

75. The point is made in Karen Kennelly, CSJ, "Foreign Missions and the Renewal Movement," *Review for Religious* (May–June 1990): 445–63. As will be noted in the next chapter, even those who went to Latin America primarily to teach responded to many other needs.

76. On the origins and development of the Sister Formation Conference, see Richardine Quirk, BVM, "The Evolution of the Idea of Sister Formation, 1952–1960," *Sponsa Regis* 33 (April 1962): 223–33; and Marjorie Noterman Beane, *From Framework to Freedom: A History of the Sister Formation Conference* (New York: University Press of America, 1993). For an analysis of the ecclesiology and theological assumptions of this group, see Angelyn Dries, OSF, "Living in Ambiguity: A Paradigm Shift Experienced by the Sister Formation Movement," *The Catholic Historical Review* 79 (July 1993): 478–87. For specific references to SFC engagement with Latin America, see Beane, 107–18.

77. Beane, *From Framework to Freedom*, 118. Latin American students in particular were already the focus of the Catholic Conference on Inter-American Student Problems, whose president was Robert Pelton, CSC. For information about this group, incorporated in 1960–61, see box 10/5, CCISP File, LAB, ACUA.

78. Celsus Wheeler was provincial of the OFM Holy Name Province (New York) from 1952 to 1961. He was the executive secretary for the Conference of Major Superiors of Men and then became superior of the Franciscan Bolivian Mission in 1963.

79. The Sister Formation Conference invited Mary Anne Chouteau to edit Houtart's talks, which were published the following year as *The Challenge of Change* (New York: Sheed and Ward, 1964). Houtart had hoped to have a permanent research center in Latin America. The Sister Formation Conference was one of the places where he found an agreeable audience to further his ideas.

80. Several months after their return, Bradley met in Washington, D.C., with representatives of the State Department and the Alliance for Progress to argue for the necessity of a Church-related group's participation in teacher education in countries such as Peru, which traditionally had a religious foundation. At the time, the only U.S. program was offered through Columbia University in New York. The conference proposed its services to facilitate a program for teacher education in Latin America.

81. Confidential report on Latin American Visit, 4 March 1962, series 3, box 12, Latin American visit folder, 1961–62, SFC Archives.

82. Information about Regina Mundi obtained from Gretchen Berg, OSF, interview by author.

83. For an example of the theology of mission in the early 1950s, see John F. Clarkson, SJ, "The ABC's of Missiology," *Worldmission* 3 (1952): 337–52. Andrew Seumois, OMI, wrote an essay summarizing some of the European mission theorists, "The Evolution of Mission Theology among Roman Catholics," in Gerald H. Anderson, ed., *The Theology of Christian Mission* (New York: McGraw Hill, 1961), 122–34.

84. Edward A. Freking et al., eds., *The Church at Work in the World* (Cincinnati: Catholic Students Mission Crusade, 1961), 4.

85. Ibid.

86. This was also the point made by Robert Wood, SM, *Missionary Crisis and Challenge in Latin America* (St. Louis: B. Herder Book Company, 1964), 86. Edmond J. Dunn, a former Papal Volunteer in Latin America, analyzes a post–Vatican II theology of mission in terms of development in *Missionary Theology: Foundations in Development* (Lanham, Md.: University Press of America, 1980).

87. John J. Considine, *Education to World Christianity* (Washington, D.C.: National Catholic Educational Association, 1944), 9. Considine later presented substantially the same idea to the Catholic Hospital Association's conference. See John Considine, "Program of Promise for Latin America," talk delivered to the Catholic Hospital Association, St. Louis, 24 May 1962, box 10/5, Catholic Hospital Association File, LAB, ACUA.

88. Considine talk to Cloistered Maryknoll Sisters, 28 November 1943, Considine Writings 8/6, MMA.

89. Included were William J. Coleman, MM; John W. Comber, MM (superior general); George Higgins (director, Department of Social Action, NCWC); sociologists Thomas O'Dea and Joseph Fitzpatrick, SJ; missiologists Edward L. Murphy, SJ, and Ronan Hoffman, OFM-Conv; Frederick McGuire, CM (Mission Secretariat); Ivan Illich; Otto Shelly, SVD; and Columban Kevin O'Doherty. The conference talks were published in John Considine, ed., *The Missionary's Role in Socio-Economic Betterment* (New York: Newman Press, 1960).

90. Mulherin narrated the story of the Maryknoll women's mission prior to the Korean War in 1950 in "Brief History of the Maryknoll Sisters in North Korea, October 1924 to October 1950," Korea, Mary Gabriella Mulherin File, MMA.

91. Sister Mary T. Connell, MM, to Dear Sisters, Family, and Friends, 17 May 1993, a letter written on the death of Mulherin, Korea, Mary Gabriella Mulherin File, MMA.

92. Lernoux, *Hearts on Fire*, 201.

93. Aylward Shorter, WF, raises this question as the title of his first chapter in his *Theology of Mission* (Notre Dame, Ind.: Fides, 1972).

94. Hugh J. Nolan, ed., *Pastoral Letters of the U.S. Catholic Bishops*, vol. 3 (Washington, D.C.: U.S. Catholic Conference, 1987), 293–97, here 293.

95. Ibid., 294. The document proceeds to encourage the involvement of every diocese and parish in the work of the Society for the Propagation of the Faith and the Association for the Holy Childhood, both papal organizations for the financial support of missions. The bishops also make reference to the United States Mission Council, established in 1969 after the Mission Secretariat was dissolved.

96. Remarks in *Maryknoll* (May 1942): 3.

97. Report of the Evaluation Committee, 1946 General Chapter, typed, p. 1, MMA.

98. By 1991, the number of laity had risen again to 446, declining to 406 in 1992.

99. Nolan, ed., *Pastoral Letters of the U.S. Catholic Bishops*, 3:293.

100. *Between Honesty and Hope: Documents from and about the Church in Latin America*, issued at Lima by the Peruvian Bishops' Commission for Social Action, trans. John Drury (Maryknoll, N.Y.: Maryknoll Publications, 1970).

Chapter 9 /
A Time for Reassessment, Liberation Theology and the "Option for the Poor," 1965–80

1. Numbers of U.S. Catholic missionaries in selected Latin American countries:

Country	1958	1962	1966	1970	1975
Brazil	298	370	668	699	485
Peru	135	270	665	693	492
Bolivia	148	215	334	346	279
Chile	122	199	347	132	196

Source: U.S. Catholic Mission Council.

2. In addition to the books published from various conferences of the groups mentioned, Latin American Bishops' speeches and articles appeared in journals and magazines, such as Juan Cardinal Landázuri Ricketts, "To Be More Human," *Worldmission* 21, no. 2 (1970): 46–51, an apologia for the relationship among development, "humanization," and evangelization in Latin America.

3. Number of U.S. Catholic missionaries in Central America:

Region	1958	1962	1966	1968	1975
Central America	392	537	857	936	712

Source: U.S. Catholic Mission Council.

4. For his own analysis of his leadership in this area, see Louis Putz, CSC, "Reflections on Specialized Catholic Action," *U.S. Catholic Historian* 9 (Fall 1990): 433–39.

5. Marcos Gregorio McGrath, CSC, *The Renewal of the Panamanian Church* (privately printed, 1995), 4. This biographical booklet is a translation from the Spanish and was edited by Robert S. Pelton, CSC, on the occasion of McGrath's retirement as archbishop of Panama (copy from McGrath to author).

6. Gustave Weigel, an advocate of ecumenism in the early 1960s and colleague of John Courtney Murray, was the first North American priest to establish roots in Chile. He was popular among the American community in Santiago, even though many were not Catholic. The Chilean government presented the Order of Merit to him for his contributions in educational and social work. In 1956, he made a speaking tour of Colombia and Chile on a grant from the State Department. For Weigel's Latin American experience, see the Gustave Weigel

memorial issue of *Woodstock Letters* 97 (1968): 457–83, which provides excerpts from his letters and talks on Latin America.

7. Marcos G. McGrath, telephone conversation, 27 March 1994.

8. From 1966 to 1969 McGrath was a member of the Vatican Secretariat for Non-believers and from 1966 to 1971 a consultant to the Council on the Laity.

9. McGrath's many writings, including sermons, articles, and books, are cataloged in *Indice de Escritos del Arzobispo de Panamá, Mons. Marcos G. McGrath, CSC (1953–1988)* (privately printed, 1988), typescript. Examples of his writings in English, which indicate his theological and pastoral perspectives, are M. G. McGrath, "The Theological Foundation of Missionary Communication," in Frederick A. McGuire, ed., *The New Missionary Church* (Baltimore: Helicon, 1964), 117–36; "Theological Reflections on Inter-American Relations," in Samuel Shapiro, ed., *Cultural Factors in Inter-American Relations* (Notre Dame, Ind.: University of Notre Dame Press, 1968), 183–99; and "Church and Mission in Latin America," in Francis J. Butler, ed., *American Catholic Identity: Essays in an Age of Change* (Kansas City, Mo.: Sheed & Ward, 1994), 236–49.

10. The Maryknoll Sisters were originally in a "country" diocese of Panama and proved a threat to the new Spanish Augustinian bishop. "There were two 'powers' there and one had to go, so the Maryknoll Sisters left and went to other Latin American countries" (Catherine Carden interview).

Maryknoll had influence on another issue related to Panama. Filmmaker Robert Richter approached Maryknoll about producing a film on the U.S.-sponsored School of the Americas, which apparently taught torture techniques and destabilization processes to subvert governments unfavorable to U.S. interests. The Army training program was originally based in Panama, but is currently at Fort Benning, Georgia. Janice McLaughlin, MM, director for the Maryknoll Communications Office, became the assistant associate producer of "School of Americas, School of Assassins," a documentary which received an Academy Award nomination. Roy Bourgeois, MM, has participated in public demonstrations for the school's closure. Prior to her work at the Maryknoll office, McLaughlin had worked for twenty-two years in Rhodesia, where she was imprisoned during the war of independence before the area became Zimbabwe. She and Dana Robert summarized the report on human rights issues in southern Africa in "Mission and Human Rights," *Mission Studies* 2, no. 1 (1985): 70–72.

11. Leo Mahon, "Let the Eagles Fly," typescript in Mahon's possession. The autobiographical narrative treats of his experience as pastor and, later, vicar, of the San Miguelito area in Panama. Information was also obtained from Leo Mahon, interview by author, 17 April 1995. Mahon, as of 1996, served as pastor of Our Lady of the Lake parish in northern Chicago. Several references are made to Mahon's association with Hillenbrand and the clergy he influenced in Margery Frisbie, *An Alley in Chicago: The Ministry of a City Priest* (Kansas City, Mo.: Sheed & Ward, 1991), which narrates the life of Monsignor John Egan, another well-known "social justice" priest and leader of the Catholic Family Movement. See also Steven Avella, "Reynold Hillenbrand and Chicago Catholicism," *U.S. Catholic Historian* 9 (Fall 1990): 353–70.

12. San Miguelito grew from about ten thousand people in 1962 to 250,000 in the 1990s, with over twenty parishes. In 1996, there were over twenty parish priests, of whom more than half were Panamanians (McGrath to author, 30 October 1996).

13. The San Miguelito Reports can be found in box 21/8, LAB, ACUA. The archives for the San Miguelito Project are located at the University of Notre Dame, because Mahon feared that John Cardinal Cody would destroy the files (Mahon interview). Some missionaries and local clergy rankled at the mention of San Miguelito, because some proponents broadcast this approach as the only method to use in Central and South America.

14. An important aspect of San Miguelito was its team approach, which included priests, Sisters, and lay Panamanians (Barbara Hendricks, MM, to author, 27 February 1997). A St. James Society priest described the team approach used at the Institute for Inter-Cultural Communication of the Catholic University of Puerto Rico, which prepared North Americans

to work in Latin America, in Frederic M. Cameron, "Teamwork: A Key to Latin America," *Worldmission* 18, no. 3 (1967): 15–16.

15. Leo Mahon, "So You Think You're Ready to Work in Latin America!" in John J. Considine, ed., *The Church in the New Latin America* (Notre Dame, Ind.: Fides, 1964).

16. Emily Schug, CSA, to Mother Rosita, 9 October 1966, Nicaragua File, CSAA.

17. Leo Mahon, quoted in Gerald M. Costello, *Mission to Latin America: The Successes and Failures of a Twentieth Century Crusade* (Maryknoll, N.Y.: Orbis Books, 1979), 196.

18. Alfred T. Hennelly, ed., *Liberation Theology: A Documentary History* (Maryknoll, N.Y.: Orbis Books, 1990), xvii–xviii, after indicating some of its "forerunners," describes three key components of liberation theology starting in the mid-1950s: basic ecclesial community formation, the education method of Paulo Freire (1921–97), and awareness at universities of ideologies which legitimate injustice. The book, however, does not seem to mention the influence of U.S. missionaries on the first of these developments.

Barbara Hendricks, MM, missionary in Peru from 1953 to 1970, notes that the major sources for the new theological and pastoral movements arose from within the Latin American Church itself and that missionaries "were nourished and guided by the movements within Latin America in our interpretation of the reality and in a theological methodology of reflection among ourselves and among the small communities. Our spirituality was formed by this influence. As Gustavo Gutiérrez has said, 'Theology of Liberation is first of all a spirituality' " (Hendricks to author, 27 February 1997).

19. Capuchin presence in Central America was sporadic in the 1600s. In 1849, Capuchins came in exile from an antireligious Spain, settling in Guatemala at the request of a conservative government which sought religious to work in parishes. From 1899 to 1939 Catalan Capuchins established Cartago, Costa Rica, as a Capuchin center in Central America. After the creation of the Bluefields Vicariate in 1913, Catalan Capuchins served there until the U.S. Capuchins arrived in 1939. Information obtained from David Zywiec, OFM-Cap, and Niles Kauffman, OFMCap, interviews by author. They were missionaries to Nicaragua.

20. Frieda Folger started the association in 1899 in Lucerne, Switzerland, to aid the mission work among the Capuchins. Those who sent in money were remembered in the Masses and prayers of the Capuchin community.

The four Capuchins in the first group to Nicaragua were Francis Busalt, Regis Neeser, Henry Barth, and Richard Brunner, who had been in the mission at Allahabad, India. While not in the first contingent, Brother Gaul Neumann spent many years in Nicaragua. The departure ceremony for the first three men took place at St. Francis Church, Wisconsin, on 19 February 1939. They arrived at Bluefields on 24 March. Information from James C. Wolf, OFMCap, archivist, province of St. Joseph, Detroit. See also the official publication of this Capuchin province, *Messenger* 6 (1936–39): 279ff.

21. Niedhammer made his religious profession in 1921 and was ordained to the priesthood on 3 June 1927. He taught for two years at Garrison, New York, then became an assistant pastor of St. Michael's Parish, Brooklyn. From 1935 to 1939 he worked at St. Labre Indian Mission in Montana and was missioned to Latin America in 1939. The Capuchin influence among the people in the interests of social change is discussed in Manzar Foroohar, *The Catholic Church and Social Change in Nicaragua* (Albany: State University of New York Press, 1989), and in Michael Dodson and Laura Nuzzi O'Shaughnessy, *Nicaragua's Other Revolutions: Religious Faith and Political Struggle* (Chapel Hill: University of North Carolina Press, 1990), 127–31, which relates the influence of the *delegados* on Nicaragua's political situation.

For a journalist's overview of the Catholic Church in Nicaragua, see Penny Lernoux, *The People of God* (New York: Viking, 1989), 365–405; for the relationship of Scripture to the renewal of church and government life, see Guillermo Melendez, *Seeds of Promise: The Prophetic Church in Central America* (New York: Friendship Press, 1990).

22. Three of the pioneers wrote biographical sketches of their work in Nicaragua,

all in typescript: Sister Mary Agnes Dickof, CSA, "Mission Work in Nicaragua"; Sister Paulette Scheck, CSA, "Reminiscences of Our Work in Nicaragua," written from Leo House, New York, March 1978; and Sister Francis Borgia Dreiling, CSA, "Historical Memoirs, 1945–1977," CSAA. See also Matthew Niedhammer, "The Sisters of St. Agnes Come to Nicaragua," *The Cowl — A Capuchin Review* 10 (March 1946): 51–54.

23. Dickof, "Mission Work in Nicaragua," 7.

24. Dreiling, "Historical Memoirs, 1945–1977," 47.

25. An important lay woman in this work was Mary Hamlin de Zúniga, a volunteer from Minnesota who came to work with the Agnesian Sisters. She compiled an extensive report on the training program. See Mary Hamlin de Zúniga, "Integral Program for Leadership Formation on the Rio Coco, 1970–1974," Central American and South American Missions, CSAA. Mary eventually married a Miskito from Nicaragua, Marcelo Zúniga, and they moved to Guatemala where he received a degree in veterinary science.

Mary Hamlin is also mentioned in the story of a Mercy Sister in Nicaragua: see Julia Liblich, *Sisters: Lives of Devotion and Defiance* (New York: Ballantine Books, 1992), 30–85. Most of "Revolution of the Heart: A Missionary Comes of Age," a chapter in Liblich's book, presents the work of Mary Aileen Dame, a Mercy Sister from Manchester, New Hampshire, who went to Cartago, Colombia, in the early 1960s. After studying midwifery for a year, she moved to Panama for a year and, after more medical study and practice in Mexico, served in Grenada from 1983 to 1985; she then went to Nicaragua. The tone of the chapter is generally critical and caustic toward ecclesial authority, but more so on the part of the author than Dame.

26. Scheck, "Reminiscences of Our Work in Nicaragua," unnumbered page.

27. Florian Ruskamp to Mr. Hudepohl, Puerto Cabezas, Nicaragua, 22 December 1962, Maryknoll folder (1962–63), LAB, ACUA. He refers to a book edited by John Considine, *The Missionary's Role in Socio-economic Betterment* (New York: Newman Press, 1960). Ruskamp was born in Olean, Nebraska, ordained in 1945, and missioned to Bluefields in September 1946. In 1969 he resided in Managua and worked on religious life, pastoral renewal, and integration within the Nicaraguan Church.

28. "Chronicles, 1965–1966," p. 19, CSAA.

29. "Chronicles, 1967–1968," p. 26, CSAA.

30. Emily Schug, CSA, to Sr. John Baptist (CSA administrator in the United States), Mexico, 23 October 1969, Mexico City folder (1964–75), CSAA. Schug was in Mexico while studying Spanish and taught catechetics. Other aspects of Agnesian history in Central America were provided by Emily Schug, CSA, Rosa Inés Silva, CSA, and Patricia Hayes, CSA, interviews by author.

31. Scheck, "Reminiscences of Our Work in Nicaragua," unnumbered page.

32. "Chronicles, 1966–1967," p. 23, CSAA.

33. "Chronicles, 1967–1968," p. 28, CSAA.

34. Sister Eileen (Mahony) Waspam, 25 June 1974, to My Dear Family and Friends (copy), Historical Accounts of Missions folder, Correspondence — Nicaragua, 1962–71, CSAA.

35. A barrio team community was formed in Managua in 1971, called Barrio Riguero. Uriel Molina, OFM, three Agnesians (Nancy Chow, Bertha Bumann, and Colette Hartman), and nine male university students from wealthy families worked to form other Christian communities among the six barrios in the parish of fifteen thousand people. An example of recent emphasis on indigenous formation is Gregory Smutko, OFMCap, "Toward a New Paradigm in Spiritual Formation: One Example, The Miskito Nation," *Missiology* 20 (January 1992): 55–68.

36. Father Joe Martin to Mother Catalina, 24 January 1971, folder 662.2, no. 26, Joseph Martin Correspondence 1965–73, Sisters of St. Joseph Archives.

37. "Chronicles, 1978–1979," p. 26, CSAA.

38. Maureen Courtney, CSA, to Sister Judith Schmidt, CSA, 26 September 1982, CSAA.

This letter was written three years after the revolution, but it is clear that tensions still existed.

39. Credo, Agnesian meeting in Nicaragua, November 1979, South American and Central America Missions, CSAA.

40. "Bishops' Statement of Solidarity on Human Rights: Chile and Brazil," 14 February 1974, in Hugh J. Nolan, ed., *Pastoral Letters of the United States Catholic Bishops,* vol. 3 (Washington, D.C.: U.S. Catholic Conference, 1987), 453–55.

41. *Congressional Record,* Extensions of Remarks, 9 October 1974, E6387. See related articles and documentation on the issue of the CIA and its use of missionaries in the USCMA Archives 78/2, MMA.

42. *Congressional Record,* Extensions of Remarks, 9 October 1974, E6387. The Catholics who signed the October document were Teresita Austin, SC; Madeline Conway, SND; William J. Davis, SJ (national director, Jesuit Social Ministries); Betty Ann Maheu, MM; William McIntire, MM; Hugh O'Rourke, SSC; Mary Reynold, OP; Janet Wahl, RSM; and James Zelinski, OFMCap.

43. Philip Agee, *Inside the Company: CIA Diary* (London: A. Lane, 1975); John D. Marks and Victor Marchetti, *The CIA and the Cult of Intelligence* (New York: Alfred A. Knopf, 1975).

44. Donal Ehr, SVD, to William Colby, 29 July 1975, USCMA Archives 78/2, MMA. See also Richard L. Rashke, "CIA Funded, Manipulated Missionaries," *National Catholic Reporter* (1 August 1975): 1, 16–17.

45. *Congressional Record* 121 (15 December 1975).

46. CIA resolution reported in *Congressional Record* 122 (25 May 1976), regarding S.R. 7901–S.R. 7902. This issue includes copies of the correspondence between Hatfield and Bush on the subject from January and May 1976.

47. See Senator Mark Hatfield to Sr. Ann Gormly, assistant to the executive secretary, USCMC, 9 June 1976, box 78/2, CIA and Missionaries (1974–76), USCMA Archives, MMA.

48. In March and April 1980, Anthony Bellagamba, USCMC director, appeared before the Senate Select Committee on Intelligence with respect to the National Intelligence Act of 1980 H.R. 6588. See box 78/3, CIA and Missionaries (1979–80), USCMA Archives, MMA.

49. "CIA Recruitment and the Church," *Christian Century,* 13 March 1996, 285–86; Arthur Jones, "Same Old CIA Out to Fix Image," *National Catholic Reporter* (26 April 1996): 4–5.

50. The conference held in 1963 was published in William J. Richardson, MM, ed., *The Modern Mission Apostolate: A Symposium* (Maryknoll, N.Y.: Maryknoll Publications, 1965).

51. Lawrence Nemer, SVD, interview by author.

52. The gathering took place in Rome from 27 September to 26 October 1974. See *Synod of Bishops — 1974* (Washington, D.C.: U.S. Catholic Conference, 1975) for the "interventions" of the U.S. Bishops.

53. The August 1980 USCMC study appears in "Report on Questionnaire from Mission Coordinators Re: Returned Missioners," USCMA File 77/6, MMA. The study by Christopher Farrelly, SSC, "Missionary Spirituality in the World Today — From a Columban Perspective" (M.A. thesis, Jesuit School of Theology, Berkeley, Calif., 1987), reported that 72 percent of Columban priests ordained between 1967 and 1982 responded to questionnaires he had sent out. Farrelly sought to identify the relationship between spiritual resources and the actual practice of mission life in one mission society, especially with respect to the missionaries' original vision of mission and what had happened to them through the years. One section of the questionnaire asked for responses on emotional, intellectual, aesthetic, spiritual, recreational, communication, sexual, and work issues related to mission. Informal discussions with other mission congregations offered reason to believe that the results of this study are not unique

to the Columban Fathers, but that they could apply to other mission congregations, at least to men's groups.

54. The letter was signed by twenty-eight Anglican and Roman Catholic missionaries and dated September 1968, Record Group 20/4, USCMA, MMA.

55. William T. Wood, SJ, interview by author.

56. See Renny Golden and Michael McConnel, *Sanctuary: The New Underground Railroad* (Maryknoll, N.Y.: Orbis Books, 1986), appendix 2. The letter was signed on 23 January 1985. The Sanctuary Movement revived the medieval custom of providing safety in a church building to those who thought themselves unjustly treated by the government. For the history of developments in the mid-1980s beginning with the work of James and Pat Corbett, see Robert Tomsho, *The American Sanctuary Movement* (Austin: Texas Monthly Press, 1987).

57. Many stories of the fear, torture, and death of poor and indigenous people with whom missionaries worked appear in the early chapters of Lernoux, *People of God*.

58. Patricia Hayes, CSA, interview by author. The young man healed, and occasionally Hayes hears from him. At the time of the interview, Hayes was codirector of the Cross-Cultural Training Center sponsored by Maryknoll in Chicago.

59. Among the many books featuring U.S. men and women killed in Central America and including excerpts from their letters are Ana Carrigan, *Salvador Witness: The Life and Calling of Jean Donovan* (New York: Simon & Schuster, 1984); Phyllis Zagano, *Ita Ford: Missionary Martyr* (New York: Paulist Press, 1996); James Guadalupe Carney, *To Be a Christian Is to Be a Revolutionary* (San Francisco: Harper & Row, 1987); Stanley Rother, *The Shepherd Cannot Run: Letters of Stanley Rother, Missionary and Martyr,* ed. David Monahan (Oklahoma City: Archdiocese of Oklahoma City, 1984); and Stephen Markham, FSC, *Memorial to James Alfred Miller, FSC, of the Winona Province* (Winona, Minn.: St. Mary's Press, n.d.).

Donna Whitson Brett and Edward T. Brett, *Murdered in Central America: The Stories of Eleven U.S. Missionaries* (Maryknoll, N.Y.: Orbis Books, 1988), include Catholic and Protestant missionaries in their work. Albert Nevins, MM, *American Martyrs from 1542* (Huntington, Ind.: Our Sunday Visitor Press, 1987), contains brief biographies of 146 women and men who were martyred in the present-day United States from 1542 until 1985. "An American Martyrology," *Catholic Historical Review* 6 (January 1921): 495–516, lists by date, names, and places the persons who died (usually) at the hands of Native Americans, though Bishop John Neumann and Elizabeth Seton, who were not martyrs, are also listed.

60. The event was noted by a variety of newspapers and magazines. See, for example, "The Martyrs of El Salvador," *America* (20 December 1980): 401, and follow-up letters to the editor; Marcella Hoesl, MM, "Reflections on the Life and Death of Maura Clarke, Ita Ford, Dorothy Kazel and Jean Donovan," *Missiology* 9 (October 1981): 389–92. The deaths led also to the formation of the Religious Task Force on Central America, an organization which continued into the 1990s.

61. Emily Schug, CSA, "Personal Thoughts on Maureen's and Teresa's Death, January 1, 1990," contained in papers written by Nicaraguan or North American Agnesians who have ministered in Nicaragua, gathered for CSA history, CSAA.

62. A list of their activities, though not the names of the women, appears in the "Grail Institute for Overseas Service: Confidential Report," October 1960, Grailville Archives, Loveland, Ohio, courtesy of Janet Kalven.

63. Alden V. Brown, *The Grail Movement and American Catholicism, 1940–1975* (Notre Dame, Ind.: University of Notre Dame Press, 1989), 76–77.

64. Ibid., 147.

65. Among the places where the history of the U.S. Catholic Mission Council appears are William G. Connare, "U.S. Catholic Mission Council," *Worldmission* 23, no. 4 (1972): 19–25; and Staff of the National Office, "The United States Catholic Mission Council, 1967–80, First Draft," May 1980, USCMA Archives, MMA. For an example of the rethinking, see Donal O'Mahony, SSC, "Missions and Organization," in J. Franklin Ewing, "Global Mis-

sion of the Church," 1962 conference proceedings, typescript copy, pp. VIII-6–8, USCMA Archives, MMA.

66. The proceedings were published in Frederick A. McGuire, CM, ed., *The New Missionary Church* (Baltimore: Helicon, 1964).

67. The U.S. Bishops' 1971 document on mission activity also referred to its part in the development of the U.S. Catholic Mission Council, whose aim was "to provide a forum and organ for the evaluation, coordination and fostering in the United States of the world-wide missionary effort of the Catholic Church" (National Conference of Catholic Bishops, "Statement on the Missions," in Nolan, ed., *Pastoral Letters,* 3:296). The statement was taken from the USCMC bylaws.

68. The Grail, *The Laity and the International Scene* (Loveland, Ohio: Grailville, 1957).

69. Staff of the National Office, "United States Catholic Mission Council."

70. Simon Smith, SJ, interview by author. The unresolved issue of authority and "control" continued to bring tension among members of the council throughout its ten-year history.

71. An overview of the Inter-American Meetings of Religious appears in Canadian Religious Conference, *Religious in the Local Church* (n.p.: Canadian Religious Conference, 1981), 91–110. The book includes the major talks and conclusions of the Fourth Inter-American Meeting held in Santiago, Chile, 16–23 November 1980.

72. Segundo Galilea, "Latin America in the Medellín and Puebla Conferences: An Example of Selective and Creative Reception of Vatican II," in Giuseppe Alberigo et al., eds., *The Reception of Vatican II* (Washington, D.C.: The Catholic University of America Press, 1987), assessed the impact of the work of these missionaries and of Vatican II in Latin America.

73. In addition to Ivan Illich's 1967 critique in *America,* see James A. Clark, "Placing U.S. Personnel in Latin America," *Review for Religious* 28 (1969): 879-85, and *Should Priests Be Sent to Latin America?* (Washington, D.C.: U.S. Catholic Conference, 1971).

74. Published proceedings appear in *Priests and Religious for Latin America: Proceedings and Conclusions* (Washington, D.C.: U.S. Catholic Conference, Division for Latin America, 1971); Canadian Religious Conference, *Religious in the Local Church*; and *Inter-American Papers Presented at the VI Inter-American Conference of Religious of the Americas* (Silver Spring, Md.: Conference of Major Superiors of Men and the Leadership Conference of Women Religious, 1995).

75. The members of the planning committee were Alan McCoy, OFM, president of the Conference of Major Superiors of Men; Anthony Bellagamba; Ann Gormly; Joseph Nangle from the U.S. Mission Council; Virginia Unsworth, SC; Barbara Hendricks, MM, of the Global Ministry Committee of the Leadership Conference of Women Religious; Richard John, OSC, of the Conference of Major Superiors of Men Mission Committee; and Simon Smith, SJ.

Smith, former faculty member at the Jesuit school in Baghdad and director of the Jesuit Missions Secretariat from 1975 to 1984, was a major influence in moving the Jesuit "faith and justice" agenda from their General Chapter to the three sessions. On his strong recommendation, the USCMC, which had been asked to plan the meetings, invited the Center of Concern to develop the process for the gatherings.

76. Philip Devlin, CSC, to committee members, 15 September 1976, USCMA Archives 74/2, MMA. Information about these meetings also obtained from Simon Smith, interview by author.

77. One example occurred in 1973 in Cambridge, Massachusetts, when Howard Gray, SJ, rector of Weston School of Theology, made an impact on the Jesuit community when he chose to live with a group of returned missionaries. The men were conscious of the high level of consumerism present in the United States and decided to live an intentionally simple and poor way of life.

78. See, for example, William McIntire, MM, to Ann Gormly, 9 May 1977, USCMA Archives 74/2, MMA, and Simon Smith interview.

79. Outline appears in USCMA Archives 74/3, MMA.
80. Joseph Holland, "Background Paper for *Convivencia,*" 1977, pp. 6–8, USCMA Archives 74/6, MMA.
81. Barbara Hendricks, MM, to author, 27 February 1997.
82. Frederick McGuire comments on this in Costello, *Mission to Latin America,* 196.
83. Niles Kauffman, OFMCap, interview by author.
84. This point is made explicitly in John Considine, "New Spirit for Our Time," *A New Spirit for a New Age,* 1961, Mission Secretariat File, LAB, ACUA.
85. For an overview of these effects, see Ricardo Ramirez, CSB, "Medellín and Puebla from a U.S. Perspective," in Edward Cleary, OP, ed., *Path from Puebla: Significant Documents of the Latin American Bishops Since 1979* (Washington, D.C.: National Conference of Catholic Bishops, 1989), 10–21.
86. Information obtained from William D. McCarthy, MM, in his chronology of significant dates for Latin American missions, compiled 1 July 1996.
87. Dana Robert to author, 24 December 1996.
88. Carlotta Gilarde, CSJ, a missionary in Peru for thirty years, in referring to this phenomenon appeared skeptical of the value of such "experts." She remarked that when a person sees the effects of poverty, their vision is broadened. "You almost know more about it than those who write about it or intellectualize it" (interview by William Milhomme).
89. "Your Sisters in Peru" to "Dear Sisters," no date [c. 1970], pp. 1, 2, folder 662.3, no. 23, Letters to Congregation 1968–71, Sisters of St. Joseph Archives.

Chapter 10 /
U.S. Catholic Mission History: Themes and Threads, 1850–1980

1. For the evangelical and pastoral challenge presented by the continued diversity of the U.S. Catholic Church, see Marina Herrera, *A Strategic Plan to Prepare Ministers for the Multicultural Church: A Response to the Demographic Changes Facing Our Society and the Catholic Church in the 1990s and Beyond* (Washington, D.C.: Washington Theological Union, 15 June 1992).
2. Since 1974, missionaries themselves have identified several "trends" in mission. Among the sources noting trends, see Gerald H. Anderson and Thomas F. Stransky, CSP, eds., *Trends in Mission* (New York: Paulist Press, 1974–84), an eight-volume ecumenical and global project; and Joseph J. Shields, "Attitudes of American Women Religious Towards the Concept of Mission," research report submitted to the U.S. Catholic Mission Council (c. 1978). Mary Motte, FMM, and Joseph Lang, MM, *Mission in Dialogue: Sedos Research Seminar on the Future of Mission* (Maryknoll, N.Y.: Orbis Books, 1982), contains a wealth of insight about trends and sets an ambitious mission agenda for the future; see also Motte, *A Critical Examination of Mission Today: Research Project Report, Phase One* (Washington, D.C.: U.S. Catholic Mission Association, 1987). William Jenkinson and Helene O'Sullivan, eds., *Trends in Mission: Toward the Third Millennium* (Maryknoll, N.Y.: Orbis Books, 1992), compiled articles written over the last twenty-five years in celebration of the silver anniversary of SEDOS, an international consortium of seventy-two Catholic mission societies.
3. Anna Dengel, *Mission for Samaritans: A Survey of Achievements and Opportunities in the Field of Catholic Medical Missions* (Milwaukee: Bruce Publishing Company, 1945), 115. It will be remembered that Dengel understood medical missions not simply as a work of charity, but one of restitution, a "debt, which we, the white race, owe to the peoples subjected and exploited by our forefathers" (ibid., 5).
4. Mary Agnes Dickof, CSA, "Mission Work in Nicaragua," Historical Accounts of Missions folder, p. 12, CSAA.

5. Paul Wattson (1863–1940) and Mother Mary Francis Laurana White (1870–1935), both Episcopalians and attracted to the ideals of Francis of Assisi, founded the Society of the Atonement at Graymoor, New York, in 1898. The idea to form a society for evangelization came when, as a young man, Wattson's father heard the well-known Paulist, Clarence Walworth, speak at St. Mary's Cathedral in Baltimore. Mr. Wattson indicated to his son that the Episcopal Church needed a similar group of preachers, and the idea was born. White desired to live according to the Franciscan way of corporate poverty. Together White and Wattson understood that church unity was to be the mission of their society. In 1903, Wattson founded the *Lamp,* a magazine which appealed to Anglicans to return to the Roman Catholic Church. To hasten the reunion of all Christians, he established an eight-day time of prayer, the Church Unity Octave, held annually from 18 to 25 January. In 1909, the society was received into the Roman Catholic Church. Currently, the society publishes a newsletter, *Ecumenical Trends.* For biographical information, see D. Gannon, *Father Paul of Graymoor* (New York: Macmillan, 1951), and Mother Mary Francis Laurana White, *The Graymoorian,* 3d ed. (Garrison, N.Y.: Graymoor, 1928).

6. For the history of the Chicago Catholic mission programs, see Paul Bechtold, *Catholic Theological Union at Chicago: The Founding Years* (Chicago: Catholic Theological Union, 1993). The school started with four academic concentrations, one of which was cross-cultural transformation. James Scherer, professor at the Lutheran School of Theology, was one of the founding members of the school. The mission program at CTU was established in 1970 by four Divine Word Fathers: Eugene Ahner, John Boberg, Lawrence Nemer, and Donal Skerry.

7. For the history of the organizations, see Norman A. Horner, "The Association of Professors of Mission: The First Thirty-five Years, 1952–1987," *International Bulletin of Missionary Research* 11, no. 2 (1987): 120–24, and Wilbert R. Shenk, *The American Society of Missiology, 1972–1987* (Elkhart, Ind.: The American Society of Missiology, 1987). Donald M. Wodarz, SSC, joined Gerald H. Anderson and Ralph Winter on the first executive committee of ASM.

8. Andrew Walls, *The Missionary Movement in Christian History: Studies in the Transmission of Faith* (Maryknoll, N.Y.: Orbis Books, 1996), 221–40, here 230–31.

9. In addition to the source in chap. 6, n. 33, see also Barbara Welter, "She Hath Done What She Could: Protestant Women's Missionary Careers in Nineteenth-Century America," *American Quarterly* 30 (1978): 624–38; Barbara Hargrove, "Religion and the Changing Role of Women," *Annals of the American Academy of Political and Social Sciences* 480 (July 1985): 117–31; Ruth Tucker, "Female Mission Strategies: A Historical and Contemporary Perspective," *Missiology* 15 (January 1987): 73–89; Kwok Pui Lan, *Chinese Women and Christianity, 1860–1927* (Atlanta: Scholars Press, 1992); Leslie A. Flemming, ed., *Women's Work for Women: Missionaries and Social Change in Asia* (Boulder, Colo.: Westview Press, 1989); and Dana Robert, *American Women in Mission: A Social History of Mission Theory* (Macon, Ga.: Mercer University Press, 1997).

10. Overview articles which examine recent American Protestant mission history include Gerald H. Anderson, "American Protestants in Pursuit of Missions, 1886–1986," *International Bulletin of Missionary Research* 12 (July 1988): 98–118; Dana Robert, "From Missions to Mission to Beyond Missions: The Historiography of American Protestant Foreign Missions Since World War II," *International Bulletin of Missionary Research* 18 (October 1994): 146–55; and Mark Noll, "The Challenges of Contemporary Church History, the Dilemmas of Modern History, and Missiology to the Rescue," paper delivered at 15 June 1995 meeting of the American Society of Missiology.

11. Sister Augustine Kerby, SMSM, interview by author.

12. Bruno Hagspiel, *Wanted: Co-Missionaries* (Techny, Ill.: Mission Press, 1940), 6.

13. Born in Pittsburgh, Maria del Rey worked as a writer for the *Pittsburgh Press* before entering Maryknoll at age twenty-five. She served in Hawaii and the Philippines and took two trips abroad to produce books about missionary life. Another book in this same tradition is

Sister Mary Francis Louise, *Maryknoll Sisters: A Pictorial History* (New York: E. P. Dutton & Company, 1962).

14. *Annals of the Propagation of the Faith, Supplement to the American Edition* 66 (January–February 1903): 46, 47. A survey of 295 missionaries conducted almost sixty years later indicated that the top six missionary virtues recommended by respondents were prayer, patience, fraternal charity, spirit of sacrifice, humility, and the imitation of Christ. See Joseph A. McCoy, SM, *Advice from the Field* (Baltimore: Helicon, 1962), 177.

15. Representative sources indicating the progression from self-assurance to self-doubt include Paul Manna, translation and adaptation by Joseph McGlinchey, *The Workers Are Few* (Boston: Society for the Propagation of the Faith, 1921); Anton Huonder, SJ, "The Heroism of the Catholic Missionary," *Sermons and Lectures on the Missions* (Techny, Ill.: Mission Press, 1918), 88–96; Michael A. Mathis, CSC, "Three Marks of a Missionary," *The Bengalese* (March 1933): 24–26, 30; James E. Walsh, MM, *Maryknoll Spiritual Directory* (Maryknoll, N.Y.: Field Afar Press, 1947); Sister Jeanne Marie Lyons, MM, *Means of Fostering the Missionary Vocation in the Catholic Primary and Secondary Schools* (Washington, D.C.: The Catholic University of America Press, 1941); Paul Manna, PIME, and Nicholas Maestrini, PIME, *Forward with Christ: Thoughts and Reflections on Vocations to the Foreign Missions* (Westminster, Md.: Newman Press, 1954), which is an updated version of Paul Manna's 1921 work cited in this note; Paul F. D'Arcy, *Constancy of Interest Factors Patterns within the Specific Vocation of Foreign Missioners* (Washington, D.C.: The Catholic University of America Press, 1954); James E. Walsh, MM, *Blueprint of a Missionary Vocation* (Maryknoll, N.Y.: Maryknoll Publications, [c. 1952]); George L. Kane, *Why I Became A Missioner* (Westminster, Md.: Newman Press, 1958); Albert J. Nevins, MM, "Reappraisal of Mission Vocation," in William J. Richardson, ed., *Reappraisal: Prelude to Change* (Maryknoll, N.Y.: Maryknoll Publications, 1965); Maria del Rey, MM, *Bernie Becomes a Nun* (New York: Farrar, Straus & Company, 1957); Peter Hebblethwaite, "Why Missions?" *Catholic World* 205 (September 1967): 335–39; Graham P. McDonnell, MM, *Meaning of a Missioner* (Maryknoll, N.Y.: Maryknoll Publications, 1967); Charles J. Beirne, SJ, "Missionaries Among the Unemployed?" *Worldmission* 19, no. 1 (1968): 24–27; R. Pierce Beaver, "Missionary Image Today: Internal Pressures for Change, Self-Understanding of Church and Mission," in John T. Boberg, SVD, and James A. Scherer, eds., *Mission in the '70s: What Direction?* (Chicago: Chicago Cluster of Theological Schools, 1972); Donald J. Casey, MM, "Change in the Missioner," *Worldmission* 23, no. 1 (1972): 44–47; and Alfonso M. Nebreda, SJ, "Conversion of the Missionary," *Worldmission* 23, no. 3 (1972): 6–10.

16. J. M. Lelen, "The Missionary Vocation," *Catholic Missions* 10 (April 1916): 86.

17. See, for example, these qualities identified in James E. Walsh, *Maryknoll Spiritual Directory*, 145.

18. Mathis, "The Three Marks of a Missionary," 25.

19. Thomas Calkins, OSM, "Servites in Zululand," typescript with handwritten marginal comments by Edward Kinch, OSM, Servite Archives, Chicago.

20. James E. Walsh, *Maryknoll Spiritual Directory*, 145.

21. John Tauler, *The Sermons and Conferences of John Tauler*, introduction and index by Walter Elliott (Brookland Station, Washington, D.C.: Apostolic Mission House, 1910); John J. Burke, ed., *St. Teresa of Jesus of the Order of Our Lady of Carmel*, introduction by Walter Elliott (New York: Columbus Press, 1911).

22. For the development of body imagery in relation to the resurrection, see Caroline Walker Bynum, *The Resurrection of the Body in Western Christianity* (New York: Columbia University Press, 1995). On the propensity for images, see Anthony J. Gittins, "Missionary Myth Making," *Verbum SVD* 27, no. 2 (1986): 185–211.

23. Sister M. Pauline Grady, ASC, *Ruma: Home and Heritage, the Story of a Convent in Rural Southern Illinois, 1876–1984* (Ruma, Ill.: privately printed, 1984).

24. See, for example, the idea in James E. Walsh, *Blueprint for a Missionary Vocation*,

42, 44. The trend toward a separation of "mission" from the ordinary life of the Christian or of the parish is seen already in Joseph Wissel, *The Redemptorist on the American Missions* (1920; reprint, New York: Arno Press, 1978). Wissel asked how "wayward souls" are to be "reclaimed." He responded that the "ordinary ministry" of the parish priest could no longer reach them and, thus, the "extraordinary ministry" of religious communities was required (ibid., 7–8).

25. J. Paul Spaeth, ed., *Perspectives in Religion and Culture* (Cincinnati: Catholic Students Mission Crusade, Paladin Press, 1957).

26. Vatican II, "Decree on Missionary Activity," par. 9.

27. Michael Collins Reilly, SJ, *Spirituality for Mission* (Maryknoll, N.Y.: Orbis Books, 1978).

28. Michael A. Mathis, CSC, "Proposal for Graduate Program in Mission Formation," to Alfred Cousineau, CSC (superior general), 24 March 1941, Holy Cross Fathers and Brothers Archives. Document obtained from archivist, William Blum, CSC. Mathis, well-read in the history of mission, modeled his program on the Carmelite and Franciscan mission schools founded in Rome in the eighteenth century.

29. Ibid., 4.

30. John J. Considine, "An Outline of Missiography," *Missionary Academia* 1, no. 8 (1944).

31. "Franciscan View of Missiology," in *Franciscan Education Conference Proceedings, Washington, D.C., June 1946* (Washington, D.C.: Franciscan Education Conference, 1946), 1–19.

32. Louis J. Luzbetak, SVD, to author, 31 March 1997.

33. Cooper, a correspondent with ethnologist Wilhelm Schmidt, SVD, developed an interest in anthropology from his canoeing trips, where he met Native Americans. He did periodic work at the Smithsonian Bureau of American Ethnology. Information about Cooper obtained from correspondence with Regina Herzfeld, Cooper's student and now professor emerita, department of anthropology, Catholic University of America. For a description and analysis of Cooper's work in relation to the scientific theories of the time, see Elizabeth McKeown, "When Adam Was a Primitive Man," unpublished paper, 1995. Elizabeth McKeown, "From *Pascendi* to *Primitive Man:* The Apologetics and Anthropology of John Montgomery Cooper," *U.S. Catholic Historian* 13 (Winter 1995): 1–22, provides an analysis of Cooper's view on "social hygiene" areas (birth control, eugenics, etc.) of the post–World War I period.

34. C. Joseph Nuesse to author, 17 October 1994.

35. For his plans on this, see "The Glaring Lacuna in Catholic Education," c. 1962, 10/6 Hoffman File, LAB, ACUA. See also Ronan Hoffman, OFMConv, "The Development of Mission Theology in the Twentieth Century," *Theological Studies* 23 (1962): 419–41. Hoffman's basic premise was that there was no longer a "missionary apostolate" but only a mission of the Church, engaged in by the entire Church.

36. Louis J. Luzbetak, SVD, "Toward an Applied Missionary Anthropology," *Anthropological Quarterly* 34 (1958): 165–76.

37. Louis J. Luzbetak, SVD, *The Church and Cultures: Applied Anthropology for the Church Worker* (Techny, Ill.: Mission Press, 1963); Luzbetak, *The Church and Cultures: New Perspectives in Missiological Anthropology* (Maryknoll, N.Y.: Orbis Books, 1988); Luzbetak, "Cross-Cultural Missionary Preparation," *Trends and Issues: Missionary Formation* (Epworth, Iowa: Divine Word College, 1984), 61–79. For the Divine Word Missionary emphasis on applied science for missionaries, see a *Festschrift* issue on the Divine Word Missionaries in Papua, New Guinea, from 1896 to 1996, *Verbum SVD* 37 (1996); and Ernest Brandewie, "Ethnology and Missionaries: The Case of the Anthropos Institute and Wilhelm Schmidt," in Darrell I. Whiteman, ed., *Missionaries, Anthropologists, and Cultural Change* (Williamsburg, Va.: Department of Anthropology, College of William and Mary, 1985), 369–86. Biographical information appears in Louis J. Luzbetak, SVD, "My Pilgrimage in Mis-

sion," *International Bulletin of Missionary Research* 16 (July 1992): 124-28. Information also obtained from Luzbetak, interview by author.

38. Ewing did field work in Auriesville, New York, at the Shrine of the North American Martyrs, staking out the exact delineation of the Indian village. Little information about the origins of the Fordham Mission Institute is available in the J. Franklin Ewing Papers at Fordham University Archives, Bronx, New York, or at the Jesuit Provincial Archives, Bronx, New York. John Considine has a few items in his papers in box 9/8, 1954, John Considine Writings, MMA. Biographical information on Ewing provided to author by T. Gerard Connolly, SJ, Fordham University archivist, and Gilbert J. Scott, SJ, New York Province.

For Ewing's approach, see J. Franklin Ewing, SJ, "Applied Anthropology for the Missionary," *Worldmission* 2 (February 1951): 105-7; Ewing, "Anthropology and the Training of Missionaries," *Catholic Educational Review* 55 (May 1957): 300–311; and Elsa M. Chaney, "They Go Prepared to Foreign Lands," *Catholic World* 189 (June 1959): 11–14.

39. Edward L. Murphy (1904–73) was born in Jamaica Plain, Massachusetts, and entered the Jesuits in 1920. In the course of his studies he was sent to the Philippines and taught at the famous Jesuit secondary school, the Ateneo de Manila. After his ordination, he studied missiology at the Gregorian University in Rome. He returned to Weston, Massachusetts, and taught ascetical theology and sacred eloquence, "in both of which fields he excelled." Between 1948 and 1955, he worked in a Jesuit parish in Boston, where he became famous for retreats and days of recollection for workingmen. He was on the editorial staff of *Jesuit Missions* from 1955 to 1960, then returned to Boston to teach theology at Boston College and continued work with the laboring class. His main published work is *Teach Ye All Nations: The Principles of Catholic Missionary Work* (New York: Benziger, 1958). Information on Murphy obtained from correspondence with John Walsh, SJ, Campion Center, Weston, Massachusetts, 8 September 1994.

40. J. Franklin Ewing, "For a Better Missionary," p. 6, J. Franklin Ewing Papers, Fordham University Archives. Joseph Fitzpatrick, SJ, taught sociology at Fordham at the same time. See chap. 8 for more on Fitzpatrick.

41. Ewing, "Anthropology and the Training of Missionaries," 307.

42. J. Franklin Ewing to Vincent T. O'Keefe, SJ, 21 November 1960, Fordham University Archives.

43. For a list of titles from these conferences, see the bibliographies in the works edited by J. Franklin Ewing. For a woman's perspective on formation in the 1950s, see Mother Sebastian (Holy Rosary Sister), "Training of Missionaries for a New Era," in *Proceedings of the Mission Secretariat* (Washington, D.C.: The Mission Secretariat, 1954).

44. Joseph A. McCoy, SM, *Advice from the Field* (Baltimore: Helicon, 1962).

45. "Mission World," *Worldmission* 18 (Fall 1967): 54–57.

46. The Divine Word Missionaries were founded by intent to be international and from the start had mission houses in Holland, though mainly for native speakers of German, Austria-Hungary, and Polish-speaking Silesia (Louis J. Luzbetak, SVD, to author, 31 March 1997).

47. For current observations about the relationship between mission formation and education of missionaries, see Mary Motte, FMM, "A Roman Catholic Perspective on Missiological Education," in J. Dudley Woodberry, Charles Van Engen, and Edgar J. Elliston, eds., *Missiological Education for the 21st Century: The Book, the Circle, and the Sandals* (Maryknoll, N.Y.: Orbis Books, 1996).

48. "Mission Exhibit in Cincinnati," *Woodstock Letters* 62 (1933): 448.

49. "Lengthy Account of the Mission [of Belize]," *Woodstock Letters* 39 (1910): 335.

50. Thomas M. Calkins, OSM, *Umfundisi, Missioner to the Zulus* (Milwaukee: Bruce Publishing Company, 1959), 12.

51. An unnamed Maryknoll Sister missioned to China reflected that because women had to deal with the "humdrum" daily activities of life, they were more able to identify with the people they served. This Maryknoller viewed men as better speakers, but interested in

administration, and, thus, more lonely than the women (Penny Lernoux, *Hearts on Fire* [Maryknoll, N.Y.: Orbis Books, 1993], 52).

52. Brother Florentius, CSC, "The Missionary Brothers," in *To Defend the Cross: The Story of the Fourth General Convention of the Catholic Students Mission Crusade Held at the University of Notre Dame* (Cincinnati: Catholic Students Mission Crusade, 1924), 123, 124.

53. Fulton J. Sheen, "The Woman Who Reaches for Souls," *Worldmission* 3 (1952): 259–64, here 260.

54. Ibid., 261.

55. *Worldmission* 15 (Spring 1964): 21–30.

56. Robert Streit, *Catholic Missions in Figures and Symbols* (New York: Society for the Propagation of the Faith, 1927), 77.

57. An American Woman, "Chiefly among Women," *Catholic World* 21 (June 1875): 324–40.

58. Sister Mary Jane Knight, CSJ, to Dear Sisters, 21 March 1970, folder 662.2, no. 23, Letters to Congregation 1968–71, Sisters of St. Joseph Archives.

59. A short overview of the history of mission theology to Vatican Council II appears in Andrew V. Seumois, OMI, "The Evolution of Mission Theology among Roman Catholics," in Gerald Anderson, ed., *The Theology of Christian Mission* (New York: McGraw Hill, 1961), 122–34. See also Ferguson, "Paradigm Shift in the Theology of Mission"; Michael Amaladoss, "Mission: From Vatican II into the Coming Decade," *International Review of Mission* 79 (April 1990): 211–22; and Thomas F. Stransky, "From Vatican II to *Redemptoris Missio*," in Charles Van Engen et al., eds., *The Good News of the Kingdom: Mission Theology for the Third Millennium* (Maryknoll, N.Y.: Orbis Books, 1993), 137–47.

60. *Ad Gentes* ("Decree on the Church's Missionary Activity"), no. 2, in Austin Flannery, OP, general editor, *The Documents of Vatican II* (Northport, N.Y.: Costello Publishing Company, 1992), 814.

61. Considine to Mother Florence, SL (copy), 11 January 1961, Major Religious Superiors, Conference of 1961 folder, LAB, ACUA.

62. Bishop Harold Henry to Fulton J. Sheen, 11 September 1963 (copy), 6A 62, Kwangju Archdiocese Papers, CFA.

63. John F. Clarkson, SJ, "The ABC's of Missiology," *Worldmission* 3 (1952): 337–52; Hoffman, "The Development of Mission Theology in the Twentieth Century." Hoffman no longer used the scholastic terminology two years later in his "Ecumenism and Mission Theology," *Worldmission* 15, no. 3 (1964): 48–64.

64. William B. Frazier, MM, "Guidelines for a New Theology of Mission," *Worldmission* 18, no. 4 (1967): 16–24. This article was reprinted in Gerald H. Anderson and Thomas F. Stransky, eds., *Mission Trends,* no. 1 (New York: Paulist Press, 1974), 23–26.

65. Calvert Alexander, SJ, *The Missionary Dimension: Vatican II and the World Apostolate* (Milwaukee: Bruce Publishing Company, 1967).

66. Eugene Hillman, CSSp, *The Church as Mission,* with a foreword by Karl Rahner (New York: Herder and Herder, 1965). Hillman relates the story of Rahner's talk at Weston School of Theology, wherein he spoke of the world church as the trend of the future. "I was saying the 'catholicization' of the church, but he said the 'world church' and everyone latched on to that. In that lecture, [Rahner] talked about the problem I had discussed with him about the Masai people, who could not become Christians until they sent away some of their wives. So he addressed that very issue in his talk." Hillman commented that when he had first discussed the issue of polygamy with Rahner, the European "just laughed at me and said, 'Oh, no, there's nothing we can do about that' " (Eugene Hillman, interview by author). See also Eugene Hillman, "Towards the Catholicization of the Church," *American Ecclesiastical Review* 168 (February 1974): 122–34. For further biographical information, see Eugene Hillman, "My Pilgrimage in Mission," *International Bulletin of Missionary Research* 18 (October 1994): 162–66.

67. Eugene Hillman, CSSp, *Polygamy Reconsidered: African Plural Marriage and the Christian Churches* (Maryknoll, N.Y.: Orbis Books, 1975). See also his *The Wider Ecumenism* (New York: Herder and Herder, 1968); *Many Paths: A Catholic Approach to Religious Pluralism* (Maryknoll, N.Y.: Orbis Books, 1989); and *Toward an African Christianity: Inculturation Applied* (New York: Paulist Press, 1993).

68. Hillman interview.

69. Louis J. Luzbetak, SVD, to author, 31 March 1997.

Mission Periodicals

Nineteenth Century to 1960s,
with Emphasis on Missions Abroad,
Published in the United States
by Catholic Mission Groups

Annals of Our Lady of the Sacred Heart
1907(?) vol. 1
replaced in 1909 by *St. Joseph's Annual*
Watertown, New York

Annals of the Congregation of the Mission
Vincentian Priests and Sisters of Charity
mentioned in 1909

Annals of the Holy Childhood
1915 vol. 1, new series

Annals of the Society for the Propagation of the Faith
See *Catholic Missions*

The Apostle
monthly (by 1930)
Marianhill Fathers
articles and letters from South Africa

Apostle of Mary
1904 vol. 1–
monthly
letters from overseas Marianist missionaries
The Brothers of Mary, Dayton, Ohio

The Bengalese
1919 vol. 1–1956 vol. 47
Holy Cross Fathers and Sisters
information on and fund-raising for their mission in Dacca

The Bugle Call
1921 vol. 1–
bimonthly
Sisters of Providence, St. Mary-of-the-Woods, Indiana
fund-raising for their Chinese mission

Call of the Missions
1920s
published by the Diocese of Pittsburgh Society for the Propagation of the Faith

Catholic Missions
1907 vol. 1–1949 vol. 42
New York, national office of the Society for the Propagation of the Faith

Children of Providence
1890 vol. 1–1930 vol. 40
Sisters of Charity, Mount St. Vincent-on-the-Hudson, New York
quarterly, then annual; literary publication to obtain funds for the New York archdiocesan
    mission in the Bahamas
see also *League of Divine Providence*

The Christian Family
monthly (by 1930)
Divine Word Missionaries

Draw Net
1920 vol. 1–1949 vol. 29
Sisters of Notre Dame de Namur
information on and support of their China missions

Echo from Africa
Jesuits, St. Louis (by 1930)
letters from African missionaries and reports on mission aid by sodality of St. Peter Claver

The Evangelist
1916 vol. 1–
Albany, N.Y., Society for the Propagation of the Faith

Extension Society Magazine
April 1906 vol. 1–present
    Madonna
    1917–18 vol. 1
    combines Extension's "Order of Martha" and "Child Apostle" columns

Far Away Missions
monthly (by 1930)
Providence, Rhode Island
Franciscan Missionaries of Mary

The Far East
1919 vol. 1–
    Known in the United States after 1971 as *Columban Mission*
Society of St. Columban
St. Columbans (Bellevue), Nebraska

The Field Afar
1907 vol. 1–1959 vol. 53
    name changed to *Maryknoll* thereafter
    Maryknoll, Jr.
    1918 vol. 1–
    Revista Maryknoll
    Spanish edition of *Maryknoll* magazine, started in 1980

Franciscan Herald and Forum
1913 vol. 1–1970 vol. 49
monthly; Franciscan Missionary Union
edited for many years by Marion Habig, OFM

Good Work
1907 vol. 1–
begun by Bishop John Dunn, archdiocese of New York,
   Society for the Propagation of the Faith

Holy Ghost
1923 vol. 1–
Missionary Servants of the Blessed Trinity

Jesuit Missions
1927 vol. 1–1967 vol. 41
The forerunner to *Jesuit Missions* was the *Pilgrim,* begun in 1924, a publication centered
   on the Jesuit martyrs at Auriesville, New York

The Lamp
1903 vol. 1–
Franciscan Fathers of the Atonement, New York
"A Catholic monthly devoted to Church Unity and Missions"

LaSalette Missionary
monthly (by 1930)
missions sponsored by the LaSalette Fathers

League of Divine Providence
1890 vol. 1–1930 vol. 40
Sisters of Charity
fund-raising for missions to China
Sisters of Charity, Mount St. Vincent on Hudson, New York

The Little Missionary
1915 vol. 1–
published by the Society of the Divine Word Missionaries, Techny, Illinois, but intended for
   mission education in general, not for their society alone

Marist Missions
Marist Missionary Sisters
Waltham, Massachusetts
1936–39   published as *Alofa Malia* (Ave Maria in Futunian)
1945–50   published as *Marist Mission News*
1950–64   published as *Marist Missions*
1964–65   published as the *Marist*

Mary Immaculate
(by 1930)
Oblates of Mary Immaculate (Southern Province)

The Master's Work
bimonthly (by 1930)
missions of the missionary Sisters of the Holy Spirit, Techny, Illinois

The Medical Missionary
1927 vol. 1–1968, bimonthly; 1969–70, quarterly
Society of Catholic Medical Missionaries
scientific articles on mission method, especially medical work

Medical Mission News
(published by 1930)

Messenger of Our Lady of Africa
monthly (by 1930)

The Missionary
1898 vol. 1–1940s
magazine of the Catholic Missionary Union; begun by Paulist Fathers Andrew Doyle
    and Walter Elliott

Missionary Academia
(became *Mission Studies* which, with vol. 1, no. 2, became *Worldmission*)
1943 vol. 1–1949 vol. 7

The Mission Call
monthly (by 1930)
Sacred Heart Fathers and Brothers, Hales Corners, Wisconsin; articles on central Africa

Mission Message
1917 vol. 1–1930 vol. 14
Missionary Association of Catholic Women
Milwaukee

Our China Mission
quarterly (by 1930)
New York Province, OFMs

Our Missions
1921 vol. 1–
Divine Word Missionaries
Techny, Illinois
1919–21 published under the title, *Americanisches Familienblatt und Missions Bote*

The Paraclete
1912 vol. 1–
Holy Spirit Fathers, Cornwell Heights, Pennsylvania

The Patron
monthly (by 1930)
Holy Ghost Fathers in central Africa

St. Francis Home Journal
monthly (by 1930)
Puerto Rican Missions of American Capuchins

The Shield
1921 vol. 1–1971 vol. 50
Catholic Students Mission Crusade
Cincinnati
college, teacher, and junior editions

Sign
1920 vol. 1–present
The Passionist Fathers
Starting in 1933, vol. 13, monthly articles written by the Sisters of Charity, Convent Station,
    New Jersey, reporting their work in China

The Torch
monthly (by 1930)
Dominican Third Order members
articles on American Dominican missionaries in China

Ursuline Mission Service
1943–77
published to support Ursuline missions abroad; edited by Sister Marcella Difani, OSU; after this period publication reduced in scope

Woodstock Letters
1871 vol. 1–1969 vol. 98
Jesuit in-house publication. While technically not a mission publication, consistently provides more in-depth articles about the American Assistancy overseas missions than *Jesuit Missions*

Worldmission
1950 vol. 1–1981 vol. 33
National office of the Society for the Propagation of the Faith

Archives and Libraries

Archdiocese of Boston, Brighton, Massachusetts
    Record Group I 81, Richard Cardinal Cushing Papers
    Record Group III D 16, Society for the Propagation of the Faith File
    American Catholic Missionary Congress File

Archdiocese of Milwaukee
    Missionary Association of Catholic Women File
    St. Peter Claver Mission Society File
    St. Boniface Mission League File

Archdiocese of New York, Dunwoodie, Yonkers, New York
    John Cardinal Farley Papers
    Patrick Cardinal Hayes Papers

Catholic Theological Union Library, Chicago

The Catholic University of America, Washington, D.C.
    Annual Meetings of American Hierarchy
    National Catholic Welfare Conference/United States Catholic Conference Archives
        Record Group Executive Department VIII:
          Latin American Bureau File
        Missions File
    Charles F. Aiken Papers
    John Montgomery Cooper Papers
    Rare Books Collection: SVD Pamphlets

Columban Fathers, Omaha, Nebraska
    Hanyang, China, File
    Harold Henry Papers
    Kwangju, Korea, File
    Books, periodicals, materials on foundation of the society and its history in China
        and Korea

Congregation of the Sisters of the Holy Cross, Indiana Province, Notre Dame, Indiana
    Holy Cross Sisters in India

Diocese of Tucson, Arizona
    Henry Granjon Papers
    Peter Bourgade Papers

Divine Word Missionaries, Techny, Illinois
    Clifford King Papers
    SVD Universities File
    Catholic University of Peking, Peiping, China papers and materials
    Harold Rigney Papers
    SVD Regions, China (general) folder
    Magazines, books related to Divine Word Missionary history and spirituality

Franciscan Sisters of Perpetual Adoration, La Crosse, Wisconsin
  China File

Georgetown University, Washington, D.C.
  Georgetown Special Collections:
    Francis A. Barnum Papers
  Jamaica Missions

Loyola University, Chicago
  Catholic Church Extension Society File
  Francis Clement Kelley Papers

Marist Mission Sisters Archives, Waltham, Massachusetts
  Missions in Oceania File

Marquette University, Milwaukee
  Sister Formation Conference/Religious Formation Conference Archives
    Sister Formation in Peru Papers
  Jesuit Archives, Wisconsin Province
    Sogang University, Seoul
  Bureau of Catholic Indian Missions Archives

Maryknoll Mission Archives, Maryknoll, New York
  Foundation of Maryknoll Papers
  James A. Walsh Papers
  Bernard Meyer Papers
  Mary Josephine Rogers Papers
  Maryknoll Sisters in Korea File
  John J. Considine Papers
  U.S. Catholic Mission Association, Mission Secretariat, U.S. Catholic Mission Conference
    Archives
  Rogers and Maryknoll Seminary Libraries

Paulist Fathers, St. Paul's College, Washington, D.C.
  Alexander P. Doyle Papers
  Americanism Papers
  Apostolic Mission House Records
  Catholic Missionary Union Papers
  Thomas Stransky, CSP Collection: responses to mission questionnaire, 1987
  Proceedings of the Catholic Missionary Conferences for 1901, 1904, 1906
  Walter Elliott Papers

Propaganda Fide Archives, Rome

Radcliffe College Archives, Schlesinger Library, Cambridge, Massachusetts
  Arthur and Elizabeth Schlesinger Library on the History of Women in America:
    Lillian and Clara Westropp Papers

Redemptorist Fathers and Brothers Archives, Brooklyn, New York, Baltimore Province
  James Edward McManus Papers
  Thomas Francis Reilly Papers
  Books, papers, magazines on Redemptorist missions in the Caribbean and in South
    America

School Sisters of St. Francis, Milwaukee
  Missions among Native Americans
  Latin America Missions

Secret Vatican Archives, Vatican City
 Apostolic Delegation, United States
 Secretary of State Collection

Sisters of Charity, Bronx, New York
 Bahamas Mission File

Sisters of Notre Dame de Namur, Ipswich, Massachusetts
 Mission to Japan File

Sisters of St. Agnes, Fond du Lac, Wisconsin
 Nicaragua File

Sisters of St. Francis of Assisi, Milwaukee
 China File

Sisters of St. Joseph, Brighton, Massachusetts
 Latin America File

Society for the Propagation of the Faith, National Office, New York
 Complete collection of *Catholic Missions*

Union Theological Seminary, New York
 Missionary Research Library (incorporated into regular holdings in the Union Theological
  Library)

United States Catholic Conference Library, Washington, D.C.

University of Dayton, Dayton, Ohio
 Brothers of Mary Archives
  China File
  Africa Missions
  Hawaii Missions

University of Notre Dame, Notre Dame, Indiana
 Catholic Students Mission Crusade File

Yale University, New Haven, Connecticut
 Day Missions Library

Interviews

Berg, Gretchen, OSF. Rochester, Minnesota. 16 January 1995. Telephone interview.

Carden, Catherine, MM. Ithaca, N.Y. 21 March 1995.

Cardillo, Alice, MM. Maryknoll, N.Y. 20 March 1995.

Dodd, Michael, SSC. Washington, D.C. 16 September 1994.

Dwyer, Michael F. St. Petersburg, Fla. 3 March 1995. Telephone interview.

Eisele, Albert. Washington, D.C. 14 September 1994.

Gilarde, Carlotta, CSJ. Taped interview of November 1994 provided by William Milhomme.

Hayes, Patricia, CSA. Fond du Lac, Wis. 12 December 1994.

Hillman, Eugene, CSSp. Newport, R.I. 30 October–1 November 1994.

Holecek, Francis. Lakewood, Calif. 6 October 1996. Telephone interview.

Kauffman, Niles, OFMCap. Milwaukee. 1 August 1996.

Kerby, Sr. Augustine, SMSM. Waltham, Mass. 4 November 1994.

Kinch, Edwin, OSM. Manila, Philippines. 16 October 1995, 14 May 1996. Taped interview in response to author's questions and correspondence.

Luzbetak, Louis, SVD. Techny, Ill. 15 July 1994.

McCaslin, Richard, SJ. Oshkosh, Wis. 19 April 1996.

McChesney, Robert, SJ. Washington, D.C. 12 September 1994.

McDonald, Ellen, MM. Maryknoll, N.Y. 21 March 1995.

McGrath, Marcos (Archbishop). Notre Dame, Ind. 27 March 1994. Telephone interview. Panama, 5 May 1995, taped interview sent in response to author's questions.

Maher, Eileen, SC. Bronx, N.Y. 13 March 1995.

Mahon, Leo. Chicago. 17 April 1995.

Maurice, John. Wausaukee, Wis. 18 January 1995. Telephone interview.

Milhomme, William. Boston. 12 November 1994.

Motte, Mary, FMM. Nashville. 2 June 1995.

Nemer, Lawrence, SVD. Chicago. 15 February 1995.

Pendergast, Carita, SC. Convent Station, N.J. 21 April 1995. Telephone interview.

Runnoe, Mary Jo. Greenfield, Wis. 16 May 1995.

Schug, Emily, CSA. Fond du Lac, Wis. 12 December 1994.

Silva Rosa Inés, CSA. Fond du Lac, Wis. 12 December 1994.

Smith, Simon, SJ. Brighton, Mass. 11 and 14 November 1994.

Tikalsky, Russell. Milwaukee. 23 January 1995.

Wagner, Wilbert, SVD. Cuernavaca, Mexico. 25 May 1995. Taped interview sent in response to author's questions.

Wood, William T., SJ. Bronx, N.Y. 20 March 1995.

Zywiec, David, OFMCap. Milwaukee. 1 August 1996.

Selected Bibliography
The Overseas Missionary Movement of the United States Catholic Church, 1850–1980

Agnes Immaculata, SND de Namur. *Profile History of the Ohio Province: Sisters of Notre Dame de Namur, 1901–1970*. Cincinnati: M. Rosenthal Company, 1974.

Ahlstrom, Sydney. *A Religious History of the American People*. Garden City, N.Y.: Image Books, 1975.

Alderson, Sister Julian. *Franciscans in Shantung, China, 1929–1949*. Milwaukee: Sisters of St. Francis, 1980.

Alexander, Calvert, SJ. *The Missionary Dimension: Vatican II and the World Apostolate*. Milwaukee: Bruce Publishing Company, 1967.

———. "Twenty-fifth Anniversary of Jesuit Missions." *Woodstock Letters* 80 (1951): 320–26.

Alexander, Richard. *A Missionary's Notebook*. Philadelphia: Catholic Standard and Times Publishing Company, 1908.

Alumnus. "An Impressive Aspect of the Catholic University of America." *American Ecclesiastical Review* 85 (November 1931): 520–24.

American Jesuits in Shanghai. *Portraits of China*. New York: Herder, 1950.

Anderson, Elizabeth Vanderzell, D. A. "Images of China for Americans, 1927–1950: The Missionaries' Dilemma." Ph.D. diss., Carnegie-Mellon University, 1990.

Anderson, Gerald H., et al., eds. *Mission Legacies: Biographical Studies of Leaders of the Modern Missionary Movement*. Maryknoll, N.Y.: Orbis Books, 1994.

Arbuckle, George. *Missionaries, Anthropologists, and Cultural Change*. Studies in Third World Societies. Williamsburg, Va.: College of William and Mary, 1985.

Arens, Bernard, SJ. *Handbuch der katholischen Missionen*. Freiburg and St. Louis: Herder, 1920.

Astore, William J., "American Catholic Encounters with Polygenism, Geology, and Evolutionary Theories from 1845 to 1875." *Catholic Historical Review* 82 (January 1996): 40–76.

Bacigalupo, Leonard, OFM. *The American Franciscan Missions in Central America: Three Decades of Christian Service*. Andover, Mass.: Charisma Press, 1980.

Bannon, John Francis, SJ. *The Missouri Province of Jesuits: A Mini-History*. St. Louis: The Missouri Province, 1977.

Barrett, William E. *The Red Lacquered Gate*. New York: Sheed and Ward, 1967.

Barry, Colman. *Upon These Rocks: Catholics in the Bahamas*. Collegeville, Minn.: St. John's University Press, 1973.

Bassham, Rodger. *Mission Theology, 1948–1975: Years of Worldwide Creative Tension — Ecumenical, Evangelical, and Roman Catholic*. Pasadena, Calif.: William Carey Library, 1979.

Bays, Daniel. *Christianity in China: From the Eighteenth Century to the Present*. Stanford, Calif.: Stanford University Press, 1996.

Beane, Marjorie Noterman. *From Framework to Freedom: A History of the Sister Formation Conference*. New York: University Press of America, 1993.

Beaver, R. Pierce. *American Protestant Women in World Mission: History of the First Feminist Movement in North America*. Grand Rapids, Mich.: Eerdmans, 1980.

————, ed. *American Missions in Bicentennial Perspective.* Pasadena, Calif.: William Carey Library, 1977.

Bechtle, Regina, SC, and John J. Rathschmidt, OFMCap. *Mission and Mysticism.* Maryknoll, N.Y.: Maryknoll School of Theology, 1987.

Bechtold, Paul, CP. *Catholic Theological Union at Chicago: The Founding Years.* Chicago: Catholic Theological Union, 1993.

Beidelman, Thomas O. *Colonial Evangelism: A Socio-historical Study of an East African Mission at the Grassroots.* Bloomington: Indiana University Press, 1982.

Bellagamba, Anthony. *Mission and Ministry in the Global Church.* Maryknoll, N.Y.: Orbis Books, 1992.

————, ed. *Baltimore 83: Experiences and Reflections on Mission.* Washington, D.C.: U.S. Catholic Mission Association, 1983.

Berbusse, Edward J., SJ. *The United States in Puerto Rico.* Chapel Hill: University of North Carolina Press, 1966.

Berg, Servatia, OSF. *A Cross in China: The Story of My Mission.* Fort Wayne, Ind.: Cuchullain Publications, 1989.

Berrigan, Daniel, ed. *Between Honesty and Hope: Documents from and about the Church in Latin America.* Issued at Lima by the Peruvian Bishops' Commission for Social Action. Translated by John Drury. Maryknoll, N.Y.: Maryknoll Publications, 1970.

————. "The Modern Concept of *Missio.*" *Woodstock Letters* 93 (1964): 11–29.

Boberg, John T., ed. *The Word in the World: Divine Word Missionaries Black Apostolate.* Techny, Ill.: Society of the Divine Word, 1976.

Boberg, John T., and James A. Scherer. *Mission in the 70's: What Direction?* Chicago: Chicago Cluster of Theological Schools, 1972.

Bonk, Jonathan J. *Missions and Money: Affluence as a Western Missionary Problem.* Maryknoll, N.Y.: Orbis Books, 1991.

Bornemann, Fritz, et al. *A History of the Divine Word Missionaries.* 3 vols. Rome: Collegium Verbi Divini, 1981.

Bosch, David J. *Transforming Mission: Paradigm Shifts in Mission Theology.* Maryknoll, N.Y.: Orbis Books, 1991.

Bouffard, Adrien. *Propagation of the Faith: Insight into the Missionary World.* New York: Society for the Propagation of the Faith, 1958.

Bowden, Henry Warner. *American Indians and Christian Missions: Studies in Cultural Conflict.* Chicago: University of Chicago Press, 1981.

Bowie, Fiona, ed. *Women and Missions, Past and Present: Anthropological and Historical Perceptions.* Providence, R.I.: Berg Publishers, 1993.

Bradshaw, Susan, OSF. "Religious Women in China: An Understanding of Indigenization." *Catholic Historical Review* 68, no. 1 (1982): 28–45.

Brandewie, Ernest. "Ethnology and Missionaries: The Case of the Anthropos Institute and Wilhelm Schmidt." In Darrell L. Whiteman, ed., *Missionaries, Anthropologists, and Cultural Change.* Studies in Third World Societies, no. 25. Williamsburg, Va.: Department of Anthropology, College of William and Mary, 1985.

————. *When Giants Walked the Earth: The Life and Times of Wilhelm Schmidt, S.V.D.* Fribourg: University Press, 1990.

Breslin, Thomas. *China, American Catholicism, and the Missionary.* N.p.: Pennsylvania State, 1980.

Brett, Donna Whitson, and Edward T. Brett. *Murdered in Central America: The Stories of Eleven U.S. Missionaries.* Maryknoll, N.Y.: Orbis Books, 1988.

Breunig, Jerome, SJ. *Have You Had Your Rice Today?* Chicago: Loyola University Press, 1964.

Brown, Alden V. *The Grail Movement and American Catholicism, 1940–1975.* Notre Dame, Ind.: University of Notre Dame Press, 1989.

Brown, Arthur Judson. *One Hundred Years: A History of Foreign Missionary Work of the Presbyterian Church in the U.S.A.* New York: Fleming H. Revell, 1936.

Brown, Stephen J., SJ. *Catholic Mission Literature.* Dublin: Catholic Central Library, 1932.

Burke, Thomas J. M., SJ. *Sinews of Love.* New York: New American Library of World Literature, 1959.

———, ed. *Catholic Missions: Four Great Encyclicals.* New York: Paulist Press, 1957.

Burrows, William R. "Needs and Opportunities in Studies of Mission and World Christianity." *International Bulletin of Missionary Research* 19 (October 1995): 172–78.

———. "Tensions in the Catholic Magisterium about Mission and Other Religions." *International Bulletin of Missionary Research* 9 (1985): 2–4.

———, ed. *Redemption and Dialogue: Reading* Redemptoris Missio *and* Dialogue and Proclamation. Maryknoll, N.Y.: Orbis Books, 1993.

Burton, Katherine. *According to the Pattern: The Story of Dr. Agnes McLaren and the Society of Catholic Medical Missionaries.* New York: Longmans Green & Company, 1946.

Bynum, Caroline Walker, Stevan Harrell, and Paula Richman, eds. *Gender and Religion: On the Complexity of Symbols.* Boston: Beacon Press, 1986.

Calkins, Thomas, OSM. *Kisimusi, the Story of a Zulu Girl.* Milwaukee: Bruce Publishing Company, 1962.

———. *Umfundisi, Missioner to the Zulus.* Milwaukee: Bruce Publishing Company, 1959.

Cameron, Frederic M. "Teamwork: A Key to Latin America." *Worldmission* 18, no. 3 (1967): 15–16.

Campbell, Debra. "Catholic Lay Evangelism in the 1930s: Four Models." *Records of the American Catholic Historical Society of Philadelphia* 95 (March–December 1984): 5–14.

Campbell, Robert Edward. *The Church in Mission.* Maryknoll, N.Y.: Maryknoll Publications, 1965.

Camps, Arnulf, OFM, and Patrick McCloskey, OFM. *History of the Order of Friars Minor in China (1294–1955), with Special Reference to the Years 1925–55, Based on the Research of Friars Domenico Gandolfi and Bernward Willeke, OFM.* St. Bonaventure, N.Y.: Franciscan Institute Publications, 1996.

Canadian Religious Conference. *Religious in the Local Church: Fourth Inter-American Meeting of Religious.* N.p.: Canadian Religious Conference, 1981.

Capuchin Mission Unit. *India and Its Missions.* New York: Macmillan, 1923.

Carbonneau, Robert, CP. "Life, Death, and Memory: Three Passionists in Hunan, China, and the Shaping of an American Mission Perspective in the 1920s." Ph.D. diss., Georgetown University, 1992.

———. "Passionists in China, 1924–1929: An Essay in Mission Experience." *Catholic Historical Review* 66 (1980): 392–416.

Carney, James Guadalupe. *To Be a Christian Is to Be a Revolutionary.* San Francisco: Harper & Row, 1987.

Carpenter, Joel A., and Wilbert R. Shenk, eds. *Earthern Vessels, American Evangelicals, and Foreign Missions, 1880–1980.* Grand Rapids, Mich.: Eerdmans, 1990.

Carrigan, Ana. *Salvador Witness: The Life and Calling of Jean Donovan.* New York: Simon & Schuster, 1984.

Case, Howard D., ed. *Joseph Dutton [Memoirs]: The Story of Forty-four Years of Service among the Lepers of Molokai, Hawaii.* Honolulu: Honolulu Star-Bulletin, 1931.

Catholic Foreign Mission Society of America. *Christianity, a Personal Mission: A Symposium of Contemporary Christian Thought.* Maryknoll, N.Y.: Maryknoll Publications, 1964.

Catholic Students Mission Crusade. *China, a Mission Investigation.* Cincinnati: Catholic Students Mission Crusade, 1925.

———. *The Church at Work in the World: Selections for a Readings Course on the Theology, History, and Methods of the Mission Apostolate.* Cincinnati: n.p., 1961.

———. *Lay Apostolate: Some Fundamental Principles from the Writing of Our Holy Father, Pope John XIII.* Cincinnati: Catholic Students Mission Crusade, 1960.

———. *A Missionary Index of Catholic Americans.* Cincinnati: Crusade Castle, 1942. Subsequent editions appeared in 1944, 1946, and 1949.

———. *To Defend the Cross.* Proceedings of the Fourth General Convention of the Catholic Students Mission Crusade at the University of Notre Dame. Cincinnati: Crusade Castle, 1923.

The Catholic University of Peking. Beatty, Pa.: The Archabbey Press, n.d. [c.1930].

Caulfield, Caspar, CP. *Only a Beginning: The Passionists in China, 1921–1931.* Union City, N.J.: Passionist Fathers, 1990.

Celebrating 25 Years, 1971–1996, Cooperation and Support, Mission of Friendship. Erie, Pa.: Diocese of Erie, 1996.

The Century of Mary of the Passion. Translated by Joyce C. Dunphy. Saint Brieuc, France: Studium Châtelets, 1984.

China and the Churches. Techny, Ill.: Society of the Divine Word, 1981.

Christensen, Torbin, and William R. Hutchison, eds. *Mission Ideologies in the Imperialist Era, 1880–1920.* Denmark: Christensens Bogtrykkeri, 1982.

Clark, Francis X. *The Purpose of Missions: A Study of the Mission Documents of the Holy See, 1909–1946.* New York: Missionary Union of the Clergy, 1948.

Clark, James A. "Placing U.S. Personnel in Latin America." *Review for Religious* 28 (1969): 879–85.

Clarke, Peter. *A Free Church in a Free Society: The Ecclesiology of John England, Bishop of Charleston, 1820–1842, a Nineteenth Century Bishop in the United States.* Hartsville, S.C.: Center for John England Studies, 1982.

Clarkson, John F., SJ. "The ABC's of Missiology." *Worldmission* 3 (1952): 337–52.

Cleary, Edward, OP. *Path from Puebla: Significant Documents of the Latin American Bishops Since 1979.* Washington, D.C.: National Conference of Catholic Bishops, 1989.

Clifford, James, and George E. Marcus, eds. *Writing Culture: The Poetics and Politics of Ethnography.* Berkeley: University of California Press, 1986.

Cogan, Mary de Paul. *Sisters of Maryknoll through Troubled Waters.* New York: Charles Scribner's Sons, 1947.

Coleman, Mother Mary, MM., ed. *Discourses of Mother Mary Joseph Rogers, M.M., 1912–1925.* Maryknoll, N.Y.: Maryknoll Sisters, 1982.

Coleman, William J., MM. *Latin American Catholicism.* World Horizon Report. Maryknoll, N.Y.: Maryknoll Publications, 1958.

Collectanea Commissionis Synodalis 1 (May 1928) — 7/12 (July–December 1947). Microform.

Colonnese, Louis M., ed. *Conscientization for Liberation.* Papers from the 1970 CICOP Conference. Washington, D.C.: U.S. Catholic Conference, Division for Latin America, 1971.

Congar, Yves. "Theology of the Apostolate." *Worldmission* 7, no. 3 (1956): 283–94.

Considine, John J. MM. *Africa: World of New Men.* New York: Dodd, Mead, 1954.

———. "African Gods in Catholic Bahia." *Worldmission* 8 (Winter 1957): 78–95.

———. *Call for Forty Thousand.* New York: Longmans, Green & Company, 1946.

———. "The Church and the Unity of the Human Race." *Catholic Action* 26 (October 1944): 6–7.

———. "The Church's Teaching on the World Apostolate" (1944). John J. Considine Papers. Considine Writings. MMA.

———. "Education to World Christianity." *Journal of Religious Instruction* 14 (December 1943): 405–9.

———. *Fundamental Catholic Teaching on the Human Race.* World Horizon Report, no. 27. Maryknoll, N.Y.: Maryknoll Publications, 1960.

———. *God So Loved the World.* Maryknoll, N.Y.: Maryknoll, 1950. A 1960 version was adapted by the Maryknoll Cloister Sisters and privately printed.

———. *March into Tomorrow.* New York: Field Afar Press, 1942.

———. "New Faces in Africa." *Worldmission* 10 (Summer 1959): 71–81.

———. *New Horizons in Latin America.* New York: Dodd, Mead, 1958.

———. "An Outline of Missiography." *Missionary Academia* (New York: The Society for the Propagation of the Faith) 1, no. 8 (1944).

———. "Some Points on the Place of Mission Education in General Catholic Education." *Catholic Education Review* 4 (April 1943): 229–33.

———. *The Vatican Mission Exposition.* New York: Macmillan, 1925.

———. *When the Sorghum Was High: A Life of Gerard Donovan, M.M.* New York: Longmans, Green & Company, 1940.

———. *World Christianity.* Milwaukee: Bruce Publishing Company, 1945.

———, ed. *The Church in the New Latin America.* Notre Dame, Ind.: Fides, 1964. Papers from the first CICOP meeting.

———. *The Missionary's Role in Socio-economic Betterment.* New York: Newman Press, 1960.

———. *The Religious Dimension in the New Latin America.* Papers from the fourth CICOP meeting (1967). Notre Dame, Ind.: Fides, 1967.

———. *Social Revolution in the New Latin America: A Catholic Appraisal.* Papers from the second CICOP meeting (1965). Notre Dame, Ind.: Fides, 1965.

Considine, John J., MM, in collaboration with Thomas Kernan. *Across a World.* New York: Longmans, Green & Company, 1942.

Conway, Bertrand. *The Question Box.* New York: Catholic Book Exchange, 1903.

Conway, Robert Louis. "A History of the Chilean Vicariate of the Precious Blood Fathers, 1947–1972." Ph.D. diss., Loyola University, Chicago, 1980.

Cooney, John. *The American Pope: The Life and Times of Francis Cardinal Spellman.* New York: Times Books, 1984.

Costello, Gerald M. *Mission to Latin America: The Successes and Failures of a Twentieth-Century Crusade.* Maryknoll, N.Y.: Orbis Books, 1979.

Cotter, James Patrick, SJ. *The Word in the Third World.* Woodstock Conference on Mission Theology, under sponsorship of Jesuit Missions. Washington, D.C.: Corpus Books, 1968.

Cushing, Richard. *The Missions in War and Peace.* Boston: Society for the Propagation of the Faith, n.d. [c. 1944].

———. *The Modern Challenge of the Missions.* Lowell, Mass.: Sullivan Bros., [c. 1962].

———. *Multiplying the Missionary.* Boston: Society for the Propagation of the Faith, n.d. [after 1944].

———. *Questions and Answers on Communism.* Boston: Daughters of St. Paul, [1961].

Daley, B. E. "In Ten Thousand Places: Christian Universality and Jesuit Mission." *Studies in the Spirituality of Jesuits* 17 (March 1985).

Davis, Cyprian, OSB. *The History of Black Catholics in the United States.* New York: Crossroad, 1990.

Dease, Alice. *Bluegowns: A Golden Treasury of Tales of the China Missions.* Maryknoll, N.Y.: Catholic Foreign Mission Society, 1927. Published from stories from the London Catholic Truth Society.

Decker, Charles F., SMSM, ed. *Saving the Solomons: From the Diary Account of the Reverend Mother Mary Rose [Decker], SMSM.* With a foreword by Richard Cardinal Cushing. Bedford, Mass.: Marist Missions, 1948.

de Jaegher, Raymond, SAM, "The First Chinese Bishops and Father Cotta." *Worldmission* 6 (Fall 1955): 267–77.

de Jaegher, Raymond, and Irene Corbally Kuhn. *The Enemy Within: An Eyewitness Account of the Communist Conquest of China.* Garden City, N.Y.: Doubleday, 1952.

de Mijolla, Marie Cecile, SMSM. *Origins in Oceania: Missionary Sisters of the Society of Mary, 1845–1931.* Rome: n.p., 1984.

Dengel, Anna. "A Catholic Medical College for India." *Worldmission* 3 (Autumn 1952): 277–86.

———. *Mission for Samaritans: A Survey of Achievements and Opportunities in the Field of Catholic Medical Missions.* Milwaukee: Bruce Publishing Company, 1945.

Dever, Joseph. *Cushing of Boston, a Candid Portrait.* Boston: Bruce Humphries, 1965.

Donders, Joseph. *Charged with the Spirit: Mission Is for Everyone.* Maryknoll, N.Y.: Orbis Books, 1993.

Donovan, John F., MM. *The Pagoda and the Cross: The Life of Bishop Ford of Maryknoll.* New York: Charles Scribner's Sons, 1967.

Dougherty, Dolorita Marie, CSJ, et al. *The Sisters of St. Joseph of Carondelet.* St. Louis: B. Herder Book Company, 1966.

Douglas, Mary, and Baron Issherwood. *The World of Goods.* New York: Basic Books, 1979.

[Doyle, Alexander.] *The Apostolic Mission House for the Training of Missionaries to Non-Catholics.* Washington, D.C.: n.p., 1902.

Dries, Angelyn. "The Hero-Martyr Myth in United States Catholic Foreign Mission Literature, 1893–1925." *Missiology* 19 (July 1991): 305–14.

———. "The Legacy of John J. Considine, MM." *International Bulletin of Missionary Research* 21 (April 1997): 80–84.

———. "Toward a U.S. Theology of Global Christianity: John J. Considine, MM (1897–1982)." *Records of the American Catholic Historical Society of Philadelphia* 103 (Winter 1992): 23–31.

———. " 'The Whole Way into the Wilderness': The Foreign Mission Impulse of the American Catholic Church, 1893–1925." Ph.D. diss., Graduate Theological Union, Berkeley, Calif., 1990.

Dudink, Edward, ed. *The Word in the World: Ghana.* Techny, Ill.: Divine Word Missionaries, 1972.

Dunn, Edmond J. *Missionary Theology: Foundations in Development.* Lanham, Md.: University Press of America, 1980.

Dussel, Enrique. *A History of the Church in Latin America: Colonialism to Liberalism.* Grand Rapids, Mich.: Eerdmans, 1981.

Eleanore, Mary, Sister. *On the King's Highway: A History of the Sisters of the Holy Cross of St. Mary of the Immaculate Conception, Notre Dame, Indiana.* New York: D. Appleton and Company, 1931.

Elliott, Walter. *A Manual of Missions.* Washington, D.C.: Apostolic Mission House, 1922.

———. *Mission Sermons.* Washington, D.C.: Apostolic Mission House, 1926.

Ellis, John Tracy. *The Life of James Cardinal Gibbons, Archbishop of Baltimore, 1834–1921.* 2 vols. Milwaukee: Bruce Publishing Company, 1952.

———, ed. *Documents of American Catholic History, 1493–1986.* 3 vols. Wilmington, Del.: Michael Glazier, 1987.

Ewing, J. Franklin. "Anthropology and the Training of Missionaries." *Catholic Educational Review* 55 (May 1957): 300–311.

———. "Applied Anthropology for the Missionary." *Worldmission* 2 (February 1951): 105–7.

———, ed. *Christian Living in Mission Lands.* Proceedings of the Fordham University Conference of Mission Specialists, 1957. New York: Fordham University Press, 1959.

———. *The Global Mission of the Church.* Proceedings of the Fordham University Conference of Mission Specialists, 1962. New York: Fordham University Press, 1962.

———. *Local Leadership in Mission Lands.* Proceedings of the Fordham University Conference of Mission Specialists, 1954. New York: Fordham University Press, 1954.

———. *The Role of Communication Arts in Mission Work*. Proceedings of the Fordham University Conference of Mission Specialists, 1956. New York: Fordham University Press, 1958.

———. *Social Action in Mission Lands*. Proceedings of the Fordham University Conference of Mission Specialists, 1955. New York: Fordham University Press, 1955.

———. *The Training of Converts*. Proceedings of the Fordham University Conference of Mission Specialists, 1953. New York: Fordham University Press, 1953.

Fairbank, John King, et al. *The Missionary Enterprise in China and America*. Cambridge: Harvard University Press, 1974.

Father Price of Maryknoll. Maryknoll, N.Y.: Catholic Foreign Mission Society, 1923.

Ferguson, James J. "A Paradigm Shift in the Theology of Mission: Two Roman Catholic Perspectives." *International Bulletin of Missionary Research* 8 (1984): 117–19.

Fields, Kathleen Riley. "Anti-communism and Social Justice: The Double-edged Sword of Fulton Sheen." *Records of the American Catholic Historical Society of Philadelphia* 96 (1988): 83–91.

———. "Bishop Fulton J. Sheen: An American Catholic Response to the Twentieth Century." Ph.D. diss., University of Notre Dame, 1988.

Fischer, Edward. *Light in the Far East: Archbishop Harold Henry's Forty-two Years in Korea*. New York: Seabury Press, 1976.

———. *Maybe a Second Spring: The Story of the Missionary Sisters of St. Columban in China*. New York: Crossroad, 1983.

Fisher, James T. "The Sign of Contradiction: Catholic Personalism in American Culture, 1933–1962." Ph.D. diss., Rutgers University, 1987; Ann Arbor, Mich.: UMI Dissertation Service, 1991.

Fitzpatrick, Joseph P. *The Stranger Is Our Own: Reflections on the Journey of Puerto Rican Migrants*. Edited by Madeline Moran. Kansas City, Mo.: Sheed & Ward, 1996.

Flanagan, Padraig, SPS, ed. *A New Missionary Era*. Maryknoll, N.Y.: Orbis Books, 1979.

Fleckner, Johannes. *Thomas Kardinal Tien*. St. Augustin: Steyler Verlag, 1975.

Fleming, Peter Joseph. "Chosen for China, the California Province Jesuits in China, 1928–1957: A Case Study in Mission and Culture." Ph.D. diss., Graduate Theological Union, Berkeley, Calif., 1987.

Flemming, Leslie A., ed. *Women's Work for Women: Missionaries and Social Change in Asia*. Boulder, Colo.: Westview Press, 1989.

Ford, Francis Xavier, MM. *Come, Holy Ghost: Thoughts on Renewing the Earth as the Kingdom of God*. New York: McMullen Books, 1953.

Ford, John T., CSC. " 'A Centre of Light and Truth': A Century of Theology at the Catholic University of America." *Catholic Historical Review* 73 (1989): 566–91.

Foroohar, Manzar. *The Catholic Church and Social Change in Nicaragua*. Albany: State University of New York Press, 1989.

Franciscan Missionaries in China: Province of the Most Holy Name. Paterson, N.J.: St. Anthony Guild Press, 1934.

Franciscan Missionaries of Mary. *For the Mission and Its Risks, 1877–1984*. Privately printed, 1984.

Franciscan Missionary Union. *American Franciscan Missions at Home and Abroad*. New York: Franciscans, Province of the Most Holy Name, 1955.

———. *Statutes of the Franciscan Missionary Union*. N.p.: privately printed, 1922.

Franciscans, Province of the Most Holy Name of Jesus. *The Departure Ceremony*. N.p.: privately printed, 1945.

———. *In Honor of the Occasion of the Departure of the Franciscan Missionaries for Their Mission Field in Shasi, Hupeh, China*. Paterson, N.J.: St. Anthony's Guild, 1936.

Frazier, William B. "Guidelines for a New Theology of Mission." *Worldmission* 18, no. 4 (1967): 16–24.

Freitag, Anton. *The Catholic Mission Feast*. Adapted for America by Rev. Cornelius Pekari and Bruno Hagspiel. 2d ed. Techny, Ill.: Mission Press, 1914.

Freking, Edward A., et al., eds. *The Church at Work in the World: Selections for a Readings Course on the Theology, History, and Methods of the Mission Apostolate*. Cincinnati: Catholic Students Mission Crusade, 1961.

Freri, Joseph. "Native Clergy for Mission Countries." *American Ecclesiastical Review* 57 (1917): 113–28.

————. *Native Clergy for Mission Countries*. New York: Society for the Propagation of the Faith, 1917.

————. *The Society for the Propagation of the Faith*. Baltimore: Society for the Propagation of the Faith, 1902.

————, ed. *The Catechist in Mission Countries*. New York: [Society for the Propagation of the Faith], n.d.

From Generation to Generation: The Story of the Nigeria/Ghana Mission of the Society of Jesus. New York: privately printed, 1993.

Fujita, Neil S. *Japan's Encounter with Christianity: The Catholic Mission in Pre-modern Japan*. New York: Paulist Press, 1991.

Fundamentals of Missiology. Cincinnati: Catholic Students Mission Crusade, 1957.

Gaffey, James. *Francis Clement Kelley and the American Catholic Dream*. Bensenville, Ill.: The Heritage Foundation, 1980.

Gauci, R. P. Juan, CSSR. *Redemptorist Apostolates in the Caribbean of the Nineteenth Century*. Santo Domingo, Dominican Republic: privately printed, 1989.

Gier, Ann. *This Fire Ever Burning: A Biography of M. Leonarda Lentrup, SSpS*. Techny, Ill.: Holy Spirit Missionary Sisters, 1986.

Gilkey, Langdon. *Shantung Compound: The Story of Men and Women under Pressure*. New York: Harper & Row, 1966.

Gillard, John Thomas. *The Negro American: A Mission Investigation*. Cincinnati: Catholic Students Mission Crusade, 1941.

Ginder, Richard. *With Ink and Crozier: A Biography of John Francis Noll, Fifth Bishop of Fort Wayne and Founder of Our Sunday Visitor*. N.p.: Our Sunday Visitor, 1953.

Goyau, Georges. *Missions and Missionaries*. Translated by F. M. Dreves, SSJ. London and Edinburgh: Sands & Co., 1932.

————. *Valiant Women: Mother Mary of the Passion and the Franciscan Missionaries of Mary*. London: Sheed & Ward, 1936.

Grady, Sister M. Pauline, ASC. *Ruma: Home and Heritage, the Story of a Convent in Rural Southern Illinois, 1876–1984*. Ruma, Ill.: privately printed, 1984.

The Grail. *The Laity and the International Scene*. Loveland, Ohio: Grailville, 1957.

————. *The Laity Look Eastward*. Loveland, Ohio: Grailville, 1950.

Grassi, Joseph A. *A World to Win: The Missionary Methods of St. Paul the Apostle*. Maryknoll, N.Y.: Maryknoll, 1965.

Gray, Francine du Plessix. *Divine Disobedience: Profiles in Catholic Radicalism*. New York: Alfred A. Knopf, 1970.

Greene, Robert W., MM. *Calvary in China*. New York: G. P. Putnam's Sons, 1953.

Groell, Sister Clare. *White Wings in Bamboo Land*. Emmitsburg, Md.: St. Joseph's Provincial House, 1973.

[Grondin], Sister Marcelline [Therese]. *Sisters Carry the Gospel*. World Horizon Report, no. 15. Maryknoll, N.Y.: Maryknoll Publications, 1956.

Guider, Margaret Eletta. *Daughters of Rahab: Prostitution and the Church of Liberation in Brazil*. Philadelphia: Fortress Press, 1995.

Gutteres, Antonella Marie. *Lorettine Education in China, 1923–1952: Educational Activities of the Sisters of Loretto in China, Hanyang, and Shanghai*. Taipei: United Publishing Center, 1961.

Haas, Roger M., OFMConv. *A History of the American Province of St. Anthony of Padua of the Order of Friars Minor Conventual, 1906–1982*. N.p.: privately printed, 1984.

Habig, Marion, OFM. *Heralds of the King: The Franciscans of the St. Louis-Chicago Province, 1858–1958*. Chicago: Franciscan Herald Press, 1958.

———. *In Journeyings Often: Franciscan Pioneers in the Orient*. St. Bonaventure, N.Y.: Franciscan Institute, 1953.

———. *Pioneering in China: The Story of Rev. Francis Xavier Engbring, OFM, First Native Priest in China*. Chicago: Franciscan Herald Press, 1930.

Hagspiel, Bruno, SVD. *Along the Mission Trail*. 5 vols. Techny, Ill.: Mission Press, 1925–27.

Hanley, Philip M. *History of the Catholic Ladder*. Edited by Edward J. Kowrach. Fairfield, Wash.: Ye Galleon Press, 1993.

Hanley, Sister Mary Laurence, OSF, and O. A. Bushnell. *A Song of Pilgrimage and Exile: The Life and Spirit of Mother Marianne of Molokai*. Chicago: Franciscan Herald Press, 1980.

Hart, Sister Mary Francis Borgia, SSF. *Violets in the King's Garden: A History of the Sisters of the Holy Family of New Orleans*. New Orleans: privately printed, 1976.

Hartig, Mary C., ed. *Greetings from the Land That Time Forgot: Letters from Reverend Francis P. Swift, SVD (1915–1982)*. N.p.: McNaughton & Gunn, 1989.

Heller, James, and Richard Armstrong, eds. *Apostolic Renewal in the Seminary in the Light of Vatican Council II*. New York: Christophers, 1965.

Hellwig, Sister M. Cuthbert, SCMM. "The Language-Learning Problems of the Ordinary Missionary." *Worldmission* 15, no. 3 (1964): 27–32.

Hendryickx, Jeroom, CICM, ed. *Historiography of the Chinese Catholic Church, Nineteenth and Twentieth Centuries*. Louvain: Ferdinand Verbiest Foundation, 1994.

Henkels, Joseph, SVD. *My China Memoirs, 1928–1951*. Techny, Ill.: n.p., 1988.

Hennesey, James, SJ. *American Catholics: A History of the Roman Catholic Community in the United States*. New York: Oxford University Press, 1981.

Henry, Antonin Marcel. *A Mission Theology*. Notre Dame, Ind.: Fides, 1963.

Henzel, Francis X., SJ. *The Catholic Church in Micronesia: Historical Essays on the Catholic Church in the Caroline-Marshall Islands*. Chicago: Loyola University Press, 1991.

Herlihy, Francis. *Swords and Ploughshares: Fifty Years of Mission in Korea*. Blackburn, Australia: Dove Communications, 1983.

Hickey, Edward J. *The Society for the Propagation of the Faith: Its Foundation, Organization, and Success*. Washington, D.C.: Catholic University of America Press, 1942; New York: AMS, 1974.

Hill, Patricia. *The World Their Household: The American Woman's Foreign Mission Movement and Cultural Transformation, 1870–1920*. Ann Arbor: University of Michigan Press, 1985.

Hillman, Eugene, CSSp. *The Church as Mission*. New York: Herder and Herder, 1965.

———. "Inculturation and the Leaven of the Gospel." *Commonweal* (11 January 1991): 21–23.

———. "Maasai Religion and Inculturation." *Louvain Studies* 17 (1992): 351–76.

———. "The Main Task of the Mission." In *Rethinking the Church's Mission*. Vol. 13. Concilium. New York: Paulist Press, 1966.

———. *Many Paths: A Catholic Approach to Religious Pluralism*. Maryknoll, N.Y.: Orbis Books, 1989.

———. *Polygamy Reconsidered: African Plural Marriage and the Christian Churches*. Maryknoll, N.Y.: Orbis Books, 1975.

———. *Toward an African Christianity: Inculturation Applied*. New York: Paulist Press, 1993.

———. *The Wider Ecumenism*. New York: Herder and Herder, 1968.

Hinton, Mary Louise. *Sister Xavier Berkeley (1861–1944), Sister of Charity of St. Vincent de Paul: Fifty-four Years a Missionary in China*. London: Burns & Oates, 1949.

Hoffman, Ronan, OFMConv. *The Mission Theory of Cardinal Brancati de Laurea.* Hoboken, N.J.: n.p., 1960.

———. *Pioneer Theories of Missiology.* Washington, D.C.: Catholic University of America Press, 1960.

———. "The Priest and the Worldwide Mission Apostolate." In Joseph Cevetello, ed., *All Things to All Men.* New York: Joseph Wagner, 1965.

Huber, Mary Taylor. *The Bishops' Progress: A Historical Ethnography of Catholic Missionary Experience on the Sepik Frontier.* Washington, D.C.: Smithsonian Institution Press, 1988.

Hunt, Darryl L. *Go, Tell It Everywhere: Modern Missioners in Action.* Maryknoll, N.Y.: Maryknoll Publications, 1965.

Hunter, Jane. *The Gospel of Gentility: American Women Missionaries in Turn-of-the-Century China.* New Haven: Yale University Press, 1984.

Huonder, Anton, SJ, ed. *Sermons and Lectures on the Missions.* Adapted from the German by Cornelius Pekari, OFMCap. Vol. 1. Techny, Ill.: Mission Press, 1918.

Hutchison, William. "Americans in World Mission: Revision and Realignment." In David Lotz, ed., *Altered Landscapes: Christianity in America.* Grand Rapids, Mich.: Eerdmans, 1989.

———. *Errand to the World: American Protestant Thought and Foreign Missions.* Chicago: University of Chicago Press, 1987.

Hyde, Douglas. *One Front across the World.* Westminster, Md.: Newman Press, 1956.

"Ignatian Spirituality and Mission." *The Way* (London), Spring 1994.

Illich, Ivan. *Celebration of Awareness: A Call for Institutional Revolution.* Garden City, N.Y.: Doubleday, 1970.

———. "The Meaning of Cuernavaca." *Jesuit Missions* 41 (April 1967): 19–25.

Inter-American Conference of Religious. *Priests and Religious for Latin America: Proceedings and Conclusions.* Washington, D.C.: U.S. Catholic Conference, Division for Latin America, 1971.

International Mission Council of the Order of Friars Minor. *Proceedings of the First International Mission Council of the Order of Friars Minor, 16–21 November 1981, Rome.* Rome: Curia Generalizia dei Frati Minori, 1981.

Jacks, L. V. *Mother Marianne of Molokai.* New York: Macmillan, 1935.

Jenkinson, William, and Helene O'Sullivan, eds. *Trends in Mission: Toward the Third Millennium.* Maryknoll, N.Y.: Orbis Books, 1992.

A Jill of All Trades: The Life and Experiences of Sr. Mary Leclerc, SMSM. Waltham, Mass.: Marist Missionary Sisters, 1984.

Johnson, Stephen W. *Companion to the World Mission Rosary Map.* New York: National Office of the Society for the Propagation of the Faith, [1952].

John XXIII. *L'Oeuvre Missionnaire de Jean XXIII: Textes et Documents Pontificaux, 1958–1963, presentes par l'Union pontificale missionaire.* Paris: P. Lethielleux, 1966.

Jonas, Thomas Joseph. *The Divided Mind: American Catholic Evangelists in the 1890s.* New York: Garland Press, 1988.

Just, Mary, Sister. *China, 1925: A Mission Investigation.* Cincinnati: Catholic Students Mission Crusade, 1925.

———. *Immortal Fire: A Journey through the Centuries with the Missionary Great.* St. Louis: Herder, 1951.

Kane, William T., SJ. *A Memoir of William A. Stanton, S.J.* St. Louis: B. Herder Book Co., 1927.

Kauffman, Christopher. *Ministry and Meaning: A Religious History of Catholic Health Care in the United States.* New York: Crossroad, 1995.

———. *Mission to Rural America: The Story of W. Howard Bishop, Founder of Glenmary.* New York: Paulist Press, 1991.

————. *Tradition and Transformation in Catholic Culture: The Priests of Saint Sulpice in the United States from 1791 to the Present.* New York: Macmillan, 1988.

Kazel, Dorothy Chapon. *Alleluia Woman: Sister Dorothy Kazel, OSU.* Cleveland: Chapel Publications, 1987.

Keeler, Floyd. *Catholic Medical Missions.* New York: Macmillan, 1925.

————. "Missionary Organization and the Mission Societies." *Ecclesiastical Review* 74 (February 1926): 124–29.

Keller, James. *The Priest and a World Vision.* New York: The Christophers, 1946.

Kelley, Francis Clement. *The Story of Extension.* Chicago: Extension Press, 1922.

————, ed. *The First American Catholic Missionary Congress Held Under the Auspices of the Catholic Church Extension Society of the United States of America Containing Official Proceedings.* Chicago: J. S. Hyland, 1909; New York: Arno, 1978.

————. *The Second American Catholic Missionary Congress.* Chicago: J. S. Hyland, 1913.

Kennedy, Camilla, MM. *To the Uttermost Parts of the Earth: The Spirit and Charism of Mary Josephine Rogers.* Maryknoll, N.Y.: Maryknoll Sisters, 1987.

Kennelly, Karen M., CSJ. "Foreign Missions and the Renewal Movement." *Review for Religious* (May–June 1990): 445–63.

Kent, Mark Leo, and Sister Mary Just. *The Glory of Christ: A Pageant of Two Hundred Missionary Lives from Apostolic Times to the Present Age.* Milwaukee: Bruce Publishing Company, 1955.

Kersbergen, Lydwine Van. "African Journey: What Pattern Do the Africans Evolve When They Are Free to Express Themselves?" *Commonweal* 59 (20 November 1952): 159–61.

Kettl, Sister Mary Rosalia, MM. *One Inch of Splendor.* New York: Field Afar Press, 1941.

Klaiber, Jeffrey, SJ. *The Catholic Church in Peru, 1821–1985: A Social History.* Washington, D.C.: Catholic University of America Press, 1992.

Koppenhafer, Aimee Julie, SND. *With Dedicated Hearts.* Privately printed, 1963.

Koren, Henry J. *The Serpent and the Dove: A History of the Congregation of the Holy Ghost in the United States, 1745–1984.* Pittsburgh: Spiritus Press, 1985.

Kroeger, James, MM. *Living Mission: Challenges in Evangelization Today.* Maryknoll, N.Y.: Orbis Books, 1994.

————. *Mission Today: Contemporary Themes in Missiology.* Hong Kong: Federation of Asian Bishops' Conferences, 1991.

Kselman, Thomas, and Steven Avella. "Marian Piety and the Cold War in the United States." *Catholic Historical Review* 72 (1986): 403–24.

Laberge, Roy L. *Manual of Missionary Action: A Translation.* Ottawa: University of Ottawa Press, 1948. Translation of Pierre Charles, SJ, *Les dossiers de l'action missionaire: manuel de missiologie.* 2d ed. Louvain: Editions de l'Aucum, 1938.

LaFarge, John, SJ. *A Report on the American Jesuits.* New York: Farrar, Straus, and Cudahy, 1956.

Lan, Kwok Pui. *Chinese Women and Christianity, 1860–1927.* Atlanta: Scholars Press, 1992.

Lanahan, Mary Francesca. *History of Notre Dame Mission, Wuchang, China, 1926–1951.* Sisters of Notre Dame de Namur, Ohio Province. Cincinnati: Privately printed, [1983].

Lane, George L., ed. *Why I Became a Missioner.* Westminster, Md.: Newman Press, 1958.

Latourette, Kenneth Scott. *History of the Expansion of Christianity.* 7 vols. London: Harper, 1939–45.

————. *Missions and the American Mind.* Indianapolis: National Foundation Press, 1949.

LaVerdiere, Eugene, ed. *A Church for All Peoples: Missionary Issues in a World Church.* Collegeville, Minn.: Liturgical Press, 1993.

Leahy, William K., and Anthony T. Massimini. "Missionary Activity of the Church." Pt. 11 of *Third Session: Council Speeches of Vatican II.* Glen Rock, N.J.: Deus Books, Paulist Press, 1966.

Leonard, Henry. "Ethnic Tensions, Episcopal Leadership, and the Emergence of the Twentieth Century American Catholic Church: The Cleveland Experience." *Catholic Historical Review* 71 (1985): 394–412.

Lernoux, Penny. *Hearts on Fire: The Story of the Maryknoll Sisters.* Maryknoll, N.Y.: Orbis Books, 1993.

———. *The People of God: The Struggle for World Catholicism.* New York: Viking, 1989.

Lima Methods Conference of the Maryknoll Fathers. Maryknoll, N.Y.: The Maryknoll Fathers, 1954.

Loretta, Sister Mary, AdPPS. *Amazonia: A Study of People and Progress in the Amazon Jungle.* New York: Pageant Press, 1963.

Luzbetak, Louis J., SVD. *The Church and Cultures: New Perspectives in Missiological Anthropology.* Maryknoll, N.Y.: Orbis Books, 1988.

———. "Cross-Cultural Missionary Preparation." In *Trends and Issues: Missionary Formation.* Epworth, Iowa: Divine Word College, 1984.

———. "Understanding 'Cross-Cultural Sensitivity': An Aid to the Identification of Objectives and Tasks of Missionary Training." *Verbum SVD* 16 (1975): 3–25.

———. "What Can Anthropology Offer to the Missions?" In Joachim Georg Piepke, *Anthropology and Mission: SVD International Consultation on Anthropology for Mission, Puna/India, Dec. 29, 1986 to Jan. 4, 1987.* Nettetal, Germany: Steyler-Verlag, 1988.

Lyons, Jeanne Marie, MM. *Maryknoll's First Lady: The Life of Mother Mary Joseph, Foundress of the Maryknoll Sisters.* New York: Dodd, Mead, and Company, 1964.

———. *Means of Fostering the Missionary Vocation in the Catholic Primary and Secondary Schools.* Washington, D.C.: Catholic University of America Press, 1941.

McCahill, Bob. *Dialogue of Life: A Christian among Allah's Poor.* Maryknoll, N.Y.: Orbis Books, 1996.

McCarthy, Raymond P., CSSR, and Robert E. O'Leary, CSSR, eds. *Grains of Wheat: South American Mission, C.SS.R.* Privately printed, 1973.

McCaslin, James. *The Spirituality of Our Founders: A Study of the Early Columban Fathers.* Society of St. Columban, Maynooth Mission to China, 1986.

McCormick, Sister Rose Matthew, MM. *The Global Mission of God's People.* Maryknoll, N.Y.: Maryknoll Publications, 1967.

McCoy, Joseph A., SM. *Advice from the Field.* Baltimore: Helicon, 1962.

McDonald, Ellen M. "Maryknoll's Fifty Years in Latin America." *International Bulletin of Missionary Research* 16 (October 1992): 154–56.

McDonald, Sister M. Grace, OSB. *With Lamps Burning.* St. Joseph, Minn.: Saint Benedict's Priory Press, 1957.

MacDonnell, Joseph F., SJ. *Jesuits by the Tigris: Men for Others in Baghdad.* Boston: Jesuit Mission Press, 1994.

McGlinchey, Joseph F. *A Catechism on Catholic Foreign Missions.* 12th ed. Boston: Society for the Propagation of the Faith, 1921.

———. *Conversion of the Pagan World: A Treatise upon Catholic Foreign Missions.* Adapted from Paul Manna. Boston: Society for the Propagation of the Faith, 1921.

———. *Mission Tours: India.* Boston: Society for the Propagation of the Faith, 1925.

———. *The Workers Are Few.* Translation and adaptation of Paul Manna. Boston: Society for the Propagation of the Faith, 1912.

McGlone, Mary, CSJ. *Sharing Faith across the Hemisphere.* Committee on the Church in Latin America, National Conference of Catholic Bishops. Maryknoll, N.Y.: Orbis Books, 1997.

McGrath, Marcos. "Church and Mission in Latin America." In Francis J. Butler, ed., *American Catholic Identity: Essays in an Age of Change.* Kansas City, Mo.: Sheed & Ward, 1994.

———. "Theological Reflections on Inter-American Relations." In Samuel Shapiro, ed., *Cultural Factors in Inter-American Relations.*

McGuire, Frederick, CM, ed. *Mission to Mankind*. New York: Random House, 1963.
———. *The New Missionary Church*. Baltimore: Helicon, 1964. Papers from the 13th annual meeting of the mission-sending societies (1962) with three papers from the 1961 meeting.
McHugh, Peter, SVD. "The Development of the SVD Brother Formation." *Verbum SVD* 35, no. 3 (1994): 241–58.
———. *The Spirituality of Our Society: A Theological Reflection*. Manila: SVD Manila Province, 1975.
McQuaide, J. P. *With Christ in China*. San Francisco: The O'Connor Company, 1916.
McSorley, Joseph. *Father Hecker and His Friends*. St. Louis: Herder Book Company, 1952.
Maestrini, Nicholas. "Lay Missionaries: Their Role and Goal." *America* 80 (2 April 1949): 715–16.
———. *My Life with the Chinese: Laughter and Tears, 1931–1951*. Avon, N.J.: Magnificat Press, 1990.
Magner, James Aloysius. *Latin America Pattern*. Cincinnati: Catholic Students Mission Crusade, 1943.
Maguire, Theophane, CP. *Hunan Harvest*. With a foreword by Richard Cardinal Cushing. Milwaukee: Bruce Publishing Company, 1946.
Mahon, Leo T., and Sister Mary Xavier O'Donnell. *A Catechism of the Family of God*. Maryknoll, N.Y.: Maryknoll Publications, 1965.
Mahoney, Irene, OSU. *Swatow: Ursulines in China, 1922–1952*. Bronx, N.Y.: Ursuline Sisters, 1996.
Mainwaring, Scott. *The Catholic Church and Politics in Brazil, 1916–1985*. Stanford, Calif.: Stanford University Press, 1986.
Manion, P. J. "West to the East: Hanyang, 1923–31." In Ann Patrick Ware, ed., *Naming Our Truth: Stories of Loretto Women*. N.p.: Chardon Press, 1995.
Mann[a], Paul, and Nicholas Maestrini. *Forward with Christ: Thoughts and Reflections on Vocations to the Foreign Missions*. Westminster, Md.: Newman Press, 1954.
Marcelline, Sister M., OP. *Sisters Carry the Gospel*. Maryknoll, N.Y.: Maryknoll Publications, 1956.
Maria del Rey, Sister. *Her Name Is Mercy*. New York: Scribner, 1957.
Maritain, Jacques. "The Church and the Earth's Cultures." *Worldmission* 1, no. 1 (1950): 41–48.
Mary Francis Louise, Sister, MM. *Maryknoll Sisters: A Pictorial History*. New York: E. P. Dutton & Company, 1962.
Maryknoll Fathers, ed. *Christianity, a Personal Mission*. Maryknoll, N.Y.: Maryknoll Society, 1964.
Mathis, Michael A., CSC. "Three Marks of a Missionary." *The Bengalese* (March 1933): 24–26, 30.
———. *With the Holy Cross in Bengal*. Washington, D.C.: n.p., 1925.
Mauss, Marcel. *The Gift: Forms and Functions of Exchange in Archaic Societies*. London: Cohen and West, 1970.
Medicine in the Service of Foreign Missions. Cincinnati: Catholic Students Mission Crusade, 1939.
Melendez, Guillermo. *Seeds of Promise: The Prophetic Church in Central America*. New York: Friendship Press, 1990.
Members of the Province. *Congregation of the Sisters, Adorers of the Most Precious Blood, Province of Ruma*. Techny, Ill.: Mission Press, 1938.
Mennis, Mary R. *Hagen Saga: The Story of Father William Ross, Pioneer American Missionary to Papua, New Guinea*. Papua, New Guinea: Institute of Papua, New Guinea, Studies, 1982.
Merk, Frederick. *Manifest Destiny and Mission in American History*. New York: Alfred A. Knopf, 1970.

Meyer, Bernard F. *Lend Me Your Hands.* Chicago: Fides, 1955.

———. *Like to Leaven: Mission Methods in China.* Hong Kong: Catholic Truth Society, 1950.

———. *The Mystical Body in Action: A Workbook of Parish Catholic Action.* Herman, Pa.: Center for Men of Christ the King, 1947.

———. *The World Is My Neighbor.* Notre Dame, Ind.: Fides, 1964.

Michenfelder, Joseph, MM. *Gringo Volunteers.* Maryknoll, N.Y.: Maryknoll Publications, 1969.

The Mission Book. Baltimore: Kelly & Piet, 1862.

The Mission Movement in America, Being the Mind of the Missionaries Assembled in the Third Washington Conference at the Apostolic Mission House. Washington, D.C.: Apostolic Mission House, 1906.

Mojzes, Paul, and Leonard Swidler, eds. *Christian Mission and Interreligious Dialogue.* Lewiston, N.Y.: Edwin Mellen Press, 1990.

Motte, Mary, FMM, "The Role of Women in the Church." In Padraig Flanagan, SPS, *A New Missionary Era.* Maryknoll, N.Y.: Orbis Books, 1979.

Motte, Mary, FMM, and Joseph Lang, MM. *Mission in Dialogue: Sedos Research Seminar on the Future of Mission.* Maryknoll, N.Y.: Orbis Books, 1982.

Murphy, Edward L., SJ. "Mission Activity of the U.S. in Our Time." *Studia Missionalia* 8 (1954): 3–30.

———. "The Purpose of the Missions." *Missionary Academia* 1, no. 2 (1943).

———. *Teach Ye All Nations: The Principles of Catholic Missionary Work.* New York: Benziger, 1958.

Murrett, John C., MM. *Tar Heel Apostle: Thomas Frederick Price, Co-founder of Maryknoll.* New York: Longmans, 1944.

Naber, M. Vera, CSA. *With All Devotedness: Chronicles of the Sisters of St. Agnes, Fond du Lac, Wisconsin.* New York: P. J. Kenedy, 1959.

Naidenoff, George. *Pauline Jaricot: Heroic Lay Missionary.* Dublin: Pontifical Missionary Aid Societies, 1988.

National Office of the Society for the Propagation of the Faith, comp. *The Mission Apostolate.* New York: Society for the Propagation of the Faith, 1942.

Nemer, Lawrence, SVD. *Roman Catholic and Anglican Attitudes toward World Religions.* St. Augustin, Germany: Steyler, 1981.

Nevins, Albert. *The Meaning of Maryknoll.* New York: McMullen Books, 1954.

Nicaragua Was Our Home: Relocation of Miskito Indians. (Lee Shapiro Productions, 1985), videocassette.

Nolan, Hugh J., ed. *Pastoral Letters of United States Catholic Bishops.* 3 vols. Washington, D.C.: U.S. Catholic Conference, 1983–84.

Official Guide and Program of the First American Catholic Missionary Congress. Chicago: Catholic Church Extension Society, 1908.

O'Rourke, Alice, OP. *Let Us Set Out: Sinsinawa Dominicans, 1949–1985.* Dubuque, Iowa: Union-Hoermann Press, 1986.

Osborne, Francis J., SJ. *A History of the Church in Jamaica.* Chicago: Loyola University Press, 1988.

O'Shea, David. "The U.S. Laity in Latin America." *Apostolate* 10 (Spring 1964): 2–9.

O'Sullivan, D. J. *A Life Sketch of Mother Mary Lawrence, F.M.M.* Boston: Society for the Propagation of the Faith, 1919.

Our Lady of the Angels Fraternity, Third Order of Saint Francis. *History of the Tertiaries' Mission Circle.* Cleveland: privately printed, 1933.

Paulin, Eugene, SM, and Joseph A. Becker, SM. *New Wars: The History of the Brothers of Mary (Marianists) in Hawaii, 1883–1958.* Milwaukee: Bruce Press, 1958.

Payne, Robert S., ed. *College Readings on Africa: A Collection of Discussions on the Cultural, Economic, Political, and Religious Aspects of Present Day Africa.* Cincinnati: Catholic Students Mission Crusade Press, 1963.

Pendergast, Mary Carita, SC. *Havoc in Hunan: The Sisters of Charity in Western Hunan, 1924–1951.* Morristown, N.J.: College of St. Elizabeth Press, 1991.

Phillips, James M., and Robert T. Coote, eds. *Toward the Twenty-first Century in Christian Mission.* Grand Rapids, Mich.: Eerdmans, 1993.

Pontifical Council for the Pastoral Care of Migrants and Itinerant People. *Solidarity in Favour of New Migrations: Proceedings of the III World Congress for the Pastoral Care of Migrants and Refugees.* Vatican City: n.p., 1991.

Power, John. *Mission Theology Today.* Maryknoll, N.Y.: Orbis Books, 1971.

Powers, George C. *The Maryknoll Movement.* Maryknoll, N.Y.: Catholic Foreign Mission Society, 1922.

"The Proper Role of the Foreign Missionary." In *Between Honesty and Hope: Documents from and about the Church in Latin America.* Issued at Lima by the Peruvian Bishops' Commission for Social Action. Translated by John Drury. Maryknoll Documentation Series. Maryknoll, N.Y.: Maryknoll Publications, 1970.

Rabe, Valentin H. *The Home Base of American China Missions, 1880–1920.* Cambridge: Harvard University Press, 1978.

Redinger, Matthew Alan. " 'To Arouse and Inform': American Catholic Attempts to Influence U.S.-Mexican Relations, 1920–1937." Ph.D. diss., University of Washington, 1993.

Reed, James. *The Missionary Mind and American East Asia Policy, 1911–1915.* Cambridge: Council on East Asian Studies, Harvard University, 1983.

Reher, Margaret Mary. "Denis J. Dougherty and Anna M. Dengel: The Missionary Alliance." *Records of the American Catholic Historical Society of Philadelphia* 101 (1990): 21–33.

———. " 'Get Thee to a (Peruvian) Nunnery': Cardinal Dougherty and the Philadelphia IHMs." *Records of the American Catholic Historical Society of Philadelphia* 103 (Winter 1992): 43–52.

Reid, Elizabeth. *I Belong Where I Am Needed.* Westminster, Md.: Newman Press, 1961.

Rent, N. Rosa, "Insiders and Outsiders in the Study of Religious Traditions." *Journal of the American Academy of Religion* 51, no. 3 (1983): 459–76. Followed by four responses, 477–91.

Reuter, Frank T. *Catholic Influence on American Colonial Policies, 1898–1904.* Austin: University of Texas Press, 1967.

Richard, Lucien, OMI. "Vatican II and the Mission of the Church: A Contemporary Agenda." In Lucien Richard, OMI, et al., eds., *Vatican II, the Unfinished Agenda: A Look to the Future.* New York: Paulist Press, 1987.

Richardson, William J., MM, ed. *The Modern Mission Apostolate: A Symposium.* Maryknoll, N.Y.: Maryknoll Publications, 1965.

———. *Reappraisal: Prelude to Change.* Maryknoll, N.Y.: Maryknoll Publications, 1965.

———. *Revolution in Missionary Thinking.* Maryknoll, N.Y.: Maryknoll Publications, 1966.

Rigney, Harold, SVD. *Four Years in a Red Hell: The Story of Father Rigney.* Chicago: Henry Regnery Company, 1956.

Robert, Dana. *American Women in Mission: A Social History of Their Thought and Practice.* Macon, Ga.: Mercer University Press, 1996.

Roche, Aloysius. *In the Track of the Gospel: An Outline of the Christian Apostolate from Pentecost to the Present.* New York: P. J. Kenedy, 1953.

Roche, Douglas. "The New Boom in Lay Missionaries." *Sign* 38 (April 1959): 36–38.

Rother, Stanley. *The Shepherd Cannot Run: Letters of Stanley Rother, Missionary and Martyr.* Edited by David Monahan. Oklahoma City: Archdiocese of Oklahoma City, 1984.

Runnoe, Mary Jo. "Building a Movement: The Volunteer Missionary Movement." Master of Theological Science thesis, Catholic Theological Union, Chicago, 1992.

Ryan, Joseph P. "American Contributions to the Catholic Missionary Effort in China in the Twentieth Century." *Catholic Historical Review* 31 (July 1945): 171–80.

Ryan, Thomas F., SJ. *China through Catholic Eyes*. Hong Kong: Catholic Truth Society, 1941; distributed in U.S. by Catholic Students Mission Crusade.

Rybolt, John E., CM, ed. *The American Vincentians: A Popular History of the Congregation of the Mission in the United States, 1815–1987*. Brooklyn: New City Press, 1988.

Rynne, Xavier. *The Fourth Session: The Debates and Decrees of Vatican Council II, September 14 to December 8, 1965*. New York: Farrar, Straus, and Giroux, 1967.

Sacrae Congregationis de Propaganda Fide Memoria Rerum. Rome: Herder, 1975.

Saint Jacques, Bernard. "The Society of Jesus, an Essentially Missionary Order." *Woodstock Letters* 83 (1954): 47–64.

Salamone, Frank A. "Feminist Mission Sisters: Nurses, Midwives, and Joans-of-all-Trades: The Dominican Sisters in Nigeria." In *Women Missionaries and Cultural Change*. Studies in Third World Societies, no. 40. Williamsburg, Va.: College of William and Mary, 1989.

Sanneh, Lamin. *Translating the Message: The Missionary Impact on Culture*. Maryknoll, N.Y.: Orbis Books, 1990.

Scherer, James A. *That the Gospel May Be Sincerely Preached throughout the World: A Lutheran Perspective on Mission and Evangelism in the Twentieth Century*. Published on behalf of the Lutheran World Federation. Stuttgart, Germany: Kreuz Verlag, 1982.

Scherer, James A., and Stephen B. Bevans, eds. *New Directions in Mission and Evangelization*. Vol. 1, *Basic Statements*. Vol. 2, *Theological Foundations*. Maryknoll, N.Y.: Orbis Books, 1992–93.

Schmalz, Norbert, OFM, and Boniface Pfeilschifter, OFM. *Shen-Fu's Story: The Memoirs of Two American Missionaries in the China of Yesteryear*. Chicago: Franciscan Herald Press, 1965.

Schmidlin, Joseph. *Catholic Mission History*. Edited by Matthias Braun, SVD. Techny, Ill.: Mission Press, 1933.

———. *Catholic Mission Theory*. Translated by Matthias Braun, SVD. Techny, Ill.: Mission Press, 1933.

Schwager, Frederick, SVD. *The World Missions of the Catholic Church*. Techny, Ill.: Mission Press, 1914.

Schwartz, Aloysius. *The Starved and the Silent*. Garden City, N.Y.: Doubleday, 1966.

Seager, Richard Hughes. "The World's Parliament of Religions, Chicago, 1893: America's Religious Coming of Age." Ph.D. diss., Harvard University, 1986.

———, ed. *The Dawn of Religious Pluralism: Voices from the World's Parliament of Religions, 1893*. Peru, Ill.: Open Court Publishing Company, 1993.

SEDOS, ed. *Foundations of Mission Theology*. Translated by John Drury. Maryknoll Documentation Series. Maryknoll, N.Y.: Orbis Books, 1972.

Seumois, Andrew, OMI. "Lay Missionary Organization." *Worldmission* 1951 (4): 78–87.

Seventy-fifth Anniversary, Fifty Years in America: Society of the Divine Word. Techny, Ill.: Mission Press, 1950.

Shapiro, Samuel, ed. *Cultural Factors in Inter-American Relations*. Papers from the 5th CICOP Conference. Notre Dame, Ind.: University of Notre Dame Press, 1968.

Sheehan, David M., SSC. *A Columban Missioner: Forty Years in Korea*. Kwangju, Korea: Chonnam National University, 1996.

Sheen, Fulton J. *Missions and the World Crisis*. Milwaukee: Bruce Publishing Company, 1963.

———. "A New Theology of Missions." *Worldmission* 22, no. 3 (1971): 20–25.

Sheerin, John B. *Never Look Back: The Career and Concerns of John J. Burke*. New York: Paulist Press, 1975.

Sheridan, Robert E., MM. *The Founders of Maryknoll*. New York: Catholic Foreign Mission Society of America, 1980.

————, ed. *Very Rev. Thomas Frederick Price, Co-founder of Maryknoll: A Symposium, 1956, with Supplement, 1981.* Maryknoll, N.Y.: privately printed, 1981.

Shields, Joseph J. *Attitudes of American Women Religious towards the Concept of Mission.* Research Report Submitted to the U.S. Catholic Mission Council. Washington, D.C.: 1978.

Should Priests Be Sent to Latin America? Washington, D.C.: U.S. Catholic Conference, 1971.

Shower of Roses upon the Missions: Spiritual and Temporal Favors Obtained through the Intercession of Blessed Teresa, 1909–1913. New York: Society for the Propagation of the Faith, 1924.

Shuster, Robert. "Documentary Sources in the United States for Foreign Missions Research: A Select Bibliography and Checklist." *International Bulletin of Missionary Research* 9 (1985): 19–29.

Sisters of St. Benedict. *Beyond the Horizon.* Taipei: Ou Yu Publications, 1980.

Smith, Simon, SJ. "Creating a New Missiology for the Church." *Missiology* 10 (January 1982): 97–100.

————. *Hopes and Concerns for Mission.* Washington, D.C.: U.S. Catholic Mission Council, 1976.

————. "Refugees, 1983." *Studies in the International Apostolate of Jesuits* 8 (January 1984): 1–13.

————. "Reverse Mission: Two Catholic Models." *Missiology* 7 (January 1979): 116–19.

Smith, Simon, SJ, and J. G. Donders, WF. *Refugees Are People: An Action Report on the Refugees in Africa, Spearhead No. 88.* Eldoret, Kenya: Gaba Publications, 1985.

————. "Witnessing to the Kingdom in a Dehumanizing World." *Donum Dei* (Toronto: Canadian Religious Conference), no. 22 (1975).

Society for the Propagation of the Faith. *Proceedings of the Annual Meeting of the Mission Secretariat.* Washington, D.C.: The Secretariat, 1957.

Society of the Divine Word. *The Word in the World: Divine Word Missionaries, 1875–1975.* Techny, Ill.: Divine Word Missionaries, 1975.

Spaeth, J. Paul, ed. *Ecumenism and Universalism: A Collection of Readings on World Outlook for the Sixties.* Cincinnati: Catholic Students Mission Crusade, 1963.

————. *Perspectives in Religion and Culture.* Cincinnati: Catholic Students Mission Crusade, Paladin Press, 1957.

Spieler, Joseph, PSM, comp. *Lights and Shadows: Scenes and Sketches from the Mission Field.* Translated by C. Lawrence, OFMCap. Techny, Ill.: Mission Press, n.d.

Srambical, Clarence, SVD. *Mission Spirituality.* Indore, India: Divine Word Publications, 1975.

Steward, George C., Jr. *Marvels of Charity: History of American Sisters and Nuns.* Huntington, Ind.: Our Sunday Visitor Publishing Division, 1994.

Steyler Missionswissenschaftliches Institut: Divine Word Missionaries in Papua, New Guinea, 1896–1996. Nettetal: Steyler Verlag, 1996. Festschrift volume, *Verbum SVD* 37.

Straelen, H. J. van. *The Catholic Encounter with World Religions.* Westminster, Md.: Newman Press, 1966.

Streit, Robert. *Catholic Missions in Figures and Symbols, Based on the Vatican Missionary Exhibition.* New York: Society for the Propagation of the Faith, 1927.

Suenens, Cardinal. *The Gospel to Every Culture.* Translated by Louise Gavan Duffy. Westminster, Md.: Newman Press, 1957.

SVD Word in the World. Steyl, Holland: Steyler Verlag, Society of the Divine Word, published annually from 1960 to present.

Synod of Bishops — 1974, Rome, September 27–October 26, 1974. Washington, D.C.: U.S. Catholic Conference, 1975.

Tennant, Joseph J. "The World Is the Mission." *Worldmission* 6, no. 2 (1955): 240–42.

Thomas, Evangeline, ed. *Women Religious History Sources: A Guide to Repositories in the United States.* New York: R. R. Bowker, 1983.

Timp, Frederick N., SVD. "Foreign Mission Interest and Activity in the Archdiocese of Chicago to 1940." Master of Divinity thesis, Catholic Theological Union, Chicago, 1971.

Trettel, Efrem. *Rivers, Rice Fields, Souls: Memoirs of My Mission in China.* Chicago: Franciscan Herald Press, 1965.

Tucker, Ruth A. "Female Mission Strategies: A Historical and Contemporary Perspective." *Missiology* 15 (January 1987): 73–89.

——. *Guardians of the Great Commission: The Story of Women in Modern Missions.* Grand Rapids, Mich.: Zondervan, 1988.

Turner, Frederick C. *Catholicism and Political Development in Latin America.* Chapel Hill: University of North Carolina Press, 1971.

Un Si a la Vida, A Yes to Life: 25 Year Celebration of the Sisters of St. Joseph of Carondelet in Peru. N.p.: Sisters of St. Joseph of Carondelet, 1987.

Unsworth, Virginia, SC. "American Missionaries and Communist China: 1941–1953." Dissertation, New York University, 1976.

Van Bulch, Gaston, SJ. "R. P. Pierre Charles, 1883–1954." *Studia Missionalia* 10 (1960): 3–56.

Van Engen, Charles, Dean S. Gilliland, and Paul Pierson, eds. *The Good News of the Kingdom: Mission Theology for the Third Millennium.* Maryknoll, N.Y.: Orbis Books, 1993.

Varg, Paul A. *Missionaries, Chinese, and Diplomats.* Princeton, N.J.: Princeton University Press, 1958.

Verstraeten, A. M., SJ. "Catholic Missions in India." *America* 26 (1921): 33–35, 57–58.

Walls, Andrew F. *The Missionary Movement in Christian History: Studies in the Transmission of Faith.* Maryknoll, N.Y.: Orbis Books, 1996.

Walsh, Flavian A., OFM. "Holy Name Province in Mission, China: 1913–1932." *Friar Lines* 3 (Winter 1991): 17–24.

——. "The Shasi Mission: 1932–1945." *Friar Lines* 6, no. 3 (1994): 25–40.

Walsh, James A. *A Modern Martyr, Theophane Venard.* Translated from the French by Lady Herbert. Revised and annotated by J. A. Walsh. Boston: Society for the Propagation of the Faith, 1905.

——. *Observations in the Orient.* Ossining, N.Y.: Catholic Foreign Mission Society, 1919.

——. *Thoughts from Modern Martyrs.* Ossining, N.Y.: Catholic Foreign Mission Society, 1912.

——, ed. *Maryknoll Mission Letters, China: Extracts from the Letters and Diaries of the Pioneer Missioners of the Catholic Foreign Mission Society of America.* New York: Macmillan, 1923.

Walsh, James E. *The Church's World Wide Mission.* New York: Benziger Brothers, 1948.

——. "Description of a Missioner by One." *Worldmission* 6 (Winter 1955): 402–16.

——. *Maryknoll Spiritual Directory.* Maryknoll, N.Y.: Field Afar Press, 1947.

——. *Mission Manual of the Vicariate of Kongmoon.* Hong Kong: Catholic Foreign Mission Society, 1937.

Walsh, James J. *American Jesuits.* New York: Macmillan, 1934; reprint, 1968.

Walsh, Marie de Lourdes. *The Sisters of Charity of New York, 1909–1959.* Vol. 3. New York: Fordham University Press, 1960.

Weber, Elizabeth J. *Celestial Honeymoon: The Story of Sister Catherine Bushman, S.C.* New York: Benziger Brothers, 1950.

Wedge, Florence. *Franciscan Nun in China: Sister Mary Joseph Hubrich (1886–1962).* Pulaski, Wis.: Franciscan Publishers, 1963.

Wegener, Herman, SVD. *Heroes of the Mission Field.* Techny, Ill.: St. Mary's Mission Press, 1924.

Welter, Barbara. "She Hath Done What She Could: Protestant Women's Missionary Careers in Nineteenth-Century America." *American Quarterly* 30 (1978): 624–38.

Whiteman, Darrell L. "The Use of Missionary Documents in Ethnohistorical Research." In Darrell L. Whiteman, ed., *Missionaries, Anthropologists, and Cultural Change.* Studies in Third World Societies, no. 25. Williamsburg, Va.: Department of Anthropology, College of William and Mary, 1985.

Wiest, Jean-Paul. "Lessons from the Work of the Paris Foreign Mission Society and Maryknoll in the Guangdong and Guangxi Provinces." *Missiology* 10 (April 1982): 171–84.

———. *Maryknoll in China: A History, 1918–1955.* Armonk, N.Y.: M. E. Sharpe, 1988; Maryknoll, N.Y.: Orbis Books, 1997.

———, editorial advisor. *Collectanea Commissionis Synodalis: Guide to the Microfiche Collection.* Bethesda, Md.: Academic Editions, 1988.

Willeke, Bernward H. "Documents Relating to the History of the Franciscan Missions in Shantung, China." *Franciscan Studies* 7 (1947): 171–87.

Wiltgen, Ralph M., SVD. *The Rhine Flows into the Tiber: The Unknown Council.* New York: Hawthorn Books, 1967.

———. *The Word in the World, 1969.* New Guinea: A Report on the Missionary Apostolate. Techny, Ill.: Divine Word Publications, 1969.

Wissel, Joseph. *The Redemptorist on the American Missions.* 1920. Reprint, New York: Arno Press, 1978.

Wojniak, Edward J., SVD. *Atomic Apostle: The Life Story of Thomas Megan, SVD.* Techny, Ill.: Divine Word Publications, 1957.

Wolf, Ann Colette, SP. *Against All Odds: Sisters of Providence Mission to the Chinese.* St. Mary-of-the-Woods, Ind.: Office of Communications, 1990.

Wood, Robert, SM. *Missionary Crisis and Challenge in Latin America.* St. Louis: B. Herder Book Company, 1964.

World's Parliament of Religions. Chicago: World's Parliament of Religions, 1893.

Yates, Timothy. *Christian Mission in the Twentieth Century.* New York: Cambridge University Press, 1994.

Index

Abenakis tribe, 13
Accra, Ghana, 152
Acer, Paul, 151
adaptation of missionaries, 78, 138–39
Ad Gentes, 237, 268
Adorers of the Blood of Christ, 120, 127, 180, 326n.5
Africa: attitudes toward, in the 1950s, 176–77; effect of World War I on missions to, 151–52; *Fidei donum* and, 149, 171–74; as an important mission territory, 247; increase of missionaries sent to, between 1940 and 1963, 2; Jesuits in, 325n.91; lay women from the U.S. as missionaries to, 174; Marianists in, 324n.90; mission statistics for, 213, 273, 304n.2; racist view of, in U.S. textbooks, 170–71; Society of the Divine Word in, 317n.9; Spiritans in, 324n.85. *See also specific countries*
African Americans: bishops' lack of support for, 40; Catholic attempts to censor racism in the 1940s, 173; nineteenth-century mission to, 27–31; racist view of, in U.S. textbooks, 170–71; Vatican documents on treatment of, 283n.36
Afro-American Congresses, 30, 39, 48
Agee, Philip, 230
Agnes, Mother, 291n.14
Ahner, Eugene, 341n.6
Aiken, Charles F. (1864–1924), 75–76, 288n.17, 294n.49
Alaska, 35, 286n.53, 304n.2
Alemany, Archbishop Joseph, 109
Aleuts, 35
Alexander, Calvert, SJ, 152, 154, 270, 320n.41, 322n.70
Alexander VI, Pope, 6
Algonquins, 13, 14
Alliance for Progress, the, 182, 207, 224
Alvarado, Isidoro, 234
Amadeus. *See* Dunne, Sarah Theresa
America (magazine), 87, 160
"American": use of the term, 3
American Board of Catholic Missions, 82; change in plan for, 299n.27; the Columbans and, 118; formation of, 106, 247, 298n.25; funding of China missions by, 148; overview of history and work of, 92–95; self-definition of, 299n.34
American Board of Christian Foreign Missions, 75
American Board of Commissioners for Foreign Missions, 111

American Catholic Missionary Congresses, 70–71, 78, 80, 111
American Catholic Tribune, 30
American Colonization Society, 43
American Committee for China Famine Fund, 147–48
American Federation of Catholic Societies, 41
Americanism, 57, 65–67, 78–80, 288n.17, 291n.17, 296n.72
American Professors of Mission, 252
American Society of Missiology, 252, 341n.7
Anciaux, Joseph, 283n.36
Anderson, Gerald H., 252, 307n.28, 341n.7
Anderson, William T., SM, 173, 324n.90
André, Gabriel, 288n.17
anonymous Christians, 257
anthropology, 81, 82, 91, 168, 169, 260–61
anticommunism: Catholic, in the 1930s, 320n.44; the CIA urging missionaries to promote, 230; Latin American Bureau and, 189; the Pontifical Commission for Latin America and, 187; of U.S. Catholic institutions and leaders, 212. *See also* communism
Antigonish Movement, 210
Antillach, Father, SJ, 56
Antilles, the, 50–51
Apostolic Mission House, 67–68, 74, 259, 296n.67
archaeology, 313n.99
Argentina, 181
Aristotelianism, 268, 270
Arizona, 11
Ark, Joseph Fie, 111
Asia: number of U.S. missionaries in, in 1968, 213; world religions of, 246. *See also specific countries*
Asian American studies, 3
Association for International Development, 155–56, 230
Ateneo de Manila, 65, 85, 344n.39
Augusta, Mother, 112
Augustinians, 8, 11, 277n.18
Aurea Xavier, 141
Austin, Teresita, SC, 337n.42
Avery, Martha Moore, 292n.35
Ayde-Curran, Georgiana, 288n.4
Aztecs, 8
Azusa Street Revival, 28

Badin, Stephen, 281n.3
Bahamas, the, 45–49, 288n.4